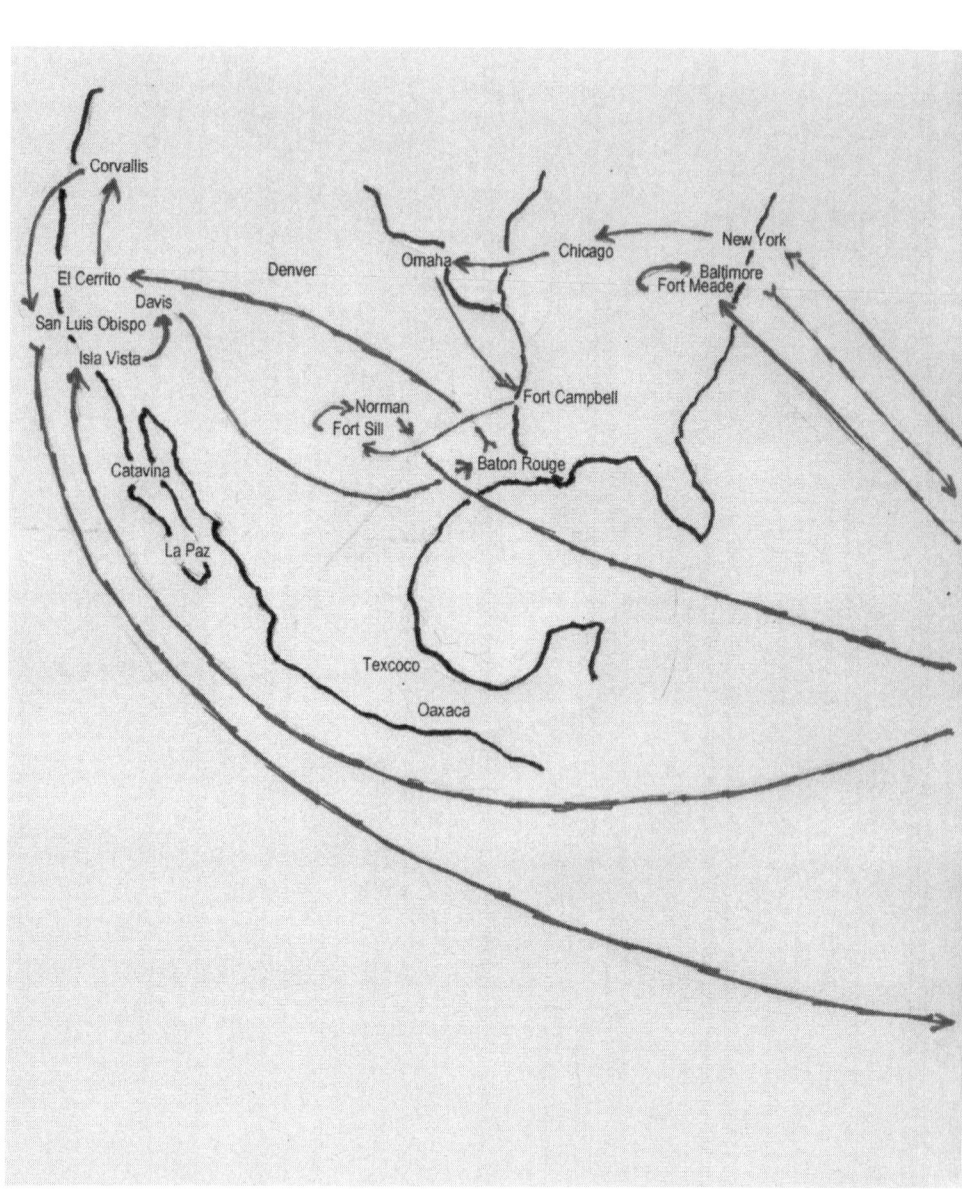

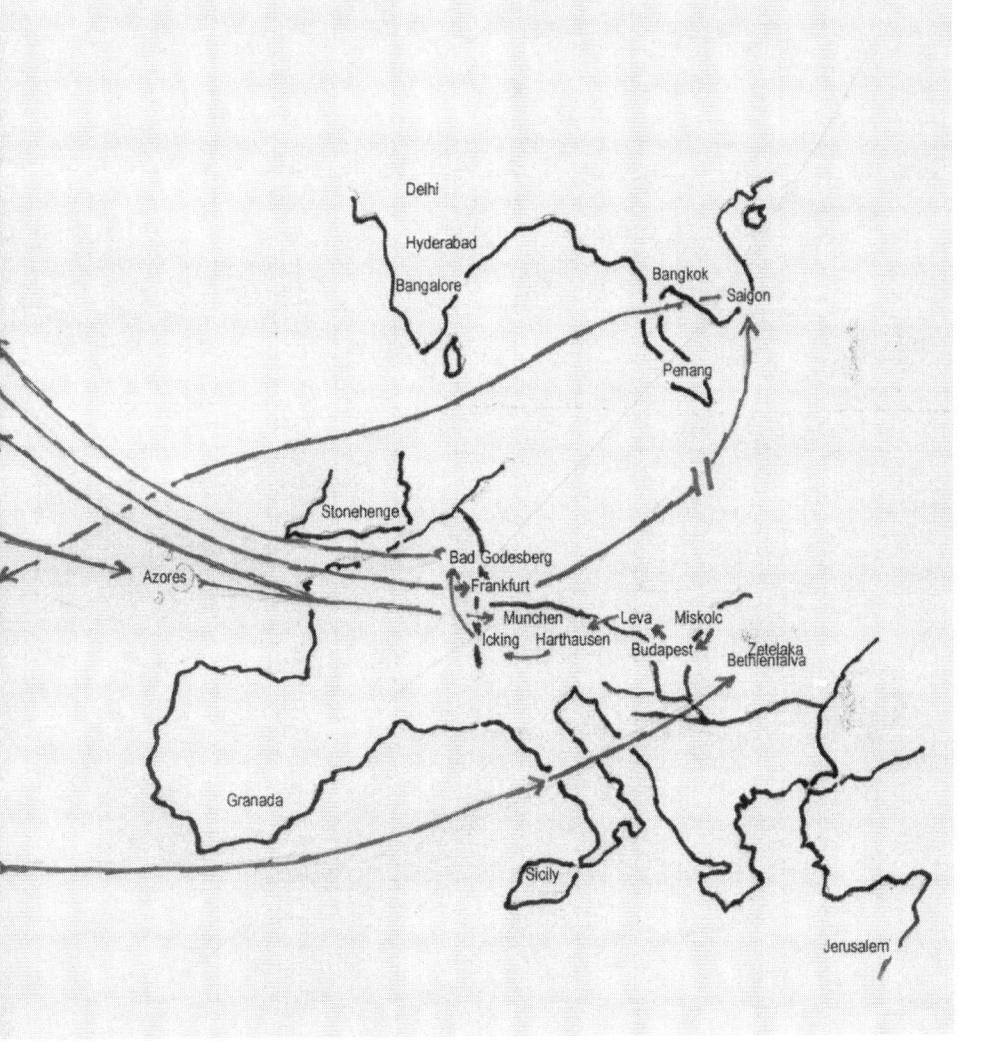

In Search of
an America

In Search of an America

An Introvert on the Road

Gabor Bethlenfalvay

Copyright © 2011 by Gabor Bethlenfalvay.

Library of Congress Control Number:		2011908912
ISBN:	Hardcover	978-1-4628-8049-2
	Softcover	978-1-4628-8048-5
	Ebook	978-1-4628-8050-8

All rights reserved. No part of this book may be reproduced or transmitted in any form or by any means, electronic or mechanical, including photocopying, recording, or by any information storage and retrieval system, without permission in writing from the copyright owner.

This book was printed in the United States of America.

To order additional copies of this book, contact:
Xlibris Corporation
1-888-795-4274
www.Xlibris.com
Orders@Xlibris.com
94182

Contents

Motivation 19
Előszó—Vorwort—Prologue 21

Chapter 1-Daybreak 25
    Snapshots of childhood 26
    War clouds 29
        On butterflies 30
        More war clouds 31
        Home 32
        Tribulations 33
        Childhood memories 34
        Back to the war 36
        The end of innocence 37

Chapter 2-The Refugee 39
    The first leg of the long road 39
    The first-way station 40
    The bear 42
    The smiling god 43
    Stalingrad 45
    The rooster experience 46
    Bombs, hornets, and more bombs 47
    Linzer torte and the first glimpse of America 50
    On to Mauthausen 50
    The mammoth 52
    At the Bahnhof 54
    The concentration camp 55
    Samu *bácsi* 56
    Asombroso 57

Chapter 3-The Exile 59
    Middlegate Corner 59
    Yellow june bugs 60
  Werfen 62
    How Magyars relate to the Russians 65
  Harthausen 67

Tonsils, Indians, and the end of the day	68
There is more to life than memories	69
Freedom and frogs	71
Dies irae	72
Life goes on	73
Icking	75
The *Ickinger Schule*	77
On cost-benefit ratios	78
The potato eaters	79
Saving a year	79
On consequences	81
The crow convention	81
Mei Ruah	83
The third consequence	83
First love	85
Bad Godesberg	87
On the way to the AKO	88
The *Collegium*	90
Social order at the Stella Rheni	91
Self-searching	94
God versus principle	95
On photosynthesis	96
Still on topic, but on a lighter note	96
To stay or not to stay	98
The open window	99
Chapter 4 - The Emigrant	102
Austin, Nevada	102
A bit of botany	103
The International	104
At sea	105
The promised land	107
The Sabbath	109
Eureka!	111
Chicago	112
A lesson in American	113
Cornstarch	114
Baseball	116
The first beer	119
Omaha	120
Soot and soap	120
American Christmas	122
Life in cold storage	123

Skid row	125
First stab at college	126
The guillotine	127
One more immigrant	129
The milkman	131
Chapter 5-The Soldier	**133**
On the road again to Grass Valley	134
The enlisted man	135
Why put on the uniform?	135
Not in uniform yet	136
Basic training	139
On morale, discipline, and patriotism	141
Jump school	142
At the Eleventh Airborne	146
The 'trooper	147
The NCO Academy	148
Yolanda	149
The past intrudes	150
The officer candidate	151
The officer	155
The second lieutenant	155
The old emigrant	156
A letter from home	157
The first lieutenant	157
Boss for a change	159
The uprising of 1956	161
Sergeant Hamilton and a short course in politics	161
Back to the Magyar uprising of 1956	163
Decisions, decisions	165
Back to his element	165
Quanah Parker and Geronimo	166
Paris	169
Chapter 6-The Student	**172**
Meandering	172
On the road to the Gund Ranch	173
Causes and consequences	174
Grass Valley insights	175
Norman	176
Career choice gone wrong	176
College town ambiance	177
Physics as drudgery	179
On physics and the mind	180

The controller and the Self 182
The uprising of 1956 revisited 184
Interlude on the Azores 186
A time of doubt 188
Some thoughts on schools 189
An engineer! 191
Munich 192
Physics in Munich 193
Fugit Amor 195
The russet mantle 196
Light in October 197
Physics, one last time 200
Amor omnia vincit *201*
Farewell to physics 202
Getting acquainted 203
Back to the renewed search of an america 204
Chapter 7-Soldier Again 206
On politics, coal, and intelligence 207
Herding pigs 208
Back to the facts: coal and intelligence 209
Military intelligence 210
Maryland 211
Fort Meade 211
Getting married 212
Distant thunder 213
College Park 214
The job 216
Fort Holabird 219
About his father 221
Recycling some of the past 223
Frankfurt 226
The brat: on raising children 226
On the job in Germany 227
Off the job in Germany 229
Re-education 232
Italy 236
Brave new world 239
Resignation 241
Closing out Frankfurt 243
Thoughts on soldier's pay 246
The fox 247
Karma 249

- Packed and ready to go 250
- Saigon 252
  - On war 253
  - Tan Son Nhut 254
  - Back to intelligence once more 256
  - The daily routine 259
  - Saturday off 260
  - On R&R 262
  - Bangkok 262
  - Penang 265
  - Figmo chart finished 267
- Chapter 8-Student again 268
  - Grass Valley: almost there 269
  - Isla Vista 271
    - The counterculture 271
    - Biology 273
    - On the road again 274
    - On the grand principles 283
    - Robin 285
    - Gardening, *Katze,* and goats 286
    - The Child Care Center 287
    - Child rearing 289
  - Davis 289
    - Botany at Davis 291
    - A digression on tenure 293
    - Defining the dissertation 293
    - The thesis 295
    - Hiking, trespassing, and private property 297
    - More on hiking 298
    - Nuggets in the sand 300
    - The ashram 301
    - A vision 301
    - The postdoc: nitrogen fixation 303
    - Problems at home 305
- Chapter 9-The Biologist 307
  - The job market 307
  - Louisiana 309
    - Blackjack 309
    - Going back east 310
    - The Hopis 312
    - The Deep South at last 313
    - The workplace 315

- On climates ... 315
- The concept ... 318
- Alone again ... 319
- Soybeans and the market ... 321
- Soybeans, sacrifice, and self-deception ... 323
- Reenter Marc ... 323
- Sacrifice ... 324
- The present intrudes ... 326
- Involvement ... 327
- The magnet of the Black Mesa ... 329
- On coincidences ... 331

California ... 332
- Starting the trek back West ... 332
- Okeene ... 334
- Bud ... 335
- The Menonites ... 336
- Romilda ... 337
- The Llano Estacado ... 338
- Solitaires ... 340
- House hunting ... 341
- The job scene ... 342
- Symbiosis, tongue-in-cheek ... 344
- The home scene ... 345
- Baptizing Robin ... 347
- India ... 350
- Free market ... 355
- Cuernavaca ... 358
- Family storm clouds ... 360
- On being cooped up ... 361
- Suran, Reno, and economics ... 362
- Austin: an Eden? ... 366
- The birth of the story ... 367
- Collaboration with Ronald ... 370
- Texcoco, Walmart, and the *mercado* ... 372
- *Un poquito sobre la ciudad de México* ... 376
- Jerusalem ... 379
- First trip home ... 382
- Léva revisited ... 385
- The real Mexico ... 388
- Four highlights ... 390
- Ash Meadows ... 395
- Karma ... 396

- Oaxaca 398
  - Totóntepec Mije 401
  - The vision 403
  - An in-law 406
  - Past revisited 407
  - Léva 411
  - Jet lag 415
  - Birds leaving the nest 417
  - Ambiance 417
- Oregon 420
  - The big picture 420
  - Closer to home 424
  - Granada 428
  - A bit of *turismo* *431*
  - Fülek 435
  - More soil biology 437
  - Black clouds 438
  - The false friend 440
  - Times of yore 441
  - *Hazatérés*—Homecoming 442
  - The Sumerian connection 444
  - How to get to Baja and stay for a while 448
  - The recurrent Dream 450
  - On to La Paz 451
  - El Comitán 454
  - Is work that is fun work? 458
  - The subtropical tip of Baja 459
  - Family visits 460
  - On self-deception 463
  - Poor road 464
  - The road imp again 465
  - Decisions jelling 467
  - Phasing out 469
- Chapter 10-Twilight 471
  - Big decision 472
  - On greed and bubbles 473
  - On the way to the roots 475
  - The Mártons 478
  - On the road to Bethlenfalva 479
  - Paradise lost 481
  - Settling in for good 481
  - Austin, an america 483

    Nine eleven 485
    The neighborhood 486
    The neighbors 488
    One more trip to Bethlenfalva 490
    Bush era politics *493*
    Las Vegas 495
    The demon reappears in Budapest 497
    Relating to realities 499
    The cloud is lifting 501
    The days dwindle down 502

Epilogue--Nachwort–Utószó 505
Hungarian Pronunciation 509
Glossary 511

These memories are dedicated to my Family:

To my Father, whose undaunted spirit in the face of the tragedies in his life has always been an inspiration to me in my own

And to my Mother whom I did not know well for her smile left me early

But I found it again on the face of my Wife who is the source of my strength and the joy of my being. It is a smile that now lives on in my new little Granddaughter

And to my elder son who had seen trouble and battled it bravely

And to my younger son who is my bridge to the New World

And to my brother, my anchor to my World of Old, now gone with the wind.

Motivation

From the founding document of the Abbey of Tihany, on the peninsula in Lake Balaton:

Minthogy némely halandók elméjükben elgyengülve, akár lustaság folytán, akár vétkes hanyagságból, s igen gyakran a világi dolgoknak hamarosan múló gondjai miatt is tudatlanúl, mert nem emlékeznek rá, könnyelműen feledésnek adták át, amit láttak és hallottak; ezért a tudósok, bölcselők s atyáim igen sokan tanácskozással és okossággal és iparkodásukkal rájöttek, hogy amit az emberi nem fiai helyesen elhatároztak, azt mindig szorgalmas írnokok keze által betűk emlékezetére bizták, nehogy annak avúltsága folytán nyoma se maradjon későbbi kor utódaiban.

Az Úr 1055-ödik esztendejében, András, Isten kegyelméből a magyarok győzhetetlen királyának parancsára Béla herceg állitotta össze, és Miklós főpap írta.

Sintemalen manche Sterbliche, geschwächt in ihrem Geist, sei es aus Trägheit, sei es aus sündhafter Nachlässigkeit, oft aber auch unbewußt, bedingt durch die schnell wächselnden Sorgen der weltlichen Geschäfte, sich nicht mehr an das erinnern, was sie gesehen und gehört haben und diese Dinge leichsinnig der Vergessenheit überlassen; deshalb haben die Gelehrten, die Weisen und die Ältesten meines Hauses, die in ihrer Vielzahl hier versammelt sind, zufolge ihrer Beratung, Klugheit und Bestreben befunden: dasjenige, was die Söhne des menschlichen Geschlechtes rechtmäßig beschlossen haben, sei immer durch die fleißigen Hände der Schreiber dem Gedächtnis der Buchstaben anzuvertrauen, damit die Spuren seiner Kunde duch Verjähren nicht ausgelöscht werden für die Nachkommen späterer Zeiten.

Anno Domini MLV, auf Beschluss des Andreas, von Gottes Gnaden unbesiegbarer König der Ungarn, verfasst von Herzog Béla, geschrieben durch die Hand des Bischofs Miklós.

Whereas some mortals, enfeebled in their mind, be it for sloth, be it for sinful lack of care, and often also unknowingly, due to the rapidly shifting worries of worldly affairs, forget and carelessly surrender to oblivion all that which they have seen and heard; therefore the scholars and the wise men and my elders here gathered and, debating with wise counsel, prudence, and endeavor, have decided that the things that the sons of humankind rightfully decreed should always be entrusted to the memory of letters by the diligent hand of the scribe so that such matters would not be lost without a trace to the descendants of later ages due to their transience.

In the year of the Lord 1055, by command of Andrew by the grace of God invincible King of the Hungarians; composed by Prince Béla; given by the hand of Bishop Miklós.

Előszó—Vorwort—Prologue

Driving along the highway is like a relationship without commitment. The driver is a crab in his fiberglass shell. When in need of a recharge, he ventures out furtively. A coke, a candy bar. Fill 'er up. Then back to the road. An illusion of action; speed means mastery over the curtain that controls the changing scenes of the scenery. Never bored but not involved either, yet always expectant, for any bend in the road might explode with the unexpected, the challenge, the adventure, encounters that he fears as potential might-have-beens or should-have-dones that then live on unfulfilled under the surface of his semiconscious pool of disquieting self-searchings. What he really fears is his bent for thinking the promise of the next adventure to death.

This is not to say that the scenes he contemplates from behind his windshield are not alive. Each is a siren call. Stop! Get out of the cage! Touch us, feel us, live us! He senses what his eyes see as if with all the cells of his body, but he drives on under the hypnosis of the road's center dashed in yellow. True, there are always places he must get to, deadlines, and commitments, binding even if only self-imposed. Still, in passing, he is good at soaking up sheen and shadow of view and vista. Hues and tints of distant hills that on this trip, have already started to transfigure in anticipation of the outcry of climax that will be the desert's suntide. The wistful olive greens of sage, juniper, and pinion pine about to grade to subdued blue-gray in obeisance to the high heat of the year's fulfillment that for him is midsummer.

Beyond the wind-glad, heat-open creosote bushes of the flats, the foothills steepen, and then the crags leap to their blue limit in jagged, sun-shimmering shades of gray ending in black at the skyline where the road then curves up to the next pass, the next summit. The Loneliest Road has many of those. All different and, for him, heart-tuggingly desolate, all hiding untraveled valleys behind their foothostile curtains of cliffs but with promises of unknown, beckoning treasures hidden behind the shifting, wavering outlines of heat-painted rocky imaginings.

But there is no time to pause and to unlock those secrets. And so the potential of each vista point to stop and to turn illusion to life is erased by the next turn along the transience of time that is the road. Mesmerized, he is only conscious of his helplessness that something in him that is lord over his will controls his remembering and forgetting and keeps a silent, subconscious record of each stop with gratitude and each lost nonstop with regret. This is his reality of the road, compelling, inexorable, and ineluctable, and yet with all its detours and switchbacks fatefully one-dimensional and plotless.

Of course, the story of a life run by the road may be a lament, but it is not a lamentable one, for lamentation can be its own redemption, self-therapeutic as this story is for me. If life is the road, then the road is life, and in the end, it is fun driving along it while the going is good, ever-present storm clouds and unforeseeable roadblocks notwithstanding. You see, the oneness is the clue. Once he understood his oneness with the road, he was on his way.

>Afoot and light-hearted, I take to the open road,
>Healthy, free, the world before me,
>The long brown path before me, leading wherever I choose . . .

This road that I took or which has taken me and to which I belong was and still is formative, as I sit here working on words while looking out at Bishop's Peak. *He*, the one who I have been along my road, was and still is formed like a piece being turned on a lathe to a shape that is never final until it finally is. And even then, perhaps, the flow of this tale, which may have eddied into the lives of others should they have taken an interest in it, may go on in its search for that elusive rainbow on the horizon, that never-never land of legend and fantasy that he came to call "an america."

But for now, I am using the Loneliest Highway (US 50) as the metaphorical road along which the echoes of my past resound as if they were alive in my present as I drive to an actual place of work in the desert. At least I started my story that way until the lengthening road no longer admitted this mnemonic device for further use.

It must be understood that his views, as he held then along the stages of his road that are my past, are not necessarily mine anymore at my current level of insight into all the things that make up the great causeway that all of us travel together.

Some of these views of his or even the events that he thought he saw unfolding may be questioned, but that was the way how he experienced and understood them in their time, and so, that is the way I have to report them now.

These views may be different from yours, as some that he held then are different from the ones that I hold now. This is especially true for the events of ethnic strife that were tragic in their consequences for the ones to whom he belonged and on whose side I still find myself. His views on this matter must therefore be reported the way he—and many others like him—felt them to be true, no matter how politically incorrect they may seem at this moment in time. For this moment, hopefully, is one of concord, one of the healing of new and ancient grievances. But these have to be stated the way they were and still are felt, for only if they are known and understood can they be resolved and laid to rest.

To record the process of these growing pains is the reason why I feel that I have to take the views and the sights of my road, like so many faded pictures, off the walls of that storehouse of my mind and re-store them in this marvelous, new, magnetic memory machine of mine.

San Luis Obispo, California, November 2010

vitéz Bethlenfalvay Gábor

Chapter 1

Daybreak

So then there he is on the road, the tires of his old red Toyota Civic happily hugging the hot pavement heading east. He loves to drive. On the roadside, turkey mullein and wooly *Encelia* rush by quickly. Further back, rabbit bush and sagebrush pass more leisurely, while the junipers on the distant slopes do a slow waltz with their pinion-pine partners. What his eyes take in is a palette of multicolored form, but his mind instantly transmutes this collection of shapes into a functional whole, the desert ecosystem that is his job as well as his hobby. As always, its stark, complex simplicity spellbinds his consciousness; his thoughts wander until they are no longer refining the design of his field experiment at the next station of his long string of self-imposed commitments.

This one is a research site of the Agricultural Research Service, or ARS, in the middle of one of those vast north-south passages of the Great Western Intermountain Basin, a valley flanked on both sides by mountains adorned in the spring by snowcaps at their highest north-facing slopes and peaks. But right now, he is not there yet; he has still a long way to go to get there. He becomes aware of his car radio blabbing and he turns it off. Blessed silence. Images of his plants at the work site pop back up and fade out again.

Then, as if given free rein by the silence, the internal dialogue, the despot, takes over and goes its own way. Fleetingly, as he often does, he muses, Who is doing all this thinking? Is it I or is it my brain? But as he makes no effort to follow up on the logic (or the lack of it) of this imponderable split in his identity—the controller, the boss, that inner punch card of a bundle of nerve cells—independent, autonomous, and programmed benignly to make the mechanisms of his mind manageable, opens a circuit of its own choosing and connects to an archetypal flashback.

Snapshots of childhood

And before he knows it, he is singing. A hymn, prayer, confession of his fun-loving but tragically challenged ancestors:

> Isten áldd meg a magyart   God bless the Hungarian
> Jó kedvvel, bőséggel,   With joy and abundance,
> Nyujts feléje védő kart   Grant him succor
> Ha küzd ellenséggel . . .   When he faces his enemies . . .

With that, he is off the road of the here and now and back into that bittersweet, now increasingly shadowy world that his father, who dared the big leap to the New Country as a destitute old man to join his two struggling immigrant sons, used to call the *az-ami-volt*, that-which-was, home, home, the paradise of the past that it was, while he was pushing his janitor's broom with the melodies of gypsy-band violins in his ear and daydreaming about flying home on *táltos* stallions:

> Szép vagy, gyönyörű vagy Magyarország,   Full of splendor you are, Hungary,
> Gyönyörűbb mint a nagyvilág . . .   More glorious than the wide world . . .
> Táltos paripákon odaszállunk . . .   On winged steeds we shall fly home

What is a Magyar? he muses. Is he a human being, a concept, flesh and blood, or an aberration of history, praying (always in vain) that God may bless him with good cheer and abundance? He sings the words of his old national anthem to his faithful friend, the steering wheel. This is the only time he dares to do this, for his voice is flat and toneless; he knows from early on that he cannot carry a tune. *Botfülű*, his father used to call him lovingly, referring to the unmusical arrangement of the bones in his inner ear.

Maybe if somebody had encouraged him or just let him sing along with the others in grade school, back in the Léva of his childhood memories, he would not have turned into such an introvert. Into a true introvert. An introvert transplanted now into a culture that reserves the epithet of esteem, the "true" for those it approves of, the extroverts. To a culture that glorifies competition and derides introspection.

But his friend does not mind and tune after tune bubbles up freely from some dark recess from below the gray matter of his brain. Where do they come from? From his mother's singing at her beloved piano or from dark nights lit by Boy Scout campfires or from listening to *honvéd* (homeguard) soldiers sing on the march?

The controller left no traces of their origin in his consciousness, and so as soon as his fledgling knowledge of biology permitted him to think of his mind in molecular terms, he decided that these songs, words, melodies, and the whole Magyar world woe that cries out from them were imprinted on his genes through long generations into that part of his DNA that geneticists, still lacking the data, the insight, and the foresight, mistakenly call "redundant" and that he is destined to carry through life as part of his inheritance like his brown eyes and high cheekbones, as if any of these things had some hidden survival value.

The steering wheel becomes aware of his lack of attention to the details of road imperatives and takes over to autopilot the car. No big deal; it is used to it, and it does not mind, for traffic on the Loneliest Highway is benign. The controller itself (himself?), very much part of the scene now and subject to his own innate, inalienable Magyar world woe, vacillates. It seems undecided to what room in its storehouse of memories to lead his minion's meandering mind. Discordant currents of thought fragments swirl in eddies, each trying to come out on top. Childhood images finally win out.

Like an evening of late spring. His mother is playing Liszt's *Liebesträume*. The garden is enveloped in the fragrance of lilac and acacia in bloom all over the small town where he first found himself to be himself, now a long lifetime ago. The plaintive chords of a distant bugle call wafting through mild waves of dusking evening air. They are the call to quarters of the Seventh Infantry Battalion, soon to be transferred to Kolozsvár in Erdély, Transsylvania, newly liberated from Romanian occupation but really training, without knowing it yet, to end up joining future battles somewhere on the Don or Volga. In Léva, however, the moment is still one of peace in the here and now as night is falling after a day of work:

| Este van, este van, kiki nyugalomba. | It's evening, it's evening, a time for repose. |
| Feketén bólongat az eperfa lombja... | The mulberry branches are nodding darkly... |

All of that is still palpably present for me. All I have to do is close my eyes, and that ever-present past of mine surrounds me as if it were now. Now! My brother, in far away Denver, do you remember this evening, all those evenings like this one? If you die now, I will be the only one left to know that that world ever existed. For our town is shattered, destroyed by the rages of ethnic cleansing approved by the victorious enemy. The lilac is gone, the acacias are gone, the garden is gone, the house is gone, and the melody of our mother tongue is gone from the lips of the new people who live there now, gone with the whirlwinds of war, defeat, and hatred.

Stop smoking, please, so that you may go on breathing a little longer, so that I may share this treasure with you yet another day, another week.

Distracted by his brother's illness, his thoughts are bouncing back and forth for an instant like a kayak in the rapids but then smooth out again, back to that enchanted evening with the lilacs and the bugle call, where his father is standing behind his mother at the piano. He is wearing the dark brown gold-embroidered dress uniform of a colonel of the Royal Magyar Horse Artillery. They are about to go to a reception but are delayed by the magic of the moment. He is silent and looks pensively at his wife with an expression of tenderness, trust, and respect and a unity of purpose. That look is his inheritance as is the memory of that evening. It is the way men are meant to relate to their women.

Within that fold, the boy is secure; belonging, he has no questions, no doubts. Everything will always turn out fine. Paradise owned for a moment. God is good, and His world is whole for He cares; He knows when a sparrow falls from the roof. So clearly, life can only hold love, trust, goodness, the joy of learning and knowledge, all leading to wisdom. A world view that he could not think and speak of in such terms back then, of course, but that was how he felt about it. It was a certainty, a wordless longing with the confidence of the innocent experiencing nirvana without having a name for it yet, felt with all the cells of his body like with a trillion-eared antenna receiving vibrations of an as yet unthought-of form of energy from universes that exist only in word and sightless visions.

Who knows? I sometimes wonder now that perhaps such a childhood is a detriment from the point of view of storytelling. An unrealistic, deleterious kind of preparation for what life's real world ends up holding later when the words are there to tell about it. Perhaps the *jó kedv* and *bőség* that the Magyar anthem is praying for is a double-edged sword, a cudgel that blunts the impulse, the need, and the compulsion to tell its story. Is it so perhaps because a pleasant, contented life is a story not worth telling? Who wants to hear what good fortune the writer lucked into in the midst of all the Dickensian woe of the world?

The controller, of course, did not know yet back then what I know now, as I am conspiring against the past with my accomplice, this keyboard. But as it is prescient, it must have been participating in such musings with furrowed eyebrows. For it is concerned with real life and gets goose pimpled by all that Magyar nostalgia, none of which can contribute to the essentials of life-effectiveness about which to decide is its function and competence. And so to return to the elements that make up real life (economy of effort, allocation of resources, control of competition, and the like: survival, for short), it picks up on that uniform and that bugle call and promptly the dreams of a midsummer night merge seamlessly and timelessly into the storm clouds of another set of memories.

Einstein was right (mostly). Time, as we think of it, does not exist. It is a figment of our minds. It is not constant. Only permanence is. The world always was and is, and the big bang of our universe was only a moment of singularity in

Brahma's awakening day some ten billion or more years ago. When God's eye sees past, present, and future all at once, it must all seem to be at rest to Him, while the illusion of change is reserved for us who, unlike Him, are part of the system, while He is the system itself. Everything is always there. Peace and war. And those images of war are as present for me now as they were real for him (the boy) when they happened in that "time" now "past."

That is why my story starts there, with the time when war turned into reality, slamming the gates of the first decade of innocence of his childhood shut.

War clouds

In the fall of the penultimate year of what was for him the "Great War," school was interrupted more and more often by the call of air-raid sirens in Léva. Classes were then called off for that day, but the sun of unearned freedom somehow seemed to shine coldly and reluctantly, as if uncertain of its ability to dispel the menace of that siren call. For it was not really a call. It was the shriek with which the fell specters of a child's dread of the dark tear him out of a nightmare. What the siren warned of was well known after some five years of war, although the horsemen of the apocalypse had not yet descended personally from their winged four-engine steeds that used to fly unchallenged over his peaceful little town.

While there was gradually less and less school and more and more air-raid warnings, refugees from the East started arriving in increasing numbers. All homes were opened up to these homeless home-losts, who brought with them tales that had been experienced earlier by others and that were incarnated on canvas in the visions of the Black Goya. The Guernica tales of war, of torture, rape, arson and looting by the subhuman beasts of the invading hordes as they were described by the media. And all of that was coming his way now irresistibly.

Then the Romanians surrendered, and the Red Army poured through the gap so opened in the Southern mountains along the Danube into the Nagyalföld, the Great Plains of what used to be Nagy-Magyarország, Hungary, before it lost two-thirds of its territory after the First World War. With that, Erdély, his ancestral land of forests, was cut off, and overnight, Bethlenfalva became inaccessible—the village where the big house of his summer vacations stood, where Nannyó, his Székely grandmother, was always waiting for the next visit, the house surrounded by the meadows of wildflowers that ended only in the distant forests around the jagged rocks of the Szarkakő, where the butterflies that he and his brother would follow all day came from.

The *nappali pávaszem*, the peacock's eye with its deep red rainbow wings! Mikes Kelemen must have dreamt of this meadow while walking alone on the shores of the Marmara Sea, where he followed his leader, Prince Rákóczy, into exile after their struggle for freedom was crushed by the might of the Hapsburg Empire some three hundred years ago. Zágon, the village where Mikes had been at home, was just across from Bethlenfalva, in the county of Csíkszék, on the other side of our Székely mountain range, the Hargita. He wrote home letters of loneliness and despair, as all his companions had died by and by and he was left alone to live in the distant past reality of his meadows of Zágon, replete with the vision of his childhood's butterflies.

Erdély felé mutat egy halovány csillag,	A faint star blinks over Transylvania
Hol a bércek fején hó korona chillog	Where snow-crowned peaks gleam and glitter
S a bércek aljában, tavaszi pompában	And in the valleys in spring's splendor
Virágok feselnek. Zágon felé mutat	Flowers bloom. It points towards Zágon
Hol minden virágon	Where on every flower
Tarka pillangóként első ifjúságom	Like colorful butterflies
Emléki röpködnek . . .	My childhood memories flutter . . .

On butterflies

The magic of those butterflies! Back in Léva that fall, browsing through his grandfather's library, he had found a magic book. It was kind of old even back then, dated "MDCCCII". With the meticulous, painstakingly loving effort of a less hectic era, craftsmen had prepared the woodcuts to present in minute detail the butterflies and the moths of Central Europe as described in the work of artists and of historians of nature. The caterpillars were also all there; the chrysalises hung from the appropriate plants, and the pupae of the moths rested snugly in their cocoons. Most intriguing were the largest moths, the nocturnal ones, whose caterpillars pupate in the soil, and among these, one stood out prominently, the *halálfejes*, the huge moth that bears the image of an ominous orange skull on the black background of its thorax.

He was completely enamored with those colorful creatures that could have flown off those pages had they wanted to. The book then disappeared, only to reappear later under the Christmas tree that year, with a note from his grandfather exhorting him to guard it well. He himself had collected most of its denizens more than six decades ago, the note said, and he hoped a great-grandson of his would also be able to continue the tradition using that same book.

The magic book became a bible and was studied all winter. Next spring, he no longer netted butterflies (their wings were always damaged in the process) but searched the greenery for the caterpillars. The activity was so contagious that his brother and his friends could not help but join in, forming the Society of *Nyűvészők* (caterpillarers). Knowing that the caterpillars blended in among the leaves to become near invisible, the *Nyűvészek* looked for the droppings on the ground, checked them out for freshness, and then invariably found their elusive prey in the branches above. The caterpillars were fed daily with fresh leaves, and their growth, molting, and pupating habits were observed and recorded.

Finally, he watched with awe the emergence of the metamorphed final imago, the winged wonder, from the constraint and confinement of its last imperfect stage. Now he no longer used the grooved wooden plate that his father made for him earlier to help impale the insects in preparing them for the collection. He let his charges fly off in silent little farewell ceremonies.

Don't cling, don't cling, the butterflies advised while taking wing. Clinging is losing. Cling to objects at your peril! We are not a butterfly collection. We are free spirits. We are life. Pondering the unfathomable schism between life and nonlife became a lifelong preoccupation for him. Was life perhaps an interface, the connection between some unknown primary realms that are inaccessible to our limited senses, and an elementary realm that contains all the building blocks of the material world as we know it and as we are able to measure it, which includes our own bodies and even the substance of our brains where that mysterious controller seems to reside?

"*Praestet fides supplementum sensuum defectui,*" they used to sing at church at the hour of evening devotions. But how could faith supplement, round out, or even fill the gaps of the defects or limitations of the senses? Is faith not just a wishful acceptance without proof of a phantom reality beyond the senses? Reality! Proof! He was busy with his butterflies, which were reality enough without need of proof in his childhood's Garden of Eden. But an early serpent of doubt was already lurking out there somewhere as yet unexpressed and insubstantial. Like a question mark.

Like that adder in the oak forest of Sándorhalma. He was picking chanterelles—those dark, egg-yolk colored, fragrant mushrooms—and found a group of particularly nice large fresh ones half hidden among the dry leaves at the edge of a clearing. He squatted down to start taking them when his eyes met those of the snake, the *keresztes vipera*, the viper with the pattern of the cross on his back. He was coiled up like a whole collection of question marks right in the middle of *his* newly found treasure of mushrooms and was within striking range. They looked at each other for a while. His eyes were not hostile or evil; they were cold and indifferent. He seemed to be appraising the boy. After a while, he slowly uncoiled and disappeared unhurriedly among the leaves. "You can have your mushrooms now," he said in parting.

More war clouds

But I digress. The late fall of that year, the last full year of his Great War, wore on, and as if the sky itself wanted to participate in it with an endless deluge of cold tears, it rained all the time through November. He would sit at the windows of his favorite alcove jutting out from the living room of his grandfather's house, watching the large trees of its small park sway in the wind that made the cold, dreary cloud fragments chase each other in the already wintry sky. It was still warm and cozy inside, with fire lighting up reassuringly the chill gloom of forebodings that was creeping in through the windows. But that gloom was now not only a result of the weather. Some days earlier, the first murmurs, whisperings, and sighs of the war could be discerned ever so vaguely, maybe more like a gentle trembling of the earth than a sound.

However, that mournful though still distant mutter made the battlefield a palpable reality for the first time. That by itself would have perhaps come across more like the unease that a war movie always evokes in those with a firsthand acquaintance with war had it not been accompanied by sightings of the Stalin Organ.

Now the Stalin Organ was well known from the German war films. Not nearly as lethal as the pride of modern warfare, the blockbuster bomb nor nearly as accurate as today's sophisticated guided missiles, but a fearsome sight it was to behold in the dark nevertheless. A dozen or so of these rockets could be fired off rapidly from their parallel tube launchers, and on their way together to their destination, they described high arcs in the black sky, giving off a hellishly scary red glare. Those rockets' red glare had no association yet for him with the gallantry of streaming flags in the night back then. Those rockets were not poetic, just deadly. His search for America was not yet on.

Still the rockets were not only deadly; they were also beautiful like fireworks are beautiful, if I may dare now, with the insight of all these years of hindsight, to combine esthetics with terror in the same sentence. Of course, those red-glaring rockets were not spectacular and entertaining like Fourth of July fireworks are, but still they held a fearsome fascination, the sort of sensation that young men experience when they sign up to go to war, immersed in that gloriously exulting flush of feeling, of valor in action beyond the call of duty, of a hero's return home from the gates of hell, and of that blissful denial of the terror that lurks when that blood red rocket in the air finally comes down and hits home.

Home

Home, that warm, sunlit house of his summers in Sándorhalma, only a couple of hours drive by horse-drawn carriage from Léva. It is surrounded by a huge, parklike garden inhabited mainly and ruled over decidedly by his little bantam rooster with that blood red comb on his head. Beyond the garden, on the one side, was a vegetable garden with long rows of beds interspersed with fruit trees and with a greenhouse complex at the far end. On the other side, the *tyúk udvar*, with its fifty or so Rhode Island red hens (whose eggs he collects every morning) and with the pigeon coops on high poles that would provide the most delicious part of a Sunday feast. Ah, roast pigeon . . .

Then uphill, behind the house, were fields sown in poppies that last summer before those blood red rockets came to usher in Christmas. Beyond the fields was his oak forest, large enough to get completely lost in (and endless fun to get lost in first so that one may then find one's way out later) and full of red *szamóca*, wild strawberries, in the clearings in the spring and with profusions of *rókagomba*, chanterelles, mostly anytime but especially in the fall.

Now let's linger on for a moment with the *rókagomba*, for it is a true gift of the gods. It is a fragrant, deep orange mushroom whose savor is most pungent when its hyphae are associated with the roots of oak trees (a *datum* that he was not yet aware of then). When prepared with sour cream and paprika, with a few chunks of *kolbász*, the hard Magyar garlic sausage thrown in for flavor enhancement, it is ambrosia for gods and Magyars alike. It is savored best as a second course after soup. Followed but not to be outdone by, ah, that roast pigeon as the next course.

Little did he know then of (or about) things like being hungry. And when you are hungry as a habit, you tend to face strings of other hardships also as if to keep the growling of your stomach company. Marina knows or senses when I am about to write a sentence like this, and then she gives me background literature to read up on the subject. Like that book by Székely János about the tribulations of an orphan, composed in the Dickensian style. Such tales are visceral and seem to be—who knows why—highly readable.

Tribulations

And that will bring me to tribulations as one of my next, hopefully readable subjects. You see, when you see those red rockets, it means that the front lines are very close. And so they were by the end of November, but then there was a counter offensive. The Magyar Szent László Division and two German Waffen-SS divisions drove back the Soviets in the sector north of the Danube from Léva toward Losonc and Kassa, and there was a moment of respite. Of course, remember that such data like all else that he saw and heard and would someday (now) try to relate and pass on, are not an accurate researched report on history but a matter of memories, and this particular one is that of a child, at that point in time not yet eleven years old.

A child, however, who had an army brat's fascination with the wall-size situation map in his father's study and who followed avidly all of the grown-ups' discussions of the front lines as they moved back and forth on that abstraction that was a huge map of Russia. The Prut, the Dniester, the Bug, the Doniets, the Don, the Volga! The victorious dash of the anti-Soviet armies toward Stalingrad and then perhaps on to the oilfields on the Caspian Sea? That was how they all felt about it at first. Except for his father.

The war had not even started yet when at some meeting of the general staff, he explained to everyone's consternation that it was impossible for Germany to win it. And Magyarország, tragically sandwiched in between the two great powers of the East and the West, had to choose between them. It chose what it saw to be the lesser evil, Germany, for things look different from close up than from far away like from across an ocean. "No dedication, bravery, and patriotism could stand up to what was delineating itself as the great enemy alliance," he said, "for that alliance would have a superiority of ten to one in personnel and a hundred to one in matériel. Numbers do not lie, only people do," he went on. "And it is the numbers that win wars."

So what could they do with a maverick like that? They retired him and sent him in an administrative function to Léva (though still in uniform) to captain the *Vitézi Szék* there, the regional chapter of the *Vitézi Rend*, the Order of Valor. As a member, he had been granted land at Sándorhalma, near Léva, for bravery in the previous Great War.

Léva had been a Magyar settlement since the conquest of the Carpathian Basin some eleven hundred years ago. It was also the birthplace of his (the boy's) mother and the home of his grandparents. It was the bright, to this day, sunlit stage of his childhood years until in early December of that fateful year (1944), the front lines moved back to hearing range again.

Childhood memories

Those were five blessed, magical years that wafted by on the wings of his butterflies and will linger on lightly, sweetly, and gracefully, without the need of clinging, to his last breath. How such realities of the past can come to life again miraculously, if their memory is not permitted to get lost in the rush of the moment to be covered by the garbage of daily chores in the landfill of oblivion, was brought home to me by an unexpected gift.

Those five years of his in Léva were resurrected even more vividly during the course of this writing by a set of notes of his grandfather, completed and dated seventy years ago (in 1936, when he was going on eighty, seventy-eight to be exact). I had these notes for quite a while, hidden somewhere among my books, unread. Then rummaging around for something insignificant, I ran across them.

Well, the process that followed in my mind upon reading them was akin to something that he had observed once in a high school chemistry lab. Upon slowly and carefully cooling the disorganized mix of ions of a warm saturated salt solution, all of a sudden the bright, smooth, and perfectly aligned reality of a crystal emerged in the beaker, quick as a flash of lightning as if from nowhere. Reading those notes of my grandfather's was like that instant of phase change in the beaker for me by revealing my early years in a new light. This is how he had come by those ancient notes, and this is how the notes survived like a message in a bottle floating from coast to coast at sea.

After he left Léva on his family's Odyssey westward, his grandfather's house was sacked and plundered by a mob in the wake of liberation by the Red Army. What the looters did not take with them was trampled and left on the street. As fate would have it, however, a former patient of his grandfather (who identified himself as Siepak Miklós, resident of Léva, on the book's first page) passed by and picked up a bound volume that turned out to be these handwritten notes of my grandfather's childhood memories.

How the soiled manuscript then found its way to my aunt, Zsuzsi *néni* in Losonc, I do not know. But her daughter (Zsuzsi II, my cousin) passed it on to her daughter (Zsuzsi III) who transcribed them later to a CD, and her daughter (Zsuzsi IV) sent it to me when she came to study in the United States. I then ran off a hard copy of it and filed it away somewhere. Until at the prescribed moment, the notes emerged from the recesses of my bookshelves at the right time like Bilbo's Ring of Doom and bade me add some of my grandfather's lines to mine (which were really provoked by his) as his contribution to the ongoing family saga.

"Soborsin!" my grandfather writes (and I translate from Magyar). "How dearly this word echoes from the soul of this old man, my soul! The name of this small provincial town! Dearly, since those four years that we spent there in undisturbed peace, were the brightest years of my childhood. I was six years old when we arrived there, at the age when new impressions root most deeply in a child's soul. This is the reason why my thoughts like to return there like a bird to its nest . . . Oh, where is the Gligania with its centuries-old oak trees . . . Where are you, the *Cukorhegy* [sugar-loaf mountain], with your crags hidden among the sloe and hazelnut bushes . . . Where are the meadows on your slopes full of fragrant flowers . . . and where are you, radiant sunshine, that suffused all those things with a golden glow, with a radiance that still warms my old heart and soul whenever it finds its way back into those years of yore . . ."

You see, my grandfather described in this way my own magic years in Léva, mirror images of his own, which he lived and enjoyed some seventy years before I was born! Following this passage come details upon details of that small child's memory fragments, and I cannot help the eerie feeling that I had once lived those very same details myself, although the events that come to life upon my reading them had lived and died many decades before he was reexperiencing them in his own here and now then, in his own new present that is now yet another seventy years past and that was ending in those days in the convulsions of war.

Back to the war

Although those ominous front lines were like black storm clouds overhead, like the lingering thought of a seriously ill loved one overshadows all the routines of a busy everyday day in one's mind, today was a day like those bright ones before the cloud. Even the rain had let up for the occasion, and school was on since there was no air-raid alarm. As the Latin teacher came in, the class snapped to attention, for he was a war hero. He had already been popular when they called him up, a man in his early fifties, to go and fight the enemy. At that time in May, the front seemed still far away, somewhere near places whose names sounded like Orel, Kursk, or Kharkov.

In his class, nobody minded memorizing Latin irregular verbs. "Latin is important," we would say. "To be really articulate, you need to know some Latin to understand the structure of a language, either to learn a foreign one or to use your own properly. But Latin is more than that. It is a construct of logic," he used to repeat. "If you know its rules and exceptions, you can solve the puzzles that each complex sentence represents, sentences written two thousand years ago by Julius Caesar. And you will need this method of deductive reasoning for math, engineering, and business, everything in the life of an educated person." He explained the why, and the class liked it.

He was gone all summer, and in September, when school started, he was back. With one leg missing. How he made it back, a convalescing cripple, through the convulsions of defeated, retreating armies and through hunger, fear, incessant partisan attacks and air strikes, outrunning the ever more rapid enemy advance, he would not say. What he said on that day was that prepositions were crucial parts of a sentence, and since in Latin, prepositions governed different cases, one would have to know which ones required the accusative, dative, or genitive. "And to be really adept at that, you must memorize them. For the next time, therefore, you will have mastered the ones with the accusative by heart:

> Ante, apud, ad, adversus,   Contra, erga, extra, infra,
> Circum, circa, citra, cis.   Intra, inter, iuxta, ob, . . .

The next day also started cloudless. The first class was math. Equations with one unknown, standard fare for starting sixth graders. But there was no second hour. The Latin teacher came in and spoke quietly. "Everybody outside, into the yard. Formation in military columns by class. The principal wants to speak to you." Then the principal spoke. It was a short speech. "The enemy is near. You are not safe here. Go home. Make yourself useful there. Read your books. That way, you will not fall behind when we open up again. God bless Magyarország and our brave soldiers. See you again soon."

But that school never opened again. The region with its Magyar population was awarded by the vindictive victors as a prize to the neighboring state that had positioned itself on the winning side. The town was thereupon ethnically cleansed. Latin, or Magyar for that matter, was not taught there again, and his teacher, whose name, I shamefully admit, I cannot recall, was on the road again. *Vae victis*, woe to the vanquished, he might have added as an afterthought to the director's speech.

The end of innocence

A few days later, he (the boy) made his first real acquaintance with what was to become the road. Not that he had not moved before. He was born in Miskolc, where his father commanded the Seventh Royal Magyar Artillery Regiment. Three years later, his father was transferred to Budapest to head the artillery school of the military academy, the Ludovika Akadémia, and from there, they moved on to Léva. But these moves did not involve the road as he came to know it later; the controller left him with no memory of any of their details.

But then there came Léva, the town of lilacs and acacias, the town of his memories, the town folk songs speak of:

Tele van a város akácfa virággal,	Our town is awash with acacia blossoms,
Akácfa virágnak édes illatával...	With the sweet fragrance of acacia flowers...

This was the stage of his life that fixed itself in his mind as if his town had indeed been always awash with the white petals of acacia flowers blowing in the wind like snow.

Léva, home of deep family roots! His grandfather, Máriusz Karafiáth, was one of the founders of the town's first modern hospital, where he practiced as chief physician till his death. Everyone in town knew him and his children and even his grandchildren after they moved back there. The Karafiáths are first mentioned in 1618 and had migrated to Magyarország from Moravia. In the course of the rapidly passing years, they became as Magyar as Magyar can be (or maybe even more so as is often the case with newcomers to an old country). And *ópapa* married a woman of the local aristocracy whose ancestors had come with the last (the third one after the Huns and the Avars) conquering wave of Magyars from the East more than a thousand years ago and had settled near Léva in Kereskény. So he had heard the story told by his grandmother.

Those were always happy outings to that old ancestral family mansion with its vast park that had been the home of my grandmother, Majláth Borbála. Roaming all day in the fields and the forests was one thing, but being minded like celebrities everywhere by the peasants who had been serfs in earlier times but who still were (and felt like being) integral parts of the estate was an entirely different feeling. Magyarország was a living anachronism in this respect, one that had remained pseudo-feudal in many aspects of its societal structure all the way into the twentieth century along its rough and rocky road through the adversities of its history until its road as a kingdom came to its end with the end of the Second Great War.

Chapter 2

The Refugee

The first leg of the long road

When he hit that road, the road that ended the fairy-tale kingdom of his childhood on that cold and frosty morning two weeks before Christmas 1944, there was nothing really very unusual about it at first. The going was good by car on a strangely deserted side road like other trips in the past to Losonc, Babád, or Budapest. But this time, the driver, a sergeant assigned to his father (a young lawyer in real life, for everyone was in uniform in those days), advised that their gasoline would last only till Szenc, the last Magyar village this side of the Slovak border. Slovakia, you may want to recall, was a brand-new concept created by the Germans after the dismemberment of Czechoslovakia in 1938. The redrawing of the borders returned an area inhabited by close to a million Magyars to Magyarország and established Slovakia to the north as a quasi-independent state.

But there was a matter of greater urgency right now than the perennial agony over the shifting of the border, that artificial demarcation line on the ground that for a brief moment in history at that time reflected quite fairly the distribution of ethnicities on either of its sides. That matter was the fact that there was no more gasoline to be had.

Few things were more precious than gasoline in those days. Gold, maybe, but you could not use it to make your vehicle move. By the martial law, that was the rule; if there was any to be found, it could be used only for military or essential civilian administrative purposes. But somehow, maybe because of his father's uniform, their move to Szenc fell into one of those categories. He was well aware of the inconsistencies of the situation, and so, in an ominous way, this move did not seem to fit after all into the pattern of previous vacation trips. It would end in Szenc, wherever that was, and then what with those Stalin Organs following closely behind? It felt like an adventure, but it had eerily discordant overtones to it.

They got to Szenc by nightfall and occupied a desolate, little decrepit room at the edge of the village. That room was the first real break with life as he used to know it. It was dawning on him gloomily that he had no inkling of what was coming up next, except that it was bound to be an ill wind, and a cold one, that was going to blow from now on. And it was more than an inkling that told him that it was going to be up to him to make it blow any good for him, pampered, *bourgeois*, upper-class mama's boy that he was or rather had been up to then.

How can I get anybody to understand that feeling, that mood, that break in the cosmic eggshell that the windings of his gray matter had been conditioned to recognize as whole and inviolable for those long, first almost eleven years of his? For those who shared those times with him and later times also for that matter, his friends and classmates, are now all gone probably, resting, sleeping, no longer sharing their bygone memories.

> Where are Guisztó, Arnold, Erwin, Klaus, Tell and Dieter,
> The weak of will, the strong of arm, the clown, the boozer, the fighter?
> All, all, are sleeping on the hill.

Are any of those old geezers like me still hanging on? Do you remember that feeling, my brother, across the Rockies in faraway Denver? Do you remember that room in Szenc, empty except for those few suitcases, the remnants of our glory life of old? What do we, you and I, recall of those first days on the road?

The lake with that fish frozen into its foot-thick layer of ice on the outskirts of Szenc? Remember the *Török Ház*, the manor in the middle of the village whose owner asked us to move there, seeing the plight of our mother, but more likely because he felt that the edge of town was for gypsies, not recognizing yet that that was what we actually had become already, homeless refugees, notwithstanding the uniform of the Royal Magyar Army that our father still wore? What you surely remember is how bravely our mother bore this unbearably light new state of being, lying on that wooden army cot, dying slowly of leukemia.

The first-way station

In the meantime, against all odds, the young lawyer-sergeant unearthed a bucketful of gas somewhere in exchange for some pipe tobacco that they had with them as an exchange medium, for paper money had lost its meaning by then. He duly reported this remarkable feat to his (the boy's) father. They could then have gone on at least to Pozsony, the capital of the new Slovakia, just across the border, but they had a covered wagon coming behind, driven by their stable master, an old soldier of his father's from the previous Great War who had settled with them at Sándorhalma, their new estate near Léva.

He had been told to find them in Szenc when he got there. The wagon was important, for it held the provisions and trunks packed with the necessities for what might become a long journey, although they could not possibly imagine how long it would turn out to be in the end. So they decided to wait for that wagon in Szenc rather than to go on to Pozsony. And so his father nodded his appreciation to the sergeant. "Take the car, my son, consider it to be yours. Go back to your family in Léva, take off that uniform, and mind those Stalin Organs on your way back."

The wagon actually found them soon afterward, and what was left of their earthly goods accumulated through generations found its way into the basement of the Török Ház. Then his father embraced his old comrade-in-arms. "*Siess haza fiam mielött a muszka megint elvág*," he told him. "My son, hurry home before the Russians cut you off again. The Russians had done that once before somewhere on the eastern front in Galicia some thirty years ago. They were the same age, going on sixty, but that was how Magyar social classes related to each other back then: cordially and respectfully, especially if they could look back on shared experiences of hardship and danger.

"The horses and wagon are yours, *Isten veled kedves öreg katonám*. God be with you, my dear old soldier." They both acted as if they did not see that they were crying, although showing emotions was acceptable behavior in that society. Kocsis István was the man's name. He became a member of the *Vitézi Rend* (the Order of Valor), although he had started out in the previous Great War in 1914 as a private, as the officer's servant of the boy's father. Officers were gentlemen then and needed someone to serve their coffee and shine their boots even when they were actually in combat. They went through that war together; Kocsis István made sergeant in time and later continued to work for his father at the estate in Sándorhalma.

But for him (the boy), this simple giving away of things (cars and horses were things of great value) as an act of shaking them off when they finished serving their purpose was a lesson for life. Not that things had no value. He was soon to learn the value of things like a change of dry socks after sloshing through wintry slush. Objects, possessions, are a fleeting, incidental, ephemeral aspect of one's path, encumbrances that come and go, appear and vanish, like the milestones along the road passed by a speeding car. *Don't cling*, the road was lecturing. *Don't cling, for possessions crush your spirit.*

When the time came, they moved on to Pozsony after all. It was only a short stretch of the road there, and the controller did not make a record of the details of this move. They stayed till the end of March or early April. I am not sure now how long exactly they tarried in that beautiful old city on the Danube, capital of

Magyarország, for a while in the Middle Ages. Then, in the winter of 1944—1945, it seemed to be about equally divided of tongue between Magyar, German, and Slovak.

It was resistance to the bloody siege of Budapest by the Red Army that had stabilized the front that long. It lasted over two months, and it left its scars on that city to this day, more than sixty years later. Pozsony was spared the bombing, but armadas of the four-engine monsters flew over it almost daily with impunity. As they flew, the German flak would pump out hundreds of rounds at them that exploded in midair like puffs of little black clouds. But during the entire war, he never saw a single one of those bombers hit and brought down.

The bear

Then time came to hit the road again, although there was no rumbling to be heard yet in the east. But there was a window of opportunity to move. The German area commander, a friendly sort of fellow and an old acquaintance of his father from bygone days of peace, offered to help evacuate the Magyar Embassy in Pozsony. That was how he found a place in the back of that large German Army truck. The truck had one curious aspect, and because the controller recorded it in such detail, it must have ascribed significant survival values to it, so my keyboard agreed to record it also.

That truck had no gas tank. Having suffered from the prolonged dearth and then total lack of gasoline to feed it, it must have decided at one point to reabsorb that now useless organ. Or else it sloughed it off (don't cling) at one time of crisis or other and then regrew it as a curious appendage on the side of the driver's cabin. This new appendage was a largish, perforated, cylindrical metal container in which dry wood shavings would start to slowly roast and simmer whenever its masters were asking the truck to move, or more precisely, the process seemed to be a precondition for moving. The heated material then gave off some form of flammable wood gas that was somehow conducted and piped to the pistons to explode there like gasoline (or diesel) would have. But significantly and perhaps that is how the controller got involved in all this, this contraption had an unintended but, for him, benevolently foreordained survival effect: it served as a splendid space heater as he was leaning against the cab of the truck, back there in the icy wind of that unseasonably cold early spring.

So it was that he made it through Bécs (Vienna), the once-proud capital of an empire now clouded in the dust and the smoke of yet another carpet bombing that must have rolled through it not long before his truck did. A few people were emerging from the basements of the ruins, dazed but somehow inured like soldiers must look after years in the trenches. Although fires were burning everywhere, the main component of the reek that forever incrusted itself on his brain's olfactory center was not the stench that is given off when the contents of peoples' homes burn (including the people themselves) but that acrid quality that air has when pulverized particles of cement are suspended in it. Nothing evokes memories as strongly as odors, and he will meet this same stench again in Léva decades later at the ruins of his grandfather's house. Except for the thick air, however, the road was empty, cleared by the bombs for the time being so that all the truck had to do was to maneuver around the new craters.

The driver, a *Wehrmacht* corporal with that air of death-intimacy of the cannon-fodder foot soldier about him, remarked chuckling that they were lucky; rarely would one find one's way through Vienna traffic so easily. As the truck roared and sputtered out of the suburbs (as if that wood gas were giving its innards chronic indigestion), the road, apparently the main highway west toward Linz, was gradually filling up with an outlandish assortment of humankind that reminded him vaguely of Romanian gypsy caravans he had seen in Erdély, only vast, seemingly endless in scope and robotlike in nature.

It was a spring tide of refugees fleeing west. Moving like a river does after a flash flood, hurling and dragging with it the washed-away debris of humanity's pitiful possessions. Occasionally military convoys would hog their way eastward in the center of the road, pushing carts, coaches, horses, mules and foot plodders into the ditches. Occasionally also, military police would demand his truck's marching orders, eyeing him and his brother with their civilian-looking belongings in the hold of the truck suspiciously. But they never failed to salute politely his father's colonel's insignia in the cab.

This was, as I remember it now, the road to end all roads. It was the quintessential road, the distilled essence of the road experience. He had the feeling that not even his father, who up to this point in time, had been a rock of purposeful forethought in his eyes, had any idea where they were heading and where they might end up. It was as if the road itself was leading the way. And strangely, it occurs to me as I am writing this down that I never asked him later whether he knew or at least had some thought of a plan, and so I do not know it now as I pause to look out of my study's window on Bishop's Peak to think about it. Perhaps the truck's papers contained a destination clause, giving it a purpose in the torrent of purposelessness that was raging all around them, in the middle of which, the truck, like a bear chased by a pack of dogs, suddenly veered off the road into a position of defilade next to a deep road cut, with trees protecting it from the front and the rear.

The smiling god

The corporal with his dry chuckle (that was actually hard to tell from sobbing) must have been well used to this sort of maneuver in quick-think, for the bear hadn't even come to its screeching halt when he was already out of the cab and in the ditch, as if to demonstrate to his passengers by wordless personal example what the correct military posture was in situations like this. Clearly his ears were calibrated to the sounds that fighter planes make on the chase. Then they all heard the staccato chatter of that machine gun, and instantly the ditches filled up brimful with humanity.

As he (the boy) lay there in the cold, smelly effluents of that ditch, his main feeling was incredulity. This could not be. That plane had a star painted on its wing, but it was not a red star. Those with red stars were capable of anything, and that was exactly the thing, he knew, that they had decided to escape from. Maybe it was trying to get the bear, mistaking it to be some menace to its own kind? That kind, sputtering old bear that was only trying to take him to safety, wherever safety was! But he was well camouflaged, hidden by the road cut and the trees. The bullets were meant to hit elsewhere. They hit the people in the ditch. And when it was all over, some of those people, it seemed to him, just thoughtfully decided not to crawl out again. But then some of the horses were hit also, and those horses did not hold their horses' tongues. The sounds a dying horse makes are mind curdling, and there were several of them shrieking out the accusations of their death agony, while the people were mostly, as it seemed to him, quiet. Silent.

As for him, on the other hand, the world was in turmoil. This was his first experience in denial. He simply could not believe it. He wanted to go to the cadets' school in Kőszeg and become a soldier, an officer, himself when he grew up. Soldiers had a code of honor. Soldiers respected a brave enemy. Soldiers were chivalrous. Attacking the unarmed was outrageous. Shooting at civilians was unthinkable.

Then there it was again. Swooping by with guns blazing and flying so low that he could see its face. Could he really see the face of that which sat at the controls of that plane? Stressful situations can play tricks with your senses and perceptions. But he did not feel stressed. He was not even scared, for he did not have time to become afraid; so sudden was the onslaught of this new aspect of the universe happening to him.

Everything was happening so quickly that he only had time to feel puzzled, for he was encountering an intrinsic contradiction of the kind he had never experienced before. For what the controller in his brain, the amygdala and the hippocampus, had recorded was that that face was smiling. Not even maliciously. It just seemed to be enjoying the sport. Perhaps for it, sitting safely up there, the world that it saw down here had lost its reality.

Perhaps that is the essence of power. The powerful live by different rules, march to different drums, answer to different standards, and are judged by different codes. What they do is right by definition. Their definition. When they do it, it is right and good. When others do it, it is wrong and evil. When they win, they become heroes. When they lose, they are hanged.

Of course, he did not think of all this in such terms then, lying in that ditch, but that must have been the concept that his mind was beginning to form nonetheless, in the same slow, hesitant, exploratory, and yet ineluctably and undeviatingly goal-seeking manner in which caterpillars have no choice but to form pupae on their way to their fulfillment as butterflies.

Stalingrad

With the incident over (*noch einmal glimpflich davongekommen*, the corporal chuckled), they moved on and made it to the outskirts of Linz. It was a hill, a flat-topped rise, from where the city and the Danube behind it could be seen clearly, especially with his father's military binoculars. The site was actually a farmyard overgrown with weeds, spacious enough for the three well-positioned, medium-sized bomb craters that somehow missed the farmhouse and the barn that, in that part of the world, forms the rear end of those two-story farmhouses. The *Wehrmacht* sergeant, the other member of our escort, took us there because it was the home of his best buddy, a soldier who went on to Stalingrad while he himself was granted emergency leave to bury a bomb-victim family member.

With Stalingrad mentioned, the sergeant and his father fell to discussing the fate of the German Eighth Army, and neither of them had kind words for its commander, Generaloberst Paulus, who had begged Hitler to let him move his overexposed positions back from the Volga. But nobody won arguments with Hitler, and the front remained in its untenable position until it finally met its doom and was crushed. "*Wo der deutsche Soldat einmal steht, da bleibt er*" was Hitler's position on the matter, and yes, the sergeant said, Hitler turned out to be right, his buddy did stay in Stalingrad. Frozen to stone in the ice storms ravaging Russia in those days or shredded to mincemeat by the Soviet artillery. "*Ja, Stalingrad . . . Dort haben wir den Krieg verloren*," mused the sergeant. I remember his words clearly after half a century. "Yes, we lost the war in Stalingrad," he said.

Many historians would agree with that, but now as I write this down, another related snippet just surfaced from the pool of my mind's scrapbook. Someone asked Eisenhower, by then president, what the greatest achievement of his career had been. "The defeat of Nazi Germany," he declared pompously.

While he was out there, somewhere on the Don, the sergeant continued to relate, he met up a couple of times with soldiers of the Magyar Second Army that was annihilated by the same Soviet winter offensive in its positions north of the German Eight. He could not understand how those *Madjaren* made it out there to the Don. They had no ammunition, no vehicles, no tanks, no winter clothes and no food. Their horses had died or they ate them along the way out there—*alles war verrückt, verrückt, verrückt.*

All this *Verrücktheit*, lunacy, reminded him (the boy) of his high school teacher, making his way home through that same crazed world back there in order to assign those Latin prepositions with the accusative for him to memorize. And he felt determined more than ever to know them when school would open again. "*Penes, pone, post et praeter, prope, propter, per, secundum, supra, versus, ultra, trans*," he repeated over and over again like an incantation to exorcise the demons that were about to materialize above them.

And sure enough, presently, the air-raid sirens started wailing down there in Linz. The corporal chimed in to add his two cents' worth to the conversation: "Maybe they'll manage to hit another strategic target this time," and pointed across the craters to a few scrawny chickens with a rooster and the cow in the barn that the wife of the sergeant's dead buddy was milking to be able to offer her guests something to drink. The rooster, hearing the sirens, decided to participate and crowed. Wonder what my little rooster is doing back there in Sándorhalma, he thought. Is anybody left there to feed him?

The rooster experience

Relating to his rooster had been a soul-core-forming experience during those formative years of his. The rooster had appeared one day in the garden of his house in Léva. It was not a present expressly for him; his mother just thought one day, seeing it for sale somewhere, that it (along with that little black hen) would be a nice addition to the garden. But the *kis kakas*, the roosty, was not just another pet. It was a jewel, and it soon became the apple of his eye. A little bantam jungle fowl, he had a blood red comb and big snow white eyespots on the sides of his face. His hackles flowed down toward his back like molten gold, and there the feathers turned into a deeper, redder mantle of glimmering bronze. Black wings and a jauntily curved black tail all suffused with iridescent emerald hues set off its whole magic apparition as the incarnate fragment of a rainbow.

He was entirely enchanted with this newcomer. They started to speak to each other on first sight. The roosty wore an earnest but friendly expression in his benignly clever eyes and had the demeanor of a gentleman of high birth. Then one day in spring, they both (Pityu, the roosty, and Kati, his hen) disappeared, and he was disconsolate. There was no nook that he did not search, but all crannies came out empty until he decided to climb down into the basement (accessible only from the outside) to derive some consolation from one of the leftover pears from last year's harvest that were stored there, as they kept well through the winter down there in that cool, dry darkness.

There he was greeted by that subdued "kotkot*kot*kotkot" that he knew by then to mean, "Here I am and make no fuss about it." Pityu sat on the edge of the shelving that held the pears, and behind him sat Kati in a basket filled with twigs and dry leaves. Pityu did not think it necessary to stand up; he just looked at him with his head inclined sideways, the way roosters do when they want to look at something closely, for chickens cannot focus forward with both eyes (just to let you know this factoid in case you are not familiar with them). Then he went on to say something else that is hard to transliterate verbatim into people-speak, but what he did clearly mean to say was that what he (the boy) was witnessing was a significant event to be appreciated accordingly, namely that Kati was sitting on a clutch of egglets and that she was really hungry and thirsty by now, after five days of hiding.

He (Pityu) would not budge from guarding and defending (if necessary) his family, but since he (the boy) could be trusted, why didn't he go to provide some victuals right now? He (Pityu) told him all these still sitting down. Later, as he continued to guard his chicklets in the garden, he (the boy) asked him once if he had given it any thought how those downy little feather balls of his would have negotiated the steep stairs of the basement without his (the boy's) help. But Pityu sidestepped the answer as he had scratched up some juicy bit of live chicken feed just then and had to call the family urgently with a loud *tyuk-tyuk-tyuk* (*tyúk*, by the way, means "hen" in both Magyar talk and rooster talk).

Yes, that's the way he was. Chivalrous. All the tidbits he found he turned over to his family, and when a cat or a dog chanced by and became interested in the family, he would fight them off with a flash of purple fury that they learned to respect like the sharp spurs on the back of his legs. The only thing he feared were the raptors of the sky that he was an expert in spying out with one eye turned upward. He then sounded his warning, a shrill but low-pitched *krrrrrrr* that sent the family scurrying for shelter. He (the boy) did not even have to look up anymore to see the hawk wheeling high up there when he heard the warning, for the hawk was always there when Pityu warned.

Bombs, hornets, and more bombs

Just as they were always there when the sirens called. Up there like those four-engine raptors whose presence evoked those siren calls just then. The raptors (liberators, as he later learned they were called) seemed to come from the southeast this time (judging by the direction the bear had come from and by the course of the river down there beyond the city), and they were flying directly over that hill with the farmhouse on their way to their target down below. Then the flak opened up. As the shells burst in air, the sky was again painted in that pointillist technique with the little black dots of the smoke puffs that always reminded him of his mother's Seurat print over her bed at home. Again, like so often in Pozsony, none of those raptors were hit as they flew on inexorably undisturbed, like fate itself, in their imperturbable formations.

It seemed to him that they didn't even need to unleash their load of terror to commit their carnage; so overpowering was their mere presence. There were (seemed to be) hundreds of them. Space itself was rent into its individual particles, all vibrating at random by the din the raptors made, and he had the feeling that the ground under him picked up on those deep, quaking waves of menace and was quivering in sympathy or defiance or just with the impersonal disdain of the inanimate for the flesh. Yes, those airplanes were not at all like birds of prey that soar silently and gracefully, it came to him; they were not at all like hawks or eagles. What they resembled much more were huge insects. They were like hornets.

Yes, that is what they were like, hornets. The hornets. The hornets of that old hollow willow tree on the far side of the Bolgár Truck Farm, way beyond his house on the edge of town, at the end of the Kákasor (the street where he lived) in Léva. It was a hollow road, more like a path, lined with willow trees that formed one of the boundaries of this truck farm that supplied all the vegetables for the town.

The path ended at a small chapel next to the Rákóczy fa, the ancient linden tree under which Prince Rákóczy Ferenc, the revolutionary hero of the eighteenth century uprising against the Austrians, had slept during one of his campaigns. In those days, it seems, princes not proletarians were the revolutionaries, but then that was not yet class warfare but a war of national liberation. It failed because the nation was divided, and its defeat left the Austrians to rule the land liberated from the Turks previously by yet another Christian coalition of yore.

That coalition got rid of one tyrant, the Sultan in Istanbul, only to replace him with another, the *Kaiser* in Bécs, just as our present "coalition" got rid of Saddam in Baghdad to replace him most likely with a new dictator whose name we do not know yet. But even back then, the Western armies probably did their deeds in the name of higher values and virtues. "For freedom and democracy," we would say today, although I do not know how history recorded such things over two hundred years ago. Maybe then they did not mind turning their phrases more truthfully after all: "We took it because we wanted to and because we could." Someone like Metternich might have said it that way. You see, whichever way you turn your phrase, what always happens is a power grab when would-be liberators lose their way.

Well, as I was saying, that hollow tree had this hornet's nest in it, and the comings and goings of those hornets intrigued him to no end. Now, hornets, if you have not seen one, are about four times bigger than wasps; otherwise, they are clad in the same black—and yellow-striped jackets as their smaller kin. They have the deep, sonorous voice of a bass viol when they fly, and if two or three of them sting you, you might die. He knew this, but he just could not help but throw that rock into the hollow of that tree. The tempest that came out of that hole then was a vivid foretaste of the liberators (the airplanes, not the Austrians). The normally placid drone of the individual hornet gave way to the angry, high-pitched, vengeful onslaught of the swarm.

Drawing from its evolutionary past, the controller instantly summoned up the instinctively correct course of action. Before he could think, *What now?* he was already half submerged in the patch of swamp grass on the other side of the path. The winged menace checked him out, but it failed to identify him as the culprit, and eventually, it gave up and settled down again. But there was no evolutionary precedent to counter the new menace that droned up there in the air now. He could have cowered down into some hole again, into one of those bomb craters, maybe, but the spectacle that enfolded down below held him standing up, spellbound.

With the binoculars, he could see the hatches of those flying fortresses open and then follow the graceful parabolic path of the released cargo down to its destination. The utter unreality of what he saw almost gave him the feeling that the spectacle that ensued then was somehow meant to entertain or educate or indoctrinate him as war films did in the past. Pictures like those black and gray medieval etchings swirled up in his mind like the one by Dürer called *Ritter, Tod und Teufel* (*Knight, Death and Devil*), which impressed him deeply when he saw it first. But he had not been informed yet by any spin doctor that the holocaust he was watching, that scene down there from one of the very last acts of the great tragic play of his time, was rather meant to serve the benevolent and humanitarian purpose of shortening the war and to save (American) lives thereby.

He would not have understood then and I must admit that he never really learned to understand later that lives have different values depending on the pigment of their skin, the language of their tongue, the color of their uniform, and the purposes of their masters. What mattered at the moment was the spectacle. It was different from fireworks in that it lacked color (to start with, at least). Most of the explosions produced a monotonous, grayish black, almost bluish kind of smoke that differed in hue depending on where exactly the bomb went off. If he could have picked out individual vibrations from that continuous, rolling thunder down there, the voices of the black clouds might have reminded him of the high-pitched cracking sound that thunder makes when lightning is directly overhead. A few of the explosions, however, were snow white. They had a softer voice upon blowing up, and very soon afterward, they would turn their surroundings red.

He learned later when he himself got to find himself in the explosives business at the Artillery Center in Oklahoma that these were the incendiaries. White phosphorus. WP for short, but normally they were dubbed with the endearing nickname of "Willie Peter." Now to really understand all this, you must know that when a fleck of WP falls on you, you cannot put it out. It burns right through you, your flesh and your bones, and the odor that this process gives off is something you do not want to think about.

The other kind, the HE or high explosive, had no nickname that he knew of or can now remember, perhaps because they are more prosaic, direct, and straightforward. "Clean," we would call them in today's military parlance. And that was the way those HE bombs went about their business down there in Linz. Cleanly. Matter of fact. Businesslike. Wave after wave of liberators took out block after block of city. Churches, hospitals, everything. Centuries of creative effort reduced to rubble in minutes. Nature loves entropy. As it was, Linz could be grateful that it got only a sprinkling of the Willie Peter and escaped the fate of Dresden. Only, at the moment, the good Linzers could probably little appreciate their luck. Yes, those lucky Linzers! Linzer? Isn't that the place where *linzer Torte* comes from?

Linzer torte and the first glimpse of America

Yes, linzer Torte, that was his mother's favorite dessert, a delight that came from his mother's kitchen back in Léva. All those goodies that would emerge from that kitchen! She liked linzer torte so much that when the spirit moved her to have a taste of it, she marched out to the kitchen herself, bade the cook to sit down and watch, and proceeded to create the whole thing herself. If you are not acquainted with real linzer Torte, I don't think I can help you, for what you might get at your local bakery (even if it is a very good bakery and even if you are very lucky) is not likely to be the real thing.

He was never very partial to pastries of the dryish, more brittle variety. He prefers (to this day) chewy, fluffy, and creamy sweets, but he was born to know a good thing when he tasted one, and his mother's linzer Torte was a dream. It was not taken as dessert after dinner but at the midafternoon coffee ceremony. Coffee with sweet whipped cream floating on top, a slice of that linzer Torte, homework already done, long cross-country hikes in the woods coming up on the weekend, and now curling up with a good book on Magyar history. Or with tales of the Wild West about brave Indians defending their land, their buffalo herds, and their freedom, which were his first glimpse of *the* America.

The Wild West, the Llano Estacado, home of the fighting Comanche. All that was so far away that it probably lived only in storybooks written by romantics who had never been there. But he, like all the kids of his culture, identified with the Indians. The Indians, who were all brave and lived in the land of the free. Their land. He dearly wanted to see and experience that land.

He liked the story of Quanah, the great warchief of the Comanche best; Quanah, who resisted capture to the last. When he finally surrendered with the remnants of his starving little band, there was a white woman with them and the cavalrymen were proud of having liberated her. That was Quanah's mother, Cynthia Ann, who grew up with the Comanche and had become one of them. She helped Quanah mount his final escape by leading the cavalry astray in a snowstorm, risking her own life in the snowdrifts. Was that story really true? It almost sounded a little like sentimental fiction, but that did not matter.

An early-spring snow flurry started mixing its flakes into the clouds of smoke and dust below. The liberators (not the cavalry) had done their job and were gone.

On to Mauthausen

The two German soldiers did not seem to take much note of the scene below. They were drinking the hot milk prepared by the woman whose husband Hitler had posted forever in Stalingrad. She brought a cup of it for his mother, who was lying on the wooden army cot that had become the most important item of their equipment. His father was clearly ready to move on. But he (the boy) and his brother were stunned. They did not feel the chill gusts that were starting to move the smoke toward the west, for they were chilled to the bone by the experience.

The horror of it. Terror incarnate had focused all of its evil on the quivering, defenseless flesh of innocent human beings whose hearts, naked to the dread of annihilation, cried out to a deaf god for mercy. The horror of it!

Oh my god, the experience must have set off something in him, a new process of questioning and searching. Like searching the database for answers on Google nowadays—oh my god, who and what are you really?

Some years later, he was sitting at his desk in the basement of Mrs. Eastep's rooming house on College Avenue in Norman, Oklahoma, fighting another hopeless war, this time with differential equations on his way to a degree in engineering physics. His roommate, a decent, witty, and wordy guy, son of oil company executives from the oil company town of Bartlesville but proud of working his way through college on his own by flipping hamburgers at the Brown Owl around the corner, was also working at his books.

Nepper, I remember only this nickname of his, (will he read this if it ever sees the light of print and send me a comment by e-mail?) had a record of Nazi marches playing, for he was preparing to become a media man, an anchor maybe, one knowledgeable of politics and history. Prompted by that music, he looked up and mentioned what he had seen in Linz. Nepper's comment was quick, casual, and matter-of-fact as talk-show hosts are expected to talk: "So what?" he said. "So what? They asked for it, and we gave it to them." That's what he had said: "They asked for it, and we gave it to them!"

If you now feel indignant and angry about all this uncalled-for commentary by the narrator, ready to string him up for his nerve of not participating in the adulation of this sacred cow (America's last just war), consider an important thing here. That crucial factor is the position of the observer. As any physicist knows, when the observer is part of the system that he observes, all his observations are intrinsically biased. The system (any small well-defined part of the universe) that he felt challenged to deal with there in Mrs. Eastep's basement was the mindset of the Neppers of the world that is shaped by the ruling paradigms of the society into which they are born, that inculcates them with the values they learn to hold holy, that supplies them with their needs and wants, and that in the end, irons their minds smooth and pliable like a cotton handkerchief.

Are people whose life experience is to observe the world from a position of power capable of seeing the world like it really is? You decide. No belief is as strong as the one that we have convinced ourselves to be true. No error is more tenacious than denial, and denial is nothing but the ripe fruit of the self-righteous ignorance of a closed mind. What did his father teach him? "A decent man is a chivalrous one, and a chivalrous man sides with the underdog." What can you do then if you are doomed by birth to be the overdog? Does that entitle (or condemn) you to give them what they ask for, as if it were your birthright to sit in judgment over others (the losers)?

But he did not pursue the matter. He felt overwhelmed by the utter futility of trying to explain. There was no time, the pressure was on, final exams were coming up, and he knew that he was not good at debating anyway. He was an introvert. He shrugged and went back to struggle with his differential equations. He was well on his way to discovering America by then.

But that day back in Linz, momentous as it had been in the morning, was not over yet. The bear was soon on its way and lumbered on, all cylinders moaning as if its guts were being fed with beans rather than wood chips. He had lost interest for everything at the moment, however. His eyes were turned inward, with his mind trying to cope with what he had just seen. Pyburg. There was the road sign that said so, with two bullet holes in it as if cowboys had been using it for practice like they do in Oklahoma (as he learned later). They were passing through or by or past Pyburg (he did not know or care), and it must have been already midafternoon, for the low-flying, wet snow clouds were turning dark gray. There was a stop sign at that double-track rail crossing, and they stopped at a sidetrack to consider things.

The mammoth

Then comes the siren of that police car. A man with military police insignia gets out. "All military vehicles must report immediately to the assembly point near the Sankt Pölten *Bahnhof*," he barks. The sergeant unfolds his travel orders and tries to explain that he is on a special mission: evacuating the Magyar Embassy from Pressburg (Pozsony). "*Zum Teufel* . . . to hell with the Magyar Embassy in Pressburg," he is shrugged off impatiently. "All previous orders have been summarily cancelled. The Russians have broken through the front lines southeast of Vienna. You have half an hour to get to the *Bahnhof*. Move it." And he jots down the bear's vehicle number.

His father knows that there is no argument here. The laws that govern soldiers at war are of the same stuff as those that move the planets in their orbits. The Germans unload their belongings by the roadside. They salute, the corporal refrains from chuckling, and the bear disappears in the gathering dusk. A snow flurry kicks up again as silence falls.

There are some houses in the distance, perhaps two kilometers away. His mother is too weak to walk, and they cannot carry her that far. They are at the mercy of wind and weather, abandoned to the growing cold and dark. There is no traffic, no human presence, no hope for help, just the vast gray indifference of the snow clouds in the sky. He does not turn to his father for reassurance because he knows there is none to be had but even more so to spare him (his father) from being looked at at the hour of his despair.

A train filled with soldiers moves by, going east at a fast clip. Some of them wave. Night is falling and the snow persists in falling with it. After a while, another train comes into view, going west this time. It slows! A man jumps out and sets the switch. The train moves off the main line to the sidetrack. The great, big black steam locomotive hisses by, slowly now, making noises like mammoths would have in their day. Yes, she is like the prehistoric lead female with her gray wooly clan following close behind, one whom he knows well from his favorite animal book.

Then with brakes screeching, the procession of passenger and baggage cars comes to a halt, right there in front of them. I am not asking you to trust me with this, go ahead, don't believe in miracles if you want to be that way. But the fact remains that the train had not quite come to a halt yet when the door of the nearest baggage car had already flown open.

A big red-faced man with an enormous mustache, clad in the khaki uniform of a Magyar staff sergeant, jumped out first, creating a flurry of activity in his wake. Piles of charcoal were sprinkled with 180-proof *slivovic* to help them catch fire. Large kettles were soon steaming over the ensuing blazes, spreading the aroma of chicory-*ersatz* coffee and *gulyás leves*. Real Magyar goulash (you should know this) is not the thick vegetable stew that Western cuisine has made of it, but a *soup*. It consists mainly of *krumpli* (potatoes) and *kolbász*, the hard Magyar sausage. When sliced into boiling water with a lot of paprika and a good helping of *disznó zsír* (lard), the *kolbász* becomes ready to eat at the same time as are the potatoes. And bingo, there you have it: *gulyás leves*.

He and his brother could not wait for this to happen soon enough, for it had been a while since that warm milk among those bomb craters back in Linz. And that staff sergeant, the head cook, with the sharp eye of the professional combat-support specialist, had not only noticed them; he had already provided them also with army mess kits.

In the meantime, though, he was not unaware of other happenings of major import. As the train's passengers alit to inspect the kettles, a lieutenant colonel ambled over to salute his father, introducing himself as the train commander. (To him and to his brother, he became known as Csicsa *bácsi*). It took Csicsa *bácsi* no time to understand their situation. He barked a few orders to that effect, and instantly, a compartment in one of the passenger cars was cleared, their trunks were tagged and loaded on to a baggage car, two soldiers picked up his mother on her cot and lifted her into their new compartment, and the *gulyás leves* was barely all eaten and gone when the mammoth was already moving out with great huffing and puffing again, with the snow outside and with them inside that cozy second-class (nonsmoking!) compartment all for themselves.

Their savior was a Magyar army supply train provisioned to feed the soldiers of the Second Army, surviving units (or bands) of which had fought their way home from the Volga and then retreated clear through Magyarország into Germany and kept on fighting until they finally met the Americans on the far side, to whom they then obligingly surrendered. In reality, perhaps, members of the general staff who had sat through the war in their offices in the Ministry of War had a hand in commissioning this train to utilize it as a refuge for themselves and their families. People of authority and in positions of power are wont to do such things, taking advantage of profitable situations wherever they can find them.

At the Bahnhof

It was night by the time they stopped at some Bahnhof. He looked for the bear but it was too dark to see. What he saw from his window instead was an animated discussion with a lot of pointing and gesticulation, mostly up in the air, by officers from the train, including his father and the station master with his red cap on and his assistant (without one). They must have come to an agreement, for they looked all satisfied in the end. When his father had come back to the compartment and the train was moving again, he related what happened.

The station was bombed out regularly every day around midnight, and so their train had to move, for its wreckage would otherwise have hindered the reparation of the tracks for the next day's military traffic. The problem was that their train could not move out on the main track, for that was damaged and there was only one lane going west at the moment. Since it had become impossible to maintain schedules and reliable communications, going that way would risk a head-on collision in the night. So the stationmaster had briefed them on the situation.

"*Schlechte Zeiten*," the assistant without a red hat lamented mildly and compassionately, but blinking and winking profusely, he added that people of good will could sometimes find a way out of a predicament even if it was really *verboten* and too risky to consider. The stationmaster nodded knowingly, and Csicsa *bácsi* understood immediately.

He barked an order, and the supply sergeant, as if he had been expecting this (he was apparently used to it already), was immediately at hand to produce two large sacks of white wheat flour, a barrel of lard (with the bacon cracklings frozen into it), and a bale of that mixed-fruit army marmalade that was wrapped in foil and hard enough to be cut with a knife. All were treasures worth more than gold in those days (to this day, you still cannot eat gold).

The two Germans nodded. "*Alles in Ordnung*." The hatless assistant climbed up to the mammoth's cabin to show the way, and off she rumbled into the night—on a sidetrack. It was slow going for quite a while in pitch darkness. When they came to a halt, there were no points of light anywhere, but there was a strange smell that reminded him vaguely of the passage through Vienna.

The concentration camp

Sleep came quickly for it had been a long day, but it was a wistful, uneasy sleep full of dreams, forgotten and suppressed soon afterward, except for the winking of those indifferent, blandly smiling blind eyes of the deaf god in that fighter plane. "See, I am almighty. I can send you a mammoth to replace your bear, if I happen to feel like it," they were suggesting.

What tore him out of his semidormant intercourse with the higher powers of providence was the sliding door of their compartment being yanked open. To his relief, it was not an incarnate emissary of an evil dark lord but only Csicsa *bácsi*'s adjutant, a first lieutenant, who stood there to announce: "*Ez a mauthauseni koncentrációs tábor. A vonatról kiszállni nem szabad, az ablakon kinézni nem szabad.*" Then he slammed the door shut and went on to make the same announcement from compartment to compartment, his stentorian voice echoing all the way up and down the train. He had been polite. Speaking to officers and their ladies, he did not say *tilos* (forbidden); he just said that you may not leave the train or look out of the windows, being, as they were, within the secret confines of the Mauthausen Concentration Camp.

The adjutant could not have encouraged him more if he had offered him a Korfu bar. He immediately crawled to the window and poked a hole into the heavy canvas curtain. His eyes had to adjust slowly to the dusk. In the shifting black shadows of the early dawn, the world looked as if it were uncertain whether it wanted to awake to what was awaiting it.

Then he started to make out the outlines of the scene outside, each minute with increasing clarity. It was a meadow with a line of trees in the distance. From where he was, he could see two (perhaps there were more) round, black buildings like large Quonset huts, with smoke coming out of the center of the roof. A jagged row of humanoids stood in line, in rags, but apparently no longer feeling the cold or were oblivious of it, judging by their demeanor. Ever so slowly, they shuffled into the buildings, and he could see nobody coming out. Nothing and nobody except for that acrid smoke. It was beyond his ability to grasp.

Was he awake? He never had had a nightmare this chokingly intense. Then he thought of those winking blind eyes and was transcoursed with fear. There was a power at work or at play here, he felt, whose malice or maybe indifference knew no bounds. Only, what was the name of its game? People need words to shore up their thoughts. Then, all of a sudden, the controller flicked on the switch that connects disjointed neural circuits to create as if *de novo*, hitherto unimagined but often desperately sought-after insights. My God (whatever you are), could Samu *bácsi* be down there in that line? It could not be. Nothing was known of the scene that played itself out in front of his very eyes. Nothing, certainly not to him but to nobody he knew either, not even hints. But there it was, right outside his window.

The horror of it. Terror incarnate had focused all of its evil on the quivering, defenseless flesh of innocent human beings whose hearts, naked to the dread of annihilation cried out to a deaf god for mercy. The horror of it!

Samu *bácsi*

Around the corner from the Petőfi *utca* in Léva, the quiet side street lined with ancient, wild walnut trees, where his grandfather's house used to stand, was a little shop on the town's main street that led from the steam mill up to the main square dominated by the three-story *városháza*, the city hall and courthouse that contained his father's office and that of Majláth Laci *bácsi*, his grandmother's cousin, the county's *főszolgabíró* (district judge) or maybe *alispán*, I forget which. That little store was not unlike an American drug store. It was always open, and it was always the owner who stood behind the counter or sat in an easy chair, a man in his midfifties.

Among the treasures in that store, he held nothing in greater esteem than the candy it had for sale, and within that nice selection, nothing stood out more clearly than the only two types of candy bar (choice was still easy for kids in Magyarország in those days) that were available then: Oxford and Korfu. He would go there when he had a ten *fillér* coin to buy one or the other, always in alternating order, for they were equally scrumptious. But this time, he could not find his coin. The man watched him for a while as he searched for it in his pockets and then walked out from behind the counter.

"You can call me Samu *bácsi*," he said. "I know your grandfather. He healed my eyes when I was going blind with a cataract. I had no money then, and so he told me, "Don't worry, my son, pay me when you can. Right now, I am glad that I could help you. Yes, that's what your grandfather said. So I will now extend credit to you. Take your candy bar and pay me when you find your coin."

Then one day, he found that Samu *bácsi* was wearing a yellow star on his sleeve. Once aware of it, he saw that star on other people also. He saw it only on simple people, shopkeepers, and artisans. One doctor, maybe. The higher folks, officials, officers, his professors, the good society of that little town, and friends and acquaintances of his parents and grandparents did not wear one. Something kept him from asking Samu *bácsi* about those stars, so he turned to his father.

He, as always, explained it as if he were talking to a grown-up. "Those people with the yellow stars are Jews. People who are different or just feel different and show it, and those who choose to stay different from most of the other people of a country are called a minority. If such a minority grows to be greater than about five in a hundred ("Percent," the boy chimed in, "we had that in math last week"), they somehow become visible to the majority. If they are hardworking, talented, and intelligent, they rise in importance and that makes them even more visible. Then they start being resented and envied. Now, all may go well as long as times are good and the country is strong and prosperous. But let hard times come and the mood will change. Then the majority finds scapegoats and vents its anger on them. So it has happened through all of history. I am afraid it is happening here now."

Then one day, he (the boy) chanced to pass by an out-of-the-way small square in town. A group of people was milling around there. They were being loaded into German Army trucks, each of them carrying one small suitcase or a bag. Samu bácsi was among them. When he saw the boy, he turned away. After that, the yellow stars had disappeared from Léva until they reappeared in Mauthausen. Those ragged people lined up in front of those smoking black buildings wore them on what remained of their clothes.

Asombroso

Outside the train, a man in gray uniform showed up and signaled the mammoth to move. The nightmare faded. Then they were back on the main track. The controller did not record the rest of the day. It, ever solicitous, must have been worried about an overloading of his right hemisphere's circuits. He was probably dozing most of the day anyway; it was slow going with many stops and changes of direction. He woke up the next morning being shaken mercilessly by his brother.

"Get your butt in gear! *Amit látni fogsz, az nem is igaz!*" What you will see is not even true! But it was true. It was awesome beyond words, for even now I am tearing up Webster in search of adequate ones in vain. The train stood on the right-hand side of the Salsach River facing downstream toward Salzburg. From its high vantage point near the *Bahnhof* of the town of Werfen, the slope fell steeply down to the river, and on the other side, in its full glory, in the blinding morning sun, thrusting its snow-covered peaks vertically into the sky was the range of the Riesen Gebirge, the *Eisriesenwelt*.

What he had taken for mountains back home in Erdély were molehills compared to this "Ice Giants' World." It was overpowering. At my stage in life now, I have started mixing up my languages. *Asombroso* is one of the words that fits the bill well here, maybe because of that sonorous, exotic quality of it. I picked it up, contemplating Popocatépetl and the Sierra Nevada of Granada. But the Eisriesenwelt was bigger, badder, and well, more *asombroso* than anything else, perhaps because it was the first of this kind of an experience for him.

An altogether new experience. That glorious sight mercifully blotted out the ghosts of those dreadful blind and deaf gods of yesterday, but it also inexorably pushed back into the misty distance those cozy, warm, and peaceful realms of old where his rooster and butterflies used to live. Something new was taking shape. He did not know it yet, but childhood was over. From that childhood, he took with him two bits of wisdom, although at that time, those bits were far from being as ripe and clearly distilled yet as a *Stamperl* (shot) of fragrant, transparent-yellow *barack pálinka* (apricot brandy) can be. They were more like data still waiting to be evaluated by the statistical analyses of variance of the rest of his life.

He knew that the best in life was not only possible but could be tangibly real. But he also knew equally well that the worst not only could happen, but that it did happen. Later, people would often call him a pessimist rather than the realist that he knew he was, and this would always irk him. But he would easily forgive people this modicum of vexation, for how could they know what he knew?

Chapter 3.

The Exile

The drive on the Loneliest Highway from Reno to that T-junction where a side road leads south to Goff and Luning through some lunar landscapes is pleasant and not far, at least not in terms of the vast, empty expanses of the Intermountain Basin. He loves that emptiness free of dogs and people, and driving through it is anything but a chore; it is fun, something he really likes to do. But the controller had worn him out with all that delving into the past, so that now he is good and ready for an icing to his cake: he is partial to a cup of coffee and a slice of cherry pie with a generous scoop of vanilla ice cream on top of it. At one of his favorite watering holes, for part of him has become what one may call an American, but the other remaining part is alien, it takes the ice cream and lets it float on top of the coffee like the *tejszinhab*, the sweet whipped cream, did back in his days of yore in Kereskény. Now, have you ever seen a real American do that to ice cream?

Middlegate Corner

When in need of rest, he really looks forward to that cherry pie *à la* and especially so at that old-fashioned mom-and-pop coffee shop that is about to materialize like a tangible mirage along the roadside. And none other than the one at this particular T-junction. It is not just any run-of-the-mill watering hole! It is historic. A relic of the days of the Pony Express, a true Western corner. Not old, though, like them thar hills yonder across the flats, to be sure, no such claims, so let no foreign tourist shake his head in amusement at the pretension of a historic marker that it deserves.

It is its isolation and endurance that make it venerable, and the antediluvian motel cabins with their outhouse of pre-infernal-combustion-engine times reinforce that impression in its hot, tired, and thirsty customers like him.

How did those pioneers pick this exact spot on the edge of this plain encrusted in such picturesque dreariness to offer solace to future migrants who might chance by? Pony express stop? Well, as you heard me say before, this is no researched account of history, but the memory fragments of a survivor. Somewhere, though, there is an answer to be found for everything. Maybe that grove of elms behind the inn promised easy access to the water table below, to some deep upwelling sweet water spring. Yes, I guess, that could be an answer, don't you? Although maybe those trees came in later. I will ask about it if I ever pass though through there again.

Inside, it is cool and dark. The aged wood paneling exudes an air of comforting reassurance. An oasis. A place of safety, if not of solace in an unforgiving, hostile, unfathomably glorious semidesert. The center of a little universe of a few cabins and trailers in the back among the trees, where vagrants have found a foothold to catch their breath for a moment at first, but then to stay out the times of their life there in contraposition to all that beyond the hills that made them flee its fumes and fluster in the first place. And also its rules, regulations, taxes, and maybe even its enforcement of the law.

This time, he is hungry enough to opt for a cheeseburger though, saving the pie for later. And a cold, frosty Coke instead of that coffee. There will be a choice piece of pie to be had later at Carol's Country Kitchen. Carol is a totally unlikely establishment to be found in a that most alive of ghost towns, where he aims to bed down for the night. *Haute cuisine* (country style, but *haute* all the more) and appointed with a touching, dainty, imported elegance of, unpretentious Western down-to-earthness that anyone's favorite grandmother could be proud of. Could have been, rather than could, for it is not there anymore, you see. The old, ramshackle building is still there, but Carol's restaurant isn't. Not anymore.

Yellow june bugs

For it was twenty years ago now that he had been planning his experiments in Grass Valley as I write this here in the shadow of Bishop's Peak in that ever-shifting now of time. And in the meantime, Carol gave up one day on the long-gone clientele who worked those abandoned silver mines and moved to Reno, and Austin was never the same again (for him at least). Yes, it was twenty years ago in the swiftly fleeting course of the decades that he first started spinning the yarn of a (then) very vague and irresolute resolve to relate his story while his red Toyota did the driving and his controller unfolded the pages, by then musty with old age, of his beginnings that had been so very alive four decades before that "time" that was now twenty years ago! Twenty years ago . . .

Úgy mentem el mint egy kis gyermek	As a small child I left
És most mint meglett ember jöttem meg.	And as a grown man have I come back.
Húsz esztendő, az idő hogy eljár...	Twenty years, how time flies by...
Cserebogár, sárga cserebogár.	June bug, yellow june bug.

I know all this Magyar poetry may sound abstruse to you who are reading this, but you see, I am doing this vita-thing for myself. Not for self-therapy anymore by now but for fun, although it is becoming a bit of a yoke of a hobby I must admit, like a treasure hunt gone obsessive or an archeological dig for the unneeded and yet much-desired skeleton of the missing link. And when long-lost fossils like this one surface, wash up on these lengthening lines of my memories' pages, they just have to integrate themselves, like it or not, into the *corpus* of the saga's slow morphogenesis, if only for the sake of the link itself, for the completeness that each link contributes to this research on *le temps perdu*, the time lost, almost forgotten, or just simply gone by.

Okay, those twenty years of yours, you may say, "Why not fit them in if you must, but what do yellow june bugs have to do with it?" The yellow june bugs? Well, everything! Petőfi Sándor wrote these lines at the time when his (the boy's) grandfather's uncle enlisted in the newly formed *Honvéd* (home defense) army of the *Szabadságharc* (fight for freedom) against the Austrian emperor in 1848, at the same time as the great poet himself. His grandfather noted down the exploits of his (the boy's) great-granduncle in his own aforementioned memoirs as he (the grandfather) had heard them related by his father, for that war was fought before he (the grandfather) was born.

But all this is merely tangential. What matters here is that Petőfi clearly wanted to pat me on the back and tell me personally and confidentially that he felt the same way about yellow june bugs eight score years ago as I did myself only three and a half-score years ago. And as I still feel the same way about them now (although they may have become extinct, thanks to modern pesticides), while you may never have seen one and most likely never even have heard of one until now. That is where our sad discontinuity lies, the great divide between my organically passed-down past and your pastless present, you, my sons and descendants, and I deplore this and feel for you deeply, as nothing, not even your ability to double click on Google, can compensate you for your loss.

Therefore, let me tell you, "June" bugs rise to aboveground life in Magyarország (or did back then, before global warming) in May (*Maikäfer*), after about four years of a dark, wingless, subterranean, root-chewing existence as ugly large white grubs. But when they emerge, they become a country kid's delight (though a farmer's bane). They are compact, hard-shelled, copper-colored toys (just ask Wilhelm Busch), and when you shake them off your plum trees, they hit the ground like large hailstones. What you do with them, then, depends on the kindness of your kid's heart, but they have cousins (a different species) that are smaller and lighter in color (yellow).

And these used to fly at dusk in Léva in late spring, about that hour of eventide when the bugles of that infantry battalion sounded their plaintive tunes of retreat that calls soldiers to quarters, in the season when the lilac and the acacia bloom (no doubt I told you about all this already). And as they fly, they produce a melodious, barely audible buzz and appear to give off a faint lemon glint of stored sunlight (it certainly seems that way), and they are an irresistible magnet for kids to chase after. And when you follow them, you forget everything else and feel as if you could fly yourself. That is the meaning that the poet meant to convey, but how can you understand that if you have never chased a june bug? My brother in faraway Denver, do you still remember that meadow above the *szőlőhegy*, our vineyard in Léva, where that tree with the yellow cherries and the big walnut tree stood? How we used to fly there, soaring along with the *sárga cserebogár*?

Werfen

He apparently skipped the thinking about the upcoming experiment at the Gund Ranch while cooling off at the Middlegate Inn and is back behind the steering wheel now. But the cheeseburger was good, thank you. They were offering (or were then, perhaps only experimentally) tasty sourdough and not those unspeakably bland hamburger buns that an incomprehensible America is still addicted to, as if it had not discovered Europe lately. In fact, it (America) ran across it (Europe) quite a while ago by now, so its explorers have had plenty of time to see the light.

The earliest of these explorers, within the scope of his own experience and lifetime, appeared in Werfen, riding high in tanks in May of 1945, and that is no less than three score and two years ago now. Now, at the moment of this writing, that is. The column stopped near the *Bahnhof*, and as their helmeted heads peeked out from behind their armor, they seemed to appraise his mammoth-train uneasily.

Of course, they had never seen khaki uniforms cut in such a foreign fashion before, so how could they know what to make of them? Were those people in those odd uniforms, with their red-white-green flag flying, anti- or pro-American? They (the ones in the tanks) had all attended schools where world history and geography are not exactly the daily diet (he did not know this yet), so they had no ready reference points to orient themselves by in such a potentially consequential matter.

Also, to shed more light on their possible predicament, just the day before, a truck full of SS troops, armed to the teeth but, strangely, not appearing to be war worn, had stopped in that same spot, and their leader, addressed by a local as something like *Herr Obersturmgruppenführer* (I cannot vouch for this, it was purely a phonetic pickup), riposted angrily to a sentence in which the name Admiral Dönitz had occurred by saying, "*Solch eine feige Kapitulation kommt garnicht in Frage. Wir kämpfen bis zum letzten tropfen Blut.*" (Such a cowardly capitulation is out of the question. We fight to the last drop of blood.) This was apparently in reference to the final act of the Third Reich by Hitler's successor.

This reply impressed him (the boy) so much that his controller recorded it verbatim, and he could therefore understand the uneasiness of the explorers who may have faced this dragon of a warrior the day before, even though no sounds of battle had come from the direction of the pass that the black-clad hero in his impeccable uniform and spit-shined jack boots had sworn to defend to his soldiers' last drop of blood and where the explorers in the tanks had just come from.

But the explorers, upon seeing the khaki-clad ones waving at them, interpreted this action correctly as nonmenacing and waved back so that they ended up sitting on top of their tanks, tossing edible tidbits to the local children who had assembled around them. He himself did not make an attempt to garner any of the things being thrown. For one thing, the German kids probably were hungry and he was not (the mammoth was still well provisioned), but more importantly, the scene reminded him of a visit to the Budapest Zoo and the reaction of the monkeys there to the peanuts flying at them.

The peanuts! They were the connection, the mental bridge between past and present, for peanuts are called *Amerikai mogyoró* (American hazelnuts) in Magyar. So now, it was American *mogyoró* that came flying from real American hands, aimed not at monkeys in a zoo but at him, and this was something that something in him decided not to participate in. Maybe it was an ill omen, an early hint of a distance that would stand between him and what was to become the object of his search. But as it happened, there was no further temptation along those lines anyway. Catching a candy bar, even one of only C-ration quality, would have become irresistible with time, but the tanks soon moved on.

Other than that, the few weeks in Werfen, a month or two maybe, for no exact record survived of this episode on the road, were like a vacation. It was a little gloomy when it started, for they were assigned quarters at the old Hotel Post and there, once again, they had to deal with late-spring snow flurries. Those came to visit, this time from the Ice Giants' World, through the broken windows of their cold, dingy, musty, and empty hotel room. A hotel it was in name only, for there was no staff and no guests, and it had clearly served through the last years of war as quarters for troops passing through. It did have a *Speisesaal* downstairs, but that was closed, for food was rationed and there was no provision in the ration cards for things like eating out. However, the owner (or maybe manager) of the hotel, accustomed, nonetheless, to making her daily rounds, chanced by to check on them, and it did not take long before she was back with a dish of steaming *Wiener Schnitzel* with everything else that goes with it, like in the best old days of Imperial-Austrian hospitality.

It was for his mother only. They were touched, for they knew by then that the German meat ration was a pound per month. Seeing their surprise, she spread her hands in a gesture of good-hearted I-give-up-so-don't-ask-me. "I can see that the lady is ill, and I can tell that you are good Christian people," was what she ended up saying, pointing to the small, elaborately worked bronze cross that had been blessed by Pope Pius XI and that his father always hung, first thing, over his mother's bed (that wooden army cot) since they had left home. "There are few good people left in the world," she commented sadly on her take on world affairs. "This is all I can do for you now. But tomorrow I will find a better place for you to stay," and with that she was gone.

By noon of the next day, she had found a sunny, warm, and friendly room for them in a house across the street. Do I make this up? No, it is the gospel truth. They were not even Christian, or if so, in name only. That with the cross was just some family ritual whose origin escapes me. If anyone of that little nuclear family was Christian at that time, it was he, although his bouts with that deaf god had made it clear that he was facing some serious reevaluation of his understanding of the ways the universe worked and was designed. There was simply too much haphazard chance in it to be purposeful, it started dawning on him. But more on that in its own good time. Right now, he was still the one who went to church to pray.

And this Catholic church in Werfen was the scene of remarkable ecumenical services. One of the pieces of the flotsam of war, the Budapest Opera Company, had somehow also washed up on the slopes of the Eisriesenwelt, though not as members of the Military Order of the Mammoth, which had become a loose-knit community by now. "I am grateful to be able to go to that church and sing to an audience," the prima donna told his mother when she dropped in for a chat, "otherwise, I could lose my voice." And sing they did, but not Rigoletto or La Traviata. They sang the hymns of an ancient Christian-nationalist-chauvinist culture, like "Boldog Asszony Anyánk" ("Our Beatific Lady"). But the one he liked best was

Miatyánk Úristen, ki vagy a mennyekben	Lord God, our father, who art in heaven
Add, hogy hazánk újra szabad s nagy lehessen.	Let our country be free and great again.
Szárítsd le a könnyet, vess véget a jajnak	Dry up the tears and bring an end to woe
Nyujts reményt, biztatást annyi sok mártírnak,	Give hope and solace to so many martyrs
Idegen hazában szenvedő Magyarnak . . .	Hungarians suffering on foreign soil . . .

This one expressed the feelings of this congregation perfectly. It was plaintive, and the suffering it spoke of was deep, heartfelt, and sincere. Those were certainly his feelings then as they are now. But yes, there was also something petulant in it; I have to admit now. We had been wronged, Lord God, and as we call you our father, how about some solace? Can't you see how we are suffering out here in this wide, wild, foreign, and hostile world of Yours?

You must understand that so many of these exiled refugees were the upper stratum of a society where they had led the good life of the intelligentsia, the leaders, the rich, the overdogs. *Extra Hungariam non est vita, si est vita, non est ita* (Outside of Hungary there is no life; if there is life, it is not like that) was an old adage. Life, like it can only be at home. It was meant as a pun but was felt as the truth. And importantly, you must also understand that when a Magyar speaks of his country as *nagy*, a word that one may translate as "great" in this context, he does not speak of a concept that the French would call the "*gloire de la patrie*." No, he thinks of its size, of the historical, geographic Magyarország before the Peace Dictate of Trianon in 1919 after the war of 1914—1918, when it lost two-thirds of its territory that had been bounded by the crest of the Carpathian Mountains and bordered on the Adriatic Sea for over a thousand years, not counting the years of Turkish occupation.

How Magyars relate to the Russians

Time passed just fine in Werfen, quickly like a thousand and one days would if you didn't count them one by one: without school, as if that institution had never even been invented. Endless hikes into a new world of mountains, along trails following the creeks swollen with rushing ice water fed by the glaciers above, to the fortress on the hilltop above the town, the likes of which could not be found in Magyarország, for what survived the Turks had been blown up by the Austrians out of spite following the Fight for Freedom at the turn of the eighteenth century.

The Magyar officers continued to wear their uniforms and continued to be saluted by the enlisted men as if the authority of their society, which is the basis of all military discipline and etiquette, had not vanished utterly by then. Then a rumor came up that the Americans were preparing to go to war against the Russians as the exiles continued to call the Soviets.

You see, old grievances die slowly (if ever). This particular one came into life as a result of a letter sent by the *Kaiser* of Austria, Franz Josef, to his cousin, *Tsar* Nicholas of Russia. They had close family ties, those two, but their realms were also politically connected as members of the Holy Alliance of the time. This was an alliance of countries headed by Christian monarchs who ruled by the grace of God (hence the epithet of "holy") and who maintained that the peoples under their authority belonged to them personally.

The Magyars, for their part, felt that this was something that did not apply to them, and they rose up to shake off the yoke. This maverick attitude and behavior became their undoing. For at the end of this war of 1848—1949, in which the

Magyar freedom fighters led by General Görgey defeated the Austrians and chased them out of their country, Ferenc Jóska (as the Magyars called the *Kaiser*), fearing that his erstwhile subjects would not stop at the border but kick him out of his residence in Vienna to boot, sent that fateful letter to his cousin, requesting his help in putting down the uprising of the Magyar freedom fighters. Nicholas was more than happy to oblige and unleashed a fresh army on the double to shore up their common holy cause.

Attacked from the rear and facing overwhelming odds, Görgey had no choice but to stack arms, lower the flag, and surrender his exhausted, bloodied troops to the Russians. As an avid student of the American Civil War that he became later, he could never separate this event in his mind from General Lee's appearance in his dress uniform at Appomattox.

The Austrians on their part, anxious to save face and show their mauled mettle, executed a dozen of the freedom fighters' top officers by hanging. These then entered Magyar history as the *aradi vértanúk*, the martyrs of Arad (the Magyar town, today in Romania, where the atrocity took place). Now, whether this version of this footnote to European history is factual to the last iota, he did never dare to question, for this was the way his teacher, a Magyar patriot with the good Slovak name of Pekarik, beloved and respected director of the *Lévai Református Elemi Iskola* (Calvinist Elementary School of Léva), had related the story in the history curriculum of the third grade. And I am satisfied enough that at least the gist of it is true that I will not undertake further historical studies of it.

The point here is that oddly enough, it is not this Ferenc Jóska who remained the villain (as he should have) in Magyar national consciousness but the Russians, the archenemy.

And now, as a rift was opening between the rising, rival superpowers with their clashing ideologies, a mirage arose on the far horizon, an unhoped-for window of opportunity to turn back, face to the east again, and fight the Russians together with the Americans! What a sad delusion that soon turned out to be! He had heard of the Crimean Peninsula, of course; he had seen it on that situation map of the War in his father's study; he had even heard Hitler himself rant about it on radio as "*dieser drohende, rote Flugzeugträger mitten im Schwarzen Meer.*" But he had not heard of the one spot on "this menacing red aircraft carrier in the Black Sea" that was to have the most menacing meaning for Central Europe during the next half century: Yalta!

What happened there at that conference of the Allied Powers I do not want to get into here; it is too painful. But there was talk at that time among the refugees, many of whom had been highly placed and had close connections to the Vatican in the past, about a conversation between the pope, the successor of the one who had blessed their brass cross, and Roosevelt. "How can you give up, turn over, sell out, and betray ancient Christian nations and cultures to evil, atheist, Bolshevik tyranny, you who profess to be the global protector of freedom?" so asked Pius XII. "Give them time, and they will get used to it," so answered the president of the United States of America.

Historical fact? How could I possibly know? Let historians search the archives for it if written proof is what you need. What matters here is what actually happened as a consequence of that highhanded abrogation of the hope and the right of a hundred million people to freedom. That is what happened at Yalta. So what? They asked for it, and we gave it to them: The Russians. For fifty years! America, America, where will I find the real you? Where do you hide the grace that God has shed on thee? The British, at least, call a spade a spade: "England has no eternal friends or enemies, only eternal interests," so observed one of their honest leaders of yore.

All right, so they did not have their chance to go back to fight the Soviet army all over again after all. Instead, the Allied Military Government of what later became West Germany went to work in the wake of the war and did its best to do what it is good at. A slow, well-planned, well-financed, goal-oriented, detail-focused rejoining of the fractured joints and limbs of the body politic and economic of what lay there in shambles, floundering in the murky pools that had collected in all those bomb craters. The Marshal Plan. The re-creation of markets to better serve, as soon as possible, what the business of America is all about: business. In addition, of course, it had its redeeming grace. It gave Americans a chance to feel good about doing good.

Harthausen

As far as they (he and his family) were concerned within this grand design, things were far from good, but they could have been much worse. By the time-honored business principle of the efficient grouping of like units, the millions of refugees of a Babel of tongues were sorted out, and most of the Magyars found themselves grouped in a vast, barbed-wire-less, open "concentration" camp in the villages around Bad Aibling in Bavaria. Trucks, US Army douce-and-a-halfs, driven by Pfc's of an all-black, segregated unit took them there from Werfen, and Harthausen, a village irregularly criss-crossed by muddy dirt roads then, would in time begin to feel a little like home.

It is the habit of people to make a home for themselves even if it is in hell, as the adage goes (I might have occasion to use this one again). And believe me, it is true, for it began to dawn on them by this time that they had better get used to their refugee quarters in Harthausen, as going home was no longer in the cards. The new Bolshevik puppet government installed by the Soviet overlords in Budapest was requesting extradition of officers and politicians from the US military government: to be hanged, as fighting the Russians was apparently a war crime. Or maybe fighting on the side of the Germans was the offence, I forget.

More important, though, than all these geopolitical developments and events was, for them, the steadily deteriorating health of his mother, who was becoming more transparent every day like a loosely woven, much-worn, white silk scarf. He and his brother did not know that she had only a few months left to live, for their father kept that to himself; he did not want to burden his sons unnecessarily, although their load was really a remarkably light one in those days.

It was a glorious, warm, early summer, and they took possession of their new roaming grounds with gusto, exploring the meadows and forests of the wide countryside. These were blessedly free of No Trespassing and Violators Will Be Prosecuted signs, nor was there any barbed wire in evidence, as there is, sad and sorry I am to say, everywhere in the "Land of the Free."

It was a free and civilized country, as it is to this day. The only crimp to his newfound joie de vivre was the time of the year, that month from mid-May to mid-June, when the grasses bloom in abundance in rain-soaked Southern Bavaria. And the pollen that they shed then are like clouds in the wind: bad news for him, for hay fever would hit him like the plague in response to grass pollen ever since that year (he was eight years old then) when they took out his tonsils at the army hospital in Budapest.

Tonsils, Indians, and the end of the day

What a fun trip that had been, that one to Budapest (apart from the loss of his tonsils, and that was no big deal). It was a peaceful Budapest long before the siege. There was no hint of war anywhere for that was far away somewhere in Russia, and it would be won before long. He stayed at the hospital for over a week, and to help him recuperate from what was really a Mickey Mouse operation, he got a book, a huge, heavy tome bound in gray canvas: *A Nagy Indiánus Könyv* (*The Great Indian Book*). It contained all five volumes of the complete, unabridged Leatherstocking tales by James Fennimore Cooper (in Magyar, of course).

It was the treat of his lifetime, and it would revisit him at the end of it. He had finished it by the time it was time to go home. He had sensed, and he did not have to be a literary critic to know it, that this book was different from the other popular Indian stories by the likes of Karl May or Donászy Ferenc, who had conjured up imaginary worlds of the Wild West from many thousands of kilometers away.

Deerslayer and his friend, Chingachgook, were real people. Their setting, the endless, trailless, virgin wilderness of what would become New England later, was something one could contemplate only with closed eyes in wondrous awe from a comfortable hospital bed in faraway Central Europe.

Most poignantly, the first story dealt with one who was the last of his kind, and with his passing, the age of unspoiled nature, that of the free, civilized Mohican nation, would come to an end, irrevocably. As he lay there snugly in his bed but under the spell of the story, flashes of forebodings troubled him sometimes when he thought of his father's assessment of his Nation's chances in the war. What if the Bolsheviks did win? Would his world then also pass like that of the Mohicans?

He completely identified with Deerslayer, the hero of the tale, and with his pointless—and goalless pilgrimage through the rapid passing of the age of the free Indians and the inexorable westward movement of the frontier. He accompanied this survivor, this introvert and loner, in all his adventures and in his rites of passage through the foreign and hostile spaces of a changing world. A world that was becoming more bewildering with each stage of his move further into the unknown that was the Wild West, and that would become less and less his as he followed the setting sun.

What touched him most deeply, though, in all these tales, is how their hero, Natty Bumppo, died. Or maybe that was not how it was told at all, but it was rather how his mind internalized it. I do not know, for I have not reread the story in its original and probably will not do so anymore until my own time comes. So the old trapper—that's what they call him now—sits on a log alone, except maybe for his blind dog. From there he contemplates a cold, alien land of wind-blown grass at the foot of a range of forbidding, bare, and jagged rocky mountains. Gone are the trees of his forests and the faces of his friends; he is alone. Alone in a place and in a land that does not hold his memories. Sitting there, he awaits his end.

My father also died that way on the shores of the Missouri River in Omaha, Nebraska, where everything was alien to his eye, to his mind, and to his heart in his present's merciless reality, where he died alone. I did not think that he would die that night, and I left him to get some sleep. And so he died alone. I also will die that way when my time comes. Will it then help that for me this land, in the meantime, holds so many memories?

There is more to life than memories

Back in Harthausen, there was a sanatorium at the far edge of the village, and not far from it, across the fields, there was a jewel of civilization, the public swimming pool. And one that worked. You probably cannot imagine a general, all-pervasive, permanent set of conditions where nothing works. The windows are broken; the roofs leak; the fountains are dry; the trains are late if they come at all; the stores are closed, and when open, they are empty; you have a lot of money, but it is worthless; you are always hungry; when it is cold, you freeze; your socks consist of holes; and even the vending machines at the *Bahnhof* are only broken and desolate reminders of bygone times of normalcy that are not showing any signs of ever returning.

But this swimming pool worked; it was sizable and had clean, swimmable water in it. Although it was an hour's walk from town, along the *Birken Allee*, the walk lined by birches, at a time when very few lucky people had bicycles and nobody even dreamt of owning a car. He proceeded to teach himself to swim there, for admission was free; there was no fence, and he felt that he owned that pool. All ages used to show up there, even an occasional American soldier with his local lady friend, although the clientele was mostly teens, and these were not the rowdy, rebellious ones of today but well-behaved, good-natured kids, as if the discipline of Hitler Youth training had imbued them with a cohesive and constructive sense of community, whose jagged, command-tone edges of the recent past had quickly and mercifully died away. They (he and his brother) and their Magyar buddies (Eisele Peti, Vitalis Laci, and all the rest of them) fitted in seamlessly in a spirit of mutual tolerance. Spite is a product of plenty, while need teaches comradeship.

The roaming in the forests produced some entertainment in addition to the gathering of mushrooms and raspberries. The ammunition from an old dump could be pried open to yield black powder and other explosives for some gorgeous fireworks, and at one time, poking into the depths of a thicket, he espied something that looked like two large, well-hidden metal cans. He would have gone on, but his brother insisted on checking this out, and unbelievably, the cans turned out to be full of gasoline. Now, that was a treasure, for only the occupation army had access to gasoline. They took those cans home under the cover of darkness in their indispensable, all-purpose, hand-drawn, four-wheeled cart and hid them in the barn.

His father appeared impressed. He contemplated this boon silently for some time and then shook hands approvingly. Before the week was over, the olive-green Magyar military ambulance vehicle with its red crosses on top and sides (from that large guarded lot that held the sundry collection of the Second Magyar Army's surviving motor park) pulled up in front of Resi Meyer's farmhouse, where they had been assigned quarters. The driver and a medic (still in uniform) lifted his mother into the back on a stretcher. His father also climbed in there to be next to her during the trip, and off they went. There was just enough gas for the ambulance to make it to Tegernsee and back.

How his father found out about that little Pension (lodging) by the lake, where everything was so untouched by war as if that had been nothing but a bad dream, and how he was able to arrange and pay for it, I will never know. He (the boy) had never been much into asking questions. "If you ask many questions, you will get many answers, and then you will get all confused," his favorite teacher, Doktor Schlusnus, would soon advise him at the *Oberrealschule* in Icking. But that comes later.

Father and sons had an emergency meeting the night before. He explained that the gasoline would make it possible for him to take their mother to a beautiful, peaceful, and peaceable place, at a resort that he knew of, in hopes that she might recover there (regretfully, accommodations were available only for the two of them). "Full recovery of your mother might take a while," he said, "and I trust that you will take care of yourselves and of each other like the adults that the times have made you before your time."

All that was communicated in a matter-of-fact, military manner, as behooves a unit well trained in the contingencies of the road. The love, the sadness, and the worry for their well-being were all there but only between the lines and were felt all the more deeply, and their pride in his confidence in them was strong. With that, his grown-up days had begun, although he was still just a little boy, really.

Freedom and frogs

But what heady days (several months, really) of freedom those were that the parting of his parents ushered in! He became so imbued with freedom during this time that no amount of regimentation that followed later could ruffle the smooth feathers of his self-confidence. Subliminal pangs of guilt about missing school had no chance to surface, for there simply were no books around to remind him of the confines of a classroom. Instead, he spent a lot of time hunting frogs with his trusty slingshot (a relic of the home that had already started to recede into the past) in the round pools formed in the craters of bombs near the swimming pool. Bombs that may have been meant for the sanatorium nearby or were just dropped to produce a little collateral damage.

They engineered a move with all their stuff to somewhat more commodious quarters out of Resi Meyer's old farmhouse, where their room had been damp and cold even in midsummer. Then they needle-nosed their way into the distribution channel (as distributors!) of surplus (throwaway) army supplies, food rations that American troops turned over to the Magyar refugee camp.

This was a most welcome complement to what was on their German ration cards, for that was hardly enough to stay alive on. Reliance on the hard, black bread that those cards provided was reassuring as a last resort, but they had to be on their toes to know when their old pal, the Magyar head-cook staff sergeant (now more and more out of uniform and less and less a sergeant), would rustle, catch, and slaughter a wayward cow, and so share in the bounty since the meat ration on those cards was a pound per month.

Getting firewood for their little iron stove was always an adventure, for it had to be fir if they wanted it to burn without drying it first. The trees had to be small enough to be sawed by hand while hiding in one of the nearby stands, and the operation had to avoid the vigilant eyes and ears of the farmers who guarded their trees closely. The tree trunks had to be cut to size to fit in that small, trusty aforementioned cart to be smuggled home. No wood? No cooking! And as winter came, this fuel became a conditio sine qua non, as fragments of Latin from home reminded them sporadically of school. And so the days passed one by one, uncounted, although he even kept a diary, which, unfortunately, did not make the long leap to Chicago. But that comes later.

Dies irae

They made it to Tegernsee once by train. The little Pension where his father and mother stayed was like a time warp. Clean, snow white, fresh-smelling sheets and cushions; feather beds; shining, transparent window panes; bright sun reflecting up from the smooth surface of the lake; waxed hardwood-panelled floors; a smiling, polite landlady; breakfast with white toast and butter and jam. *Miraculum miraculorum.*

They would have been so glad for their mother had she not been pale as the linen she was lying on. Then they knew without having to be told that her time was almost up; this was the last visit, the time to say good-bye. His father had kept a little black notebook of that time in Tegernsee. Short notes of agony, I expect, for theirs was a great love story. I shied away from reading them: I have not had the courage to do so to this day. And now that I could face the thoughts that he wrote down, intending to share them with me, I cannot find them. The time might come when they would be a solace: knowing that others have been there also may relieve a little the black emptiness of being alone in the face of death, that of a loved one or one's own.

Three weeks later, his mother was back in Harthausen in a coffin. There was no church ceremony. No relatives came because there were no relatives. His father arranged for the service like he must have for battlefield burials on the Russian front. The military chaplain, a good friend of his, kept the officiating to a minimum. Then six soldiers sang the ancient Gregorian chant from the Mass of the Dead:

Dies irae dies illa	A day of wrath, that day
solvet saeclum in favilla	turneth the world to ash
teste David cum Sybilla.	as foretold by David and Sybil.
Quantus tremor est futurus	What trembling there will be
quando judex est venturus	when the judge cometh
cuncta stricte discussurus.	to deal sternly with the doubters.

How strange. On the one hand, singing the "Dies Irae" puts the mourner in his proper place if he has been familiar enough with Catholic liturgy from early on, that is, to be able to relate to it deeply. It is a solemn rite that takes the individual out of the denial of his imagined uniqueness and offers him unity with the community of saints.

On the other hand, the harshness of it! The threat of fire and brimstone for cardinal sins, of which being a doubter is one of the worst. He really did pray to a Heavenly Father for his mother's life, having listened often enough to sermons on the ability of faith to move mountains to actually believe it. Only, perhaps, that deaf god had already left seeds of doubt behind by then that were growing in some recess of his soul, whispering, "Let's check him out, this Heavenly Father! Let's see if he can really deliver."

For the mountain to move, the transaction, the quid pro quo—I trust you, and you, you do your miracle—the deal with the Good Lord, must apparently be pure and clear as double-distilled water. Otherwise, no deal, as far as He is concerned. Or else perhaps "god" was just busy somewhere else at the time of the deal when he (the boy) was praying for his mother's life. Was He perhaps off, watching galaxy clusters collide in one of his parallel universes? More likely, though, in the wisdom of His judgment, time had come, and for reasons known only to Him this was the right time.

So I should be fair about this. In my case, whenever I have been really remiss, there was no excuse. Have I lived and learned enough by now not to be judgmental? I am thinking of an instance that surfaced in conversation just the other day. I was not even aware of its importance until now, and so its record must fit in here, next to God's not answering my own prayers. I was negligent to my everlasting regret. This is what happened: I went to a meeting in New Orleans instead of attending my son's high school graduation. It was an important meeting, and no one was there to come to my own graduation since I did not graduate. No big deal. But I chose to think of my son's graduation as I did of my own nonexistent one at the time, being wrapped up in the demands of the moment.

At any rate, that was how I tried to excuse what turned out to be a grievous omission, for my son was left with the feeling that his event, a big one for him, was unimportant to me. He wanted to prove something to *me*, and my absence made him feel that I did not appreciate his effort. I should have known it. I should have felt it. But I did not. I did not! I let him down, while what God did was something that was not up to me to judge.

Life goes on

Just like the moon, each era has its time of waxing and waning, its time of sowing and harvesting, and its time of being in full flower. Like a vacation, for instance. On the first day, you still have a great two weeks ahead of you, but after the first week is over, what remains is no longer of quite the same quality.

After his mother's burial, the great vacation of freedom in Harthausen continued as before, his father, having returned to share their small room did not interfere with the established routine. In fact, he and his brother tried to comfort him as best as they could, for he was much more deeply affected than they were. He had now lost everything that had meaning for him in life: country, vocation, beloved wife, and going on sixty, the future must have looked to him like to a survivor of a shipwreck floating on an ice floe in a fog bank over an arctic sea.

Am I over-emoting? What you may not fully understand if you think so is what country and vocation meant to a Magyar army officer of those days. The uniform was not a set of overalls put on for the nine-to-five workday like it was for the soldiers at Fort Sill, Oklahoma. Wearing it meant that you were a member of an exalted, elite class that identified itself with the defense of nationhood, traditions, music, language and literature, and the memory and cult of a thousand years of mostly tragic history of an island nation set apart from all others on the continent by its different language and origin.

Defense not only against all enemies, armed foreign and self-serving domestic, but even more so against relentless political pressures and hostility from all sides and the threat of obliteration by assimilation. And now, all of that gone in the whirlwind of war, and with it gone also the soothing comfort of the sharing and understanding heart of his adored wife. He (the boy) and his brother were a lifetime away yet from understanding this level of pain; they were callow and were focused on their own future.

And yet I can say that his father did not sink into any sort of depression. Instead, he slowly picked up the few pieces that were left and went about the business of each new day an hour at a time. He (the boy) could only vaguely be aware of the great effort and strength that went into this process, but sense it he did with a not fully comprehending, muted sense of admiration.

Thus, the days of this summer slowly trickled out. There was a half-hearted attempt on the part of some concerned grown-ups to organize something like school, for there were quite a number of kids who, by now, had missed a good year of it. Soós *bácsi*, a Latin and German high-school teacher—professor they were called in Magyarország, where teachers (as I must have mentioned before) were held in high esteem—was the driving force behind it, and he (the boy) and his brother volunteered to attend these sessions with good-natured consent. But this activity did not last very long, as Soós bácsi opted for going home to Kecskemét as soon as the opportunity for that arose since he was worried that all director's positions would be filled if he did not hurry. Such was the ignorance of the refugees of the true nature of the tidal wave that had swept away their old way of life! Neither Latin nor German would be taught again in Kecskemét until the Red Empire crumbled fifty years later.

Other than that, a most noteworthy innovation that was introduced to Bad Aibling that year was the American movies. Humphrey Bogart, Gregory Peck, Clark Gable, and Gary Cooper made their debut to this new adoring audience (Jane Russell, Rita Hayworth, and Doris Day also). The novelty of it! One thing that really stood out among all the remarkable things that these gents were doing (besides showing off a world of enviable opulence) was their manners. They were into putting their feet on tables, and instead of standing up straight, they kept their hands in their pockets and slouched in strange, contorted ways against walls and furniture while blowing cigarette smoke into peoples' faces.

All teens immediately fell all over themselves in assiduous attempts to imitate the new idols to the grave disapproval of their elders. As for him, his sense of freedom had become so strong by that time that he did not think it necessary to resent authority. So he stood up straight when that was called for and slouched when he felt like it. But he resented the Westerns, and for that reason, he never became a fan of their chief idol, John Wayne, a regular sort of guy though he was.

Those Westerns used to focus on two things. First, on the Indians who were savage brutes characterized by their bent for scalping innocent white men and by stupidly riding around circled wagons emitting whoopy yelps while being shot down one by one. And second, on the US cavalry that always appeared on the spot with gallantly streaming guidons at the last moment to rescue said innocent white gunmen who coveted the Indians' land to set up "little homes on the prairie" on it and their women, who were always dressed up like Victorian dolls in the middle of the dust-choked ruts of the emigrant trails.

Something was wrong with this mindset, he felt. How could this be? Why did all those smart directors and producers and actors go along with this and show it in this patently untruthful way? And why did the Americans, good and decent folks, all of them, not side with the underdog, the Indians, who bravely defended their home and freedom? Would it not be quite something, he often thought, to experience this America live, in person, if only to verify that its reality was not as wrong as some of its movies?

Icking

Then September came as the Central European summer turned slowly into the warmest, kindest, most gloriously halcyon days of an Indian summer in living memory (his own rather short record of memory, that is). And with that, the era of freedom came to an end. With his full consent, of course, for school was a necessity, a must; no one had to lecture him on that.

Whence the car came from that took them to Icking is another one of the many small data lost along the road. His brother does not remember it either. But when it deposited them at the door of the *Schülerheim* on the Walchstätter Höhe, there was a strong, fresh wind in his sails.

This Icking was (and is) a power spot. The ancients had a clearer feel for the convergence of tectonic lines of force than we do, for their minds were less encumbered with minutia than ours are. And so I do not doubt that Icking, and specifically the spot where the old Catholic church still stands, was a focal point for the celebration of timeless Druidic rites for ages. I do not need supporting documentation to know this. If you want proof, just go to Icking, sit down in the tall grass in the small, walled cemetery around the church, let your back rest against the church walls, release your mind of its constraints, and you will feel it without the need of any old parchment attesting to it.

Now, Walchstatt is another village about a twenty-minute walk away from Icking, and this *Schülerheim* stood on the "*Höhe*" of it, that is, on the "heights," on top of a rise of what was at the edge of the village then. All of this is well within the range of the power that emanates from around the old church in Icking, and you yourself can become part of that power as you gaze down from the heights on the valley of the Isar River below and, beyond that, at the panoramic vistas of the Alps in the distance. From there, you can also make out the outlines of the great road that starts in Munich to the North, leading across the mountains toward the distant realms of the magic South.

The road that was the very path that led Goethe (the inns along it, where he stopped for the night, all have historic markers to proudly proclaim this) to that most distant island—land that still haunts the dreams of men condemned to bide the times of their lives in the cold and wet regions north of the mountains:

Kennst du das Land wo die	Know ye the land where lemon
Zitronen blühn	trees bloom
In tiefgrünem Laub die	And in deep-green foliage gold
Goldorangen glühn?	oranges glow?
Kennst du das Land?	Know ye that land? Thereto,
Dahin, dahin . . .	thereto . . .

You can tell by now that nostalgia overcomes me as I think of my few years in Icking. So do not mind; let me reminisce. On the edge of the meadows where the land drops off steeply toward the river, you can still see (if you know how to look) traces of the old Roman Road, the *iter militaris septentrionalis*, that the legions followed north to the *limes*, the wall that marked the end of the civilized world.

But what was most important to the here and now of the denizens of the *Schülerheim* were not the lemons and the oranges of Sicily (ten thousand *Reichsmarks* could not have bought them, for there weren't any to be had, not so soon after the war) nor the dismal fate of the legions north of the *limes* in the Teutoburger Wald (where they had no business to go back then two thousand years ago) but that lasting monument to the benign side of the defunct Nazi regime, the *Staudamm*, the dam on the Isar that gave rise to the *Stausee*, the large, shallow, artificial lake with its intermittently reedy or pebbly shores and surrounded by stands of willows and alders that made a fine home for ducks, geese, swans, frogs, water snakes, and every other small creature that longs to find a refuge from human population growth, and served as a paradise for swimming and exploring to the students living in said *Schülerheim*, their home away from home.

That this same *Stausee*—that one reached via a covered bridge crossing the weir—was to become three decades later the favorite vacation haunt of his sons also is a strange repetition of personal history in this ever-changing world.

The boardinghouse itself was a splendid little institution up there on that flat-topped hill in Walchstatt, no more than a half hour's quick jog away from the lake. It was homey in spite of the twice-daily mandatory Bible reading and interpretation and Psalm singing—Lutheran style. But the lake was frequented on weekends only, for the *Schule* down there in Icking, that the *Schüler* attended was a school not to be taken lightly.

The *Ickinger Schule*

It was also a splendid little institution. Its physical plant consisted of two parts: a private villa converted to this new purpose for the upper grades and a wooden barracks building that held classrooms for the lower grades and a hall for gym and ceremonial purposes. It was all quite primitive and makeshift, for this was not a regular state-run institute of learning but one founded and supported by the parents of kids living in the Isartal, who when living out of walking distance from the school, took the *Isartalbahn* (yet another splendid institution), the local Isar Valley Railroad, to get there from the neighboring towns. And when they got there, they faced a demanding curriculum and a formidable faculty. Formidable only in class but kindly friends outside.

"School is not a building but an event for dedicated givers and takers," said Socrates (although this *dictum* of his may not have been preserved in writing). "You can have the best of school under an oak tree or on the steps of the *agora*." The teachers in Icking had either passed the *Staatsexamen*, a state examination after many years of university training both in the subject of their specialization and in the methods of presenting it, or they held doctorates in their subject (or both). They were inspired givers to eager takers.

The curriculum (8:00 a.m. to 1:00 p.m., Monday through Friday; 8:00 a.m. to 12:00 p.m. on Saturdays) consisted of some ten major and three minor (music, art, and sports) subjects, and you had to pass *all* of the major ones (math, Latin, English, history, physics, chemistry, etc.) to advance to the next higher grade. There was no picking and choosing the easy ones. Under this system, each grade was a self-contained society; no one did or could take courses pertaining to a higher or lower level, and when you failed any one major subject, you had to repeat the entire year and were relegated back to a group made up of your juniors. This was a powerful incentive not to slack off, I can tell you that!

Yet for all its demands, it was a school without books at that time, for just like the lemons and the oranges that could not be had because they were not on the ration cards, textbooks could not be printed because the binderies and paper mills were all burnt out by the thorough-going liberators and also (I think) because the educators had to rethink their "denazified" new pedagogy first. So there was endless dictation from books that only the teachers had.

And here, he hit on a system that made remembering things easy at a relatively small cost of extra effort. He took his notes, scribbled hastily in class and immediately after lunch while the memory of the spoken word was still fresh, and copied improved and complete versions of the dictation into a notebook.

The result was near miraculous. The process of rethinking the subject matter apparently fixed the information into a memory bank, and it did so in a goal-oriented, mindfully controlled manner. It was apparently crucial not to leave it up to the controller to pick and choose information to remember depending on its own criteria of emotional or other survival value. The extra effort of regurgitating *all* the information was what did the trick.

So for instance, I still remember to this day that a red blood cell has to be coin shaped rather than spherical to permit the resulting large surface per volume ratio to facilitate biochemical exchanges with its surroundings more effectively. The controller, left to its own devices, would have immediately relegated this *minutium* of a detail to oblivion.

On cost-benefit ratios

Well, this bit of extra effort soon bore fruit for him in more ways than one. What happened was that he got good grades, and this attracted the attention of the *Praefect*, the academic and disciplinary supervisor of the *Schülerheim*. So he (the *Praefect*) called him aside one afternoon during the mandatory study hall that lasted till dinner for everybody without exception. "What's your secret?" he asked, looking at the group sitting there. "How can we(!) help them to do better?"

He (the boy) felt very good about the compliment and the man's thoughtful approach. "I appreciate your confidence, sir," he said politely, explaining his method. "The first thing you can do is to dispense me from study hall. I do not need it. I think I can schedule my time well enough myself. But should anyone ask you then why I am an exempt while he is not, you can tell him that it depends on his grades and how he can improve them."

The man *schmunzelte*. *Smiled* is a translation of that word that comes to mind, but that is only an approximation. *Schmunzeln* has a quality of *Verschmitztheit* to it, and that is based on an undertone of a hidden, cunning, conspiratorial understanding. He was, like so many men of his age, a frontline survivor (half of his right hand was missing). He was also the proud owner of the Iron Cross First Class. He knew the definitions of leadership and discipline well and was not worried about student rebellions. He only wanted to see for kicks how he (the boy) would react to what almost amounted to flattery, but he seemed satisfied by the result.

So he just made a brief gesture of agreement (it looked a little like an aborted *Heil-Hitler Gruß*). More was not needed, and bingo, there he (the boy) was roaming in the forests much of the time again (homework permitting). Such are some of the secrets of freedom as he had learned to appreciate early: do willingly what cannot be avoided anyway and things will tend to work out well for you.

The potato eaters

But no roaming in the woods let him ever forget a mealtime. You see, the Magyar past was rapidly receding, displaced by the reality of the German present. The villages around Bad Aibling where the refugees were quartered, Harthausen, Elmosen, and Kolbermoor, still resounded with Magyar-speak; they still felt almost as if you were back home on the Puszta, the great plains of the Danube, but here in Icking that seemed far away. And at no time was this distance more palpable than at mealtime. For even at the worst of times in Harthausen, he and his brother managed somehow to scrounge up some things worth eating. One could trade something for eggs with the Bichlmaier kids, whose farm was across from Resi Meyer's house on the Harthauser Straße. Or a dozen of those frog legs from the bomb-crater ponds could be fried for a splendid protein supplement. And they knew what mushrooms were edible at a glance. Whatever. There were always ways.

Here at the Schülerheim, however, there was no room for such latitude; the fare was strictly potatoes and turnips. Once a week, red beets came on the table, or green cabbage (the proverbial *kraut*). It was harsh. What made it worse was that the German kids did not think there was anything wrong with that. They were inured to this kind of fare through years of habituation and had come to expect that this was the way things had to be. They would *motzen*, or grumble, sometimes and say vacuous things like "*Die Nazis brachten uns Vitamine, die Amis brachten uns Kalorien, wer gibt uns endlich was zu essen?*" ("The Nazis brought us vitamins and the Amis calories, but who will give us something to eat?") But that was only talk to relieve the *Kohldampf*. And although that means "cabbage steam" if you translate it literally, what it really means is hunger.

He and his brother, on the other hand, suffered. Every Saturday, two students were detailed to go with a handcart to the village of Dorfen and return with two large milk cans of *Buttermilch*, the stuff that is left over after the butter is churned out of the cream. The thin, cottage cheese—like dish that was prepared from this was the Sunday feast. They were always hungry, not starving-hungry to be sure, just hungry-hungry. Their chemistry teacher, Doktor Grotensohn, calculated that you had to eat ten pounds of potatoes to get your normal daily requirement of protein from that source.

However, not even having to eat a ton of potatoes could have deterred them from getting on with their future, which took a leap forward when their teachers decided that they were misplaced in their current grades and should skip one by doing two grades' worth of work in one year. So they proceeded to do that.

Saving a year

What made this not only possible but made it feel like fun was the presence in Icking of an inspired teacher. She did not like standing in front of classes, so her students came to her as patients would go to their shrink's private office. Dr. Tilla Kratz was a genius but not the kind that has her feet in the clouds. With the social fabric of her place in society having been rent by the war (like most everyone else's), she needed to earn a living, and she did that by bringing laggards in school up to snuff.

She accepted the two Magyar grade-hoppers as a fun assignment. Her background was somewhat mysterious. She must have alit in that little wooden cottage of hers in Maina Bachman's garden right next to the school, tossed there by the winds of war from some high, distant academic peaks and circles that she did not care to talk about.

But I have read not one but two novels playing on stages reminiscent of the Icking cultural scene (had I not forgotten their titles and authors, I would cite them here). Both were written in the style of an intellectual elite playing the esoteric Game of Glass Pearls, and I could distinctly recognize the Magic Mountain backdrop of Icking and the unmistakable overtones of Tilla's personality in them, although neither of these had been mentioned explicitly in those books. If my pen is less discrete, it is only to do homage to my teacher.

Tilla could open her prodigious Latin dictionary exactly to the correct page on first try; she would make a game of complex Pythagorean proofs; she introduced him to Dostojevsky, Plato and Hermann Hesse; she made English and French sound easy; and she took him not only to the opera but also to hear *Die Fledermaus* fly at the Theater am Gärtnerplatz and to celebrations of *Hausmusik* at her friends' homes in Munich. With all this, she managed to convey the idea to him that the subject matter of the eighth grade, the one to be skipped in class, was not a hurdle of hard work but a cakewalk with time left over for roaming in the woods.

The other students in the *Schülerheim* watched these strange goings-on (when they were not busy playing soccer) with an attitude that he recognized to be a none-of-my-business shrug, but they also accepted it with the innately tolerant comradeship that people are capable of who do not feel threatened and at the same time are too hungry to be hostile.

He and his brother, although recognized as different, were not seen as a minority to be ostracized. They were refugees like most of the inmates of the *Schülerheim*, and as such, they were as much part of the scene in all the ways of this openly closed community as all the others. So when the time came next September, with the new school year to make the switch from the group they skipped out of to the one they moved up to, it was a non-event, although he did wonder at times why no one else ever tried to do this grade skipping also.

The new classmates were all as normal people as the old ones were, but two of them I need to single out here who stood out as good friends, Erwin Weiss and Wilhelm Schüler, the latter only known as "Tell." I hope they will live to see this in print and to forget about suing me for not having asked for their permission to name them. For I have lost track of them, even though Erwin had invited me repeatedly to class reunions, which I never attended for reasons so obscure that not even I myself could understand them. I do not have the knack or endurance or the vitality to keep up with lost-but-maybe-still-alive dear ones. I am a frigid fatalist, and I am afraid that that may be the deaf and blind god's childhood legacy.

On consequences

Getting good grades that lead to a freedom to roam the woods sounds like a good and even clever consequence of rewriting one's classroom notes. Jumping over an entire grade is a little more far-fetched, but saving a year that way is a consequence that still follows the same logic.

But there was a third consequence of all this extra effort that was so fateful and long lasting that I find myself squirming around to find a way to face the need of reporting it. So I will interrupt the sequence of events here. The chronology that was scrolling down on his controller's screen as he was driving east on the Loneliest Highway to his work site. Instead, I will push the fast-forward button to the present for a change. Much of this flash-forward has little to do with the third consequence itself, but is, in its own convoluted way, a preparation for it.

The crow convention

I stopped at this town on my way north to my favorite water hole, a hot spring in the Northern California Coast Range. It was not in order to refresh the memories of those intensive years of mine there at the University of California at Davis, years that prepared me for a future that is now years past already as I write this, but because it was getting late and I did not like to drive in the dark anymore.

After settling into my motel room, my feet led me to the edge-of-campus shopping center at Russell and Anderson streets, a couple of blocks from where I had lived then, for a mug of beer at The Graduate. Well, the graduates must have all gone on to drive taxicabs, for that establishment was not there anymore. What I encountered instead was a major regional convention in the parking lot. It was convened by the steering committee of that other sapient species, *Corvus brachyrhynchos*.

There were some sixty or seventy small trees in that large parking lot, and each one of them had fifty to a hundred crows crowded in it. There was also a multitude of large trees, pines, and oaks mostly surrounding the lot, all packed with crows, and in the light of the street lamps that fell on three of those trees, I could count in each of them up to three hundred busy, raucously cawing birds all moving about in a state that felt like joyous excitation mixed with concerned agitation. Conservatively speaking, there must have been, all in all, some fifty thousand of them at the very least. The thing is that I have witnessed this same event before at the same place and the same time in midwinter, so I infer that it is a planned, annual event, a mate-meeting celebration, perhaps in honor of the lengthening of days.

Now, crows are territorial in a loose way, although not strictly so like many of the songbirds. Still, they need a given territory to support each one of them separately. If such an individual crow-support area approximates, let's guess, ten acres, that will come to half a million acres that the participants of this convention needed to distribute themselves back to after they had finished discussing this year's topic.

But the real question is whether these annual gatherings are nothing but a social fiesta, or is there perhaps something more to it? The crow (and if you did not know this, it is a good time to take note of it now) as well as the other members of its family, the *Corvidae*: the ravens, the rooks, the magpies, the jays, and the mockingbirds, are a chosen people among birds.

They have an area in their brains, the dorsal ventricular ridge (modestly comparable to our laminar isocortex), and the intelligent designer of the evolutionary process outfitted them with that (in play or on purpose?) in such a way that they are not only capable of episodic memory but may also integrate disjointed events into concepts for use in planning future agenda. But at the same time (and here is the rub), since they do not have much (or any) of a cerebral cortex to speak of, their ability to relate to the universe and to receive messages from it is not shielded by the activity of the regrettably incessant internal dialogue that we (*Homo sapiens*) are enslaved to by virtue of possessing such a cortex.

So in their way, I would venture to guess that they are able to meditate without recourse to prayer wheels, mantras, or rosaries and without the laborious Yoga practices that we need to prepare us for it. What then may have been this year's message from the universe that they were exchanging with each other so excitedly? What answers did they find; what new plans, and alternative strategies did they arrive at? And will they do something about it this time, or will they just table it again for later? Or will they be satisfied with a nonbinding resolution?

Shake your head, if you like; ours is still a free country (as we speak). My problem is, you see, that I hold degrees in physiology and physics, the sciences of life and nonlife. And as the lessons from these merged and gelled, a synthesis arose that reinforced earlier thoughts along these lines. This synthesis suggested on the one hand and denied on the other that there is a "force" (for lack of a better word) outside the realm of our sense experiences, a force that is a function of a primary realm not accessible directly to the elementary one that is the home of our bodies, one that consists of everything that our senses and our instruments can perceive. And where the two realms overlap, at their interface where life exists, this force can make itself be felt and, perhaps, even interpreted by living beings and especially by those who, like the crow, are sapient without having been condemned innocently to be weighed down by the original sin of incessant thinking, like us. To the incessant chatter that acts like a barrier and prevents us from accessing the force while at the same time, the crows are free to get their message from the universe.

Next year, maybe they will let us know what it was. But not now because this time, overnight, all the tens of thousands of them, ghosts on black wings, were gone by sunup, vanished as if they had never been there. Was their convention just an apparition, a spook, a midnight musing of my mind (*Mensch! Gib acht! Was spricht die tiefe Mitternacht!*)? Maybe, but the parking lot and the streets around it were as white with bird shit the next morning as fallen snow.

Mei Ruah

Next, still on my way to the hot-water spot, I stopped in Middletown, as I always do, and wandering around in the time-forgotten part of its few streets, I ran into a sign over a rickety wire-mesh gate to a time-and use-worn yard and cottage, clearly the property of someone of my age, that said, "This is where I belong." The time frame of it? The Old Saint Helena Creek Bridge next to this cottage is dated 1906, about the time my mother was born.

That is so long ago now that even the street on which she learned to walk has vanished in the wake of those ethnic-cleansing bulldozers in Léva. Here in Middletown also, right across the street from my fellow traveler who did find his place where he belonged on earth, spanking-new houses of a subdivision had arisen during the year since I had last seen it. That reminded me of that other sign on a house in Pullach that he always watched out for when looking out of the window (on the right-hand side going toward Icking) of that wooden-benched, third-class car of the *Isartalbahn* of the immediate postwar years.

That sign said in Bavarian what the sign in Middletown said in English. It said: *Mei Ruah*. With the strong premonition already of owning the road as well as being owned by it, the mindset of someone who could declare his position on earth with such lapidary certainty affected him, the teenager, with a sense of awe. Years later, looking out from a now softly upholstered second-class car, he never stopped searching for that sign, although even the house had disappeared and given way to a high-rise. Its erstwhile owner, I hope, found his *Ruah*, his rest, his peace, his permanent angle of repose at a slope of zero degrees in a nicely manicured Bavarian cemetery, before his home was razed by the bulldozers of progress.

The third consequence

What must go on in the minds of crows and in the minds of people who actually find their place on earth seemed akin to him, for he did not understand either of them. Instead, what he understood from early on was the search. Back then in Icking, of course, that was not yet defined as a quest of "The America," a place not in the clouds but a real one on the ground, not one conjured up only by his imagination like This Place Where I Belong or Mei Ruah. He did not know yet that it was not his lot to find such a place. And with time, reality shrunk America down to the size of a mere continent, which as the aim of his quest, lost its capital A. The real place on the ground moved back up into the clouds and became "an america." A place that was akin to what he liked to read about in the Mahabharata and the Vedas in the library of that hot-spring spot a few miles north of Middletown, where he had arrived in the meantime.

The *Upanishads* are not easy to read. They sounded to him at first as if the crows or, at least, minds equally different from his had composed their contents. What those lines might say can easily sound garbled. Maybe this is so because the manner in which the channelers of divine intuition rendered those foreign concepts into their original language sensitized the brains of their audience in certain ways, and this language cannot be readily remolded into something like English because the new audience finds it difficult to interpret the old meaning, no matter how bravely the translator struggles with the text.

This reminds me of his own futile attempts to teach his roommate Nepper, in Norman, Oklahoma, to pronounce the German vowel *ü* as in *Führer*, for they were sometimes discussing Hitler and the war. For the life of him, wordy media man though he was, Nepper was not able to reproduce the sound; it always came out as *furor*. Finally, he realized that it was not Nepper's tongue but his brain that balked. Although his ear perceived the sound correctly, the auditory centers of his brain were not sensitized to process it. So also may it be with some of those Eastern concepts. We need to get sensitized to them through practice to get their deeper meaning.

To be of help in such an impasse, one or another prophet or even the incarnation of a concept (Krishna is the one I like best) has always jumped into the breach. I can almost see him smile when he sees me pondering over the imponderable: "Hold it! Use your head since you are a person and have one. The idea is simple, so try to get it right: it is neither good nor bad what we, the gods, send you, for you, the receiver, determine the value of the gift. It is up to you to make of it what you can."

And that brings me at last to the gift, that third consequence of those good grades in sixth grade. It has found for itself the proper cosmic environment here by this digression into transcendence. And that befits the discussion of it, for the skipping of the eighth grade had no less of a consequence for him than falling in love for the first time. And that is a cosmic event indeed. Only, it took the universe more than a decade to decide whether that cosmic event was reward or punishment for him, for he was quite helpless to decide for himself what the value of the gift was at the time.

First love

And puppy love it was not, this first love, although in the ninth grade you are a puppy, and so was he basically, in spite of the already lengthening path that took him there. And he knew it and suffered from it, for the last thing you identify yourself with when you fall in love for the first time is puppyhood.

Now, you must not confuse that ninth grade in Icking in 1948 with a freshman high school class in the US. The lessons of the times that have shaped those ninth graders were very different from what I gather those lessons are nowadays. The war had an impact on everything and everybody. Like a drought will hasten the ripening of fruit, the war had encouraged an early understanding of the precious precariousness of the moment and a sense of responsibility for that present moment's consequences for the future.

Those in the *Schülerheim*, mostly from places like Breslau, Hermannstadt, Danzig, and Karlsbad, whose homes (like his) had fallen into the claws of the victors, felt this more deeply than the local Isartalers, but those also had seen the liberators at work in Munich and understood the realities of their times. The girls especially, for girls tend to be ahead of boys at that age. They were good and wholesome and, at the same time, mysterious and exciting company.

Uta and Sylvia were like that, and one could have gone to steal horses with them; as Lehner, the art teacher, would express it: "*Gelt, man kann mit ihnen Pferde stehlen gehn.*" But then there was the *femme fatale*. The Lara of Pasternak, the Eula of Faulkner, the one with the mysteriously oriental and yet blue eyes that she would close slowly and keep closed for a moment like Siamese cats do. Before he knew it, he was lost, sunk beyond the reach of a lifeline in the cold mountain lakes of those blue eyes.

Why try to tell you here, how it is to fall into a cold mountain lake before you have learned to swim? If you know how it is, you know it, and if you do not, no words can help. As I sit here in the café of my hot-springs haven and look out on the steep mountain slope on the other side of the valley, rain is washing down the dusty digger pines, blue oaks, manzanitas, and mountain mahogany bushes that still are footed in brown grass, for this was, up to today, a winter of drought.

The top of the ridge is cloaked in fog whose long white fingers reach deep into the gray-green-turquoise-mottled foliage of all those xerophytes as if to hug them reassuringly with a wet kiss, and this embrace creates such a closeness between the earth and the sky that there would be no telling how high the mountain might rise, if one did not know it already. But as the fog now connects seamlessly with the rain clouds above, the whole horseshoe-shaped valley seems to be one, separate, self-contained, live but unconscious being that does nothing and has no purpose other than to echo the music of the raindrops.

And in this way, the whole scene before me helps me a little to speak of the way he related to those mountain lakes. For you are really helpless in that regard.

Your heart feels like a vast, resonant echo chamber with its walls lined with the hundred thousand words of the tongue you speak, and you are possessed with this overwhelming desire to reach up and pluck the right ones off and fit them together so that they might paint and compose the world that all of your trillion sentient cells were deeply involved with at the time you were submerged in those cold, blue mountain lakes. Good luck! Great poets have tried it, and the fewer words they plucked, the better they are remembered.

Well, now. Within the constraints of the situation, the relationship was essentially one of distance. There was no mechanism to narrow this physical distance. The Icking of that day had no cars, no movies, no cafés, or any conceivable places where to get together out of the weather. Walking her home from school now and then along that forest path (one that is still there!) was the limit of intimacy, but it was a fragile, new, and unexplored type of intimacy whose very likelihood he did not really dare to take for real (shy introvert that he always was).

Also, he was encumbered (*belastet* would be the word with the most correct connotations here) with the image and the concept that his parents' relationship had engendered and nurtured in him that women, though very real in their own right in this man's world, were yet somehow creatures from different realms and that this difference of their being that surrounds them with an aura of dignity could only be approached very gingerly and, yes, in its own way, reverentially. Therefore, such down-to-earth approaches as holding hands, for instance, as a first step in bridging the distance was a thing he did not even think of. Imagine that in today's world!

How strange this pattern of behavior must have appeared to her, who came from a family of a more robust social fabric! Her models were those of a different society and country that are given to *Sturm-und-Drang* values of robust domination and possession though, at the same time, are couched in the genteel and romantic traditions of their great art and music. And those values were very different from those of the chivalrous sophistication of people like his father, who dominated his limited child's field of vision. But none of this troubled him, for it never entered his mind—back then.

Still, puzzled as she must have been at such times of togetherness, she was always cheerful, friendly, compassionately though sometimes perhaps exasperatedly interested, and very talkative in a comradely sort of way. She would bring him books to read like the *Buddenbrooks*, the *Idiot*, and *Björndahl*. Given to a spontaneous outpouring of everything that came to her mind, she would unabashedly relate secrets that others may have entrusted to her *sub rosa*, in confidence, so that he could not help wondering how she might talk to others about him, maybe poking fun at his odd ways.

Silence was something that she was quite incapable of, and this was a thing he missed most acutely in her company. When silence between people feels awkward, it is a sign of distance, a sign that he did not yet know to properly read and appreciate. Real or imagined, however, there were enough times of sharing and exchange that permitted and encouraged a depth of feeling to blossom, if ever so guardedly, to become a significant and, for him, long-lasting reality.

Nothing could exemplify this reality more than the subtle, subliminal signs of discord that she could probably feel (if not outright read) quite clearly, while he, if aware of them, would deny them resolutely. There was this children's play that her father had written, where she played the star role of Lilo Fee, the human princess, who is seduced by a nature spirit—the well meaning but ominous *Wassermann*—and carried off to his castle at the bottom of the lake. And yes, it was he, of all possible people, who reminded her of this Waterman, and she related this to him cheerfully without noticing his consternation and disappointment during one of the dancing lessons that her mother had organized at her house.

Her mother, a woman with equally blue but warm eyes that saw everything that was happening in the world around her and with the wholesome wisdom of people whose world is cheerfully secure, arranged for those dancing classes in her living room. She did it because she liked to dance herself, as she would smilingly admit when describing that great dance floor at that mysterious hotel-castle where she had learned to dance before the war.

This *Schloss* stood at the foot of the Wetterstein Mountain, and in its great hall, people would dance nothing but the Viennese waltz, the *Rheinländer*, and the *française*. Sylvia, whose grandfather had built it, knew it well, and it was Tilla who undertook the pilgrimage to it with him one weekend, explaining its *zauberberg*-like essence and history during the train ride to Klais. It was quite a hike up from the station below in the valley to Elmau in those car-free days, and this visit was to be the first of a long sequence to come, though at long intervals and in different, changing circumstances.

Meanwhile, back at that living room in Irschenhausen, there were some seven or eight of them learning to do the foxtrot, Uta and Sylvia, Tell from the *Schülerheim*, and maybe Arno Kolbe of Irschenhausen, all from the ninth grade. He walked with Tell the three kilometers, miles from the *Schülerheim* to Irschenhausen, for these occasions through the dark wintry forest lit a little by the snow from below, taking the pathless detours on the way back that he is still so fond of, testing his ability not to get lost. Tell was great company; he had a budding *Weltanschauung* on school, women, and politics that was reassuring and compatible. He was not yet at the stage of falling in love, but he shared his friend's predicament with amused understanding. I wish I had kept up with him through the years.

Bad Godesberg

However, as the Vedas also teach, no pebble is thrown into a lake without causing ripples and waves. The ripples of this infatuation, the consequences of attention and concentration diverted from Athena to Aphrodite, soon washed up on the prosaic entries of his report cards, and they were not exactly those someone who lives on a scholarship-grant based on good grades needs.

Change was needed, and when the roots of the situation that demands change go deep, the best medicine tends to be radical. Such was the medicine that his father prescribed for him with his own full understanding and concurrence, seeing that it was necessary. His father then mobilized what connections he could command from his refugee's room in Harthausen, and in the end, a few letters bearing the signature of names of import tipped the balance in favor of his acceptance at one of the most prestigious prep schools of the country.

His last days in Icking were true lessons in the wisdom of the butterflies: "Don't cling." He walked every path that he knew with the page of her poem in his shirt pocket written for him as a parting gift (the piece of paper on which it was written disappeared in the course of the decades that followed), and I remember now only one of its verses:

Du hast begonnen mit dem Spiel der Blicke	You started with the game of glances
Und wußtest plözlich immer wo ich war.	And suddenly you always knew where I was.
Jetzt spiel ich mit.	Now I play along.
Und heute über's Jahr?	And in a year from now?

She was very honest and prosaic in her poetic assessment of the status of affairs. "I play along now." It is all a delusion, the wish to know the unknowable, to see the future, the essence of another person, life in the castle at the bottom of the sea. I play the game now. But "now" is nothing but the blink of an eye as ripples spread only until they abate at the edge of a mountain lake.

On the way to the AKO

Then time came to bid Icking farewell, and soon those woods between Walchstatt and Irschenhausen were in the rearview mirror of his mind as he got on that train headed for the Rheinland. But his heart was a different matter; the time spent there was already deeply embedded there with its multilevel meanings and memories, to be never uprooted again. But the wind was blowing briskly from the east so that his sails were again spread taut on this next leg of the journey: westward, ho!

He was on his own for the first time, and for an introvert, he was curiously unconcerned. Even the ride itself was a novelty, for the commute between Bad Aibling and Icking via Munich for the summer vacations was made up of short hops on local trains, but this new stretch of the road, this new *vasút*, this iron road, was one that led into the great world well outside the postwar concentrations of the Magyar diaspora.

Bad Godesberg, the goal, was already in the reaches of French-influenced Western Europe, a world of unknown dimensions, unexplored. A *Katzensprung*, a mere cat's leap, by the measures of his later travels, this first trip to the Aloisiuskolleg was a major journey then, lasting all day on the still hard, wooden benches of the third-class carriage that he could just barely afford, interrupted by a change of trains at Frankfurt. That is a city that was to become well known to him later but was now experienced only as a *Bahnhof* of portentous proportions with an entirely bewildering (for one who had never seen the like of it) maze of possible connections from which the right one to Köln had to be found promptly from arcane schedules seemingly written in cuneiform, for back then, there was only one train available a day, and it had to be found if he did not want to spend the night at the station.

From Frankfurt on, the road was one of pure joy. By luck, it was not at night but in the afternoon of a clear and bright spring day (in the Rheinland, the school year starts in April not in September as everywhere else in the world), and from his window seat, the Great River of song and lore opened up suddenly to his enchanted gaze, embedded between slopes covered by vineyards with picturesque medieval towns below and ancient, weather-worn castles above on the hilltops,

Die Luft ist kühl und es dunkelt	The air is cool as night falls
Und ruhig fliesset der Rhein;	And placidly floweth the Rhine;
Der Gipfel des Berges funkelt	The peak of the mountain sparkles
Im Abendsonnenschein.	There in the sun's setting shine.

as his mind's eye had seen it as a vision in the beginning of his time in Miskolc. His German governess had sung it for him when he was less than three years old. This song was one of the very few memories of his earliest years, and the controller had apparently embedded it deep in his consciousness, perhaps because of its haunting melody.

This resurfacing of the song from the depths of oblivion at the sight of the river that it describes reminds me as I sit here looking out on Bishop's Peak of the seeds of corn that my friend and colleague, Boone, had found in a cave on the dry highland plateau of Oaxaca in Mexico. They had lain there for about twenty five hundred years (he had them carbon dated at the Instituto Tecnológico de Oaxaca), and under Boone's skillful touch, a few of them could be coaxed back to life. It was quite a find, for the origin of corn is still a hotly debated subject of dispute, and these could have become a link between the Olotón landrace that grows there now and some ancestral form of it like *teosintle*. But the seedlings did not survive, leaving the mystery of their evolution in the hands of Centéotl, who gave these magic plants to mankind in the first place.

Such a magic gift was that song for him, however, for it created a bridge to this new world on the Rhine, and he did not feel so lost and alien in it anymore. In the end, all those reveries of past and future did not prevent him from noticing the signs announcing Godesberg and from getting off just in time, for the stop was very brief. And so he was able to climb up the hill and knock at the gate of the Aloisiuskolleg (AKO) well before dark.

The *Collegium*

Saint Aloisius, a fifteenth-century Italian nobleman, was noted for his involvement with the education of children and the care of the sick. He was given to chastity of thought and action and died young, but above all, he was a member of the Jesuit order, the Society of Jesus. So fittingly, he was chosen as patron saint of this *Collegium*, an institution in some respects not unlike a British "public" school and one of the most prestigious schools in all of Europe (as I have always suspected but just now saw it confirmed by clicking into Google).

A "college" in European usage, you must know, is not the American institution of higher learning typically with a four-year curriculum of studies, where students make up for much of what they should really have learned in "high" school. Instead, it is a community of scholars usually who live and work together in furtherance of some common goal.

He felt at home there immediately, although there were no woods to roam in. Had there been, that type of activity would not have fitted, not seamlessly at least, into the lifestyle of this *civitas collegialis Societatis Jesu*. For roaming in the woods is basically indulgent however wholesome a pastime it may be. And self-gratification is not compatible with a worldview that holds that all thought and action is to be *ad majorem Dei gloriam*, the motto of the order.

Lest you misunderstand this, I must hasten to explain the meaning of this tenet and the subtle dichotomy in its realization as far as the conduct of affairs at the AKO was concerned. On the one hand, there were remarkably few rules of the explicit do-this and don't-do-that kind. There were certainly no rules against enjoying oneself. Having done the homework (yes, the study hall), one could do what one liked, sports, reading, playing games, whatever; one could even go and swim in the Rhine. Back then, one would still do that hanging on to a boat to be towed upstream and then float back with the current. These days, one might dissolve in the caustic solution the water has become. So there was no self-abnegation of any kind; having fun was encouraged (tacitly), perhaps, as part of the development of a healthy self-image. It was almost as if having fun would also contribute to the Greater Glory of God.

On the other hand, there were all kinds of things that everybody did as if under compulsion, in unison, and yet freely, without being told to do so. These related mostly to the rites and religious observances, morning mass at 7:00 a.m., evening devotions, the rules of school and house etiquette, nondisturbance, and helpfulness.

I cannot help but enthuse about my couple of years at the AKO; feeble though my attempts can only be to describe its spell on me. It was like living in a great Gothic cathedral but one whose wide glass windows (colored and transparent at the same time) are open to the sun and the wind and, for a select few like for Saint Aloisius himself, to the Holy Spirit. There were a few classmates who felt like this, although for most, the AKO was probably just another boarding-school experience.

In reality, the accommodations were not unlike his metaphoric cathedral. The upper grades lived in a small chateau, the Stella Rheni, surrounded by a huge park from where a filtered view opened on the Drachenfels, a medieval fortification on top of one of the seven peaks of the Siebengebirge, the range of hills on the other side of the river. In this castle lived a community (*collegium*) of students organized into two essentially self-governing groups: the three upper grades and the three middle grades of the nine-year gymnasium (a designation that denoted mental exercise rather than physical, as the word is understood in America).

Each group had an elected representative who served as a liaison to the *Pater Praefectus*, a smiling, soccer-playing young priest in his final stages of becoming a full-fledged member of the Jesuit order (after a decade or so of studies in theology, philosophy, the natural sciences, and everything else that may be known under the sun) in his present assignment as an advisor and leader of young people. He was ever present, but it was the lightness of his touch rather than the firmness of his grip on community discipline that was discernible. That was the way in which the hierarchy of the AKO moved (glided, I am almost inclined to say) through the performance of their functions in their black cassocks. Each of them had an aura, which always served, though invisibly, quietly, and unsermonizingly yet all-pervasively, to remind all those teenagers around them of the *ad majorem Dei gloriam* spirit of the institution.

Social order at the Stella Rheni

Apart from these transcendentals, the community living at the Stella Rheni was very much down to earth. In fact, it represented in a stylized way the society of grown-ups on the outside. There were distinct social classes whose characteristics were not displayed in community settings: in school, at meals, at sports, and at devotions. But in play and recreation, in "social life" that is, subtle and subliminal yet intransgressible barriers seemed to arise that were no less real than the Berlin Wall, whose concept and reality were to take shape some ten years later.

There was the aristocracy, the old money, the new money (*die Neureichen*), the intellectuals, the independent unclassifiables, and a few token representatives of the *misera plebs*, the proletariat (*die Kumpel*, they called them). He often wondered, whether the *Patres Praefecti* and the hierarchy were aware of this stratified caste system.

He first ran into it while playing bridge. As if by a process of natural osmosis, he got to be a member of a subgroup that habitually practiced this fine mental exercise together. The foursome consisted usually of a prince whose family still owned the estates of their formerly sovereign little domain, a count from the Eastern lands now lost to the enemy, and a baron who lived within bicycling distance in a castle surrounded by such a genuine, medieval moat that it still could have deterred many an enemy. When visiting at this castle, they played bridge there also at times (when not picking cherries) and learning new tricks of the game from the baron's mother, who was as great a player as she was a kind lady.

Sometimes others of the larger clique replaced one or the other of the foursome who happened to be busy elsewhere, but the replacement was always from the same group, the nobility. One of them was a red-haired fellow who had such a historic name that one of his ancestors along with his principality were mentioned in Schiller's historic play, *Wallenstein*. But unlike them, he (the lad) was also in close communion with the intellectuals, and so he came to know how one of them, a lanky, earnest, polite but somewhat tense guy (whom he met again at Elmau later) felt about this bridge club.

Andreas would have given ten years of his life to play cards with the titled ones, but there was no way for him to jump over his shadow. It was not that someone told him that he could not, that he was not welcome. No, it was more like one of these force-field shields in science-fiction movies that you run up against headfirst without seeing it because there is nothing material to be seen. Having noticed this, he started studying the phenomenon and was amazed by the strength of it.

The intellectuals liked to speak French and read Tacitus and were into proving geometric theorems. No outsider thought them to be uppity because of this, if that was their bag, it was their business and no one else's, even though the baron, a robust type of martially oriented lad, was not above calling them *Bücherwurm* (bookworm*)*, but he did so only out of their hearing, so as not to offend.

He (the lad) was busy at this time making up for two years of French that they did not have yet in Icking. Here again a fine teacher came to help, whose nickname was Pater Mac, for he also taught English, and at one time (so the story went), he gave such a memorable presentation of Macbeth that the name stuck (but was applied only affectionately).

This Pater Mac had been a prisoner of war in England and, in covering the prescribed material, sometimes wove his own experiences into what the *Lehrplan* (the curriculum) required, making his English and French lessons events of enjoyment. He often picked out words to explain their origin. So at one time, he stopped at the French word *bougre*, denoting something like a bungling wretch, a bugger, and explained how it originated from the Medieval Latin *Bulgarus* (Bulgarian). That kind of lost him in thought, and so he went on to explain that there is a similar etymology for *ogre* (the mean ones that populate fairytales), which came from the French *hongrois* (*Hungacicus* in Latin), an *ogre*, being a fierce, warlike, maybe even bloodthirsty type of brute.

Seeing a grin light up his (the lad's) face, Pater Sonntag could not help remarking,: "*Na, sie sind wohl stolz auf ihre Vorfahren*" ("So you seem to be proud of your ancestors"). But then, as if attempting to mitigate what he might have thought of as an unintended edge in his words, he went on to liken the olden ways of the Magyars to those of the Vandals and the Vikings, folks of his own ancestry. Little did he know that he (the lad) was quite satisfied with being identified with *ogres* rather than with *bougres*.

But from this time on, a bond was established between teacher and pupil, and the *Pater* supplied him so well with books and advice that he (the lad) got inspired and embarked one day on learning English in his old no-pain-no-gain way. He first took up *Julius Caesar* and then *The Midsummer Night's Dream* and looked up and wrote out every unknown word, a hundred of them a day, and memorized their meaning. Each day, the text containing a hundred unknown words became a little longer, and by the time he had some ten thousand of them in his notebook, he gave up on his dictionary, for it was not needed anymore.

The intellectuals took note of this activity, and that was the way he became a member of that group also. He had a couple of good friends among the independents. Fritz Bayer stands out, but again, it was not in him to keep up with what could have been a lifelong rewarding friendship. The old money with names from the great industrial dynasties of the Ruhr Valley did not take note of his presence, but some of the new-money folks were hostile for reasons that he could not fathom. This led to the only little incident of this type during his entire stay at the AKO: one of the *Neureichen* called him a *Zigeunerbengel*, a gypsy brat, in the course of an argument whereupon the baron gave the guy such a resounding slap on the cheek that everybody within hearing took note of the mumbled apology that followed. But this was entirely atypical, and he was accepted as a casteless entity ("above caste" he liked to flatter himself).

He also related (no one else did) to the two *Kumpels* in the group. The term, as it came across to him there, had the derogatory connotation of a put-down, although *Kumpel* really means something like a comrade or buddy, as used by miners, who rely on each other in their dangerous work. They were nonpaying inductees (like he himself) into the ranks of the elite, where they felt acutely and painfully out of place. He could feel that they were suffering, like fish out of water, and this disturbed the overall harmony of the place for him, for it did not contribute to a greater glory of any sort.

He thought about discussing the *Kumpels* with one of the *patres* with whom he talked about his own problems at times, but he did not do it for fear that it might be interpreted as criticism of a decision made by this great teaching order. The *Kumpels* were clearly there as a generous gesture to further their advancement, but the alien environment was shredding the fibers of their self-esteem. He felt flattered by their confidence in telling him their woes of rejection by their companions who were not their peers and were lacking the sense of comradeship one might learn in the coal mine.

Self-searching

His own problems were of a different kind. He did not partake in Holy Communion. It would have been easy to do so, and had the *patres* made an issue of it, it could have cost him the precious opportunity of his stay at the AKO. But they did not, and so he did not take the sacrament, for it would have been a dishonest gesture. To qualify for receiving the transsubstantiated body of Christ in communion, one must first confess and repent one's sins, and not believing any of the teachings of Holy Mother Church is one such offence.

Well, if you are at a stage of your development where you simply cannot believe in or relate to God the way "He" is described in detail in the creed, what can you do? You may be sorry for not seeing it that way, but you certainly cannot repent it! So he did the only thing that he felt was open to him: he participated in all the rites (he actually enjoyed the liturgy, the rituals, and the Gregorian chants very much) and strictly refrained from communicating his doubts about matters of faith to his peers. The hierarchy, keenly aware of every small detail within its purview, did not object. But he did discuss his problem with this one *Pater* who had his special confidence, usually when walking in the park.

Being near big trees is a good place to discuss God or the gods, for plants are every bit as alive as we are (the biochemistry of most of their metabolic pathways is the same as ours, as he was to learn in great detail later) and yet are ever so much more humble even when they are a thousand times bigger than we are. So he would look at that huge elm tree while posing the perennial questions like "Herr *Pater*, how can we with our finite minds presume to know anything whatsoever about an infinite god? And how can the world be divided by an abyss between this omnipotent Creator and lowly creation groveling forever abjectly at 'His' feet when the world is clearly one? And if 'He' is all-good, how come 'He' created this world with evil so real in it (and please spare me the cop-out about 'free will' as God's gift to man)? And if 'He' is infinite, how can he be male, when sex is an attribute of 'created' matter and not of an unknowable principle?"

He did not expect specific answers, for he knew there were none, but the answers that he got were reassuring, such as they were. "We ponder all these mysteries as long as we live," the *pater* said. "And when grace comes, it obviates further pondering. So live your life so that grace may come. Make the best of your gifts. Be decent and side with the underdog. If it is your station, teach others to side with those who are weaker than they are. Don't get bogged down with futile details more than you must. But remember, some minds live by such details for they need them to support their futility. Who are we not to provide crutches for the lame?" That may have been the gist of all those years of studying theology and philosophy, and he (the lad) understood that this meant more than counting the angels that could dance on the head of a pin.

God versus principle

But they did get into esoterics anyway, just for the fun of it. They liked to turn the creator-creation enigma round and round. There was the importunate inconsistency of postulating a creator as the starting point, the origin of all things, the *per quem omnia facta sunt*, but who by the logic of the same circular argument must have started somehow himself, namely created by a previous creator (and that's why that circumspect sect in India, the Jains, denies the creator concept, as he learned later). Nevertheless, they both agreed that a mysterious "other," namely other than that which is accessible to the senses, be it person or principle, was indispensable for the completeness of the universe. The person-or-principle choice, they agreed, was a matter of personal preference, and the *Pater* was, by virtue of grace, very definitely a person person, while he (the lad), graceless as he was, had no choice but to be a proponent of the principle.

Later, as time went on, he took to calling this "other" the primary principle. The *Pater* called his "other" God. But while this God was unambiguously defined as the causal agent in his capacity as the creator of matter, the lad's elementary principle was not defined as subordinate to the primary principle. As these chains of thought took form in the course of his search for meaning, he started realizing that such definitions were arbitrary or even presumptuous, for they were based on wishful thinking, on a yearning for a benignly motivated, sensible, and purposeful presence in midst of all the pointlessness that for him was the result of all honestly evaluated observations.

Still, he could not help pondering the possibility or perhaps the necessity of a relationship between his intrinsically unknowable primary principle and his elementary principle, which encompasses everything accessible to the senses or derivable from such accessions, everything from the galaxy clusters in parallel universes to the nuclei of the atoms in our own cells. For he felt that even if everything were really as pointless as it appeared to be, the world still had to be one and the principles could not be disjunct. They could not ignore each other's presence. They could not go through their paces, express their meaning, and exert their being without interacting with each other.

Then a form or mechanism of such an interaction presented itself once, and it came across to him almost gracelike. It came years later, when he was working on his dissertation. It had to do with the first step of energy conservation in photosynthesis. And since that fits here well, let's digress, do a fast-forward, and discuss it for a moment.

On photosynthesis

Photosynthesis, you must realize, is an imponderable miracle. It takes place in genetically semi-autonomous organelles, the chloroplasts, within plant cells. The host cells and these endobionts have developed a mutually obligate interdependence with each other through the eons of evolutionary time.

The process depends on all four elements of ancient alchemy: fire, water, air, and earth. As the driving force, it utilizes *fire* in the form of photons of light from the sun. The energy so captured is channeled to split *water* into its constituent parts and then drives cascades of electrons liberated in the process to create a gradient of charged particles (protons) across lipid biomembranes within closed subsections of the organelles, the thylakoids.

Energy conserved within this physical system of separated charges, in turn, becomes the source needed for the synthesis of the chemical "energy currency" of the cell, using a key mineral from the *earth*: phosphate. The resulting compound, ATP, then becomes a crucial ingredient needed for the fixation of carbon dioxide from the *air* to produce the reduced-carbon compounds that are the ultimate energy substrates of all life (as we know it on our planet).

What we have here, he realized, is a sequential transsubstantiation of nonlife energy (light) and nonlife matter (water, minerals, and gases) to more and more complex forms of life energy and life matter (the proton gradient, ATP, and sugar) for the purpose of serving life itself.

But having accomplished that, does living matter become its own purpose? Something in him negated this possibility. Living matter is made up of lifeless constituents of the elementary principle, and the process of their becoming alive is one of transfiguration into an entirely new state of being. The result of this transcendence is *life*. And it dawned on him then that *life* does not have the same meaning as *living matter*. If so, what is it? Could it not exist perhaps at the outermost *limes* of the elementary principle? Part of it still yet different from it already in its essence, as if it were *at* an interface or perhaps as if it were *the* interface to something else. And what else is there? There is nothing else left there but that mysterious "other." Life, the interface between the principles between the godhead and matter, part of both, but by itself neither of the two.

Still on topic, but on a lighter note

About the same time as these photosynthesis studies took a hand in shaping his thought, some two decades after those discussions in the park of the Stella Rheni, a countercultural revolution of social consciousness was at work throughout the lands of the New Country with focal points at power spots like Telegraph Avenue in Berkeley and the Haight-Ashbury of San Francisco.

A mover and shaker of import of this movement in the Haight was Steve Gaskin, at San Francisco State University, the guru of the *Monday Night Class*. Gazing down across the bay at the blinking lights of the Campanile of UC Berkeley, he wrinkled his brow in mock disgust one evening after class and opined, "The greatest stumbling block on the way to enlightenment is a college education." Or so did the episode and the words get stuck in my memory.

Steve, of course, had nothing against the joyous process of learning that leads to knowledge, for he was reputed to be a great teacher. What might he have meant then by this apparent indictment of a system of which he was part? Certainly not the imparting of knowledge! I think it was rather the relevance of the offerings and their disjointed, piecemeal way of presentation that he had problems with, for he was searching for something more meaningful to present to his students of semantics than just a collection of textbook facts and examples.

It must have been the both yes and no dichotomy of preparing his charges for a job in the world or for a meaningful life in it. And if that meant the difference between just surviving in the world or being able to relate to the god principle, then he chose to redefine what he felt was relevant given those two choices. He was dissatisfied with the direction where the country was going, and so he set out to show by example what could be done about it. That was "The Farm" in Tennessee that he founded: it was a palpable demonstration of meaningfulness to a world of college courses attended by those who could get themselves deferred from having to serve in a senseless war (Vietnam). The Farm was his new course in semantics; it was the road that led to a new definition of enlightenment.

So in a way, he thought of Steve's farm as an interface when he visited it a few years later. It was not an abstract place like the one between his two principles but a real one between the world as we know it and the utopia as we all would like it to be. An interface where a life lives, one that is conducive to miracles, and none of them more holistic than the wholesome, farm greenness of plants they cultivate there without the use of poisons.

Of plant leaves specifically, for now we come to that aforementioned gracelike insight again. I can tell you, that when you have labored long to learn to isolate your chloroplasts from those leaves by centrifuging them from all that ground-up cell debris and then broke them and washed them in nonbuffered isotonic solutions to reduce your system to those minute, green, lifeless, lipid pouches that the proton-pumping thylakoids are; common sense would call for nothing to happen when you shine the light, the fire element, on them.

But no, what happens is not what common sense calls for. What happens is the miracle. The lipid membranes of those lifeless pouches spring to life, and yes, they perform the cosmic dance of Krishna on the point of a pin. They pump themselves so quickly full of protons that your expanded-scale pH meter can barely follow the resulting change in the charge saturation of the suspension in which your thylakoids swim. It is an event confined to a little glass vial, but it is mind-blowing when you first witness it. There is something at work here that neither of the two principles alone can accomplish. They need each other; they are joined at this point where matter becomes living matter to bring about life.

So there, Steve, this sort of thing also comes from a college education and is far from being a stumbling block on the path to enlightenment. But now back to the present. His college education to come was still far away and was slow in coming, for the road leading to it would be rocky (choppy to be exact). It would lead across the waves of a stormy ocean in the wake of well- or ill-considered decisions pro or con the big leap across it. For the time had now come to push aside the luxury of metaphysical speculations in the rarefied atmosphere of elite scholarship at the AKO and face the necessities of reality. Those of the road, for all of a sudden the road was beckoning again.

To stay or not to stay

The decisions for the future that ripened in that small, square, world-isolated corner room in the Harthausen farmhouse where his father still lived had been engendered by global developments far away, concocted and then signed into life in quite another type of room, oval in shape and world-wide in character. These developments were part of the consequences of his Great War.

You see, if countries are like dough, then wars are like the yeast that makes it rise to new and sometimes unexpected heights. The vast young country that had been basking quietly and mostly peacefully in its splendid isolation between sea and shining sea, mostly innocent of any natural enemies for almost two hundred years, had been shaken (or shook itself?) out of its somnolence by the rising waves of violence raging beyond and across both of those seas. Its decision to take part in, to become part of, those age-old cycles of violence then changed its way of life and contorted the peace of its soul. Its proud promise to become the *Novus Ordo Saeculorum* remained printed on its most powerful weapon, its almighty currency, but the words started ringing hollow as its newfound power went to work on this New Order of the Ages, doing what power always does.

Back there in that room in Harthausen, inhabited by those three persons displaced from their home were interested only in their own future and cared little for any distant and intangible *Novus Ordo*. The future effects that newfound power would eventually bring to bear on this nascent superpower were in no way discernible yet. Those effects would come home to roost later in Hué, Can Tho, Fallujah, Sadr City, and Kandahar.

What they could see clearly, however, was the hostility that had arisen between their two erstwhile enemies, the old empire in the East that they had long known to be evil and the new empire of the West that they hoped was good and that seemed to be willing to oppose the former. When this opposition came to be written in stone in the National Security Act of 1947, there was a bit of short-lived rejoicing sparked by the hope of immediate action. But as that new, cold sort of war that was officially inaugurated by the NSA47 started its slow march month after month into what seemed to become a state of permanence, the displaced persons of Harthausen started focusing on another act also conceived far away but of more immediate impact on them: the Displaced Persons Act of 1947.

The DPA47 was an economic outgrowth of his Great War and was intended to affect America directly, while the Marshal Plan was tailored to address the needs of war-torn Western Europe and to affect America indirectly by creating markets for its products. At home, the war effort had revolutionized the productive capacity of American industry that was now used to turning out untold thousands of tanks, jeeps, airplanes, and ships with never before experienced rapidity and efficiency. This was an effort that in view of the emergence of a powerful permanent enemy (a newfound gift) could not be abandoned but had to be modernized, augmented, serviced, and funded.

This and countless other aspects of capital creation, the provision of exports in support of the markets being stabilized by the Marshal Plan abroad, the rise of demand by the newfound wants of a higher standard of living, the growing dependence of the nuclear family on two cars rather than one, and the plans for an explosively growing interstate highway system, to mention but a few, put stresses on the labor market that could not be relieved without a new wave of cheap immigrant labor.

So it was only natural that the gaze of the brokers of power on Wall Street and on Pennsylvania Avenue turned to the millions of displaced persons like him and his brother in Harthausen that had flooded the Western remnant of the old Germany from the lands now under the yoke of that other superpower that was belatedly becoming recognized as evil even in America.

And these DPs were not "the tired and huddled masses" that the Statue of Liberty spoke of. No, these were persons of initiative and intelligence like others before them who, homeless and tempest-tossed now, had displaced themselves by calculated choice not to become victims of the Red Tide. And now the power brokers were to give them a chance to become the lubricant to grease the skids and to oil the cogs of the great industrial machine that was beckoning, over there, over there, over the seas, at the feet of the skyscrapers of New York and Chicago. Of course, they (the lad and his father and brother) did not look at the situation in these exact terms back then. They looked upon it as you look out of a window whose shades have suddenly been raised in a formerly dark room.

The open window

And it was truly a window open now but one that could and certainly would be closed soon. Magyarország had an annual immigration quota of only a few hundred heads per year, and the DPA47 temporarily lifted that limitation. What to do? Let the golden opportunity pass? At first, the question was academic, for one needed a sponsor and they did not know anyone over there. Also, when the *Pater Direktor* at the AKO first heard of this possibility (with hundreds of students he found time to concern himself with him), he would shake his head and advise earnestly against it. "America is a land that cares for money and profit only," he would say. "That is not your place. You will not fit in well there. As I have come to know you, *du bist du eine rein theoretische Begabung*. Don't do this. Your classmates, your friends that you have made here are priceless assets and connections for your future here in Europe, and we (the order) will smooth your path after you graduate from the AKO."

That was a heavy argument. Having been pegged as one with "purely theoretical talents" by the *Pater Direktor*, what could he, the introvert, do, ten thousand words of useless Shakespearean vocabulary notwithstanding, with zero training in spoken English, on the dog-eat-dog streets of an American city? For that was the way the future loomed, unknown and from afar, on the Western horizon. They hashed and rehashed all the pros and cons, enthralled by the powerful attraction of the challenge. Facing the challenge, that was where the future was, pure and simple. The challenge is a force that inhabits no cozy nooks among the neurons of the amygdala. It is stronger than the controller.

As the clock was ticking closer and closer to high noon, everyone was advising Gary Cooper on what he should do. That making a stand staring down half a dozen gun barrels alone was not a good idea. But the sheriff's ears were not tuned to the talk around him but to the haunting melody of "I'd lie a coward in my grave." The point that High Noon makes is pertinent, if not doing is the same as cowardice; it is a crucial factor that went into their decision to go. After all, they were fixing their sights on a challenge, on conquering the Wild West of their storybooks. Then, in the middle of all those theoretical deliberations, a sponsor materialized from thin air all of a sudden. In Chicago.

And that was that. That spring (the year was 1951), when he (with his brother this time) got on the train in Munich going west, it was not to Bad Godesberg but to Bremerhaven. Since the assembly-line processing of all those multitudes of DPs could not have been accomplished efficiently at Ellis Island, the military government set up an emigration camp at Vegesack, near Bremerhaven. They spent some two weeks at this center, waiting, processing, and saying good-bye. They had time to explore the strange novel sights of the towns and villages of this North German environment, so very different from the home away from home that Bavaria had become.

But the straw-thatched roofs of many of the houses in Vegesack looked homey like those he knew from Kereskény and Babád. Places that already seemed as small and far away as what you see when you look backward into binoculars. But they were not in the mood of looking back; they looked at the gray river that led to the gray ship that would set sail for the boundless gray sea, under a drizzling gray sky into the gray fog of a future glimpsed then like through a glass darkly. Tolkien's elves felt like that when they arrived at the Grayhaven to leave behind them the long ages of their past on Middle Earth. It is what the crane feels when he leaves behind his native nest for the first time to venture into the unknown, under the spell of a compulsion he only feels but does not understand.

> Darumadár útnak indúl, búcsúzik a fészkétől.
> Bús-panaszos hangja hallik tovaszálló felhőkből.
> De ha én is útra kelek, én még sokkal messzebb megyek,
> Nem jár arra madár sem, nem hallatszik sóhajtás sem odáig.

> The passing clouds resound with the crane-birds plaintive cries
> As he sets out and takes leave from his nest.
> But the Far Land where I will go is beyond the sound of sighs.
> No birds fly there, only grey clouds in the sky.

To mourn or celebrate the parting with their past in the Old Country in style, the last evening they went out to the best restaurant in town, ordered a bottle of Chateau Lafitte, and had an *Abschiedsschmaus*, a farewell feast of the best they could afford. His brother paid, for he himself did not have the money to buy even a pencil for years now. But that would soon be the past. Soon they would be in the land that flows with milk and honey, where all you have to do is shake the trees a little and the greenbacks fall into your lap like leaves.

Chapter 4

The Emigrant

When people who do not know the plants that grow along that road from the T-junction to Gabbs and Luning to the next town east by their first and last names, they think they are passing through an empty desert. And they are right, for the area is classified (technically) as arid to semi-arid. So it is kind of a desert-ish technically. Only, it is as far from being empty as a cactus is from being smooth. You simply do not see the things whose names you do not know, for your controller pays them no mind. How could it? The controller is the granddaddy of all taxonomists and in taxonomy, the name is the name of the game.

Austin, Nevada

In long-distance travel on the road, on the other hand, it is the spacing of eating places along the route that matters to goal-focused drivers. Now, he is anything but a goal-focused driver, but that feast with that bottle of Chateau Lafitte in Vegesack scrolled down his mind's computer screen just in time to remind him of Carol's Country Kitchen, the last outpost of civilization before dipping into the depths of the remoteness of Grass Valley. That is the next great north-south running valley on the other side of the summit named after the town of Austin, and it is the site of his upcoming experiment.

Checked into the Pony Canyon Motel, an establishment whose level of amenities remind him of bygone days when a good night's rest on the road cost no more than three bucks, but one that is overhung by shady trees and whose wood paneling creates a feeling of rustic restfulness, he first does his predinner constitutional walking up and down the town's quaint, semidesolate streets that are now cooling down in the gathering dusk.

The twenty-year silver boom about a hundred years ago lasted just long enough to leave behind it some now crumbling stone buildings that line Main Street. These days, an eighteen-wheeler will thunder by now and then but at mercifully long intervals, for this main street is part of the Loneliest Highway. Carol's, at the bottom of the south-facing slope of this vertical-V-shaped, canyon-configured town, is sandwiched in between the Masonic-Odd Fellow's Hall and the Lander Lumber and Supply hardware store.

The hall, by the looks of its upkeep, appears to have been deserted since the last miners left town, but the store is still open (it finally closed down this summer of 2009) even at this hour. It connects to Carol's and is clearly the commercial, if not also the cultural, center of town, for the culture that it has flows down the steps to it through the always open door from the dining establishment some ten steps above, which (as I may have mentioned before) is such a jewel that even its most demanding patron's favorite, cultured grandmother couldn't have created a more endearing Western Victorian atmosphere.

Carol serves mountain trout that evening, and he can tell by the freshness of its tender, flaky flesh that it had been caught that same day somewhere in a lake on the upper reaches of the Reese River that feeds off the snow from the high peaks of the Toyabee Range south of town.

After the long-delayed apple pie à la mode, he strolls out to the west end of Court Street, up slope from the canyon bottom. The small, red brick house there is like one of those houses that he glimpses now and then from all those roads that he travels, and which he imagines he could inhabit blissfully to the end of his days. Never mind the ugly heap of junk that is piled up around this one now and forget that it doesn't even have a window looking out on the valley below.

Just lean against the fence next to it and look out west, where you have one of the grandest views that the planet has to offer, right there from the end of Court Street. All right, maybe not quite as grand as the Grand Canyon, but when the sun has just set like now, over the distant range of the Shoshones across a good twenty miles of the wide-open, serene, and uninhabited Valley of the Reese, and in parting has thrown a russet mantle of glowing cumulus clouds over the black shoulders of the mountain peaks, your eyes wish the moment would never pass.

A bit of botany

The Reese River itself is the kind of secret reference line drawn in disappearing ink on a treasure map that you have to know about beforehand or you might never notice it. Most of the time, it is no more than an ankle-deep trickle in the places where it actually connects the mud puddles along its course. But up-valley, there is enough of it to supply a University of Nevada Research farm with water. Its presence also indicates that there must be indeed a treasure, a water table somewhere not too far below the soil surface of the valley, a surface of sandy loam that serves as the substrate for the roots of what looks to the untrained eye like a random collection of grayish shrubs. Plants that look pretty much all alike and that blur into a uniform, dry, olive-drab background not unlike the rough strokes of color dabbed onto a canvas by an impatient impressionist brush, and if you drive by this exhibition too fast, you can indeed make out the individual, rough brushstrokes only if you know well what you are looking at.

But should the spirit move you to slow down to find out the first thing about those shrubs you take at first for unsightly, you could not help noticing how carefully they space themselves. With a highly individualistic regularity, they keep each other at arm's length. Their distances depend on the size and kind of each plant, and the obligate nature of this standoffishness suggests a purpose, or maybe even a compulsion.

If you examine the leaves of the plants of greatest frequency in the vegetation, you will find them to have an elegant, three-furcate venation pattern. Pleased to have caught your eye then, these plants introduce themselves by first and last name as *Artemisia tridentata*, aptly named after Artemis, the Greek goddess of wild nature (as well as of other things also like the moon and hunting) and tridented because their leaves are shaped a little like Neptune's fork. They are the dominant species of the "big sage brush-grassland community," and community, in wild nature as in domesticated life, implies complexity (as well as order, competition, cooperation, and more of the like).

But it has turned dark by now, and that is not the best time for him to think about deep things like purpose, compulsion, and complexity. They yield their secrets to examination more readily after breakfast by the light of day after a good night's rest. So he wanders back to the Pony Canyon Motel and turns in.

The International

No, that is not the anthem and marching song of the socialist workers' brotherhood. It is the old hotel across the street. This International Hotel you have to see to believe. The upstairs, where the rooms used to be for rent, is no longer open, for the rats have gnawed suggestive patterns into its walls. But the spacious eating area downstairs continues to serve the heartiest of omelets for breakfast that can keep you in energy till the next morning, easily. There used to be a sign on the wall that suggested in self-mockery the easy pace of the place: "Eat less and chew it better—you have all day." You could almost see the author of this advice laugh at himself as time seems so timeless in this town, well alive under its cloak of ghost-townness, a life only barely apparent to the transients.

Next door, the saloon proves the motto. At the great, red-mahogany, huge-mirror-adorned, made-in-England, shipped-around-the-Cape bar, under walls papered with dollar bills, some folks seem to be camped out permanently as if tethered to their endless supply of Bud Lites emerging from behind the counter.

Not for him though, not today. It is quite a stretch to the Nevada Agricultural Experiment Station's Gund Research Ranch where USDA-ARS maintains a trailer for workers and visitors like him. And it is slow going on that rutted gravel road that veers off from the highway to the north on the far side of the pass. But just before the summit, at a good seven thousand feet of elevation, a narrow dirt road leads off south along the "military crest" of the ridge. It crosses small stands of quaking aspen and is immersed in spring flowers. You can see it plainly when you drive up the curves of the grade, and as it disappears behind some craggy outcroppings in the direction of the snow-capped peaks of the Toyabee in the distance, it promises to lead to realms of adventure waiting to be explored. One day, I will have time to walk that road, he tells himself every time he drives by it. But this time, it is another as yet unfulfilled promise of adventure that slips him back into reverie mode.

At sea

The adventure whose pictures projected themselves next on his mind's screen were those of that short bus ride from the processing camp at Vegesack to the waiting gray ship in the harbor on the Weser River. They were intensive, a medley of past and future, of introspection serving as spontaneous, self-therapeutic panic prevention. For that bus ride was the very end of the road to the *Finis Terrae*, land's end, the end of the world that he thought he was beginning to know well. The Old World, the Old Country. *Az, ami volt*, that which was,

Zúg-búg a szél Késmárk felett,	The wind is sobbing over Késmárk,
Édes hazám, Isten veled	My dear home, God be with you

as the exiles, the Kuruc warriors fleeing the looming Austrian domination, used to sing after their freedom fighter's flag fell on the plains of Nagymajtény almost three hundred years ago.

Then they arrived and there was a wait at the dock before boarding. A light, misty rain was falling, driven by squalls coming from downriver, from the sea! It was evening and the whole world consisted of nothing but different shades of gray tempered into cold shapes and patterns by the cries of the sea gulls, cries he had never heard before. Then he heard the foghorn, a real one, for the first time. It sounded exactly like it did in that black-and-white movie he saw back in Bad Aibling, where Humphrey Bogart (or someone like him) is gazing out on a black-and-gray harbor exactly like this one in its somber mood and calls the foghorn the saddest yet most exciting sound in the world.

While all those DPs, hundreds of them, went through the boarding process, it conjured up another long-forgotten memory fragment, that of cattle being loaded onto railroad cars, back years ago at the railroad station in Léva. But there was no time to dwell on things not relevant to the momentousness of the moment, for the gentle roll of the deck under his feet soon announced unequivocally that the die was cast, the tether was cut, the part of his passage that he had lived and knew so well was irrevocably over. That which was. My beloved home, may God be with you.

That gray ship was the USS General Muir, a troop transport. It had served well some years back, ferrying bodies East, and since some of those never returned home, it now had a chance to end its service honorably by ferrying live replacement ones back West before being mothballed in Suisun Bay. Years later, looking down from the tall bridge connecting Benicia to Martinez at that rusting fleet put to pasture in the estuary of the Sacramento River, he always wondered if the Muir was one of them.

Right now, however, it was time to settle in. The navy was well organized. Sailors led groups of DPs in single file down below and, having arrived at their point of destination, pointed with mute authority to the next person in the file and then to the next empty bunk, and with that, both person and bunk understood that there was no need to mill around; the union between habitant and habitable space was formed for the coming week. And a close union it was! The bunks were three feet wide with two—and-a-half feet of vertical distance between bunks stacked on top of each other, seven or eight bunks high. No one could think of complaining, for they were all volunteers (unlike many of those bodies before them going the other way), and above all, the passage was free.

But for him, the inescapability (especially for the night) of that extreme closed-in-ness brought on such a dread of being confined to a small space that it lasted the rest of his life. Imagine the benign intent and foresight of the engineers who designed this type of transport to produce built-in nausea and claustrophobia to keep the minds of the soldiers off the impending landings on the beaches of Normandy.

One of the last books he had read at the AKO was a collection of stories by Edgar Allan Poe, one of which described what it feels like to be buried alive. So when the screamies came upon him, he would sneak upstairs, under the free, dark, cold, wet, salt-sprayed sky. Strictly speaking, this was against the rules, but the young tars or old salts that moved about up there doing their chores did not mind. The one time they wanted to know (using gestures) why he was not down there in his bunk, he used his Shakespeare on them. Taken aback by this, they put him in charge of a clean-up detail below.

The promised land

Military etiquette is strict, and on a ship, it calls for an inspection every day. To pass it in his assigned area of the cavernous, dark, labyrinthine hold, he had to do a lot of coaxing in the German that was the lingua franca of the DPs who had all spent years in West Germany since the end of the war. So he got to know a few of them.

One who stands out is a man, a good thirty years his senior, who actually helped him in getting the chores done every morning. His name was Fridman, and he had served time in a Magyar military labor camp. So he knew all about inspections. He also had learned his lessons in cruelty there, and he knew all about the big and petty atrocities that people in power delight in meting out upon their victims. Among other indignities, he had been compelled to flutter by beating his arms like wings outside his barracks at dawn, stark naked regardless of the temperature, to rouse the other inmates by loud crowing.

He (the lad) was heartbroken to hear that Magyar noncoms could commit acts like that and secretly preferred not to believe what *zsidó bácsi* (as he and his brother called Mr. Fridman) was telling him. Uncle Jew was going to the Bronx, where he had some distant relatives. "Why not to Israel?" he (the lad) would ask. "Isn't that the new homeland?" Mr. Fridman had clearly considered this, but he was slow and thoughtful in explaining as people are when they try to articulate a new concept that is still in its formative stages in their minds.

"Let the young ones go to the kibutzim," he said. "People who have gone through what I have are needed elsewhere. I and those like me—we go to America because there we can serve Israel better. America is becoming now the most powerful country in the world. We must do what we can to make Americans identify with us Israelis, for only that way can we secure Israel's future. And I can work on that better in the Bronx than in Beersheba. After all, we Israelis and we Americans live by the same Bible. We must also use the same weapons. And being smart and successful is the strongest weapon. We are smart and success leads to power."

Such was Mr. Fridman's general run of thought, and he (the lad) was listening to it and actually felt pangs of shame. This man was just a stateless emigrant like him, and yet he already spoke like the dual citizen of two powerful countries. And he himself was hardly a Magyar anymore and certainly no American yet. And certainly, he was not really going to America to work there single-mindedly for a sacred cause. Like the cause of liberating Magyarország from the Russians or Léva and Bethlenfalva from its foreign occupiers, for he had never gotten over thinking of those who own them now as squatters on his land, no matter how anachronistic and politically incorrect this may sound today.

He was going there to mind his own business and to make his own way. If that was all that there was to it, why did he then not stay in Germany? Well, for one thing, he was not a German. His national identity was already written in stone when he left home. It was a feeling that was fostered further by his surroundings, for although accepted by his classmates as one of them, he also remained always an exotic foreigner nevertheless, both in their and in his own eyes.

Germany was not home, and he could not see that it could ever become that. Having been born one kind of European meant carrying such a load of historical baggage that becoming another kind (like a Magyar turning into a German) could simply not be managed emotionally. So since he could not go home to Magyarország and could not stay in Germany forever as a foreigner, what was he to do? You see, the Pan-European spirit had not come to life yet then. Why, clearly the answer was go to the only place in the world where everyone was a foreigner. The place that now opened its doors to him and that was now welcoming him: America!

Still, this America was very much more than just a last resort, a door opening when others had closed. It was an adventure, a land shrouded in a controversial cloak of mystery. It was a land buffeted by crosscurrents of good and evil. The economy of its infancy was based on genocide and slavery, and yet it claimed for everyone the fundamental right to have been born equal. It was apparently populated by kind, good-natured people, for the few contacts he has had with its officials always surprised him with their friendliness and civility, in sharp contrast to the uppity and often cynical conduct of German bureaucrats.

And yet these people who sent CARE packages to unknown sufferers could also rain bombs on innocent civilians. It was the land flowing with the milk and honey of opportunity limited only by your own ability to make good in it, but it was reluctant to offer a safety net in case misfortune befell you. It cherished charity but, in the same breath, also glorified ruthless competition. Such were some of the colors of the rainbow that painted the promise of an unknown America.

Opposites attract, and the mystery of this attraction was like a magnet. One of his favorite books had been *Az Aztékok Kincse* by his favorite storyteller, Donászy Ferenc. The treasure of the Aztecs was a mystery; nobody knew for sure if it was really there, somewhere in a pathless mountain redoubt hidden and forgotten. It was a perilous search for those who wanted to find it, and legend had it that what the search would lead to in the end was not gold but sharp-edged pieces of obsidian. I think the moral of the story was (I last read it seventy years ago) that this search was one for the sake of the search itself and that any treasure that one would ever find was nothing but the effort put into finding it. And so he determined to make that effort. That must have been what really got him on that ship.

Such were the thoughts fleeting through his mind, and they may have occurred to some of the people also who were sitting and chatting there on deck in what would have been called a "dayroom" in an army camp. They were people like him who needed to escape from dozing in their bunks. But *Zsidó Bácsi*, who was always a member of the group, did not seem beset by any such doubts. There was such a deep undertone of loyalty, of solidarity forever, of identification with his historic homeland, so young and so ancient, that he (the lad) could not help wondering how he (*Zsidó Bácsi*) would deal with problems of mixed allegiance once he was facing the oath of allegiance to defend the constitution of the United States against all detractors wherever they may lurk. For America did not yet recognize and admit dual citizenship.

The Sabbath

At the next table, by himself, a white-haired fellow DP with the long bushy beard of a patriarch was listening with half an ear, looking up sometimes from the old books and scrolls that he seemed to be immersed in. Then, when a cocky, brash, youngish fellow who formed his *r*'s the uvular German way (which sounds so out of place in Magyar that there is a special word for it: *raccsolni*, and which all true Magyars take for a snobbish affectation of worldliness) cut into a discussion on religion to assert that "we" certainly do not pray to the same God as you who crucified the Messiah, the rabbi opened both ears ready to join battle. He (the lad) was not interested in this type of exchange and moved on but was determined to hear what the old guy had to say about the matter another time.

That time came on the fourth day of the voyage. The choppy seas of the first night and day had quieted down, and it was "smooth sailing" now, as one might have called it in bygone days. Four days moving out at a fast clip and still nothing but endless water. Water, water, everywhere, an experience lost to present-day travelers locked up in their airplane cabins!

Never having seen the ocean before, this was an experience beyond words for him. He could stand there and gaze at it until all words vanished from where they are stored. The controller closed shop; the waves flooded in and washed out the details that had accumulated there and that the Jesuit *padre* had warned him against. The effect of being in the middle of the ocean is different from just looking at it from the shore. The enormity of the sea swallows you whole even when you are standing on the deck of a troop ship, and if you let it happen to you, it will hypnotize you out of your mind. Then, when your fellow DP with the books and scrolls finds you clutching the railing with white fingers and moves his hand back and forth in front of your eyes, he might find that your pupils don't follow it. That is a good frame of mind to talk about things that matter—after you have come to again and settled into a nook on deck protected from the wind.

"Religious bigots think every word of the Bible is the 'gospel truth,' but they know nothing about the Messiah, and it is little use arguing with them," he started out without having to be prodded, picking up the chain of thought where the sentence was left floating back there in the dayroom.

"The Messiah is just a symbol. He is only a personification of a greater concept, that of the Messianic Age. The Messianic Age is the rebirth of the age of innocence, the time before the "tree of knowledge" had born fruit. The time before good and evil, before sin, which are human inventions, not creations of God. The time before analytical, teleological thinking. The time when the cerebrum was young. But everything that is born to life must pass through its growing, living, and dying pains and bring its life to fulfillment along the road that we, you and I now, and mankind through the ages, have traveled in the past and must travel in the future. This journey is a process that each of us should master now, and mankind also will and must master eventually.

Dealing with good and evil is the purpose of this process since good and evil are both our genetic heritage. This process is the price of our consciousness. No pain, no gain. Each small painfully achieved victory along this road is part of the gain that leads to the fulfillment of the promise. That promise is the Sabbath. The Sabbath is not a day on which you may not do work under threat of some temporal punishment. The Sabbath is the ever-recurring reminder that there was a time and that there will be a time again when mankind rests in God (for it does not do so now)."

These may not have been the rabbi's exact words, but this was the gist of what he has said. Perhaps a link or two of my own have crept into his chain of thought along the long road since then. That reminds me that I must read Buber again. Or was it maybe Erich Fromm's *Forgotten Language* where I ran into this type of thought again?

The silence that ensued then was a signal that some question or comment on his (the lads) part was now appropriate. He had heard similar thoughts (though interpreted differently) in the park of the AKO. "So," he asked, "is that why the Pharisees could not accept Jesus as the messiah? Based on what you say, they might have said unto him, "Verily, we urge thee, look about thyself. Where dost thou behold ever so small a sign of any Messianic Age here under the Roman yoke? So what makes thee think thine time as the messiah hath come? Thou art a charismatic leader, rabbi, no doubt about that, and we see that the people follow you, but beware, the Romans have no sense of humor and they are harsh with the rousers of the rabble (and we, ourselves, are not all that keen on competition either)."

The rabbi (the live one) smiled and nodded. "Let's not be facetious now," he said. "This is a serious matter. And as I hope you have noted when I was talking about everything that lives and the road that life must travel, I did not include unconscious life. This is a problem for me. Unconscious life travels our road, I have no doubt about that personally, but I think it is like a side road that they have taken. Or a parallel one. It does not fight its way toward enlightenment. It seems it does not have to. It seems unconscious beings got there naturally as if they had always been there. If I could have a wish fulfilled, I would want to be able to chat with a cat. Or listen to a tree. Or help a chloroplast conserve energy. The things I could learn! I sometimes feel as if they, everything that lives, were a link, a key, to something 'other' out there, something, that is beyond our grip."

I (the recorder) do not remember what in the troop ship's routine broke up this exchange. But now that I am piecing the puzzle together for myself, it occurs to me (all of a sudden) that my rabbi on the USS Muir was watering a seedling that is still growing.

Eureka!

Then one morning, that of the sixth day of the voyage, the skyline of New York City emerged from the fog. It is an experience the poor natives are denied. For him, it was almost like hearing a booming voice from above announcing, "This is the sixth day. So let there be dry land and let it have structures on it that scrape the sky." He had seen NYC in some of the movies in Bad Aibling. Some of the ships arriving with celebrities on them were greeted with great foaming arches from the water cannons of fire ships. His ship was not so greeted. Instead, there were lines to stand in for inprocessing upon arrival. The key to this welcome ceremony was a paper to be signed: the all-important "First Paper." This was a declaration of intention and of gratitude to become with time, if well behaved and also otherwise qualified and found worthy, a citizen of the United States of America.

The significance of this paper was underlined by the fact that one could change one's name on it. Yes, one could put any name on that paper and it would become one's own, real, new name henceforth. It would supersede one's birth certificate! One would be born again, as if into a new identity, a new state of grace, that of a future American citizen. He decided to keep the old name. His old name, his old identity.

"Hey," the official at the signing table said, "how about Gabe Bentley? That has almost all the letters of the old one but is half as long. And it sounds American! Not only that, it sounds Anglo! You'll spend half your life spelling your name otherwise. Now is your chance. Take it!" The guy was nice and friendly: he was personable. He came across like a person, almost like a friend, not like an official. It was a good omen, and that was the way Americans turned out to be for him whenever he met them as people. Having guns in their hands, it seems, is what Americans cannot handle.

So the name stayed the same. But the identity? They say that in the course of every seven years, all the molecules of one's body are completely replaced by new ones. Does that not change one's physical identity every seven years? If so, I have become a different object, I have been born again in seven-year cycles more than ten times. Strange things, all these objects. All these objects around me will survive me indefinitely, even if all they do in the long run is getting buried in a landfill upon being of no further use to me.

My gold ring with its coat of arms in bloodstone/heliotrope that my father wore all his life may be around for thousands of years after me until somebody melts it down, perhaps. The pictures that have crystallized onto the walls of my house in the course of a lifetime, who will look at them after I am gone? Like the one I am looking at now, my dear wife's big, blue Hundertwasser print with its red ribbon spiraling concentrically into the ever-tightening black tunnel of a wormhole leading out into that "outer" space where all my past spiritual identities are already floating around, waiting for this last one to join them?

Faced with such uncertain possibilities, nothing is more reassuring than a permanent record. A record of identity, a picture. And so, in the true American spirit, a young reporter with a camera surfaced just in time after he signed his first paper, took him and his brother to a bull's-eye window of the ship and made a snapshot. It was published the next day in a New York City paper with the caption: CHICAGO NEXT STOP. The caption shows his old name under the picture of his old identity halfway between his second and third rematerialization. If you are interested, you may find this picture along with its caption in one of the NYC newspapers printed on or about May 8, 1951.

Chicago

The coach of the Nickel Plate Railroad Line that whisked them to Chicago had a good number of other DPs loaded into it. The World Church Service, which sponsored the transit, must have been well organized, for the conductor knew which ones of the newcomers had to get off at what station. They all waved good-bye to the ones still going on before they got off and did so with a breathless, wide-eyed, expectantly concerned air about them. The train ride was uneventful, but looking out of the window was interesting. The towns and cities were particularly so, for the train always went smack through the middle of them, so that one could look through the windows into the bedrooms and living rooms of the houses.

Unlike in Europe, where the stations are at the edge of town or in town but at a dead end so that the train has to back out first before going on, here it seemed that the station (and the tracks) came first and the settlement grew up around it with it as the center. *So*, he thought, the center of this American way of life here must be one of mobility, while over there, the center was the church, a haven of stability. Such were some of the thoughts evoked by observing all those new, unaccustomed sights outside.

But as far as I can remember now, he never wondered for a moment what he would have done had his sponsor not shown up at the end of the line, the station in Chicago. How he could have been so unconcerned is a mystery to me now (having turned into a worrier in the meantime), for all he had on him was the ten-dollar bill that his father had given him for the road, who probably sold his last gold coin for this purpose (the last one that was left after paying his bill at the Pension in Tegernsee?).

Everything you do can be like a game if you know the rules, but this arrival in Chicago felt like coming from another planet, the security of ten dollars of folding money notwithstanding. However, it never came to their wandering around in the streets like an extraterrestrial, for the sponsor did show up. He made sure of that because he was also a DP from the refugee camp at Bad Aibling and had experienced the feelings that accompany an arrival in Chicago personally not too long ago.

It was Sunday afternoon by the time the taxi had deposited them at 2460 Iowa Street. The sponsor had rented an apartment for them in the rear of a three-story wooden building that had nine apartments in it. The building itself was identically replicated from one end of Iowa Street to the other. The door led into the kitchen, which had a refrigerator, a gas stove, a table, and two chairs in it. A calendar showing the days of July 1950 was hanging on the wall. There was a door to the bathroom (shared with the neighboring apartment) and another one to the bedroom, which was equipped with two single beds, complete with mattress. The whole thing was not dilapidated in a strict sense of the word, but it was well along on the downhill slope of its use cycle.

After the ride through some of the busy thoroughfares of Chicago, the landing on this quiet side street of the Promised Land could have been classified as a non-event had it not had all the emotional undertones of that landing long ago at the beginning of the road in Szenc. After all the excitement of the journey, this landing felt like what an inflated rubber balloon must feel when it is pricked with a pin.

The sponsor explained that he had paid the rent to the end of the month and expected to be paid back by then. "So you have ten dollars," he said. "That's great. That should last you till your first pay. You get paid here weekly. Now, let's go. I will show you the way to work." That way took an hour and a half, changing buses and streetcars at least twice. California Avenue and Belmont Street stand out as memory fragments along the route. The goal was the Curtiss Candy Factory on Eighth Street and Farman Place. Work would start the next morning (Monday) with the six o'clock shift. That meant leaving "home" at four thirty and earlier the first time to allow for check-in. By the time they got back to the apartment, it was turning dark.

There was a corner grocery store down the street run by a second-generation Polish family (remember, my brother, we used to call the owner the *lengyel shopos*), and there they made their first acquaintance with the American brown paper grocery bag. When they got back to their kitchen, they rejoiced proudly in their functioning refrigerator and the stove that turned on and produced a gas flame, obeying the flick of a switch, without the need to feed it wood like in Harthausen. They had never seen a refrigerator before, so they just called it the icebox like the one back home.

A lesson in American

The next morning, they made it to The Curtiss Candy Company in time and were admitted in a few minutes. The foreman took him to his post at the business end of one stretch of the assembly line and gave him his instructions, which he understood because they were accompanied by an appropriate set of hand-and-arm signals. Here is a fragment of one of the sentences that the boss barked at him, remembered to this day.

It went like this: "And then flush the mess down the sink." The words *and*, *then*, *the*, and *down* he knew well enough. But *flush* from his readings in English literature at the AKO had two meanings: one was "to take on a reddish color"; the other was "to cause birds to fly up." *Mess* was a group of people eating together like the officers' mess. And *sink* was a very common verb, one of the mercifully few irregular ones in English grammar (sink, sank, sunk), meaning something like "move to a lower position." As the sentence therefore presented a puzzle, he kind of shook his head, muttering to himself, "Sink? Sink?" "Yes, yes, the sink," shouted the boss impatiently, pounding on the large, industrial-size drainage basin with his fist, "down this sink."

To this day, I cannot imagine what the mess was that he should have flushed down that sink, for his duties were limited exclusively to handling cornstarch. But he said dutifully, "*Ach so*, okay, boss," and then proceeded to start making his own money, sixty-eight cents an hour. A small step for Chicago but a giant step for him, for it was his first actual self-earned cash.

Cornstarch

The job was simple, basically. All he had to do was to take large, flat, shallow wooden trays filled with cornstarch and put them on a moving belt but making absolutely sure that there were no empty spaces left on the belt between trays. The trays were delivered in stacks about two yards high and left standing next to the elevator about ten yards from the point in space where they had to be put on the moving belt. The trays, two by four feet in area and about two inches thick, were not heavy (basically) but, as the hours of the day ticked by, became more and more so.

The trick to this whole operation was that the belt, although it did not move at break-neck speed, never stopped, the trays had to be moved from the elevator to that which had become for him his nightmarish "point in space" where they were to be downloaded from their stacks onto the belt. The stacks were moved over those ten yards by means of a dolly in such a way that they did not tip over en route, no matter how hasty the move had to be due to the relentless advance of the belt. This would have also been a simple feat (basically) had it not been for the time-crimp attached to it. That time factor was not leaving a space on the belt vacant during the transport! There should have been two people doing this really, but the civic-minded company preferred not to be saddled with extra expenses that they would have felt obliged to pass on to the consumer.

The matter with the empty space, on the other hand, was not discretionary (like passing on expenses) but peremptory. The starch in the trays had evenly spaced, finger-sized grooves in it. In the exact time intervals that the belt moved the trays along their course, a large vat was lowered over the trays. It was filled with hot, molten caramel, and it squirted streams of this sticky goo into those grooves at precisely prescribed time intervals. Had the next tray not arrived at its correct space at the predetermined time, the goo would have been squirted onto the chains moving the belt, goobering up the gears and cogs that kept it moving and bringing the production process to a sticky, sugary, and messy but otherwise blissful halt.

And that would have been an event for which the language of the Anglo-Saxons borrowed with foresight from the French-speaking Normans the word *désastre* after the lost Battle of Hastings. To prevent such a disaster from happening, there was a red panic button at his station, designed and programmed to bring the coordinated movement of belt and squirter to a screeching halt. Well, he scurried so conscientiously between elevator and loading point that he never needed to activate the button. What would have been the punishment provoked by the high crime of button pushing? Perhaps, it occurs to me as I write this, the boss might have flushed that mess of a perpetrator down that sink.

It also occurs to me now that curiosity never moved him to explore all the steps of the morphogenesis of the Baby Ruth candy bar (before and past the stage of his contribution to it) that he helped produce and dump on innocent children by the untold thousands during the two months of his stay there. Either he was too exhausted to go to the trouble or it was not interesting enough to find out. I guess, however, that the trays containing those sticks of caramel cooled along their travel on the belt were dumped onto screens that collected the sticks while the starch dropped through below to be reprocessed onto fresh trays. The sticks might then have been passed through a twirler that incorporated roasted peanuts into their still warm and pliable mass. Finally, they were then coated with a chocolate-flavored glazing.

I cannot swear to the process, but I know that I have never looked at a Baby Ruth bar since then, although I heard that they have been a consumer's favorite since 1920. There were trays of it available without wrappings for anyone to eat to his heart's content, but it was forbidden to take any of them out of the building. The mere smell of the stuff had become sickening to him by the third day.

These two months at the Curtiss Candy Company yielded two important insights for him for the rest of his life. One concerned his brother, a charismatic, six-foot-three-tall, Yankee-doodle-dandy good-looker, with manners that he could sport endearingly to good advantage. Astute and sharp-eyed management soon picked him out of the menial-labor line and advanced him to office standing, while he (the lad) was forgotten at his point in space with cornstarch and sink.

The lesson: if you are a plain, run-of-the-mill, five-foot-nine introvert, it does not suffice to do your job well to get ahead. You must do more than just not push the red button. The second revelation came later when he no longer fell into bed physically and emotionally exhausted as soon as he got home and, used to the rote now, started thinking again.

This was the utter precariousness of his situation, a hand-to-mouth existence, one of total self-reliance without any glimmer of outside help should he need it like when getting sick. No work, no money and you're out on the street. He was completely unaware of any social safety-net provisions that a civilized society, even a dog-eat-dog one, may offer to its members in need of them, if any such existed in the Chicago of the early 1950s at the boundary line between the East European Immigrant and the Negro Quarters.

This compulsion of having to report to his point in space at the relentlessly moving belt or else he would be out, destitute and hungry on the street, was somehow not part of the picture he had made of that exciting challenge of conquering the Wild West back in Harthausen. America, the home of the dollar, had begun its process of morphing into "an america." This new concept was no longer a place. It was rather the set of conditions that define the quality of one's existence. Elusive conditions, in whose search you spend your life.

Baseball

Nevertheless, times were so good back then that out of his $27.20 weekly pay check, he could and did buy, on the spur of the moment, a gray woolen double-breasted suit as he was strolling down Division Street with his brother one Saturday afternoon on their way back from the Lakeshore. A suit, a tie, and a white shirt. It was meant to be a precaution against being caught short by that unforeseeable yet firmly expected chance and occasion when such a garb would be called for. That such a chance might not come never entered his mind, and I do not remember where he abandoned that suit that he had never worn, not even once.

He simply never felt that he was poor, he never identified with that state of mind, and it never occurred to him that he would not climb out of his present economic depression sooner rather than later. So instead of dwelling on such things, he went to the movies a lot. Back then, the double features complete with cartoon and newsreel ran continuously, and once inside the theater, you could watch the same fare all day until you decided that you had enough. So he and his brother spent entire Saturday and Sunday afternoons watching the same movies, each time understanding what was said a little better. With time, he had enough confidence in his American to quit the candy business and switch to a job polishing brass ornaments for coffins.

This activity took place in an otherwise deserted red brick factory building. Each morning, a large bin full of the raw material was delivered to a cavernous, dark, half-dusty, half-dank room with rusting equipment of forgotten purpose along the walls on the second floor. The task was accomplished with the help of small electric machines that moved a thin strip of sandpaper like a belt. There was no time constraint; he could reach into the bin for the next piece at his leisure, making sure only that each finished work of art would be exactly like the previous one. There was an incentive for keeping up a good pace, however.

Each acceptably turned-out end product was worth two cents to the artist. At a self-imposed rate of a piece per minute, he could therefore almost double his take-home pay compared to that at the candy factory. Piecework is the cleverest ploy of capitalism, and it succeeded in turning him into a robot while he was there. A robot and a security freak. It was this time, this place, and this job where he developed the urge and the need to lay in a little security cushion of cash for a rainy day. For the road had taught him (as I may have mentioned before) that the worst not only could happen but actually did happen ever so often.

This short, second, and last chapter of his passing through Chicago at the red brick factory was supervised, as jobs always are, by a boss. He (the foreman) also had a sandpaper machine, but he used it only to demonstrate the job to a new arrival or when boredom otherwise overpowered him. He was soft-spoken with a toothy grin and his off-the-job topic of conversation was entirely on an arcane subject that he (the lad) knew nothing about: baseball.

When checking and weighing a finished batch of pieces, he (the boss) would throw unacceptable ones at the perpetrator, but in a baseball-like way, expecting the piece to be caught with one hand. The catcher then would throw the discarded piece at one of the rusty machines that stood for a base. If the throw produced a loud clunky noise, that was a successful run, and the thrower was applauded. The discarded piece would stay where it fell, waiting to be pondered over by archeologists of some future age.

The management style of this boss was both prescribed and simplified by the circumstances of the work. The bin had to be finished by day's end. If the crew of artists was slow and tardy, everybody had to stay until the bin was empty. If somebody did not want to stay, that was up to him, but then he was automatically fired and was not accepted for work the next morning. Since there is no pay for overtime in piecework, there was community pressure on the team members to finish on time.

The boss was in his midtwenties, married with two children: the prototypical American nuclear-family man. To practice his English (and to fight his introversion), he (the lad) tried to make conversation, for unlike his solitary post at the candy place, the dozen or so sandpaper men here were arranged in a circle, side by side together, with the bin in the middle. "Why did the boss leave Baltimore to come to Chicago?" he asked. "Why not?" the man answered. Was he not sure or could he not articulate it or did he not care to do so? "Where was he headed in life?" That made the boss think for a moment, but he just ended up shrugging. "Why was he doing this type of work, he, a high school graduate?" At this, the boss wrinkled his eyebrows and shook his head suspiciously. "What's wrong with this work? And what does it have to do with high school? And what's the matter with you anyway, with you and with your questions? You a philosopher or something?"

It was all by way of friendly banter only, but among all the inconsequential platitudes that made up these exchanges, he picked up on the curious way the boss pronounced *philosopher*. Back in history class at the AKO, the teacher had remarked at one time that when Karl Marx pronounced the word *bourgeois*, he did it contemptuously, as if he were spitting out a glob of phlegm. Well, the boss uttered the word *philosopher* the way Whittaker Chambers or Senator Joe McCarthy must have said *communist*.

There was distrust, aversion, unease and perhaps even a touch of fear and hate in his tone of voice. Fear and hate, perhaps, of all things that he did not know, all the things that high school did not teach him, all the things beyond his grasp. He was like a balloon at a fair that a child's hand had let go, but one not pumped full enough to let it rise into the sky. The way he talked and even the way he moved was like the drifting of deadwood in the backwater eddies of a slow-moving stream. But when not seeing himself confronted with philosophy, he was not only a nice person but also a good and considerate boss.

Then, when he tossed a reject at him the next time and the lad happened to catch it with his left hand, the boss's misgivings vanished quickly, and he said approvingly, "You a second Babe Ruth." Reminded of his candy bars, he almost threw up. But clued in by the reference to the great athlete, he then took to quizzing the boss on the historic feats of the Orioles of Baltimore, and the boss, feeling good on this firm footing, took to telling stories about the World Series of American baseball. He (the lad) was tempted to ask why they called this particular tournament the "World Series" when no one outside the United States had ever heard of it, but then he reconsidered, for he saw no point in making a point of it.

He did not pick the boss to talk to because he was the boss, but because he was the only one inclined to talk. Most of the time, the only sounds in that circle were the clicks of the finished pieces and the whirring and whizzing of the sandpaper belts. There was no general exchange of thought. There was no community, and the men who drifted in and out shared little, as if they had nothing to share. Maybe, if they really did have thoughts on their minds, they had just never learned to communicate them or perhaps they had learned not to, perhaps having experienced sharing as risky, as something that is best avoided.

They stayed a few days, never longer than a week. They were Americans, born in country, as he could tell by their native accents when they were bitching occasionally about the poor lighting, the cold draft, the dampness, the dust, the rats, the cockroaches, and the pay. Nothing beyond the surrounding minutia ever came up, no politics, not even the war, although Korea was still going strong. He felt a strange sort of kinship with them, for they seemed to be introverts like him, but these were encounters like those between fish in an arctic ocean who glance at each other with glassy eyes and then drift on.

Only, they were not the same kind of fish that he was. Instead, he felt they were formed and deformed by the culture that brought them up to become what he experienced in meeting them. And that was an alien culture. Or was the culture of the marginalized poor the same in Magyarország as it was here? They were not into letting people share the insights of their solitary travels. He really wanted to know more about the stations on their road, for he saw no other way to find out about the potholes that he would have to avoid if he were ever to climb out of the rut that he already started feeling stuck in. One of them, an older fellow with the watery red unfocussed eyes and the transparent gray reptilian skin of one suffering from the terminal psychosomatic illness of the inveterate boozer turned to him unexpectedly one day as the bin was emptying out and said, "Let's go have a beer."

The first beer

Why not? he thought, Let's go and see what that is all about. You may have frequented bars yourself, or at least you may have seen some in the movies. But this bar in this factory area that was declared a blight on the city and therefore about to be razed for the mayor's next urban renewal project, was something you may have been lucky to escape. Its chemistry once identified, the smell could have led you there from blocks away by your nose alone, with your eyes shut along deserted streets and empty lots overgrown with weeds. The simile that this memory conjures up in me now (having studied pest-control biology in the meantime) is the erratic but goal-oriented flight of the medfly that is drawn to its doom by the pheromones released by the death traps set up for it.

The sun was still high on this summer afternoon, but inside, it was dark enough to take some time for the eye to adjust. Not that there was much to see, the scene was stark in its simplicity. The bar, with a fat, tattooed woman with a wig on her head working the taps. Three tables with a couple of chairs, half a dozen men sunk into themselves drinking beer and smoking.

There was something else there also, but I cannot describe it, for it was not material in nature. It was the desolation of hope lost by those people who sat there in that stale bar reek. It wasn't even hard liquor, just beer, factory-produced beer, Budweiser, for microbrews were not even thought of yet. But there was a meaning to that reek, and he could feel its reality, only he did not understand it, for it was written in a language whose dictionary he had not yet opened. Yet its language spoke to him in unknown words, casting long shadows of ambiguity ahead on pitfalls lurking on an as yet untraveled road.

It would be wrong to say that they were warnings, for had they been warnings the interpretations of those words could have come only from his own head, which was of no help, for he was as yet totally lacking in street wisdom.

He knew, however, with that noncerebral certainty of the things you know to be true without need of proof, that it was the morbidity of those end-of-their-line people that exuded that language, and he was suddenly afraid. Afraid not only of their message but of the very reality of it that had found a home in that reek. The message was one with the reek, and the reek was the message of reality.

I must say to his credit that he did not run away. Beer he had been invited to share, and he had come to have it in hopes of listening to something, and if it had to be, well then, to the message of the reek. What came in the words, though, the words that he had already learned to understand, was no message at all. It was a sequence of incoherent sobs and hiccups, on abuse, exploitation, gangs, dope, women, trying and failing and trying and failing again, and then booze. And a few gestures that included the others who sat there sunk into their mugs in this communal fate.

Omaha

His brother was first to recognize that their existence in Chicago was a dead end. They did not discuss the foolhardiness of having plunged totally unprepared into their great adventure. They did not have to, for it was all too evident. They knew that they had no talent for business. So with the Korean War still going strong, the GI Bill for veterans was the only way out. Without further ado, his brother enlisted in the Air Force. He himself, not yet ready for such a decision, got on a Greyhound bus and took to the road. To Omaha, where an older cousin had arrived with family sometime before.

These were people with training that they were able to turn to their advantage. And they were lucky to have had a substantial sponsor who set them up for a good start. Soon they had a down payment for a little house. It was a street that dead-ended literally onto some railroad tracks, and that should have been a pointer or a warning. But those were strange American sidetracks on which he had never seen a train pass while he was there, and so it took him a little while to get restless again, for Burdette Street was in one of those pleasant, dreamy, 1950s American, tree-lined, fragrant-with-flowers, next-to-a-block-size-park, clean-swept, backwater neighborhoods that Ronald Reagan may have grown up in and into which he seemed to have retreated emotionally during his later years, those of his presidency. He had a feeling that a cozy, protected, hopeful, whole, and unbroken world surrounded that lower-middle-class ambiance of Burdette Street.

Soot and soap

Promptly, he found a job with the Holland Furnace Company as a chimney sweep. An American chimney sweep, you should know, is not one of those sooty folks whom he used to watch climb the roofs back home in Léva, with a huge brush attached to the end of a stiff but elastic roll of tough wire on his shoulder that he (the sooty one) then unrolled into the chimneys to be scrubbed free of soot. Meeting one of them was thought to bring luck, although they looked black like the devil himself.

In Omaha, in contrast, the chimney sweep moved about in a truck equipped with a vacuum machine whose big hose was funneled upon arrival into the basements where the furnaces were (for that was still the age of the coal furnace), and the sooty and ashy obstructions were then sucked out of the chimney from below. Such a chimney sweep was expected to be able to fix anything that may have gone awry with anything connected with the furnace, and he was so cluelessly baffled by this immediate high-tech demand on him (he had no on-the-job training whatsoever and had never even heard of such contraptions before) that his senior sanitary-engineer partner who drove the truck, having recognized him for the theoretical talent that he was, did not tarry in getting him fired within a week. The parting was a relief for both of them, and what he could chalk up to experience from this lesson was that seeing, not being, a chimney sweep was what brought you luck.

But there was a feeling of luck and well-being vibrating in the air of that halcyon summer in Omaha. Vibrating because this was the year of a major cicada cycle. There were untold zillions of them everywhere, and the racket they made took over the world, every nook of which was brim-full of their din. Maybe it came from the energy of those vibrations or from some unknown kind of a contact high with his new surroundings that produced this feeling of wellness that he had. A hundred-monkey effect that rubbed off on him from all those confident 1950s Americans who went to work to their stores and offices from Burdette Street, sure of a safe and prosperous future and ensconced in a secure and well-provided-for American Dream. Things were just fine now, we won the war (we had never lost one before and never would in the future), and each new generation could only have it even better than we did.

He too felt good, and having escaped from that bar in Chicago must also have contributed to his self-confidence. So checking through the ads and drifting through half a dozen hiring offices, he was a wage earner again within two days, selling soap from house to house. It was not exactly a merchandize-for-money type of real salesman's job (that is the hardest of all ways to make a living unless you are born to be good at it), but rather it was part of an ad campaign: "Here is your free sample of Cheer, Procter & Gamble's new washday discovery," he was expected to say after having rung the doorbell. It was not very cerebral for a come-on, but there was no high-tech prerequisite knowledge weighing it down like he had faced in the chimney business.

What he found difficult in the end was the repetition. Going from house to house in that pleasant fall weather was fine, but declaring the same thing over and over again all day was soon a nuisance. Nevertheless, this was the sentence that P&G's market research had come up with as the irresistibly effective one, and there was an area boss who directed the sales force from block to block, and he checked with the recipients to see whether the offer was made correctly.

No poetic pleasantries and courtesies, no embellishments and variations on the theme like he would have liked to dish out by now: "Here is your free ticket to cheer. It will smooth your gullet like a swig of beer. It will keep your sheets white like snow. Trust pee and gee. It's in the know." He caught himself dreaming of variations on this theme, a new one to greet each new homemaker with, but it was *verboten*. In the end, here again, both parties soon agreed that it was time to part.

American Christmas

But winter was coming and his safety cushion of cash was still more of a concept than a reality to be cheerful about. When it came (winter, not the safety cushion), it was like one we don't have anymore these latter days. The snow fell one day in December, and it stayed for the duration. The city's chimneys tried their best to take the gleam off of its sparkling surface and dull it into agreement with all those smokestacks that he had escaped from cleaning, but then more blizzards refreshed its spirit of well-scrubbed, gleaming-white resistance with a clean, snow-white cheeriness as if it had been discovered and developed by Procter & Gamble itself.

Bitter cold though it was, it was a cheerful type of winter wonderland in Omaha that year, with bells jingling for weeks and weeks and weeks in all the stores. This was an entirely new aspect of Christmas for him. Back home in Léva, the stores attended to business and did not meddle with the tree that went up at home secretly in the afternoon before Christmas Eve, nor did they try to interfere with the spirit that the tree was meant to represent. It was as if some unwritten, self-understood, extra-constitutional separation between faith and commerce had been the law of that now half-forgotten land. The stores there were places of business, and Christmas was Christmas, and "never the twain shall mix" was people's approach to the two worlds.

At any rate, he found that he did not dislike the fuss. Even if he was puzzled by it, the novelty of it was captivating. Then there was Bing Crosby's voice crooning out the cheer that was decreed to reign with the promise of presents, and that voice sounded real here, not far away like in that movie house in Bad Aibling. No, all those warm, well-lit places where the presents were stacked up were so cram-full of all those goodies that Bing himself could have easily come around a corner, bumping into you with a big Santa Claus smile on his face. But while he was watching it and while he found himself liking it secretly, deep down, he also found himself to be a spectator of it only, an alien, unlike and separate from the crowd around him that seemed to be an integral part of the fuss.

With a shudder, he started realizing that not only did he not belong into what he felt was less of genuine cheer and more of an artificially stirred-up flurry of shopping excitement but that he was also somehow becoming less and less malleable in his efforts to adjust to this new environment. He was simply not renewable like the surface of those snowbanks; the lad in him was ossifying into a man with a growing sense of the knowledge of what he was and what he was not. What he was not was easy to grasp. What he was, on the other hand, was hard to see, for there was not much there to see. What he could see were unfinished shapes abandoned in midcourse like the snowmen on Burdette Street that children had left standing without a carrot for a nose and pieces of coal for eyes.

His life so far was made up of *Gestalten* that have had no chance to mature. This was the time of year, just before Christmas, when time had come to leave behind the pupae of his caterpillars in that large carton under his bed in Léva, a chapter of childhood left forever unfinished. He had never stopped wondering what had become of them. Were they thrown out on the street by the mob with all his other treasures, or did they die in that box after they turned into butterflies?

The child was left behind, abruptly, with those butterflies. The same way, time had come to close his books at the AKO and to leave the lad behind there and let what was left of him metamorphose into something new in this hospitable but harsh new land, where there was nothing for him to do but search for an america in hopes of finding the right one.

This was "a man's world," but I can still remember well how he clung to not being a man yet, even though he knew that his lad phase was over, abruptly again, when he climbed on board that troop ship. The grown-up reality that reigned here was an unforgiving taskmaster, notwithstanding the one-horse open sleighs and the dreams of a white Christmas that were vibrating through the ether like the cicadas had done a few months before. The truth of this reality was marching on and marched him soon to other edifying experiences that led nowhere in terms of material advancement but helped him to flesh out his experience of the American way of life from the bottom up. This road to experience, not from rags but neither to riches, took him next to a job at the Omaha Cold Storage Company.

Life in cold storage

Dodge Street ran, back in those pre-Interstate Highway System days, from the University of Omaha at the western end of town to where the Omaha Cold Storage building stood on Farnam Street, on the eastern edge. These were the two poles of his life that winter. The OCS (not Officer Candidate School, which came later) was a landmark in a dreary, run-down industrial area called the Jobber's Canyon Warehouse District, right on the river, before urban renewal replaced much of the site with a park. But then it stood there like a huge square cement bunker, three or four stories high within its redbrick *facade*, large as a city block (so it seems to me now), and maybe it was really that big.

Its influence on the area outside was such that there the snow could never stay white, even though the winter kept much of the Missouri River, right next door, under ice. The nature of the building, by the design of its builders or as a result of its own, independent volition, was so ingenious that it sucked up those icy temperatures of the winter and conserved them within its layers of insulation all summer.

That was the way he felt about it emotionally, for he had as good as forgotten by then what he had learned in Icking about the nature of energy from the physics teacher, the new director who had come to transform that school into a modern institution after he (the boy) left for Bad Godesberg. "*Die Temperatur ist keine Eigenschaft der Materie,*" Dr. Niklas (whom they nicknamed "*der Boss*" as if by premonition that the world would become full of bosses later) would explain. "*Sie ist lediglich eine der Möglichkeiten ihren Energiezustand zu messen.*"

Well, if temperature is not a property of matter but serves only to measure its energy content, he could measure it well with his constantly frozen extremities. It was hellishly cold inside that building, as Eskimos no doubt imagine hell to be. At any rate, the passing from the outer to the inner ice ages across the doors and gates of the OCS always reminded him of the Magyar saying: "*Csöbörből vödörbe esett*," for he felt like falling from a pan into a pail (both full of ice cubes) upon entering that building. And in fact, a pail it was on which his activities focused at the OCS at first.

I can relate his activities there only cursorily, for his mind seems to have blanked out on much of the finer detail that filled his time there day after day. The controller apparently repressed most of it as having negative survival value, as something that he would have avoided in the wilds during the hunter-gatherer phase of his phylogeny.

The pail that he was assigned to handle was a connecting link between two separate centers of activity. One was a large room where a multitude of women were kept busy over what seemed like the entire egg production of the inhabited universe. The eggs kept rushing in on conveyor belts and were promptly cracked open. Some were separated into yolk and white; others were dumped whole into appropriate containers. He neither knew nor cared what happened to the product next (he heard egg powder mentioned); for it was his lot to deal with a side product.

There were so many eggs that although having an occasional rotten one in a lot is relatively rare, here they aggregated into respectable amounts quite rapidly. The critical mass of rotten-egg substance was a pailful, and this he collected from the women along the belt who placed this side product in special pans designated for this purpose. He then toted these pailfuls into another small room where he collected his harvest in a good-sized drum and beat it with a huge whisk as you would do with scrambled eggs while adding a powder that transformed the resulting mix into a viscous substance. He then rolled the full drum into the next room, and again he did not know nor did he care what they did with it there (but he heard glue mentioned in that context).

While the complexity of this whole operation in and by itself may make it appear appealingly challenging as I describe it here, there was a sensory (olfactory) drawback to it, and that was most intense in that small egg-scrambling room. "Never mind," the boss would encourage, "the sulfur in the air will clean out your lungs." I do not know anymore how long this phase lasted exactly. But one day, the boss came by to tell him that he considered his (the lad's) lungs now to be clean enough and that he would be moved elsewhere, where his proven, pertinacious talent was equally needed.

Skid row

To desulfate himself before facing other people, he did the few miles back to Burdette Street on foot in the evening, taking a different route every time. This being a walk through a good-sized city almost from one end to the other, there was a large variety of choices in route selection, and he did it without a street map to train himself in not getting lost. This cost him sizable detours at times when he ran into impassable stretches like railroad yards or fenced industrial areas. Nevertheless, these were the walks that helped develop in him a fascination for observing the expressions, both of desolation and delectation, that city people produce at and around the places where they live and work. These were also the walks that let him stumble by chance into Omaha's skid row where he saw his first real, live Indians.

It was an area of only a few blocks. The streets were wide and open like those of the downtown from which it was not all that different, except for the size and the state of maintenance of the buildings and the amount of trash in the streets and on the sidewalks. It looked old and shabby. It looked like a man who had drowned his youth in an excess of drink and drugs. It was hard to imagine that it was only about four score and ten years ago that President Lincoln had stood up there on the Bluffs where the free native nations used to hold their sacred councils on the other side of that Great River and gazed down on an open ocean of waving prairie grass that stretched unbroken all the way to the escarpments of the Rocky Mountains. As Big Elk, the last real chief of the Omaha, described it:

> There was a time when the land was sacred and the ancient ones were one with it. A time when only the children of the Great Spirit were here to light their fires in these places with no boundaries . . .

Now, there was nothing left of those places but their new boundaries. The drunken Indians that squatted in the gutters outside the bars of skid row did not have the fierce eyes and the sharp aquiline profiles of the storied ones of his childhood's books. Their skin was not a coppery red but a sallow, pallid earth tone, their faces round, their noses flat and their eyes glassy as if they were sightless.

Of course, these were not descendants of the fighting, undaunted, and indomitable Comanche, Apache, Blackfoot, Dakota, and Cherokee tribes that the sagas of his childhood's stories sang about. But still their name, Omaha, that is said to translate into something like "those who go against the wind" or "those who swim against the current" makes a clear statement of their spirit of old, of the days of yore when they moved from the forests of the East into their new home as masters of this endless open land on that Great River.

They had been hunters and farmers; they had grown beans, corn, and squash; and they had minded their daily business without making a great name for themselves on the warpath like the others whose fame crossed the ocean all the way to Léva for him to read and dream about. And here they were now, with their spirits broken, in the gutter. "Who speaks for us," the extinct light in their eyes seemed to plead, "in a culture of dogs where the size of the fangs is the only thing that counts?" The disconnect between them and the cozy, Christmassy ambiance of middle-class Omaha seemed abysmal. The breaking of the spirit is the most dreadful thing there is in human experience. He would live to see it happen to some of his very own. Will it happen to him also in the end?

First stab at college

Three nights a week, he would wander down Military Avenue on his way to Dodge Street and there take the streetcar west to the University. That was at the western edge of the city; the trees of the campus served as an interface between the upscale neighborhoods there and the farmlands and prairie that followed, if I remember it right. On that main road leading out west past the campus, there was a sign: Five Miles to Boys' Town.

That was a real link to the past, to Bad Aibling, to the movie *Boys Town* he had seen back there, starring Spencer Tracey and Mickey Rooney. That movie was one of the first hints, a premonition that America might become a reality for him. I do not remember the story, really (one of these days, I'll check out a video cassette to run it by my controller again), but I think it must have shown Mickey as a drifter and Spencer as the benign padre-director-vagrant-boy-rehabilitator like his (the lad's) mentor had been at the AKO. Seeing that sign and thinking of taking that same streetcar going east to the OCS at the crack of dawn the next morning, often made him wish, I must admit, not to have embarked on a career of globetrotting vagrancy himself.

At the University of Omaha, he enrolled in a course of public speaking. Not knowing what sort of profession to aim for (he still felt that he was born to be an officer and a land owner like his father), he thought learning to face audiences, besides being a start in academics without a hasty commitment to some specialization, might be another way to take a crack at the shyness and introversion that were his lot. Also, it was a good medium to practice the sort of spoken American, of which his Shakespearian vocabulary (now rapidly going dormant) was not exactly a kissing cousin. But when he tried to go through the course catalogue with its graduation requirements to get a feel for what might lie ahead in terms of a degree, he found that at this rate, one evening course per semester, he was looking at twenty years of night school until he could earn a bachelor's degree. He found that prospect discouraging.

The guillotine

Fortunately, the next morning's streetcar ride would not give him much leisure for wallowing in discouragement. The activities of the OCS were many-faceted, and the next facet of this diamond in the rough of a storehouse of experience came to him on another moving belt. One, that this time was aflutter with wildly beating wings. Those belonged to large, sturdy, if not all-out powerful, ill-tempered Tom turkeys, heads hanging down and with feet tied to metal hooks on that chain belt at eye level.

The leadership of the OCS, good at measuring the capabilities of their employees, promoted him to this new task carefully so that it would not surpass the level of his competence. To enable him to perform it, they supplied him with a sharp knife but no goggles (of whose existence and availability he was as yet unaware). All he had to do then was to dive with eyes closed to a narrow slit into a fierce storm of feathers, wings, and beaks that were desperately flaying the skin off his arms and face, search for the neck and cut the throat close to the head so that only the head would come off.

Success was demonstrated by a gush of hot blood that spurted everywhere, especially on his face if he did not "cut and run" from the reach of the wings fast enough. The beheaded bird kept on struggling even more desperately (as poultry will do) but then promptly disappeared through the hole in the wall provided for the conveyor belt's further progress. *C'est tout.*

As a result of a bizarre association with what he had learned about the *guillotine* in history classes at the AKO, he spoke French to the birds, and as the next one to be beheaded approached, he (the lad) informed him (the Tom) in this foreign and therefore impersonal and, for him, unsentimental tongue that this was the end of his line. "*C'est tout pour vous, pauvre shlemiel!*"

Simple, *n'est ce pas*? Quick and easy it was indeed, this quintessential American exposure to the businesslike approach. Off with their heads, and no dillydallying about it! In comparison to this, his prior experiences with French as a mode of expression were, well, like exercises in diplomacy. For at the AKO, where his first serious encounter with the language of diplomacy took place, *Pater* Sonntag exposed them early to the gamut of what it had to offer, although that was, of course, not even the scratching of the surface of that treasure trove, as Marina discovered later on her way to a Ph.D. in French literature. But the pace was fast enough that he soon started taking stabs at serious readings in some of those masterpieces.

None of which, unfortunately, prepared him for his ongoing tête-à-tête dialogue with his turkeys. But there was one little gem that did prepare him for the mood of that gruesome scenario. It was a poem, a poem of poems, whose melancholy, sonorous melody wove itself into that bloody turkey experience for him and which I will therefore reproduce here in full (may Verlaine forgive me) so that you may better understand the mood of that episode:

Les sanglots longs	Tout suffocant	Et je m'en vais
Des violins	Et blême, quand	Au vent mauvais
De l'automne	Sonne l'heure	Qui m'emporte
Blessent mon cœur	Je me souviens	Deçà, delà
D'une langueur	Des jours anciens	Pareil à la
Monotonne.	Et je pleure.	Feuille morte.

The long sobs	Suffocating	And I set off
of autumn's	and pallid,	when in the stiff wind
violins	the clock strikes	that carries me
wound my heart	I remember	hither and thither
with monotonous	the days long past	like a
languor.	and I weep.	dead leaf.

Yes, he often felt like a fallen leaf himself when facing a particularly suffocating, pallid, and desperate turkey and remembered the good old days not so long past but had no time to feel overly sentimental, for he had to deal urgently with a few aggravating circumstances of the job at hand. First, he had to try not to nick his knuckles or maybe even cut a digit of his own off instead of the gobbler's guzzle for fear of contracting psittacosis or *Salmonella* infection. Next, he had to approach the kill with the sixth sense of a blind matador or that developed by a troglodyte whose lamp has gone out, for as I have said, he shut his eyes to the narrowest of a slit for fear that the endeavor might otherwise "permanently vitiate" his own eyesight. Finally, he had to see to it that his motivation did not flag, for the pace of the belt was not designed to permit Mac the Knife to lapse into daydreaming between turkeys; it was relentless in its determination to maximize profitability and the CEO's bonuses.

To enhance this motivation, the boss explained that he would consider the appearance of an intact turkey on the far side of that hole in the wall a major breach of businesslike conduct and professional competence. This would therefore be dealt with harshly, he said, since no mechanism existed to recycle a live bird from the outgoing belt (with the others already on their way to become turkey ham) back to the incoming belt, short of assigning an extra person to physically accomplish the transfer, which would constitute an unacceptable inroad into said profitability.

He ended his instructions and admonitions with a gesture that he (the lad) had first seen in Werfen. One of the American explorers in those tanks there had made it when a German kid was jokingly signaling a desire to steel some of the C rations.

It was a hand moving around the neck and then up behind the nape: better watch out or we'll hang you. A gesture understood instinctively by everyone of Western culture and upbringing.

One more immigrant

By spring 1952, his father had made it across the Atlantic to Omaha also. The DP Program was ending, and the old man wanted to be close to his sons. He (the lad) and his brother had serious misgivings about this by this time, but what could they say? Don't come? Crossings of the ocean were rare and expensive back then and very much unlike the ease of hopping on an airplane nowadays. Obtaining an immigrant visa outside the DP program was more like a daydream. He therefore availed himself of this last opportunity, or else it might have been "See you later in the happy hunting grounds."

So they sponsored him. Sponsoring meant an assumption of full responsibility for the immigrant in order to avoid his becoming a ward of the state should things go wrong somehow. Given their own precarious financial situation, this sponsoring business that they took on was akin to today's practice of giving credit cards to teenagers or subprime mortgages to anyone without even a cursory credit check. At the time of his arrival, his father did not know any English at all. He had no training in any sort of work other than commanding troops and supervising the managers of his land at Sándorhalma. In Omaha, the name of this type of preparation for the local job market was called "unskilled labor." His decision to come was as courageous as it was foolish for someone at the age of sixty-four:

> Doing the garden digging the weeds
> Who could ask for more
> Will you still need me
> Will you still feed me
> When I am sixty four

and ultimately it even had a bit of tragedy attached to it, for shortly after he left Germany, the German government, in a singular show of generosity and loyalty, awarded full retirement rights to military officers of countries that fought with the Germans against the Russians to the end. But you had to be a resident of Germany and classified as a "stateless person" at the time the law was enacted. So instead of drawing a colonel's pension in a country whose language he spoke and whose customs he knew, he became the janitor and digger of weeds at the Lutheran Church on Crosby Street in Omaha.

This in and by itself did not have to be the end of the world. A suburban protestant church of the America of the 1950s was like a social club. Sure, there was an actual room there with an altar and a pulpit, and a sermon and psalm singing on Sunday were the routine, but the physical plant of the church, its meeting and sitting rooms, its community kitchen, in short, its entire make-up, seemed to be designed more to draw in people for a good time of communal well-being than to communion with a transcendental God.

So it seemed to him at least, being used to more austere and hereafter-oriented church buildings back home in Europe. The more affluent the neighborhood from which such a church drew its clientele, or flock, the more cozy (and big) was its physical plant, and for the resident janitor (this was a time before outsourcing), that meant a lot of constant care and devotion. And his father was neither born nor conditioned by his life up to that point for sanitary engineering.

The enormous furnace had to be freed of its slag and ashes every day in season, supplied with coal, and stoked expertly for it to provide the proper climate control upstairs. Trash and garbage that mushroomed like a rapidly growing organism in every nook of the building where the flock was grazing had to be collected, removed, and cleaned up. Fixtures bent and broken had to be righted and fixed again. The place was a born handyman's delight.

But the old colonel of artillery was no handyman and his DNA seemed to be coded to read that cleaning up after others was servant's work. This may sound haughty and uppity to most natives (an immigrant who does not know his place) and especially to those of us who have, taught by necessity, either learned to jump over our shadows or have always led lives where such a worldview was never an issue. But he (the lad) could see how his father, born and raised (like an oak tree) to brave storms of a different kind, was breaking under the kind and mellow breezes that wafted through those cheerily pious church rooms all the time.

Charlie, do this. Charlie, do that. It was akin to what we call identity theft today. The trouble was that he could not complain, for he had volunteered for it. He was too old to become a gofer, and I am sure that he could never have become one at any other time of his life either. And neither could I have become one, for that matter, wordless acquiescence to the demands of the assembly lines notwithstanding. But it could not be helped. He (the lad) could barely keep his own nose above water, and his father had to make do as best he could. Do or die.

But then there came stroke of unhoped-for good luck: the Air Force assigned his brother to Offutt Air Force Base, near Omaha, after he completed his training as a medical technician at Fort Sam Houston. He (the brother) declared his father as a dependent and so became eligible for a military "housing allowance." With that they rented a little apartment together near the church, and the brother commuted to Offutt every day with colleagues (for he had no car) who luckily lived nearby.

The milkman

There was one final episode in his (the lad's) training to become a good immigrant. Still with the OCS, he declared his unwillingness to practice his French any longer and was thereupon assigned to be part of the plant's dairy operations.

Upon being unloaded from trucks, huge, solid-metal cans of cream came into the basement from the outside on a metal track equipped with rollers to facilitate the cans' movement. The track slanted down at a slight angle, so that movement was powered this time not by a machine with a preset speed but by gravity. Nevertheless, the cans came on after they passed through a plastic curtain at such a constant rate that not only he, but two more colleagues were employed there to lift them up to a ramp, about four feet high, to send them on their way to a steam chamber for cleaning and disinfection.

As pleasingly and unassumingly simple as this job was, it had, like all the others before it, its rough side. The cans were very heavy. In fact, they were heavier than he could handle, and by the rules of this particular game, they were meant to be lifted up to the ramp not by collegial cooperation (like two people per can) but singly and individually. This was necessary, for the cans arrived so fast that three people had barely enough time to lift them off the roller track.

Although lifting with astonishing ease themselves, the colleagues showed understanding for his plight and taught him to use his legs to do most of what they called their practice in "pumping iron." After a couple of woeful days (and nights with all his muscles aching), he made rapid strides in becoming an expert lifter of cream cans. In becoming adept at it, he learned to accomplish the task with such precision that he ended up doing it without spilling the cream all over his white work overalls, as did his colleagues. This was apparently one of the workings of the theoretical talent that the *Pater Direktor* at the AKO had discovered in him, and it was also the circumstance that had caught the eye of the boss.

Assiduous, diligent, unremitting lifting apparently went unnoticed, but keeping one's overalls clean and white must have stood out like a sore thumb, for hardly had three weeks gone by before he was yanked out from under that unending sequence of cans and assigned to a desk equipped with cream-testing instrumentation to sit there comfortably in his new capacity as cream tester—under the disapproving glares of his erstwhile colleagues who went on lifting cans.

Bacterial contamination, fat and protein composition, acidity, and a few other qualities were quite carefully spot-checked and even more carefully recorded and related to the dairy farms of the product's origin. He was being broken in as a tester with a 100-percent pay raise for no apparent reason other than not splashing the cream on his overalls.

This was a promotion, the first nod of approval by the new world, a wink of the blind eye, a hint that one may get noticed after all, if lucky. Lucky in the sense that the outcome in this case was not the result of premeditated planning but of a fortunate coincidence. More than that, it was an eye-opener. You had to do a little more in this society than just doing well what was expected. How small that little extra really was did not matter as long as it was noticeable. After the first day of sitting at his desk, he walked home not looking at the sights of the new route that day, for he was calculating the time it would take him to become director general of the OCS.

It took him another week of pipetting cream on Petri dishes to realize that to become general director of the OCS was not really one of his childhood dreams. Over the weekend, he took the bus out to Boys Town for the first time, and there he thought that he recognized some of the sights he had seen in that movie in Bad Aibling. He sat on the bench in front of the admin building, looked out at what was still pretty much open prairielike countryside, and tried to recall his old dreams about the kind of an america, no longer the country but the concept, the goal, and the dream, that he was searching for. The Indians. The buffaloes. The Wild West. The utopia of its clean, pure, benevolent, charity-for-all-and-malice-to-none promise. Next Monday, he went in to work for the last time and to give notice to quit. On Tuesday, he was at the Omaha Recruiting Station and signed up for the army. With that, his days as an immigrant were over. He was to become a full member of the club.

Chapter 5

The Soldier

In basic training back in those days, the twenty-mile road march was one of the primary stratagems that the army put to use to win the hearts and minds of new recruits for soldiering. This march is a maneuver that is executed by the buck private with a pack containing his full field equipment on his back, with a carbine (if in the artillery of the early 1950s) on his shoulder, with a steel helmet on his head, and with his feet (hopefully) already broken in to his government-issue (GI) boots.

In case of rain, he is directed to put on his poncho, but only after the fact, for the march goes on in formation three to five abreast and you do not break such formations lightheartedly, based only on some premonition of upcoming discomfort. You do that only after the consequences are already fully all present and accounted for, namely after you are soaking wet. The planning and the conception of such marches includes the selection of the dustiest dirt road available on whatever military reservation happens to serve as the proving grounds for the development and the nurturing of a spirit of service and patriotism. The guiding principle in this endeavor is no doubt the ageless wisdom of the motto "No pain, no gain."

For him, who had adopted this principle as his very own a long time ago, the army's methodology therefore came on like second nature. He also knew, from many marches on such roads, foraging for food back in the Harthausen area, that in case of said rain, such roads would turn from the dustiest to the muddiest and would therefore become the most gainful of training vehicles. There were a good number of such roads back in the boondocks of Camp Chaffee, Arkansas, and the walking of more than a few of them (the twenty-mile march was a dawn-to-dusk job) did not fail to do the trick with him, for it led to the first budding of his love affair with his US Army uniform.

On the road again to Grass Valley

He would not forget those roads as long as he lived, and so now that it was his little red Toyota and not a drill sergeant that took him along on just such a memorably dusty road with potholes rivaling it in size, his controller whisked him back easily and naturally to those days of yore and forward again to the here and now. This new road that led now (but actually more than twenty-five years before this writing), northward through Grass Valley to the USDA-ARS research site, about halfway between US-50 and I-80, turns left from the Loneliest Highway after passing Austin Summit, going east, and is actually, come to think of it, quite unlike those at Camp Chaffee in its overall ambiance except for the dust clouds common to both.

Anyway, this gravel road meanders North between two mountainous ranges of hills that are not as exciting as the high Toyabees to the South but are in their own simple and serene way maybe even more beautiful, if you are receptive and attuned to their attractions. Timeless though the valley itself is in uplifting the spirits of the contemplatively minded observer, it is nonetheless a survivor of recent adversity, for at the turn of the last century, sheep were herded up and down its bottomlands by Basque immigrants.

Now, if the land does not belong to you and you are only interested in using it to squeeze the last drop of profit out of what is the national treasure of all of us, flocks of sheep can bring about amazing changes in the vegetation growing on the fragile and endangered soils of a semi-arid climate. Deep-rooted native bunch grasses that remain green through most of the dry season and provide forage for deer and rabbit, like Indian ricegrass, squirrel tail, needle-and-thread, and Thurber's needlegrass are taken out to be replaced by less palatable or outright inedible species like fleabane, prickly phlox, thorny skeleton plant, Jimson weed, and brome grass.

The dust bowl that is created by such abuse takes a long time to recover somewhat, if it does so at all, as it fortunately did over many decades in Grass Valley. Why does this intricate process of recovery take so long? That was one of the puzzles that the ARS permitted him to help exploring, and that which you (as anyone interested in the survival of life on our planet) might want to get interested in as a hobby. The key to this puzzle is the nature of that unique living organism: a healthy soil.

You see, the soil, as most people view it, is there for us to step on. It is something we plough up, something that we hardtop over with roads and parking lots and subdivisions. Dust-bowl soil, like that of Grass Valley must have been a hundred years ago, becomes such a lifeless mass of mineral matter upon prolonged abuse to be blown away by the wind or to be washed away down to the bedrock by an occasional deluge. But the soil that supports the plants that provide us not only with the food we eat but also with the very air we breathe, is not some dead agglomeration of compacted sand, silt, and clay. It is (as I will keep repeating) a living organism.

Only its mineral matrix, its skeleton, is lifeless, but this matrix provides countless habitable pore and capillary spaces to house myriads of interacting and interdependent organisms, most of which we have not even named yet, but all of which perform some vital function, or else they would not be there. This "soil food web" is organized in a multidimensional trophic pattern starting with unicellular life-forms, bacteria so small that they are barely made visible by the most powerful light microscope, all the way up to the indispensably important though often unwelcome mole and gopher.

Within these unseen and little-known realms of underground life, run, not unlike the arteries of our own bodies, the roots of plants, which supply the denizens of this live soil with their sustenance: organic compounds derived from photosynthesis, a process that takes place in the leaves above that are bathed in air and sunlight. To further facilitate this movement of nutrients from plant to soil, an ancient symbiosis had developed some four hundred million years ago at the time when plants first ventured out from the oceans to colonize the dry land.

This particular symbiosis (a "living together" of different life-forms to perform mutually useful functions) is one made up of the roots of almost all plant species and soil fungi that colonize the live cells of those roots. From these cells that provide the fungus with food and energy, a network of delicate fungal hyphae branches out into the soil, permeating the open spaces of the soil matrices where the soil organisms live. These fungal hyphae work for the soil like our own capillaries work for the maintenance of the cells that make up our own tissues. They are the ultimate supply line of food to the soil biota. And this soil biota is an essential requisite for the establishment, functioning, and survival of plants in nature (although they may do without the fungi under controlled, experimental conditions).

The enlisted man

Why put on the uniform?

His mission in all this complex biology was simply to try to find some of the missing pieces of the soil-restoration puzzle by running experiments with or without one or the other of the soil biota's living components. Simple perhaps, but it was quite an advance compared with the simplicity of the mission that he envisioned for himself when he reported to that recruiting station in Omaha some thirty years before he undertook this work in that Valley of Grass. Back then in the early 1950s, his geopolitical world view was one of opposition to the menace of monolithic communism that had lowered an Iron Curtain over his homeland, cutting it off from the Free World.

The war in Korea that was still going on at that time was only one local aspect of this greater struggle, so that it mattered little to him whether the enemy on the other side of the curtain spoke Russian or Chinese. He would become an honorable part of the greater cause by putting on the uniform of the good guys, while at the same time doing what he could for the advancement of his own limited, selfish purposes by qualifying for the educational offerings of the GI Bill should he live to see that.

While this concept was quite pragmatic and could hardly be faulted, he could nevertheless not help feeling uneasy about the lack of clarity in this approach. Was he committing himself to fight for a cause, or was he simply aiming to secure a good deal for himself in the end? In practice, however, the resolution of this quandary of conscience was made easy for him by a basic fact of life. He had to eat. And at the moment, the only way open to him to satisfy this need was working hand to mouth. There was no room for failing at this for a single day; there was no margin of error. That was what he did not like, and knowing that most people on earth live reduced to that condition was no consolation. It was an existence akin in many ways to slavery.

Not that he had any problem with work as such. On the contrary, he found that work was something like a backbone for life; it gave life support and structure. Even more than that, it cut to the very basics in an important way, in one where he agreed with the views expressed in the manifesto of the enemy's theoreticians: "He who does not work, neither shall he eat." There was convincing justice in that statement while he wondered about the logic in a system that declared all men equal and then made some of its members work while others did not and still ate. But even that was all right with him, as long as this elite state of eating without working was honestly earned by the eater earlier, and he wanted to find his way to that kind of an america himself.

Not in uniform yet

That way, though not yet in uniform, started with the train ride from Omaha to Joplin, Missouri, where the army operated an induction center at Camp Crowder. Come to think of it, "induction," the noun form of the verb "to induce" is a fine word. Like so many other English words, it is rooted in Latin (*in* + *ducere*). It is used to express "the leading or moving of another [person] to act in a certain way" and implies "an influence over someone's reason or judgment." Webster, the one who arrived at this definition and etymology, must have been a first sergeant for a good stretch of his natural life to come up with this depth of understanding of it. For the truth of it was made clear to the recruits upon disembarking from that train by the first uniformed bearer of authority who waited for them at the station. This robust father figure started exerting said strong influence over their reason and judgment without delay by explaining that those certain ways of action that may have been right ones or wrong ones in their past were now irrelevant, for from now on there would be only one way for them to act that mattered: the army way.

Before he embarked on internalizing this army way in earnest, however, good fortune provided him with an unexpected boon, a mentor. This was a ruddy redskin with a pockmarked face, about his age and height, fresh in town from the reservation up North on Blackbird Creek, who happened to sign his papers at the recruiting station at the same time as he did. He and Joe, the Omaha, had both stipulated as their condition for enlistment that they be assigned to the paratroops after basic training. The recruiter promised this, but upon seeing Joe's name, he became convulsed with laughter. "Hey, looky here," the SFC with a master parachutist's badge over his left breast pocket was screaming in his best parade-ground voice for the whole shopping center to hear. "We got a natural-born 'straightleg' here who thinks he can become a 'trooper.'" For Joe's name translated into English from his native Cegiha, the language group of such folks as the Pawnee and the Osage besides the Omaha, meant nothing less than "Straight Leg."

Now, paratroopers, who wear their trousers bloused into their distinctive, spit-shined paratrooper's boots even when in dress uniform, condescendingly call all those unfortunate soldiers whose jackets are not adorned by the winged medal, the badge of honor of their elite outfit "straightlegs" or simply "legs," but with the vowel pronounced drawlingly (l-a-a-g). Of course, neither Joe nor he could understand what was going on, but he could distinctly feel how every muscle in Joe's body and every neuron in his brain were tensing up, ready to explode in violence and to hell with the consequences.

The only thing that Joe could see at this point was that they were making fun of him and probably because his skin was red. His eyes were glazing over like those of a bull in the ring might upon seeing the matador's scarlet cloth. He stepped aside to avoid getting involved in something that was none of his business, but the incident was a lesson of import for him nonetheless. It was one of those insights into the spirit of this New World that was still such a new world for him. A world of the fistfight and the revolver where you don't resolve differences by polite social intercourse but where you apply your brawn first and ask questions later.

But the sergeant did not get to be "first class" (SFC) for being a blind fool either. He also could see what storm was brewing there, and besides, he got his points not by alienating prospective recruits but by signing them up. So he got a grip on his mirth and piped down. Next, he got a couple of cold beers out of the fridge and explained to Joe what was up. "Your name just cannot be 'Straight Leg' if you want to serve in an airborne unit. That is a contradiction in itself. An airborne soldier is not a straightleg. Why not use your real Indian name instead? Don't fret it. Others have long, weird names too, just look at this one" (and showed him mine). And a fine, well-sounding name Joe's Cegiha name was. I forgot it, but I think it had four syllables and thirteen letters. He probably spent the rest of his army career spelling it (like I did).

After that, they went to see a movie together that night, and Joe kept exclaiming in wonder, admiring breathlessly the tall buildings of downtown Omaha, "And you were really roaming these same streets all the time?" He deduced from this that the village of Macy, where Joe came from, must have been home to a wholesomely simple way of life with its small collection of one-bedroom, government-furnished cottages. Joe, however, turned out to be anything but simpleminded. By the mysterious mechanisms of atavism, the spirit of his lord-of-the-prairie ancestors had broken through again in him, and he was fierce like that swarm of hornets in Léva.

His new buddy, the white man, had started thinking of himself by this time as the fortunate product of quite some special training in facing the vicissitudes of life in the great wide world. Joe taught him humility. Joe demonstrated to him that he was basically still a gentle, genteel, introverted romantic at heart. Joe did not get any training in street wisdom out there on the reservation in Macy; he had it in his blood.

He did not even need it apparently, for his understanding of our dog-eat-dog world was that of a natural. At the movie's ticket counter, he pulled out his enlistment papers and shouted with determined authority, "We are new army volunteers, and we are entitled to a free show." Then he (Joe) dragged him (me) inside, papers in hand, head held high, and eyes defiant, before anybody could think of anything to counter. When the group of that week's recruits, mostly draftees, was given the signal to board the train, Joe dragged him into the coach ahead of the others to occupy the only sleeping compartment (the trip was overnight from Omaha to Joplin) that turned out to be vacant and available. And so it went: the best bunks in the barracks once at Crowder (in the cadre room, no less), volunteering to police the grounds to escape from KP, and helping with the issue of clothing to get the best-fitting boots. Others were assigned to tasks; Joe picked his with an endearing but at the same time defiant grin.

He could never hope to match Joe's talent. He knew he would have to cope with the army way in his own introverted manner. But it was an education, and it helped him over the initial hurdles of this new way of life. Sitting on the stairs in front of their barracks door in the evening, they would chat and watch old soldiers, veterans, fresh back from Pusan or Pohang-dong, brass shining and medals gleaming, walk by in step, heels clicking smartly on the pavement. That was what they wanted to be like too.

Then they were issued their uniforms and were permitted to try them out and put them on. The first thing, once in uniform, was to take the assignment test. It consisted of a few simple questions. Joe, the mentor, did not do well with the abstractions that the world of letters represented for him. He was a true extrovert and did not have a penchant for theory like his new buddy. The test must have shown this, for Joe was assigned to the infantry where the ones with the fewest correct answers were sent. He was sent to Camp Chaffee, Arkansas, to the Five-Forty-Second Armored Field Artillery Battalion to be reinvented as an artilleryman, like his father. This Camp Crowder experience was crowded into less than a week and was over almost before it started.

Basic training

There are times in life that are so full of substance, happenings, and experiences that they seem to fly by like an arrow. Looking back at them, however, they appear to be long, and one savors, in retrospect, every fleeting hour of them. On the other hand, there are those that drag on tediously day after day, hour after hour, while their present lasts, only to have their past expunged from memory or condensed into a moment by the controller, not unlike the clearing of a blackboard full of scribblings to produce a clean slate for something more worthwhile.

The latter scenario held true for him for the next four months. Or were there six? Or two? Actually, I could look this up in my files, for one of the few memory fragments the controller did permit to become part of the filing cabinet between his ears were a few remarks of the first sergeant during the in-briefing: "You are doing really well here if I don't get to know who you are," he said, "and save a copy of all your assignment orders while you are on active duty." And so he did. Therefore, I could look up this datum, but why? It does not matter. And maybe I could not, for maybe the moths and bookworms have chewed up these musty files; I have not looked at them for almost forty years.

So I know, not from memory but by deductive reasoning, that those months must have been spent learning to perform a number of tasks. To handle the 105 mm field howitzer, the all-purpose work horse of the field artillery; to use army communications procedures with radio and field telephone; to help surveying the position of the firing battery; to internalize rudimentary Fire Direction Center procedures; to read maps and use the compass; to fire the carbine accurately, and more of the same; in addition to road marches, close order drill, calisthenics, saluting, and all the minutia of everyday soldiering. Only, I simply do not recall the live, detailed, colored, sharp contours of any of those military things; I do not even have a mental image left of the streets of Camp Chaffee, Arkansas, or of its surroundings on the fringes of the beautiful ancient Ozark Mountains.

What I do remember are things like the housekeeping as the essence and the aura of that life that has disappeared from actual army routine long ago but remained immortalized by the *Beetle Bailey* comic strips, which seem to continue to haunt our newspapers to this day until the papers themselves give way in the end to some electronic medium one day. And this essence expressed itself most clearly by two activities: white-glove inspections and kitchen police (KP).

Recruits do not get three-day passes, those coveted rewards (Friday, Saturday, and Sunday off) for not letting the first sergeant know that they exist. Instead, they practice endlessly to learn drawing their blankets over their bunks so taut that the inspecting officer can bounce a quarter off of them. At night, until lights out, they spend scrubbing the floorboards of their barracks until the wood turns white, often using their tooth brushes on the spaces between boards (because of this, housecleaning remained for me a sort of curse ever since). They learn to abandon any and all aspiration for privacy. Their clothing (uniforms only) hangs on open racks behind their bunks and their footlockers are open with contents arranged uniformly throughout the barracks for inspection on Saturday mornings. The barracks, two-story wooden buildings, house some twenty double bunks on each side of the center isle upstairs and downstairs, for a total of about a hundred and sixty people.

Crowding breeds strife; it is therefore imperative that no minds be permitted to go idle. To relieve the burden of regimentation a little, competition is practiced. After evening chow, while it is still light, ponchos are spread outside between barracks and the carbine is disassembled (field stripped) and re-assembled, a process that is timed by the platoon sergeants. The best man gets his name scratched from the list that shows his next turn on KP. Then competition advances to the inter-platoon level. There, the fastest field strippers from each platoon do their act with eyes blindfolded. The winner gets to be invited by the field-first sergeant to call the cadence at the next road march or to lead the "daily dozen," the twice-daily calisthenics.

He even thinks that he understands the basic rationale behind all this activity. You must keep them busy to make them fall into their bunks exhausted when their day is over. But the inner workings of group psychology are interesting, as it is all new and unknown to him. His unit is a hodge-podge mix of what in Europe would be called lower-class humanity but with two main groups predominating here: Dagos and Niggers, as they call each other, from the slums of Chicago, most of them draftees, none of whom want to be there.

None are anxious to go to Korea to get their arses flamed. They would just as soon fight each other right here if they had a chance. But they are not given a chance. KP is a sixteen-hour job. Those with enough gigs or demerits during Saturday's inspection pull it that same Sunday in addition to their normal turn on the duty roster. In this way, the endless bitching and moaning about the fucking army slowly and subtly (by chance or on purpose?) displaces the internecine bents of the initially hostile ethnicities and bestows on them something akin to an esprit de corps, if only in united opposition to the oppressor of the moment. An important first step in building armies from a mob, he reflects, remembering half-understood discussions in his father's office back in Léva.

On morale, discipline, and patriotism

He would sit there in the corner, looking down from the third floor of city hall on the great square below. Sometimes, on holidays, there would be a market that would fill up the square with tents and activities ranging from the auction of sheep to amusement booths for children. He then would appropriate his father's binoculars, the same ones he later used to watch the carnage in Linz, to observe the details of these folk festivals. But with half an ear, he would always listen attentively to everything being said. His father liked to expound on the principles that govern the formation of a selfless, patriotic spirit in simple people who are otherwise preoccupied only with eking out a meager living in the face of odds stacked up against them by their betters, the ruling class.

A ruling class, like the old, entrenched, pseudo-feudal one that ruled Magyarország back then, has no problems being patriotic. The way it defines that lofty-sounding word is straightforward. Patriotism is that type of feeling, behavior, and activity that enhances the wealth, well-being, security, and glory of one's country. One's country, mind you, is an abstract notion. It seems to be the same on the surface but actually is quite different from the reality of "the people of that country" and, in practice, is very different from "*all* the people of that country."

The "country" in Magyarország was the old nobility, the foremost beneficiary of actions contributing to its wealth and well-being. Also, the members of this nobility were the ones who felt primarily entitled to benefit by the security and to bask in the glory that were the results of the sacrifices of all the others. Not far behind them, however, was an already solid middle class, whose social standing was based on money or on education. Its members were also proud of "their" country and benefited accordingly. But how about the rest, the "masses," the Dagos and Niggers of his battery, that the enemy's founding theoreticians called the proletariat? How would this toiling class (if it was lucky enough to toil and not mired in hopeless unemployment) define patriotism?

I do not know. Neither did the officers and officials know who discussed this conundrum in his father's office. Yet it was urgent to find an answer, for the peasants from the fields and the workers from the factories are the stuff that the patriot class needs on distant battlefields to perpetuate its rule at home. And the attitude of this stuff matters, for if it is not (or is only reluctantly) enthusiastic about giving its last full measure of devotion to whatever patriotic cause the patriot class asks (or orders) it to sacrifice itself for, then the outcome of the fight for that cause is in grave doubt.

This was the unfortunate quandary of the Magyar proletariat. The officers found it difficult to convince the men that their lot would be worse under some unknown, future red rule than under the feudal form of capitalism that had them under its yoke in the here and now. For to fight for "their country" was something too remote from reality for the Magyar peasants and workers to get wildly enthusiastic about. And so it seemed to be also for those conscripts from Chicago. Kocsis István, the old soldier who lugged those trunks to Szenc with the Stalin Organs at his back, did not fight his way through world wars for his country. He did it out of loyalty to his master, my father. Was he therefore less of a patriot than the master whom he served so loyally? You decide; I don't know.

What I do know for sure, however, is that no road march, close-order drill, white-glove inspection, or KP was able to ignite in the hearts of the Coles and of the Carbones of "Baker" Battery of the 542nd Armored Field Artillery Battalion enthusiasm for going to Korea. A tour of duty in Korea—that was simply not part of the world of their childhood dreams if childhoods in the slums of Chicago are able to produce many dreams. What about the urgent need to stop evil, atheist communism, where it happened to be at the moment (in Korea, for instance), before it could hop over the Pacific Ocean to threaten freedom and democracy in Chicago?

Come on, be serious. None of the men of B Battery (except perhaps for him) could see a threat to their country, and so they went unwillingly. Was that unpatriotic? But they went anyway. Did that transform them miraculously into patriots? Remember, this was the early 1950s, still a time when elders could lecture young ones successfully. "We landed on Omaha Beach and on Iwo Jima. Just who do you think you are to question the wisdom of your commander-in-chief? It is war now, and in war, we Americans stand by our president. My country, right or wrong."

As you may know, if you really did take a history class in school, that particular war in Korea ended in a draw. The first one that America did not win. But the country of the Coles and Carbones did win decisive battles in the barracks of those basic training camps, even if it did not do so at the demilitarized zone of that peninsula at the far end of the world. These victories led to the emergence of a *corps* with its own newborn *esprit* from what looked to him like a hostile mob of disaffected gangland dwellers in the beginning. Not quite an esprit like that of those legendary elite formations, of the Light Brigade at the Khaiber Pass, or of Pickett's Division charging up Cemetery Ridge, to be sure, but they became credible and cohesive "units" nonetheless, with a veneer of discipline strong enough to make them stand up to enemy fire, even in the absence of the kind of courage that only conviction can give.

Jump school

Well, now that this story makes me think of it, I see that I have even forgotten if graduating from basic training made him automatically an E2, a PFC, a first-class private that is. At any rate, first class was the way he felt when he next reported in at the orderly room of that storied training outfit at Fort Benning, Georgia, known in its own vernacular simply as "Jump School."

Georgia, if you have never been there, has a climate blessed by its Maker. In the winter, it is not very wintry by more Northern, continental climate standards, but in the summer, it can indeed be very summery if you judge that by its two main guideposts, heat and humidity. Now, of special interest among the life-forms that thrive there naturally under those conditions and that have an impact on people constrained to move about the landscape in marching columns are gnats.

The authorities charged with running Jump School, well versed in the art of training for war, took due cognizance of this phenomenon of nature in their desire to turn out a product worthy of its name, the Airborne Soldier. Seeing that there was little leeway left to improve on the methods already perfected in basic training, they did do nonetheless what little they could and focused their attention on that hardy mainstay of their trade, the road march. Only now, as befits this higher, advanced level of training, the march was done on the run or, to use the appropriate vernacular, on the double or in double time.

But also, to emphasize the kind of mental and physical balance that the Airborne Soldier needs to cultivate so that he can make up his mind properly to leap out into the propblast of an airplane without hesitation and then bring his physique into the proper bent-leg alignment for the landing fall (to use the vernacular again), the trainers added a minor little refinement to the mode of this double timing. No doubt only to balance the rearward pull of the full field pack on the back, the M1 (infantry) rifle (twice the weight of the artillery carbine) now had to be held at port arms (with both hands in front) while double-timing in formation. This was certainly a fine way to build up stamina in this future elite. Also, it was in perfect alignment with his own long-held conviction of the truth in "no pain, no gain."

But this was where said gnats came into the picture. They are fond of moisture. They cannot help it, it is their nature, and they are therefore drawn, like by magnets, to anything that is damp. As a double-timing column of the future elite then passes by their breeding grounds, they rise up in clouds that literally darken the sky (like November rain in Harthausen). And he, with both hands glued to his M1 rifle in front of him, knew instinctively that if he wanted to become part of the airborne elite, he had to learn to breathe, instead of O_2, a pure airborne suspension of gnat.

Yes, as his Latin teacher in Léva used to say, "*Per aspera ad astra.*" Hardships make reaching for the stars look more like an accomplishment in the end than something that you get for free. Every roadrunner chick worth his canteen of water and his ration of salt tablets, upon becoming a fledgling, must eventually learn to fly, if he really wants to become airborne. This next feat of learning was accomplished in Jump School by a painless yet gainful method (exceptions prove the rule).

To serve this end, a number of tall metal skeletons had been erected that reached up into the sky, in aspect not unlike the Eiffel Tower in Paris, France. At the top, these towers had two long horizontal crossbars spreading out toward the four points of the compass, and these, in turn, were equipped with pulley systems at their ends. These pulleys accommodated long metal cables to which circular steel frames were attached, the size of an open parachute. And yes, open parachutes were rigged onto these frames so ingeniously that upon having pulled the fledgling as high up into the air as the towers permitted (already strapped securely into his harness, which was a step in the learning process while still on the ground), the silk canopy released itself automatically from the metal frame, and yes, the erstwhile straightleg was on his way down, being borne by the air.

From not quite as high as the *astra*, the stars, but that was on purpose also. For paratroopers are not dropped from the lofty heights that skydivers are fond of for a good reason. The closer they are to the ground when jumping out, the shorter is the time that enemy riflemen down below have to pick them off while they are floating down helplessly. Other tactical considerations also influence this relatively short float, the main one being control upon landing. The wind usually has a nasty way of kicking up in the middle of a parachute drop, which then lands the 'troopers scattered all over the terrain. If the 'trooper is an artilleryman, like he was, the equipment of his unit that is also dropped includes big items like howitzers (these are guns that zap the enemy using indirect fire) and trucks that pull the howitzers. Now, these items weigh tons and therefore have different rates of descent and wind drag from that of the personnel that have to scurry upon landing to secure them before the enemy does. The shorter the float, the less the scatter, and consequently, the assembly process becomes more efficient. But even so, a major drop can be a hilarious mess, like ants milling around, even on a training jump at a well-known home base.

All of which is quite reasonable tactically speaking, but it has its drawbacks emotionally. As I hinted already, paratroopers are not skydivers. Although all volunteers, they are typically apprehensive when awaiting an up-coming jump episode. They huddle around on the tarmac sometimes for lengthy periods until the all clear (weatherwise) is given and then load into their airplane. Once in, they attach the hooks on the rip chords of their chutes to the cables that run along both sides of the plane above their heads, and as they sit in their canvas chairs, about thirty of them on each side, they face each other. After takeoff, the plane is flying at a low altitude (that of the impending drop) and is therefore subject to the air pockets and turbulence that occur there and that most air travelers hardly ever encounter nowadays.

These are conditions that tend to suddenly lift and lower stomachs and their contents within the chest cavity, and they do so regardless of how tough, lean and mean the disposition of the veteran 'trooper is who happens to experience the feeling. So you sit there staring into the green faces of the folks on the other side and wish it were over—you don't care how, but over *pronto*. Then finally the warning light comes on, they get up, face backward, toward the exit door that is behind the wings and the propellers, the jumpmaster makes a last check to see if they are all hooked up properly, the green (sometimes red) Go light and that insistent beeping tone come on, they shuffle (so as not to lose their footing and stumble) to the door, they shout Geronimo, they think they jump but are really sucked out by the prop blast, the ripchord (it better be attached to the cable inside) pulls their chutes out of the bags on their backs, and finally comes that hellish yank of catharsis that they experience as the chord rips free from the chute and tells them that the moment of truth has come, that it (the 'chute) had better open, and immediately if not sooner.

And this is where the aforementioned emotional drawbacks of a drop at a low altitude come into play. If the chute opens as is expected and hoped for, you know it immediately. You look around you, and what you see is sheer, numinous joy. You are a bird! The tension, stress, and earthboundness have fallen off like the prison that the chrysalis is for a future butterfly. The only thing that is lacking is a little more time to prolong the exuberance of this delivery from the evil of not having permanent wings.

But on the other hand, if the chute does not open as expected and hoped for, it becomes what is known as a "cigarette roll" in the vernacular, and you start streaming down quicklike. There is no way of telling what the total experience is really like, for there are no authentic accounts of it extant, but they all know that the reserve chute that is attached to the harness in front is more of a morale factor than a second chance. They cannot open it immediately for fear that it would entangle with the main one, and if they wait one count longer, well then, "that's all she wrote," as the saying goes. In the vernacular, what she wrote (or might have written) is paraphrased in the refrain of the 'troopers' marching song: "Gory, gory, what a helluva way to die, he ain't gonna jump no more" (to the tune of "Glory, Glory, Halleluiah").

How can I best treat you to that complex of emotions that a paratrooper, by definition, the antithesis of an introverted intellectual, harbors in his breast as the essence of his pride in being an airborne soldier? That mixture of bravado, temerity, and self-indulgence, which at the same time is an honestly devil-may-care joy in the challenge and in the daring of danger, just for the hell of it? Maybe a couple of stanzas from the 'trooper's "Blood on the Risers" song will help a little:

> He hit the ground, the sound was "splatt," his blood went spurting high
> His comrades then were heard to say "A helluva way to die!"
> He lay there rolling in the welter of his gore
> He ain't gonna jump no more!
>
> There was blood on the risers, there were brains upon his 'chute
> Intestines were a'dangling from his paratrooper's boots,
> They picked him up, still in his 'chute and poured him from his boots.
> He ain't gonna jump no more!

You get the idea now. In a way, this was a fraternity closed to those who did not feel the way they felt, an assemblage, yes, a "college" of the select with their own secret codes and rituals.

At the Eleventh Airborne

There were some twelve thousand of them, all volunteers, all screaming, devil-may-care extroverts, in the Eleventh Airborne Division, Fort Campbell, Kentucky, that was to be his next home for about two years after Jump School. How in sweet hell did he get himself into a fix like that? But nobody minded him, as long as he did not freeze in the door so that the rest would land in the trees off the drop zone. One had to be an all-out leg by heart, one who did not wear the winged badge, to be made to feel odd by that community. For it was a community, even though it was one without any human cohesion that he could detect. The spirit of community was, as far as he could tell, all resting on external appearances and a circular logic. You were sharper, better, and braver than a leg because you were a 'trooper and you were a 'trooper because you were all those things.

The fifty dollars a month of hazardous duty pay seemed to be incidental, although it was big money then; it almost doubled a PFC's pay, and at a nickel a soft drink, you could buy a thousand bottles of coke for it (one extroverted math genius figured it out exactly that it was thirty-five bottles a day). No, these folks were not in this for that extra money that is for sure. But neither were there any friendships nor any group cohesion among more like-minded subgroup members nor any doing of out-of-uniform things together. On three-day passes, everybody went off in search of women on his own and often far afield, for the two small towns nearby were saturated with single soldiers. Even when sitting in the bars during the weekend, the conversation, if you can call it that, was not a form of sharing but more a rowdy, mutual shouting each other down.

He participated in all of it, and he did not suffer from its vacuous loneliness, for his ways were solitary anyway. But he remembered the intimate comradely chats of his scout-uniformed campfire days back home, and he was astounded how different things were here. Even though his main preoccupation at the moment was simple mental survival, he still needed time to search for and find the words with which to describe this self-selected environment into which he had lost his way. And he now had to find a way to fit himself into it, for he was not about to admit that it was he who was the misfit and not the environment. One key word that he came up with was *surface*.

Interactions, whether personal or institutional, seemed to move at the level of slogans like the advertisements on billboards. It seemed that there were a number of tenets indelibly ingrained on some subconscious level in the minds of these extroverts and that these were floating around unanchored, unreflected, and undigested intellectually. When he attempted to engage them in conversations about important topics for soldiers like war or *the* war (the current one), the outcome was always the comment that he had already heard before in Chicago: "You a philosopher or something?"

At best, they would dig out one or the other of those slogans that then obviated any further dialogue: "We are the best. We paratroopers, we football players, we Americans. You (not he in particular but all the rest of the world), you are lucky to have something to look up to. Us." All right, maybe he was still a foreigner and had not learned to understand—yet. Maybe. But then, he was also somewhat of a maverick, though only inwardly so. He was not there to feel macho and show it. It was only to himself that he had to prove himself. That he could be like them or at least that he could act like them, outwardly, for show. And that in the end, being like this elite, he would find a chance to go and face the enemy and prove to himself, whatever uniform he wore (and they wore). That he would not run away when facing the enemy.

The 'trooper

He was assigned to the Detail Section of Able Battery, Eighty-Ninth Airborne Field Artillery Battalion. The detail section of an artillery battery does everything combat-oriented that the "Firing Battery" (that handles the battery's six 105 mm field howitzers) does not, such as surveying, communications, reconnaissance, forward observation, and the like. The chief of detail, SFC Herrera, who had been an officer in the Mexican Army and therefore himself an outsider, watched him (benevolently) struggle for a while (he could not even drive a jeep yet!) and then had him sent off to Radio School at Fort Sill, Oklahoma.

Those were good months. He found a couple of good buddies. These folks talked about their families, their aspirations, their place in the United States as the Southerners that they were, and their plans to go to college. They were informative, and their company felt like his first foray out of the "lower depths" of that America that he had been in touch with so far and that was not the one he was searching for. They went dancing at the USO in Lawton and even attended ballroom dancing classes together.

He came back to Fort Campbell without really knowing how to fix a field radio, though with a good understanding of how Kirchhoff's and Ohm's laws worked on paper. Relating to the theory behind it rather than to the object itself was and would always remain his bag. However, he had learned army communications procedures thoroughly, including the use of code systems, and that sufficed to earn him his corporal's stripes. But although he was now exempt from KP and could go to the mess hall for a cup of coffee whenever he liked, he somehow did not learn yet to feel safe and sure in that sea of extroverts. As a (very) junior NCO, a noncommissioned officer, he was still quartered in the main room of the barracks, a place that took him over a year to get used to.

Even things like that little clique of four or five Negroes that would get together every night, two bunks down from his, to spend the night playing nickel-dime poker by flashlight after lights-out, became a routine part of that scene for him. They carried on a lively though tolerably muted chatter till dawn. At first, he tried to understand what they had on their minds that kept them so busy chattering, but the only fragment of speech that came through to him clear enough was "motha fuckaah." They used it all the time; it seemed to him that every second utterance of each member of the clique was that and only that and that it was the pitch or intonation of that phrase that contained the meaning that they wished to impart and not the incidental non-expletive that accompanied that phrase. As he learned to appreciate with time, people who use expletives routinely to express themselves are almost always culturally challenged. But again with time, he became so accustomed to the lullaby of these poker players that he could not fall asleep anymore without their steady, low-pitched drone.

In order to advance his cause of getting to prove himself in combat, he would go to the orderly room repeatedly to ask about the status of his application to be sent to Korea. At first, First Sergeant Mahan was patient and explained that there was only one airborne regiment over there and that every real paratrooper wanted to go so that there was a waiting line.

Was that really true? Sergeant Mahan was the mother of the battery. He was as tough and mean as anyone, but he was the epitome of the finest of career soldiers: "Mission first and foremost" (of course), but "take care of your men" not second but almost as first as the mission itself. He always called a spade a spade and always told the truth, and if not, what he said was as good as the truth or maybe even better. Maybe Mahan just did not think that he should go to Korea and, after several inquiries, kicked him out of his orderly room. "Damnit, Corporal, wait your turn. Can't you see I am busy?"

The NCO Academy

Then the division commander decided to start an academy to train promising 'troopers to become real noncommissioned officers. So Mahan got the old man (the battery commander, First Lieutenant Rozsypal, an OCS graduate) to send him to attend that first NCO course. I wish Mahan were still alive, for I would like to ask him why he sent him there. Did he see some hope in extroverting him? At any rate, it was there that both he and the army discovered his talent for orientation in the field by map and compass. He graduated first in class, was promoted to sergeant, and was detailed from the battery to the NCO Academy as an instructor of reconnaissance, night patrolling, and map reading.

With the newfound feeling that he was really good at what he was doing, he gained a firm footing among the extroverts, along with a new voice of confidence and authority. He would truck groups of his students out to some nondescript point in that vast military reservation at night, send the truck back, and then let them fight the mosquitoes till dawn (to get them into the proper mood for the exercise).

At sunup, he would point to some coordinates on the map and inform the group that if they got to the abandoned farmhouse that stood there within twenty-four hours, hot chow would be waiting for them. To the somewhat anguished—"But, Sarge, where are we now?"—he would only offer that finding their way (maybe upon being dropped behind enemy lines in some much hoped-for near future) with only a map and a compass was a crucial part of their training as noncoms. But then, along the way to that farmhouse, he would be helpful, giving pointers on how to recognize terrain features and how to triangulate their exact position using those features and their map and compass. In short, he strove to make his students the best map readers in the army.

Yolanda

Next, he bought a car, a big, used but still badass Super-Rocket V-8 Oldsmobile. You are not a real American if you don't have a car. That opened up new worlds. Up to then, all his worldly possessions had fitted neatly and without the need of undue stuffing into his army-issue duffle bag (I still have it), and when he wanted to get somewhere, he walked or hitchhiked. Now, there was the trunk of his car for things not subject to Saturday morning inspections, and exotic places out of walking distance became accessible. To appreciate the impact of this new dimension, consider this simile: if you have a space rocket, you can go to the moon (or Mars). He could go places, and others who did not have a car came to *him* to ask him for a ride. One of his new adjuncts (fellow travelers) taught him to drive.

At the USO, he met a lovely girl chaperoned by ladies of the local aristocracy. Yolanda was a good dancing partner (she did not seem to mind excessively when he stepped on her toes) and fun to be with. She attended the local college to perfect her English (she was from Peru) while visiting relatives in the United States. It was from her that he picked up his first bits of Spanish, among them the schmalzy "*Schlager*" tune that became for him the theme song of that short epoch of his life:

Te quiero, dijiste, poniendo mis manos	I love you, you said, putting my hands
Entre tus manitas de blanco marfil,	Between your small hands of white ivory,
Y siento en mi pecho un fuerte latido	And I feel in my breast a fierce beating
Y luego el chasquido de un beso fevril	And then the spark of a fervent kiss

Well, there were few *besos fevriles* (if any), for Yolanda, though sweet, lively, and warmhearted, was very definitely upper class where she had come from, and here, in Clarksville, Tennessee, she unmistakably projected that aura of conditional approachability that must surround young ladies like her back in Lima like a stone wall. And the condition, it was clear to him, was commitment, although she did not say so, for she did not need to. Now, it was also clear to him that he was in no shape or form either ready or fit for any sort of commitment, and she, in turn, seemed to sense and accept that. So it was one of those truly sunlit and fragrant but transient episodes that are as rare and precious as that fleeting season of the lilacs' and acacias' bloom back home in Léva. It was like when two butterflies meet over a flower and they spiral up around each other high into the air in the weightless dance of their rainbow wings till a gust of wind separates their moment of eternity. A moment as brief as life itself.

The past intrudes

Still, he might have pursued the matter in earnest—and Yolanda was not above intimating that she would not have minded that at all—had not all of a sudden the blue-eyed past of those cold mountain lakes intruded into the present and ruffled the smooth surface of those dark brown eyes until they could no longer mirror the image of the Southern Cross for him. Letters started arriving from Irschenhausen. Nothing significant, nothing very meaningful, pleasant chatter, "How are you doing over there in the Wild West? Are you still alive? We here are graduating from school this summer, and would you believe it? Muschi [one of their class mates] got herself engaged."

Now, they had been corresponding before, even from the AKO, where the mail was censored by the *patres*, so this was not an earth-shaking first. But she was also asking why he did not hurry up to become an officer, for "wouldn't it be nice if you would come back so we could talk about things again?" And all of a sudden, believe it or not, that world seen through the pink glasses of first love that I tried to describe for you while looking out on the fog and rain in Harbin Springs stormed back into the present and blew away the dust of time that was beginning to settle on the yellowing pages of its memories. These letters injected a new sense of urgency into his life, a life made simple by the solid string of basic necessities that people struggle with who do not have the means that afford them the luxury of choice.

Of big choices, that is, for little choices there were aplenty. He could go to see a movie, play pool in the dayroom, read a book in the library, or drive around a little in his big car, all of this duty permitting, of course. He could choose to go and drink Schlitz, Pabst Blue Ribbon or Miller High Lite in one of the innumerable bars of Clarksville or in Hopkinsville over the state line in Kentucky. There was always plenty of company there for that, and by now, he had learned to sidestep the brawls that drinking will provoke in some people's behavior. He could never understand this, for beer made him only mellow and sleepy.

There was also another choice; he could go and have dinner at the mansion of those old ladies who made a pastime out of organizing dances for "our soldier boys" at the USO (and who had introduced him to Yolanda). Clarksville, though just barely south of the Mason-Dixon Line, considered itself very Southern, and Southerners, especially if they also belong to the Daughters of the American Revolution like his old ladies, are fond of cultivating military traditions and doing things for the soldiers. And these dinners were special, for the old Negro butler himself served the dishes, offering the plates correctly in his black-and-white uniform every bit as properly as his (the soldier's) mother had learned from her mother to expect this service to be performed by her servants.

Now, introverts are born musers, and he invariably lapsed into musing when dishes like cervelle à la meunière or a strawberry parfait appeared on their plates from behind his right, ready for him to pick out his choice helping. This was exactly like it used to be at home. "*Méltóztassék, tálalva van*," a servant used to announce there that everything was set for the meal—a short phrase that is difficult to render in a non-feudalist, democratically spirited idiom, for it means something like "may you graciously condescend [to come to table], for the dishes are waiting." That old Negro butler with his veiled, unfocused eyes and faraway, benign demeanor would have fitted perfectly into that scene at home, gone with the wind now also. But while musing, he would carry on the chat over comparing etiquette in different countries since this was a favorite subject of his hostesses.

But the climax of these high-society episodes came during the annual horse-show, when the whole family from Nashville and from their country estate was assembled in their booth right above the arena. He was also invited to come, and he did so in his sergeant's uniform, for they knew (and perhaps they also liked to show that they knew) that it was not an officer's commission and an act of Congress that made a man a gentleman. Now, as it happened, the booth right next to theirs was that of the division's commanding general, and the sergeant had a rare chance to explain to the general how his father's horse artillery battery succeeded in breaking up the attack of a Cossack cavalry squadron in Galicia some forty years ago, to which the general then good-naturedly offered reminiscences of his own.

The officer candidate

But then, when the time came for a real choice, it wasn't really a matter of choosing. At least the occasion did not present itself that way when the old man called him into his office. "I am sending you to OCS" (not Omaha Cold Storage this time but Officer Candidate School), Lieutenant Rozsypal said. "You will like it there." That was not an order, of course; no one had to become an officer (and a gentleman) if he did not choose to. And in this terse, lapidary form, the offer sounded more like a compliment than an order, anyway. The Poles, you see, for Rozsypal was one, somehow retain a sense of the genteel ways with which they are born even after they become second-generation Americans.

He had a couple of months until the course was to start, and he had to pass a General Educational Development (GED) Test of High School Equivalency first as one of the conditions for admission. So he spent every off-duty hour in the Post Library, reading and soaking up every bit of information within sight and hearing. He read the three great novels of Thomas Hardy, reviewed world history and economic geography, refreshed his mind on analytical geometry, and even went through a chapter of *Bellum Gallicum* by Julius Caesar.

Then he went to take the test with trepidation when the time came, only to experience the surprise of his life. There was also a bit of disillusionment mixed in it, for it turned out that he did not have to know anything at all to pass this GED test. They made him read a page of some text, and by checking true or false answers, he only had to show that he had understood much of it. In math, if I recall this right, they asked how many nickels and dimes should he get back if he bought a hamburger for thirty-five cents and paid with a half-dollar coin. My, oh my, really!

He had always been ashamed of not having had time to take the *Abitur, die Reife Prüfung*, the Examination of Maturity, that closed out school back at the AKO before leaving for America. Now he was declared a high school-graduate equivalent by virtue of his being able to read! He could hardly believe it. But it was okay, for if these were the standards by which American schools operated, OCS would have to be a snap.

In this, however, he was proven thoroughly wrong. The drive to Fort Sill was his first long-distance experience at the steering wheel, and the stay overnight in Broken Bow, Oklahoma, recalled one of his childhood stories of the tragic struggle of a brave people for the right to be free. Even though in this case, the story was not quite accurate, for Broken Bow was not named for a massacre of Indians.

This trip was also the start of his enduring love affair with the open, great American road. To this day, I get the goose bumps when I hear the melody of

> On the road again,
> Goin' places that I've never been,
> Seein' things that I may never see again.
> And I can't wait to get on the road again

But for the next six months, there would be no more road open to him. It was back to regimentation but at a level of perfection that has perhaps been only rarely achieved anywhere since the Spartans had passed on the tradition to future military cultures. It started well enough, for when he got to the barracks of his officer candidate battery still clad as a sergeant with his green leadership tabs on his shoulder straps, the officer-candidates-to-be who were milling around there waiting for time to pass mistook him for some higher being and snapped to attention, which gave him a good laugh.

It was a good omen, but in two more days, when the full class was assembled, things would change. The sergeant's stripes came off the sleeves to be replaced by the round OCS patch, and with that, the system took him (and his fellow candidates) into its vise, screwed tighter every day, to reinvent him as someone who could be addressed as "sir" if he could prove that he wanted it badly enough to endure the torture.

The torture was subtle. No one wants to be constantly badgered, harassed, and shouted at; no one wants to be reminded all the time that he is gross, sloppy, and nothing really but a hopeless flop of a wet dishrag. But of course, the intimation behind all this was that "you too may be able to overcome your present condition of total inadequacy if you make a superhuman effort." And they all made that effort. There was a daily routine of classes interspersed with field exercises. So I think at least, for just as with the basic training routine, I really cannot remember anymore what the specifics were to fill up six long months.

But to give you a glimpse into the art of the artillery anyway, consider for a moment its basic premise. You want to hit a target with "guns" whose operators, the gunners, do not see the enemy. To accomplish this, you need three groupings of personnel.

First, the "firing battery" that is made up of the six howitzers. *Gun*, you should know, is a generic term used by laymen. For the pro, *gun* is a destruction delivery vehicle that is used for high-velocity, directly sighted fire as practiced by tanks, for instance, while a howitzer would typically fire at the enemy indirectly from, say, the other side of a hill. The position of the howitzers is known (surveyed) exactly and pinpointed on the tactical contour map. They must be "laid" (oriented) in a predetermined direction.

Second, there is the forward observer (FO). He and his crew are the ones who do see the enemy maybe from some elevated vantage point. The coordinates of the FO's position should also be determined as well as possible on the map.

Finally, there is a Fire Direction Center (FDC) that receives the "fire mission," which is the information regarding the enemy's disposition from the FO by radio. The brains at the FDC then calculate with great speed (for the enemy may be moving) and accuracy (to avoid collateral damage by friendly fire) two directional must-haves. Namely, the deflection (the horizontal, angular deviation of the howitzer's barrel from their preset direction) and the elevation (the vertical orientation of the barrel). This elevation, along with the amount of gunpowder used, determines the trajectory and the range of the projectiles. If done right, the rounds then usually end up near enough to the intended target.

As he sees the first impact, the FO then radios back follow-up commands to the FDC, which in turn directs the adjustment of the gun-sight settings (that control the direction of the barrel) for the next salvo. He does this either directly from the map or relative to a known reference point, until the target is "neutralized."

The venerable and legendary reference point that all beginners' classes were using at Fort Sill was and maybe still is the Blockhouse on Signal Mountain, a landmark known and fondly remembered by all artillery officers not only as a terrain feature but also as a milestone in their professional development. So it was either in the bleachers looking out on Signal Mountain or in the classrooms of that new, huge, windowless, fortresslike building that was and perhaps still is the Artillery School where he spent much of his time, for there was much to learn.

An artillery battery is a little universe, with some two hundred men, a half dozen or so officers, and hundreds and hundreds of pieces of equipment, all of whom and all of which demand of a good officer an expert's touch in the Zen-like mastery of knowing, handling, caring, and commanding, so as to earn and obtain the loyal cooperation of his men and the reliable functioning of his equipment. Now, all of this was fine and even propitious; the problem was with the extracurricular shit that the system dumped on the candidate on purpose to make him suffer so that he could prove being worthy of a second lieutenant's gold bars by his mute endurance of this chicanery.

I will leave the details of all the well-meant and goal-oriented sadism to your imagination and to similar and more vivid accounts in the pertinent literature, if any of that exists. Let only one example suffice here. One drizzly winter night, at 2300 hours (eleven o'clock in the evening), after a long day in the bleachers, the alarm rang in the barracks.

"Everybody and everything outside, into the open space in front, including bunks and footlockers and get set up for open-air inspection. In fifteen minutes." They were already sound asleep when the order came and getting dressed and dragging everything outside within that time frame resulted, as expected by the *marquis*, whose idea of character testing this was, in the kind of pandemonium that even Pan himself could have watched with glee back in his day when he let his cattle stampede by blowing his whistle.

Well, it took a whole hour. The barracks door was just wide enough to let one bunk pass at a time, and everyone was in everybody else's way. So they stood in formation out there finally, freezing, bewildered, and highly pissed off, only to be told that candidates must never shiver or appear to be cold no matter what the temperature may be if they had the stuff to become officers. Then the *marquis*, the tac officer in charge of all this sadism, inwardly every bit as gleeful as Pan but outwardly severely reproachful and judgmental, told them how miserably they have failed in this simple task. "Everything and everybody back into the barracks."

No sooner were the bunks (blankets now moist with the drizzle) lined up in the prescribed precise order that the alarm sounded again. "Repeat." A great moan went up, but this time purposeful organization and cooperation were also blowing in the wind that was all ill before. They made it on time this time. Nevertheless, it was well past 0100 hours (one o'clock) the next morning that they finally got to bed. On their bunks that day, they found notices that their resignations from OCS would be accepted without prejudice. But there were no takers.

This type of thing was his main beef with OCS. His minimum sleep requirement must have been well above the OCS norm. So he would have dozed through many a class had not his best buddy's sharp elbow sent him urgent wake-up messages. Jim Harris was never sleepy. Although already an intellectual, a college graduate, he seemed to have morphed successfully into a natural OCSer. He finished with distinction and was assigned, you guessed it, to the OCS staff. I met up with Jim again some fifteen years later in Saigon. He came in from the field for a visit at MACV headquarters where I was. They were both seriously disaffected with that war by then. But more of that later.

Let me just add here that almost forty years after that, three weeks ago to be exact, Jim found me on the Internet, climbed into an airplane in faraway Tampa, Florida, and came to see me. I was touched to tears. Nothing like that had ever happened before to an introvert like me. Then last week (April 2010), we met again at Fort Sill. He flew in from Florida; I drove in from California. The OCS we knew was gone; only the wooden building that housed the staff remained. It was now the OCS Hall of Fame, with the pictures of graduates who made colonel or above on the walls. Six of his class (January 1955) made it there.

The officer

What followed were three more years right there at Fort Sill. Now, Oklahoma, if you don't know this because you have had the misfortune of never having been there, is not one of the most scenic and touristy places in the world. But that is highly deceptive. You stick around, and it grows on you rapidly, and before you know it, you are a dyed-in-the-wool Okie. You cannot describe the process easily. But if you have spent your early years with the kind of Indian lore that he did, then the ghosts of the past materialize for you readily, and pretty soon, you think you are an avatar of Geronimo. What he did for the army during that time (and what the army did for him) appears to me almost incidental now, important though it was, compared to what Oklahoma did to him.

The second lieutenant

So there he was, a second "Loui," assigned to a school-support unit, the Five-Forty-Eight Field Artillery Battalion, where he did nothing else for a year, day in and day out, but check the settings of his howitzers' aiming devices so that none of the rounds fired from them would be lobbed accidentally off course to explode outside the target area. Even though that never happened while he was checking the sights, the bosses, the battery commanders, never thought it called for a commendatory acknowledgement. The first was a somewhat less than gentlemanly captain, then an even less-so first lieutenant, and they did their best, as bosses can, to keep his high level of enjoyment of being saluted by enlisted men within limits by detailing inane chores on him. But that was just as well, as he learned to shrug that sort of thing off in time.

The rewards came out in the field at the firing positions. There, while waiting for the next fire commands, the troops would dig up tarantulas and train them to fight each other. He liked to watch that. Incidentally, this was the first time that he observed an actual, natural symbiosis. The tarantula holes always contained small, short-legged toads that apparently lived on the remains left over from the bounty provided by the huge spiders' nightly foraging. The toad cleaned house in exchange for its keep.

No one cleaned house for the fresh-baked officers at their BOQ, like officers' servants did in the more gentlemanly days before World War I, when his father was a second lieutenant. In these latter-day quarters, the Louis spent their nights playing cards, bridge, or poker, a pastime that he enjoyed. Playing cards gives you an illusion of individuality in action and freedom in judgment and decision making, while in reality, it is governed by strict rules and the tyranny of random chance. Now, if you are an extrovert, you may be surprised to find that the former is the state of affairs that introverts long for, but the latter is where they feel at home.

The old emigrant

This was the time that his brother in Omaha got married and his father, no longer capable of enduring the Charlie-do-this, Charlie-do-that routine at the church (and of paying the rent by himself now), moved in with his younger son, him. They set up house in Lawton, the town adjacent to the Fort, their economy being based on his salary of a tad over 200 dollars per month. It was a good time for both of them. Having a dependent was quite a restriction on his finances and his freedom of movement, but the old man was good company, and they were compatible.

His father had slowly (and miraculously) recovered from the devastating losses that he had suffered at an already advanced age, and although he chafed under the sense of being a burden on his son, he accepted the inevitable with the smile of resignation. Now, that I am older than he was then, I understand better what he was doing. He was fighting the last hopeless battle gracefully and under immeasurably harsher circumstances than mine are now, although he had not heard of Krishna as I have. He had not read the Bhagavad Gita; he did not even know it existed.

He was not a true extrovert, but he was outgoing and sociable, he enjoyed company, he liked to talk with people, and so he made friends, as an old soldier himself in that military environment, much more easily than his tongue-tied son. By now he could express himself in English in a manner that people found endearing. Even Jim Harris remembered him well, as he was telling me before he flew back to Tampa three weeks ago in this latter-day point in time.

A letter from home

Then, along the convoluted paths that fate is fond of taking to spin its webs around its unsuspecting victims, his father received a letter from faraway Székelyudvarhely. It was from Rösler Kari, who owned a beer brewery there and was a family friend. "*Szervusz, kedves barátom*" ("I am your servant, my dear friend"), he wrote. "I just got a letter from the Siegmunds, emigrants like you, from a place called Norman, Oklahoma, wherever that may be in this wide world. Remember Max Siegmund? They owned a store on the street leading to Bethlenfalva, and your father used to stop his carriage there on his way home to take a refreshment. It seems his sister, Trude, has been living in this Norman for ages now, married to a professor of physics at a university located there. But your address has Oklahoma in it also. Are you anywhere near this Norman?"

Now, this Trude *néni* had been a secret admirer of his father's back in their school days. Then she left to study medicine in Berlin or Coppenhagen where she met and married Jens Rud Nielsen. Or maybe she made her way to the shores of the Pacific Ocean somehow and met Uncle Jens Rud there, at the California Institute of Technology. At any rate, together they decided that they would rather be big fishes in a small pond than the other way around and moved to the University of Oklahoma.

That must have been a backwater then, in the 1920s and 1930s, in physics and perhaps in most other aspects of the Nation's life as well. Well, this Norman was only a two-hour drive away from Lawton, and the university had become a bustling, modern, up-to-date institution by this time. Father and son went to visit. The campus was impressive, and the Nielsens and Siegmunds were hospitable. The elders could not stop reminiscing about their *temps perdu* in Erdély. And while soaking up those memories of a vanished world with one ear, his other ear started picking up vibes of the future. Here was a place that promised real advancement, for he was starting to feel uneasy about his GED at the high school equivalency level. And that was the opening to the next chapter, coming up promptly. But let's finish this one first.

The first lieutenant

He moved up in status to battery executive officer and, along the way, decided to add a ranger tab to his uniform to accompany his parachutist's badge. Wearing this bright orange-on-black shoulder patch identified you to all those in the know as a select member of an elite that thought highly enough of itself to undergo some arduous training in the swamps around Eglin Air Force Base in Florida, and in the Great Smoky Mountains near Dahlonega, Georgia. You need not know all the details of this memorable experience, so I will recount only two minor episodes that somehow stuck in his mind.

For the survival training part of the course, upon getting off the trucks in the very middle of a shrubby, swampy, mosquito-ridden nowhere on the Eglin Reservation, the trainers released a bunch of sturdy, freedom-minded, full-grown chickens as a wish-you-well gesture to the soon-to-be-starving trainees. As if on cue, as a matter of reflex, everybody who had his wits about him set out instantly in a mad dash to grab one of these fowl adapted through evolutionary ages to outrun on foot would-be captors—birds that turned out to be true masters in the art of dodging. He did succeed in tripping one up with a stick and twisted its head off immediately to let it bleed out before gutting it. With this important detail accomplished, he looked around and saw that the majority of the class was setting out toward the river to the tune of "I'm Going Fishing."

He then took the initiative so rare for an introvert (but natural to an exNCO Academy drill sergeant) to call out "Hey, you guys, wait a minute. In an hour it will be dark. The riverbank, if there is one, will be swampy, and the mosquitoes will soon suck you dry. You will stagger back to this high ground wet, cold, muddy, itching, and bitching. Stay here, gather some firewood, and roast your chicken. Tomorrow will be a better day for fishing."

A few of them did not have to be told. His good buddy, Bill Riley, and the two marines, Murphy and Rice, smiled and nodded and went off to gather fuel for their campfires. The rest acted as if they had not heard. What followed turned out as he had predicted. The stragglers that had found their way back to the high ground, all self-declared pretenders to out-of-doors expertise (but all fishless), took their chickens (if they were lucky to have one) and stuck them in the middle of the flames (if they could still find fuel in the dark), only to pull them out after fifteen minutes burnt black on the outside and bloody raw on the inside (all pain but no gain).

He and Bill Riley shared a fire, let it die down to a hot, glowing, smokeless bed of embers, and then turned their birds over it slowly for a good hour. It was one of the best meals of their lives, they agreed. Bill was a West Pointer, and I hope he made general in due time. Murphy and Rice were the first Marine Corps officers to attend an army ranger course, and their mission was to learn and observe and then to become the core cadre of a similar course to be started soon by their organization.

The second memory fragment was part of a three-day cross-country trek to blow up a dam and then return evading a simulated (but in fact nasty) "enemy." The details of this exercise (not elaborated on any further here) were all of a nature that led to some very gainful outdoors experience, especially considering that it was late November in the Smokies, with cold and blustery mornings and equally chilly evenings without fires (for simulated stealth and secrecy).

Well, when it came time to call it a day late the first night, the "bedding-down" process was indeed quite makeshift. Equipment had been kept to a minimum for speed of movement, and there were no sleeping bags and only one blanket. The poncho was the main source of comfort. He, unfortunately, was prone to catching colds and to having cold feet, something he was only too well aware of. But he also was the owner of a small store of old old-country proverbs and adages, and he decided to put one of them to use here: "*Die Köpfe kühl die Füße warm, das macht den besten Doktor arm.*"

Yes, he knew, he had to keep his feet warm, not to make any doctor poor but to be able to sleep. So he took his boots off, emptied his backpack, wrapped his woolen shawl around his feet, and stuffed them into the pack. Not a good recipe for taking off in a hurry in case of a sneak enemy raid, to be sure, but he did sleep through what was left of the night with cozily warm feet. At dawn, he was awakened (it was not his turn to lead the group) to the crunching sound that breaking ice makes. There had been a drizzle apparently, and a small pool of it had crept under the fold of his poncho freezing his right shoulder into its crust. He went on to feel its effects for many years, foretelling a change in the weather, until a deep massage at the aforementioned hot springs eventually loosened it up.

Boss for a change

Then he was given command of his battery. Being battery commander was his first experience at being the boss, and don't you think for a second that that is a cakewalk. He could order the some two hundred people under him around, to be sure, but with the weight of responsibility on his shoulders, he soon learned that the standard army "yes, sir" for an answer was a surface effect only. Below that, there was a whole spectrum of reservations and resistances differing from individual to individual subordinate, and he knew that all these pent-up feelings were always bubbling up in the barracks bull sessions like a kettle full of witches' brew, an unstable, explosive *fluidum* that is also known as "unit morale." He was well aware of these intangible undercurrents that are so crucial in the military from his days as a denizen of the barracks himself, but from the commander's point of view, this aspect of the trade took on an entirely different dimension.

I hate to tell you this but if you have never been a unit commander in the army, you have missed out on something very special. To explain the concept briefly (or you won't have a clue as to what this is all about), in the military, only authority can be delegated to subordinates but command responsibility cannot. For a unit to be a good one, the commander must be an all-pervasive, positive presence. If something bad happens and he did not know about it, he is relieved of his command with prejudice, for it is his job to know everything. Ignorance is sufficient proof of incompetence. If something bad happens and he knows about it but does not correct it immediately, he is court-martialed and convicted in shame.

Civilians seem to have a hard time grasping this concept, and so commanders-in-chief sometimes turn crooks, lie, and cheat and even do so publicly but always go scot-free in the end. It is their aides who may go to jail, unless they get pardoned, a loophole that is mostly closed to lesser mortals. Remember that those grandiose gestures declaring "I accept full responsibility" are not enough. If you are responsible, you are the one who should suffer the consequences and not everybody else (Watergate is a prime example). These days, leaders are no longer in the habit of following this recipe, and whenever they do not, the evil precedent gnaws perilously at the delicate fabric of the soldier's and the whole nation's morale.

But to return to my chain of thought, for a young fellow to become all of a sudden father, mother, judge, priest, and maybe even undertaker for a bunch of people most of whom are older than he is and to try to exercise this responsibility as humanely as his still callow wits permit is a veritable neurosensory uplift, not unlike smoking pot. And this, as I said before, I wish all of you could have shared, for it is psychedelic. His second year as a first Loui went quickly and was full of the joy of learning at the life of the battery, the unit that was *his* now. He learned how to chew out people severely who did not cut the mustard cleanly enough. And he also studied the ways to tap those on the shoulder who deserved it without making them uppity.

All the little daily ups and downs of his unit's life were significant for him. There was the "revolt" of the junior NCOs against a tough field-first sergeant who took no back talk and demanded perfection from the gunners of the firing battery. He put that down by backing the field first, whom he set up as an example for the young buck sergeants. "You just try to be as good a soldier as he is," he told them, "and I will back you up against your crews as I back him up against you now."

Then there was the old SFC in charge of the motor pool who had seven children, could not make ends meet, and went deeply in debt. When the merchants from town came and demanded that he freeze the sergeant's pay for what he owed them, he explained to them patiently but pointedly that they had made themselves culpable by having extended credit recklessly to a member of the military. "We could sue you for that, and then you lose all of it," he advised them. "Let's forgive some of that debt, cut it down to size, consolidate it, and then let's talk again." The man never thanked him in words, but he started running a motor pool that became the pride of the post.

There was also an instance where he balked the system. That was with the practically mandatory collections of money for the annual charity drive. Unit commanders were rated for their ability to extract the most money from the troops for such seemingly irreproachable enterprises as the Red Cross and the Army Emergency Relief. The ability to do this well was considered to be a sign of leadership. Only, in his experience, these do-good agencies had never come through with help for his soldiers when it was needed. He deduced from this that they were overhead supporting bureaucracies, and so he refused to collect. "Let them prove their worth, and then the donations will beat a path to their bank accounts," he would say. "That is the American way." The chain of command frowned at this attitude, but deep down, it might have agreed, although it did not admit it.

The uprising of 1956

One noteworthy sequence of historical events occurred during this time that affected his outlook on life. Rumblings could be heard from the other side of the globe on the shortwaves of Radio Free Europe and the Voice of America by the few who were interested and concerned. But these rumors also traveled along the semi-official grapevine and whispered furtively that the US government was encouraging Magyarország (and perhaps also other Soviet satellites) to rise up against the brutal occupation imposed on Central Europe by the Evil Empire as a result of the decisions made in Yalta by the victors of the last Great War. Although this talk was all nebulous and vague on this side of the Iron Curtain, he could vividly imagine how eagerly it was accepted, believed, and trusted as a serious promise and commitment on the other side.

Now, the Magyars, as I told you at the very beginning, are a strange, emotional lot. They are no good at all at bending circumstances to their own advantage when it comes to the power plays that govern international relations. So unlike their neighbors, they keep ending up on the losing side. The gamut of their disposition can range from submission to inexorable fate (though not for long) to exuberant enthusiasm for a cause. Conditioned by their tragic history, freedom has always been such a cause. And with the (purported) promise of help from that great global champion of freedom and democracy, the United States of America, they did rise up like they did a little over a hundred years earlier against yet another hegemon.

The news was electrifying, at least to him. With what looks to me now as a piece of incredible naïveté, he informed the battalion commander, his boss, that he wanted to go to Budapest to join the freedom fighters "in our common cause." "Sit down, Son," the colonel said and, in a very unusual gesture, brought out a bottle of Scotch, something he probably had never done before in dealing with subordinates during duty hours. "Let's think this through."

Sergeant Hamilton and a short course in politics

Let me regress here back in time for a moment to show where his mindset was then within the framework of his very limited understanding of the realities of power and politics: back to the barracks that housed the cadre of the Eleventh Airborne Division's NCO Academy. He was bunking in the NCO room with one SFC Hamilton, a man some twenty years his senior. The old sergeant was a paragon of proper military etiquette when dealing with the trainees, but he was of Scots-Irish extraction and was fiercely proud of that. And so he was not above calling people Dagos and Niggers in private, and perhaps because of that same pride in his ancestry, he made a point of not noticing his roommate with the weird, long non-Anglo name.

Not until the "kid" caught him one evening immersed in a book of Kipling's poetry. "Hey," said the kid (as Hamilton called him thereafter), "I know Kipling. I read the *Just So Stories* when I was seven and ate them up." "Seven?" Hamilton looked up with raised eyebrows and then suggested musingly, "I thought you were a foreigner, and now I know it for sure. We here don't start reading books until we are in high school, if we ever do. Do you know this poem about the Fuzzy-Wuzzies? It is my favorite, and I know it by heart."

These Fuzzies in question, he soon learned, were the tall, proud Hadendoa warriors of the Beja tribe of North Africa. Their claim to fame that Kipling then so famously celebrated was their achievement in breaking a British square. This was the first time that he had heard of such a square, but he had no problem deducing from the verses that Hamilton did not tarry to recite, that it was a defensive military formation made up of stalwarts like the seasoned, disciplined, unwavering, undaunted, stone-hard veterans with the stiff upper lips of some legendary Scottish regiment of the theretofore invincible British Colonial Armies.

And (or but) as Hamilton's presentation made clear, the essence of the story was not that the Fuzzies were strong and valiant in their own right in facing and overcoming an adversary that did not spare the ammunition from his superior modern fire arms. No, as interpreted by Hamilton, the measure by which the Fuzzies were judged by Kipling (although admiringly so) was not their own, absolute worth but how that worth stacked up against the keystone of values, the bearers of that white man's burden, which the men of that British square represented in the world (and apparently still do for some).

Now, what do the Fuzzies and the British square have to do with those Magyar students defending the royal castle of Buda and other strong points in the city of Pest, whom he wanted to join and against whom those three thousand Russian tanks had descended to punish their audacity of demanding their freedom? A lot. The fleeting associations that arise when important decisions based on novel thought processes are gelling are often the ones that the controller records, and when it does so unasked and on its own, they have a meaning worth considering, especially when the connections are as momentous as they were then.

The Magyar freedom fighters broke an early, although transient breach in the Russian square, the Iron Curtain. They had demonstrated that it was possible. The consequences then were just as disastrous, though different, for Magyarország as they were for the Fuzzies. The Fuzzies were cut to shreds in the process by those repeating rifles. For Magyarország, the bloodbath was even worse, for the cream of the crop of its population, the students, the intellectuals, and the elite such as was still left there, was able to escape through the hole in the mine fields that opened up for a brief while as a result of the uprising, to be sucked up and assimilated by the West. An irreparable loss for the loser. *Vae victis*. Some of them even ended up in Norman, at the University of Oklahoma. But more on that later.

The exchanges of thought that ensued thereafter with Sergeant Hamilton were all pertinent to his understanding of the realities of power and politics. They gave him a first conceptual background for the discussion with the colonel, the battalion commander, at the moment. But they were even more important in a broader sense, for they were educational. What the old sergeant had to say about the Fuzzies and the British seemed to lie at the core of his political worldview, which was the kid's first real glimpse into an existential area of American political thought.

Back then, you must know, professional military people, officers, and NCOs alike, were conservative, registered Republicans (maybe they are that to this day), and Hamilton was one of them, even though he was an exception of sorts, for he read books and knew a lot about history. "Since the rise of the modern menace in the East," he would intone, "real, red-blooded Americans are left with no choice but the *right* choice. When I say the 'right choice,' that means now to follow General Eisenhower's lead. And that of John Foster Dulles, his handpicked secretary of state. We cannot let those dominos, all those little-bitty countries that don't know what's good for them fall to the Reds; we cannot afford to make any concessions to that alien creed. It is contrary to everything that we are and to all that we are proud of and that we hold holy.

They, the professor types, like Adlai Stevenson, theorize this way and vacillate that way. They don't know their ass from a hole in the ground, yet they think they are so much smarter than we are. We are the real Americans. Look what Roosevelt and Alger Hiss did to Central Europe in Yalta! Look what Truman did to McArthur! If left alone, old Mac would have cleaned up China by now. We, on the right, know who we are and that we are right. How could we be wrong? We cannot. We are patriotic Americans."

All this sounded a bit uneasily dogmatic to him, but it also sounded convincing, and besides, it was right down his alley. It appealed to him enormously, in fact, even though it was not the redness of the menace that was so much on his mind. That was something abstract and therefore distant. It was the Russian boot besmirching Magyar soil. Or Polish soil or Latvian soil for that matter. He was a citizen now, and clearly he would vote for Eisenhower as the right choice and the only choice and as his patriotic duty.

Back to the Magyar uprising of 1956

But it did not work out that way. Back in the colonel's office, he got the facts of life explained to him: if he left cold for Budapest like he wanted to, he would be

AWOL, absent without leave, and if he took up arms in a foreign land, he would be a deserter. To avoid that, the colonel went on, he would have to get a discharge first, and that would take time even if he recommended it to the system, and he would not, the colonel stressed, because it made no sense. For the struggle would be long over by the time he could get there. Those thousands of Soviet tanks that were on the move right now would put down the uprising in no time. The freedom fighters could not hold out for more than a few days and would soon be crushed in blood and despair.

And of course, that was exactly what happened. Making shameful use of this tragedy as a smokescreen, the British and the French attacked Egypt to grab the Suez Canal, but although they were driven off, their ill-advised adventure diverted world attention from Budapest at the crucial time.

In the end, Eisenhower shrugged his shoulders, stated that he was so very sorry but there was really nothing he could do, and that was the end of the matter. This somehow reminded him of the *Great Gatsby* (one of the books that he had read in preparation for his high school GED test), where the very rich are shown to venture out sometimes from their walled and gated lairs and latifundia to meddle carelessly, in passing, in the affairs of the poor and after having done their mindless damage, recede again behind their moats or oceans, remote and inviolate in their own secure world as if in a separate reality.

Realistically speaking, he could not (and did not) blame Eisenhower, for he knew that the United States could gain nothing from helping the Magyars (except for flaunting its favorite image as the selfless champion of freedom and democracy). A president's job is, after all, to protect and advance the interests of his own country. "*A pénz beszél, a kutya ugat*" ("Money talks, dogs bark") is the realist's creed known in Magyarország quite as well as in America; he had no problem with that.

But for him, nonetheless, this experience was like seeing a candle burn out in a church while celebrating midnight mass. The world becomes a little darker afterward. Was Hamilton's absolute faith in the Right's being always right, right? Was that which Eisenhower symbolized truly trustworthy? Was the insight of Dulles into the minds of Asians sane?

He found himself not able to go to the voting booth that time, although it was his first chance to do so. Certainly not to vote for Stevenson, the liberal know-it-all, whose nature it was to do nothing but throw the taxpayer's hard-earned money at any problem he might fancy. Democrats could not be trusted with the country's finances, and even more importantly perhaps for those from whom he gleaned his incipient political wisdom, they were not pro-army as were the Republicans. But he could not vote for Eisenhower either. Not after the president had washed his hands in innocence over the Magyar uprising (like Pontius Pilate did before him in disavowal of a different cause) when his chance had come to show his quality. There was a crack now in the smooth, white shell of his newfound faith in America as the champion of liberty. The truth of it had all of a sudden become elusive.

Decisions, decisions

This episode contributed significantly to his decision to quit the army and to go back to school. There were other, more rational reasons also. A practical one was that promotion boards looked more favorably at officers with college degrees. He might return yet to active duty after college but far better qualified. Another one was that he simply did not see himself as someone at an intellectual level defined by an American high school equivalency GED test. Then again, emotionally, he was dissatisfied by the subordinate social status of the American officer corps. Subordinate to the commercial and political power elites, who seemed to him more self-serving than patriotic.

While this particular stratification of the hierarchy may appear to be as natural to American civic consciousness as the tides of the oceans on earth must appear to the moon in the sky, his consciousness was rooted in a different society, in one where the elites considered it their patriotic duty to serve as career officers in the unending defense of their country and where the sons of that elite would have felt ashamed not to have worn the cloth of honor, the uniform, before going on to some other more lucrative though less noble task.

Here, officers took their uniforms off after work like plowboys take off their overalls after a day in the field. "The business of America is business," said Calvin Coolidge. "Not war!" he might have added as a warning had he known what was coming in those untroubled pre-superpower days.

The Founding Fathers saw and understood the world of their present clearly. They separated church and state. Had they foreseen the future as well, they would have, no doubt, separated the worlds of peace and war also. But it would take many more scores of years before this was to become a problem. Before the unholy alliance of those two worlds would become a stranglehold on the country and on the world.

But at that point in time, when he was pondering his own need to choose between a business suit and his uniform, this concept had not yet become a conscious reality in his mind, nor was it so in the minds of people in general, for it was still nameless. Eisenhower had not yet coined the term *military-industrial complex*.

Back to his element

But mostly, life went on smoothly for a few more months, filled only with small episodes, each of which took time and effort and was a worthwhile experience. A battery commander is a minuscule wheel in the army, but down there, where he goes about his business, he is a big one. So he could afford to come in late and expect everything to be in place and running smoothly by the time he showed up. In this, he had the invaluable support of his "exec," George Russell. George was completely exceptional. He was a Stanford graduate and came from an important, upper-class business family to do his patriotic stint in the military. All his actions, his demeanor, and his contact with subordinates and superiors alike reflected the security and harmony of character that such a background can impart to a young man.

He was of help in many small, personal ways also. At one time, they were discussing his (the soldier's) plan to go back to school to study engineering. Another lieutenant, also a former sergeant but a true high school GED type, overheard and was commenting cynically, "What makes you think you could pass college?" George was laughing. "Why, of course he could," he said. "He does not have a fossilized brain like some people around here." He was rarely this testy, but when something really rubbed him wrong, he let it be known. He was a good friend. I should have kept up with him. While he was there, he was minding the shop so well that he (the soldier) had time to roam the great outdoors again.

Not the forests like in Icking, for there were none in that part of Oklahoma, but there was a vast area abutting on the military reservation of Fort Sill to the West, the Wichita Mountains. Mountains was an overstatement, but the red granite hills, often only huge boulders of naked rock, clad throughout the landscape with the dark green mantle of the shrub oak, were pleasing to an appreciative eye. Unlike the high ranges of the Far West, they let the cool (sometimes hot), wild winds that came from everywhere in the endless continent blow with lung-filling, direct unfetteredness. Grassy leas enjoyed by buffalo, prairie dog, and rattlesnake alternated with a few large lakes hidden among the hills that were like jewels of blue-green turquoise in their golden, dry prairie settings.

The lakes had been dammed up in bygone days by the people-friendly, liberal initiatives of Roosevelt's CCC, and now, fringed by willow, cottonwood and cattail, were his favorite and mostly solitary swimming holes. He would cross them in his slow frog-kick and dog-paddle types of self-taught, introvert-style swimming (extroverts crawl), often accompanied by water moccasins, whom he had to learn not to mind too much.

Quanah Parker and Geronimo

In the course of his off-the-road explorations of this still wild-looking and wild-feeling Oklahoma, though in reality it was only a refuge remainder of what it must have been less than a hundred years ago, he discovered Post Oak Mission. That was only an abandoned, time-worn but solid wooden building, used perhaps for meetings when there still existed some kind of a community around it. Now it came with a historical marker, and the words on the marker told the story of Quanah and Cynthia Ann Parker. Some of that story may have played itself out right there, perhaps under the very same post oak trees that were only a little younger then, measured by their long lifetime. They could have been witness to the surrender of Quanah and his band after a relentless pursuit by the Texas Rangers and the US cavalry (the actual venue of Quanah's story and that of his white mother were a little different, he found out later).

So then—and the marker left no doubt about it—this old tale of his childhood, ten thousand miles away in space and what seemed to him now like ten thousand years away in time, was really a true one! He felt overwhelmed by an upsurge of emotion. Looking out from the top of that knoll over the harsh, fate-tested ancestral Indian land undulating like the waves of the endless ocean itself to the far horizon, he found himself in tears with the dirge of *Dies Irae* echoing around him like in an ethereal cathedral whose ceiling was the now darkening sky above him, and he fell to praying without knowing to whom. Quanah lay buried here!

The next day, at lunch at the officers' club (on his last trip to Fort Sill with Jim Harris just a week ago, he found to his dismay that it was no longer functional, not by its old, distinguished, traditional standards, the way he and Jim remembered it), he was telling everyone within hearing of his discovery, only to find that none of his fellow officers had ever heard of Quanah Parker and that none of them were really interested.

But the other local story, that of Geronimo, as the Mexicans had named him, was quite well known to everybody. Not far from the housing area on post, there is a hill that rises gently on one side but falls off abruptly as a sheer cliff on the other. This is Medicine Bluff. The fearless and legendary leader Goyathlay of the Chiricahua Apache, being chased by the cavalry one day, rode up the soft side of the hill laughing all the way, only to leap, horse and all, down deep into the lake below. That is a body of water that is not there today and may not have been there then, who knows? But in doing so, he shouted out his name aloud so that not only the enemy but also the Great Spirit could hear it and know that it was he, and none other, whose spirit was indomitably free. That is why paratroopers, to this day, yell Geronimo when they leap out into the propblast.

Only, this story (unlike that of Quanah), well known and true as it may be, is not fact. A fact is something that you have seen happen with your own eyes and that has been recorded faithfully in writing for others to know it also. How different is this from the truth! Truth is not something you believe in; truth is resting in itself at the core of your being; it is the essence of what you are, like the impersonal Brahman is the essence of existence. So you see, he did not have to fret over the factuality of the Geronimo legend. Geronimo's leap into the abyss was for him a given, a *datum* unquestioned.

> My name is Geronimo.
> I, too, called it out many times when leaping out into the deep.
> Only, I was not tested like he was.
> That is my curse.
> He was the wind; he was the rain.
> He was the law; he was the *logos* of his land.

And I, I am now only old.

I am also Quanah.
I am a half-breed like he was.
My grandmothers were of Magyar blood.
My grandfathers had foreign names but were of Magyar spirit.
So, like Quanah, I lay claim to my being's unity.
Like he, I was captured by my fate.
But he rests where his fathers lived, while I am not at home anywhere.
That is my curse.
And now, I am only old.

But there is nothing wrong with being old, I assure you.
Therefore, let me tell you something now,
that only those who have survived at least seven decades know
and who have gained from the pain of all those years.
Fame, wealth, success and accomplishments: All are vanity.
Only the happiness and the sorrow of your weekdays count.
To know that is my blessing.
Sour grapes? No. The truth.

Geronimo does lie buried in the Indian cemetery at Fort Sill, although Quanah is no longer at the Post Oak Mission. His bones do not rest there anymore, for as an eloquent sign of how things have changed since the times when genocidal megalomaniacs like Custer denigrated the good name of honor of the US Cavalry in the West, "we" reburied him (not Custer) with full military honors in the Old Fort Sill Cemetery in the year of the Lord nineteen hundred fifty-seven.

I say *we* because as aide-de-camp of the commanding general of the Artillery Center during his third and last year there, he was involved in some modest way in many a ceremonial function. He would be assigned, for instance, to take care of luminaries like Eleanor Roosevelt or Otto von Hapsburg (the perennial heir-in-waiting for the crown of the Kingdom of Hungary) while they visited the area.

Quanah's disinterment was necessitated by the expansion of the Center westward to accommodate its new missile capability, and Post Oak Mission was in the way. The general did not like the idea of a warhead busting open the hallowed grave of the old chief, who had served as an example for the successful adjustment of the red man to the white man's ways, and so he ordered the ceremony of reburial to be solemn and dignified as befits the memory of an erstwhile brave adversary and a newfound friend.

Paris

Finally, the day of his emotional, melodramatic separation from the uniform was approaching after six long years in the service. But just ahead of that, there was yet another brief episode of note. The letters from Europe were coming again; she was going to school in Chartres now to learn to speak French *courrament*, and "It would be so nice to study the stained glass windows of that great cathedral together." Okay, he thought, now or never, I must check this out. What was the advice of old Dr. Schlusnus, his favorite teacher in Icking, on matters like this? "You may end up regretting what you *have* done now and then, but you will *always* regret what you have not done."

So without much further ado, he took leave and hitched a ride on an Air Force plane from the base near Oklahoma City to the one at Dover, Delaware, and from there to none other than the City of Light, Paris, France (in uniform you could do that for free). Having kept his high school French current with the turkeys in Omaha, he had little trouble finding his way to a hotel room in Chartres, and from there, the next morning, to the house of the family with whom the beauty with the mountain-lake-blue eyes stayed. How strange it is, by the way, that I even remember the name of that family, Morissey, although I have forgotten so many other, more important ones.

The ensuing week was enchanting. The season was on its way to turn cold, but they did not notice that. They walked the boulevards and byways of the City of Light, marveled at the Palace of Louis XIV in Versailles, and feasted on *paté de fois gras* in Trianon (he told her that that was a sadly important place in Magyar history). A highlight was dinner at the Restaurant Hongrois (see there, it might have been called something else, but I forgot it) where he had the gypsy band play for her:

Csak egy kislány van a világon,	There is only one girl in the world
Az is az én édes, drága galambom	And that one is my very own sweetheart

Each hour of each day was full of some now mostly forgotten memorability like that *jongleur des mots*, who asked the diners during the meal for twelve randomly chosen words, from which he proceeded (and instantly so) to craft a well-rhyming poem with the words coming up in the correct order, only to top it off with another equally accomplished poem with the same words but in reverse order, as entertainment for better digestion, as it were. Although the days were replete with such diversions, in the evening they always took the train back to Chartres, for the affair, though far from platonic, had an air of purity about it that was not to be touched prematurely, before its right time, with rash hands. It was so for him, and I am sure it was so for her also.

Today's culture of sexual liberation might shake its head uncomprehendingly vis-á-vis such a vestal attitude. The one night they did spend together was a most delicate game of unconsummated fulfillment of a dream of both past and future, for it resulted in a tentatively firm commitment for an as yet admittedly very uncertain future together. Believe it or not, they spent some of that night reading together in bed, pondering such significant passages as "*tu deviens responsable pour toujours de ce que tu as aprivoisé.*" That is what Saint-Exupéry had the Fox say to the Little Prince. I think now that each of them thought that he (or she) was the one being tamed, and the other the one who became forever responsible for the taming. Could you imagine today such an innocent approach to a love affair and its first night of love?

However, like ominous chords of fatefulness in the music of movies that forebodes unhappy endings, some motifs of discord cropped up during that week that spoke only to him and that were beyond her field of vision.

They bought a 45 cm record of Yves Montand at a store on the Rue de Jenerappel-la that related, on one side, a brief episode on the cold, dark, rain-swept Atlantic coast of France. The piece started with "*Il pleurait sans cesse sur Brest*" and went on to describe two lovers standing on a wind-swept pier at night in the cold rain, being watched by a man agonizing in his loneliness. The man punctuated the dark thoughts of his own longing for love by repeating the phrase "*Rappelle toi, Barbara*" ("Remember, Barbara"). Well, she could not play this record often enough, as if she were reveling in the sound of her name. It reminded him of the Narcissus myth and that made him feel uneasy. It made him feel shut out, not as the lover but as that lonely introvert observer.

There was also a flip side to that same record. For her it did not seem to exist, she did not pay any mind to it, but for him that *chanson* became, though only subconsciously at first, the theme song of the whole affair:

Oh, je voudrais tant que tu te souviennes	Oh, I wish so much that you would recall
Des jours heureux où nous étions amis.	The happy days when we were friends.
En ce temps-là, la vie était plus belle	In those days life was more beautiful
Et le soleille plus brûlant qu'aujourd'hui.	And the sun shone brighter than today.

It then speaks of the autumn leaves that get raked up together with souvenirs and regrets and goes on to describe their common fate:

Et le vent du nord les emporte	And the north wind sweeps them away
Dans la nuit froide de l'oubli . . .	Into the cold night of oblivion . . .

L'oubli. Do "we" have a word like that in English? It is not *forgetfulness*, and it is not *the forgetting*. Lapse of memory or oblivion, maybe. L'oubli, that is the end result of a process of loss after which only cold, black emptiness remains in the place of something that had been live and bright and real in its own time, as if it had never been there. Remember how that poem by Verlaine had it? "I recall the old days, and I weep." That is what you must feel like before the oubli covers up your memories along with yourself in the end.

And lastly, there was the visit to the Rodin Museum. They took in all the marvelous creations there like *Le Penseur* and *Le Baiser*. Hidden somewhere on a shelf among other perhaps minor pieces was one that leapt out at him, although she did not even notice it. Its title was *Fugit Amor*. Go and see it the next time you are in Paris, and only then will you understand the effect it had on him. But don't make too much of these dark undertones that I am mentioning here; they were vanishingly peripheral, and on the whole this bright interlude ended in a happy, confident, upbeat, joint-future-oriented spirit.

They agreed that he would go back to school and get his degree as fast as he could to provide them with an economic basis (the promise of a job, that is), and she would wait for him, although separated by an ocean in the meantime. He flew back, got his discharge papers, and within a few weeks, he was enrolled in a course of studies at the University of Oklahoma in the demanding field of engineering physics.

Chapter 6

The Student

Finally and belatedly, a university had opened its doors for him! And in one of its most demanding fields: physics! Why physics and not biology, his fascination and his hobby since childhood? In his free time, he always caught himself reading about the interdependence of life-forms and never about cold, lifeless laws like those that govern thermodynamics or electromagnetism. But he knew a lot now about the laws of the job market, and the applied kind of physics that he meant to delve into seemed to offer better chances to make a living than the science of life. And making a living was the condition on which the promise he made in Paris rested.

Meandering

His overall game plan to accomplish this was an outright extroverted one. While he anticipated that natural laws formed logically intertwined, inescapable sequences, links in chains enmeshed in each other three-dimensionally like amino acid sequences in proteins, he also knew by now that all rules have exceptions. One rule, not of nature but of the American academe, was that it took four years of serious application and devotion to earn a bachelor of science degree. He, however, burdened by the Paris promise, could not diddle around that long. He had to be an exception. He would do it in two.

They were quite a chore, those two years, only to turn out to be a *Holzweg* in the end. If you like to hike in the woods, you must have been on a *Holzweg* at one time or another. You know the general direction where you want to end up and march along on that *Holzweg* at a good clip. And before you know it, you are at a large clearing choked with impenetrable shrubbery, and the *Holzweg*, the logging road, dead-ends in the middle of that. Then, if you are lucky, it is not too late to turn around and find a better way. He was lucky. You see, in the end, things sometimes sort themselves out.

Although he originally started out in physics for reasons of practicality, the road eventually lead him back to his childhood passion. But that sorting process meant meandering over three continents in space and over a decade in time until he got back to where he really was meant to be. But all that comes later. When it came, he found that while he was keenly interested in the subcellular and molecular aspects of life, it was only on a reading level and not on a working one. He was really drawn, for the purposes of finding new insights by way of his own work, to whole organisms and their relationships and to the rules and systems that govern and describe the living together of different life-forms.

And that is where his little red Toyota was taking him now, skirting the potholes on that gravel road going north in the middle of Grass Valley, to a place where such insights could be gleaned.

On the road to the Gund Ranch

There is no better place for studies on life-form interactions than the desert. It is the relative simplicity of life in arid lands that lets you peek into the secrets of plant-community interactions more easily than would be practicable in a rain forest, for instance, and that gravel road from Austin to Beowave leads to some good sites where work like that can be done. The University of Nevada has a station at one of them, but the mission of universities is only to acquire, catalogue, and pass on knowledge.

For his organization, the ARS, on the other hand, all that is only a by-product en route to its actual goal, the solution of agricultural problems. Now, for the ten past millennia of the age of agriculture, the perennial, central endeavor had always been the production of more food to sustain ever-growing human populations. It was only in his day, at the end of the current, second Christian millennium, that this age-old problem was being eclipsed by a new one. One even more ominous than what the threat of famine was to hundreds of past generations and still is to the one living today.

This is the steady, apparently unstoppable loss of the productive base, the soil, by erosion and desertification as a result of mismanagement, greed, and uncontrolled population growth. What happens, for instance, when you herd too many heads of cattle on lands that the Good Lord had not intended for profit-oriented grazing in the first place because he chose not to irrigate them sufficiently for that with rain. The crux here is how many is "too many," and that depends on the circumstances. Further back east, where the buffalo used to roam on the short-grass prairie, a given size of land might accommodate comfortably many more heads of cattle than at that ancient, dried-out lakebed where the ARS had its site in that dry valley of Central Nevada.

Causes and consequences

It just seems to be human nature to rush in foolishly, to do the damage first, and then to pay for it dearly and ruefully afterward, be it the raping of ecosystems and the senseless unleashing of unprovoked wars in general or the overgrazing of desert land like the Grass Valley of Nevada, in particular. "*Quidquid agis, prudenter agas, et respice finem*" is an old admonition that the Romans already had heard from the Greeks and the Greeks from the Sumerians, who first invented agriculture ages ago in their land between the two rivers that is called Iraq now. A warning that he was called upon to memorize in Icking: whatever you do, do it prudently, and think of the consequences.

If you are an introvert, you inevitably drift into such musings while your trusty little red Toyota navigates the potholes. Has anyone learned to act prudently and to consider consequences since the times when those Sumerians dug their first irrigation ditches to make themselves independent of having to pray for rain? It does not look like it. Even though the first lessons of history were written down in those ancient cities, where the harvests made possible by those ditches created the wealth that eventually demanded and permitted the invention of the written record. First lessons that tell us of a brutal invasion by outsiders that left those cities in rubble and parched the green fields to be blown over by sand shifting in the hot desert wind.

That was a very long time ago, but did anyone have time to learn history lessons since then? History is there to be repeated over and over again, it seems. The causes are always the same, and so are the consequences. The only thing that changes is the justifications. These become more sophisticated with time, as it is easier to justify misdeeds when hypocrisy flows fluently out of your keyboard instead of having to imprint it laboriously on moist clay with a stylus. But how did I get into this anyway? He was thinking about soil erosion sitting in his little red Toyota, but now, as I am writing this, the word *Iraq* popped up by accident, and since that is where all the action is at the moment, I simply cannot help expressing my feelings about it.

We went there heedlessly and mindlessly on worthless, contrived intelligence, unleashed an unprovoked war, are in the process of wreaking destruction on that country, and are doing so on borrowed money rending the fabric of our own society at the same time by amassing debts that can only lead to bankruptcy in the end. Why? It is the delusion of power. Others have whole litanies of explanations that range from the rational to the romantic, but for me, it boils down to this simple cause. Power. The delusion of being empowered to do whatever we like.

Acquiring a pristine, beautiful but fragile piece of land like what that valley in Central Nevada was a hundred years ago and grazing it into a dust bowl worked along the same set of principles. After us the deluge. But there is a ray of hope. We are better than that. Only, we are so always after the fact. First comes the mindless rushing in, then comes reflection, and finally there is remorse and atonement. And will that really be followed up by paying in atonement with money borrowed now from our grandchildren?

Enough of that. On a lighter note, speaking of Iraq, of the Sumerians, and of war and history, as a Magyar American I simply cannot help going off on a tangent to dabble a bit in something that is not my field and that I should therefore better leave alone. And that is nothing less than the etymology of the word that the Sumerians supposedly used to call their home: *Mezopotamia*.

That is a Greek word, and in Greek it has a perfectly good meaning that fits the facts. It means "land between the rivers." Only, since the Greeks did not arrive on the stage of history until over a thousand years after the rise of Sumerian culture, they either gave that land an entirely new name that fitted their own tongue, or more likely, they adopted the original one and distorted it to make it fit. You will hear a little more about the Sumer-Magyar connection later; let me only give you here a derivation of *mezo-pot-am-ia* in the briefest possible way, assuming that its origin was in fact Sumerian and not Greek.

Here are the meanings of those syllables in present-day Magyar, based on the sound shifts that naturally occur in the course of time in all languages (Sumerian→Magyar): mezo→*mező*: grassland; pot→*főd*: soil (with the shift of p→f, d→t); am→*hon*: home (the unaspirated *h* omitted in Greek, m→n); and ia→*ja*: the postposition that designates *hon* as the genitive object of *mezőföd* [the Magyar *j* is pronounced as *y* in yet]. This results in "prairie soil home," a fine name for a people's place in the Grasslands at the dawn of history.

Grass Valley insights

And all this puts us squarely into the middle of Grass Valley of Central Nevada with its problems of soil degradation. "Soil death" is not an expression that you will find in the literature of its field, for many experts do not accept the notion of the soil as a real, living organism. Still, that was what his interest focused on nonetheless: the interface between soil physics and soil biology since it was becoming clear that successful replanting (i.e., the efforts at atonement after mindless destructive action) depends on a recreation of habitable soil structure in substrates pulverized by too many trampling hoofs. *Habitable* in this context refers to the open pore spaces of a well-structured soil that are used by microbes to live in.

As the work progressed and as the theory that was to accompany it started jelling, it was becoming clear that sticking plants (or seeds) into dead soil did not work well. Roots prefer a structured base in which to grow. And its restoration, the recreation of its capillary and aggregate structure, depends on the handiwork of many cooperative and interdependent types of organisms. Of these, he chose to work with symbiotically associated roots, fungi, and bacteria that form a system of pleasingly comprehensible functionality.

The plant roots provide the fungi with food and energy. Enabled by this input, the fungi grow a pervasive network of hyphae in the soil, a mycelium, and penetrate even the finest soil pores where they provide exudates to feed members of the soil microbiota, such as bacteria and actinomycetes. These then make mineral nutrients available to the system; they solubilize phosphates and fix nitrogen among other things, and the fungi take these up and translocate them back to the roots in return for the organic nutrients received in the first place.

While the end result of this mutual give-and-take is basically better plant growth and stable soil structure, in reality, this idealized system turned out to be vastly more complex (the simplicity of desert life notwithstanding) than he envisioned originally. There were unknown preferences between different species of plants and fungi and between fungi and bacteria, and all of these myriad interactions were affected in little-known ways by the multitudes of the other members of the Soil micro- and mesofauna and flora, all of which could help or hinder the problem-solving goals envisioned by the experimenter. To top it off, all these imponderable complexities depended on and were affected by the environmental conditions that could be imposed on the system by him on purpose or were unleashed by the vagaries of nature by chance.

Norman

Yet complex as all this was, it was a benign, hospitable, ever-changing sort of complexity, that of life. A complexity very different from what promised to be the enticing simplicity of the stern equation-ruled security of the world of immutable natural laws of physics at the University of Oklahoma (OU) in Norman (for that's where we have arrived now). Or so it seemed to him at first; in the beginning, things tend to be easy. He had been good in math in school, and he thought that would help him through the hurdles. At least, that was what he counted on when he decided on engineering physics as his path to a job during that long ride on that propeller-driven airplane across the Atlantic on his way back from Paris.

Career choice gone wrong

There was more to the decision than the promise of the job market only. Physics, contemplated from the outside, has a ring of prestigious, abstract scholarship to it; it is a realm populated by the brightest of human brains. This made intellectual snobbery an aspect of his decision, as I can readily admit today. But since the job market for physics below the Ph.D. level did not seem very promising and that would take far too long, he added the practical twist of engineering to it. The combination of the two is a separate, more down-to-earth discipline, and it was also offered as a field of study at OU. For someone, who had never ever opened a book on this type of subject voluntarily in his spare time, the choice is very difficult to rationalize in retrospect. But he had no one to advise him how to choose the right field of work. That field, as I know now, is one about which one likes to read for fun in one's spare time.

But there he was, charging full of irrational exuberance and temerity into a four-year curriculum, which he was determined to complete in two to shorten the waiting time on both sides of the Atlantic. What can I say? The lessons of life are easy to read at the end of the day. They come down to short, pithy findings like "how ye sow, so shall ye reap." The recommended number of credit hours per semester in engineering physics at OU was twelve. If he took twenty-two and put in extra quarters of study during the summer breaks, he might make it in two years instead of in four.

College town ambiance

Norman was typical for a public, land-grant university town in the great American heartland. Its downtown was perhaps five blocks long and contained all the businesses. The side streets, if I recall this right, were already mostly residential. He went there rarely for there was nothing to do there in the first place, and he was very busy. Only on Saturdays, after midterm and final exams, did he walk over from university town, some half-dozen residential blocks away, to enjoy a favorite dish, Kentucky fried chicken. This was a reward for passing the test, so to say.

The KFC place was a pleasant little restaurant that proclaimed proudly on its printed napkins that it was only the second in what was envisioned by its founder to become a nationwide chain someday. So it was at the ground floor of a bit of entrepreneurial history in the making. The chicken was good. It tasted like the free-running ones from back home in Sándorhalma. Only the *rántott csirke* there did not come with biscuits and honey like the ones *à la* Kentucky. What were the side dishes with *rántott csirke* at home? he would ponder. Rice, maybe, or *tarhonya*? He was startled to realize that he could not remember. He would ask Siegmund Elsa *néni* the next time when she prepared her famous *töltött csirke*, chicken replete not with store-bought "stuffing" but with a mixture of secrets that equaled in savor the delights that used to emerge from his mother's kitchen.

Then he would walk through the shady, quiet streets, always mindful of that historic marker on the main street (was it Main Street?) that reminded its readers of the time not much more than some fifty years ago, when a small group of educators first stood on that spot that was then bare and desolate, commissioned by a brand-new state to build an institution of higher learning there.

Back then this was a spot without a tree in sight as far as the eye could see. So that first university president, noting that his small tribe of a handful of pioneers of the chalk and blackboard trade was all ready to retreat to civilization, squared his shoulders and declared, "We are going to create an oasis here. Anybody can go to Yale and drink his beer there in the shade of the ivy trees. But we, we are going to create here a great grove of elms, oaks, and sycamores. We will plant them and water them so that when students come here fifty years from now, they will not miss the ivy. So that when they finish here, ready to get on the road to discover new worlds, they will remember us in the tales they might tell or the stories they may write. So let's get to work."

Or he would sit by the tracks waiting for an occasional freight train to pass and as it thundered by, he would hum the tune to the words of a melancholy, wistful Western that he picked up while exploring the towns and countryside around Fort Sill. Although he certainly had not spent his younger days in a lonely shack, this was a song that he could relate to as completely as if he had done that:

> In a lonely shack by a railroad track
> He spent his younger days,
> And I guess the sound of the outward bound
> Made him a slave to his wand'rin ways.
> Oh, a wayward wind is a restless wind,
> A restless wind that yearns to wander . . .

and there he was, a slave yearning to wander while chained to his galley of a desk and to his classrooms a good twelve hours a day, seven days a week. Except on some of those postexam Saturday afternoons.

Then he would also wind his way out of town to the edge of the North Canadian River. Edge rather than bank, for the "river," hundreds of yards wide in places, was shifting its course from season to season and was mostly just an ankle-deep trickle of rivulets crisscrossing its sandy and pebbly bed. While the few willow trees framing the wide, flat Central Oklahoma horizon could be picturesque and reminiscent of the *fűzfák*, the willows that flank the Tisza River crossing the great Magyar plains back home, care had to be taken here with the hiking, for those dry sandbars could be hidden death taps of quicksand, especially for solitary wanderers.

For he was a solitary wanderer, even though the crew in Mrs. Estep's boarding house at 416 College Avenue, all motivated, mostly GI Bill financed fellow students, was a compatible one. Stan, his first roommate who came to Norman from Fresno, California, because of the Sooners' football fame, as well as Napper of the "they asked for it, and we gave it to them" view of America's place in history stand out. I wonder if they are still alive. It was not because he was so very busy then that he did not keep up with them later. Introverts are just naturally boxed up in their own little worlds.

Physics as drudgery

And his new world of engineering physics was becoming more and more a prison as the courses were getting to be more demanding. The fun pretty much went out of it, and it was more dogged determination than the joy of learning that carried the day, day after long day. But he still had the feeling that he understood it all, although not as convincingly as he would have wished. Even partial differential equations were okay until he finally hit a stone wall with quantum mechanics during his last semester.

I like to tell myself now that it was the lack of time for the proper digestion of all that information, of all those half-chewed courses gulped down on the double. Maybe. But I still have exam nightmares, and they are often related to QM, to the feeling of helpless incomprehension of what the esoteric operators of the math peculiar to that subject were meant to mean. The professor was young and inexperienced; this was the very first course he was assigned to teach, and there was no textbook.

Worst of all, some of the others in class appeared to grasp what was going on! Maybe it was the six years that he had been out of school during which his mind had forgotten how to internalize externalities. Maybe the return to the discipline of learning was too abrupt. He got away with a D in QM (the prof was generous) and was able to graduate on time, in half time, in two years. He should have known better than to try to go on with physics. But more was still to come later.

Here again, as with other courses of instruction earlier in this saga (I start to see the consistency of it as I write this), his controller seems to have thought little of the subject matter, for it has wiped the slate of his mind quite clear of all that clutter by now. Instead, little snippets still managed to hang on. Like the reaction of the class, when Dr. von Engel (visiting from Oxford, England) mentioned at one point in passing what had been obvious to physicists for fifty years, namely that nothing can go faster in the universe than the speed of light.

The skeptical OU undergraduates (to their credit dubious of everything) were not convinced. "How come?" they wanted to know. "Maybe we just can't measure everything quite well enough yet?" The prof put the matter to rest curtly: "Because Einstein and I agree on it, that's how come." Then Dr. Nielsen would weave graduate stuff into an undergraduate course on thermodynamics. He would mention things like "the dilatation and contraction of time" and "the anisotropy of timespace" and blink smilingly with one eye as if to indicate "Just wait, the best is still to come. You haven't heard anything yet." This was the kind of stuff his controller liked to frown on while at the same time some other entity in his mind or brain relished it as if it were anticipating a dangerous adventure.

On physics and the mind

I am afraid I need to go off on a tangent here as I am in the habit of doing. It is this bothersome dichotomy between me and my controller that makes me digress again this time. As so often, this happens when something extraneous crops up in the course of writing that asks to be included for the sake of completeness. It is not really extraneous, this dichotomy, for its emergence from I do not know where is like a real event every time it occurs. And it is important to me because it is about my internal argument with the controller.

As I have suggested tentatively in the beginning, the controller is a function (but also a part) of the brain that seems to act independently of the mind in dealing with such matters as memories, emotions, and survival information. But this turns out to be a touchy subject, for philosophers and physiologists alike tend to disagree with each other over the meaning of the words that need to be used when thinking about the mind for lack of better and clearer ones.

This may be so because the mind defies definition; at least it does so for me. Is it, when its workings suggest that it is conscious both of itself and of the outside world, some nonphysical construct, one out of this real world as we think we know it, or is it nothing more than the sum total of the neural processes of the material object that the brain is? While both views have merit, to me the first choice is more appealing emotionally; and the second one more reasonable realistically.

Experts on the subject, however, fight over this distinction, and some even go to an extreme and claim that the problem is moot, for we are not able to decide it in the first place. We cannot, they say, since we do not have the mental faculty to access both our consciousness and our brain simultaneously. This is so because we access consciousness through introspection but the brain through our senses.

Is this a problem mainly within the domain of the physiologist or the philosopher? He, of course, was neither, but because he had been asked, and always disparagingly, since he came to America if he were "a philosopher or something," he developed a feeling that it might not be cool for anybody but certainly not for somebody like him, with his skin-deep americanity, to be a philosopher.

But philosopher or not, it was back then at the University of Oklahoma that he first became aware of the question about the physical or nonphysical nature of his mind in the course of that class in physical chemistry.

What became a real nuisance then was that he could read pages in his textbook, even highlighting important passages in yellow, without remembering any of it a few minutes later. It was as if somebody in his brain had taken control and decided that all that reading was hogwash, had no survival value for him based on his evolutionary history, and therefore was not worth recording and keeping.

It was somebody who looked like Darwin with a bushy, white beard maybe, somebody worthy of reverence even, but somebody who needed to be tricked out of the rut of his dominance. For things like Brownian Motion and Avogadro's Number were not only interesting but under the circumstances had some definite survival value. Times had changed; he was a student at OU and not a caveman. So something else in him, within his brain or outside it, had to swing into action and exert control over that aboriginal caveman's controller.

In practice, he succeeded in gaining this upper hand by stopping after each paragraph in his textbook and repeating the contents as if he were explaining them to a class. The result of this activity was clear-cut in overriding the controller's efforts to forget. You may call this successful process nothing but the activation of long-term memory, but the point still is: who was the controller of the controller that accomplished this feat? If it was nothing more than another part of his brain, that poor organ must have been acting at cross-purposes to itself at the same time, and this seems to me an unlikely state of affairs. Could the controller of the controller therefore have been outside the material object that is his brain?

Such outside-of-the-object phenomena are well known in physics, as he soon found out. For instance, when you apply a potential difference to a conductor of electricity to make a current flow in it, an electromagnetic field is created around that conductor. That field has no material reality, but it is clearly real physically, for you can measure it. A compass needle gets deflected when you stick it into this field. Then, when you turn the battery off and the current ceases to flow, the field collapses, apparently into nothingness.

Now, for all practical purposes, this *field* did not exist, at least not for theoretical, human cognition, before Maxwell, the father of electrodynamics, described its reality in his seminal equations. Thereafter, however, electromagnetism became an often-used term in common parlance whether or not its precise meaning was understood by those who used it. Such people have became "aware" though not quite "cognizant" of the concept, one might say.

But using the birth of this electromagnetic phenomenon as an example, may one not reasonably postulate the possibility of other out-of-the-object phenomena that we do not think of as real simply because their essence is not yet an accepted scientific concept since we must first learn to measure their reality? Measure it with instruments that we use as extensions of our senses to access otherwise inaccessible reality. Ideating a concept first and then quantifying its measurable aspects are the conditions for the recognition and acceptance of a new mental reality that may then take shape all of a sudden in real life like a spirit may be made to appear on stage dressed up as a *deus ex machina*, a god out of a machine.

So let us consider this miraculously constructed machine of interacting organic molecules and cells, be it a bacterium or a human being, that exhibits the properties that we sum up as "life." One that at its highest level of development, becomes conscious by producing a mind. This machine sends electrochemical signals within itself in all directions to regulate its rate of growth, its reactions to the outside world, or simply its state of existence as a living entity. When it is then subjected to some extreme condition that disrupts the interactions of its constituent parts so that these cease to function as a unit, it "dies." It becomes a blob of inert material, still identical for however short a time with what it was before but without its distinguishing trait of vitality like that wire without a current flowing through it.

Does this *machina* produce, while it is alive, a kind of modern *deus*, a surrounding force field, one with a physical reality that either collapses into nothingness when its machinery fails to function and dies but, alternatively, one that continues to persist in some as yet unknown and unmeasured state of being? I vote for the latter, but this will remain a mere chimera until we find a way to measure that field and then follow its fate.

As the history of that other force field of physics elucidated not so very long ago strongly suggests, this one may be next, waiting and ready to be discovered. And when we do discover it, it could well turn out to be the *locus*, the place, the realm, where consciousness, the controller of the controller resides. A realm of immaterial physical reality, like the electromagnetic field. A realm that exists outside of the material confines of the brain's neural circuitry, but which can directly influence its progenitor, the brain, nonetheless.

Quite a conjecture, isn't it? But that is not the main stumbling block for me. The problem I have with such a force field is not whether it exists, for I am, subjectively, quite satisfied that it does. But what happens to it after it collapses? Does it really disintegrate into nothingness? Since it is brought about or caused by the underlying biophysical activity within a material object, a transfer of energy into it must occur from that object that imbues it with its physical reality in the first place.

Now, in that class on thermodynamics, Dr. Nielsen liked to expound (this time with nonwinking seriousness) on that essential quality of energy: its propensity for self-preservation. So since this field contains energy and it must contain it to exist, where does the energy go when the field collapses? It cannot go into nothingness without violating the law of energy conservation.

Where does the realm of consciousness go then when its originator, the brain, dies? Is the energy contained in its field reassimilated in some form by some mechanism by elements of the elementary principle of our known, finite, material universe from which it emanated originally? Or does it perhaps (dare one suggest it?) self-preserve? To go somewhere, maybe, where matter and antimatter go after they "annihilate" each other upon meeting in this universe of ours? Or does it perhaps transcend to some greater, unknown infinite universe, in which our known one, however rapidly its size may be expanding, is but a speck, that of the vibrating, immaterial strings of untold dimensions that are the music, the mirth, and a manifestation of the primary principle of which it then becomes part?

The controller and the Self

These posits bring me back at last to that extraneous event that, as I mentioned earlier, brought about all this digression into metaphysics. That event was triggered by my reading of a passage in the Bṛhadāraṇyaka Upaniṣad, where the word *controller* popped up unexpectedly just minutes after I finished writing it down in my own story in one of the preceding paragraphs.

Upon turning off my computer, I went to bed and picked up the book, as I often do before going to sleep. And I immediately ran into this word in the following context. The sage Uddālaka Āruṇi was asking a fellow Brahmin, Yājñavalkya, the question of the ages: "[Who is] the inner controller of this world and the next, as well as of all beings, who controls them from within?" The answer was lengthy, but an essential, small part of it was: "it is this Self (Ātman) of yours who is present within but is *different* from the mind, whom the mind does not know, whose body is the mind, and who controls the mind from within—he is the inner controller, the immortal."

Needless to say, the use of the word *controller* in the two different contexts may be purely coincidental. I picked the word originally because the question "Who is the boss, you or your brain?" makes me feel uncomfortable and even resentful of being possibly under the tutelage of someone or something whom or what I do not understand. But Marina, my dear wife, who patiently, lovingly, and even with interest reads installments of this tale as it unfolds, suggested *gatekeeper* as a preferable alternative to name that function of our mind that sifts our perceptions and experiences and decides which ones will be preserved in our memory bank. Had I used her word, this juxtaposition with the Upaniṣad would not have presented itself to make me think about a possible relationship between the two concepts. Also, who knows what the real meaning of the word may have been in ancient Sanskrit that found its way into English as the "inner controller"?

Be that as it may, the reality of the "Self," the *Ātman*, as experienced by the Eastern mind is unquestioned (at least it may have been so back in the times when the Vedas made their appearance). This attitude of acceptance does not exist (yet) for the energy field that surrounds living matter, which for me is equally real but which will have to be measured and quantified first before it can become part of a universal Western experience. Reading the entire passage of the Upaniṣad then suggests (to me it makes it clear) that *mind* is a word that the ancient authors used in this context to stand for that part of the body that does the thinking, the brain, since the passage deals with material parts and faculties of the body and not with abstract concepts.

So let us now try to compare the Upaniṣad's definition of the *Self* with a physically real force field around us. In doing so, we find remarkably close similarities. First, the Upaniṣad says that the Self (like the field) is "present within (permeates) the mind" (brain), from which it is inseparable, but "is different from it!" Next, "the mind (brain) does not know" the Self (the field)! And how could it? The field that contains consciousness (or *is* consciousness) is beyond the grasp of the electrochemical processes of the brain's neural circuitry.

Furthermore, the "body (only the body!) of the 'Self' (i.e., of the field) is the mind (brain)," but the Self is clearly more than just the brain for "it controls the brain." Like the field does, like consciousness does, and like my controller of the controller does by being the master of the various phenomenal functions of the brain, which it permeates "from within" (like the Self does).

Finally comes the last *dictum* in Yājñavalkya's answer that is troublesome for those of us who are not religious: "He (the Self) is immortal." Can epistemological Western thought cope with a notion of immortality and integrate it with a construct of physics, a force field?

Should we decide that it can, we would first have to postulate that the field of consciousness does not collapse into nothingness upon the cessation of the brain's functioning but continues to persist without being reabsorbed amorphously by matter. But if this persisting energy packet were to retain its essence, its content of consciousness after death, it could not do so within the current, confined state of our grasp of the natural world. It could do so only as a form of energy that is as yet unknown to us. A field that is forged into a new, permanent (immortal) reality by the fire of the processes of life, a fire that may be thought of as the creator of consciousness. This consciousness, then, could be the property of life that resides at the interface between the principles.

The way I see it, there is agreement between the Upaniṣad and physics. One declares that the Self is immortal, while the other postulates that energy is conserved forever. But there is also a difference. Energy conserved in a lifeless physical system does not take its acquired intelligence, like the specific laws it obeys, with it upon transformation to a new state. The Self, the Atman, the force field of consciousness, on the other hand, should carry with it its content of consciousness immutably. Why? According to the Upaniṣad: because it is an integral part of the Brahman. According to me: because I hope so. According to physics: give it time, and it will declare itself.

The uprising of 1956 revisited

A diversion from all that relentless learning and a welcome throwback into the past was the intercourse with the group of Magyar students who had made their escape after the uprising of 1956 through the barb-wired minefields on the Austrian border that were deserted for a few days by their uniformed armed keepers. Some of the refugees, students who opted to come to the United States, were apportioned by some deciders within the INS to one institution or another, and OU's share was about a dozen of them.

The new homeland treated them much better than it had treated him when he first arrived. They were provided with all the necessary living and learning expenses until graduation, and that would take a few years, for they spoke no English when they arrived. They accepted this largesse with an aplomb that surprised him. There was an attitude of "you owe us" about it, although they never mentioned the reason for it. Was it the betrayal of their cause by the West? Maybe they did not see it that way, and he did not press the question.

But now he could practice his native idiom with them, and he did this with relish. He took a course in vector calculus together with Imre, and a nice friendship developed in the course of it. Imre was a born engineer, and I heard later from Trude *néni* that he made good and realized the American Dream by becoming rich. If so, it seems that Imre pursued happiness successfully. I should have kept up with him, for he was good company. Then there was Ildikó, who studied medicine, and Tóni, the pharmacist.

He liked thinking and talking about politics and history as did the Magyar newcomers, and so they would often sit in a booth of the student center's cafeteria and discuss such topics by a glass of beer. At the center of interest at that time was the overthrow of the US-supported strong man of Cuba. They all greeted the rapid collapse of that dictatorship with jubilation, for they identified with the rebels marching down into La Havana from the Sierra del Este. Freedom and democracy at least somewhere, even if not at home, in Magyarország!

Then, as those events developed, they watched them with growing consternation. They were glued to the television set in the lobby of the fraternity house where some of them lived and, with their nascent understanding of English, pieced together an unexpected story from those early reports about the relationships developing between the Cuban freedom fighters and the American ruling class.

To buy the assets of the sugar industry from the absentee owners, the new Cuban regime offered the official price, the one shown on the assets pages of cooked company books. "Unfair," the owners cried from abroad where they lived, "those fields, factories, and refineries are worth much more than what you want to pay us." Fidel Castro shrugged. "Those are your own numbers, and if they are too low, " he replied, "it is because you kept them that way to cheat the Cuban people out of the tax revenues you owed it. Fine, we will pay a fair market price for the assets, but then you owe us back taxes with compound interest for all the decades of your reign of exploitation."

In the end, their worlds were too far apart to reach an agreement, and the rebels who had morphed into the leaders of the new system declared their country's means of production to be the sole property of their people. With that, they were soon declared communists by the vested interests of the dispossessed landlords on the mainland. With no one else to turn to for support, the country of the erstwhile freedom fighters ended up as a satellite of the Kremlin.

This turn of events, for this was the way they saw it, was bewildering for the Magyar student freedom fighters who identified with Che Guevara. It was interesting for him to see how their decade of exposure to Marxism had left its marks on their minds. That the means of production, the sugarcane in the fields, belonged to the hands that cut it and not to some absentee landlord was a matter of course for them. They had no problem with that. What they were opposed to and what they revolted against was not the red doctrine, as long as it really represented a just and fair distribution of their country's assets, but the Red Army that enforced it.

But here, in what was to become their new home, people seemed to think and feel differently. What ruled here was the law passed by the people's will and consent, and yet these laws were on the side of the absentee landlords. And as long as the law sided with the landlords, it was only just and proper to enforce it, both at home and also in places like Cuba, where it was done by proxy, by dictators like Batista. "My god, what is going on here?" the exiles kept asking him. Communism, no—that is un-American—but exploitation and dictatorship, yes? A fine way to demonstrate freedom and democracy to the world!

However, the reality of their daily struggle in asserting themselves in this strange New Country took all their energy; they felt that politics were not their concern, not at the moment at least. They were too busy with survival and with becoming assimilated into this new system so full of contradictions, to let ideological scruples trouble them.

Interlude on the Azores

All the while, the correspondence with Irschenhausen or by now München, was voluminous. And it must have been gushy in a single-minded, simple-hearted, devoted-forever way. I wish I had kept it, to see if I would find it touching or amusing now, or if it could conjure up the deep and sincere feelings of that era in his life. I did not. But the feelings then were strong enough to result in a previously unplanned *Wiedersehen* at half time and at the halfway point between the continents in the Atlantic Ocean, on the Azores.

Coming from different directions, they met up at the airport at Lajes Field on Terceira Island (I think that's where it was). It was late at night when they got to their hotel room, exhausted from the excitement of anticipation, for the entire exercise seemed a little otherworldly. That is the only word that can describe it, although they had read about something like this in books of romantic adventure. In fact, that was where he got the idea for it in the first place, although he knew that neither of them could afford it financially. Those were not the days yet, like today, when people think nothing of continent hopping.

For him, this undertaking was a veritable emotional maelstrom. His views on how to relate to the opposite sex, in theory and practice, were formed by how he had observed his father relate to his mother. Of course, he had experienced the whole gamut of sexual behavior patterns during his soldier years, but that was a different matter, it had nothing to do with the code of conduct that applied to his *grande passion*, his own great love affair. And that conduct, dictated by the archaic values of his past, was that all desire of consummation, no matter how overwhelming, had to be kept strictly within bounds by respect and chivalry until the proper time had arrived for it. It did not even occur to him that she might have had a different and more liberal outlook on the matter. But apparently she sensed his feelings somehow, even though she may not have fully understood them.

Apart from the enchantment of being with her, he was deeply affected by the feeling of being in an environment that reminded him of home. The Azores were very different from anything that he had seen in Europe before, but still, the layout of the fields, the hedgerows, the architecture of the buildings, the irregularity of the streets, the comportment of the people, the lack of traffic, and many other small details all contributed to an incredulous wonderment that was like a time warp. That this should be happening to him! Meals in the elegant, high-ceilinged dining room of their stately old hotel were formal. There was no menu; it was understood that a fish course should precede the main meat course; the most appropriate wine was presented for tasting with each, and the local goat cheese to end it all (after *flan* as dessert) was, well, for those who appreciate and understand goat cheese, exquisite.

I think the town's name was Angra, but see, I cannot swear to that. What I do remember is that elderly gentleman in coat, tie, and hat walking in the street—barefoot. I also remember the owner of the hotel coming to chat solicitously in the course of their third evening meal, expressing delight in seeing them content with the offerings of his establishment but also commenting that the Azores have much more to offer than the modest sights of his town and that most foreigners move on to the Furnas Resort on Saõ Miguel, "which is a world-class attraction." So they decided to take the little, one-prop commuter plane to the main island and found that Furnas really lived up to its fame.

One can only describe it the way tourist guidebooks do: "You must visit the valley of Furnas, a paradise, with its crown jewel of a sky-blue lake surrounded by flower-adorned shores and the emerald green hills for a backdrop, inspiring tranquility or excitement and romance." All right, all of that was quite accurate. And it was even better than that, for back then there was only one hotel there, at least I remember only that one. Also, there were no hordes of tourists that I am sure crowd the place today.

This hotel was more like the mansion of a billionaire who liked to have dozens and dozens of guests with him all the time. The mayor domo himself picked the two of them up at the grassy airstrip (no buildings, just a giant orange sock to indicate from where the wind was blowing) and then the two modest little people ("*les petits fiancés*" a lady had called them a year before in the Paris Métro) were welcomed like royalty at the castle and had a splendid time there.

Then, however, came that excursion to the coast. It was an exciting venture, for they were landlubbers, and walking a few miles to a fishing village on that traffic-free road lined with an abundance of blue hydrangeas was very special, another first for both of them. He lugged a feast of a lunch with him in a wicker basket, and the picnic and their mood and the view from a cliff over the ocean and everything else in the world felt as if it were veiled by a cloth woven from the golden rays of the sparkling sunlight around them.

But on the way back, he decided on a little detour to see some more of the countryside and this took them to a fork in the road. Although he had no map, it was perfectly clear to him, which turn he had to take. But she wanted to ask some men working in a nearby field for directions. He insisted that it was not necessary, and she insisted that it was. She went and asked anyway. Not understanding what she wanted, they pointed in the wrong direction, and she decided to take their advice.

What could he do? He could not let her go alone in a strange foreign land and then in the wrong direction? So he went along, but the sun was no longer glittering in her black hair. She trusted a stranger more than him. The sign was there, clear as day itself, and he refused to read it. But in the end, the glorious light of the now westering sun was still too bright for this shadow to persist.

In parting at the end of their stay, they did not promise to be faithful to each other until the end of the waiting time (they knew enough of the world's realities already for that). What they did promise was absolute honesty. If they had a change of heart, they would report it immediately, without fail.

A time of doubt

It seems the controller is keeping a tight lid on all memory fragments of the remaining waiting time that second year in Norman, for none of them are surfacing from the deep strata of the *oubli* where they are mercifully buried. Nothing worthwhile seems to be bubbling up, as if covered up by thick layers of the dull drudgery of the seemingly endless sequence of courses and exams required for graduation.

On the positive side, he did move from Mrs. Eastep's dank basement to Trude *néni*'s house on University Boulevard, and that was a good move. It was a pleasant little room facing toward the sunset and away from the traffic (although that was tolerable in sedate, sleepy Norman). It also was paneled in honey-colored pine, and sleeping in a room with wood paneling always worked like magic for him: it eases tensions and reduces stress.

And he needed that for about two months after the Azores, the tone of the letters from München changed. It started with a rather detailed report of a party at her attic apartment at the Odeonsplatz that she shared with a friend. Siegrid was her name. She usually described things exhaustively so that was in itself nothing unusual. But one of Siegrid's acquaintances had brought along a new guy, an air force lieutenant, and she described him in great detail also. He did not think much of it at the moment, except that this was a bit unusual, really. Now I wish he had not thrown her collected letters into the Isar soon after he met Marina, for the change in the way she (not Marina) expressed whatever she wanted to tell him before and after that party was remarkable. Those letters were a real little study in the psychology of relationships that have to endure an extended period of separation. And in a way, a shifting in one's emotional closeness or distance from someone changes the tone of the words that describe even mundane, insignificant, little things. *C'est le ton qui fait la musique.*

The new remoteness and the new lack of music in those letters that continued to arrive nonetheless, though less frequently now, soon became a source of quiet desperation for him. If that relationship was an addiction, then his attitude toward those letters was one of denial. He had gone to hear Rigoletto back ages ago in Munich, and after his years of soldiering, he knew quite a bit about the subject of *la donna è mobile.* He was by no means a naive newcomer himself to the realities of life. But his very own love affair had to be clearly different from the things that other people do all the time! She promised she would tell if there was something to tell. And since she did not tell, there was nothing to tell! Wouldn't she stop writing if there were something to tell as a substitute for telling if she could not make herself tell?

So he would convince himself time after time. The worst of it was that there was nothing he could do. He could not go and climb on the next ocean liner (that was the usual mode of transatlantic transport then) to check things out. So it was that endless sequence of courses and exams that became his remedy or narcotic for the time being that carried him through the rest of that year. And with each exam, the light at the end of the tunnel crept closer, although under the circumstances somehow, it did not seem to become brighter.

Some thoughts on schools

For those of you who got your education in American colleges, my dwelling on all those courses and exams must appear odd. "What's wrong with that maze of requisites and prerequisites that a college catalogue is made up of?" you will say. That's the way it has to be, for how else could the system function? If the courses of your curriculum were not required, you would not take them, and if the prof did not assign the pages in the textbook for you to read for the next quiz, you might end up having to read the whole book (heavens forbid) to avoid flunking them. This was an attitude toward learning that took him a while to understand. It was an outlook of schoolboys, and all of his classmates at OU had it, so now I cannot help but expound on all that a little here for the next two pages, tedious though it may be.

Why was all this so different from the attitude of university students in Germany? Why are high school students so much freer to choose their classes in the United States and college students so much more regimented, when in Europe it's the other way around? Eventually, he started to understand this, watching his own children go through the American school system.

That was a system conceived to prepare children to become citizens of a country that was proud of its lack of regimentation from above. And so American public schools came to operate under local control, subject mostly to the dictates of school boards that are elected from the members of their own community. All children (except for those who can afford to go to private schools) are required to attend the twelve years of instruction offered, and they do so in what I would call a rather carefree, free-floating spirit of freedom.

By contrast, in countries like Germany, all children go to the same elementary schools, but when they reach fifth grade, a selection process based largely on aptitude (and also on social status) divides those who want to go on to advanced studies from those who do not. And those who do, go through their next nine years of school in a strict spirit focused on learning rather than the *laissez faire* ways that prevail across the ocean.

Ten-year-olds who wish to go on to the university after secondary schooling take a test of admittance to the Gymnasium, an institution similar to a "college-preparatory high school" in the United States. It offers choices with different specializations: emphasis in modern or ancient languages or in the natural sciences, but requirements that are basic for a claim of being an educated person, such as history, geography, mathematics, economics, music, art, and philosophy are mandatory for all students. It is a rigorous course of study, which ends with a tough, nationally standardized and supervised written and oral comprehensive test of all the subjects. This is called the "*Reife-Prüfung*," the "Test of Maturity," to indicate not only that the graduate has passed his courses but also that he is now a responsible, mature adult. This test is his pass for admission to the university.

And so, since he has proven his ability to think, the graduate of the Gymnasium is now given a high degree of freedom to think for himself as far as the choice of courses is concerned. Of course, there are guidelines as to what must be mastered, but it is entirely up to the individual when and how he wishes to accomplish that. The two semesters of instruction per year alternate with two lengthy "semester vacations," which are times of independent study to read all the books available on the subjects of his choice in preparation for the next semester. After their tightly regimented Gymnasium days, university students have freedom to explore not only their chosen field but also everything else the academic environment has to offer. And for doctoral students, this broad exploration of human culture is something like a moral mandate. Or so things were back in the days when he was there. Today, this level of freedom is not attained in the United States until the student has achieved advanced postgraduate status.

Here, unlike in Europe, everyone goes to the same type of school until the age of eighteen. While there may be general agreement nationwide as to what a basic curriculum should include, what is actually offered may differ from state to state, from school district to school district, and even from school to school and is often determined by factors like the philosophical orientation of the school board that rules its school district and the local availability of funds upon which such essentials as the teacher/student ratio, the qualification of teachers, and the composition and kind of courses depend.

The apparent equality within a given school is modified somewhat by the students' ability to choose a "track" from eighth grade on, emphasizing one or another general orientation, such as science or home economics so that they may graduate with different levels of achievement in specific subjects. Students who are less academically inclined may opt for whatever electives their school can offer (like shop if resources permit), as long as they can fulfill some minimum graduation requirements in reading, 'riting, and 'rithmetic. The result (or the price of this premature freedom) is that American graduates of public high schools are not as well prepared academically as those of European Gymnasia. Of course, those who are motivated enough can always beat the system and excel on their own.

In reality, tensions and hostility between different groups within the student body are the rule. Discipline problems that result from this can tax to the limit the ability of the teachers to cope. They are expected to teach skills and disciplines that require concentrated attention in an atmosphere where book learning is often dismissed as the province of geeks and nerds and philosophers. Rather, the old adage "Those who can, do; those who can't, teach" expresses admiration for the man of action and a kind of contempt for intellectuals.

But these are problems for future education presidents to ponder, even though every one of them likes to call himself that. Right now, in 1959, that is, everything was still prescribed. If you want us to certify you as a bachelor of science in engineering physics, he was told, these are the requisites, in this sequence, and if you don't do it that way, you do not graduate.

An engineer!

And so that was what he did, exactly the way they wanted it. In the end, the dean of his school declared him a bachelor of science in a ceremony that he did not attend. This was on a Friday, and next Monday morning, he went to work as an engineer for the air force at Tinker Air Force Base, where some of the planes of the B-52 Bomber Fleet were being maintained, repaired, and modified.

There he was assigned to a desk equipped with pencil and paper. But there was nothing for him to do there. If you are not aware of the *Dilbert* comic strip in the business section of your newspaper or if you are aware of it but do not read and follow it (as you should), you will have difficulty in appreciating what that experience was like. There were bosses around, but they seemed to be in a daze also and therefore did not constitute a menace. Still, he could not bear just to sit at his desk and drink coffee, and so he would browse around in the enormous library of folders and binders full of incomprehensible stuff, logistic tables, weight and strength statistics, supply catalogue notations, engineering specifications of all the enigmatic inner workings of airplanes, and the like.

He could not go and check out the airplanes themselves, for one needed a specific work order for that. But during the two or three months that he was there, he actually succeeded in getting to design a little plexiglass panel for the instrumentation board of the B-52. It was nothing but a simple drawing exercise. But this bizarre scene was all for the good, for it was dawning on him that after two years of concentrated, diligent work, he knew nothing about engineering. He also developed an eerie feeling that it was not the rush-rush nature of the effort that he forced himself to put into it, nor was it the system's fault in the way it had tried to impart that knowledge to him. The system was fine, for lo and behold, there were those giant birds of metal out there in a hangar that were capable of climbing up into thin air, and somebody trained like him had been able to build them. It was he, whose cerebrum was not designed to deal with any sort of competence with this specific demand.

Fortunately, he knew that this was only a limited stay for him at Tinker, sandwiched in to make a little money while waiting for the next semester of physics to start at the University of Munich. Had he faced engineering as the way to spend the rest of his life, he would have despaired.

It was spring again when he took that train to New York City to climb aboard the ocean liner USS America. The crossing was pleasant, very much unlike the one on the General Muir. There were a lot of young people down in the third deck of tourist class who were eagerly awaiting their first chance to explore Europe. There were dances and, believe it or not, a typical, little five-day shipboard romance. His cabinmate was a well-mannered German lad who had spent a year at a college as an exchange student. He was a serious sort and wanted to talk about US-German cultural influences all the time. "Hey," he heard himself say, "That is a deep subject. Cool it now. You a philosopher or something?"

Munich

It was dark by the time the liner docked in Bremerhaven. There was a cheering crowd waiting at the dock, and those who were being picked up disembarked. He had gotten a telegram that she would come, but she was not there. The ship emptied out in the course of the next morning, and the last ones went to board the ship train that was made up of cars marked with the names of the main German cities as their various destinations, with Munich among them. The train was to leave at two in the afternoon, and he was sitting in the bleachers watching the scene, ready to get on the train in case she did not show. But then, there she was with nine full minutes to spare.

For anyone observing the scene, the meeting was not unlike a business traveler being picked up by an agent of a foreign affiliate. For him, it was like a cruise ship full of vacationers expecting and hoping for a happy and exciting journey running into an iceberg. The controller took careful note of every small detail, and I will spare you all that. You cannot blame an iceberg for being an iceberg. If rain falls on the North Pole, it freezes; if it falls on the equator, it evaporates again. Who tells the wind where to blow the dry autumn leaves? The wind has no moral code like medical doctors or lovers do, who have one primary obligation (do no harm). How often he would ponder that during the next two years!

Intimacy with the loved one is what the lover longs for; intimacy with the erstwhile lover is what the one who fell out of love flees. *Fugit Amor*. She made sure that every minute for the first couple of days was a social affair. They went to visit friends of hers in Hamburg, forcing him to try to make polite conversation when all he wanted to do was to run away. Why didn't he? It is not easy to step away from your *persona*, the person you perceive yourself to be. Part of this person is the image you present to the world, which may include the way you comb your hair, what type of clothes you wear, what kind of car you like to drive, and how you think that your imagined personality fits into the social framework where you choose or are forced to live.

But the world that your emotions and your imagination creates for you, the world outside of yourself, the work that you enjoy or can barely tolerate, the friends that you like, the enemies that you loath, and the loved ones that you think you adore can also become part of who you imagine yourself to be, and these things are then no less real for you than the color of your skin. This persona, when fully developed, can become a prison cell. You set up shop in it and eventually you cannot imagine living anywhere else.

That was where he was then. His small mind would not and could not accept that his glorious love affair that had survived so many years was *Schluss, Kaput, Strich darunter*, over with. Something miraculous would happen; don't give up now; stick with it; never say die. His heart knew well already, without having to drag it out for another year or two, that the damage was irreparable. It was a matter of trust. She had promised that she would tell, and she did not. Whatever she could say to him after trust was broken would always be open to doubt.

Physics in Munich

The *Universität München* is not one of the oldest in Europe, but it is venerable nonetheless. The liberators laid it in ruins, in *Staub und Asche*, during the war. His brother had studied chemistry there for a semester or so before they emigrated, studies that consisted mostly of hauling bricks as part the reconstruction effort. But this was after he had already moved to Bad Godesberg. The Germans wasted no time in rebuilding, for by the time he got back to Munich in 1959, the university had long been fully functional again.

He first went to see Prof. Doktor Bopp (famous for his statistical treatment of quantum mechanics) to have his OU transcript validated for admission to the First Institute of Physics, where Röntgen had discovered x-rays. Bopp scrutinized the white-on-black photocopy of his transcript with a magnifying glass and, noticing the only D thereon, wanted to know with raised eyebrows why he did not "like" quantum mechanics. But he did not pursue the matter and, uncharacteristically for a famous German professor, found a moment to chat. At the end, he offered (an honor of imponderable magnitude in a land where people stand up when a professor looks at them) to guide him past the endless queues of registrants to the Registrar's Office to have his admission papers stamped (since he was going that way anyway, Bopp said, almost as if he were apologizing for his courtesy).

With that, he was enrolled, and it was high time to study the course catalogue. That study was an education (no pun intended), for nowhere in that book was there a hint of what courses a student was required to take to become a *Diplom Physiker*, a master of science in physics. It just described the offerings for that semester.

At a loss for this utter lack of guidance, he went to seek advice from Munker Jancsi and Peter Bäumler, friends from the good old days back in Léva and Pozsony, also students of physics at the UM. They were amused by what they thought was the "American *naïveté*" of his questions. "This is a university, not a grade school," they chuckled. "You take any course you like and read any and all the books you want, whenever the spirit moves you to do so. As long as you can pass the orals at the end."

He found a room in the Barer Straße, a street only two blocks away from the old university complex where the *Erstes Physikalisches Institut* is located, and started attending the lectures. He relished the leisurely pace of it. Luminary nobelists like Heisenberg and Konrad Lorentz were lecturing, the one on field theory and the other on animal behavior. He found himself sneaking into the biology courses with increasing interest. He bought a blue VW bug, for being able to be on the road had become a must for his well-being. Fortunately, the dollar's exchange rate at that time was so good that his GI Bill benefits and savings made this luxury affordable.

He made trips to Harthausen, by car now, and he rediscovered Icking and reran all his old byways in the forest. The old building of the *Schülerheim* on the Walchstätter Höhe still stood, although it no longer was a home to schoolboys. The return to the scene of this formative period of his life had an emotional impact on him that in today's fast-moving world, where everything is in easy reach, might be difficult to appreciate.

It was much more than a mere rediscovery of the past. The Icking experience had been a new world for him back then, and internalizing a new world's ways is an intensive process that leaves deep imprints on one's self-awareness. And when such a past world reemerges but is now viewed from a different level of consciousness, with a new set of imprints from yet another new world weighing on one's back, it feels like stepping down to the earth again after having gotten used to walking on stilts for years.

Fugit Amor

But there was a more palpable difference than all that. The difference between what had been an uncertain world of struggle and discovery for the refugee lad ten years ago and what was now more like the relative security tourists enjoy when visiting a civilized country was something he had to deal with, but he could take that in stride easily. She was the real difference. She had been such a central point of his old Icking experience that he found it impossible now to reconcile the bright hope for a future that she represented in the past, with the shattered shards of disillusionment that she meant for the present.

Ironically, they had been talking about those same shards while walking by the shores of that lake in Furnas. "How fortunate we are," they both agreed, "that we found each other while still in one piece. Let's not let our story break to pieces." And now it was in pieces. Had she written him something like "I have met this other guy, and now I cannot keep my eyes from him. There is nothing I can or want to do about it, so you are free, and I wish you well," he would have felt lousy for a while, but he would have gotten over it quickly. Her way of handling the matter correctly would have helped.

Correctly! Is it odd to use this cold, businesslike word in this context? Think about it! Correctness in emotional matters is like Aloe for a sunburn. Correctness chokes off resentment; it does not let it arise in the first place. And that matters a lot, for resentment is the father of many diseases; it can fester on for a long time, and it can beget ugly children. But correctness is not an easy trade to ply; it takes courage sometimes and always consideration for the other guy.

Self-centered people do not look at it that way or cannot, maybe if their vision is blurred enough, enamored with what they see in the mirror of their pool's surface as Narcissus was. But see now, the horse's hoof of resentment is starting to show from under the cassock even after all these years (*kilátszik a lóláb*), and I better stop before I'd run the risk of becoming judgmental again.

To escape the problem, he spent many a night in his favorite dark, dank, booze-reeking basement bar in Schwabing, crying into his beer in the company of a few other lonely downbeats like him, to drown his hurt and, yes, resentment. Drinking did not help, and he knew it, but he could not help it. Whenever he thought of her, it was like experiencing a permanent solar eclipse. Just light enough to see what he did not want to see but dark enough to know that there was a short in the circuit of his life, that his fuse had burnt out, and that something was dreadfully wrong. And when something is that wrong, you cannot concentrate on anything else, even if it is your favorite pastime like quantum mechanics. You cannot read in the dark, especially after you had lost your rose-colored glasses.

Luckily for him, he was not born to be an escape artist but a realist. There had to be some gain somewhere in all this pain, and all you had to do is look for it and find it. To add to all of this misery, however, it was that summer of the century in Germany when the sun hardly ever shone. He counted the days when it had broken through the clouds, and they added up to four or five for the whole season. *Il pleuvait sans cesse sur la Bavière. Merde.*

The russet mantle

As a remedy, he turned to reading Shakespeare again, and it helped a little. It reminded him of the Aloisiuskolleg and the clear, calm here-and-now above-worldliness of its spirit. And so, slowly and hesitantly "dawn came in a russet mantle clad." The role of "Dawn" was played by Hans-Peter, and the russet mantle was his sister, Evchen. HaPé had been a student at the *Ickinger Schule* after he (the lad) had left, but he acted as if they had always known each other and had been the best of buddies from way back. His courtesy knew no limits, and he was outright self-effacing in being of service to his (very few) friends. He was a true gentleman, although he could be facetious if he forgot himself. To shock his friends (and because he enjoyed doing it), he was given to singing schmaltzy arias from Viennese operettas. One of his *facetiae* was his definition of a gentleman: "A man who treats a whore like a lady and really means it."

He was a law student and had a room in the Türkenstraße, just a block away from his pad, and as I just mentioned, he also had a sister. Evchen was no real replacement for his loss, and she knew it, but she was sturdy and had a healthy dose of self-esteem, strong enough not to suffer from the situation that she was well aware of. Instead, she went about playing the role of the Russet Mantle during that cold and clammy summer, as if she had been training all her life to be a warm, woolen blanket.

She was not an intellect, but she did not have to be one. It sufficed perfectly for her to be clever, cheerful, competent, and *unternehmungslustig*. And that she was; she had a talent for initiatives. There were concerts, plays, and trips to the countryside in his blue VW beetle; to Garmisch, where her very well-to-do parents lived; and to the Castle of Elmau, where he rediscovered the Viennese waltz with her, although he was not good at it. Like Napoleon, he had to think about each successive step. She also liked to attend amusement and entertainment activities of the American Military, to which he had access since he was in the US Army Ready Reserve and had an appropriate ID card to show for it.

But all along, resentment was still very much with him, although he did not let it show when Evchen was around. He was trying to resolve a psychological puzzle that continued to hang like a millstone around his neck. The lady of lost love, whenever they met, and that was not infrequently, alone or with Evchen, never let an occasion pass without trying to put him down, smiling but with a sharp, unkind tongue, without provocation and without any motivation that he could understand.

Why was she acting like that? he kept wondering. Had he not kept his part of the bargain? She had deprived him of his right to choose after she had made her own choice; she let him come from another continent as if she had wanted to place him side by side with his replacement to be inspected and compared for adequacy. He wanted to think that perhaps she did not feel very good about her broken promise after all, and proving him unworthy in her own eyes could justify her behavior and assuage her conscience. His continued preoccupation with the dying and crumbling affair only showed that it was not over yet and that he was still stuck in that tight cocoon of his imagined persona, which either did not want to release him from its clutches or to which he still clung in spite of himself.

Then, one afternoon, the emotional tangle he was still caught in took another long step toward its *dénouement*. She came to report that her German air force lieutenant, Lutz was his name, had crashed during a training flight and died. That finished banging the door shut. The sound of it reminded him of the man in one of Kafka's stories who waits patiently all his life in front of a closed door. In the end, old and decrepit, he is ready to die. Before he kicks the bucket though, the warden opens the door, steps through it, and tells him, "This door was destined to be yours alone. I am now closing it forever." You see, you can win a competition only against a live rival. If he quits before the outcome of the bout is decided, the prize becomes irrelevant. Some may claim it by default, but that is a hollow victory, and he was not one who could live with such an outcome. His rival's death had closed the door that otherwise might have been reserved for him after all.

Light in October

Harsh though it may sound to put it that way, this tragic event turned out to be a stroke of luck for him. It cleared the air; it resolved remaining doubts. And then, one evening, all of a sudden, it was over; it was like when a *Föhn* blows over the Alps and sweeps a whole season's rain clouds away. It was HaPé who produced a real *deus ex machina* this time on the stage of his room. He had been talking about Marina a number of times already, but now he was all excited about her, for she had reappeared. "None other than an unreal, ideal female being, a bouquet of roses, pure poetry, supernatural is no exaggeration," he would gush, "a paragon of grace, beauty and intellect. She is pure poetry."

HaPé had first met her sometime ago at a sailing course on the Chiemsee, and now she had surfaced again, here in München of all places, to study medicine. "You better watch out," he would warn his friend. "You declare fealty to Aphrodite, and Justicia will let you fall flat on your face at your next exam, HaPé was a law student. Are you not too old for this kind of gushy puppy love? What you describe there is unreal indeed." But it was not, as it turned out.

He had come back with Evchen from an outing, and they dropped in on her brother for a cup of tea. And there she sat in the corner, a little tense, back very straight, taking in the scene with a mien as if questioning her good sense in being there in the first place. She was not making any conversation, and her comments were monosyllabic. She was ready to leave. You can tell when someone has lost interest is about to get up and leave but is hesitant about it for fear of appearing curt and impolite. He sat there too and let the siblings do the chatting while his own mind lapsed into that strange, quiescent state that is wide open to the sensory perception of the present while integrating the just perceived moment with important imprints of the past.

If this sounds too abstract and complex to describe the point in time when you see the real dream girl of your life materialize for the first time, that is all right because it *is* a complex matter. So let me explain. The science of language holds that it is impossible to think without using words, and this may be true for a logical, goal-oriented type of thinking. But no one can tell me that there is no wordless thought. Such a nonverbal process uses real images as its medium of reflection, images all imbued with an emotional content of their own. These shapes, clear or shadowy depending on how complete and ripe the mental framework is where they are at home, turn and twist around each other until they come to rest like the colored crystals of a kaleidoscope. But when they are finally at rest, all the fragments together present a new composite image. One whose parts need to be integrated to provide an acceptable interpretation for the new, nascent whole.

This was what his mind must have been doing while his eyes took in that new apparition in the corner. All the people he had known in his life were there together for an instant, like those colored crystals, men, women, friends, enemies, lovers, role models, detractors, disappointments, and even the indifferent ones, all with their bright and their shadow sides, with their strengths and shortcomings in a pantomime of the jumbled, fading reality of the past. What was emerging was a picture not mirrored artificially to reflect a pleasingly symmetrical composition of something desirable and desired but simply a whole new, unknown world, all of its own.

And the one thing that this picture of wordless reflection told him was that this new form sitting in the opposite corner and on the verge of leaving was something entirely outside of the host of his past experiences. After a quarter of a century on the road, he thought he was past the likelihood of ever encountering something so completely new. But it was happening now: the apparition in the corner all of a sudden smiled. At him? He could not tell. Perhaps she just remembered something funny. Or had she gone through a similar process with a similar conclusion? She will let me know when she reads these lines, maybe. More likely than not, she will say, "Cut the convoluted cerebral stuff. Delete it. It is distracting. Try to say what you mean in plain English."

And why not, would it not be better, if I followed her advice? No, it would not be. Like it or not, this is the way introverts process their sensory intake when they are about to discover a new world. That's why. When she was first intending to leave, she did not mean to come back. But that smile turned the tide. A smile can be like pent-up water reaching the top of an earthen dam, and then the first tentative rivulet, unsure as yet what it is up to, carves a tiny little channel on top of it, on its way to end up washing out the entire dam of reservations.

At first they were a foursome doing things together like getting lost in his VW bug on a snowy *Holzweg* in the forest with the tank on empty and night falling so that he could barely meet those large, soft questioning hazel-brown eyes in the rearview mirror anymore. But they made it somehow to the nearest village inn to recover from the scare with *Semmeln und Leberkäs'* and mugs of *Spatenbräu Bier*. They also would go to Elmau together to take in the culture and the music there, for the "*Schloß*" was still very much a power spot like Thomas Mann's Magic Mountain and not just another commercial luxury hotel as it has become in the meantime.

Climbing the Wetterstein was a big attraction, but also that cozy house, the only one within the valley besides the *Schloß,* where Ragnhild, Marina's best friend from college days, spent her vacations with her family, Martin, Maren, Klaus, and Helke. So time was again passing rapidly, while the siblings, slowly at first, became less and less part of the action, and soon there was no doubt anymore that their new world was becoming all of their exclusively own.

What really sealed the deal for him was the excursion to Wasserburg one Sunday. About a two-hour drive from Munich, this little medieval town sits on a hill where the Inn River makes a horseshoe-shaped loop around it. Memorable though the details of the day must have been, and we have a genuine, old Merian etching of the town hanging on the wall to prove that they were indeed memorable; the only one I remember now was the interminably long trip back to Munich on the *Autobahn*.

The entire population of the city seemed to be coming back from outings like theirs, for it had been a halcyon day. The drive was bumper-to-bumper most of the time, but instead of experiencing the nerve-wracking frustration that traffic jams like that can evoke in him, he actually felt like you do when you sit in a warm Jacuzzi, watching the snow falling outside. The miracle that she was working was the conversation. There was none. There was no need for it. They were together and that was enough.

Only a true introvert can understand how refreshing and invigorating it is when your heart is full of things to say but you can save it for the recipient of all that gets it without the need for words. He thought of the lady with the cold, blue mountain lake eyes. Was that lake deep or shallow? Funny, it occurred to him, as it does to me now in retrospect, he could not tell, for the surface of the lake was always rippled.

With her, there was no peace without a gusty wind of words always astir. Eureka, he thought in the middle of that traffic. I found what I was looking for.

Physics, one last time

That was well and good; in fact, it was super, but in that large, old lecture hall in that venerable, historic old building of the Ludwig-Maximilian Universität that apparently survived the liberators, there were three huge blackboards, each of them in two enormous parts, and when Professor Bopp scribbled the part in front of him full of hieroglyphics, he would jack it up on its pulley system and then proceeded scribbling the second part of it full also. Then he would go on to the next one and then to the third one, and by the time those too were all covered with his hieroglyphics where Greek letters are corralled and whipped into obedient marching files by mystical math operators, the first one was again ready to receive more of all that knowledge, wiped clean by an assistant.

Yes, it was quantum mechanics, and that foretaste of it in Oklahoma was preschool stuff. Bopp used no notes; he had it all in his enormous head. Equation after equation, formula after formula, all with a running commentary that was beyond grasping even if it could have been heard, for he had his back to his audience all the time. What he was doing on those blackboards was in no book, he knew that, for there were any number of books to be had on the subject by now and he had read into quite a few of them. I still think it was all voodoo, and you could not check on it, for the Professor Doktor's lecture style did not entertain questions.

But it was not all an exercise in futility. There where Heisenberg and Gerlach, very good and stimulating in their presentations, and at times he thought it was outright uplifting to be part of the great intellectual hubs of the world, even if only at the lowly receiving end. But with general relativity, the physics show was over for him; there was no more doubt about it, for it was truly incomprehensible.

To cap it off, he took a trip with Peter Bäumler (who was job hunting by then) to IBM's regional headquarters in Zürich, Switzerland, to get a feel for what the job scene in physics might look like. The place was a state-of-the-art, gleamingly sterile monument of a monastery, designed for the adoration of technology. They met the chief abbot himself. The guy was interested in the electrogenic impurities in solid-state media and wanted to hire someone who was ready to devote his life to that so that the resulting ever-faster business machines could grease the skids of unlimited growth more noiselessly.

He, for his part, did well to remember another fragment of his Latin (*si tacuisses, philosophus mansisses*), and so he wisely decided to remain a silent philosopher (or something) and let his friend do the talking. Let's face it, and he was facing it somewhat anxiously for his resources were running out, the bits and pieces of physics that he devoted four years of his life to by now were leading up to the dead end of this *Holzweg* of his. That was okay. *Strich darunter*, but how was he going to explain it to Marina?

Amor omnia vincit

I do not remember how he did it. Was the situation communicated verbally or nonverbally? I really do not see how he could forget it, for this was such a crucial juncture, a decision for the rest of their lives. I think now that she just picked up the vibrations in the ether and when the decision was ready to present itself, she was already aware of it and ready to face it and graciously so. This ability of hers to patch together seamlessly pieces of cloth as if they were made of the same fabric and then use the resulting quilt as a blanket for the security and well-being of her chosen loved one(s) remained a lasting miracle for him.

And because miracles do ask for explanations for the doubters, this one prompts me to add a few words in exegesis. You see, the need for a profession like marriage counseling is a visible symptom of the disfunctionality of our society. With all due respect to the dedicated folks who practice it and to all the good they are doing, the place for intensive counseling in intergender relations is not after a mismatch has produced its intractable problems but before people ever tie the knot.

So prüfe, wer sich ewig bindet	So, let him, who ties the knot forever
Ob sich das Herz zum Herzen findet:	Test the valence of the bond.
Der Wahn is kurz, die Reu' ist lang.	Illusion is short and repentance long.

That would take a good dose of pragmatic authoritarianism that our society, alas, does not have. Far from being an intrusion into some sacred, secret, untouchable sphere, if done well, it could teach the infatuated eye of the lover to recognize real values rather than focusing on imagined ones, and by now, he thought he knew more about this than anyone. You can theorize till doomsday about all the reasons why some matches work while others do not. If they do, is it just an equilibrium of power that accounts for it? Or rather a deep compatibility that comes from sharing the same education, the same values, and a similar view of the world? Or all of those and many more? It is a mystery, and so is the reality of simply feeling at ease with one another.

And that reality had to be strong, for it was going to be tested for them right now, from the very beginning. Putting the uniform back on again was not only a sigh of relief for him; it was the return to a way of life he liked. But she did not grow up with the bugle calls of reveille and retreat and with all the arcane ceremonies of military life that might be nothing but a nuisance to her, coming, as she did, from a

Menonite family that went to the extremes of trouble because of its refusal to bear arms.

She was brought up on European customs and culture and had opposed her father's plan to send her to college in the United States because America felt alien to her. This new turn of events might well have felt like menace to her, a trial that she did not bargain for. If so, no trace of it was showing. She was facing this new challenge, his decision to quit physics and rejoin the army with a confident, come-what-may smile. And he knew that what he had on his hands now was *the* mystery, this beautiful woman who chose to spend the rest of her life with him, something not to be fathomed but simply to be happy with.

Farewell to physics

What had facilitated his return to active duty was the Second Berlin Crisis. The army was welcoming reservists who were willing come back on active duty, and since the matter by that time had come down to a choice between Einstein or Eisenhower, he opted for what seemed to be the lesser evil at the time and expressed his willingness to return to the fold.

He finished his master's thesis with time to spare. It was on an aspect of Raman spectroscopy. The phenomena studied by the methods of RS are fundamental to atomic physics. A given substance will absorb a certain discrete wavelength of light depending on the spatial configuration of its molecules' constituent atoms. The interactions between the atoms' electron shells depend on the nature of this arrangement, and so do the kind of photons that can be absorbed by the molecule. This input of light energy raises the state of excitation of the substance. The energy absorbed is briefly stored at the several metastable levels of the excited electrons. When it is released (emitted) again, it is not in one packet the way it came in, but in several smaller ones, so that the light that comes back out has different wavelengths (colors) from the one that went in.

An analysis of these events is helpful in determining the structure of the molecule. Simple, isn't it? Anyway, it was really a fun piece of work, and because it was fun, it was well on its way, waiting only for the finishing touches when the army decision became final. He always lived under the compulsion to be well prepared in order to avoid being a "last-minute Charlie."

Actually, it was not so much the scientific involvement that the thesis demanded but the surroundings where it took place that had really turned him on. As you pass by the statue of The Owl, companion of Athena and a symbol of wisdom, under its heavy stone baldachin in the inner courtyard of the old main university building, there was (and still is) a door, on the left-hand side of the underpass and accessible only from it, to a basement room. Arched in solid, raw, unplastered stone, cold, damp, and dark, it was a physics lab that survived the bombs. It was crammed full of arcane scientific gear, for he shared the place with two more students.

It was a near exact replica of that legendary, mystical, medieval alchemist's laboratory in Bártfa, which the favorite book of his childhood described in poetic prose. The book's title is *Egy Magyar Diák Élete Mátyás Korában* by Donászy Ferenc. It is that only book, *ex libris* Bethlenfalvay, that made it all the way from home to the foot of Bishop's Peak, and I still read in it when I am in need of solace, although I have known it by heart for a long time now. It describes the life of a Magyar student in the time of King Mátyás, who reigned just before that disastrous, genocidal Turkish invasion and occupation of Magyarország in the sixteenth century.

Getting acquainted

There was not much need for seeking solace in old books in those heady days full of a new zest for life. I cannot go into great detail of its individual events for I do not remember much of it. This is a sure sign that things were going very well; it is the misfortunes that you have to deal with that the controller etches deeply into the memory banks somewhere in the limbic system of your brain. The good times are full of living and doing. He who can, does; he who can't, writes. And he who does not remember has nothing to write about, unless he makes it up. He lived in the Ainmillerstraße during this last phase of his stay in München, and last year, when I was back for a visit, I tried to find the house. I could not even find the street; so thoroughly had the *feuilles mortes* of the *oubli* covered over that *temps perdu*. But nonetheless, I do remember three minor events there distinctly.

One was the first evening they spent alone together. He went up to her room, not totally sure of the reception yet but not worried either. She was pleased. "Let's play a game of chess," he said, not as an exploratory gambit in starting the interaction but with the full intention of doing so. And so she introduced him to her Chinese checkers version of the game. She did not want to see any pieces knocked out, but this had to be done within the rules of the game, without flagrantly disregarding one's advantage when it came. So the chessmen had to slide past each other in ways calculated to avoid confrontation. That was manageable with the nobility and the royalty who could move back and forth; it was the pawns, the cannon fodder, that have no choice but to advance, which resisted their benevolent general's idea of mock warfare. It was a message: she wanted no winners and losers. It was an omen for the future.

Another was a visit to her mother's house in Meererbush, up north in the Rheinland, near Düsseldorf. She wanted to see the great old house in Kaiserswerth again where they lived while her father was still alive. She had told him a lot about that house, described every room in detail, and spent time on reminiscing about a sour-cherry orchard that never failed in its springtime bounty of her favorite fruit.

Well, they ventured through the gate, trespassing flagrantly, but she simply wanted to see her garden again. Then a couple of American-clad and

American-mannered young men issued from the house and very curtly and imperiously ordered them to leave the premises immediately. They did so in English and seemed to assume that the whole world naturally understood that idiom. She tried to explain that she had lived there as a child, but they were not interested. He noted that on his own, he would never have entered a strange garden like that and that she apparently did not share some of his inhibitions.

The third one was the occasion, early in their acquaintance, when she initiated the institution of the *Haushaltskasse*. This was nothing more than a black leather pouch, a purse, into which each of them deposited cash to be used for jointly incurred expenses. The *Haushaltskasse* is a concept that avoids a lot of minor social hassles about who pays for what, but at the same time, it is also a statement full of *gravitas*. It means "we are traveling together."

Gravity is the most mysterious (physical) force that we are aware of in our universe. Its waves are so subtle that they defy exact measurement, but its more gross effects suffice for keeping our feet on the ground instead of floating off into space. Once this *Haushaltskasse* had become a firmly established institution, their feet, in addition to being firmly grounded, acquired also a sense of direction and gravitated naturally, with the unconscious singlemindedness of somnambulants to the *Standesamt*. That is the office where the knots of unions for life are tied officially.

The brief ceremony was anticlimactic, for their knot was already tied as squarely as any knot ever was. The fun came afterward, when she helped him discover Venice. Up to that time, Venice had been a small, old, black-and-white photograph of his parents for him, on their honeymoon, standing in San Marcos Square surrounded by the obligatory pigeons. A picture that stood in a simple silver frame on his mother's desk back home in Léva. Now it came to life in vivid color. Venice is entirely unlikely, and I will not attempt a description of it and of the details of that glorious week, for it was too long ago, although it seems like yesterday now that I think of it. There was a fresh breeze blowing on that wide square under the watchful eye of the great Campanile, and an orchestra played the snappy tune from the movie *The Guns of Navarone*. Go and see Venice before it, like life itself sinks into the sea of oblivion.

Back to the renewed search of an america

In the end, time came for him to get into his blue VW beetle, in uniform now, to drive to Bremerhaven. Once again, he said good-bye to a girl who promised to wait for him. Only this time, there were no portents of gloom and doom of any kind. He would find a place to live for the two of them somewhere near Fort Mead, Maryland (but not on post), where he was to be stationed, and then come back to get married again in earnest, in church. When things are clear, they tend to be simple and easy. Instead of the details of the planning and parting, I remember only an irrelevant little incident en route clearly enough to report here.

It was about four thirty in the afternoon after an all-day drive from Munich, already on the outskirts of the city of Bremen, when he noticed that his speedometer needle no longer moved. That is no problem on the *Autobahn*, where there is no speed limit, but back across the Atlantic, in the Land of the Free, the eye of the law is vigilant and frowns on any over-exuberance in motoring, even if unintended. So he stopped at a garage whose sign promised quick, courteous, and reliable repairs and said *offen* in spite of the advanced hour on a Friday afternoon. Let's get this done, while still in the Land of the VW, he thought. And there he got his last bit of education in German customer relations from the owner-foreman, who had already washed his hands in preparation for the weekend. "*So, und das ist ihnen gerade jetzt eingefallen, wo ich eben Feierabend machen wollte,*" the man said, winking at his assistants.

This kind of attitude Germans seem to soak up in school, where the teachers, although (or because) otherwise highly qualified, often act out rituals of cynical superiority in class. "No. I know it's late, and I know you are ready to call it a week. This did not pop into my mind just now. It happened now," he replied, shaking his head. "The car will be loaded for transport overseas tonight, and I would appreciate that quick and courteous service of yours since you are still open." He pointed at the sign. "*Aber sie sind doch gar kein Ami, sie sprechen doch deutsch,*" sputtered the man while he got his crew to install a *Tachospirale* that brought the needle to life again. It took them ten minutes. "Yes, a few *Amis* do speak German, and *Ami* businessmen treat their customers as kings," he offered in parting.

Why do I remember this episode when I do not even recall whether his ship was military or civilian? Ask the controller himself, for the controller of the controller does not know. But the departure scene was radically different from that momentous farewell some ten years before on that troop transport full of emigrants. This second departure to continue his search felt now like an established routine.

Chapter 7

Soldier Again

Remember the "Coal Miner's Anthem" by Merle Travis, which was revamped into a number-one hit song in the mid-1950s by Tennessee Ernie Ford? He heard it first in a bar in Lawton, on one of those rare weekends off as an OCS upperclassman.

> You load sixteen tons and what do you get?
> Another day older and deeper in debt.
> Saint Peter don't call me, for I can't go:
> I owe my soul to the company store

Once you have heard it, its melody will haunt you forever, especially at times when some inescapable impasse has got you up a dead end. Well, looking back at his most recent past from his desk at the Foreign Language Interpreter's and Interrogator's Section of the 525th Military Intelligence Group, Fort Meade, Maryland, he did have mixed feelings sometimes about the way he had been husbanding his passing years lately.

> Four years of physics, and what do you get?
> Four years older and nowhere yet.
> Einstein, don't haunt me, for I can't go:
> My arse is in hock to the Army now

That is, if being a captain of US Army Intelligence in the early 1960s means being nowhere. It is easy but futile to shake one's head about the past in retrospect. But military intelligence, the place where he landed upon being recalled to active duty? That asks for a bit of a commentary right here, up front. So let's stop and compare for a second the hopelessness of mining all those tons of coal a day with the futility of spending all those hours of the day in the offices of the 525th MIG, doing essentially nothing. What about the merits of either of those two ways of spending one's life?

On politics, coal, and intelligence

One can be of one school of thought about this today and claim that having burnt those sixteen tons of coal a day for all those years is what is melting the polar ice caps now. Folks at the opposite end of the political spectrum see our priorities differently. What worries them is a sinister, foreign menace (then slant-eyed, now rag-headed), and they bet all their money on guns to save us from it. They place all our money, whether we have it or not, on this one chip. They call it money well spent, and never mind if it bankrupts the country in the end. How in hell can we afford not to spend it (even if we have to borrow it) when it is spent for the sake of freedom and democracy?

You might take all these political polemics for page-filling, irrelevant moralizing as they switch back and forth between his uninformed and dissatisfied pre-Vietnam stage and what he knows today after a long road of watching and listening. And of living and learning, for a road of learning is important, especially for a brand-new officer of military intelligence who finds himself not finding much intelligence in what he is doing.

So let us consider the meaning of the words we use for a moment to make sure we are talking about the same thing. *Intelligence* is "the ability to apprehend the interrelationships of presented *facts* in such a way as to guide action towards a desired *goal*," says Webster. That makes intelligence a whopper of a word and one with consequences. To deal with consequences, you must first decide what the *goal* is. Next, you have to face the *facts*, which have a bearing on that goal.

The first one, the goal, is easy. At least, it was so for a relatively still young Army captain, a registered, conservative Republican like him. The goal, as he internalized the concepts of *his* American citizenship, was simple to grasp. It was the conservation of democratic freedoms guaranteed by the Constitution, which he had sworn to defend. Even though he was not a sufficiently sophisticated Republican yet at that time to fully understand the nature of the proper way to pursue collective happiness: a way paved by free, unregulated markets without tax-and-spend, big-government interference. High values worthy of being conserved, tads of whose benefits ultimately may trickle down to everyone. But about this time, he had an ominous dream, a rare one that remained clear in his memory.

Herding pigs

Kereskény had been a large estate, that of his maternal grandmother's family. Spending a few weeks of the summer vacation there was always a treat, for it opened gates to worlds closed to city kids. One of these worlds was that of the pigsties. There were many pigs there, always milling around especially when they fought their way to the troughs at feeding time to get at the slop that trickled down to them from the various and sundry leftovers and by-products of the estate's economy. To watch all that squealing, snorting, and jostling was an attraction, but the real attraction was to accompany them on their run to a swampy patch in that ancient oak forest about half a mile from the sty, a forest whose limits were too vast to be known.

This was a daily exercise under the supervision of the swineherd, a small, stocky man with a bushy mustache, a Slovak who spoke little Magyar but who could understand it well. He knew every one of his charges, possibly by name, and although there was no swine dog to help him (the pigs would have eaten such a nuisance alive), he always got them all back to the sty in the evening after they had their fill of the bitter acorns and of mucking around in the mud to their hearts' content in their search for truffles. No mean feat that, for pigs, unlike sheep, have their own minds. But then, maybe, they had just got used to spending the night indoors. This was the backdrop of the dream, this and Árpád *bácsi*'s smiling compliment of a headshake. "Some city kids who go herding pigs in the forest!" his granduncle's gesture seemed to say.

Then one time, that strange, atonal melody from the old swineherd's five-holed, reed-stem flute was interrupted by the terrified shriek of a piglet in the distance. They all took off in that direction, and he was the one who stumbled on the scene first. There was a large, brown animal sitting in a lotus position in the middle of the clearing. He knew him well form zoology; he was a puma. One, who was called a mountain lion in his books about the Wild West. One who did not belong in a forest at the foothills of the Carpathian Mountains. And this one had a human head that looked down on the bleeding piglet between his front feet. Then he looked up. He looked up at him or rather through him, and his eyes shone with aggression while expressing something like self-satisfied, cold contentment.

The dreamer, the kid in that long-ago forest and the soldier in the present, one person as they were, felt a little puzzled as they realized that they were not even startled; it was as if they had somehow expected to see what they saw. But as the vision itself faded away from his perception, he found that he kept searching for recognition. That round, beefy face on that beast! Whom did it resemble? He had seen so many faces by then. He thought he heard Jung's voice admonishing him to try harder, for it mattered; dreams had a meaning. It was the smirking face of a powerful, fat man full of malice and menace. He tried harder, but he could not recognize the face, and the effort woke him.

But waking up did not end it, for the dream lingered on before it finally went dormant. While it lasted, he tried his best to interpret it and to relate it to what was going on around him, for he knew it had to be relevant somehow. Was there a way to apprehend some relationship, maybe between the warning that the dream image conjured up and the facts of his new position as an officer commissioned to deal with the menace that the secrets of war are?

By Webster's definition of intelligence, it was the facts that should guide action toward a goal, uninfluenced by premonitions, omens, and dreams. But that face! That face! Was it maybe a face of some unknown consequence lurking in the future? Some consequence that might be avoided if one only saw the facts more clearly even if guided by a well-interpreted dream?

Back to the facts: coal and intelligence

Those pesky, elusive facts! They render the bag of intelligence so bulkily intransigent. But they are the ones on which everything depends. I will not try to list them all here, all those that should have been considered in those years leading to the Vietnam War since this is my own life's story and not history. Let me just stick with the two that I already mentioned, the mining of coal and the value of intelligence, for they are relevant not only to my personal tale but also to that wider outlook that all of us faced at the time. Facts that were relevant to Vietnam then as they are to this Second Iraq War now, the tragedy of this decade, the one that occupies my thinking now and therefore keeps working its way into my discussion of the past.

The mining of coal exemplifies the conundrum of our impending environmental catastrophe. It is the chief pollutant of the air we breathe, but it produces most of our electricity, and without electricity our modern life would come to a halt. Which is more important? That was still easy to decide at the time, back in the early sixties, some fifty years ago. Then, that decision depended entirely on where you came from.

"The need for power is real," the realists said, and he was one of them. "Not burning coal would impede the economy. Banks would lose money, so they would stop lending it, and that would strangle business. Pollution is only pesky, and we can control it. We realists are not simple minded. We do not get upset over imaginary horrors like *Silent Spring*, global warming, and *Inconvenient Truth*. Science does not support all that. Let scare-mongering leftist ideologues fret over their environment. We need power. Like power from coal. Power to support our military. For that is what deters real trouble. Trouble like what the Reds are stirring up now in Southeast Asia.

"But look at it another way," the other side, the idealists, would argue plaintively. "Consider an apple. It has a thick, waxy, impenetrable skin, and that keeps the worms out. Good. But what if it then rots from the core? Would not safe bridges, secure jobs, good schools, affordable health care, and less debt be a better way to keep trouble at bay than tanks and atomic submarines? Not to mention clean air, water safe to drink, and poison-free food."

Who knows? All this was not as clear in the early sixties as it is today; at least it was not to him. He had a copy of *On War* on his desk, a present his father had given him, *Vom Krieg*, by Carl von Clausewitz. But he had not read it; it was forbiddingly voluminous. It may have explained it all, how coal (along with steel) and war are related to each other and to the present and future well-being of a country and also how analytical intelligence (based on solid facts) is needed to unravel the riddles that this relationship poses.

He certainly did not know, nor did he care all that much. He was busy hoarding up a bit of cash as a cushion for a rainy day. The answers depended then, as they still do now, on what sort of fixed ideas populate the murky realms of politicians' preconceived concepts and partisan minds. And that was too bad (as it continues to be), for the *facts* on which a successful attainment of good goals rest, cannot come from guesswork or wishful thinking.

Facts are statements without question marks: a point that Webster might have stressed had he foreseen this postmodern, neo-American, partisan political gridlock of ours. Attitudes that are based on unpatriotic bigotry and on the negation of facts. He (Webster) also might have added that all this is moot in this context anyway, for he did not mean his definition to apply to any military type of intelligence in the first place.

Military intelligence

But unfortunately, there is still more to "intelligence" that *does* apply to the military. Intelligence has a bearing not only on one's own conduct but also on the planning and the execution of the affairs of a society that affect all of its members collectively: intelligence in this sense is "the power of meeting any situation successfully by proper behavior adjustments!" This is the crucial part that the powers that steer a ship of state (including the military) must heed, if they want to avoid getting stuck in an armed foreign affairs quagmire. In "a vietnam" one would say today, but that concept had barely started to develop back then in the early 1960s.

If we want to approach this type of intelligence right, we must meet the challenges or "wars" of our times (those on poverty, crime, drugs, terrorism, and the like) by a dispassionate examination of the causes and a realistic consideration of the remedies, basing both processes on all pertinent facts. You do not falsify facts emotionally, as we did both for Vietnam and the Second Iraq War, for if you do, they will lead to the jungles and deserts of defeat, if not militarily so, at least morally. And on the way there, an instrument that was designed to provide insight into the facts of the present and foresight for the future, like military intelligence, might become nothing but an oxymoron.

Back then in the early 1960s, he, of course, did not yet engage in this sort of harrowing internal dialogue that for me stems now from a comparison of those two wars four decades apart. He was still untroubled then. A misuse of intelligence is not new, but this flagrant, new style of it, that of the new millennium's first decade, the one that we suffer from right now, is stuff that streams (or rather creeps and crawls) into my consciousness at this moment of writing and does not let go.

Instead of using the inferences drawn from the facts honestly, we jumped to preconceived conclusions willfully, judgmentally, and irresponsibly, one could almost say compulsively, and having decided on our tragically misguided course, we used fictitious "military intelligence" after the fact to back up and justify what we did. And today, as I am working on this very last revision of my story, some three months after I signed off on it as finished, the current president of the United States bestowed the Medal of Freedom on the previous one for having done all that.

Maryland

He was to discover and encounter the abuse of military intelligence himself within a few years, but right now, he found himself floating in what was a placid, peacetime backwater, far removed from the rapids of history. Those currents were already running strong elsewhere, as they always do somewhere, and that somewhere at the time was on the far shores of a wide, war-ravaged but now pacified ocean, the one way out West. But that comes later.

Fort Meade

Right now, at the 525th MI Group, he had to deal with this curious new sort of army that was so very different from the straightforward business that he was familiar with in the artillery. In the artillery, things are clear-cut. Whether there happens to be a real enemy in front of you or not, the daily training routine focuses on all those varied activities that ensure that in the end, you can hit that target when the time comes. In peacetime, it is a game only, but it is a serious one. The intelligence business seemed to be a game also, but the way it was played at the 525th, it was difficult for him to take it seriously.

There were folks who played at "Order of Battle." That is the name for a pastime that pieces together the formal structure of the enemy army, the organization of its units, its equipment, and its disposition. Folks who do this thoroughly, honestly, and in earnest in a real world would then be able to report things like "The bad guys have all sorts of units but also some that can deploy weapons of mass destruction, and we know for sure where they hide them." But the 525th had no such mission;

the toys we played with were old, historical ones like the Soviet units of the last Great War.

Then there were others who were trained to recognize objects from stereoscopically superimposed photographs. These folks interpreted and analyzed the results of aerial surveillance. If you do this thoroughly, honestly, and in earnest, you can then come up with insights like "They have all sorts of equipment but also some large, covered trucks, and we *think* that they *might* concoct chemical and biological agents in them because those vehicles have such a strange, special configuration, and because they are so secretive about them. They move those trucks about furtively all the time, and so we ought to send a live agent in there to verify this. Alas, we do not have anyone who can speak their language." But again, we were just playing with pictures left over from World War II.

Then there were still others (including him) in the business of interpreting, translating, and interrogating. Only none of this type of activity was actually going on. And had there been, it would have been in tongues of Eastern Europe, which reflected the strategic thinking of the time, the direction from where the menace was expected to come: Soviet armored divisions pouring into Western Europe through the Fulda Gap. Why think ahead like learning Farsi or Arabic? Or Vietnamese for that matter?

There was only deafening silence at the 525th about the "Nam," and he was not all that interested in the subject either. A study of the conflict in that faraway land was simply not on anyone's agenda where he was, and so he was blissfully ignorant of it also, interested though he had always been in history. Eisenhower was gone by then, and his successor, the chief politician of the moment, seemed to have inherited some of his predecessor's scruples about committing his country to a venture in the jungles of the Far East.

But Kennedy was also under the wing flaps of hawks like Ike had been. His top advisor on the matter at the "Defense" Department, an erstwhile head bean counter at a big car company, was itching to get the feet of other people's sons wet in that upwelling of red nationalism on the southeastern fringes of Asia. So there were sporadic references to Vietnam in the media, but these were not of the kind that his controller chose to file away in any sort of orderly fashion. Dealing with omens and premonitions is not the controller's business, and the controller of the controller was focusing on other things at the moment, on ones closer at hand and very much more important.

Getting married

The most important of these was flying back to Meererbusch, where Marina still lived, to get married again, this time in church with all the accompanying pomp and circumstance. Mother-in-law arranged for a beautiful wedding party. Family and close friends only. His father flew over for the wedding. He was his old graceful, gentlemanly, loving self for the occasion and proud of his lovely daughter-in-law. She reminded him of his own experience in finding the love of his life. "*Ismerem az esetet*," he told him. "I know the case. She is very much like your mother was. You can see the devotion in her eyes, but there is no gushy outside showing of affection. I am glad you came to your senses. Now I do not have to worry about you anymore. She will take good care of you."

The service was dignified and took place in an ancient, medieval chapel nearby. The priest, an old World War II military chaplain, chuckled and shook his head when he read the bureaucratic note the archbishop of Baltimore's office had provided to permit him to marry an infidel (only if she promised to hurry up with becoming a good Catholic). Even HaPé was there and played the best man (his brother, Miklós, a medical doctor by then, could not shake loose from his patients). HaPé, as always, was a paragon of tact and showed no resentment for having lost the prize of his life to one whom he might well have regarded as a false friend. I am truly sorry for not having kept up with him. I hope he found the happiness that he so thoroughly deserved. There were a couple of days of honeymooning in Paris on the way back to the United States, but the army is stingy with leave, and they were soon back in College Park to start a new life in earnest.

There was nothing earnest about it though. It was more like a permanent sequel to that outing to Wasserburg in slow motion. It had the promise of a bright, cloudless morning about it. They felt like they were "one piece." "*Wir sind ein Stück*" they would call their place in this new life, for having met in Munich, they continued to use German as their family-speak. They went to Fort Meade to shop at the PX and the commissary. When there was a unit party or a ceremony or parade, they would attend it together. But they lived off post, and the army's tentacles did not reach all the way to College Park, where she was busy with her French classes at the University of Maryland.

Distant thunder

Nevertheless, there were reminders of what the army's business is. Remote though they were at this point in time, fragments of info filtered down through the layers of bureaucracy now and then. Like General Ridgeway's staff study of a couple of years back on Indochina: "Don't send American boys into that quagmire," it admonished. Eisenhower was good at reading and understanding army staff studies, and so he stood his ground on this one against his other advisers. Had he (the soldier) given any thought at the time to such matters, he might have imagined scenes in the Oval Office with John Foster Dulles doggedly harping on the imperative of not letting that first domino fall to the reds. Then there was the question of the free elections for both the North and the South of Vietnam. Those that Ho Chi Minh had been promised in Geneva in 1954 after General Giap trounced the French at Dien Bien Phu, ending the French colonial adventure in Indochina. Elections that were subsequently thwarted by none other than the great global champion of freedom and democracy. This was such an important footnote to history that his controller should not have overlooked it at the time, for its consequences came home to roost in earnest ten years later.

The problem then was a question of principle for US foreign policy. Can elections be free and democratic if their outcome is unlikely to be pro-American? This must have been the great quandary and dilemma of the policy makers of those relatively still untroubled times. But he did not find out about that Geneva Conference until some fifteen years later, when it was too late. Must I wonder now how he could have missed this crucial bit of information, the terms of the Geneva Accords? Busy as he was with becoming a paratrooper in 1954, at a time before television and without newspapers in an apolitical place like Fort Campbell, replete with its twelve thousand screaming extroverts. Could it be that the media did not consider Geneva newsworthy? Or maybe the government saw no merit in having it publicized?

College Park

After the mental stresses of physics, the daily routine would have been like a permanent vacation had it not been for the requirement to appear at his desk physically, in person, each and every *workday*. But he liked wearing the uniform, and he liked the saluting, the courtesy, the parades, the bugle calls, the belonging to something big, strong, reliable—to the club of the good guys. He did not mind taking orders (there was little of that, and what there was was done in a collegial way in the MI), while giving orders had always been something (let's admit it) that he liked.

There was another circumstance that contributed to his general well-being, namely that they did not actually live on post. Before Marina followed him across the Atlantic, he had found a neat, sunny, little south-facing apartment on the top (fifth) floor of a new apartment building on the southern edge of the University of Maryland Campus, in the town of College Park. Their windows were so oriented that on the Fourth of July, they could see the fireworks over the Washington Mall in the distance above the College Park tree line.

Marina, whose doubts about her aptitude for medicine had led to a reevaluation similar to his own regarding physics, had started on a graduate program in French literature while teaching beginning French as a teaching assistant. This connected them to the campus not only as her workplace but also through the friends they made among the students. And on their evening walks on the rolling green lawns of the University of Maryland, they discovered some of their favorite mushrooms, the meadow Agaricus, which no one else dared to pick. Thus, the university environment provided reminders of Europe and the intellectual stimulation that was lacking at work.

To make the transition in lifestyles easier, though, he did actually have to wrestle with physics a little longer, for his oral exams for the master's degree, diploma, were still pending. Marina encouraged him to bring his years of fighting physics to a formal close. And that this particular *Gestalt* could be completed, lived to fulfilment, only by going back to Munich and facing Professor Bopp and his colleagues eye to eye to tell them what he remembered about physics. So in the fullness of physical time, they took a quick flight to Munich where he was then actually declared a *Diplomphysiker*. With *Ach und Krach* I might add, but passing is passing, and that was the end of it, *Strich darunter*.

Marina herself was quite busy with her studies. She already spoke French with native fluency, but dealing with the intricacies of literary criticism was an exacting new experience. Reading and enjoying a novel is one thing, but mastering the craft that leads to an understanding of its form is quite another. A novel is like an edifice; it has structure, and putting its parts together must be learned. A bio, (like this one) on the other hand . . . well, it seems to me, its structure is nothing but a stream that finds its own bed to flow in. Still, they had time to explore the offerings of the Washington area.

There will be a hiatus of a month or so here in my efforts to dredge the grown-over channels and streambeds of my memory for relics. I will undergo a cancer operation tomorrow. I wonder if I will resume this effort afterward. What happens to my priorities when my presence down here is no longer a continuum but becomes something measured in discreet units of time: a counted number months left? This reminds me of a poem that I read a long time ago and now, suddenly I understand its meaning. It is *"Die Gestundete Zeit."*

Es kommen härtere Tage.	Harder days are coming.
Die auf Wiederruf gestundete Zeit	Time borrowed subject to repeal
Wird sichtbar am Horizont.	Looms now on the horizon.

Then I understood *gestundet* as *"Zeit in Stunden geteilt,"* that is, "time divided into hours." But the verb *stunden* really means something else like "to grant a respite for something" or "to borrow time." Both meanings seem to apply here well. See, even at such a juncture of my life as this one, I am still entrapped in nugatory efforts of quibbling about the meaning of my vocabulary. So if I do go on with my story, will my focus on the words that I work so hard to find be different? Will my outlook on life, my views of past and future, change radically, or will my currents of habituation be strong enough to let me (or make me) just go on as before?

Those offerings were varied and bountiful. There was a small theater that showed foreign movies and a delightful little French restaurant in Georgetown, among many other things. There were the Chesapeake and Ohio Canal for hiking.

There were the concerts and lectures at the U of M. There was downtown D.C.: one could actually visit the White House back then after a bit of standing in line. There was the antique hunting for a chest of drawers (but mostly just looking and touching) at New Market, Maryland.

How that quaint little town must have changed since the 1960s! Maybe next summer, we will pass through there again, if our last, long, glorious around-the-whole-country road trip actually comes about as planned. And all this on a military salary that was, by civilian standards, something like the minimum wage is today. Being in the army was a service then rather than the mercenary business that it is becoming today.

A vivid little memory fragment in this regard is their first grocery shopping at the Fort Meade commissary: nine dollars for three huge bags of goodies, enough food for ten days. What made all this possible was simply that Marina was the ideal person to be living with, practically speaking also. She had a sense and appreciation for the good things in life, but she was frugal and was well aware of the limits of the family budget. So there was never a word said about money, for the family bank account, like the *Haushaltskasse* of the past, was an open book to be read with a lot of good, common horse sense.

The job

After a while, he was promoted from the Language Unit to Group Headquarters as assistant operations officer. This was tricky, for the group was not "operating" in any strict or loose sense of the word. But there is always routine training in any army, and he was mainly in charge of that. If his time at work was actually pleasant, that was due to the personality of his boss, the operations officer.

Major James Caldwell was tough. He had come up through the ranks and had seen combat in World War II. He was black (the term "African American" was not in use yet) and had the speech, deportment, and character of a fierce Zulu warrior. Not that he (the soldier) had ever met a live Zulu warrior, but no matter, the lack of a live image to serve as a comparison made Jim's martial identity even more perfectly profiled. He called him "Jim" off duty, for the major did not have to worry about familiarity eroding his status of respect as a superior, as is true with any strong and good leader. He was the man. The two of them got along famously.

But then came the first real reminder that an army's business is war. It was like the music in thriller movies, like the ominous notes presaging the appearance of the shark in *Jaws* or the appearance of the clock ticking off the last minutes to "high noon." Jim got his orders for Vietnam. He tried to buy a house off post for his wife to live in while he was gone and to settle into afterward, but folks at the new housing development at Laurel, although it was built with federal aid, did not seem to want Negroes as neighbors.

After exhausting his legal resources and running short on time, Jim wrote to President Kennedy for help. The next day, he had the answer under a "The White House" letterhead. After that, he had no trouble moving into the house of his choice unopposed, but he did not get his chance to go and serve out his career in honor and to be promoted to lieutenant colonel in the Nam. "I am packed and ready to go," he told the assignment people at the Pentagon. "You are not going anywhere, Caldwell," they riposted. "You are retiring right now." Yes, the army does not like political interference, even if it comes from the POTUS, the commander-in-chief. But "I am packed and ready to go" became a stock phrase in the family for the next half of a century. And there was occasion to use it often.

There were also breaks in all that drudgery. That is why the army offers a way of life that is basically very satisfying. You are not locked into the same, unchanging rote of doing the same things to make profit for someone else forever—if you don't quit or are not fired. That is how a soldier imagines work for a private-sector business must be like, as depicted by the *Dagwood* and *Dilbert* comics of the newspapers. In the army, the next assignment is bound to be something new, while still providing a secure paycheck, although that was very modest in those days. Some of the breaks in the routine of the 525th came as assignments where he could utilize his ability to speak German.

At one time, he took five German generals to all the major combat arms service schools and to the National War College. The visit to West Point was the most memorable event on this trip for him. West Point is awesome. If you are not a West Point graduate, you might as well give up dreaming of becoming a first-class officer, he felt after having experienced that fortress on the Hudson River. There was lunch at General Westmoreland's table at the eagle's nest-like balcony high above the huge cadets' mess hall below which it overlooks. General de Maizière, his chief German charge, and he were chatting while observing the scene on the ground floor from above, waiting for the host to appear.

As the cadets came in at a slow double time in single file, they continued running in place after they arrived at their tables until they were all there. Then on command, they all stopped, came to attention, and again on command sat down abruptly as one, moving their chairs around them with the same predetermined, fluid motion. They were too far below to see if they also started chewing their food in rhythmic unison. "We too were good at chicaneries like this at the Prussian Military Academy," de Maizière mused. "But that was before the world wars. It would be unthinkable now to expect German citizen soldiers to act like this in our present, democratic *Bundeswehr*."

Another time, in the fall of 1963, it was a group of Austrian field-grade officers interested in air defense matters. After having visited the Army Air Defense Artillery Center at Fort Bliss, they were sitting in a briefing room overlooking the runways of nearby Biggs Air Force Base on the outskirts of El Paso, Texas. Time was passing, and there was no briefing. "We are little people and they forgot us," said a major.

"Or something very bad has happened," suggested a lieutenant colonel who always had a more positive outlook on things.

Barely had he uttered those words when the B52s started taking off from that endless runway that Biggs has. Rapidly, one after another, hardly any space between them, as if in fear of being caught on the ground. He had seen a few B52s back in the hangar at Tinker AF Base in Oklahoma, but those had been just sitting there, tame and lame compared to these. There is nothing man-made that can compare in frightfulness with an angry B52 bomber. The shriek of their many huge engines is deafening. They are an untamed menace of apocalyptic proportions. And they were zooming off into the air now under the pressure of some unknown urgency. After a while, the briefing officer remembered them and came in. He apologized and explained that all personnel without the appropriate security clearances had to leave the base immediately. President Kennedy had just been assassinated.

The next stop after that was a day off in Dallas, Texas. This was meant to give the visitors free time to form an impression of a typical American city. They were grumbling, for they would have preferred Chicago. They had heard of Al Capone, so they wanted to see some real, live gangsters and tell about it at home. But as fate would have it, they were ambling by the court house the next morning at just the right time to witness the assassination of Lee Harvey Oswald, right there in front of a television camera, from the fringes of the crowd.

"He must have known too much. He must have known what special interests organized the attack on the president so he had to be silenced, " the Austrians all agreed. "Now, with the presumed assassin dead, no one will ever know what really happened. The gangster spirit seems to be all-pervasive and working at many levels here, in this country." Austrians are a suspicious lot, for the history of the imperial politics of their country with its long centuries of dark, Machiavellian machinations is part of their blood heritage. But now they were all quite satisfied with Dallas, where things happen like in a typical American city. They could go home with a story to tell.

Another trip was to Lüneburg, where the *Bundeswehr* was conducting armored operations. The United States and the German armies were thinking about jointly developing a new generation of tanks, and this was a great palaver about the two sides' tactical preferences. Once agreed on those, the engineers would come up with the specs for the new *Panzer*. There was a roomful of US and German armored officers busily disagreeing on most everything with an interpreter doing an incredible job of turning everything said in German into English simultaneously. He (the soldier) knew nothing about tanks, but that was not his job. He was there to pick up on the informal conversations about the subject matter by the Germans who did not know that they were being overheard.

The Lüneburger Heide is scenic. It should be a natural preserve, and it pained him to see some of that pristine, fragile heath landscape torn up by the tank tracks. But it was still a relief to be out there after the indoor sessions where the Americans, almost without exception, made a show of smoking huge, black cigars. He, near suffocation, could not help thinking of it as an inane form of demonstrating virility. The Germans saw it that way also and were commenting about it with discreet amusement among themselves. Only, the air in the conference rooms was not amusing. It was unbreathable.

Outside, however, where some of the activity took place in spite of the bitter-cold northeast gale that seemed to come directly from Siberia, it was icy. There the Germans produced a spark of amusement for the Americans. When everyone was properly frozen stiff, contemplating the imaginary on-site maneuverings of Panzer armies, a corporal came running up, assumed an impeccable military posture, and reported in a voice loud enough to be heard by all, "*Herr General, der heiße Kaffee wartet unten im 'Funkahbunkah.'*"

Now, no one in any NATO army today (especially when frozen stiff) needs an interpreter to know that *heißer Kaffee* means hot coffee, but *Funkahbunkah* was a word that had something hilariously funny about it, especially when reported in earnest to the steely eyed major general in charge of the German Armored Forces. The *u* in this word (you must know) is pronounced short, as *oo* in book, and the word itself is written properly as *Funker Bunker*, the warm, underground signal corps bunker, the communications center. Once inside, Funkahbunkah quickly became a byword. "Let's do this the funkahbunkah way" and "Man, aren't you all funkahbunkah about that." It was always accompanied by mirth, and in the end, he had to explain to the Germans what the hilarity was all about. That, of course, blew his cover, but the meet was over by then anyway.

I do not think the joint-effort, international tank ever materialized; it was simply too inauspicious an undertaking. The Germans were not above reminding the Americans that they, after all, knew all about fighting the Soviets and that they were the ones who knew what sort of weapons the "Ivan" is afraid of. The Americans, for their part, chafed under this assertion, for we simply cannot stand other people who have a claim to knowing something better than we do.

Fort Holabird

In due time, maybe after a year and a half at Fort Meade, the army saw it fit to transfer him to the intelligence school at Fort Holabird, Maryland. This was not so much a "fort" as a large, abandoned factory-warehouse complex in the Dundalk suburb of Southwestern Baltimore. To give it an atmosphere of mystery, intrigue, and secrecy, there sat a statue of a female sphinx in front of the main building's entrance. A barn with a pair of large boobs in front of it, the denizens of this cavernous warehouse called their place of work.

Yes, intelligence, as far as the army is concerned, is not an innate or even mandatory characteristic of its members but is something actually taught as a diverse series of subjects. For him, it turned out to be a long sequence of courses that lasted for over a year. Like with most everything that he learned in school, he did not retain any of this classroom intelligence. But he took with him a vivid memory of the small, brand-new, two-story apartment complex where they lived.

There was a seemingly abandoned Jewish cemetery in the back, the unkempt gravesites with headstones inscribed with Hebrew letters. There were trees around the house, for it was built on one of those rare, forgotten undeveloped, rural-looking bits of land that can sometimes be found unexpectedly, like a bright, sunny break in a heavy bank of rain clouds, in American cities. In front, to the east, there was a large open space, a hill that up to then had somehow also resisted development. Marina remembers it differently. We will go and check this out on that last road trip we are planning for next spring, before gas prices make driving prohibitive. They are going on four dollars a gallon now. But then, I cannot imagine America without driving, without the open road.

Two more things I remember about this time. One was a storybook vacation on a farm in Pennsylvania, near Scranton. It was not a guest farm but a real farm where guests could also stay. The third-generation young farmer still knew a little Hungarian. But it was Hungarian and not Magyar anymore, if you can dig what I mean. There was a picture-postcard lake on this farm, completely hidden and fringed by meadows that graded into a regular forest. All the animals were there, down to the long-quilled porcupine. It must have been part of a much larger nature preserve and looked and felt exactly like the primeval North American woodlands that James Fennimore Cooper had described for him in the *Last of the Mohicans*, back in that hospital room in Budapest.

Another memorable thing was his brother's orders for Vietnam, and unlike Jim Caldwell, he did go. He was a captain by now, a doctor in the Army Medical Corps. He was in charge of a field hospital somewhere near Cam Ranh Bay. He (the soldier) somehow had always thought, although he was an intelligence officer in the very same army that was already fighting that war, that they had only advisory functions in the Nam to support the ARVN, the Army of Vietnam, an organization that was always referred to as "allied" troops rather than the paid mercenaries that they were.

But the way his brother described the scene there, his was a real field hospital, with real Americans wounded in combat to be taken care of or to be sent home in body bags. The way Miklós spoke of his assignment there, it was very similar to the tragi-comical story told on the television. It was like *M*A*S*H*, only without any of the TV-series humor. Vietnam was apparently turning into a war in earnest, picking up speed slowly like a runaway freight train. As for him, he got busy talking to the assignment people at the Pentagon and arranged for a tour of duty in Germany for himself.

About his father

That was 1965. But tonight, some forty years later, I talked to my brother, who was asking about my recovery from the blood clot in my lung following my prostatectomy that I mentioned before, and we came to talk about our father. And all of a sudden, I realized that I had forgotten to mention that he died while I was still stationed in Fort Meade. I simply forgot to mention it! That is a sign how marginalized my father had become in the end, in the course of my American life.

But that is, of course, my fault, not that of my American way of life, even though it prompts me to include a line of lament about the latter. What is it that really sets this Way apart from the life that people lead whom I had occasion to observe in other lands? It is not our shopping-spree-inciting malls, gas-guzzling SUVs, ad-ridden TV broadcasts, unaffordable health insurances, in short, our enviable standard of living, but family fragmentation. It is a scourge. It is not that family members do not care for each other here. They do. It is more that the circumstances of their lives all too often act like millstones, grinding to pieces the parts that are meant to stay united. And the pieces are then blown away to distant parts of this vast land by the cold, market-made winds of job-search-dependent survival. What do the poorest of the poor, the migrant Mexican farmhands have to say about this? "We are different from the *gringos*. We play with our children and take care of our parents."

After the wedding in Meererbush, his father stayed for a while in Germany, visiting with friends and revisiting his old haunts in Harthausen. When he came back, Marina's favorite aunt, Daudau, picked him up in New York, and there was a family meeting at the house of Daudau's daughter, Dorothy. Then the three of them, father, son, and daughter-in-law, drove back down to College Park, to their little one-bedroom apartment. It was most fortunate that Marina and his father got along together just fine, there was no problem with that. The problem was that the place was too small for the three of them. His salary did not suffice to rent a second apartment, and his father's income was thirty-one dollars a month from Social Security.

After a few pleasant days together, they all agreed to keep searching for a permanent solution, and his father went back to Omaha, where he had carved out an existence for himself previously in the basement of three very hospitable and Christian-Catholic old ladies who took care of him. Before a solution materialized, however, there was a call from the hospital in Omaha, where his brother had served out his internship. Miklós got there about the same time. He, a doctor, did not think there was an emergency, so they left their father's bedside around midnight to get some sleep. But he died that night, alone, at an hour when darkness is at its deepest. So they did not receive the all-important *apai áldás*, the paternal blessing. Not receiving the paternal blessing leaves a gaping hole in one's life that nothing can fill.

But life did go on without it, and time has the fateful quality that with its passing even the most vibrant and live personal presence eventually fades into an unreal, spectral transparency, after it is gone. But just because I failed to put my father's passing into the proper chronological order in the course of my writing, it does not mean that he has become a specter for me. He is very much present, even if not all the time anymore. But whenever something goes wrong, he is there. "*Nem szabad mindjárt elszontyolodni*," he will then admonish me kindly and reassuringly: "Don't let things get you down."

There are other things also about him that did not fade out with time. Those are the insights of wisdom both about the beauty and the ugliness of the world as he had experienced it. One particular example that stands out for me is that penciled line on the first page of that book that I keep mentioning, the one that made it all the way to the foot of Bishop's Peak from Bethlenfalva. It says simply: *1901 karácsonykor kaptam ezt a könyvet.* I received this book for Christmas 1901.

The chapters of the book all start with a pertinent stanza of poetry, and as the boy started reading it himself forty years after that Christmas of 1901, his father called his attention to this particular one:

Tudás? Nem! Sem a becsület,	Knowledge? No! Nor is it honor,
Erények, vitézség s a hazaszeretet	Virtue, valor or patriotism
Uralkodnak e véges sártekén . . .	That rule this finite globe of mud . . .
Hanem a hatalom s egyeduralkodó	Instead, the ruling power and sole master is
Az arany, e sápadt, sárga fém!	Gold, this pale, yellow metal!
	(my retranslation, with apologies to the author)

The book attributes the poem to Wordsworth, and its title is given in Magyar as *A Világ* (*The World*). It may have been a little early to call an eight-year-old boy's attention to the reality of the world's ways, and I am sure the boy did not quite grasp what it all meant then. But there was occasion for his father to repeat it often later: "This is how it is, but do not let it get the best of you," he advised and showed him by his own example that he did not let it get *him* down. He was truly a man of honor. While still in his own world of old, he fought for the rights of the disadvantaged. He was brave in battle (World War I) and was dubbed a member of the *Vitézi Rend*, the Order of Valor. And his love of country was matched only by his devotion to his family.

But the culture that nurtured him to become what he was is gone with the wind, collapsed as if it had been a house of cards in the wake of those wars that ravaged his corner of this globe of mud. And as he was forced to flee his country, he learned the bitter lesson that all those high virtues, honor, valor, and patriotism that societies create to protect their souls from that pale, yellow master were blowing in the wind like autumn leaves, blowing in the wind like life itself that those virtues are meant to uphold. In the end he also learned to eke out a living on his pittance from Social Security that he became entitled to after he could no longer bear to wield his janitor's broom.

What will happen to that old book of mine when I die? Of all my possessions, it is my dearest. Yet I have failed to teach my sons Magyar as my father had taught me, and so they have no cognitive connection to it, let alone an emotional one. They will throw it into the recycling bin. And I, why should I care what happens to it or to anything else of mine for that matter after I am dead? But I do, unreasonable as that may be.

Recycling some of the past

Anyway, back to the book. He started reading it, I remember it so well, at that time of the year when the cold, gray, waning days of wind, rain, and then snow caused the great, tall tiled stoves to be lit in the rooms of their house in Léva. These were not the open fireplaces that one finds in most older houses in America; they were built to be functional, to hold their heat all day after the fire in them had died down in the morning. But while the red glow was dancing and playing inside them, their doors were kept open, and he would sit there watching the flames raptly, for he thought of them to be alive as they slowly advanced, consuming the sturdy logs of wood piled up inside.

Then, in the inexorably cycling course of the Christian Lord's years, it was time to celebrate His one thousand nine hundred forty-second birthday. As to the boy, he had passed his own ninth half a year ago. The November storms had exhausted their fury by then. It was vacation time, and so he could stand all day by the windows of the veranda, watching the season's first snowfall with the same transfixed wonder with which he watched the flames. From early on, he had always related to such wordless happenings more than to people. He was then and was to become even more so later an interested but uninvolved watcher of the world. Snow came in mid-December and did not melt until the end of March back then, before pollution and global warming changed the hitherto sempiternal sequence of the seasons.

Christmas was always special, but this one was made extra memorable for him by an unexpected circumstance. The custom was, since they moved to Léva in 1939, that he and his brother would walk down the hill from the Kákasor to the Petőfi *utca*, where his grandparents lived, to spend the day there so as not to see the setting up of the Christmas tree, which was meant to be an annually recurring surprise. They would come home after it turned dark and struggle through a light dinner full of expectation of the great event.

Then, finally, the door would open to the magic tree lit brightly by many candles as if it were the source of light itself in the otherwise dark room. It would glitter in silver and gold and reflect the hue of some deep red, matted glass globes. Maybe there were ones of other colors also, but my mind's eye sees only the red ones now. There were also glass birds and other shiny ornaments, but most importantly, there were tons of *szaloncukor* hanging from the branches. This is a kind of Magyar Christmas candy of three different flavors, each piece in its appropriately Christmassy wrapping designed to make it an indispensable part of any proper Christmas tree. Once he got over the magic of the visual moment of surprise (remember, there was no trace of a tree before that door opened), it was time to turn his attention to the realities under the tree. Slowly, of course, no undue haste, no greedy rush, savoring the expectation of good things to reveal themselves.

And this time, sure enough, there was something there in the pile of presents that was to be clearly his that looked entirely different. It could not be a toy in its long, grown-up-looking box! Believe it or not, it was a 22-caliber rifle, a real weapon, and clearly meant for him, not accidentally left on his side of the tree. He was to have the rifle, not his older brother, who was more into things like chemistry sets at that stage. He glanced back at his father to make sure, and he nodded. He was watching his son's joyful awe and consternation with the kind of faraway smile that reaches back into the past while taking in the present and glimpsing into the future at the same time. Seeing that smile, he (the boy) remembered having seen a similar rifle in the gun collection on a wall of the house in Bethlenfalva, and he suddenly understood that family history was repeating itself at that moment.

The ammunition, of course, was to be under paternal control though dispensed freely at special occasions. Such an occasion came a couple of days later. It was on the day before school started again that the *főispán* dropped in to discuss some matter of public concern with his father. Such visits by the *főispán* were rare, for he was the highest-ranking official of the county. In the old Magyarország, the *főispán* was appointed by the king from the high nobility to that mainly ceremonial though highly influential post (after World War I, when the country no longer had a king, he was named by the regent).

The real executive power of the county was the *alispán*, elected by the people to take care of things. The *alispán* at the time was Majláth Laci *bácsi* of Kereskény, the one whose office was on the first floor of the *megyeháza*, the county governance building. Uncle Laci never let him pass his door (when he happened to notice the boy) without a bar of Lindt chocolate to take along for the road ahead.

However, lest I digress even further, let me get back to the point here, the special occasion mentioned above. This visit by the county dignitary happened to coincide with another visit, one that was always a momentous event for him, namely nothing less than the rare appearance of a pheasant in the vineyard on the hill behind the house. A pheasant, if you have never seen one, is a big bird, and the male of the species is the size of a large Rhode Island Red rooster. His plumage is spectacular, and he can and does fly vigorously; yet he seems to prefer spending most of his time running on the ground pedestrian fashion, even though he does it in a more decorous and stately fashion than the roadrunner of the American Southwest.

What's more, it was hunting season, and he had a gun now, although it hung habitually among other, more vintage guns on the wall in his father's study. So he chose to appear quietly, so as not to disturb the discussion of the grown-ups, in the large, open double door to that room where they were sitting. He just stood there simulating patience, but he was very ready for action, for he knew quite well that a pheasant cock is restless and does not stick around in one place forever. Also, the winter sun was already westering, and soon it would be too dark to see and aim at his quarry properly.

At length, his father looked his way. "*No, mi az, fiam?*" ("Well, what's up, Son?"), he said kindly, although he normally did not like a business meeting to be interrupted for any reason. "*Fácán kakas van a szőlőhegyen,*" he replied quickly, pointing to the gun to clarify the situation. "So a pheasant cock is in the vineyard," said the *főispán* who was a great hunter and who organized the annual foxhunt for the local gentry. "But surely you do not think to bag him with that little 22-caliber? The best you could do is to break his wing, and then a fox would get him in the end." He shook his head. "I will aim for that red patch around his eye. So I need only one bullet. If I miss, he will run away unhurt."

And with that, off he was with his gun, sneaking up furtively through the snow among the grape vines up to the meadow at the top of the hill where in the spring, the yellow june bugs fly (remember?) and where he hoped his prey would still be around waiting for him. And there he was, busily looking for something in the snow-free patch under the yellow-cherry tree. But as is the habit of his kind, he was jerking his head up and down spasmodically, as if beset by a nervous tic. Nevertheless, it was a lucky shot.

As he was slowly walking down the hill, with his rifle cocked open resting on his right arm, barrel pointing downward, and with the pheasant, headless and bleeding, dangling down from his left hand, he met the two grown-ups who were coming up to check on the situation. The *főispán* did not even look at him but said to his father (but so that he could hear it): "*Gratulálok. Ez a gyerek egy valódi stüszi vadász.*" I can guess now with all the hindsight that I have accumulated since then that his father must have derived even greater pleasure from being congratulated on his son's being a real "*stüszi*" hunter than the kid did from getting the gun in the first place. But to this day, I do not know what *stüszi* means and what its etymology might be.

This was the father whose death I almost forgot to mention. I revered him before he crossed the ocean and admired him afterward. For he fought the hopeless fight here so well that even Krishna would have been proud of him. He had lost all that had mattered to him but had to live on while life lasted. That was the way he saw it, and he told me so sometimes, when he could no longer repress his suffering. And he did it as cheerfully as he could manage, for he was no introvert.

But in the end, his spirit did break, and when that attack also broke his heart, I was not with him. We flew back to Omaha, my brother and I, when we got the bad news. He was already in the hospital. His lips and fingernails were blue. But my brother and I thought he would make it through the night, and we left to get some sleep. So he died alone that night. We did not get our last paternal blessing. I too will die alone.

Frankfurt

In due time, the army intelligence school decided that he was now intelligent enough to be turned loose on the Red Menace on the Eastern Frontiers of Freedom. This time the army took care of all the pesky details of the move to Germany. They packed his growing stock of household goods and shipped it to Frankfurt (am Main), care of the 165th Military Intelligence Company, his new assignment. This was not really a company (that is an infantry term) but a military intelligence region responsible for counterintelligence operations in the German state of Hessen, including that chunk of the border that included the Fulda Gap, the expected invasion route of the Red Army.

The brat: on raising children

But first, there was an episode en route that the controller recorded carefully. The rest of the passage on that curious mix between troop transport and ocean liner, although it must have been pleasant like the other pages in the diary of their lasting honeymoon, got blurred and buried in the shifting sands of time. But this one is worth recording, for its message will resound later.

For meals, they were assigned to a table that they shared with the family of an army chaplain. He had the airs of a kindly, mild-mannered man in the uniformed service of the Lord with the insignia of a cross on his lapels and the gold maple leaf of a major on his shoulders. He had a wife along who seemed to bear the burdens of her station with dignity though not always with perfect equanimity. There was something in her conversation, perhaps some discontent with her unassuming husband, that kept reminding him of that strong, old male myth that women prefer the company of masterful men. But maybe she was just unhappy about his new assignment and afraid of life in a foreign country where everything would be unfamiliar and alien to her.

He had observed this attitude later in Frankfurt, where most American military families spent their entire tour cooped up in their fenced housing area with their PX, their commissary, their chapel, their movie theater, and their miniature golf course without ever venturing out to take advantage of their glorious chance to experience something really new and different.

However, this couple at their dinner table also had a real and immediate trial to endure. It was their preteen son. It was a little brat who had mastered the art of infuriating, sassy obnoxiousness to a most remarkable degree of perfection. I say this as judgmentally and unkindly as I can to reflect on the importance of the situation: it could have been a rare "teachable moment." One that they should have studied and taken to heart to store away the lessons for future use.

The kid refused to eat anything but peanut butter. But that he did all day, in spite of his parents' desperate entreaties, which then only pushed new buttons known only to him. Perhaps it was his way to protest this move, punishing his parents for it and for who knows what other perceived injustices. He certainly succeeded in making them miserable, and they were visibly embarrassed in front of the young couple at their table that observed the scene with perhaps not well enough masked astonishment and disapproval. "We," their inexperienced faces might have been telling the parents, "will make sure to do a better job raising our children when our time comes."

Looking back now at that episode that they both remember well, they regret their aloof and judgmental attitude. Had they been less callow and inexperienced (they never even babysat), they might even have tried to draw out the kid to see what was bugging him so deeply. That way they might have learned something during that ocean crossing that would have stood them in good stead a few years later. Instead, it would take them a very long time to realize that children can feel "culture shock" and react with resistance and even panic to unavoidable changes and unreasonable attitudes, the reasons for which they have no way to understand.

And this apparently happens to children when they are raised within a culture that is foreign to their parents (as America was to us), to whom the rules of that culture's game feel alien. The parents, and this was our own lot, then try to swim against the current of their environment, while the children want to accept the culture that surrounds them as their natural element and swim with the flow. A lack of understanding, of closeness, and of mutual confidence can result from that, a feeling of alienation right there in the middle of the struggling little nuclear family.

Such children might then search for identities that set them apart from their parents. And when that happens, it takes a lot of work to bridge the culture gap in the end. But how could they see that coming while they tried to make small talk with the chaplain and his wife? They were young and self-assured, and above all, they felt different and were probably even proud of it. In time, they would learn what life does to such differences: "*Das Schicksal setzt den Hobel an, und hobelt alle gleich*" ("Fate applies the plane and cuts them all down to size").

On the job in Germany

The name of the game he was to play in Frankfurt at the 165th was border operations. The "Company" was responsible for counterintelligence activities within the state of Hessen. There, the US Army's V Corps, whose headquarters occupied the huge, old IG Farben Building in Frankfurt, rode herd over a considerable concentration of American soldiery, with the mission to stem a Soviet invasion through the Fulda Gap. Also, it was charged with watching a good stretch of the uneasy border with East Germany. The strip of land on the other side of this border was then a fortress of minefields and barbed-wire installations studded with watchtowers manned by guards under orders to shoot first and think later. His job as border operations officer was to know what was going on along it and to evaluate and report any suspicious activity. To help him with this, there were three field offices under his supervision in towns close to the border. One was located in Fulda itself.

Fulda is and had been now for some twelve hundred years, a small but important focal point of European civilization. Founded at a time when a squirrel still could hop from one end of the continent to the other without leaving the canopy of a primeval forest, it was first a monastery tucked away in a hidden valley not all that far (relatively speaking) from the site where in the middle of the god-forsaken, cold, wet, endless northern wilderness, some of the last elite legions of the Roman Emperor Augustus were annihilated by an army that must have looked to the lords of the proud empire like a motley horde of inconsequential barbarians.

That is the kind of pride that makes empires crumble and fall. Then, in time, it became the seat of the ancient and venerable see of the Lord Bishops of Fulda. The focal point for him, of what was now a charming town largely untouched by the last war, was Saint Michael's, a pre-Romanesque chapel built in the early ninth century. It is the oldest sanctuary of the then new (now old) religion northeast of the Roman *limes*.

He would often go to Fulda to maintain liaison with the S-2, the intelligence officer, of the Eleventh Armored Cavalry Regiment stationed there. But it was not only business, the call of duty, that drew him there; he simply enjoyed the spirit of the quaint old town as well as its fine culinary offerings. And it was a relief from traffic-choked, big-city Frankfurt. He loved this job. The mission, the gathering of intelligence, was not arduous, for nobody along the chain of command seemed to be anxious to read a lot of reports, but it gave him an official excuse to do what he liked to do: walk the border and chat with the German customs officials and members of the *Bundesgrenzschutz*, the German border guards. To a man, they were always amazed to meet an American who did not have a German name but could talk to them in their idiom with ease.

They were conservative, belonged mostly to the right-wing Christian Democratic Party, and were very pro-American. In view of the harmony of their mutual political and professional views and expertise, there was little need for shoptalk. Instead, the conversation revolved mostly about things like the various ways to hunt rabbits and the ability of government-issue boots to stand up to cold mud and snow slush. But when they looked at the guard towers on the other side of the minefields, the German officials sighed. "Those are our kinfolks over there.

They are like us, and yet we are starting to think of them as the enemy," they would venture to say. "Sometimes we think we hate them."

Could it be that creating this kind of alienation within a people was a conscious part of the grand design for a better future world that the victors envisioned in Yalta? Or was it simply the age-old victor's and occupier's stratagem of divide and rule, a power-political *agendum* that may work for the overlords of the moment for a moment in history. But it is a sowing of this kind of ill seeds that always ends up in the reaping of a bitter harvest. As for his professional purposes, however, these German border officials were really the source of most information on all the little incidents along this new American *limes*, for his own staff at the border stations, not being able to communicate with the locals, only made perfunctory and fruitless ventures out into the "field."

Off the job in Germany

That tour of duty in Germany was not work only. They also took two memorable vacations. For him, both were inspired by glimpses into the future that he first had long ago, in Icking, about a world that was back then only one of fantasy, a world *az óperenciás tengeren is túl*, beyond the Sea of Operencia. What lay even beyond this sea was for Magyar consciousness—at a time when the country was locked into the confines of Turkish and after that of Austrian imperial hegemony—was not unlike what one could expect after falling off the edge of the two-dimensional, flat world of medieval times before Copernicus had published his seminal book on the movements of heavenly bodies: *De Revolutionibus Orbium Cælestium*. That is, the world that existed beyond the upper course of the Austrian river Enns (*Oberenns = óperencia*) was mythical, inaccessible territory for most everyone except for a tiny, privileged upper class.

By now, of course, the curtains of the mythos had long been lifted in theory, but in practice, places like England and Sicily were still beyond reach during that time of war in Léva and during that time of austerity in Icking, immediately after the war. And it was there in Icking that he had read *A Child's History of England* by Charles Dickens in the seventh grade and memorized the poem "*Kennst du das Land* (Sicily), *wo die Zitronen blühn*" by Goethe.

The first one, that concise yet comprehensive, gripping story by the great storyteller started in the times now shrouded in the cold mists and fogs of a past beyond memory, that of the Druids of Stonehenge. A few years later, this impression was reinforced for him by descriptions of that island in the faraway Northern Seas by the likes of Thomas Hardy and Emily Brontë. The second one, the poem about "the land where the lemon trees bloom" also refers to an island, but a warm, sunny, Southern one, so completely different, at least in his child's imagination, from the one in the North. "A land, where the golden oranges glow in the deep-green foliage." Oranges that appeared in Léva only at Christmas time, if at all.

Yes, he wanted to go there and experience it like Goethe did, ever since he had internalized that poem. And now the time was ripe to see both those northern and southern ends of the world. For today's *blasé* traveler, to whom every place is within the easy reach of an airport, this slow lifting of the curtains of accessibility to faraway stages of the world must be a feeling difficult to understand.

For Marina, there may have been childhood associations with these vacation plans also, although given the differences of their paths up to this point, those would have to be quite different. But now they were both ready to go and explore, and before long he drove their trusty green VW station wagon off the ferry at Dover on the left-hand side of the ramp. England! I sit here, helplessly trying to muster the courage to say something about it.

> Oh, to be in England
> Now, that April's there
> And whoever wakes in England
> Sees some morning, unaware . . .

It was not April but June when those towering white cliffs first bade them a politely gracious welcome. But they were forbidding at the same time. They were a reminder that this island was a fortress, ready to defend all its unique, esoteric, inbred ways and treasures against all comers while tolerating them for a moment with an indulgent and civilized but nonetheless skeptical smile. As I must have said before (perhaps even repeatedly), he was not all that fond of the legacy of the British Empire to the world, and so he was ready to look at things with mental reservations.

He had read the story of the Boer War (written by a Dutchman) when he was ten and found himself totally on the side of the valiant, losing underdog down there on the southern tip of the Dark Continent. He had always wished that the quintessential white men that inhabited England had left the burdens of others alone, for their incessant selfish and self-righteous meddling was like the proverbial ill wind that blew no one any good around the globe in the end. Like those bloody borders that dismembered Magyarország at the peace dictate of Trianon after World War I!

But once there, he was captivated by everything that came his way, and his reservations were washed away without a trace. They started with the Cathedral of Canterbury and drove on to Stonehenge the next day. In between these two mind-blowing experiences, there was an overnight stay at what turned out to be a typical English bed-and-breakfast place. The church and the cult site were quasi-religious, transcendental experiences of the same kind, for it did not matter to him what the people who built these two so very unlike monuments were worshipping now or two thousand years ago. What mattered was that the grandeur of these creations reflected a spirit of worship in ways that were timeless, as if not from this world and yet firmly rooted in it. That was what awed both of them in a way beyond my ability to describe.

The memory of the bed-and-breakfast place, on the other hand, though a dimension apart (string theory has it that the universe has eleven of those), remained no less vivid. It was the first contact with a live native of the land. Their hostess was a charming woman of the kind that floats on a smile like dervishes do on magic rugs who welcomed them as if they were long awaited, lost family members. She was full of good advice about how not to get lost in England, geographically and culturally. "And what may I serve you in the morning? I bet you want a good English breakfast!" And that's what they got, the whole package of a treat for only a pound (sterling)!

It was a good start, one that set the tone for the rest of the trip, a glorious twenty-one days full of sunshine with only one day of rain, as if England wanted to remind them that it was capable of that also. Stonehenge was still open and uncontrolled; one could stop at the roadside and walk up to it. Next came Salisbury, after which they doubled back to the Cotswolds. Then live Shakespeare at Stratford: Coriolanus. Lake Country, with a genuine pouring of cats and dogs all day: textbook England.

In the evening of that day, they found another B and B, an age-old, two-story house of thick stone walls, thoroughly cold and damp. The family acted subdued but friendly—they tried their best—and as if in apology for the weather, brought in not only an electric heater but also hot tea and some exquisite pastry glazed in different sugary colors. Nevertheless, it was a *Wuthering Heights* experience for him. The heater did not quite cope with the cold, and as the gale was rattling the shutters all night, he expected the specters of Katherine and Heathcliff both to climb in through the only small window any minute.

Then Scotland, all the way to the northern coast. Loch Ness. The Highlands were the highlight for him. There was something in those melancholy, deserted hills with their abandoned, gray stone homesteads that spoke to him in words that he had always known. It was not some kind of childhood-memory association, and it was certainly not a place where he would have liked to stay for the rest of his life. It was more. It was a kinship. It was a deep, essential similarity of being. The highlands were like a mirror in which he could recognize himself.

> My heart's in the Highlands, my heart is not here
> My heart's in the Highlands a-chasing the deer . . .

Edinburgh. York, the walled city. Most probably even London on the way back, though strangely, that is the one I have a hard time locating in my memory bank. Three weeks only but enough for him to understand now how those descendants of Celts, Romans, Anglo-Saxons, Normans, Vikings, Picts, and Scots, those intrepid conquerors of the steamy-hot plains of the Ganges River, of the sere sands of the

Sahara, and of the barren cliffs of the Khaiber Pass, must have felt when they remembered, in some uncharted, godforsaken corner of the world that

> the lowest boughs and the brushwood sheaf,
> round the elm-tree bole are in tiny leaf;
> while the chaffinch sings on the orchard bough:
> In England—now.

Re-education

Meanwhile, back at the shop, his good days of freedom to roam the border came to an end as all good things come to an end eventually, when he was promoted to major and assumed the responsibilities of the MI region's operations officer. As I mentioned before, responsibility in the army is not a vague notion. It is clearly defined as a command function. The commander is responsible for the honor, dignity, and integrity of his command and for everything his unit does or fails to do, and he cannot delegate it to a subordinate. But in the MI setting, the operations officer is, in a special way, responsible for the unit's intelligence activities, and those were varied and quite complex. To make matters worse, the war in Vietnam was going into high gear, and with that, the image of "the American," as perceived by the local populace, was becoming tarnished.

All of a sudden, it seemed, anti-American sentiment was welling up everywhere. "Like sewage does in the gutters during a cloudburst" was the way one of his more conservative NCOs described it. It was the era of the peace marches. Part of the mission relating to such demonstrations was to take pictures and voiceprints of the leaders while the march was going on, and to identify them afterward with the help of the German Political Police. Voluminous card files were kept current on such people so that one would be able to "take them out of circulation" rapidly in case of "trouble."

What trouble really meant was not well defined, but it was taken for granted that peace-march leaders made common cause with the sinister Evil Empire on the other side of the minefields. You are with us, or you are against us was the rule. You are either pro-American or anti-American. You are either capitalist or communist. You are either good or evil. There are no other categories. And as it turned out, it was exactly this categorical denial of freedom of thought by the system that started to shake him out of his unthinking acceptance of the doctrine of "us or them."

Was there anything wrong with having your own mind? That was the subversive thought that occurred to him one day. That is, why could you not stand up for values that you yourself came to recognize as true rather than live enthralled by a ruling paradigm created by others? That was the question that he soon started asking himself under the pressure of this novel peace-march ideology. And it was not an easy proposition for him. Immigrants, newcomers to an established order, you see, tend to feel compelled and obligated to accept the tenets of that order as a condition of admission to membership.

While some of his soldiers, officially designated as "special agents" and recognizable from afar by their Holabird-issued dark American business suits and briefcases (they looked like Mormon missionaries or Witnesses of Jehova on their rounds of proselytizing), did the work of getting the lead troublemakers on file, he was moved by personal curiosity to mingle with the crowd. To submerge into the throng and ask questions on things that puzzled him. Questions that all that schooling he has had on intelligence never touched on. Questions that were either studiously avoided or that, perhaps, simply did not occur to the MI mind as being relevant.

"We are here, spending our time and treasure protecting you from the Red Menace," he would ask the peace marchers, "and all you can do is demonstrate against us in the streets and call us murderers? If it were not for our sacrifice, you would all be crushed into the dirt by the Russian boot. Instead of hating us, you should be grateful! Don't you see that we are the hope of the world? The generous uncle that gave you the Marshal Plan? The selfless donor of foreign aid to the hungry world? The shining example to all of you how to run a free-market economy, the only one that really works? Why can't you see the light and aspire to be like us to pursue happiness freely like we do? Are you all smitten with blindness, or what?" Of course, not in these same words exactly, but this was the gist of his line.

He got more answers than was good for him. Remember what Dr. Schlusnus told him back in Icking twenty years ago? "If you ask many questions, you get many answers and then you get all confused."

Some of these answers ran like this: "You designed in Yalta the biggest ethnic cleansing operation the world had ever seen that drove many millions of Germans from their homes after the war. The Marshal Plan a generous gift? Bunk. It was the quickest way for you to create new markets to peddle your wares in Europe. Foreign aid to the hungry? A fairy tale. Your aid builds armies and police for tyrants and potentates. The profits from all that then flow back into the pockets of your military-industrial complex to the merchants of death. Free market? Nothing but the ruthless exploitation of the weak and the poor." And so it went on and on. He did not argue. His goal was not to enlighten or to convince. He just wanted to know what it was that moved them to the street to show their anger and disillusionment with their erstwhile role model.

But apart from all these accumulated grievances that seemed to have washed up at this time like so much flotsam on the tides of discontent, there was the new outrage that had become the central theme: the War. Vietnam. After all, these were peace marches, protests against what they saw as mindless, misguided, unprovoked, brutal aggression. Aggression against a people, the Vietnamese of both the North and the South, that had been fighting for decades now with unparalleled determination and valor for its freedom from foreign domination.

Maybe it was a case of unrequited love: the revered role model, America, had shown its true colors at last. So there was no *Novus Ordo Saeculorum.* What America was doing was the same old imperial power play. That was the way those people on the street saw it. Sending a French occupation army to Vietnam in US Navy ships to reestablish colonial rule there. Sabotaging the Geneva resolutions that guaranteed free elections for the entire country. Artificially dividing the country into North and South. Setting up a puppet regime in Saigon to supply American-paid local mercenaries to fight for American interests. But most important, the increasing brutality of the US military involvement: Napalm, carpet bombing, mass use of agent orange, and condoning the use of torture practiced by the mercenary allies to save American lives.

One of the peaceniks gave him a little Suhrkamp-edition book by Horleman and Gäng: *Vietnam, Genese eines Konflikts* (*Genesis of a Conflict*). He read it and was appalled not only about the story it told, but even more so by his ignorance of the specifics of that story. Incredulous, he researched similar sources compiled by Americans (e.g., United States in Vietnam by G.M. Kahin and J.W. Lewis), for the story sounded too incredible to be true. Because if it were true, there would be no escape from its consequences. His side would be that of the bad guys. And he would be one of them.

Guardedly, he mentioned his findings to his commanding officer. "That's all bullshit" was the man's take on the matter. "We have an ally in Saigon, and if we do not stand by him loyally, no one in the world would ever respect and trust us again. We have a job to do there, so let's do it and let the POTUS do the thinking."

Now, forty years later, I hear the identical arguments trying to justify our latest tragic "mistake." An eerie *déjà vu.* Only, what makes it even more eerie is this feeling I have, that this time it is different, for these troops that we are sending to Baghdad are the last legions that we have. Like Caesar Augustus did two thousand years ago. He (Augustus) could not understand why those barbarians up north were not happy to become civilized like he was. Perhaps those barbarians thought the august emperor was the incarnate devil. Just as we and our leaders cannot seem to fathom the Muslim mind and its reluctance to accept the blessings of what they see as the Great Satan.

But our current debacle is different from Vietnam, for this time, we cannot afford our escapade (we could not really afford it then either). It is not "guns and butter" now, as it was in Lyndon Johnson's time. This adventure in the Middle East now is all on borrowed money, while our society at home is falling apart for the lack of it. Health care is too expensive; the war is not. Thus do empires fall in the end. Senator McCain and his soul mates in the US Senate do not see it that way now, and neither did the Roman Senate see it that way two thousand years ago. But more on that later if I ever get there.

In the meantime, closer to home, the plot was thickening for him in Frankfurt. His doubts were rising and gelling. Was he still with the "good guys"? Was the commitment of his army and of his country in the Nam morally supportable? "My country, right or wrong" was again the favorite slogan in the professional, volunteer part of the military that was becoming increasingly uneasy now. But it was not understood in the sense used first by Carl Schurz a hundred years ago ("If right to be kept right and if wrong to be set right"). It had acquired a much simpler interpretation. The patriotic thing now was to follow blindly whatever the orders were (even if wrong), for they came from one's "country." *But how can my country be wrong?* he kept asking himself. My country is made up of millions of kind and decent people. My country is the reality of all those people on the one hand, while it is also an abstract concept on the other, one of high values, virtues, and ideals.

His country could not be wrong, ever. What could be wrong and what was wrong now, he was in the slow and tortuous process of concluding, were the politicians who decided the country's fate based on a kind of misguided motivation that was a mixture of perhaps sincere but ill-informed convictions, of personal pride and prejudices, and of shrewd maneuvering to keep getting elected in order to stay in power.

Like President Johnson, who repeatedly reassured him on television during his election campaign that he would never send American boys to Vietnam. But once elected, he changed his tune: "I will be damned if I am the first American president to lose a war" (that's the way I remember his words). And in he sent the American boys to serve not the country's best interest but his own bloated self-image.

About a year after this last sentence was written, I must add an amendment here. I just saw a splendid presentation by Bill Moyers on Public Television. Bill was remembering his time in the Johnson White House and showed the president in conversations with his advisers agonizing over his decisions on what to do or not to do about that war. That show changed my mind about Johnson. He really did some heavy soul searching before he sent the troops in (including me). But it was the wrong decision, and in his heart of hearts, he must have known it. That was why he agonized so much. He must have known that his decision was based on politics and not on the courage of his innermost convictions. And that was what broke him in the end. I think. Was President Bush the Second capable of agonizing over right and wrong? I wonder.

While his own agonizing was slowly taking shape, he was given command of his unit. His boss, Lieutenant Colonel Parker (one fine role model of an officer), had left for the Nam, and he became the new boss. By then, he had learned most of the ins and outs of the job, felt secure in it, and enjoyed it tremendously. He had thirty-two officers and over two hundred enlisted men under him and was quite free to operate within the loosely defined limits of the mission.

The next higher boss was in faraway Stuttgart, a highly respected "full-bull" colonel with whom he had an easy, cordial, professional relationship. And his new job was a battalion-level, lieutenant colonel's command position, which he was privileged to hold as a major. Command positions are coveted in the army, for they are the most prestigious ones and lead to recognition and promotion. He was on his way up. Only, the milestones of such a road leading upward had to be marked by unquestioning obedience to orders and a wholehearted agreement with the mission, whether right or wrong. And Vietnam was wrong, tragically wrong; it was now dawning on him painfully.

Italy

But by this time, a year had gone by, and it was time for another vacation. Sicily, "the land where the lemon trees bloom." Just getting there was like an adventure in wonderland, but unlike that of Alice, each stage of this one had expectation-filled associations. Verona! His brother Miklós had played the lead role of Valentine in the *Two Gentlemen of Verona* back in Icking, an event that had the brothers study up on that wondrous city at the southern feet of the Alps, that great, forbidding, cold, and snowy barrier to the fairy-tale land of the South.

And Verona did not disappoint; the great annual outdoors production of Aida included. Bologna! That was the place whose renowned medieval university had sent its best scholars and artists to the court of King Mátyás to help him create a castle and a culture at Visegrád on the Danube. A storied lifestyle in the renaissance spirit back in the country's Golden Age before the Turkish invasion and the disastrous, lost Battle of Mohács in the early fifteen hundreds. The age that was described in detail in that often-mentioned favorite book of his.

Rome! The associations were too numerous. They started with fifth-grade Latin grammar (*agricola terram arat . . .)* in Léva and then moved on to Caesar's exploits (*Gallia divisa est in partes tres . . .*) in Icking, and finally to Cicero (*Quo usque tandem abutere, Catilina, patientia nostra . . .*) at the AKO in Bad Godesberg. The main emotional tie, nonetheless, was that huge tome of a book by Felix Dahl: *Ein Kampf um Rom*. No matter that this "Battle for Rome" was fought more than a thousand years ago, that was his Rome until he saw the real one and had lunch on the steps of the Fontana Trevi. A Lucullan feast of fresh white *pane*, mortadella sausage, and pecorino cheese, all washed down with a glass of cool Est, Est, Est, the wine of emperors. All planned, procured, and provided by Marina. Of all the glories of Rome, the controller saw fit to save this one clearly, while erasing the slate of all the others more or less completely. Cosenza! Calabria is dry country even in the spring, and its river was more of a trickle than the torrent

Nächtlich am Busento lispeln	Dark of night on the Busento
bei Kosenza dumpfe Lieder,	Mournful chants murmur at Cosenza,
Aus den Wassern hallt es Antwort,	Answers echo from the waters,
in den Wirbeln klingt es wieder . . .	And resound from the eddies . . .

described by von Platen in his poem of the burial of King Alarich of the Goths. But it did not matter that the Busento was no whitewater like the one in the poem, for the *corso* of Cosenza made up for it in the evening. It was a turbulent multitude of streaming and eddying happy humanity, going nowhere and everywhere, all talking, laughing, and gesticulating in their exuberant, Italian communal celebration of the end of the day.

The ferry took them over the Strait to Messina, and then they finally settled into a picturesque little inn at their main destination, Taormina. That was a tourist town, but a special one, before cheap charter flights had started taking untold thousands of sun-seeking northerners there to flood out the enchantment. They could see Etna send up its signals from the bowels of the earth in plumes of steam and even flashes of fire as seen from their flower-studded balcony. For flowers were everywhere, even though it was early April, but those "mild winds from the azure skies" of Goethe's poetry were, alas, quite chilly most of the time.

Oh, to be in Sicily in June! That would have made the experience ever so much more perfect for him, for he had always been partial to warm weather, the hotter the better. Sicily was still a lofty adventure into whose details I will not delve here, challenged, as I am by my recalcitrant, forgetful controller. Enna, Caltanissetta, Agrigento, Palermo, Selinunte . . . Yes, it was in Selinunte that they came by a memento they still have.

On the shrubby edges of the excavation area of the ancient Greek settlement, a secretive, bearded young fellow stopped them and pulled a perfect little piece of twenty-five-hundred-year-old pottery out of his sleeve with a sly smirk on his face. It was, of course, strictly forbidden by law to purloin art treasures out of the country, and so he wanted only twenty German marks for it, for he was in a hurry. He got them. Marina, who speaks Italian, could have bargained, but it did not come to that for the guy was a good actor and appeared to be on the run and super nervous in scanning the area for imaginary customs agents. Later they made the mistake to have their treasured contraband checked out by a museum. Had they not done that, it would still be a genuine relic. Even so, it is a piece no less beautiful and a fine souvenir of a wonderful time.

Syracuse. For some reason, they decided not to go there. No doubt it was a long detour on their way to Palermo, and they decided to spend less time driving and more time in fewer places. Maybe it also had a cloud hanging over it. A cloud of associations much more recent than the millennia of Greek history there: the invasion of Sicily by Allied Forces in the summer of 1943.

Now, the Magyars had really nothing to do with the Western Allies. Mutual declarations of war with them were the folly of governments, especially of the Magyar one, which was run by a spineless clique of the degenerate "noble" upper class that gave in to Hitler's pressure and menaces.

Magyarország declaring war on America? Give me a break! But these Western Allies made common cause with the Red Menace, and that made them an enemy regardless of the notion's lack of reality. At any rate, a second military situation map, next to the one of Russia, went up on the wall of his father's study back in Léva, and the discussions swirling around this event, with all attention focused on that landing just north of Syracuse, were somber. The Italians would soon drive them back into the sea, some said. A little later, there was only angry derision of the rapidly crumbling Italian resistance. His father contributed little to the excitement of his friends. His view on the matter was that Germany had already defeated itself on the endless steppes of Russia. The new campaign in Italy would be like a tired old horse being whipped to death.

In Léva, however, these events seemed still very far away at that time, and the only tangible sign of their reality was the disappearance of lemons and oranges from the main grocery store on the town square. Those had always come from Sicily, while the Magyar equivalent of pasta, known as *tarhonya*, continued to be produced locally.

So like it or not, there was a trace of a shadow over Sicily for him, for childhood memories remain formative for the rest of one's life. The feeling was subliminal, lingering only half consciously but long-lasting nonetheless, like the benefits of an early immunization against some disease.

It did not interfere with the enjoyment of the present; in Marina's company, he would savor each new experience doubly. She was like a stereoscopic magnifying glass for him, and seeing new things her way made those things not only larger and three-dimensional but also more bright and joyful than ever before. It was no one's fault that the lemons were not blooming yet and that the oranges must have been harvested, for they were not glowing in their dark green foliage like Goethe had promised. Sicily was fine, only it did not speak to him like those Highlands of the North had done.

His most vivid memory of Sicily was of the kind that cannot be shared with anyone and that is impossible to describe. They visited an old building; perhaps it was a museum or the house of some past luminary, a poet maybe, I forget. It had a broad, graceful stairway of dark wood. The bright sun outside ventured in only timidly through the stained glass windows whose dark green and blue pieces, thickly encased in lead, kept the interior in a mysterious but friendly half-light. But the visual aspect of the place was only auxiliary to the main sensory impact. The smell of that wood! There was only one place in the world that smelled like that: the stairway from a side entrance of the house in Bethlenfalva.

The old family home, forever inaccessible now in doubly enemy territory, behind a curtain of iron, abandoned and given up forever, never to be seen again. That stairway led to the guest complex, a side wing, and then upstairs to a round room with three large alcoves opening up from it. Each of these served as the private quarters of the three brothers, my father and my two uncles, neither of whom I had known, for they fell during the first few months of World War I on the Russian front. That was in 1914.

When it was his turn to sit where they had sat some forty years ago, all their possessions, their toys, books, clothes, uniforms, and riding boots were there, left in place, neatly and cleanly, as if waiting for their owners to come home again. Smell is a worker of magic. It can open up recesses of reality again that would otherwise have long been locked and passed out of memory.

When the time allotted to Sicily had run its course, they took the ferry from Palermo to Naples. But they were so overloaded with impressions by this time that their controllers, his at least, went on strike, and that meant a beeline back to Frankfurt. But not without *Kaiserschmarrn* for supper in Innsbruck, which I think, will be subject to mention again later.

Brave new world

Back in Frankfurt and during visits with the family in Munich and Berlin, his political re-education continued. A strong influence in this process, on the road to seeing the world in a new light, was his brother-in-law, Peter. Peter had studied comparative literature for a while at the University of Texas at Austin, but he was too active a person to get stuck in publish-or-perish academia for life. He was vibrantly alive, an extrovert of the best kind, the sort that does not focus his energy on himself but is rather interested in others, and not only in the impersonal troubles of the world at large but even more so in the lives, toils, and woes of real, flesh-and-blood little people.

So he returned to Germany and became active in the revolutionary movement of students that was running particularly strong in the Western Sector of Berlin at the time. Now, these revolutionaries of the Free University of Berlin (the *Revoluzzers*), very much unlike us "intelligencers," were well versed in dialectics. They knew how to debate and knew what they were debating. Their intimate knowledge of the history of recent times rested solidly on studies of the workings of the world of old. They could shore up their conclusions and prognostications with examples from ancient, medieval, and modern history, showing how the shortsighted and self-serving misdeeds of the ever transient high-and-mighty always ended up in long-term disaster.

Disaster that rarely affected the perpetrators themselves who tended to go scot-free as a rule. No, it was always the victims, the little people, who had to pay the price. The methods of presentation the *Revoluzzers* used were simple: "These are the facts. This is what they did, this is how they did it, and this is why they did it. Understand? Okay then, draw your own conclusions as to what the results will be in the long run."

"Take Iran, for example," they lectured. "Corrupt local strong men conspire with the military might of foreigners to deprive the destitute populace of the benefits of the oil, which is their only national treasure. In comes a democratically minded reformer who nationalizes the treasure for the benefit of all the people. The deposed exploiters turn to the CIA for help, and Operation Ajax soon ousts the reformer (Prime Minister Mossadegh). Then a dictator is installed with American collusion, the Shah, and he can now buy all the tanks and attack helicopters he wants with "his" oil to stifle "his" people's right to freedom while he takes his bath in a million dollar, one-piece amethyst-crystal bathtub.

Or take Guatemala. Its "Democratic Spring" that starts in the midforties comes about in reaction to virtual rule and veritable exploitation by one almighty foreign banana company well connected in Washington. The Spring is allowed to last ten years. Then the success of the CIA's "Operation Success" ends it. That end is the violent, bloody ouster of democratically elected President Arbenz.

Or take the KYP, the Central Intelligence Service of Greece, set up by the CIA's Project Pericleus, using an anti-communist terror campaign to prevent populist parties from gaining power. And so it went on and on, Cuba, the Philippines, Puerto Rico, Nicaragua, Honduras, El Salvador . . . It was appalling.

Never had he heard anything like this discussed or even mentioned at Fort Holabird, not even in refutation. Maybe the MI did not even know about what was going on in the world. But the *Revoluzzers* in Berlin did, and Peter did a good job of telling him about it. He invited him to Berlin to provide him with a first-hand exposure to the brain waves of the SDS movement's masterminds (the *Sozialistischer Deutscher Studentenbund* had an ideology similar to that of the "Students for a Democratic Society" in the United States).

There were Rudi Dutschke and his knights around an actual round table, immersed in clouds of smoke discussing incisively the issues of the time, and he could tell that the slogans of the peace marchers on the streets of Frankfurt were echoes of the thoughts formulated at that table. One of the knights even stood up and, turning to the audience gave a short, passionately dispiteous speech about the CIA. By the looks of him, he could have easily been a youthful version of the staid, reasonable, saintly statesman Jóska Fischer, the German foreign minister of our latter days.

The CIA! For him, the CIA in Frankfurt was not the fairy-tale ogre of the peace marchers' stories, but a friendly, younger middle-aged civilian with whom he was duty-bound to confer whenever a job at hand seemed to go beyond what was strictly of internal army concern. The CIA was a benevolent Big Brother who would wisely direct matters to flow in the proper channels. And now, these damned pinko peaceniks had hung a question mark around Big Brother's neck. Was the CIA what it was intended to be, the ever-vigilant eyes and ears of the Free World? Was it dedicated to be the fountainhead of all the necessary information on which foreign policy could soundly and wisely be based? Or had it really become a self-serving instrument of America's economic hegemony over the rest of the world?

Recently, I ran into those horror stories of forty years ago on US world domination again. They are neatly summarized in the book "Overthrow: America's Century of Regime Change." In it, Steven Kinzer cites Eisenhower as wondering aloud during a National Security Council meeting: "Why wasn't it possible to get some of the people in these down-trodden countries to like us instead of hating us?"

Today, one can only shake one's head over such *naïveté*. Was Eisenhower's mind so focused on the golf course that he did not see where his advisers were taking his country? After all, he was responsible for what was happening around him. Eventually though, things seem to have dawned on him, for he warned his fellow citizens in his farewell address of giving too much power to the "military-industrial complex."

But empires do not want to be liked, loved, or even respected, as anyone with the slightest inkling of history knows. Empires must be feared, for they cannot tolerate disobedience by their satellites. Are we now so far down the empire road to perdition that we can no longer disenthrall ourselves from this all-consuming national ego trip?

As for him, he was not enthralled by his place in the army by that time. He just liked his job and the army way of life. And now the very righteousness of it was coming into question. He went to see his boss in Stuttgart and discussed the matter with this good, strong, trusted, and almost fatherly old man (respected leaders in the army are called the "old man" regardless of how old they are actually). "You want to resign? That's nonsense!" the colonel said. "What you are contemplating here I would call self-immolation. This Vietnam thing will blow over. By the time your children are in high school, they will think of it as ancient history."

Resignation

Back in Frankfurt, sitting in the setting sun on the fifth-story balcony looking down on the *Gedächtniskirche*, the bombed-out church left in ruins in the middle of the Beethoven *Platz* as a memento of the previous war, he was pondering how he should approach discussing the impending family crisis with Marina. On the one hand, there was Stefan in his crib on the balcony, and he might want to know one day how many Vietnamese freedom fighters he had killed, napalmed, or carpet bombed in the performance of the job he had agreed and volunteered to do. On the other, there was the secure monthly paycheck, many years of accrued retirement benefits ready to reap in five more years, first-class medical care for life, and all sorts of small but enticing perks and privileges like free travel anywhere where military planes flew.

But the great family council did not take place. Marina came out, and glancing at the ruins, she asked, "So how much longer are we going to keep on marching with our backs to the wind?" That did it. A man cannot be a man when his manhood is being questioned by his woman. She remembers a different version of this, and I hope she will tell it one day the way she saw it.

He got up to answer a phone call and then left to meet a contact at the *Amerika Haus*. That job done, his eye caught a small volume on a bookshelf. Then again, maybe it was the book that caught his eye. It was the current course catalogue of the University of California at Santa Barbara. He opened it. There was a picture of the student center next to the lagoon that opens on the Pacific Ocean. He picked up a pencil that happened to be waiting for him on the library table. He composed two draft letters right there, on the spot. One to UCSB, asking for information about the conditions of admission. The other to the adjutant general of the US Army. Of the latter, I still have a copy:

I, Gabor J. Bethlenfalvay, Major, MI, OF106498, hereby tender my unqualified resignation from the Army under the provisions of Section III, AR 635-120.

I desire to tender my resignation for the following reasons:

a. As the officer's oath of office requires unquestioning support of official policies, the officer, whose disagreement with such policies constitutes severe conflict of conscience, must draw the consequences and seek termination of his obligation.
b. As in my conscience and judgment our present policy in the pursuit of the war in Vietnam is in violation of our ideals, as well as contrary to our interests, I do not wish to remain an active executor of this policy.
c. In tendering this resignation, I am not only sacrificing almost two decades of work, experience, promise for future advancement, and considerable accrued benefits for myself and my family's material security, but also a cherished way of life and a chosen career. Etc.

This was heartfelt but sounds today somewhat pathetically orotund, even to me. The epistle worked its way up through channels to the Pentagon. Each echelon added an endorsement, recommending approval. The army processes such a "personnel action" meticulously. While it goes up the chain each echelon offers a comment or opinion; the decision-making level decides, and then it is endorsed down the chain again. This is called the "reply by indorsement" method or RBI. It lets the originator of the action know exactly what happened along the line.

Well, the adjutant general displayed little enthusiasm or compassionate understanding for the major's plight in his decision. He just said with dispassionate unconcern, "You incurred so many years of service obligation when you accepted your Regular Army Commission, and you have to serve them out." He did not even add, "Especially now that we have a war going on and we need every swinging *schwanz* to go to the Nam." But not much later, in another letter, he did remember the major and added, "And that's where you are going next."

So that was that, a done deal now. There were three choices of action open to him. Flee to some foreign country (most, who were inclined to do so, went to Canada) and spend his years in ignominious exile. Refuse the orders and go to Fort Leavenworth, Kansas, and spend some five years of hard labor at the Federal Penitentiary there. Finally, opt for the easiest course and put in that year in the Nam.

Now there was a family council, and they decided on the Nam option. It was somewhat cowardly, in view of all those emotional convictions to the contrary, but it was the realistic choice. After all, there was Stefan to think of. His deployment to the War Zone was still somewhat removed, and so life went on in Frankfurt for a while. They did not even pull his Top Secret Clearance; his very much less than whole-hearted commitment to official policy did not faze the system in the least.

Closing out Frankfurt

But UCSB was reasonable. It wasted no time in writing back. It said everything was okay for him to come and suggested a number of courses that could be taken by correspondence that were general educational requisites for graduation with a BS degree in biology. Courses like American literature, anthropology and *philosophy*! He started on them right away. They turned out to be quite demanding. The lectors apparently took their job seriously, and the assignments that he returned for evaluation and grading were scrutinized scrupulously. He was impressed by the University of California. And he enjoyed these courses and benefited by them. The controller also took note, and I can still remember many of the details of that effort. Some would find it an obtuse idea now to spend one's evenings into the late hours with correspondence courses instead of watching television. But there was no TV set in their house yet, and Marina was equally interested in these subjects. So they did much of it together. Like deciding where the feet were in the iambic structure of a poem, writing an essay on an episode of the *Spoon River Anthology* or analyzing Kant's thoughts on pure reason.

All along, he was still commander of an MI region on the very border of the Evil Empire. But the intelligence business of neutralizing subversive enemy activity was a bit of a sideline for him because that seemed to be the attitude of his entire official establishment. "Manage your resources," the colonel exhorted his subordinate commanders at meetings in Stuttgart. The "resources" were things like the motor pool, the equipment, the funds expended in operational activities, and the like. The colonel did not say, "Catch me some spies."

And that they never did catch one must have gratified but also mystified Colonel Comrade Vladimir Putin on the other side of the minefields. He may have wondered if this was proof of his own prowess in training his agents or of his adversaries' ineptitude to sniff them out. Or maybe he (Putin) knew exactly what was the matter with the intelligence effort on the free side of the minefields. He (the soldier) was quite sure he knew also, even before that limey in Düsseldorf explained it to him.

That fruitful little exchange of thought came about as an effect of Vietnam on the MI establishment in Germany. As all experienced special agents were transferred to the new War Zone in Southeast Asia, the scarcity of resources necessitated a reorganization. So in the ensuing consolidation, another German state, Rheinland-Westfalen, was added to his area of responsibility. Since this was in the old British occupation zone, no US troops were stationed there. The lone MI field office located in that area therefore served more to demonstrate a presence and to liaise with the Brits than as a vehicle for serious MI activity.

So in receipt of the pertinent orders of reorganization from Stuttgart, he drove up to Kaiserswerth in person to take charge and possession of his new office. That meant inspecting the premises and meeting the personnel to let them know who was going to be the new boss. And surprise of surprises, the premises were none other than that big old house where Marina had spent years of her childhood and from whose yard they had been so ignominiously chased out a few years earlier by the predecessors of the very same people who were now his subordinates.

As he walked through the house, he recognized one room after another, the staircases, wood paneling, and stained glass windows exactly as Marina had described them. He must have been smiling and shaking his head noticeably in disbelief of such a coincidence, for the agent in charge, a warrant officer, mistook it for admiration of that lordly habitation and commented on their good luck on living and working there.

By teatime in the afternoon, a German-looking and German-speaking fellow dropped in and invited him for *Kaffee* and *Kuchen* to a local *Konditorei*. It was the aforementioned limey, the British liaison officer who not only knew about the timing of his visit but also about his predilection for linzer Torte. He was impressed by the man's homework and paid him a compliment on his knack for research.

"Ah, the personal touch is what counts in intelligence," the Brit said. He spoke accent-free German and looked and acted like a died-in-the-wool local. He, on the other hand, had no one in his unit like that and could not suppress a sigh thinking of his crew of dilettante "special agents." The Brit was nodding understandingly. "We do wonder sometimes about your style of playing this game," he commented. "You Yanks either don't know what you are doing or don't care about it," he smiled and gave an imperceptible wink with his left eyelid that was difficult to interpret. It could have simply meant something like "Don't mind my honesty, I mean it well." But also, calling him a Yank with his good Magyar accent could have been meant equally as a compliment or as a put-down.

"It takes seven years of work in-country to find out where the coffee machine and the outhouse are. One cannot dry-lab intelligence operations like you try to do. You must be able to think like the locals do. For heaven's sake, you guys rotate in and out every year or so. You might as well play solitaire all day back at Fort Holabird instead. Why don't you try to learn some history, geography, and a language in high school?"

He did not put up an argument to defend his shaky position. "Not bad, this Linzer," he shrugged instead. "Thanks for showing me where the coffee machine is. I fear it is too late for me to use it. I'll miss the ambiance here when I get to Saigon in a couple of months." "Oh, really, just like I thought," the Brit said in return. "See what I mean? The only one in your outfit that speaks the local lingo goes to the antipodes. Then make sure you take an extra ration of lime juice along for the voyage. Your government is so worried about guns and butter that it may forget about dealing with scurvy. And how are you going about it personally? Are you taking philosophy and literature courses to prepare you for a guerilla war?"

The guy was uncanny. He pushed all the buttons that would have made a proper Yank see red. And as it was, he did not like the British in the first place (in general, as an institution), for they had helped the French to draw up the new borders of Magyarország after each world war that exiled millions of his countrymen into hostile neighbor states, including the ones who lived in Léva and Bethlenfalva. But he could not help liking this guy who said it the way he saw it (and the way it was, unfortunately). He felt he could have learned more from him about intelligence in a week than in a year at Holabird.

"Any of you speak Vietnamese?" the Brit wanted to know next. "Or are you going to use interpreters all the time? Mark my word (old sport) you are going to use the polygraph trying to find out if your interpreter is on your side or on that of the enemy, and you will use him to interpret what he said." He (the Brit) found this last one so funny that he almost choked on his tea laughing. "Yes, I bet you are already using lie detectors over there on people whose moral codes are an impenetrable mystery to you. What if they think that lying to you is a patriotic virtue? Will your detector register that as the truth?"

He sipped his coffee with the whipped cream on top, started on his second piece of Linzer, and listened with half an ear to the lime juicer who, clearly happy to have met a patient ear, started expounding on the pitfalls of empire now. "Your problem is that you are rushing things. You rush into countries with ancient cultures, thinking that they will lay down carpets of flowers for your tanks to roll over on their way to enlightening them about the proper American way to live their lives. Empires grow slowly and must learn to rule as they grow. But you think you are above learning from anybody else. You think adopting your ways must be everybody's ultimate day dream."

An extrovert would have joined battle over all this. Instead, his controller got to musing about trivia. "Why does it take seven years?" it asked without verbalizing it. "Does it take seven years because seven is a magic number? High school does not take seven years but it takes more than seven for the Ph.D. Or maybe because there were seven Magyar tribes that conquered the Carpathian Basin?" Or because I was born on the seventh of May?" Then the interpreter's problem surfaced from his memory pool.

A colonel was questioning him back at Fort Campbell about his motivation and aptitude to become an officer as part of the preparation for assignment to OCS. He brought up his command of two foreign languages as an asset. The colonel made a little disparaging gesture with the fingers of his left hand. "We are Americans. We can always hire an interpreter if we want to talk to a foreigner," he said.

The colonel's implication was clear; we have no need to get bogged down dealing with the non-American mind. We have more tanks, airplanes, and helicopters than even the Soviets do. After we have won, wherever in the world, an interpreter will pass on our ways to whatever local police force we want to train to protect whatever government we want to take over. And then to the lucky populace that will benefit by the regime change that we have brought upon them—for their own sake, of course. Sensing his attention lapse, the limey excused himself, leaving him thinking about his profession as he did more and more often these days. And about the war he was going to join soon.

Thoughts on soldier's pay

You are supposed to go to war with the expectation of putting up a good fight for a righteous cause. *Enthusiastically* would be overstating it; the danger element that lurks in the background always dampens the warrior's exuberance a little. After all, you may get shot dead in the process. Or blown up by a landmine. Or you may step on a poisoned bamboo spike. Well then, isn't all that part of your trade? Or your racket, if you want to put it the mob way. You signed up for it. But if you do not believe in the goodness of your fight, you have problems on a different level also. And it's not only the goodness of it; what matters also is the purity of your motive.

And if your motive is not pure service and devotion to the cause, are you then a soldier or a mercenary? What is the difference anyway? Come to think of it, originally there was no difference. Back in Renaissance Italy, where the concept of paid, modern, standing armies was developed, folks were called *soldieri* if they joined such an organization not to fight for a cause like defending their homes but for the *soldi*, the pay. They were expected to fight whatever war their paymaster wished to wage, unquestioningly.

Opposed to this is the concept of (military) service. A "serviceman" or simply "soldier" in our usage today, bears arms, whether a volunteer or a conscript, to defend the interests of his country. That is, his own interests and those of his friends and family and of all the people of his kind and culture. If he does so because his house and home are in imminent danger from enemy attack, his motive is clear. If he is shipped to another continent to do so, however, things become clear as mud. Still, he may let his leaders convince him that they know what they are doing and that his sacrifice is essential and appreciated by those he thinks he serves.

The devil here, however, is in a minor detail. It is the *soldi*. Back in the days when he first enlisted, the pay was minimal. It was no more than a kid's pocket allowance. You were in the army then for the sole purpose of serving your country. You certainly did not do it for the pittance of money you got. "In the army now, you never get rich, you son of a bitch, in the army now" was a refrain like "Left-o, right-o, ring out the mop-o, left-o, right-o, left!" They marched to that sort of cadence.

But what if the *soldi* takes on respectable proportions, comparable to, or even exceeding what civilians earn? And what if that pay is clearly meant to entice you to sign up with enlistment and reenlistment bonuses in the tens of thousands of dollars as they are today? Is that still service, or is it just another paid job? And if it is just another paid job, are you not a mercenary who fights for money like the *soldieri* of old did?

The fox

Such ruminations are not very cheerful and productive companions to accompany a soldier to the battlefield (as it was called of yore). Yet they were only pale and abstract mind games compared to the real loss he was facing. That was Stefan, his one-year-old son, whose crucial second year of development and bonding he would miss out on. The baby was a sunny and cheerful little character. He already had a hard head even before the bones had time to fully set. He knew what he wanted and would loudly proclaim his displeasure if he did not get it.

He wanted things his own way and very decidedly so. But he was also a good sport and a pleasant companion. He liked to laugh, and there were two things in particular that could crack him up completely. The rustling of paper was one. In the evening, his father's folding the pages of his newspaper would start eliciting a giggle and then the sound of paper being crumbled could provoke gales of mirth that was an absolutely curious phenomenon to observe.

Another storm of laughter was brought on by the gray, tiger-striped family cat. Her name was *Bulle*, meaning "bull" in German. Let me explain this. Although cats are sleek, silky, pliable, and cool basically, there is something unflinchingly strong, firm, and single-minded in the ways they go about the routines of their lives. Now, the next time you pass by a pasture, look past the herd of cows, and at some distance from it you might see a large, dark, stolid presence standing there like a rock, different, distant, and unconcerned. That presence is a bull. That is the way he is, and that is what he has in common with cats. Hence the name of their gray, tiger-striped one who had the habit of licking people's hair with the rough, comblike tongue that she had, like all cats do. And when she did so with his then ruddy blond hair, Stefan would laugh with all the joy of creation. Because of that hair color, Marina called him *Fuchs* or fox, and although those rufous hues soon faded, the name stuck.

Maybe you can tell from all this that the family was very much into all things connected with animals, nature, and the outdoors, and that led naturally to long hikes on weekends in the woods of the Eiffel Mountains near Frankfurt. The Fox always came along ensconced in a backpack, and when they sang one of their *Wanderlieder*, hiking songs, he would join in with his kind of still wordless accompaniment. A favorite was "*Durch die Wälder, durch die Auen, ziehen wir mit dem Fox am Rücken hin and her*," which was an adaptation to the present of Max's aria from a nineteenth-century romantic opera:

> Durch die Wälder, durch die Auen,   Through forests, through the fields
> Zog ich leichten Muts dahin   I was roaming with an easy heart

But now his heart did not feel easy and unburdened like it was when he had first heard the enchanting melody of this song twenty years ago. That was in Icking, where he started in the sixth grade to perfect his German that was to become his second language. Although the situation in the *Schülerheim* was bewilderingly novel and there was very little to eat, the daily chores were simple enough (working for good grades in school that earned him a kind of scholarship) and the future lay wide open like an ocean without horizons.

The school in Icking was a makeshift operation in a converted villa and an attached barracks building. But what was lacking in facilities was made up by the quality of the teachers. School is not a building but an assembly of people (a college) where the ones in the know impart what they know to those who know less, in ways that awaken in them the joy of learning.

Music was one of the subjects of learning, and although memorizing the mechanisms of musical notation remained an insurmountable barrier for him, the study of it was often enlivened by the school piano. Under the hands of Fräulein Doktor Firling the keys of this instrument, along with her pleasant singing voice, brought to life the characters of the Freischütz, describing the struggles, sorrows, and joys of those people of a now distant age. A thorough discussion of the structure of this art form was part of the sixth-grade curriculum. Now, if you are not much into German romantic opera and never saw and listened to one, do not take that loss too tragically. Maybe you have been compensated for that *Bildungslücke* (education gap) by the eardrum-shattering acid rock of your own teen years. But if you have never heard Max's aria, your life will not be complete until you have.

Briefly, this Max is something of a confused introvert. He is in love with Agathe, and although he has won her heart already, he must still win her hand in a shooting contest, which he loses. His luck as a hunter also deserts him, and his resulting discomfiture drives him into the clutches of his fellow ranger, Kaspar. That shady character has already sold his soul to the devil, but he can earn a reprieve of three years if he finds another victim. And so he entices Max to descend into the fell Wolf's Gorge where Zamiel, the "black ranger," provides the ominous seven magic bullets for Max. These will reestablish Max's position as a respected ranger and as Agathe's suitor, but later he will have to pay the price, which the devil always demands (and mostly gets).

In the aria, Max bewails his sorrow and bewilderment over his loss of good fortune as he agonizes over the proper decision to make. And that was very much the way he (the soldier) felt as he was roaming through a forest with the little Fox on his back, for the tune of the song flashed the half-forgotten story back into the present reality of his own discomfiture. He had gotten himself into a real fix like Max had done and was on his way to the Wolf's Gorge of his own time, that still faraway free-fire zone of the not-so-magic but no less deadly bullets in the jungles of Vietnam.

Karma

Was he guilty of some omission or commission that brought this debacle on him? Yes, he lost the contest of the physics classrooms, but that was not his fault; he had tried hard enough, and after all, he did have a diploma to show for his efforts. Given the insight that he was really unfit for physics, what other choice did he have, with Marina's hand, like that of Agathe's, still to be won but to turn for a livelihood to the trade he already knew, that of a ranger who lived by the gun? How could he have foreseen that vanity and ignorance would so overpower the minds of his trusted leaders that they would lead him down the path to the Wolf's Gorge as one of the bad guys?

This time of inner turmoil kept bringing back images of those hopeful, untroubled years in Icking, which were like a golden age in retrospect. During the next school year, after the one with the Freischütz, he was busy with digesting the curricula of both the seventh and eighth grades at the same time to make up for the lost year in the refugee camp at Harthausen. That effort put him in the ninth grade, where Doktor Schlußnus encouraged extracurricular reading of literature prescribed for the higher grades. For him, Schlußnus recommended Wilhelm Meister, and after a while, he asked him to recite for the class that famous poem from it, in which mankind's resentment for its high-handed treatment by the high-and-mighty gods finds such a remarkably well-put expression in a nutshell:

Ihr führt ins Leben uns hinein	You lead us into life
Und lasst den Armen schuldig werden.	And let us wretched ones become guilty.
Dann überlasst ihr ihn der Pein,	Then you abandon us to pain,
Denn jede Schuld rächt sich auf Erden.	For all guilt is punished on earth.

This was Max's problem as well as his own and that of everybody else; he saw that clearly now. Back in Icking twenty years ago, however, they were just a bunch of lofty-sounding phrases of poetry that apparently only the teacher could understand. For Schlußnus was nodding as he listened to those lines. Then he turned his back to the class and gazed out of the window on the villa's snow-covered backyard and the dark fir forest of the Isar Valley in the distance, as if he had forgotten where he was. He slapped his wooden leg a few times with his officer's swagger stick that he still carried with him sometimes. That made a hollow sound.

Then he turned back to face the class. He looked at each one of us as we were waiting for an explanation of those lines' meaning. But what he said was "*Ja, wo nicht geschossen wird, da liegen die Minen.*" Yes, where they don't shoot, that's where they buried the landmines. No one could guess what that had to do with the poem, and the teacher did not elaborate further. But his controller saved this quote as something of potential survival value. And now he understood. There is no hostile fire in the zone where the landmines are buried to make the enemy think that the going is safe. So you venture into the minefield feeling safe. And you feel fine, until you trip one like Schlußnus had. The mere thought, it seems, that you may be safe makes you guilty in the eyes of the gods.

Packed and ready to go

Then time came for him to pack his bags and get ready to go. Marina was very courageous or at least appeared to be so. The Fox, one-year-old, was busy with coming to terms with his new world. It is easy for the one who goes, for his mind is filled with the unfolding events. The one who stays and waits carries all the weight of the burden.

On his way to Travis Air Force Base in California, he stopped in Norman to see the Nielsens. Uncle Jens-Rud had retired from physics and was writing Niels Bohr's biography. In his honor, the physics building was now named Nielsen Hall. The Nielsen home on University Avenue was still basking in the comfortable and cultured peace and quiet that back streets of small university towns provide, especially in early May when the lilacs bloom as they did in the Léva so far away now that it perhaps never even existed. Uncle Jens-Rud was ruefully satisfied that his former student had come to see politics in the light in which he had seen it all along. This war is lunacy, they both agreed, sipping sherry on the shady and screened front porch. That great and graceful institution of the American front porch that had come to life and luster in an age free of car fumes. University Avenue had, at that time, still preserved vestiges of that bygone age.

Then he took an Air Force plane from Tinker Air Force Base to Denver to see his brother, the old Vietnam hand. They had not seen each other since their father had died five years ago. The very different paths that their lives have taken became clear to him during this brief visit. As Miklós's wife, Marilyn, was carrying on incessantly about trivia, he (Miklós), whom he had known as a lively and outgoing type (a charmer, in fact) all his life, was sitting there as if he did not hear the chatter. It reminded him of Uncle Jens-Rud, who would turn his hearing aid off whenever he felt that he was through with participating.

Trying to get his brother involved when Marilyn left the room, he turned to childhood memories and switched to tell them in Magyar. Then all of a sudden, he became aware of a strange and, for him, almost eerie happening. His brother did not switch but continued to talk to him in this foreign language, the same one they had both been using before. Then Marilyn came back. She could understand that foreign language well enough, for it was English. Since she overheard some of it, she knew they had been reminiscing, talking about the "old days." "Ni-i-ick," she said, and her voice sounded cold and threatening to him. "Clear your mind of that old stuff. This here is your home now. This is where your life is. This is the best of all worlds. Forget the Old Country."

He could see a shadow of pain pass over his brother's eyes. Or maybe he (the soldier) just sensed his own discomfort in an unusual outpouring of compassion? Compassion was never a habitat where his self-centered mind did comfortably dwell. But he felt truly sorry for his brother, and seeing his plight, he now forgave him for having changed Miklós to Nicholas on that First Paper in the Port of New York. What luck he has had to find Marina, who was not only interested in his past, but was becoming part of it like she had become an integral part of his present. He tried to be friendly with his sister-in-law but could not get away soon enough.

He took the train to Los Angeles. Riding trains is an introvert's delight, like watching the fire burn in a woodstove is. Or like becoming one with the snowflakes as you watch them fall outside the windows of a warm room. You are safely ensconced in a closed little world of your own in a train, and outside, the lives of others glide by without being able to touch you. A relationship without commitment. You can see them working in the fields, you race them as they drive their cars on a road next to the tracks, and you can look into their living rooms and bedrooms. To them, the train is a lifeless object as it rushes by, one without eyes, but your eyes take them in while your mind spins out stories of their existence in their small towns while the train rolls through like the passing of time itself. Existences, drab, and lonely ones on the margins, or happy and contented ones in the mainstream. But you see them fleetingly only, for one town replaces the other just like thoughts do.

He was six when he went on his first train trip. It seemed to be a long one then; it started in his house in Léva and ended in his other house in Bethlenfalva, a one-day journey of some few hundred kilometers, not an overnight ride like this one of well over a thousand miles. But he has been hooked on the train magic forever since then. "I guess the sound of the outward bound made him a slave to his wandrin' ways." From LA he took a greyhound bus to Santa Barbara and stayed in a YMCA residential hotel overnight. That basic but pleasantly functional hostelry and the whole street were soon to give way to urban renewal and the setting is no longer recognizable as it was when he first saw it.

The next morning, he took his typed note to a notary public on State Street; the note that he was going to use as proof of in-state residence to avoid the stiff nonresident fees of the University of California. Then without further delay, he took another bus north to Travis Air Force Base, his port of embarkation to the Nam. He did not even have time to check out Isla Vista, the student town adjacent to the Campus of UCSB. Outside the air-conditioned bus, the countryside was brown. So these are the golden hills of California, he thought. And they were parched and more brown than gold, even though it was still spring time.

Saigon

As the transport plane disgorged its load of soldiers at Tan Son Nhut Air Port outside Saigon, the troops lounging in the outdoors waiting area applauded. They were going home on the same plane, their tour of duty completed. It was the civilized way to greet one's replacements. A year from now, he would be doing the clapping if all went well in the meantime. And it did, so do not expect an *Apocalypse Now* type of war story to unfold here. It was the other type of Vietnam experience, the one that goes unreported, as it is not a saga of wanton violence, valor, desperation, heroism, or cowardice; whatever war brings differently to each participant.

It was a job. It was the kind of experience that was a curse as well as a blessing at the same time. It was a curse because it denied him the ultimate test. He kept thinking of Quanah and Geronimo. This, finally, could have been his chance to find out whether he was a hero or a coward. This was important, for as an introvert, he had that debilitating, lingering fear that he was really just a coward at heart.

Now he would never know, for they assigned him to a headquarters-type desk job. But then again, had they sent him into real harm's way, the result might not have been a test of courage but rather the relentless grind into brutality that constant fear for one's life can inflict on people.

On war

Knowing that I had arrived at this stage in the writing of my tale, Marina gave me a short Vietnam story to read, one by Tim O'Brian: *The Things They Carried*. It is a fine account of how men's minds can work in the face of danger that has become a routine condition for them. It describes in great detail all the things that American soldiers carry with them in war (which is the point but not the intent of the story). The crux of interest to me in this context was mentioned only marginally as an afterthought, but maybe it was presented that way on purpose to make it stand out even more clearly.

As the infantry platoon of the story marches on from one engagement to the next without knowing where to and what for, one of the men is shot dead by a sniper whom they cannot find. In reaction to the loss of their buddy, the men burn, butcher, and obliterate the nearest village. And their commander, the officer, the platoon leader, just looks on and lets it happen. They had a job to do and this was their way of doing it. "So what's your problem with that?" the reader-spectator might say. "War is hell. That particular Charlie asked for it, so they let his kind have it."

Official as well as eye-to-eye reports of incidents like the one in this prize-winning literary account passed by his desk as a matter of routine during that year. And reading them or listening to them always made him shudder to think what he would or could have done had men under his command expected to do their job the way that platoon in the story did. The baggage of his past that he was carrying would have made him a hopeless misfit in this new type of war waged by men whose code of conduct did not include concepts like chivalry, respect for a brave enemy, and protection of the (innocent) civilian populace. Here, everything that moved was "enemy," the toothless ancients in their huts, the naked children playing in the puddles, the slender girls planting rice in the paddies, and the fat pigs basking in the mud.

The way *he* had come to see the conflict, however, Charlie had a God-given right to defend his country, his village, and his family against the unprovoked, brutal firestorm unleashed on him by the invader. The way the invader saw it was that he had a job to do. And jobs are relentless. Once a job like this war is incarnated in the heads of the powers-that-be, it relieves you of the freedom of choice. The job takes command. You don't think about it; you do what it makes you to do until you finish it. If the outcome is in your favor, it turns into "peace with honor."

Those damn little brown monkeys in their black pajamas! They just cannot see what is good for them. They simply refuse to cry uncle! What an outrage! Here we are wasting our blood and treasure trying to save them from the mistake of running their own country their own way, and instead of showing us gratitude, they insist on shooting at us!

Tan Son Nhut

But to his utter amazement, the army did not assign him to one of the combat zones, or killing fields, as he expected it to do in view of his clearly expressed disapproval of that whole unholy mess. Instead, they assigned him to plush desk duty with the Joint General Staff at the US Military Assistance Command Vietnam, or MACV for short. He was even given a choice of desk, and after an interview with Colonel Cook, whom he knew from Fort Holabird, he ended up as Chief of Information Security at the Counterintelligence Directorate of J2 (*J* standing for "joint" and *2* for "staff intelligence").

MACV Headquarters was a regular beehive. Uncounted swarms of officers, mostly field grade, were buzzing around incessantly, day and night, along endless corridors, and hidden away there, somewhere, was the king bee, the commander, COMUSMACV, General Westmoreland, although he did not get to see him until his farewell address, when he (Westmoreland) was ceremoniously fired for having seen the light at the end of the tunnel a little too often. That light for the general was military victory over a foreign national, political, and cultural ideology and identity. For him (the major) that light was the completion of his figmo chart. This figmo was the outline of a naked woman divided into fifty-two segments. Everybody had one of these charts. Each week you colored in one of those segments, and when the last one was filled in, you got to go to the airport to applaud your replacements getting off the next transport.

Right now, however, he had just finished getting off the "incoming" himself. By the time they bused him off to his hotel in Cholon, the sun was setting. He opened his door to a dark room with the shades down and a radio blaring full blast. Puzzled, he went to turn it off, which sent a man sleeping in one of the two beds fully dressed with lieutenant colonel's insignia on his fatigues to jump up screaming.

"Sir," he informed his new roommate politely, "with your kind permission, this thing is going to be off when I go to sleep here, henceforth." I forget what the man had to say to this novel approach to bed rest, for they both went upstairs to the open patio on the roof to check out what the racket outside was all about. "You just got here for the May Offensive," (that one came just after Tet) the roommate explained upon watching for a while as the fighter planes circled and then zoomed in to fire two rockets each time into an area of low buildings two blocks away.

"We are on the main drag of Saigon's China Town right here, and Charlie must have snuck in again down there along that river course. But this time it's nothing like Tet was," he added in a tone of voice that mixed disgust with grudging, head-shaking incomprehension laced with a trace of involuntary admiration. "Plucky little devils, you have to leave that to them. But why don't they just give up? We call in the jets, the attack helicopters, and the B52s and napalm them out of existence every time," he pointed at the next plane that came in screeching. "Let's go have a drink."

From then on life settled into a routine immediately and without transition. Duty hours at MACV Headquarters out at the air force base were from 0700 to 1900 hours (7:00 a.m. to 7:00 p.m.) seven days a week. Every fourth day or so, there was night duty from 1900 to 0700 hours. This was contiguous with the previous and subsequent day duty and so the whole thing went on for a total of thirty-six hours. After all, there was a war going on outside, and that could be immediately outside, for Charlie did show up a couple of times near the exercise area where he jogged out to every noon, skipping lunch. But the few people who also followed this routine, had their 45-caliber pistols with them also, and being hit by a slug from a 45 knocks you over and out pronto. That provided for a sense of safety.

So the routine had a measure of safety built into it in addition to its salutary effect on waistline attenuation. His canvas pistol belt notched itself tighter every week for the first few months, until he weighed in at 150 pounds instead of the 180 that he arrived with. With the lard gone, his weight then stabilized, and stability was important, for those long days were mindlessly endless. He took to poetry and produced doggerels of the type appropriate for the situation:

> In Tan Son Nhut, in Tan Son Nhut,
> the days are long, the nights are hot.
> You bide your time and chew your nails
> stretched out on your army cot.
> From dawn to dusk, from dusk to dawn,
> what you asked for, that's what you got.
> You suck your gums if lust you must,
> what can you do? This is your lot:
> You watch and wait and wait and watch
> your boots succumb to fungus-rot.
>   And so on.

These products were frowned upon by the colleagues, co-victims, or comrades-in-arms; however he chose to see them on any given day, for unlike him, they were all in a rapid-advance career stage (war may be hell, but it is good for promotions), and he lost the unappreciated small collection in transit home. As section chief, he had two army majors, a marine major and an air force captain under him. A lieutenant colonel was in charge of two or three little groupings like this, and a yet more senior lieutenant colonel was in charge of two or three larger groupings like that, and that LTC reported to Colonel Cook, the director of the directorate.

The colonel was a philosopher; he did not say much, and one saw him rarely. Maybe he was busy. Maybe the rest of MACV HQ was busy also. With half a million soldiers in constant rotation, he was sure that the J1, the personnel people, must have been busy buzzing like bees, asking for and processing more and more replacements. And with the mountains of equipment lost, burnt, broken, and rusted and with the mountains of HE, WP (Willie Peter, remember?), napalm, bombs, ammo, and agent orange used up constantly and with all the other needs and wants of all those people to be replenished daily, the J4, the logistics people, must have been humming like hornets.

Not even to speak of the J3, the operations folks who were the ones steering the course of military action toward that elusive light at the end of the tunnel. That tunnel! It was dark in there. America went to Vietnam to win the hearts and reeducate the minds of the owners and carriers of an ancient culture, who already had two thousand years of experience in fighting the real enemy, the Red Chinese. But in reality, we just wanted to keep that domino that they were for us from toppling in the wrong direction.

Feeling this, Charley hardened his heart and closed his mind, and with that, our cause became a job. We had a job to do. And we did it the only way we knew how—you know how, remember Linz? No need to repeat it all over again here in any great detail. There were more bombs dropped on the Nam than in all our other wars put together, so I hear. That was how we lost our way into that tunnel. We could have given a Cadillac to every man, woman, and child for a fraction of the money we spent on bombs. Imagine how their high regard for national communism would have crumbled in reaction to driving their own Cadillacs!

Back to intelligence once more

My words just ran away with me again, as they so often do. I was talking about the other sections of the joint general staff of MACV and how they might (or must) have been so very busy. But how about his section, the J2, the one of the intelligence people? While the others were scurrying around like the workers of an anthill, the J2 folks carried on like winged drones. Not involved in the mechanics of the blood and guts of the action itself, they saw it as if from a higher vantage point. They were supposed to collect the flotsam of war, assemble its bits and pieces, connect its dots, and produce from all that a big picture for the decision makers at the Pentagon to base realistic decisions on (in addition to a lot of little pictures for the troops to use in the field).

Now, if you are a city person and have never seen swarming male ants flutter around, you may not realize how fragile their wings are. Ants are not meant to fly, certainly not to higher vantage points. So it was an open secret to anyone at J2 who cared to think about it that the "deciders" were not interested in a big picture made up of observed, processed, and evaluated facts. What they wanted to read were reports that corroborated theories that they had cooked up beforehand. And that was what was breaking the wings of the drones. Their business was not serious, important business.

When you realize that what you do does not matter, it wrecks your self-esteem. Men who had worked for him in Frankfurt would come in from Can Tho, Plei Ku, Da Nang, Sa Dec, and Hué (names that ring like an army drum roll to the veteran, but mean nothing to those who have not been there) to Saigon on some business and they all dropped in for a chat. "Hey," they would offer, "just let us know what you want to hear, and we'll report it." What could he say to that? "Hate to hear you talk like that. But I am not in that line of business here, anyway. I am in security, not in collection. "But," he would add, "I have this eerie feeling that even the generals are getting uneasy by now about all those new tunnels you guys keep on finding out there in the boonies."

It was these contacts (and he felt good about his old people coming back to see him) and helicopter rides to the outlying MI stations that broke up the isolation and irreality of that headquarters labyrinth a little. The flights would be over the brown canopy where Agent Orange had done its own deadly, impersonal part of the overall job. The formerly verdant rain forest was dead and brown as far as the eye could see. It was done in order "to deny the enemy cover." But the enemy just went underground in response.

At one of the stations, they kept a tiger in a barbed-wire enclosure. Every other day or so, they would put some live animal in there, a goat or a pig, while the tiger was dozing. Then they watched the screaming terror of the animal as the tiger came to and became interested in it. One time they put a rooster in there, one of those plucky game cocks that the Vietnamese love to watch fight and to bet on. The rooster appraised the tiger but apparently did not see the cat in him. *This thing is too big for a cat*, he must have thought, for he jumped on the tiger's back like he might have done with a water buffalo. Then the dozing tiger raised his head and appraised the rooster. "Too little and too feathery to bother with" his seemingly unfocused eyes were suggesting. With a flick of his tail, he shooed the bird off his back as he withdrew to his own world to think the unfathomable thoughts that tigers think.

An RVN army intelligence captain was there too, watching this. He had come to report some info that they had tortured out of prisoners whom a US patrol had picked up and turned over to them for that purpose. "This tiger is Asia, and the rooster is you," he muttered as if to himself, but in English, meant or not meant to be overheard, who knows? He said it quietly, dispassionately and inscrutably, the way Orientals like to act and talk.

Our troops did not torture prisoners, at least they were not supposed to. It was not what civilized people did. But torture hung in the air, as rage over the impasse in the tunnel intensified the brutality of the action. Somebody may have reported having seen some VC in a village. Then the neighboring village chief may have had a spat with his counterpart and passed his spite on to the local RVN agent. That verified the VC sighting, and as the report reached the Air Force Ops Center in a basement of MACV HQ, a B52 sortie would be called in to pacify the village.

B52s fly very high. You do not hear them or see them. You first become aware of them as their blockbuster bombs hit your village. One of those takes out an area the size of a football field. If you survive, your friends may not recognize you, for the capillaries in your skin burst and your face takes on the ghastly, black aspect, that of curdled blood. Depending how close you were to the impact.

With time, reports started coming in also from the new bombing campaign of the cities of the North. This was greeted with renewed hope, for maybe this would teach Charlie the lesson he needed to break his obstinacy. Unfortunately, some of the planes were shot down, and word was soon circulating that the captured crews were tortured into signing admissions of air piracy, of having killed women and children. Well, like it or not, that is what actually happens when you bomb cities. You kill women and children. Only, the offence, as far as his team, that of the good guys, was concerned, was not the act itself and its consequences, but the admission of it. However, as the signing of confessions was under duress, it was considered to be borderline excusable.

By sheer coincidence, there is a controversy raging at this time (as I look out on Bishop's Peak) about the new, neocon-inspired, vice-president-approved legality of torture by US troops. While it is a war crime by international standards, there is a faction in the US government that defends as justified any act and atrocity (like waterboarding) that may promise to save American lives. Others hold that torture is not only reprehensible and immoral but also useless and unreliable as a basis for obtaining information. Proponents of this latter line of reasoning have recently cited as an example supporting their point of view the experience of one of our war heroes who is running for president at the moment. He was a POW for a long time and was one of those who signed such an admission of air piracy under torture. "See," says the antitorture faction, "this is clear evidence that what is said under torture is not credible. Our own war hero could not have killed women and children, yet he signed the admission."

It is a sign of our times that the uneasiness about committing war crimes seems to be abating. The signs are pointing to the Twin Towers of New York: "They did that to us, so now any response by us is fair game." But how do you handle the publicity when you are not under duress to admit? This question reminds me of an incident (back in the Nam) that illustrates what was felt to be the appropriate answer to that all along.

A well-known reporter (R. S. Elegant) published a story in the *New York Times* about our Green Berets, an elite commando outfit, tampering with the bolts of Soviet AK-47 rifles. They then left them in the jungle so that upon being found by Charlie, they would blow up into his face and blind him. An invalid like that is a double loss to the enemy, for now somebody who could otherwise fight has to take care of him. But mainly, the defective equipment was meant to lower Charlie's confidence in Soviet-made weaponry.

This report, so we heard, caused a bit of an uproar among counterculture peacenik activists at home, for vague though the concept of a war crime is, this was one by definition. So we at the CI directorate got together to decide what to do should the investigation reach us, or should we be detailed to do the investigating. And true to form, the answer was no other than "Shred the evidence and deny everything until the affaire blows over and goes away." He did not speak up. Had he, what would they have said? "Are you on our side or on theirs?" What could he have countered? "I am an American. I do not commit or condone war crimes?"

They could only have responded with judgmental disapproval, indignation, and mostly, incomprehension. For by implication, it would have meant: "But you do." It was his chance to show his quality and he blew it. The project eventually petered out when war-souvenir-collecting GIs started putting their own eyes out with pieces of this "unreliable" enemy ordinance.

The daily routine

But the daily routine at the office involved mostly things like scheduling and supervising the control of classified information, polygraphing indigenous employees, and the like. The actual job was performed by agents of the 525th MI group. It was none other than his old group from Fort Meade, but that once sleepy, stolid outfit had molted into an efficient, operational one here. The various staff sections of MACV HQ all had innumerable classified documents and MACV regulations provided for severe disciplinary action for the officers charged with their safekeeping should they lose one. Nevertheless, they always did. Every inventory inspection that he scheduled came up with several, sometimes even hundreds, of confidential and secret documents unaccounted for. He then always duly recommended disciplinary action, which was always duly disregarded. It was a school example of what an organization should never do: make laws that it cannot or will not enforce. To be sure, there was a bit of fuss and consternation on some occasions, like the one when a smelly product of the fish market turned up wrapped in a top secret document. Still, the offenders always got their Bronze Star Medal upon finishing their tour. He, in turn, learned to shrug his shoulders. This gesture of resignation applied to mostly everything he did during that year.

Like this one, for instance. There were always groups of dark little people lined up squatting near the front gate of the headquarters building. These were drivers assigned to the various sections. There was a strict rule that they all had to be tested by the lie detector. Even though all they did was to drive their jeeps, the road from TSN Air Force Base to downtown Saigon led through heavily congested shantytown areas, and had a driver decided to turn his passengers over to the Viet Cong, they could have easily lost their way into the impenetrable recesses of that maze. So their cooperation mattered. But what did that have to do with the polygraph?

Since you are probably not familiar with lie-detecting technology, let me explain. People who are conditioned by their culture that lying is a sin (or a crime) display certain physiological symptoms upon stretching the truth. Such symptoms can be measured by instruments. This is done by means of sensors applied to the subject's body. But since similar symptoms can be elicited also by simple, everyday nervousness, a reaction that would obfuscate the results, the subject is reassured prior to the test that no surprise questions will be thrown at him. Instead, to put him at ease, the entire line of questioning may be read to him before he is wired into the machine.

As question after unrelated question is then presented in a preferably monotonous manner, it is his cultural conditioning that betrays him (almost always) and makes his body react involuntarily to give him away when his answer is not truthful. But what if he had been conditioned either politically or simply by his wartime experiences that uniformed foreigners are evil and that lying to them is therefore not a sin or crime? That it may be, on the contrary, something a good patriot will routinely do? Why then, the whole exercise becomes a joke.

He tried to explain this to his superiors. "What's your problem, Gabe?" they furrowed his eyebrows. "It does not matter. What matters is that we can show that we had done everything we could, should one of them turn sour on us. And all we can do is polygraph them. So polygraph them." One of the operators, a professional expert of an old chief warrant officer, was unhappy with this attitude. "How can I certify a subject as clean if I don't even know what the interpreter might have asked him?" he wanted to know. In the end, the man quit doing the job himself and delegated it to a lowly Spec4.

Saturday off

This type of routine went on in fourteen-day cycles, for it was the free Saturday every other week that marked the passage of time. He would spend these Saturdays exploring Saigon. That is saying too much, of course, for it did not extend beyond the surface of the city, what one can see walking through it. And even of that, it was only the old, French-colonial part, for venturing into the shanty towns was not only too risky but also too depressing. It was bad enough to drive through those in a jeep, and he did these Saturday "explorations" on foot. He had always liked to do it that way.

His targets were the quiet side streets where time flows slowly with barely a ripple from the war outside, but where small signs of people's fleeting permanence still turn into veritable monuments of lifetimes or at least pieces of lifetimes they spent there. Lives engaged in leaving a lasting expression of their transience. A small shrine, the ornaments of a balcony, a group of flowering bushes, the exotic layout of a shop. So very different in aspect from those he knew from Omaha, from Godesberg, from Léva, from Bethlenfalva, but so very similar to those in the spirit of their common humanity. All of them nothing but the steppingstones of thresholds worn deep by the footfall of the one who passes by it for a day, for a year, for a lifetime. Life spends itself, its substance, its penchant for detail, and its quest of purpose the same way everywhere.

Then, of course, there was Tu Do Street, the main street of Saigon, where much of the foreign presence played itself out, mostly in bars crowded with GIs and B-girls. The old Colonial Palace Hotel was there, and the Caravelle, where the press stayed. But all that is only a blur in my memory now. What stands out are things like that time when he forgot to take his pistol with him, his trusted 45 with its ten-round clip.

He was walking along a narrow street lined with shoe stores and cobbler shops and suddenly had that strange and distinct feeling that surges up in you when you know you are being followed. He backed into a nook in the wall between shops and reached for his gun. It was not there. That provoked an acute sensation of being naked. Like a hermit crab must feel without his shell of protection. There was no traffic on the street and no pedestrians, something he had not noticed before. It was he alone and the footsteps behind him. There are moments in life when you see and perceive every little detail with penetrating clarity. This was one.

Being in constant danger like in prolonged combat probably dulls this kind of clarity after a while. I guess at this only, for I have not experienced it. So he decided to stay where he was and see what would happen. What happened after an interminable moment was a military police jeep cruising along. With that, he stepped out of his nook into the street. "Hey," he said to the sergeant, "you guys on your way to the Colonial?" The MP gave him a skeptical look. It spoke volumes. You did not expect to find field-grade officers in that type of place on any business that was kosher. "Yes, sir," the man answered with the straightest face that he could muster. "Can do, sir, though it is not on my route."

He climbed up the stairs to the rooftop patio of the hotel, where a band was playing from mid-afternoon on, and a cold drink could be had without an ao-dai-clad lady sitting on your lap the next moment. He had his VSOP Courvoisier along with a glass of ice water to celebrate the occasion, while severely reprimanding his controller for the *lapsus memoriae.* He never forgot his gun again, but the controller played mean tricks on him in retaliation for the chiding: since that day, he occasionally dreams of being caught by the military police on narrow, deserted streets—without his pants on.

You might notice that my reporting has a negative tinge to it. No need to take offense with that. It does not mean to suggest that there were not multitudes of well-meaning, honest, dedicated, and patriotic Americans in uniform in Vietnam. Remember, this is not a historical account. It depicts merely the passage of one particular introvert taking in the scenery through the shades of his own particular, personal, dark sunglasses. We all have our blinders. Blinders are what keep horses from wandering off the straight and narrow road. Extroverts have blinders also, don't they? He always wondered what an extrovert's blinders might blind out of the total human experience. Maybe it blinds out the shadows that are darkest in full sunlight?

You might know it. I do not. At any rate, many of the soldiers serving in the Nam were probably true patriots convinced of the righteousness of their cause. If so, good for them. I cannot speak for them. Those who had something good to say about what they knew firsthand about the tragedy that the Nam was for America have probably published it already. The rest is for the historians. But this much-belated reporter has an additional problem. That is the timing of his report.

A repeat performance of the Nam is going on this very minute and has been going on for years now, and it casts a shadow over what he writes. We have not learned. Fooled twice (by our politicians), shame on us (the people). But the extrovert who unleashed this renewed tragedy sees no shadows. For him, there is only the blinding light of his own righteousness. He claims to get his guidance directly from God.

On R&R

Do not make the mistake, however, of feeling sorry for the introvert. Being one has its pluses. When times are good, he can enjoy them more intensely, since for him times are not always good. And times were really good not once but twice while in the Nam: the two incredible highlights of that year, two R&Rs, one in Thailand and one in Malaysia. These one-week periods of "rest and recreation" were meant to reconcile the disgruntled, unwilling conscripts with their fate. By rights, the regulars should not have been eligible for any of it, for all were getting what they had asked for; no need to perk them up with extras.

When a professional soldier, a volunteer, goes to war, it is not some admirable self-sacrifice that needs to be adulated ad nauseam by politicians up for reelection. It is what he does for a living. Nevertheless, he was very happy with the institution of the R&R, for he could spend those two weeks with Marina. Now, recognizing my controller's odious habit of editing out the good and the cheerful from my mind while concentrating on all the less pleasant aspects of the road, I will let Marina report on these two weeks. She is not given to the tedious circumlocution that my Dell Inspiron 2650 likes to produce. She says it straight like it is. So let's let her speak.

Bangkok

A week of R&R in Bangkok, one of the destinations in the Far East available to military personnel serving in Vietnam! We chose it because it sounded like an enchantingly exotic place, which it certainly was, much more so in those days than nowadays, some forty years later, when traffic and high-rises have greatly changed the feeling of the Royal City on the Chao Praya River. We agreed to meet at the Hotel Parliament, which served as the R&R center for the US military. It felt like a precarious arrangement then and does so even now, in retrospect, for it was all by very slow snail mail: phone connections between Munich and Saigon were simply not working. Even our letters at the time show that we were a bit anxious about the link-up.

Of the flight, I remember a stopover in Ceylon at dawn, on an airfield bordered by a marsh, where flocks of egrets were fishing, and the awed feeling that the pristine beauty of the planet was still right there, wild and innocent, at the edges of human civilization, on any continent one might alight on. The signs on the taxis, waiting in front of the small airport, said TEKSI (ah yes, of course!). However, when I arrived in Bangkok, it was evening, and the car that drove me to my destination through the steamy dark was labeled in a completely unknown curly alphabet, as were all the street signs.

At the front desk of the hotel, where I attempted to sign in, giving my name and stating that my husband had made a reservation, the manager looked me over with some concern. After checking his roster and appearing to hesitate for a moment, he said, "Madam, excuse me, but I'm afraid this not so good place for young lady like you." I looked at him blankly. "I mean to say, this is hotel for GIs and their women—much drinking and loud music and . . ." Looking around the lobby, I began to see what he meant. It was smoky and noisy—not the kind of idyllic oriental haven we had imagined. I told the manager that I understood, but that my husband was to meet me there the next day and that I would have to take the room for one night to await his arrival.

The man shook his head. "Better you leave your husband letter and let him know you go to other hotel." He seemed very firm in his conviction that I should not stay there. So I made a quick decision: I asked him to phone the hotel Eriwan for me. This was a place that had been strongly recommended to me by Trude *néni* and Uncle Jens-Rud (remember Norman, Oklahoma?). They had recently visited me at my mother's house in Germany in the course of a tour around the world which had also taken them to Bangkok.

They had a room at the Eriwan, and the manager gave me the stationary for a letter to Gábor and promised to make sure he received it. It was a rather tenuous arrangement, but I trusted this man, who seemed as worried about me as if I were his own daughter. Then he called a *teksi*, and I was on my way to the Eriwan, where the rooms overlooked the wide Chao Phraya River, and I woke the next morning to the spectacle of the river traffic of hundreds of small boats carrying baskets of fruits and vegetables and fish to market. Gabor wouldn't be landing till noon, so I found my way to a market and bought flowers and a basket of tropical fruit to welcome him. Soon he phoned from the GI Hotel, and I gave him directions—and then he was there! I will let Goethe speak for me:

Ist es möglich, Stern der Sterne	Star of stars, is it you, truly,
Drück ich wieder dich an's Herz?	Do I press you to my heart?
Ach, was ist die Nacht der Ferne	Ah, the night of being distant,
Für ein Abgrund, für ein Schmerz!	What an abyss of distress!

How did we spend that week when we weren't perched in our fifth-floor room, overlooking the river with its endlessly flowing and fascinating life, while we looked at pictures of Stefan (the Fox) and told each other about all that had been happening to us for the past six months in the vastly different worlds we now lived in?

We wandered around the city, dodging motorcycles but otherwise feeling perfectly safe; marveling at the ornate temples and palaces; sampling Thai food, a delicious discovery; admiring the wares displayed in the markets: unknown fruits and vegetables, beautiful fabrics of traditional Thai prints, in a rainbow of colors, both in cotton and silk, bowls, and kitchen implements made of teakwood. And everywhere, people were smiling and friendly, the women so graceful in their sarongs, with babies on their hips. We took a boat ride to the floating market, in the middle of the river, which has since disappeared.

There was another market I remember, where among many other things they also sold tropical fish. Some of them were fighting fish that charged at each other even when in separate bowls, banging into the glass and changing colors, apparently a sign of rage! This market was right next to one of the city's biggest museums of Thai art. We spent a few hours there and observed that people from the market, vendors and shoppers alike, would come in for a little while and lay offerings of flowers and fruit at the foot of the statues of Buddhas and Boddhisatvas and bow in reverence. They would bring their children with them, and it was very moving to see their un-self-conscious devotion to these images that we had been contemplating only as art objects. It was our first encounter with Buddhism.

One day, we took a bus to a fishing village on the Gulf of Thailand, a few hours to the south. Pataya has since become a popular resort, I hear, with the same kind of high-rise hotels one finds in other seaside vacation spots. But at that time, it was still a sleepy village, with wooden houses perched on stilts at the edge of the water. It felt remote and peaceful, as we swam in the warm water and walked along the beach, looking for shells—exquisite tropical ones such as we'd never seen before—and watched the children playing in the sand and the older ones fishing in the surf with nets. The nets reminded us of a strange sight we'd seen from the bus: along the highway to the coast, which passed through wetlands and groves of bamboo, there had been enormous spider webs woven between the telegraph wires and frighteningly large spiders hanging in them, waiting for their prey—probably the dragonflies that darted about in swarms, hunting flies and mosquitoes.

We ate seafood in a restaurant in one of the thatched huts on stilts, overlooking the calm sea. To our surprise and disbelief, it was served on dishes exactly like our own set of brown Finnish earthenware plates. How could this be—out here in this remote village? It dawned on us that the Scandinavian designs that we liked so much—whether pottery or teak furniture or wooden salad bowls—had actually taken some of their inspiration from the Far East!

The five days slipped by like a dream in this strange but welcoming city, with its ancient culture so foreign to us, but intricate, graceful, and immensely appealing. A vision of Southeast Asian life, free from colonial occupation and at peace . . . and then it was over. After Gabor left to return to the war, I had a few more hours to wander the streets, drawn back to some of the places, where we had been together—the market and the museum. And then it was time for my flight too, a long one, back to Germany and Stefan and the family in Irschenhausen, where the autumn days were growing cooler and the beech trees were dropping their tasty nuts on the lawn: *Buch-Eckerln*, one of Stefan's recent discoveries and new words.

Penang

Then came the second adventure in resting and recreating. Originally, we hadn't planned to meet for a second time during the remaining six months since the flight was expensive, and I didn't like leaving Stefan (the Fox) so often, although he was taken care of by a doting grandmother and great-grandmother in Irschenhausen. But as the months passed for Gabor, in the unrelieved day-and-night tedium in the office at Tan Son Nhut Airbase, immersed in the bureaucratic routine of overseeing "security" at HQ MACV, living in a kind of unreal bubble, amid the chaos and mayhem of that poor war-torn country, his letters sounded so wistful that we began to dream about another oriental honeymoon, another memorable adventure together during that long year of separation.

As we have all experienced, periods of time in which nothing much happens can seem to stretch out endlessly while we are living them, but in our memory, they collapse and we hardly remember them at all. Whereas days filled with new impressions and activity fly by in a flash, but in retrospect they live as a wide and vivid landscape in our minds. So it was not just to share another happy holiday but to try to salvage another piece of that year from the black night of forgetting that we decided to meet again in January, on the small tropical Island of Penang, off the coast of Malaysia. So in mid-January, I again left snowy Bavaria and headed for an exotic destination.

There was definitely a British flavor mixed in with the exotic in Georgetown, the bustling main town of Pulau Pinang, as it's named in Malay, especially at the "East and West Hotel," where I spent the first night. But the next day, before picking Gabor up at the little island airfield, I found us a smaller hotel a few miles out of town, along the coastal road. It consisted of a group of bungalows under palm trees, just steps from the wide, sandy beach that stretched out endlessly. In the early morning, we would hear singing, and if we walked down to the water's edge, there were the fishermen, pushing their long canoes into the surf.

As we wandered the beach, we would come upon other groups of fishermen hauling in huge nets; they too were singing a rhythmic chant as they all pulled together. We walked along the coast and swam when we got too hot and ate seafood at little shacks and pineapples on sticks until our tongues were raw (pineapples, you may want to know, contain a digestive enzyme). The sun shone every day, and every night, there was a tropical downpour, drumming on the roof and rattling on the palm leaves. Along the base of the bungalows ran open cement culverts into which the water from the showers flowed, and at night, the rainwater from the downspouts made a rushing sound in these little channels.

We shared our room with little green geckoes that ran up and down the walls day and night and would interrupt their hunting now and then to perform a quick series of push-ups and then inflate their necks to an amazing red bubble and utter strange cries of "Geck'o . . . geck'o . . ." They kept our room free of mosquitoes; we wouldn't even have needed the cloud of netting that hung around our bed and stirred in the breeze that blew all night from the near sea.

We had rented a car, and since Gabor cannot long be happy in a new place without checking out its wider surroundings, sometimes we drove around and explored the interior of the island. I remember a temple, a Hindu temple, I believe, with strange statues and candles and incense and many offerings of fruit and flowers. Once, we took the cable car up to the top of Penang Hill, at the center of the island. It rose through a forest of giant ferns and as we passed, we were startled by the deafeningly loud, shrill call of an insect. The gondola was moving slowly enough that we managed to see the creature, perched on a fern frond, outlined against the sky: it wasn't very big at all, just a cicada, but the volume of sound it produced was incredible! From the hilltop, we had a fine view of the entire island, the Indian Ocean, and the hazy outline of the coast of the mainland.

We also have a hazy recollection of many ethnic meals on this multicultural island, Indian, Chinese, and Indonesian, but the one that we both remember most vividly is the one that began with a soup made of ducks' feet. I suppose we wanted to be adventurous and willing to try new things, but those webbed feet swimming in hot water were too strange even for our good will. On the other hand, the desert of sweet almond-flavored bean curd (tofu) was okay. And so the days passed . . . We spent the last night at the east and west again since it was closer to the airport and Gabor had an early flight back to Vietnam. This time our parting was less heartbreaking than in Bangkok. There were only two months left, until the end of Gabor's tour. That was a stretch of time that one could get one's mind around and start counting off the days and planning for the time when the three of us would be reunited again.

Figmo chart finished

Wow! Can she write! Hers is an entirely different breed of controller! And her ease in holding her pen, unencumbered by quirky theorizing! So there, the unexpected treasure, the pebble you pick up at the roadside that turns into a gemstone when you polish it. Few were the people, if any, within his reach there who turned their two weeks of peace into a gift to last a lifetime like Marina managed to do.

But by the time that second R&R had become history, he was a short timer. A bit of good luck came his way then, for one of the members of his group who left for home before him was sent to the Pentagon to fill the all-important position of assignment manager in charge of all transfers of intelligence officers. All he had to do now was to ask this man to assign him to the Army Language School at Monterey, California, the post closest to Santa Barbara. The guy promised and kept his word as well as he could: there was an open slot at Fort Ord, nearby on the other side of the Bay of Monterey, and that was where his penultimate army orders told him to report to.

The few months at Ord passed quickly, although there were some tense moments when it appeared that the paperwork of obtaining the final approvals of an honorable discharge might not be signed before school started at UCSB in September. But it all came to pass all right with a few weeks of time to spare, and then the umbilical chord to the security, that being part of a great organization entails, was cut. This final cut is the turning in of the green plastic ID card that identifies you as an officer on active duty. It was freedom at last (or rather, freedom again), but not without mixed feelings. The army was a home for him, one whose workings were strangely, in spite of everything, very compatible with the workings of his own mind.

Chapter 8

Student again

    A lot of water has run down San Luis Creek to the Pacific since I had started this tale back in Austin, Nevada, on the way to the ag-research site in the Grass Valley. Far too much, but I do not wake up in the morning all hot and eager to start adding to it. I have never been a morning person. So it drags on. It has turned into a lucubration, done in the hours creeping slowly up to and then past midnight mostly. "*O Mensch gib acht!*" Nietzsche advised, "*Was spricht die tiefe Mitternacht?*" Hark well, man, to the message of the deep midnight!

    I do my best to pay attention and listen, but maybe I would be more motivated if I knew for sure that someone might actually be interested enough to read the end product. Everybody is writing books nowadays. Selling them, that's what Tavis Smiley does all the time on PBS after the *NewsHour with Jim Lehrer*, and even Bill Moyers, bless his kind, eloquent, and erudite heart, is not above promoting the worthy literary products of the intellectual-elite sort of pioneering celebrities in the service of good causes whom he interviews on Friday nights.

    But I simply do not think there are many folks left with the gumption to peruse all that print. Shelf stuffers, that's what most of those volumes are. I don't read them, except for the ones that Marina insists that I must (lucky me, to have such a tutor). And yet, when I do, I am always better off for it, even though—should I admit it proudly or ruefully?—I am not much into absorbing other people's thoughts anymore.

    Let the message come directly from the rustlings of the birch tree in my backyard blowing in the wind. Well, in the course of this process of maturation, I also notice that as I am unrolling the musty scrolls of my *temps perdu*, the closer I get to more recent times, the duller and foggier my controller's handiwork seems to get. Maybe I should have done with it right now, as Tibor Déry suggests in Mister G. A. in X. If Mr. G. has not been translated yet into English, maybe I should try to do that instead, for it is a great tale. He says in there somewhere that you are not done with something when *it* says that you are, but when *you* say that you are. You have not climbed the mountain when you scaled the top but when you have gotten as high as you wanted to get. But how will my sons find out how a Magyar emigrant finds his private america if I do not finish telling them? So let's get on with it.

The piece of cactus that I broke off from a large plant at the foot of Morro Rock four years ago and stuck into the ground in my backyard near where the bedrock peeps out from under its thin mantle of topsoil is coming to life again this spring. It put out one beaver-tail—shaped branch the first year, and another one the next year. The result was a form reminiscent of the two large ears on the round head of Mickey Mouse in his earliest, still somewhat sinister-looking incarnations. Then it went dormant for over a year, but now a tiny, pinkish bud signals that it is waking up again. There is probably not enough topsoil on our rocky backyard slope for its roots to sop up all the water and nutrients it needs. So it bides its time and is not in a hurry to become a landmark of a plant.

Grass Valley: almost there

There was little good soil and next to no water in the scrubland upslope from the great dry lake below the USDA station on Grass Valley Road either. As his little Red Toyota got weary meandering past the potholes of the dusty road leading there, he would stop and get out to contemplate their messages. The messages sent by the road that is and those sent by the lake down slope, the "lake" whose arid surface is whitewashed in hard, bitter salt crystals now.

The water must have receded slowly, but its abatement was apparently not gradual. It came in quantum leaps like so many other things in nature. It is reassuring, don't you think, that even time hangs on, lingers for a quantum length, however minute that may be before it ticks on to transcourse its next minuscule increment? So it must have been for the ancestors of the Washoes or Payutes who lived along those slowly vanishing shores. You can still make out those increments of time, if you look closely, by the wind-sculpted shorelines now covered by scrubby, gray-green vegetation.

Apparently, there were considerable periods of stability in the climate that permitted wind and waves to leave horizontal marks on the ground that is gently rising on the eastern side of the valley, where the road runs. The people lived next to the water on these shore ledges, and there they left tokens of their transience: chipped stoneware, bones, and ceremonial rock arrangements. Until the next wave of a thirty-some-year drought lowered the water level by another couple of yards all of a sudden. Then it was time for them to move downhill another notch.

The ancient ones among them, the historians and the mythologists, told tales of the past, how their predecessors lived higher and higher up the slope in the old days. Only, because the keepers of the past were also seers of the future, they did not feel particularly reassured by what they saw coming. Soon, maybe in a hundred generations, there would be no water left. Then there would be no fish, the waterfowl would no longer fly in from the north in the fall, and the deer would migrate elsewhere. It would be so, if no miracle came about to bring more abundant rains. But there was no stored knowledge of more rain in their consciousness. Not in their bones, not in their souls, not in the aboriginal lore of their kind.

Their arrival in the valley, maybe a thousand of their short, primitive, magic lives ago, had long passed out of memory. And so they must have felt that some Great Spirit had brought them forth, them and their lake at the same time, and that the lake was deep and the valley full of water then. Then when the water was to be no more, well, that would be the end of time. The end of their time, and they would disappear, and the Spirit would let them subside back into the rocky soil covered sparsely by its sere plants now, from which they had arisen in the first place. And that is exactly what they seemed to have done in the fullness of time, time that does not exist.

He would sit there, where they might have sat, and think of them and of the road that led him to those ancient, abandoned shorelines of that lake of salt below. There was no *Weltschmerz* in those thoughts, for he felt at peace with the world. It had been good to him. Work done, the little red Toyota would take him home to that comfortable house with the glorious, full view of the Golden Gate Bridge and Hawaii and Japan beyond (hidden by the offshore fogbanks), with Marina waiting for him and the Fox and his kid brother, the little Schnucka to keep him happy. And he had a job that was a dream job in every respect, one that actually paid him for indulging in his hobby to do what he liked to do. Like sitting by that lake while others sat in their office cubicles being tortured by their computers.

The road that had got him there had never been smooth, but it had not been rocky lately either. There was that the final, brief army episode at Fort Ord, where the Fox, two years young then, made his first encounter with a strange, new tongue. The neighbor kids in the army housing area where they lived, all spoke an odd gibberish that made no sense to him whatsoever, for he spoke only German. So after some perplexed head shaking (and this was extremely funny to witness), he retaliated in kind: "Rahrahrahrah," he would say to them, for clearly, if that was the way they spoke to him, they should understand this in return.

But he caught on quickly, mixing the idioms at first. On watching the astronauts in their strange space suits bounce around upon their first landing on the moon, he would ask, "[*Was*] *machen die* monkeys?" By the time they moved down to Santa Barbara before nursery school started, however, he was in full command of his English. So much so that upon seeing the Santa Inez Mountains sprinkled in white by a freak cold front, he was able to say: "I did not know it snowed in Southern

California." That's what he said, and he was not three yet! No one believed him (the student) when he proudly boasted of his son's erudition, but I know I heard him say it.

Isla Vista

They found a little apartment in a fourplex in Isla Vista (IV). The other tenants were a student of philosophy, another of biology and an assistant professor of classics. "AyVee" was a world of its own. A loosely knit student and dropout-hippy community a square mile in size, it sat just west of the UCSB campus looking out on Santa Cruz Island some thirty miles offshore. One would have expected to find a Corvette-driving, moneyed upper-class set of students surfing and sunbathing below the cliffs off del Playa Street, considering the charms of the location. And there were some of those also; then, as now, UCSB was known as a party school.

The counterculture

But most of the folks that inhabited IV were the opposite of all that. They were counterculture not only because of their fear of being drafted and sent to Vietnam, for most of them had some sort of college deferment, I guess. No, IV was a true breeding ground and meeting place for the discontent with misguided government. Even more than that, it was a focal point of a strange sort of cultural revolution, gentle and nonviolent and yet vocal, articulate, and convinced. It was more than bipartisan: it was supra-partisan, for both political parties of the country were equally stuck and mired in their commitment to a war that was one great big war crime as defined by the Geneva Conventions.

So both of the presidents who had perpetrated it, Johnson and Nixon alike, were equally to blame, and since the two together summed up the totality of the national ideology, those opposed found themselves to be dissidents, opposed to the culture of the land itself. In IV, the counterculture was less of a movement than a state of mind that transcended mere disgust with the war and extended to the negation of such formerly cherished national creeds as rough-and-ready, ruthless, dog-eat-dog competition as the means of realizing the American Dream: an ideal, a goal, whose meaning was becoming increasingly nebulous.

Yet it was a real movement with a strong though diffuse current of thought, and it could have evolved to become an innovative business for the reinvention of American society, perhaps, had it been able to attract or engender a charismatic leader. But the charismatic leader did not arise from among the people, from streets like those of Isla Vista.

Instead, he jumped off the tarnished silver screens of the B-grade war and society movies of Hollywood to be seated on the throne of the Golden State in Sacramento by the political pundits of the power-elite who saw in him an appealing, ingratiating, and electable symbol of a happier, simpler, pre-imperial, pre-military-industrial complex past of the America that was more than just a dream. An iconic, though insubstantial presence like the smile on the fading face of the Cheshire Cat, blown up later to heroic proportions. One, whom they could equip with five-by-eight-inch, speech-prompting memory cards and whom they could groom to carry the banner of the intolerant, righteous, coat-and-tie dominance of the haves to victory over the unshaven, long-haired, mostly on-purpose-raggedy rabble of the streets of IV. For (so it came across to the student) if you were unsuccessful, marginalized, disadvantaged, or just plain contrary, a have-not in the pinnacle best of all economic systems, it was nothing less than clear-cut evidence that God Almighty Himself had judged you to be unworthy to have a voice, an opinion, a place in the sun.

And so they sat one evening, along with a few hundred others like them, in the (then still) grassy lot between the Embarcaderos del Sur and del Norte in the middle of IV, singing the national anthem. They sang it because they thought that would somehow identify them as patriotic Americans, star-sprangled as that squad of the Los Angeles Riot Police that was taking position nearby, sent in by that charismatic leader in Sacramento.

Well, he had been a war refugee and a professional soldier who had seen his share of brutality in his day, and so he did not want to expose the little Fox and his not yet born brother to what was to come when the LARP got ready to turn their night sticks loose on that Ash Wednesday choir in the grassy lot. So they left the party early. That night, the charismatic leader redefined two important words of the English language. "The heroes of the LARP," he said, "dispersed a large group of cowardly little bums."

The Great Communicator may not have communicated this bit of history verbatim exactly like that, but I think this rendition of it is sufficiently close to what he said. And now, my friends, like it or not, that was the sort of thing Himmler had been saying to his brownshirts when he turned them loose on another group of peaceful folks, whom the self-styled, new jack-booted elite of that now long-past moment in history considered to be enemies of the *Vaterland*.

I do not need Webster to know what *hero* and *coward* used to mean. A hero is someone who acts without compulsion and remuneration at great risk to his own life and general well-being for the benefit of others. By this definition, a soldier who is ordered into harm's way is not a hero when he is harmed but a victim, unless he commits some exemplary act of unselfishness in the process. A coward, on the other hand, is someone who fights using unfair and unequal means and who shirks the moral obligations of his kind and creed in order to avoid harm to himself.

By now, our understanding of these words has already shifted (or is still in the process of doing so) to mean that we are heroes whatever we may do, and whosoever is against us, why, those are all cowards, gunmen, thugs, and more recently, terrorists, no matter what their motivation may be. All are ingrates if we gave them a chance to emulate us and they did not jump at the chance. Cowards, even when they fight outgunned by overwhelming modern weaponry brought to bear against them. How else could it be? What we want and what we do is always good and honorable. We are the salt of the earth. The Founding Fathers did not get it quite right: *we* are not created equal. We are created exceptional.

This time, however, he had a clear conscience. It was not cowardly to leave the field of action early. It was for the sake of the family. Soon thereafter, the LARP had made its show of force on the grassy lot. Later, after having patrolled the streets in their armored trucks that evening and having roughed up everybody who dared to look out of a window of his home, his formerly inviolable castle, including, *horribile dictu*, even some of UCSB's super-establishment football players, they left and moved on, probably to quell other nonviolent protests by other cowardly little bums elsewhere, much like a tornado that dips down from the sky to flatten what is man-made in its path.

Biology

When the LARP had gone home to LA, peace broke out again in IV. Like it was when they (the student and his family) first arrived in the fall of 1969, just in time for classes to start. That was a wondrous time for him, paradoxically. No more signing in and out of his unit's duty roster. No more counting those precious days of leave. Freedom now. And above all, what lay ahead was what he really liked and wanted to do: delve into the secrets of life.

To his disappointment, there was no active program in entomology. He would have liked to find out how ants manage their social lives and exactly when and why neighboring colonies decide to go on genocidal warpaths against each other, even when they forage for different resources. Or he wanted to know everything about the mechanisms of metamorphosis; how a caterpillar turns into a butterfly. Or how a butterfly knows how many eggs to deposit on a plant of a given size. If she lays too many, her offspring may eat themselves out of food. He knew from his childhood observations that caterpillars are source-specific.

Back in Sándorhalma one day, way out on the other side of the oak forest, he had found a beautiful, hirsute caterpillar with black and orange bristles who was munching happily on a plant he could not identify. He brought him home and tried to feed him with leaves from every conceivable other plant, but it was no use. The caterpillar was desperately gnawing and crunching on the dried-out remnants of the leaves he was captured with, and since no new ones could be found, his (the caterpillar's) short career was soon permanently vitiated (as the crocodile would speak in the *Just So Stories*) amidst an assortment of dozens of different juicy, fresh leaves.

He could also watch raptly for hours at the foot of the vineyard behind the house in Léva how those small black ants and the large brown ones fought each other. It took three or four black ones to bring down (neutralize or take out) a brown one. Undaunted by their diminutive sizes, the little ones clamped their jaws into the legs and antennae of their foes, while streams of their sisters-in-arms poured out of three or four holes in the ground to form defensive positions on the battlefield around their underground nest.

There was an entomologist at UCSB, to be sure, but he was no longer practicing insect science. To his dismay, the man had run afoul of a ruling scientific paradigm in midcareer. He had proven conclusively (he averred, and credibly so) that bees do not find a promising source of honey when they are clued in on its location by a mysterious wiggle dance of the just returned foragers but simply by following the paths of scent. "The mechanism is strictly olfactory," he would say.

He (the student) had a chance later to check this out at the Max Planck Institute of Behavioral Physiology at Seewiesen, Bavaria. There, a former student of Konrad Lorenz explained to him loftily that they knew all about the professor from UCSB and his hare-brained theory. "Nobody, certainly no serious scientist, would think of contradicting von Frisch's conclusive proof of the bee dance," he proclaimed.

He never forgot his prof's exegesis of Karl Popper's work on the nature of the scientific paradigm. "A ruling paradigm is like a stone wall," he would lecture. "It locks lesser minds into its confines until finally accumulating evidence to the contrary makes the wall crumble into dust. But woe to those who contradict it while the wall still stands. The defenders on the ramparts, the reviewers, and the editors will destroy their careers: they will not let them publish." And so he was no longer enlightening his students about the bees. Instead, he lectured on the history of science, starting with the conflicting worldviews of Democritus and Aristotle. "If you have new, unknown effects to explain, look first for simple causes. They tend to be the more promising path to take. Also, watch out for what nature shows you, but be leery of what your own head makes up."

So lacking a guru, insects were out. But he had no time to grieve, for he was immediately sucked into another, seemingly simpler path. In the beginning, things tend to be simple, and so it was with Dr. Haller's courses in floristics. This was an introduction to the Flora of California. It also dabbled in a descriptive way in the ecology of Mediterranean-type plant communities (like the one around UCSB), and since it emphasized wildflowers, it had the additional appeal of aesthetics. Soon he found himself hooked by the study of plants. In the meantime, Marina was making progress toward her Ph.D. in French literature, and since she was too talented to do just one thing at a time, she brought forth to the world yet another bundle of joy, Fox's kid brother, Robin.

On the road again

But at this point, in the real time of the here and now, almost forty years later, we, Marina and I, are engaged in a frivolous, self-indulgent endeavor. We are on the road again. So what follows now is a flash-forward. I have wanted to do a big, long, open-ended, Kerouac-style road trip for over fifty years now, and with her gracious consent and cooperation, time for it has finally come. Only, if you can tolerate a bit of advice, don't wait for fifty years if you want to do something. When you have more time, when you have more money. When you are retired. Because if you do that, you might end up chasing a wild goose.

This trip was conceived in a time now past whose innocence has slipped through our fingers like water. In a time, when gasoline was taken for granted like air and sunshine still are. When the concept of the unrenewable resource had not even been thought of yet. When a gallon of gas was way under a buck, not US $4 like now.

It is not the money that beclouded this trip a bit, for our budget was not on a shoestring. But the prices displayed at the filling stations were ever-present reminders of a substantial, real malaise that was not there not only fifty years ago, but not even twenty-five years ago, when the yarn of this epic started unrolling on that other road trip on US 50 to the research site in Grass Valley.

Driving for fun on the open American road now felt like biting into the forbidden fruit. We have become conscious of an original sin, that of the spendthrift. The innocence is gone. The pink sunglasses with which we had been watching our not yet warming globe are broken. Our world has become fragile, and what we do matters to its precarious web of life. We are not free spirits of the open road anymore. We are now polluters, melters of the polar icecaps. But the curious fact that we are not suffering unbearably yet, not really, by taking this trip in our suburban assault vehicle, our six-cylinder, gas-guzzling Nissan Pathfinder, but instead rather enjoy sitting high above the highway in it, does contribute palpably to our very real feeling of guilty unease. We are part of the problem, you see, and we know it.

But problem or no problem, just west of Globe, Arizona (after having dropped in on Luz and Yoav in Tucson), is the place where US60 and US70 meet and diverge. Both lead back east, and we took 60 because it is the route through the Apache Reservation, which I thought would be good for me to see once more. Crossing the Black River Gorge is momentous. I wanted Marina to experience some of the sights that up to now, on my solitary rambles, I had no one to share with. She is a stop-at-every-scenic-view person. I can appreciate grand vistas well enough myself, but I am more an endless-stretch-of-the-lonely-road person, and US60 is surpassed only by US 50 in that regard. Good old US 50, the thread that I meant to weave through this report of my memories.

Then, zipping through New Mexico toward Oklahoma, she suddenly says, "I have never been to Santa Fe. Is that not somewhere around here?" Now, that is what is good about a Kerouac-style road experience. "So you want to see Santa Fe? Sure. Let's see if we can find it." Everybody should see Santa Fe, and when there, do some soul searching. Do you see it only as a tourist trap full of expensive trinkets, or does the terra-cotta earthboundness of its unique architecture evoke the timelessness of the bond between old and new, of the not-yet-encountered in you? The new city of the white man that tries to emulate the ancient Taos Pueblo under a modern guise?

Next, on to a bed-and-breakfast at the Hunter's Lodge in Padukah, Texas, a town that had seen better days. Then Broken Bow, Oklahoma, for the third time now, this time to stay overnight. Why do such little, boarded-up, half-dead, half-alive downtowns, gasping for breath like now under the summer's heat waves, speak so loudly to me? I wandered through its few streets at night and wondered, as I always do, what it would be like to live there.

Then came Oxford (the one in Mississippi), an entirely different story! Upscale, prosperous, alive. A today's town totally, university and all, but where people like me go in search of a past described so breathtakingly by the greatest writer known to me that it is a shock not to find the places and meet the people that live and breathe in his pages. I am a Southerner too, although I lived in the South only for a few years. The race problem is tragic, but the Civil War, from the Southern point of view, is like the wars that the Magyars fought for over a thousand years, defending their identity, always against overwhelming odds. That is a bond unlike any other.

Madison, Alabama, where Rob lives. He is doing well apart from being mysteriously afflicted by anything chemical. Chemical sensitivity, barely recognized yet as an epidemic, is one of God's uplifted fingers admonishing industrial civilization to curb its rampant, rapacious ravishing and poisoning of the very roots of the tree of life. Just a couple of decades ago, there was no need to buy purified water in bottles at the grocery store. Now, tens of millions of them are used every day in this country alone. If we keep going like we are, we will have to carry bottled air on our backs in another decade like the astronauts on the moon! I am not anxious to live to see that.

But otherwise, Rob is doing well. He found a good woman to share his life with. Kristen is smart, beautiful, and reserved in her ways. Although she is an aeronautical engineer, she plays the cello, and although she could be a professional musician or a fashion model (if she chose to), she helps lay the tile floors, paint the walls, and do the wiring for the house they live in and the other ones they have bought as rental investments in perfect financial family harmony.

Marina and I admire this sort of thing, for we are inept with our hands and are more into reading, hiking, and now even writing. They, on the other hand, build airplanes and rockets (real ones), do a lot of swing dancing, and keep cats. *Katze*, that was little Schnuka's first word when he was one-year young, as he lay under our green, Swedish-designed easy chair and played with our little black cat who was convinced, judging by her general demeanor, that she was a people type of person like we are. But when he started calling every living creature *Katze*, we made the mistake of correcting him: "No, that's a horse, not a cat, and that one is a bird, a lizard, or a frog." Confused by this Schnuka refused to say another word for a year.

On the way to Florida, we stopped in a town on the bluffs of the Chattahoochee River, now dammed up to a lake of sizeable proportions. There may be better-known examples of Southern gentility than Eufala, Alabama, but then Eufala is probably well known to the students, experts, and historians of those bygone times as a monument of the antebellum era, the time before the Civil War.

The mere thought of that makes me nostalgic, for he had read *Elfujta A Szél* (*Gone with the Wind*) during those stormy, wet, and cold late autumn weeks of 1944, when he was eleven years old, just before the winds of war blew his own old world away also. So the experience of the Old South became inextricably intermingled in his mind with what he himself had lived through, both written in blood and desperation, something the victorious overdog would never be able to understand even if he tried to do so.

Now, Eufala has not one but two avenues of stately old mansions that stand there as if they were ready to crumble into the dust of history but are held up in defiance of transience by the spirit of those who understand their past. So does my father's house still stand in Bethlenfalva, although the village does not even bear that name anymore and the butterfly-blessed meadows that surrounded it have turned into an industrial park.

Then, finally, we arrived at Jim Harris's house, a couple of blocks north of McDill Air Force Base in Tampa, Florida. McDill AFB, from where the wars of President Bush, Baby Bush, are being directed. Huge warplanes shriek in at every hour of the day and night in strange contrast to the otherwise peaceful setting of the place. Jim and Mary Beth are gracious Southern hosts and live in a cozy place in the middle of what feels like a village. By the third day of our stay, Jim set out to dig up our old OCS yearbook of January 1955 from the molds of storage. I was anxious to refresh my memory with names that the controller had buried under deep layers of the dust layers of oblivion.

And then it happened. It was what I have been telling you about not waiting to do what is important. The yearbook was found but with its pages glued together. Exposure to moisture, during the last move maybe, has made it one inextricable mass of pulpy, soft paper. See? Too late. Don't wait. So we could not go through it name by name, face by face to say things like "Jim, do you remember Frenchie? The one who used to do the short song and dance routines?" This is the one he liked to sing after days when the redbirds (upperclassmen) had been particularly pesky:

My heart knows what the wild goose knows   Tonight I heard the wild goose cry
And I must go where the wild goose goes   Wingin' north in the lonely sky
Wild goose, brother goose, which is best   Tried to sleep, it warn' no use
A wanderin' foot or a heart at rest?   'Cause I am a brother to the old wild goose.

But Jim did not remember Frenchie and his song and dance routines . . .

We had a few great days there. The Dalí Exhibit in Saint Petersburg. The Bok Tower on the highest point in Florida. The manatees in the zoo. Jim drove us everywhere with a running commentary on things, although he cannot be called one gifted with excessive gab. Just good, intelligent, straight talk, even though he does not like Faulkner. "I can't stand those page-long sentences he gets me lost in," he said. "Mary Beth likes to read literature. I like to read for fun." I don't mind reading for fun either; my favorite bedtime eye closers are the volumes of Tolkien's trilogy of the *Lord of the Rings*, but my involvement with literature looks more and more like rereading old favorites.

And old favorites will be the subject at our next meeting, ten days from now (this is another year later) in Norman and Fort Sill, that I am happy to insert here as I am proofreading (again) the finally finished manuscript. Marina and I are driving back to Oklahoma, so that I may rehash some of the past with my old OCS buddy who will be flying in from Tampa with Mary Beth. I also want to hear much more about his exploits in South America, where the army had assigned him after earning an MA degree in Latin American studies at OU in Norman. Jim and I are of like mind politically, so I wonder how he felt about our making common cause with the local ruling classes to stamp out indigenous movements for peace, justice, and land reform . . . I also want to hear more about his second career teaching Spanish, for that was how he met Mary Beth, whom he calls his guardian angel. It is good to cultivate close associations with angelic folks.

On the way north to Baltimore: the Okefenokee. We did not even plan it, but once we were ensconced in that charming bed-and-breakfast place, the Folkstone Inn in Folkstone, Georgia, Marina said, as is her wont: "Did you notice that sign? This town here happens to be the gateway to the Okefenokee Swamp! That's just great. Now that we are here, I want to see it." That's her. I, mesmerized by the open road, would have driven on the next morning. Instead, we spent most of the day taking a boat tour through it. I wonder what all those alligators eat. Also, did you know that it is not really a swamp but a marsh? Do you know the difference? I didn't either, but then I did not graduate from high school. All I have is a GED test.

Well, the Okefenokee is as far east as you can get, and the trouble with the East is that people are too densely packed there. And so as a consequence of that, the great, empty, wide-open roads were gone. Because, you see, you cannot count the traffic-choked eastern Interstates as the "open road," and I try to avoid the I-roads, the Interstates anyway, wherever they may be, east or west. So we meandered northward on scenic byways until at one turn of the road over the top of a hill there opened up all of a sudden, a grand view of the Great Smoky Mountains in the blue-green distance.

We had a delightful visit with the Smiths in Baltimore. Fort Sill, Fort Holabird, Frankfurt-am-Main—Keith had been there too and at the same time. We had not been close friends. He is a complex character whom I will not attempt to define. Maybe I will write a novel or at least a short story about him. Later. But my, oh my, does he have the gift of the gab! What comes into his head, out it goes right away with audible articulation. And not chatter but good, sensible, interesting stuff laced with humor and understanding. Maybe he was too clever for me to get to know him closer.

Successful people have this in common: they can outtalk others and effortlessly so. Keith did not make general, though, either. Perhaps he lacked that quality of ruthlessness that is required if you want to get to the top of the heap and stay there for a while. Well, Keith lucked out in another way: one of the most charming women that I have ever known married him. Leora (call me Lee) and Marina kept in touch through the years. So we knew that they had created varied and fulfilling second careers for themselves after retiring from the military.

They are both artists not only of the arts but also of life. Painting, weaving, modeling, raising two adopted sons, while creating a garden spot of Eden for themselves in the storybook environment of a huge lawn surrounded by forest where their house, itself a vintage antique, stands, one filled with the treasures of a lifetime of collecting the things of use and beauty of times past. Their place, a small empire of permanence, sits there with its flower and vegetable gardens at the edge of a great metropolis and at the very end of a great transcontinental highroad (I-70) as if neither existed, as if time had forgotten that it is there, as if the progress, modernity, and mechanization had granted it reprieve from being swallowed up by them. It was an enchanted visit, and we could greet the sons who were little the last time we had seen them and who were middle-aged men now.

The Smiths drove us to our old house at Court Pleasant in Dundalk. Only it was not there anymore; it fell to redevelopment like most everything else in this world. But the Jewish cemetery behind our rear windows was there. Unchanged, though a little more weather worn as things tend to get with time. Newmarket we also found. No longer the haven of antique stores on US40; its remaining historic houses perch now uneasily within easy reach of the new freeway's (I-70) noise barrier.

Then, westward, ho! If you have some training in ecology, you can observe the gradual shift in the vegetation from forest to grassland and from long- to short-grass prairie; otherwise, you might not even notice it, I guess. It is a long stretch. West Virginia, Ohio, Indiana, Illinois, Minnesota, Iowa—did I get them in the right order? If that sounds flippant, it is not meant to be. It is meant to be descriptive, geographically as well as sociopolitically, as seen from the West Coast, in perspective.

When you try to paint a picture that involves distance, you will at first have trouble getting your subject into perspective. So parallel lines, for instance, like railroad tracks, converge to a zero-dimensional point when far enough out. And that is what the Midwest looks like to a Californian. He (a Californian) does not even know where the "Midwest" properly starts and ends. But being as patriotic as anyone (if not more so), he too has heard of the American Heartland back there and feels duty-bound to think of it with a sort of reverence.

Yes, the Great Heartland, where people are not confused and led astray by the foreign, cosmopolitan influences of the wide world that lies beyond the shores of the endless oceans and that are swept in from there by the ever-shifting jet stream. Where people are stern and are bent on conserving what they think of as the essential values of their lives. Where people are principled and hold their family-value tenets more sacred than their economic interests. Like the right to life, like the right to guns, like the rejection of miscegenation, or of same-sex marriage. If the man on the ballot says amen to things such as these during the campaign (this was the summer of 2008 and candidate John McCain was on peoples' minds), he has their vote locked up even if he promises to send their jobs to China or India in the same breath and to borrow and spend them and their country into bankruptcy.

Or at least, so it seems to the Californian at the end of the Baby Bush era when this is being written. Or am I confusing this huge stretch of the land with what I heard people speak of as that mythical God-fearing Eden known as the Bible Belt? We must have driven through that one on our way going back, eastward that is. That must be Heartland also. What can I say? It is now only a few weeks back, and my memory really cannot tell Indiana, Illinois, and Ohio apart anymore, while it certainly can still do that for Nevada, Arizona, and New Mexico. No value judgment there, man, just the power of habituation.

Yet it would be patently unfair to say that all those towns that we passed through in the Midwest were exactly alike. It might appear so to a European tourist, if he ever ventured out of our great national parks that he comes to see into the real America. It is when I wander through those dark, deserted, small-town streets at night in search of myself in all those shuttered, seemingly lifeless and haunted houses, maybe with TV screens flickering through the blinds like ghosts playing hide-and-seek, that I feel how they are all different and unique underneath their surface veneer of similarity.

And it is these solitary quests for the secret of what has made me an American in spite of all my baggage of critical, judgmental misgivings and yearnings that we might give up playing exceptional and live up to our promise instead, that makes me feel like I have seen everything and have been everywhere. I am sure that Johnny Cash also lived through this search and felt the same thing. Only he had a voice, a guitar, and a great heart to express it:

> I've been everywhere, man
> I've been everywhere, man
> Crossed the desert bare, man
> I've breathed the mountain air, man
> I've been everywhere. I've been everywhere.

Then we reached the Badlands. I did not tell you about the trip back in 1965, when we saw them first. They have not changed, and it was a great homecoming. Only the tourist presence had grown, but it was tolerable. The Badlands are awesome. You can move along the undulating plains of the short-grass prairie to the north of them without any clue as to what will happen next. Then you come to the edge, and the land falls off in precipitous escarpments of jagged but soft, porous, gray cliffs to the next level of prairie below. Seen from any angle, the view is gripping. Not in the overpowering, remote way of the Grand Canyon but more directly and palpably. You can walk up to this "bad land," touch it, and see with your mind's eye how the next cloudburst will shift, realign, and right one more chunk of the entire landscape to a state of greater stability below. And this year, so the old-timers said, was the wettest in their living memory. The prairie was lush and silky and fragrant with wildflowers.

The Black Hills: of course, we went to see Mount Rushmore. There were lots and lots of people on hand to be awed by the big heads of a few of the country's past leaders. I have always wondered why Sitting Bull is not up there. After all, the place belongs legally to his people. Looking at the heads that were there, I felt that they, having been great and honorable men in their day, all seemed to say, "Had we been alive when someone decided to put us here, we would have refused." For they could not be there if one of the most shameful passages in our history had not come to pass.

He was a kid, still back home in Léva, when he first heard those fateful lines in a history class in school, whose legacy lives on written in the stone of despair: "As long as the rivers run and grass grows and the trees bear leaves, *Paha Sapa*—the Black Hills—will forever be the sacred land of the Lakota Indians." But instead, the Lakota had to flee to a foreign country to escape losing their lives and liberty. What would Lincoln have done had he been alive and in office at the time when that irresistible societal force, gold, broke the Treaty of Laramie and prospectors swarmed over the Paha Sapa? He, the kind of man that he was, would have had no choice but to commit hara-kiri. For the sacred honor of the country had been pledged in that treaty! *Wer einmal lügt, dem glaubt man nicht, wenn er auch die Wahrheit spricht*, that is the legacy of that document signed at Laramie.

But by now, our country had survived its childhood diseases and outgrown its growing pains, and some of the Lakota have also survived and are still with us. We have now become trustworthy and altruistic; we can be relied on to seek our advantage only in the greater good of our common global community in everything we do. Exceptional, as we are, are we not?

Fortunately, however, hope springs eternal in spite of everything, for a new colossal monument is taking shape in the Black Hills. It is going to be ten times larger than the four presidential heads put together. The monument of Crazy Horse. Of the victor at the Rose Bud and at the Little Big Horn. Of the defender of his people's right to life, honor, and dignity. I would not even have known that this mountain-rending endeavor was happening had not Marina done her research beforehand, as she always does. I would have driven on not knowing that a mountain is being carved and shaped to reflect the legacy of the great Ogallala medicine man and war leader to remind everyone that his spirit and that of Sitting Bull live on in the Black Hills.

The sun was westering by now, and we drove through a couple of tourist towns run over by tourists, looking for a place to stay for the night. We, of course, are never tourists. We are part of the scene; we are always locals. We are (are we not?) intrinsic brushstrokes in the painting that stylizes our surroundings as art (wherever we may be). I am afraid we indulge a bit in the presumption of elitism with that and know it. But lest our kind of elitism might be misunderstood as aloofness, let me say here, it is not so. It is really more like apartness. But am I not digressing again?

A little further south of the worst tourist traps around Mount Rushmore, the map promised one last possibility of an overnight stay still within the hills: the town of Hot Springs, South Dakota. And Hot Springs turned out to be our kind of town. Driving into it from the north, we could immediately see its symbol: a great, big blue buffalo on top of a corner building. And below it on the ground floor: the Blue Bison Café. Open, though a little late in the day, and serving cherry pie *à la*, with some of its ice cream going on top of my cup of coffee, always in memory of the *tejszínhabos kávé* of home. In fact, vanilla ice cream goes almost better with coffee than the *tejszínhab*. We enjoyed it thoroughly after all that sightseeing, before we even started looking for a room. When we found it, the manager, having one himself, wanted to know the origin of my accent.

Not all Central Europeans harbor friendly feelings toward each other, but Polaks and Magyars do, owing no doubt to similarities in their troubled histories and to the lack of conflicting economic interests. So I pulled the only Polish on him that I remembered from sixty-some years ago, the fragment of a saying I learned from the Polish officers who were taking their afternoon walks on the Kákasor, the tree-lined promenade that led by our house in Léva.

They were granted asylum by Magyarország after the partition of their country between the Nazis and the Bolsheviks, and so they escaped the fate of so many of their comrades when the Russians massacred the entire captured Polish Officer Corps in the Katyn Forest. "*Polak, Wenger dwa bratanki*," this is how far I could take it. But our host immediately completed the sentence: "*i do szabli, i do szklanki.*" Poles and Magyars are two brothers in fighting and drinking alike.

From our motel, we took a long walk along the stream back to the Blue Bison. Marina's hip seemed to be recovering well at last from her hip replacement operation. Now that she has a chunk of zirconium oxide in her, she is more precious than ever. We had dinner at the Bison: a tasty bowl of spicy chili con carne had always been a favorite of mine. The grand old hotel of Hot Springs is now a retirement home for veterans, and the impressive old school building on the hill above town is a museum. This town felt to me like I could live out my remaining years there myself.

From there, we went to stay with my brother in the Centennial suburb of Denver. It was a good visit; he is hanging on bravely, and I will talk about that later. In Delta, Utah, I got a speeding ticket in the morning after a very pleasant, quiet night at the Budget Motel. Eureka, Nevada, our last overnight stop. Brunch at the Middlegate Tavern, remember, at the T-junction to Luning. For the first time ever, I drove through Austin, Nevada, without stopping. We were simply too travel weary. Then we got home at last.

On the grand principles

Home at last, and with that, it is time to get behind my second computer (a welcome present that Fox gave me during our last visit to his house at Las Vegas) to submerge back into the past once more: into the life of the student-beginner of biology.

Their two plus years in Isla Vista were intense. There was freedom, yes; the swim-or-sink type of freedom of those who jump into cold water to get to another, distant shore shrouded in a fogbank. One of the different kinds of freedom we have here in the Land of the Free, the freedom to break if we don't make it. Not a bad kind of freedom for those who are equipped for it. Would their saved-up resources last until that much-desired next job at the serene bosom of academe—with summers off—after emerging from the smog of quizzes, tests, and exams? That was the question that concerned them. But they were still youngish (sort of) and confident, industrious and not at all stupid, although the latter postulate was severely tested in his case by organic chemistry.

Organic chemistry is to the student of biology what physical chemistry is to the student of physics. They are all-important disciplines for the understanding of the foundations of these fields, they are demanding and thought provoking, and they are the bedrock basics for further advances. But the effects of the turning of their textbook pages late at night at the library is not matched or exceeded by any sleeping pill ever produced by a chemical factory, as I no doubt have reported earlier, in the Norman phase of this pilgrim's progress.

I should not be knocking it, for chemistry (of any kind) deals, it seems to me now, with what he began to call the "elementary principle" back in those days. It is the principle of matter, whether amorphous, crystalline, or organized into life-sustaining compounds of ever-increasing complexity by their self-generated fields of energy. Furthermore, it deals with anything at all that the senses and their extensions (instruments) can perceive and the brain can conceptualize. Everything, except the mystery, the primary principle, inherent in, yet outside of everything, "other" in nature than all that can be grasped by the mind and that can be given a name or for which a form can be imagined, including the mind itself. He was quite proud of himself to have come up with such a grand worldview as that.

Yet I do not feel at all deflated to learn, again just now, that such concepts have been erected repeatedly throughout the ages. Marina gave me this fun-to-read book by Eknath Easwaran of and about the Bhagavad Gita for my seventy-fifth birthday, and there it says, clear as day and simple as truth, that there are only two categories within our universe, the pure spirit and everything else! This "everything else" it calls *prakriti*, which is the exact replica of my elementary principle.

It is not yet clear to me, though, how exactly to interpret the meaning that the Sankhya (an ancient philosophical system first taught by the sage Kapila) ascribes to the no-thing (*purusha*) that we translate as "pure spirit." Is it meant to be, or at least to include, our Self, the Atman, that is consubstantial with the impersonal Brahman in the same way as a water molecule is related to the ocean?

But let me humbly note here also that there is an added wrinkle to my own concept that the Gita does not mention. There, Krishna simply says that the universe comes about as the result of the concerted action of the Sankhya's two categories. To me, it seems rather, that my two principles are in a tug-of-war with each other when they deal with the complex that consists of our "Self" and of our "body." In this context, the two seem to act as forces pulling us in different directions, one toward a quest of sensory gratification and fulfilment and the other to the transcendence of materiality. It is as if our lives, or all life as such, were the interface between the two principles.

But how can there be an interface between essences that permeate each other? Easy. That crucial word *life* is just a metaphor forced on us by the primitive nature of our language. What life really means is that it is unlike anything else; it is where the two principles must meet because it is the only ground that is intrinsically part of both. That is where they are one. It is their battleground within us, where their cosmic fight is felt by us as suffering. Perhaps, then, the overcoming of this suffering, the way the Buddha taught it, is a victory of the *purusha*, the primary principle. I wonder if Krishna would nod agreement to this. And I also wonder why he did not explain why there should be such a battle in the first place? He did not; he was content to drive Arjuna's chariot at Kurukshetra, as if the battle were something self-understood, a part of the basic plan. Maybe the reason is simply not for us to know.

While he (the student) may have felt free to think about the cosmic implications of organic chemistry, dealing with its reality face-to-face was more taxing, and he only got Cs in it for three whole academic quarters. Neither were his grades in the other courses quite as tops as they ought to have been, which made him wonder at times if he should not have gone into ditch digging or mail sorting instead. Not that there is anything wrong with those types of activity. As anyone who has read the Gita will know, they are also part of the *karma yoga* if done in the spirit of selfless service. But most of the schoolwork was fun and fun was also extracurricular life: coming to know the creatures of the tide zone only three blocks away, exploring the condor preserve wilderness of the dry hinterland mountains, but above all, integrating Robin into the family.

Robin

For this was the time when Robin arrived, and there is no more cosmic experience on earth than an event like that. This time he was present to see his son emerge into the light and would have been dazed with the miracle of it had it not been for the circumstances. A birth would be very much like a sunrise, where the dark outlines of distant hills slowly take on the ever-brighter colors of the nascent new day of hope ending in fulfillment, as the splendor of the disc of life breaks the horizon, if it were all that easy. For it is not. Not even for the one who is only watching it happen. But for the one who makes it happen, it is something that men can only try to comprehend. They can take part in it, but they cannot be part of the happening itself. They did not feel the life grow in them, and they do not pay the price of pain that they can only wish they could share.

But when the sun was finally up above the horizon, the smile that it evoked on Marina's face was like, well, radiant; what other word would be fitting when discussing the sun. Of course, once it starts rising, life begins to settle into place, but Robin was no problem; he never sounded wake-up calls at night nor did he ever needed diapering, at least not to an extent that he noted sufficiently enough to remember later.

He had a sunny disposition from the very beginning, and it was probably the Fox who had to make the most difficult concessions to deal with this new little sunshine in the house. I wonder if firstborns ever remember their feelings about having to share their parents. He never talked about it and handled it well at any rate. But time was passing fast for they were all very busy, and before long, Robin started crawling and then walking, and by the time he had his hands free, he started using them for fondling his *Schnuckeltuch*, his security blanket. And soon he started a dialog with *Katze*, one that is still lasting with all of Katze's successors.

Gardening, *Katze,* and goats

They had struck up a friendship with their neighbors in the quadruplex, Tolya the Greek (whom they just called *der Grieche*) and his wife Ann. To show that they were wholeheartedly into the counterculture, alternative lifestyle of the times, he and Tolya went to a livestock auction one day and bought two beautiful Nubian goats. There was another reason also; Tolya brought with him an affinity for these splendid animals from his homeland. He would enlighten everyone whom he thought was in need of it, that if you had no time to bake your own bread, you had better reevaluate your priorities. For him, fresh, home-baked bread with aged goat's chese was a feast of feasts.

The goats were kept in the enclosure behind the fourplex, and the other tenants, the biologist and the philosopher, did not mind. How could they? This was IV of the late sixties, the place and time that would abrogate the war, the empire, the market, and perhaps even Mammon himself. Goats were in, bleating was beautiful, and small-minded bickering over the flies that goat shit attracted was out.

Katze had an ambivalent relationship with the comely newcomers. She did not tolerate other animals, but here she made an exception. She would contemplate them from above, from the crossbar of the fence where she liked to sit, trying to make sense of creatures that ate things like grass and alfalfa hay. She was very discriminating.

He had picked her from three other kittens by chance. The one that emerged first over the backrest of their green sofa would be their cat. And from that moment on, he had that same magic relationship with this little animal, that his distant, caveman ancestor must have had eons ago, who first crossed eyes with *Katze*'s own feral forebear. "We will share this cave," he said. "You can sit by the fire and warm yourself because I like your looks and the way you comport yourself, and I expect nothing of you except the honor of your company." No one knows what she thought, as she continued to walk her solitary ways, but she purred in response to that first invitation.

This *Katze* was an indoor and outdoor all-round companion. She would come along on long walks, not like a dog but dashing from cover to cover. When meeting another animals, she had to be whistled back (she agreed to this bit of response training) for she would have taken them apart, small though she was. She was fearless, and at one time, she took on a VW beetle, sounding her fierce battle cry. But in the house, she was thoughtful and tried to fathom the ways of her companions, the two-legged people. She was particularly fascinated by dishwashing and would reach down from her perch on the high windowsill over the basin with a long foot, trying to participate.

But her crowning feat came one afternoon when he was trying to dig up some of the heavy clay (that proved to be impervious to the spade in the end) in the backyard to start a vegetable garden. The Greeks were having a little party on the other side with the goats as the center of attention, and *Katze* was sitting peacefully on her crossbar, shaking her head in disbelief over the digging effort. Then a big German shepherd dog jumped over the gate that led from the outside to the enclosure in the back. The goats backed up nervously, the dog made what looked like a hostile move toward them, and the party chatter abated in expectation of things to come.

Then, like a streak of black lightning, *Katze* leapt off her perch and advanced slowly with a blood-curling howl, belying her small size toward the hound, whose head alone was at least as big as her entire body. That instant, the dog was a sight to see. His whole being turned into a clump of hesitancy, and his eyes exuded self-doubt that was comical to behold in view of his size. The Greek party was rapt, and Ikaros, a frequent drinking companion, had a grin on his face that went from ear to ear.

Then *Katze* paused in her advance and glanced back at him. Her eyes were a question mark. "Should I finish him off, or what?" He gave a sign with his hand: "Go for it." But by then it was too late. The hound used this moment of reprieve and flew back over the gate again with *Katze* hot on his heels now. What went on on the other side, he could not see, but they could all hear the dog's desperate yelping. When he was satisfied that the intruder had learned his lesson, he whistled, and in a few minutes, *Katze* reappeared over the gate.

The goats bleated in cheerful appreciation and ventured forward to touch noses with her. She accepted the tribute with a disinterested air. "No big deal, it's all in a day's work," her shrugging shoulders were suggesting. The party folks came over to shake hands. "If I had only heard this told as a story and had not seen it with my own eyes, I would never have believed it," said Ikaros and picked up the cat deferentially to put her back up on the fence.

The Child Care Center

Unfortunately, none of the family was there to watch the action, but they may have witnessed similar doings of *Katze* that he did not get to see. I hope that the kids will finally get around to reading these pages when they are in their own seventies and then get inspired to relate their own experiences of those days (if these pages survive all those decades to come). For by this time, the personality that Fox was going to develop was definitely taking shape, and even little Schnuka was getting to be a character of distinction. But the pressure was on, school was demanding, there was always some exam to cram for, and I am afraid he found little quality time to spend with them. That was a grave error. Time could have been made, as I know now, but he did not see it then. Except for his involvement with the University Child Care Center.

There was a group of half a dozen men in full beards (including him) and a couple of vocal, assertive women who decided to get UCSB to fund a UCCC for IV-resident students' children in the facility newly acquired by the University on the

Devereau Dunes adjacent to IV. One of this group was Dante, another philosophy student, the one with the longest beard, one who was highly adept at negotiating. Dante was only in his early forties or late thirties, but his black beard was starting to sport a distinguished silver hue. He could look stern and uncompromising like Saint Peter on Judgment Day when he chose to be like that, and this, along with the beard, surrounded him with an aura of authority when he confronted university representatives.

They got first acquainted with the "Dantes" (Antonia, Serenella, and Nino) through their philosophy neighbors in the quadruplex, Eric and Ellen. Ellen was a free spirit tuned in to all the free-floating currents of energy that wafted liberally in all directions in the rarefied air of an Isla Vista that was not only striving to break free from political authority and the consequences of all its misguided blunders but was also actively searching for spiritual alternatives to old, hardcore, missionary-style religion.

Ellen was into transferring her trust from what her philosophy-and-theology-professor father had stood for to faith in the powers of cult healers of the body and of thinkers of the free thought of the mind, things that she did not even pretend to understand herself. Ram Das, "Bucky" Fuller, the Dalai Lama, Erhard of Sensitivity Training, Zen by Suzuki. But it seemed to him that unity with the spirit was more important for her than understanding the gist of the thought, understanding things that she rightfully felt could not be understood anyway.

Unity with an elusive spirit, however, was not the problem at the UCCC. There was a more practical problem. And that was that the bearded ones who thought they had the power and authority to establish the guidelines for "their" UCCC's curriculum were carried away by the heady optimism of the times and overstepped the bounds of the ruling educational paradigm's tolerance limits.

They decided that the proper motto for the spirit to be soaked up from the start by the children of the Land of the Free and the Home of the Brave should be "Challenge authority and distrust experts." For they felt that was the right attitude for kids to have who were to become free and brave people. However, there were counter currents to this anti-authoritarian spirit. The powers-that-be at the university found allies in more conservative parents who started a grassroots counterrevolution. The bearded ones called it inquisition or counterreformation. There was a coup at one of the board meetings, and the progressive faction was swept out of office by those who saw in their peace-and-love philosophy a pinko, anti-American menace to their children.

But it was the end of his only foray into local politics, and that was regrettable for him personally, for the UCCC exposure had shown him that not only did he have time for extracurricular activities but that they were interesting and rewarding.

Child rearing

The Fox, little as he was, has good memories of the UCCC, although he cannot clearly articulate them now. As he grew up, he increasingly self-styled himself as a maverick, and that UCCC motto may have easily been a seed for that process. But I am afraid that another, probably more important, cause was his father's inability to connect with his son properly.

His own lost year in Vietnam made him also lose out on the crucial second year in his son's life. When he got back, there was this little stranger for whom the loss of his mother's undivided attention must have been painful. And when this new rival then got impatient with his inability to tie his shoelaces, the two-year-old had no other way to cope with the big stranger's lack of empathy than with resentment. The authority figure expected the unreasonable, which naturally provoked resistance, and to his credit, he (the Fox) resisted it to the best of his ability.

He (the student) should have seen and understood all this, and his lack of training and experience (the lost year maybe) can be no excuse. Neither can the fact that his attention was channeled into a quite rigorous new course, his studies that were dead-ended by his limited savings, a situation that demanded a paying job as soon as possible. No excuse. Failure is failure. Miraculously, now, so many years later, there is a real birth of mutual understanding on the way, engendered by a touching willingness of the Fox to forgive the failures of the past. He probably did not and does not conceptualize his early relationship with his father as "failure" but as a void, a lack of grounding, an unfulfilled need for easily expressed, palpable love. A feeling of loss without ever having owned what he lost.

Sure, they went on hikes to Cold Spring Canyon and had Coca-Cola-beer afterward at the Cold Spring Tavern, but he was an introvert, not a sunny, cuddly, huggy type, like Dante was, for instance, when he was not staring down university bureaucrats.

Marina, who senses when I come to points likes this, just made me read a story in the June 30 issue of the New Yorker (2007). Go, find it in the library and read it. It is about a father-son relationship and its consequences for the son. A story that does not try to find words for the psychology involved in it. It just says what happened and how it happened without distracting explanations. That's how *good* stories run. There again was a father focused on himself and on his work, blind to the most urgent needs right next to him.

Davis

The courses at UCSB could be demanding and were at times enjoyable and interesting, but they offered little preparation for anything real in the remunerative sense afterward. It was a jumble of disjointed knowledge floating in midair that did not seem to lead anywhere. When a prof went on his sabbatical, they got a grad student to replace him who did not know much more than the class he faced. He learned to realize that lectures were basically relics from the Middle Ages, a time when there were no books readily available.

Sure, a few of the profs were inspiring and the uplift was always welcome, but he felt that if a student did not carry his motivation with him, he was out of place at a university anyway. UCSB managed to get him through a BS and MS in biology in such a way that when he left for UC Davis for his Ph.D., he did not even know how to prepare a molar solution. Maybe that type of info was up to a basic chemistry lab to deliver, but his chemistry had come from Cameron College at Lawton, Oklahoma, taken as night courses during his army days there, twenty years earlier. They were on his academic record and satisfied the chemistry requirement, even though Cameron did not offer a lab for the night-shift folks.

Back in Icking, they would have called this sort of thing a "*Bidungslücke.*" A gap in one's education. Although gaps in practical things like chemistry or math were not properly part of "*Bildung*" there. *Bildung* in Germany meant a grounding in things like literature, history, philosophy, Latin, and the like. If you could not tell Bach from Beethoven, you were *ungebildet*, or at best you had a "*Halbbildung*" (that's a woefully insufficient half of the whole), but you did not have to know that a logarithm is an exponent to be *gebildet* (that is someone whom his education had turned erudite).

Well, his bildungsgaps had to be filled quickly at the University of California at Davis. The incredulous frown of the department chair's chief technician who was to read him into his duties as the teaching assistant of an undergraduate plant physiology class, upon learning that the holder of a master's degree from a sister campus of the UC system did not know how to prepare molar stock solutions for plant-nutrition demonstrations, remained unforgettable.

They picked UCD with misgivings, for they expected it to be an ugly place in the middle of the great Central Valley of California. But it was a school with a highly reputable program in biology, and among the top ones in the country in its applied, agricultural aspects. And even more importantly, they had not only accepted him but also offered a nice little scholarship that would pay a hundred-and-eighty bucks a month for two years. In 1972, when a cup of coffee was around a dime, that was still good money (that cup is going on two dollars now). But back then, he only had a cup (with a slice of chocolate-cream pie to accompany it) as a reward after those final exams that he thought he maxed.

The transfer to Davis went smoothly. They drove up there in their white Saab station wagon for house hunting on the first of what was to become a long succession of such North-South trips for decades to come. The memory fragment that stands out in this first journey were the owls of Brentwood. The Interstate Highway (I-5) was not yet functional, or they might have taken it to speed up the trip a little. But as it happened, the going was slower than they had expected and they had to stop overnight in Brentwood. There was a pleasant little downtown there, quiet enough to be home to a couple of large owls that apparently lived in one of the old houses of its main street. I passed through this off-the-beaten-path town (much) later just to see if the owls were still there. But as you can guess, owls and urban renewal do not mix well.

In Davis, the housing market was discouraging. They went from house to house on foot with the little Schnucka on his back ("Do you know of a place to rent around here?"), but found that in the neighborhoods that looked appealing to them, apartments were handed down from hand to hand. And rent was ever so much higher than back in Isla Vista. So they decided to consider buying, a big step into unknown financial waters, but they calculated the mortgage at 7.5 percent on houses in the twenty-thousand-dollar range to be more affordable than throwing good money away to enrich some absentee landlord ("*gutes Geld dem Besitzer in den Rachen schmeißen*," was the way they put it in their family lingo).

This was the time just before the start of the great, secular California housing bubble that lasted over thirty years and is imploding catastrophically as I am writing this. They had singled out three houses from which to choose. Then there was a family vote, and it was the Fox's voice that tipped the balance. "I want the grapehouse," he said, and Schnucka seconded the motion. It was September, and in the backyard of 845 North Campus Way, the Thompson seedless grapes were sweet and ready to savor. That did it.

I don't remember the details of the transaction's paperwork and the financial woes of the mortgage payments, but they moved in promptly for what was to become a six-year stay. The house was odd by today's standards but functional. There were three small bedrooms in a row along a narrow corridor. The largest was the two kids' room, the middle one was theirs, and the third became a study. At right angles to this was a large living room, with the entire house on one polished cement slab for a floor. Parallel to the living room and facing the street was a narrow, long, and dark kitchen, the *Schlauch*.

You could step out from the living room to a patio and from there to the backyard, which was really a lush, green garden. A big fig tree in the back, a group of birches in the middle, shrubs along the fences with the grapevines running all over them. There was also a silk tree that became the trellis for a muscat table grape whose stock he borrowed one night from the Viticulture Department. The whole setup was a very livable, lower-middle-class hangout, in spite of the hoarse barking of one of the neighbor's three huge, frustrated, pent-up, ill-tempered dogs.

Botany at Davis

Davis was as different from Isla Vista as tomatoes are from peppers. Student discontent in Isla Vista had its reddish streaks like tomatoes do or like fire did when they burnt the Bank of America building, for instance. That was meant to be a message to the powers-that-be of how they felt about them. And he was very much part of that historic event, even though his own bank account was in there also to burn with the rest.

Here in Davis, it was all green and crunchy, well, like bell peppers are. Davis was known to all as the cycling capital of the "world." Amsterdam was apparently not all that well known yet to American students, and Hanoi, where the bicycle rules the street, was anathema. Town and campus were level like the surface of a plate full of thick pea soup, and that made pedaling easy. And level was the political playing field also; mayor and city council were all no-growth oriented, and the mood, hopeful and progressive, hung over students, faculty, and townsfolk like a cloud of soft, warm drizzle does over a local sugar beet field after a long drought. It felt good to be there. All the vibes were resonating right.

The Botany Department was a friendly place also. They did not have room in plant ecology for him where he really wanted to be to build on his studies at UCSB, but plant physiology was open and that was where he ended up. After he was over his initial disappointment about this, he quickly rationalized his way out of it: ecologists know little about what makes plants grow; they just wander around bewildered in the wilderness of all those interacting species. Then in desperation, they end up concocting highfaluting statistical models and equations (like their kin, the ecomonists) about community theory to make their thing sound scientific. So there! You always feel better when you have a chance to put others in their place.

What he did not know, although he kind of sensed it, was that the Botany Department was hanging in a state of limbo at this particular point in time. That point was one of luxation, one at which a painful change in priority was preparing to take shape. It was the great transition in emphasis from organismal to molecular biology. Not that the latter would entirely replace the former; a plant physiologist still has to know what makes the juices of life move through the phloem and the xylem, but the juice of research, money, the funding without which you cannot do science, was ebbing out of whole-plant work and started flooding into the molecule. And with it went the prestige. He started thinking of that as intellectual snobbery, which was unjust, for it is only natural that the smartest folk like to be where the excitement (and the money) is. It is a process not unlike osmosis.

But the Botany Department was not quite ready for its subcellular future. There was a cadre of old-timers, highly distinguished, kindly, and helpful folks who were there, resting on their merits without noticing that they were standing still. They taught from their many classic publications diligently, all the while immersed in the minutiae of the academic rote. Their careers had moved leisurely along their paths of excellence, and nothing had prepared them for the quantum leap that was starting to shake the cathedras from which they were promulgating their facts. Why worry? They had tenure.

A digression on tenure

Now, tenure is a strange, historic concept. It started back in the Middle Ages. Having progressed from *doctus* (learned) to *doctor* (more learned) and finally to *doctissimus* (most learned) at those ancient, venerable centers of learning like the ones at Padua, Bologna, or Ferrara, the teacher would pass on his knowledge and insight about the universe from his high *cathedra* to students listening more or less raptly at his feet.

These masters were less concerned with fact, but professed truth (hence their title of "professor") the way they saw it. But since truth is by nature unfortunately subjective, their lectures could become controversial on occasion, and especially so, one might guess, when the truth dealt with that heady stuff that goes on in the *polis*, community life that is: politics. So to protect the *doctissimi* from undue harassment, in time they were granted the luxury of freedom from the fear of being axed for the offense of being fearless in their profession of professing. That's tenure, or what it should be.

But now, back in UC Davis, in our own day, professors do not profess truth anymore. They are paid instead to dish out facts. And since facts are, by definition, not controversial, why should their dispensers have the protection of tenure? This is only a rhetorical question here, but it was his humble opinion at the time that they should not have it. Instead, he felt, those professors who stray from the cutting edge of new knowledge, who settle into the habit of relying on their old notes year after year, should always be politely complimented out of their students' way into retirement.

Defining the dissertation

In time he had soaked up enough of these facts at the feet of his *doctissimi* that the authorities deemed him ready to be called *doctor*, although he felt only very moderately ready for the honor. Even his dissertation was a product of sheer accident. It was the product of two lucky happenstances to be exact.

His first advisor, having hailed from England where standards are apparently still medievally strict, had very healthy views on academic succession. "You got to make it on your own," he said of dissertations in general. "If you cannot, you are not cut out to become a member of the club." He (the student) had theretofore always been able to make it on his own and to make up his mind on the proper course of action in time. This time, however, he was seriously floundering and getting worried about it.

He had a hard time identifying a problem worth putting forward as a thesis to be tested and particularly one for which Bob, his professor, would be willing to advance a modicum of the money needed to carry it to a conclusion. For the project had to be of interest not only to him but also to his faculty sponsor. And then, all of a sudden and almost on the same day, two small events occurred to thicken the plot.

One of the *doctissimi*, having just reorganized his filing cabinets, hailed him as he passed the old man's door. "Look, Gabe, what I found at the bottom of a pile of papers! I don't think I understand it, all that stuff about protons and electron clouds, but as an erstwhile physicist you might want to look at it." The old man was, as accomplished, noted, and arrived people often are, genuinely modest and polite, as he handed him an original copy of Peter Mitchell's treatise on "The Chemical Coupling in Oxidative and Photosynthetic Phosphorilation."

It was not easy going at first. Mitchell's style was dense, his terminology very British, and since the subject was new, there were unexplained neologisms interspersed within it. Or so it seemed to him. But it was fascinating. The exact mechanism of the ATP molecule's (that is the chemical energy currency of life) synthesis was not well known before Mitchell. Many people had looked for a long time for some enzymatic agency, but no one could find the missing link. "*Ahol nincs, ott ne keress*," Mitchell would have said to himself had he spoken Magyar. Do not look for something where there is nothing. What he found instead of some nonexistent enzyme-substrate combination was a revolutionary, paradigm-breaking new concept.

It was a steep chemical gradient of protons across plant membranes that functioned as a crucial early step in energy conservation by the thylakoids (minute, closed pouches) in the chloroplasts of green plants. This is the first step that nature takes to use and convert the energy of sunlight to life energy. Now, a proton, or H^+, is the elementary particle whose concentration in an aqueous solution determines its pH or acidity. This is a property of the solution that is best measured with a pH meter, and in order to make accurate measurements of pH in a system, like that of an isotonic suspension of chloroplasts laboriously isolated from leaves, one needs a specialized, highly sensitive (and expensive) instrument. One that he did not have, of course.

Neither did his new mentor, the grand old scientist with his white mane curled up over his ears like a halo Einstein-style, who accepted him as his acolyte after Bob had gone back to Aberystwith on a long sabbatical. Paul was a maverick, in the positive modern sense, of course, for the original, historic one was a rustler, one of unsavory dealings. No, Paul had set himself apart from the botany faculty as an intellectual of many interests; he was involved in the teaching of religion and philosophy in addition to biochemistry. Maybe that was the reason why he (the student) felt attracted to this outstanding *doctissimus*. So the next morning, he was still sitting in Paul's empty, darkish and deserted lab in continued, open-ended, and fruitless contemplation of Mitchell's manuscript.

And then the second shoe fell. Like a *deus ex machina* on stage, there appeared out of the shadows of the hallway, pushing a lab cart heaped with assorted gear, Grant, the departmental *factotum*. Grant had a bit of a tragic history of his own. In the middle of his studies in biochemistry, he was abruptly plucked out of his life one day and transferred to one of Roosevelt's concentration camps for American citizens of Japanese origin. When he finally got out, he made a valiant effort to put the pieces of his life together again, but there had been no books to be had in camp, the years of war had dragged on slowly, and by the time he would have been ready to go aboard again, his ship had left. In short, he flunked his Ph.D. exam. A shattering experience. But as the chief administrative technician at the Botany Department, he had become a focal point of activity with time, unobtrusive though he was. "Hey, Gabe," he said standing now in the open door, "let's go and have a cup of coffee."

On his way out, he (the student) stopped to look at the lab cart. What he saw there gave him an adrenalin surge. He could not believe his eyes. "What's up?" asked Noda, looking at him quizzically. He was not a man of many words. "I cleaned out Dr. Did-Not-Make-Tenure's lab, and this is what was left of his stuff after he left a couple of days ago. Looks to me like you want to have your pick of it?"

He (the student) grabbed the pH meter like he had seen University of Oklahoma football players tuck in the pigskin under their armpits after a successful pass for the long run to the goal line. "Now wait, Norma has already asked for that one," Grant said. But then he shrugged: "You can have it. I'll give her something else." No one questioned Grant's decisions on matters like this; the department chair knew how to delegate authority.

But when doctissimus Paul, his new guru now, saw him getting set up for work on his newly materialized dissertation with the fanciest, most accurate, expanded-scale pH meter ever made and already hooked up to a recorder, he just chuckled. "From whose stockyard did you rustle up that thing? I hope the FBI won't come looking, for I sure did not pay for it." Then he shook some moolah loose from his own funds for all the other odds and ends that were still needed.

The thesis

Like a river that just broke its dam quickly finds its new course, work on the photosynthetic electron-transport chain progressed apace now. Every morning he walked down to the Chinese grocery store (that succumbed to urban renewal long ago) on Second Street a couple of blocks from the campus and bought a new batch of fresh spinach to be ground under ice, suspended cold, and centrifuged. When supplied with an electron acceptor (like NADP) and a hydrogen peroxide inhibitor (like catalase), the green suspension, stirred by a magnetic flea in its ingeniously configured (self-designed) little glass vial, would miraculously spring to life when the light was turned up on it.

The thylakoids, minute, membrane-bound pouches set partially free in the suspension of broken chloroplasts, would instantly start pumping protons from the suspension into the closed pouches, raising the outside pH by more than a unit.

Considering the enormously greater volume of the suspension in comparison to that inside the thylakoids, the difference in proton concentration inside and outside could be estimated to be a good thousandfold.

But what was most incredible to him about this process was not what it accomplished (conserved radiant energy in the form of a chemiosmotic potential) but that it occurred at all, for the agents of action, the thylakoids, could not really be considered "alive." They did not possess the standard attributes of life. Cellular life systems are considered to be alive when they are able to decrease their internal entropy at the expense of certain (reduced, organic, or inorganic, energy-containing) substrates that they take up from their environment. After having extracted the energy, the cells then reject these substrates in a degraded form.

Or to put it simply: living things assimilate and eliminate (or even more briefly: they eat and shit). Winston Churchill would have put it that way, for expounding once upon the art of good English prose, he recommended the use of Anglo-Saxon words, and among those the old ones and among those the short ones.

That said, back to defining life: life-forms must be able to reproduce, grow, and maintain themselves, and they must possess heritable genetic information to be considered alive. Now, his thylakoids were no longer part of their host organ (the leaf), nor were they part of their host cells (that make up a tissue), nor were they contained anymore in intact, endobiotic host organelles (chloroplasts) that colonize plant cells. They were simply lipid bilayers that had some enzymes embedded in them. The only attribute of life that they had was their response to a stimulus: light. So were they alive or not? You decide. But they acted alive nonetheless. They pumped protons like crazy, and he never ceased to marvel at this whenever his recorder started graphing his lifeless green suspension's eerie, otherworldly activity. The overarching experience that he took away from this (apart from a Ph.D. degree) was humility in the face of the imponderable.

And that reminds me of a political exchange on humility *vis-à-vis* the imponderable that I witnessed just a few days ago on television (this is another flash-forward). The progressive and the reactionary presidential candidates were asked about the exact timing of the onset of humanity in peoples' reproductive cells.

The liberal one carefully beat around the bush. This type of information was not within his bailiwick, he suggested. This was a complex theological question (a conundrum) that could arguably be argued forever without a resolution acceptable to most men and women who were open of mind and good of will. He carefully avoided adding (although to me he clearly implied it in his discourse) that those hands that were guided directly by an omniscient God in compiling the Jewish-Christian Bible had regrettably omitted to include a relevant passage on the subject, although God must already have known about things like the sperm and the ovum and their course of development at the time the Good Book was written. Therefore, He must have left the question open with a purpose in mind that was known only to Him.

And He left it open, even though he must have foreseen how heated the debate on this subject would become later among some of his sapient creatures.

The conservative candidate, in turn, was not beset by any shadows of doubt or humility. He knew exactly what God Almighty had chosen not to reveal. "At conception," he fired off his answer without hesitation to rapturous applause by his born-again, evangelical audience. So which man would you like to guide your country through these always increasingly perilous times? The careful thinker or the self-confident knower? The polls indicate that you are still vacillating on this, although it is only two months from the election.

Hiking, trespassing, and private property

With time, Davis turned out to be a nice, livable place. The neighborhood was quiet, the neighbors friendly, and everything was within easy biking range. They only used their car on weekend outings to the Coast Range. Salamander Canyon was a favorite place for an outing, and one time when brother-in-law Peter and family were visiting from Germany, the kids impressed their cousins, Ben and Jupp, by catching and then cooking a rattlesnake. There were also crayfish to be caught in Cache Creek, the stream that is cutting its way through the mountains about twenty miles west of Davis. They went on hikes almost every weekend into the rough countryside along Bear Creek with its Savanna-type vegetation.

Not the kind of grown-up walks along well-trodden paths with the boredom of a clearly defined goal and then back the same way, a routine that he always tried to avoid. No, these were cross-country explorations. When something came up like the bat cave or that shallow waterhole with the large California carp in it, or that well bubbling up from an otherwise dry slope that lent itself so well to mucking around in the mud, then the hike would stop there and turn into play. To add an extra dimension of challenge to all this was an element of danger of the kind that civilized America provides.

The hikes were illegal, for by necessity, they had to start after climbing over some fence with ominous No Trespassing signs on it. "Violators will be prosecuted as prescribed by Paragraph 478 of the Penal Code." Any place that was worth a cross-country hike in the Capay Valley was private property set off by barbed wire. There was the road, but it was lawful to step on it only as long as it was county maintained. But even the narrow, tertiary dirt roads that led into hiking territory were bounded by barbed wire beset by Keep Out signs.

This fixation on the sanctity of private property was something that they, he and Marina, never got used to. The forests around Icking and Harthausen were private property also, but everyone was free to enjoy them. You could gather mushrooms, wild strawberries, and raspberries and no one cared. There, the outdoors was God's gift to everyone, written in stone by laws much more ancient than those made by the interest-group-controlled legislators of free-market capitalism. Maybe the kind of vandalism, both careless and stupid and at times also mean and purposeful, that the lords of the land in America are worried about, somehow never reached a problem stage over there. Then again, maybe it is simply the dry California climate with its concomitant danger of forest fires that makes our owners here so protective.

But having confronted irate ones a few times, he came to understand that they were not angry because he might have disturbed the placid grazing of their cattle. They acted as if it was some divine right of theirs that was being brazenly violated. Their libertarian right to own the fruit of their labor. It seemed to him that Americans had a real problem with this. He tried to explain to them when they gave him a chance, that in the end, an end that awaited everyone, they would belong to the land and not the land to them and that their bones would come to rest in the land like the bones of the trespasser. He was happy to find that sometimes (twice to be exact) this line of thought made the red-necked, gun-toting, jeep-riding owner thoughtful.

Ownership fixation is an outgrowth of market mentality, and with us Americans, they are like a religion. I knew this well enough, yet I was still astounded when I first heard the other day an impressive-looking, coat-and-tie-clad male proclaim in a deep, resonant voice on CNBC, the business station on TV: "I believe in the market." After this sentence of biblical resonance first caught my attention, I started hearing it all the time on that station. Only, sometimes markets crash.

Now, that I am inserting final corrections into my manuscript with Marina's help, it is two years later. The Great Market Crash of 2008 and the Great Recession that followed mercifully purged references to any belief in the market from CNBC—for the moment at least.

More on hiking

Sometimes the hikes started from trailheads further afield like the ones at Plymouth, Volcano, or Fiddletown. They were also favorites but were less often visited destinations. Most excursions ended at the ice cream and pie place in Guinda in the Capay Valley, for that was close by. An old, retired black master sergeant whose globe-spanning career came to rest in that most quiet and secluded of spots ran it. It was more of a hobby for him, not a lifeline for he did not need one. It seemed to be simply a tie to his fellowmen for him. He (the student) liked to stop there, not only because they all liked the ice cream but also because small, off-the-beaten-track places and the lives that people might lead there held a never-ending fascination for him, although he watched them only as an uninvolved observer from afar.

There were only a few houses in Guinda, but there was also a once stately but now deserted and vandalized schoolhouse; a small, one-story, wooden, weather-beaten, no longer active hotel but with a cozy, still active saloon on the ground floor surrounded by a porch; and also a general store apparently patronized by the whole Capay Valley from Rumsey all the way down to Esparto. It was then, and maybe still is now, a storybook edition of an old American country store, one that had everything to offer that anyone could ever need. And it was dark and musty like such a store must be to be genuine. They would get their Welch's grape juice and sparkling water there.

In the years that followed since then, the winds of change blew a huge casino complex into that valley, built on the site of the dozen or so houses of the Rumsey Indian Rancheria, which could barely be seen from the road back then. I can only hope that the members of the Wintun Band did not sell their soul to the Mafia when they turned over what was left of their heritage to the market and that they get an equitable cut of the profits. And that those profits are the kind of compensation that makes them content with their lot. Nothing would make me content, though, in their place, for the whole valley was theirs before the white man imported the plague of smallpox that wiped out most of them. But that would be my problem, and I am glad I don't have it.

On the way home from the ice cream place, Schnucka (now Rob) would handle his silken cloth of a *Schnuckeltuch*, his security blanket that he used as an extra source of comfort, and launch into descriptions of the moving parts of some machinery that astoundingly arose in his four-to-five-year-old engineering mind. He (the student) could follow the description intelligently for a while as it unfolded, but as it got more and more complex, he lost track of the working of it. Then the reassuring, plump portliness of the three water towers of Davis would appear out of the gathering dusk in the east, and a good day would come to a close.

They went on these weekend hikes even during that time when Marina did her sabbatical-replacement teaching stint for a year at Cal Poly University in faraway San Luis Obispo (SLO). He would drive her to the Sacramento Airport at the crack of dawn every Monday morning, from where one of those little two-prop commuter planes flew her South to her job.

Busy as he was with classes, exams, duties as a teaching assistant, and of course, the running and the writing up of the experiments leading to the dissertation, he would have faced the impossible task of the single parent during her absence had she not have found a proxy worthy of herself. It was Ann, also a student, who would come and look after the kids much of the time during the day. They could not have managed without her. She was a godsend. The kids had a hard time understanding at first why it was not their mother who was there for them, but Ann soon put them at ease.

So much so that by Friday night, when time came to pick up Marina at the AMTRAC Station, the transition was smooth as vanilla custard. That train ride completed her weekly round-trip commuting to work three hundred miles from home. In the evening, before the train arrived, he and the kids would first stop by the tuchi-fry ([Ken]tu[cky]chi[ken]) place for the colonel's new crispy-style offerings with corn on the cob, coleslaw, and a coke; take the goodies along to the station; and then munch on them while waiting for the lights of the engine to appear on the, by then, night-dark tracks. Sometimes it was a long wait, for AMTRAC did and still does pride itself on being notoriously late. But when Marina alit from one of the cars, it was for all three of them as if their lives were made whole again.

Nuggets in the sand

Each summer, Mother-in-Law would invite Marina and the kids to Irschenhausen, where she had moved from Meererbush in the meantime. He would then lead a kind of free bachelor existence for a couple of months. The freedom focused on outings into the Sierra Nevada foothills on weekends.

The explorations consisted of rock hopping up the streams and finding new water holes that were temperate enough by this time of the year for some skinny-dipping. His routine was to find a dirt road where he would park not far from the hardtop but out of view of the traffic on it, preferably near a bridge with easy access to a stream. Then hike all day along it, hopping from one rock to the other, and having returned to the car by dusk, unroll his sleeping bag on a level spot for the night without bothering with a tent.

Route Cal-49, which skips along the western slopes of the Sierra Nevada foothills, offered endless opportunities for this. Placerville, Forest Hill, Auburn, and Grass Valley (the town, not the valley in Nevada) were all focal points, but his favorite was Washington, the little abandoned mining spot near Nevada City, California, on the North Fork of the Yuba River.

There, lying in the grass by the stream in the afternoon sun, reading the Mahabharata but dozing off ready for a snooze, he reached out sleepily to pick up some warm sand. And there they were in that handful: two small golden nuggets. The experience of this was a revelation into human nature for him and perhaps into the subtle workings of the intelligent universe itself.

Gone were all peace, contentment, and meditative contemplation of the soothing vibrations and fragrances of wind, water, trees, flowers, and butterflies in one spurt of inane activity. He was searching like a demented loco till the stars came out, dug up the sand and gravel on the riverbank, turned every stone in the shallow bed of the stream, and shattered against each other the round white boulders of quartz, a mineral that is often the bedrock wherein gold hides out. In vain. The two nuggets that the universe had sent and that came to him willingly and without effort were the only ones that were to be had, and that was that.

Finally, he was tired enough to laugh at himself, and so he went back to the ramshackle, half-abandoned wooden hotel in Washington run by a hippy family to find a cot for the night and a delicious meal of *chile relleno* for dinner before turning in. He never searched for gold again. But he bought some gold wire and crafted a pair of earrings for Marina made of braided hoops, with the nuggets in the middle.

The ashram

Instead of looking for gold, he went to visit Ananda, the ashram built in those days by Swami Kriananda on the high ridge on the other side of the Yuba from Nevada City, off the (then) gravel road that leads to Malakoff's Diggings. The Swami was born as an American who had inherited a fortune and who decided to be different from other self-indulgent scions of wealth. It seems (so he, the Swami, intimated) that the Pure Spirit called him, sent a lightning bolt of energy to his right hemisphere to defy the pull of hedonism.

Having returned from India where he had sat at the feet of gurus like Paramahansa Yogananda, he made his way to Nevada County, California, where he bought a few hundred acres of pine-forest land, sere in the summer and icy when the weather turns, up there on that high ridge. On the left-hand side of the road (going toward Malakoff's), there surged up from that poor, nutrient-deficient soil the farm for those of his disciples who were wedded to the ways of the here and now. On the other side was the ashram welcoming all seekers of enlightenment free of charge at first, and he went there often.

On one occasion, there was a festive assembly of Pure Spirit-oriented folks, and Swamiji, sitting in a canvas chair, gave a talk with the rest of them sitting on the ground as is apparently the Eastern custom. He told his life's story, which was already long, and he (the student) remembers now only one little bit of it because that seemed significant to him personally.

The Guru described eloquently how he wanted to write great plays for the stage that would show with crushing clarity how Western society had lost its way in the back alleys of the marketplace. And then, while he was working on the plot of one of them, all at once pictures of all the others that he already knew flashed through his mind, from *Prometheus Bound* through *Hamlet* and *The Merchant of Venice* all the way to the *Death of a Salesman*. He put his pen down. "It had all been said and heard, written and read already," he told his flock listening at his feet. "And not even Shakespeare had made any difference. Why should I try to reinvent the wheel?" That was when he decided to put his energy and money into his farm and his ashram.

A vision

This was also the time, in the midseventies, when he (the student) was quite seriously into meditation, and it was in the meditation cottage of Ananda that he had one of his out-of-body experiences. It was just turning dark, and the mosquitoes were out in force outside, for the wind was still. They did not venture inside because the smoke of the incense sticks that spiritual folks of the Eastern persuasion like to burn is apparently as noxious to them as it is to him (me). But there was also netting on the windows, which were open; the fragrance of the pine trees outside was free to waft in and mingle with the smoke inside.

The resulting sensory input was quite overwhelming. Nothing can conjure up forgotten sensations as vividly as an odor, and this one awakened, brought alive again from the long-dormant past a celebration of high mass held in the old church on the hill in Székélyudvarhely, the town which later swallowed up his village of Bethlenfalva. The occasion of that mass was special, for after a year of Latin in fifth grade he thought he could make out, for the first time, a few words of the liturgy chanted solemnly in the Gregorian style. "*Domine, non sum dignus ut intres sub tectum meum . . .*"

It was a cold and windy morning on that hill, but rays of sunshine broke through the clouds now and then and also through the tinted glass windows to break again in all shades of gray on the columns of silver smoke that billowed out of the censers shaken vigorously at the high points of the ancient ritual that described the self-sacrifice of the God who became man. And how, celebrating the memory of this God-Man, bread and wine become miraculously transubstantiated into his living body, which is consubstantial with his God Father.

As these fleeting images of this powerful, still present Christian mythology of the past faded into the stillness of the thought-free repetition of a mantra (he liked to visualize the swirling green suspension of his chloroplasts to help him focus on nothing), he became aware of something around him that was really a no-thing, for having never experienced it before, he had no word for it. It must have been something like a contact high emanating from the people around him who were all immersed in their own vibrant experiences of mind rest.

And then slowly, there emerged out of the closed-eye, dark formlessness a landscape. Green basically but more gray really, for there was a dense, high drizzling fog billowing up there that sometimes obscured and sometimes revealed a vague halo of the sun. This resulted in a constant shifting of the mountainside's hues from deep olive to clear emerald. There was a church of an unknown style of architecture and a village whose likeness reminded him of something that might have been in an old issue of the National Geographic Magazine, but he knew at the same time that he had never seen it in reality before, only now with his mind's eye. From the point of view where he could have been standing had he actually been there, two things stood out. A field of plants that looked like corn but were unlike any that he had ever seen before, for they were about three times taller than he was. Then there was a strange rock formation high above the village on the hillside, round and dark like a face and crowned by something like a bishop's hat, a mitre.

While the vision was quite breathtaking because it was a first, there was nothing unusual about it. Others had told him of much more startling experiences while under a trance. What made it so unlikely came later when he saw that rock again with his real eyes. But more about that later.

When such a "thing" happens to somebody else who tells you about it, you shrug your shoulders and say, "Oh yeah, sure, how interesting." But when it happens to you, you start pondering about new mechanisms for something that was previously unthinkable. What if those trillion nerve cells in your brain are one great antenna that is either turned off or just tuned out from receiving manifestations of an existence that is always there, either waiting for contact or just simply floating indifferently in its undefined spacetime but available for interaction with those who are capable of it? Like he was, apparently, for a fleeting moment in Ananda. Nothing more came of this strange revelation. It did not point to some momentous future development. It just happened; it came and went. If chance had not taken him to Totóntepec Mije later, there would have been nothing more to say about it.

The postdoc: nitrogen fixation

Not much could be said about that time either when he became so much "more learned" in the love of wisdom (philosophiae doctor, Ph.D.) that they conferred a paper with a fake golden seal on it to document the temporary conclusion of his formal learning process, for all that was left to do now, in the aftermath of this *grand finale*, to type some two hundred applications for employment to institutes of higher learning. This was before computers, and if your typewriter typed a typo into that letter, you had to type it again, for word was that smudged letters with erasures went directly to the circular file. Then you could almost bet that in the next copy, the typo would surface in another place. Patience and quality was the name of the game, and both he and Marina had to learn it, for they were both immersed in the job-application game up to their ears.

Their problem was poor timing. By the time their hard-earned skills came on the market, the baby boomers had outmolted their college stage and had left, leaving half-empty classrooms behind. The results of the population explosion that followed the war (World War II), the baby boomers, hit the university system some twenty years after the soldiers had come home. In preparation for the invasion that lasted about a decade, the universities had overstaffed their faculties, and now the administrations were facing an aging surplus of tenured professors who were not quite ready to leave. Marina had two offers, but he did not get any, and so when the chance arose for him to accept a postdoctoral slot with the Agronomy Department, she decided to stay with him and get a second master's degree in German.

His two years at the highest level of studenthood, as a "postdoctoral student," were good. Very good in fact. The Agronomy Department was an outfit wide awake compared to botany. The work was a well-planned mix of theory and practice as demanded by the nature of the mission in serving agriculture. All the people there were not only compatible and competent, but some of them were outright inspiring, and all were noted experts in their fields. In Don's lab, he finally learned how to design experiments properly, and in chairman Cal's classes, he came to understand how to evaluate the data statistically for significance. The UC system had bestowed a doctorate on him without ever having taught him these essentials, so in a way he was lucky not to have found a faculty position immediately.

The work itself revolved around the fixation of nitrogen (N) by soil bacteria that invade the roots of leguminous (bean family) plants, where they induce the plant to form nodules. In these nodules, the bacteria morph into bacteroids. That is, they lose their identity as individuals capable of independent survival and become obligate, plant-dependent endobionts. In this capacity, they turn into little factories dedicated to supplying their host plant with an essential element, N, one that is usually in short supply in the soil and therefore limits plant growth.

The way they do this is, like so many things in life, little short of the miraculous (or is entirely so). The substrate the bacteroids use for their activity is atmospheric N, the N_2 molecule, the same stuff we suck into our lungs when we breathe. For us, it just goes in and out unchanged, for this molecule, triple-bonded as its two atoms are to each other, is one of the most stable, impervious compounds known to us. But not so to the bacteroids! Rather late in the course of the evolutionary time, it became apparent to the Pure Spirit that there was a food shortage afoot on Earth, namely that of plant-available N in the soil, that needed to be remedied. In response to this need, many different kinds of bacteria, among them his root-nodule ones, developed (or were instructed to produce, if you like) an enzyme, the most complex and energy-demanding one we know, called nitrogenase. It reduces N_2 to ammonia, which the plant then is able to incorporate into amino acids, which are the building blocks of proteins.

But that is not all there is to it. As the N_2 diffuses into the nodules, oxygen (O) would naturally diffuse in with it also. Yet by some quirk of nature, O_2 poisons and disables nitrogenase. So an ingenious device had to evolve (or to be created) to keep the O_2 away from the bacteroids. You would never guess how this is done if I didn't tell you. The bacteroids induce the plant cells to provide oxygen-impervious pouches to enclose them, where they are supplied with O_2, this life-essential oxidant, in the same way all of our own cells get it: by using hemoglobin as the agent of O_2 transfer.

This hemoglobin is another enzyme, a two-part one. The plant produces the protein part, the globin; and the bacteroids, the cofactor part, the heme. Just consider now for a moment how mind-blowing this is! Neither the legumes alone nor the bacteria alone use and produce hemoglobin. But after the twain met and were faced with the necessity of moving the offending O_2 molecule across the pouch barrier in a bound, inoffensive form, they came up with the same solution that we, the mammals (among other life-forms), have found also. So let creationists and evolutionists both play their games fighting each other, and let *us* bow our heads. Life as it exists at the interface of the two great principles is imponderable.

Why does it work the way it does, and why should it exist at all? But that was the subject of his second out-of-body experience. More on that later.

Problems at home

Meanwhile, back at 845 North Campus Way, there was one significant family episode that must be mentioned. Stefan, the Fox (now Steve) was not having a good year at school. He did not notice it, but Marina became aware of the situation when she was able to spend a few days in Davis and to visit his classroom. His fourth-grade teacher came across as a pleasant-enough woman when they first met her, but then she turned out to be a teacher unengaged with her students, one cool and remote. This had an adverse effect on class discipline and also affected the Fox's attitude to learning. He appeared listless and disconnected, had no friends, and none of the enthusiasm he had the previous year. Of course, his mother's absence all week was probably a more important factor than his teacher's distant personality.

Well, rather than quitting her job for the third quarter at Cal Poly (actual teaching jobs were prized assets on one's resume), they decided to look for a change in venue to get the Fox out of his rut and into a more inspiring environment. The Waldorf School in Sacramento was one possibility, but the encounter of the Fox with the faculty was not favorable, as viewed by either side. The teacher who interviewed him related that the Fox called things that he considered hard like math "stupid." So they were not eager to accept him this late in the school year. And the Fox, in turn, was not enthusiastic about a school either that was opposed to television and believed in manual skills instead, like gardening and handicrafts. He decided the outfit was "goofy."

Feeling that dragging out the trauma of this necessary change would not help, they drove out to the other option they had, directly from the Waldorf School encounter. He could tell just by looking that his son was aware of something unheard of happening. He was too bewildered and scared to be resentful, and his father was suffering with him.

This other option was advertised as a spiritual boarding home for children in the foothills near Nevada City, California, close to a little country school that served the surrounding rural area. The home was run by Ma Deva Pria, an American woman, who had chosen an Indian name when she became a follower of Yogananda. She was a cheerful, motherly person with two children of her own, living in a spacious house on the edge of a little lake surrounded by forest. There was a rowboat tethered to the pier and a pony in the stable, as well as chicken coops and rabbit hutches. The setting was idyllic, offered a chance to live out in the country and was not far from Ananda that both they and Ma Deva were interested in. In short, it was like an extended summer camp experience for the Fox for the last months of the school year.

They were lucky. The scene turned out to be a wholesome one for him. He made an immediate connection with David, Ma Deva's older son, who was of his own age and with the good-natured baby. The kids were mellow and happy, which reflected well on their mother. And there was a color TV set! Right then and there, the Fox decided to stay there, not to miss the movie that was showing, and when Ma Deva mentioned that they were going to see *Jaws* the next day, the deal was done. Maybe it was also a deciding factor that their own little black-and-white TV set at home, which they had only gotten (after resisting it for a long time) to keep the kids from going to the neighbors to watch, was under quite strict parental control.

So in a sense, they took advantage of their son's anticipation of the movie (a rare treat) that contributed to his decision to stay; it permitted the parting to be cloudless. But in retrospect, it seems like an all too sudden and brutal separation for a little kid not yet ten from his family, for reasons that were not very well explained to him and that probably would not have been very well understood even if they had been. They did not realize that he might internalize it as an exile and a rejection, which he could only resent.

I see this now, but what he saw then was something like "I have been to boarding schools myself and survived them, so why shouldn't my son?" He set himself up as the measure of things by which he expected others to see the world. This was misguided and insensitive, and we have often wished since then that we had not taken this step. But at the time, it was working out well: the little country school gave the Fox a chance to excel academically. He won banana splits and blue ribbons (we still have them) in math tests and sports. We picked him up for weekends or stayed there with him and celebrated his tenth birthday with a piñata and his first air gun, in memory of the real one his father had received about that same age.

There was an old, sentimental, schmaltzy Magyar *Schlager*, which I remember from childhood days: "*Minden elmúlik egyszer, minden a végéhez ér . . .*" Everything is over once; everything comes to an end, and their Davis days, intensively lived and formative, came to an end with a phone call. It said that he had been accepted for a position as a research assistant professor at the Plant Pathology and Physiology Department of Louisiana State University at Baton Rouge. As it developed after they got there, Marina also landed a position with the Department of Foreign Languages. The Deep South! They had mixed feelings about it, for by this time, they had become so Californian that they wondered if there was really life east of the continental divide. He was forty-five years old in starting out in this new career. His colleagues in academe at that age were already all accomplished experts.

Chapter 9

The Biologist

They would have preferred to stay in California, and they could have, for Don invited him very cordially to stay for at least another year, working in his lab on nitrogen fixation. But he was already in the middle of being middle-aged by this time and still a student, even though a postdoctoral one. Other colleagues at this stage of life were mid-career scientists, and this was hard for him to take.

The job market

It had nothing to do with his self-esteem; it was much more his urgent need for financial security that he all of a sudden rediscovered. It was also an unasked-for gift, one of late-blooming, grown-up insight, bestowed on him by a midlife crisis that up to now he was too busy to be aware of. Fed up with being an eternal student, now it was clear that he had to take the first real job that came his way, and Marina agreed. It was not going to be a top university, that much they knew after some two hundred fruitless applications. Nor could they both hope to get a tenure-track faculty job at the same school, given the scarcity of openings.

The California State University at Chico was one of their dream choices, but alas, the biology department there advised him after several attempts that they did not expect to have a vacancy for the next decade or so. So he took out time to visit the City College of Santa Barbara, California, but the admissions officer, who offered him a cup of coffee, just pointed to a stack of 283 applications (with his among them). "You have a nice publication record, but unfortunately that makes you overqualified and specialized for the job we want to fill," the man confided.

"We need a young generalist who does not mind to teach from basic textbooks." So the seven papers that he had published under Don's expert tutelage actually worked against him! To be found overqualified for a job one really wants is a particularly irksome aggravation of the spirit. It is like being disqualified for being well prepared.

He visited the two-year college at Ganado, Arizona, somewhere between Keams Canyon and Window Rock. With its few run-down buildings, it looked like it would be the end of the line for him, but he would have welcomed the interaction with the Hopi and the Navaho lads who must have constituted the student body. It has probably grown into a presentable institution by now even without his contributions, but at that time, he was almost glad that they did not need him.

Then there was the intriguing little college of some two dozen students off California Highway 168 in the middle of nowhere, literally some *mille miles de tout terre habitée*, as Saint Exupéry described the desolation of the place where his own airplane crashed. Well, Deep Springs College was not quite a thousand miles from the nearest settled place on Earth, but it is definitely the only human habitation within the Deep Springs Valley, a huge span of sere aridity sandwiched in between the White Mountains and the peaks of the Piper Mountain Wilderness of California, an hour's drive to the nearest town of any size. Deep springs, that sounds cool and verdant with a crystal-clear rivulet playing its way downhill between mossy rocks and the roots of shade trees, but what actually surrounds the handsome though dusty little campus is stark desert. Yet there must have been a stream there, all right, for there were fields of alfalfa in evidence and even some cattle grazing in the background.

And indeed, the uniquely focused liberal arts curriculum included a holistic, hands-on exposure to the sturdy, life-sustaining wholesomeness of agriculture. The Cold Springs workday for students went from things like milking cows at dawn to dealing with Diderot at dusk. The man in charge (I forget his name and title) was austerely modest, yet at the same time, almost evangelistically enthusiastic about explaining the workings of his domain to which only the very best could have access [sic]. "The faculty is not only well-published," he said, "but it is made up of characters that would fit well into the ripples of Finegan's Wake." And indeed, the three professors on the permanent staff taught all subjects, and all of a sudden, he felt decidedly underqualified.

But he knew at first sight that he could have been happy there. The family? Maybe they would have thrived there also. Or maybe they would have run away. But there was no need to worry about that, for landing a position at Cold Springs, as intimated by its headmaster, was tantamount to breaking open the very gates of the Eastern, intellectual, ivory-tower elite, an impossible feat for a nonlegacy outsider like him.

Louisiana

Such, then, were some of the pleasures of preparing for a profession that seemed to send him urgent messages that he was not really needed. So that when word came from Louisiana State University that yes, not only was there an opening for a research assistant professor there, but also, after having heard his invited guest lecture, they were actually willing to hire him into it, there was no need for a family council. They just nodded tacitly and packed up their possessions for transport. Marina had quickly sold the house for almost three times what they paid for it six years ago.

When their departure became imminent, Rachel, their cat-loving neighbor came over and wanted to know what they were going to do with Katze. "We are not going to leave her behind. Ann is going to airfreight her to Baton Rouge after we get there," they told her. "She is a dear member of our family, and besides, the kids must learn that you remain responsible for the animals you tame." Then they were off, the Saab station wagon packed to the hilt, but with only Schnucka in the back, for the Fox was spending the summer with his grandmother in Icking and with his uncle Peter in Corsica.

It was not only a good trip; it was also his first exposure to the Loneliest Highway. They picked up US 50 in Sacramento and stayed overnight in Fallon, Nevada, after the sun had set. That was a sleepy little town then, before its boomtown explosion of the latter days. He took off after dinner at the tuchy-fry place to do his customary wanderings through the deserted, dark residential streets but instead got tripped up by the old downtown casino, the only one Fallon had then. He quickly won fifty bucks that were more than enough for gas money all the way to Baton Rouge.

Blackjack

He had no knack for gambling, but blackjack is a simple yet strange game that he liked to play. What is strange about it is that the player, not the dealer, that is to say the house with its deep pockets, has the theoretical advantage. The house has no choice, the rules of the game say that it must deal itself up to at least seventeen points, and if it goes over that, it loses. The little gambler with his shallow pockets, on the other hand, is free to calculate the probabilities in his favor.

If he sees that the odds are likely to go against him, he can stop the cards from coming, and in the long run, if he keeps himself under control, he stands a good chance to stay ahead of the game. But that is not the way it works in real life, for who, besides a mathematician or a professional gambler, can figure whether the odds are seven to six for him or against him? So he sat at the green table with the probabilities of winning about seven out of thirteen deals at the back of his mind and watched the people next to him bet.

What he observed was an education. Most of the gamers seem to have no clue as to what they are doing, but they don't mind doing it anyway. Fun, boredom, or compulsion? Who knows or cares?! They bet even when the odds are eight to five against them. "Hey, buddy," he says to the guy next to him, for egging people on is not forbidden, "the odds were eight to five against you. Why did you ask the dealer to hit you with another card? You were looking at sixteen points in your hand!" The man shoots a sideways glance at him. "Oh yeah? So where is *your* chofer? 'Cause that must be your limousine out front." Amusement all around the table.

The folks in Fallon and the ones who stop there (or used to back then) are not gamblers. Cards are a sport and a pastime like walking your dog. You lose a ten-spot. That's enough, so you fold and move over to the bar for a drink. But the real reason why the house makes money on blackjack is endurance. Luck runs in streaks. If you have the gumption to leave at the end of your lucky streak, you leave ahead. Few people have it apparently. But if your billfold runs dry before your unlucky streak had run its course, then you leave a loser and the house now knows exactly what was in your valet. For the house is like fate—it is indifferent and outlasts all streaks.

Going back east

In the morning, it was eastward-ho again. In America, there is something unnatural about going East. Going east is going back. "Back East, out West." The East is something that had been tried, done, mastered, and left behind. I hope Easterners will feel amused rather than annoyed by hearing this, but this is the way they felt. By brunch time, they were in Austin (Nevada). They had scrambled eggs and diced potatoes for breakfast, spiced the Mexican way for which the International Hotel is famous. Famous, that is, among those who are inveterate Austinites, and they did not qualify for that yet. That came later. Now it was their very first time in Austin.

Back then, the International Hotel still had rooms to rent, although it was quite as ramshackle already as it is today. It must have been those three little motels that in time sprung up on the other side of the road that finally meant the end of the road for the old hotel. The town still had a grocery store then. Now everything the locals need means a 111-mile (one-way) trip to Fallon. I wonder how gas at US $4 a gallon factors into their budgets? Austinites are not millionaires. And how did they manage before the roads got paved and before the infernal combustion engine cut covered-wagon time to a tenth of what it used to be when its silver-rush population was twenty-five times what it is today and when there may not have been much of a Fallon to get supplies from?

Just like the International is famous for its breakfasts, the two gas stations in town are famous for their exorbitant prices. He wondered why free-market competition did not curb that until he found out that the same guy owned them both.

So instead of supporting this Austin monopoly, they decided to see if their trusty Saab would take them all the way to Eureka, seventy miles further on.

But let me tell you now, do not do such a thing. It is not cool! Not when it is a hundred and ten degrees in the shade and there is none, while there is no traffic either to help you in case of need as befits the name of that road. You remember how gas gauges used to work? They moved ever so slowly at first and then zoomed to zero in a hurry. That is what happened to them half way to Eureka. The Saab was the freewheeling type; you could put it in neutral on down slopes, and it would wheel freely without using any gas.

But in Nevada, there is an upslope for every downslope, and they sweated out every one of the last several miles. They made it all right to the next gas pump; only he could not muster the philosophical detachment while watching the gauge to enjoy the dance of the pinion pines and junipers like he did before. Nor did he notice the turnoff to the Grass Valley, or all those hills that he climbed or hiked around later. You "see" everything all the time, of course, but you notice things only when your controller decides that it matters to you for reasons only he knows. And his controller was preparing himself for the bayous of Louisiana now.

There is a lot of grand scenery between Austin and Oraibi, passing through Ely, Nevada, Panaca, Nevada, Cedar City, Utah, and Glen Canyon en route, but what I remember best now is their second visit to the Land of the Hopi Indians. It was not really the shortest way to get to Baton Rouge, but he wanted to see it again.

They had visited the Black Mesa on a previous journey, in 1965, going west that time. Having seen the wonders of the Painted Desert, night fell when they reached Holbrook, Arizona, and at the southern edge of town they ran into a sign: A Good Night's Rest for Three Dollars. It was an old, Mexican-style house with a bare, large lawnless yard beset with a number of spiny and a few shady plants all surrounded by a stone wall. The night's rest turned out to be worth ten times the price; it was so refreshing. There was something about the house, the yard, and the owner's cordiality in addition to their being tired that did it. After hundreds of forgotten night's rests and unrests on the road since then and before then, that house in Holbrook has never lost its place as a standard for them of how good a night's rest can feel.

Much later—I am not sure now which trip it was, maybe forty years had passed when they passed again through this seedy town on the southern fringes of the Navajo Reservation—they looked for that house (for old times' sake) and actually found it. It was near an underpass of a now busy and loud highway in a desolate area of urban blight, abandoned by life, forgotten apparently even by the relentless forces of redevelopment, for it was still there. When an old owner dies and there are no heirs interested in the house that had been his home, it can often stand there falling apart for a long time until it finally crumbles.

So does my grandfather's house stand there in Bethlenfalva. Yes, I am interested, but it is ten thousand miles from here, and the process of suing it back from the government is endless. Their host in Holbrook, however, was generous; he took out time to tell them about the Hopi villages on the "black" mesas just north of there, and they decided to investigate. Otherwise, they would have driven on toward Flagstaff on the road that has turned into Interstate 40 since that first time in 1965.

The Hopis

The ancestral home of the Hopi tribe is the most noteworthy place in America, north of the Rio Grande. The fact that those villages on the southern edges of the three black mesas contain the oldest continuously inhabited dwellings north of Mexico only scratches the surface of their significance. Their real significance is a spiritual one. When the forebears of the People climbed up that steep ladder of their lore out from the bowels of the earth for the last (fourth) time and watched as the hole they left behind was closed up by water, they knew that they were led by the Pure Spirit into a new, clean state of being. It was into a world as yet unspoiled by man. The Spirit then led them to the Black Mesa Country, where they founded the hubs of their new universe, Shongopovi and Oraibi, perched on steep, sheer cliffs with a clear view of what is now called the San Francisco Mountains, far in the distance.

From there, the winds of the spirit world blow their way and bring the water of life for their corn plants when they ask for it. And they have to ask for it, for otherwise it does not come, and subsistence on the mesa is harsh. Dry as it may be, they were ordered to go there on purpose so that they would never forget how to ask for rain and how to maintain living contact with the Spirit, a gift that is always lost when people come to live in the midst of plenty.

Once there, they undertook pilgrimages to the four sacred directions of the sky: to the closed, icy gates of the North (contrary to much pseudo-scientific guessing they had not come from there); to the hot, steamy jungles of the South; to the cool, dense forests of the East; and to the sere, sandy deserts of the West. They were told to do this to deserve gaining possession of Oraibi.

In their wanderings, they were meant to acquire the knowledge, the good medicine needed for the healthy communal functioning of their clans and for an unceasing communication with the spirit world. The first to return to the hub was the Bear clan, whose sign you can still see on some of the genuine pieces of Hopi jewelry. As other clans arrived, a Bear shaman assigned places for the newcomers to live and to grow their corn plants, but they had to show that they also had brought with them useful medicine. In time, other villages grew up, always on the edge of a mesa and always within a clear full view of the Sacred Mountains.

As they drove up from Holbrook past the old trading post at Keams Canyon on that long-ago (1965), pre-Louisiana trip, the first village they encountered was Walpi on First Mesa. This mesa terminates in a sharp cusp as it points westward, and at its tip, it narrows to the width of a dirt road. But beyond the natural defensive position of this defile, the cliffs that make up the mesa's furthest western end broaden again, roughly to the size and shape of a battleship. And on this gray promontory high up over the surrounding desert, from where you can survey the endless landscape like you can view the ocean from the top deck of a liner, sit the rough stone-slab houses of the village, as they have sat there for long ages now.

If you have any sense of history, Walpi will tie your mind into knots of contemplation. But you cannot go in anymore like they did then. The Bahana may not pass the narrows anymore (and on our very last visit there, we didn't even find it, perhaps because of a new road that climbs the cliffs now). I am glad that the peace-loving Walpians have learned to protect themselves from tourist hordes. But that also meant that the little Schnucka was excluded, now on their way to Louisiana, from having his young mind impressed by this monument to past and present. Maybe that was just as good, for his head was focused entirely on the present mode of the passing of time on this trip. Instead of figuring out the shifting gears of imaginary machinery, as he used to before, he was counting future hoards of money based on the amassing of his newly instituted allowance.

Those visions of wealth were only interrupted in Oraibi, where they witnessed a show of generosity, a redistribution of property, as it were. It was a Kachina dance that ended with a veritable shower of all sorts of useful to useless gifts (from household goods to cigarettes) from the rooftops and from the dance floor. Schnuka was in the front row of expectant recipients, and he managed to snare something; I think it was a box of crackers. When passing through Shongopovi on Second Mesa, a passing shower made him look up and remark, "A desert is where it rains." I do not recall what other experiences led him to this generalization.

The Deep South at last

Silver City, New Mexico. Fort Stockton, Texas. Austin, Texas. Beaumont, Texas. Texas is endless. Lafayette, Louisiana. Baton Rouge. He had already bought their new house in Baton Rouge, off Highland Avenue, past the Louisiana State University campus with the help of Bill (the nicest friend and colleague you could ever wish for) on a previous house-hunting trip. As they were driving from house to house, with him shaking his head: "Not this one and not that one either." Bill was getting puzzled. "What's wrong with them?" he probed patiently. "Nothing really. They just don't have the right kind of vibes," was all he could offer in return. Next time I have to go finding a house for an outlander, I'll bring my vibrometer along." Bill chuckled. "We Americans count the bedrooms and baths and insist on a den for the pool table. But vibrations? Lord, have mercy!"

While the whole trip came off trouble-free, it was on the floor of their own garage that they found all the motor oil drained out of the crankcase of their trusty

Saab the very next morning. It could have done it anywhere on that long road, and that would have been a bummer, for small-town garages in Texas and Nevada were not known to stock spare parts for Saab station wagons. But no, like a good horse, it waited with his stomach cramps until it felt safe in its home stable.

The house was livable, although the vibes were only so-so. It was bigger than the one in Davis, and so was the yard, but that was nothing but a large square surface densely covered by Bermuda grass, with a few sprigs of poison ivy at the back fence and, scattered, low hills of fire ants half-hidden in the turf. It was definitely not the grape-house environment of Davis. The thick and high stand of nondescript vegetation behind the fence did not need any No Trespassing signs, for it was choked with poison ivy, and so no one in his right mind would have trespassed his way into it.

It soon dawned on them that hiking and exploring like in the Capay Valley were not on the agenda here. Neither was any outdoors activity very enticing on account of the humid heat, which would linger on unabated till the end of October. Then it could cool off if it felt like it, and an occasional icy blizzard that would sweep down from the North Pole guided by the Mississippi River directly to Baton Rouge kept the vegetation from sporting subtropical species. Unperturbed by the blizzards were the fire ants, although they had migrated north from milder climes relatively recently. It took them (the family) a little while to get used to them.

Ants are another miracle of nature. Just consider how small they are, and yet they are equipped with all they need not only to scurry vertically up any surface at the same pace as down while carrying loads greater than their own weight, but in addition to being brawny, they are also programmed to live by a strict code of social conduct including altruism, service, self-sacrifice, patriotism, and a discernment of the concepts of just and unjust wars, and all that without the need to make value judgments to slow them down when quick action is needed.

So ants were always more the objects of fascination for him than of distraction or even antagonism. The fire ants changed that. When you inadvertently step on their nest hidden in the springy, soft cushion of lawn grass in Louisiana, they do what other ants do not. They are instantly all over you, bite through your skin, and deposit in the cut some vile stuff from their abdomen that promptly produces painful, itchy pustules under your skin.

Maybe they are training to become terrorists. Or maybe they wish they could be the wasps again that they once were. Either way, they do not have any of the airy, buzzy, mind-your-own-business, though pesky and respect-demanding detachment of their yellow-jacketed second cousins. They are unnecessarily mean-spirited, at least so it appears to their victims, while from their point of view, why, they just do what comes to them as the right and righteous political thing to do. Things to do to those who step on their nests and so disturb their own chosen, traditional way of life.

The workplace

At the Department of Plant Pathology and Crop Physiology, however, there was next to no overt politics, only a bit of mostly good-natured politicking. The department was an important part of the LSU Agricultural Experiment Station, and its ample funds were under the aegis of its Chairman. His position was therefore one of power, for it was not a rotational one as was the custom at UC Davis. The chair was the boss, and if he did not displease the almighty experiment station director (who had a few hundred doctorate-level faculty members under him), he was the boss-in-tenure for life.

Now you cannot do any science without money, and it takes a while (and often forever) for a new professor to garner extramural funds. So you had to be on good terms with the chair. But that was not really politics, for Wes was a straight shooter and doled out the goods equitably. Accordingly, tensions within the department were only at the personal and not on the financial level. But human nature, such as it is, makes it simply impossible to find a group of fifteen some people (that's how many pathologists there were) without a commensurate level of ever-bickering, ego-tripping, low-level incompatibility.

The physiologists were an exception. They had little to suffer from all that, for they (we) were organizationally autonomous and exceptionally congenial personally. Originally there were only four of them, all inbred products of the Louisiana system like, so it seems, everyone was at LSU at that time. Then to their everlasting credit, the four managed to break down their institutional and cultural stonewalls and prevail over the system to import a New York Yid and a California Honky.

On climates

The Yid was Marc; and the Honky, none other than yours truly. There was some amicable give-and-take about the slurs (which come across only as good-natured banter when offered in a spirit of fun: "Yes, that's what I am and I am proud of it"), and he, as the originator of calling the two newcomers by what they were, proposed to give the natives medals of merit for their courageous initiative in importing this fresh blood.

But the preexistent societal climate at LSU was something else. The students not only called the professors sir, they also acted as if they really meant it during classroom-professional interactions. Afterward in the evening, however, they organized Cajun-food-munching, genuinely friendly student-teacher social get-togethers:

Jambalaya and a crawfish pie and filé gumbo
'Cause tonight I'm gonna see my ma cher amio
Pick guitar, fill fruit jar and be gay-o
Son of a gun, we'll have big fun on the bayou

Jambalaya, des tartes d'ecreuvisse, file gombo
par a soir moi j'va allez voir ma chere amie-o
jouer l'guitar, boire de la jogue et fair de la musique
tomnerre m'ecrase un va avoir un bon temp sur le bayo.

Such a good-natured, friendly, respectful, yet exuberant spirit simply did not exist in the goal-oriented, get-the-work-done academia of the University of California, where lights were always burning past midnight in the labs.

At LSU, the campus was dark and deserted after "duty hours." I do not want to sound as being down on the academic climate at LSU. It has probably changed radically since then. But then it felt, after UCSB and UCD, as if it were suffering from intellectual anemia like a desert island with only palm trees for vegetation, although it was embedded into a pool of good, bright, nice, and kind people, some of whom were clearly tops in their fields. Let me try to explain the subliminal malaise of it by use of examples.

He and Marc were on the selection committee one time for a new weed scientist. The man favored by the majority came across as knowledgeable enough, a well-trained "spray-and-pray" specialist, as people are called in the trade who douse weed-infested stands of crops with herbicides and then stand back in hopes that the application of the poison might work as expected.

But Marc wanted more than such a specialist. He wanted the new addition to the department to be somebody with whom he could engage in exchanges of thought outside the man's narrow field of preparation. So he asked him about his philosophical vision. His views of a clean, poison-free, future agricultural world. The man shook his head in consternation, as did others on the committee. "I didn't have any kind of philosophical vision when I was hired, and I don't need one now to do the work I get paid for" was a comment from one of the colleagues that my controller put into permanent storage.

Then it was he and Marc again who chose to go against the grain of the culture. This time they were members of a Ph.D. exam committee. Recalling the European tradition that a *Herr Professor-Doktor* would be expected to work ceaselessly on deepening his erudition in a wide field outside of his specialty, he ventured a question that would have been laughable at the University of Munich. "So you want to be a doctor of philosophy? That's good. Do you know then what this title means in English?" he asked the candidate. The man was visibly "shook." He had no idea.

Cohn was the only one on the committee who did, and he provided the translation. Sure, the man had prepared himself for a life in agricultural biology and knowing any classics was Greek to him, but this lack of basic curiosity in a future Ph.D. was symptomatic of the climate, and that was discouraging.

Then there was the social climate. It was not only the all-black crew sweating on top of their roof (which leaked in the first rain after they moved in) with the white foreman shouting orders on how to lay the tile from the shade of a tree below. It was more subtle, it was a persistent malaise that was still alive, lingering on, some fifteen years now after the Civil Rights Revolution of the sixties.

An example of it happened to Marina, who was teaching French language and literature at LSU during their first year there. During the second semester, a solitary black student enrolled in one of her classes, a graduating senior transferred over from Southern University, the all-black school on the opposite, northern fringes of town. As she was woefully unprepared, Marina was going to reluctantly flunk her until the department chair explained the implications. It was the established custom, it seems, that the best students of Southern U were transferred to LSU for their final term, so that they could graduate with a white LSU degree as a reward for their efforts. And so, of course, these token, prize products of the unequal system were not permitted to fail. Hopefully, both the "equal" and the "separate" in the political motto of those times have undergone a radical change of heart since then.

Of all the local climates, however, it was the climate itself that you had to be born and raised into to survive. Marc apparently learned to tolerate it, for he is still there, working hard, a respected authority in his field, editor-in-chief of an important scientific journal. He (the biologist) is a natural thermophyle himself. It simply cannot ever get hot enough for him, so that part of the climate was fine with him.

The humidity, however, was like a sledge hammer and would hit his sinuses so mercilessly that he became afraid to go outside. Marina suffered through it gamely, but she is an all-out cold-clime person, and after the first year, well, *sie hatte die Nase voll*, she had her nose full, as the saying goes in Berlin. Her nose, sinuses, and the rest of her had taken all they could take literally, figuratively, mentally, and physiologically. Her teaching position at LSU was temporary anyway, and when another one opened up at the University of Oregon in Eugene, she took the children and moved to Oregon.

That was a continent away. Yes, she wanted to continue working in her field, and yes, she was anxious to get back out West both for her own sake and that of the children, to get away from a climate where she did not feel at home, that of the still undigested, fermenting aftermath of the Civil War that the Civil Rights Revolution of her days had not yet been able heal and resolve.

But there were other reasons also, which perhaps had not been resolved to this day. For him, yes, but maybe not for her. She was concerned with family dynamics and must have felt that that a separation would be a test of the soundness of their ties. Would her husband feel freer without the burden of the family? Would the children do better under a more cloud-free sky? And could she handle the job of a single mom? In the end, they all suffered and were happy when it was over and were together again.

The concept

Work-wise, it was not an easy deal for him at LSU. There were greenhouses for whole-plant work, to be sure, but they were abandoned and in disrepair, and since they were lacking climate control, they were useless, more like baking ovens or steam saunas during the long hot season. He thought of them as the original site where the notion of the "greenhouse effect" must have been born. His lab was a bare, converted classroom lacking any of the requirements for modern physiological research at the cell or subcellular level, and unfortunately, he was not the type who is good at improvising: giving his hands leave and freedom to assemble fixtures and machinery, something that many other people relish.

In addition, he could not use preparation for teaching classes as an excuse for drawing his salary, for his job description called for 100 percent research on soybeans. Let's face it, he was not good at the piddling nitty-gritties, the detail that makes up so much of a scientist's life at work. He was a concept man, but one who was on his own now. And what was even worse, he was one not only without a concept but without any financial underpinnings to support work on the concept should he unearth one. He soon saw that he had better learn to swim quickly in the sea of academic research realities if he did not want to sink. For what could you do with soybeans that somebody else was not already busily doing?

Then just like with his thesis at Davis, an unforeseen circumstance came to his rescue. It happened at one of those annually recurring meetings on agricultural commodities, where he heard a talk by a colleague. John was not an inspired orator. He seemed to be an introvert also, unapproachable and standoffish as he came across to him at their only eye-to-eye contact following that talk. But that talk opened a door for him into a space that he was to occupy for the next twenty years. It was about a little-known organism, a fungus that colonizes the roots of most plants. The live plant is the sole source of food for this fungus (it is an "obligate biotroph" in the vernacular of the field). This fungal endophyte then returns the favor to its host plant by sending out a network of fine, thinner-than-hair hyphae into the surrounding soil. There it takes up minerals needed by the plant and transfers them to the root tissues that it also inhabits.

"In the olden days, when primeval forests and prairies covered all the land"—John got carried away with himself sounding like a true believer—"the intertwined, anastomosed, pervasive, globally distributed underground hyphal network of this fungus connected all living things rooted in the soil into one great super-organism." *Wow*, he (the biologist) thought upon hearing this: the holistic unity of life! What a fantastic concept! Exactly the one I was looking for.

He buttonholed John during lunch. Did these fungi colonize soybean roots also?—he wanted to know. "All agricultural plants from alfalfa to zucchini, except buckwheat and sugarbeets," John said, making an impatient gesture and clearly ready to shrink back into his private space. But there was no escape for him, so he eventually gave up and reluctantly opened that afternoon the floodgates of his insights into the concept.

As it turned out, the flood of information was really just a trickle in terms of useful detail. These organisms didn't even have a proper taxonomy yet and were mostly referred to by the morphological characteristics of their spores, such as "big-yellow-vacuolate" or "small-white-transparent." But it was known that they helped their host plant take up phosphorus from the soil, and P was, as he knew only too well from his work at UC Davis, in high demand by soybean root nodules whose bacterial endophytes fix molecular nitrogen from the air into compounds that the plant is able to use. That was all he needed. He felt like a soldier who had just been handed his marching orders.

John sent him a starter culture of the fungi, and sure enough, their spores, unlike those of most other fungi, were almost big enough to be seen with the naked eye. Like with anything that is new and unfamiliar, it took a while for him to get on speaking terms with them. But by and by, he did establish a comfortable, dissecting-microscope-mediated relationship with his new friends. They had to be separated in pot cultures into morpho-species (using the only available guide, *Mycologia Memoir Number 5*, authored by Gerdeman and Trappe), propagated on sorghum as the host plant and replicated to test for purity before embarking on a first experiment. It took him all the way to the latter part of his second year at LSU before he finished his first manuscript on his mycorrhizae (fungus roots), and then it was time to say good-bye and move back West.

Alone again

That second year was a lonely one. Marina was off to faraway Oregon, and he could only hope that she was taking it a little easier on lecture preparation than she did at LSU. He could empathize with that, though, for he would have prepared himself silly also had he been called upon to teach. You can never be well enough prepared to teach a really good class. But he did not have to teach, and he did not volunteer to do so. Instead, he took to exploring Louisiana.

As he was becoming acclimatized to the humidity, he started exploring towns and country on weekend trips, staying overnight at targets of opportunity.

All the towns of any size had bars, and these always offered live music on Saturday nights when the Cajun bands of fiddle, banjo, and drum helped the local talent belt out the mood and the spirit of the hinterland in the loudest and liveliest of rhythms.

> Waitin' in the front yard, sittin' on a log;
> Single-shot rifle and a one-eyed dog.
> Yonder come my kin folk in the moonlight:
> Louisiana Saturday night.

He would sit at the bar with his bottle of Bud Light and watch the scene with his by now deeply inured understanding of the split in his personality: one moment, he could feel at home as if he had been born and raised there, relating like a native to that smoky, noisy, uninhibited throng of revelers, and the next, he knew he was as foreign there as if he had landed on Mars. It was the very same thing with the countryside. The bayou land held a magnetic attraction and wonder for him, the kind that very small children must have at every new turn of the corner. The wetlands were a strange, novel, unknown world of shiny, glittering surfaces and black, unplumbed depths.

Dirt roads would lead on dry bridges of land deep into this world of the Atchafalaya Swamp. On time-forgotten, hidden peninsulas, there could be a few huts centered on a little country store, maybe. One time, as he was waiting for his hotdog to heat up, he overheard them speak French that had a strange archaic ring to his ear, as if it had been left over from a forgotten century. He could sit for hours on a log at the dark water's edge (sometimes in the moonlight) and listen to the wind in the crowns of the bald cypresses, watching the wildlife loll by lazily: beaver, otter, mink, alligator, egret, heron.

But he had no kinfolk within two thousand miles now, not even a one-eyed dog who might have made him feel a little more at home there (Katze was back on the West Coast with the family). Besides, he was a desert person, one of the dry, wind-swept prairies of Oklahoma and of the Puszta of the Great Magyar Plains

> Ég a napmelegtől a kopár szík sarja,   The barren plains burn in the heat of the sun
> Tikkadt szöcskenyájak legelésznek rajta...   Thirsty flocks of locusts are grazing on it...

and of the endless stretches of the unlimited distances east of the Carpathian Mountains, where his people had come from long, long ago. The fata morganas of distant horizons reaching to the rising Asian sun, ones that he had never seen and that lived only in his imagination.

Soybeans and the market

Meanwhile, back at work, there were times when he could see real, serious, I might even say existential, problems arise that he might sidestep at first, but that he would have to face sooner or later. These were boom times for Louisiana agriculture and for the agricultural experiment station that supported it. There was no shortage of money. A veritable mother of all refineries, the huge Exxon complex on the River at Baton Rouge made its presence felt everywhere, but especially downwind. That shifted, of course, with the whims of the weather, but the boarded-up downtown, and LSU, further southeast, were its favored olfactory targets.

If you took an excursion trip by riverboat to New Orleans (as he did once), you could not escape the exhilarating feeling of being somehow, even if only by proxy, a tiny part of a great, all-embracing industrial hegemony at the sight of the fume-belching and effluent-disgorging chemical factories that lined the banks of the Father of Rivers left and right, much like sap-sucking aphids encrust the petiole of a rose bud. Now and then, the loudspeaker would announce excitedly the sighting of an antebellum mansion that sat there in forlorn timidity, as if wondering how long this latter-day onslaught of activity would permit it to hang on. The factories, of course, and he knew this only too well, were the rock foundation of that day's good life, and when the same loudspeaker proudly interpreted the conspicuously displayed logos of great and famous names of the industrial empire that were visible from the water, he could often recognize and identify the ones that paid his own salary, even if only indirectly: the ones that produced the chemicals without which modern agriculture could no longer live and survive.

And this brings us back to his existential problem. One aspect of those agricultural boom times that concerned him as a resident soybean expert was the rapidly advancing clear-cutting of the coastal old forest to be replaced (you guessed it) by plowed, disked, and harrowed fields of soybeans. Now in the grand design of the Good Lord, soybeans were meant to inhabit Northeastern China, for the Center of Diversity of *Glycine max* is in Manchuria, where it developed its now famous root-nodule symbiosis with the (also native Manchurian) nitrogen-fixing bacterium *Bradyrhizobium japonicum*.

Because of the mutual amity of these two compatible life-forms, the soy plant is able to produce a bean that is chock-full of protein (and lipids). Protein (in case you care to know) is made up of a chain of amino acids, which are hydrocarbon molecules with their characteristic amine (NH_2) group attached to them (hence their name). This is the group, then, which contains the nitrogen (N) fixed by the bacteria, and they do so without recourse to chemical fertilizers. In fact, an excess of fertilizer-N inhibits the ability of the bacteria to fix N.

So as all you tofu lovers should appreciate, the bean of the soy had all the sterling characteristics that a good businessman can identify in the glint of an eye: those that the market demands. For corn, that other splendid source of cattle feed in developed countries, has a fatal flaw: it is deficient in two essential amino acids (lysine and tryptophan), but when combined with soybean in the trough, that nutritional gap is filled. Vast acreages had therefore been put into soybean cultivation countrywide, and Louisiana decided to make room for it also where it could: where the coastal forest used to stand.

What nobody could apparently foresee in all this were two wrinkles in this grand market design, a minor and a major one. The minor one was easy to overlook at first. It was a small, green, looping caterpillar, innocuous and invisible because it blended seamlessly into the native, pre-soybean foliage. But my-oh—my-o, did that change when it was offered all of a sudden on the silver platter of those cultivated fields, a salad dish of fresh, turgid, always well-irrigated soy leaves free of raspy, waxy, and distasteful epidermal layers of cuticle on them!

Since they could make short shrift of a soybean field in the wink of a soy farmer's eye, the entrepreneurs got concerned. They called in the experts of the experiment station, and did so, as always, after the fact. By the time he got there, they were already doubling the insecticide load from year to year, to little avail. The looper, bent on developing immunity to the poison, was well on its way to prove the theory of evolution right.

"What do *you* propose to do?" the director wanted to know. "Your immediate problem right this minute is one for the entomologist to solve," he opined wisely. "But if you want to take out time and money to train and equip *me* to do the necessary genetic engineering, in five or six years I should be able to make your plants produce a metabolite that will cause the looper to choke on it."

How do you like this fine example of sidestepping a problem? He was proud of it. For clearly the looper would have wasted no time to evolve new genotypes in time to savor those new metabolites as delicacies. To face the problem squarely, on the other hand, was more problematic, for it would have been neither in the spirit of mercenary science nor in that of the even more mercenary market. But at any rate, he was not yet ready to come out with the truth: "You have no business growing soybeans here, for the Good Lord did not create this place for it!"

And now, at last, we have arrived squarely at the existential problem. At the major wrinkle. LSU, unlike all those other land-grant state universities, is a sea-grant school. Its charter calls, among other things, for research on the strength and the stability of the coastlines and their interactions with the sea. Interactions that include frequent, devastating onslaughts of hurricane-driven monster waves that can wash those beaches away as if they had never been there. Now what protects the land behind the sand dunes from the erosive effects of the sea is none other than the coastal forest. Without the forest, the sea would eventually reclaim the land, soybeans and all. No doubt, you get my drift by now.

Some of the experts in the other departments were already discussing this conundrum. But business groups like that of the Association of Soybean Growers

(ASG) are powerful. To do what they had done requires large investments, and those are not written off easily as losses. Capital wants to realize tangible returns for the risks it takes, and so even after it recognizes that one of its schemes has gone awry, it tends to hang on tenaciously in hopes of a turnaround often until the damage is no longer supportable or reversible. If you missed seeing such an event play itself out in real life (like our present global market meltdown in the fall of 2008 and the spring of 2009), you can read up on the spurious yet fateful logic of it in the pages of *Das Kapital*, where the process was analyzed in detail by the founding theoreticians of the erstwhile enemy.

Soybeans, sacrifice, and self-deception

In the meantime, a lot of money accrued from the ASG to the experiment station, and some of that money paid his salary. And it did not do so to finance his taking sides with Marx and Engels, nor with the Good Lord's original Manchurian-soybean grand design either, for that matter. What could the director's position have been had he (the biologist) punctiliously pointed out to him what growing those exotic soybeans was doing to the fragile coastal Louisiana ecosystem, as he felt it was (let's admit it) his responsibility to do?

"Don't you think I have heard all that world-saving stuff often enough already? Now go back to your lab and do the work you get paid for and let me do mine. I understand all the implications of everything that my organization is involved in (and far better than you do)." That would have been *à propos* and would have put him in his place.

Responsibility (let's face it) can be a yoke even for directors. If you are the leader of a large organization, is your first responsibility strictly to it or is it to the good of the greater system in which it is embedded—if the two happen to be in conflict? But the director could also have reacted differently. He could have interpreted his (the biologist's) initiative as reproach or even accusation, and if the confrontation had occurred at an inopportune moment of stress, he could well have been curt: "If the soybeans must go, then we need not keep you any longer either." And that sort of thing is not one that one conjures up heedlessly, for it affects one's existence. Thus, it is an existential problem.

Reenter Marc

The only one to talk to about such things was Marc, who had a lot of time on his hands, as he was already busy those days with laying the foundations of a lifetime career as a bachelor. Otherwise, he kept himself occupied with ferreting out the biochemical mysteries of dormancy in red-rice seeds, which is a lab-bound activity. So he himself had no interest in going out to inspect the effects of coastal-forest clear-cutting, but on the other hand, that permitted him to have a clear and open mind about the matter.

Sometimes, after dinner at the faculty club or at the po'boy stand at the student union, the two of them would wander through the dark, deserted campus under the tall trees between the Union and the Biology Building, discussing abstract things like the imperatives of conscience in confronting greed like the kind that makes money on soybeans while damaging the environment.

"Don't be stupid." Marc chuckled about his scruples. "What makes you think that it is you who has to save the world? Besides, if I get your story right, the damage is already done out there and the ones who count know it. The soybean folks may be deceiving themselves about the consequences, for they have a lot of money at stake. But if you go public now and make an issue of it, it would be nothing but self-immolation. A senseless sacrifice. It would not change anything." I mentioned this conversation to Marc thirty years later, and strangely, he did not recall any of it, while for me it is still all clear as day. It just shows you again how the controller functions: he selects judiciously from the everyday jumble of life to suit his own needs.

But Marc was a good buddy. He was like a firewall from which one could bounce off the tennis balls of one's concerns. "A fat lot of good did it do the world when you sacrificed your army career to your principles. What higher goal did you attain? It was a trade-off—that's all it was. You traded some material benefits for peace of mind. Well, was it worth it?" Marc's adept backswing of bouncing his thoughts back at him over the net of his scruples was annoying but therapeutic. Soon they eased out of the soybean problem without even noticing it and slid into discussing the abstract nature of sacrifice as such. I do not recall anymore which one of them supported which side of the argument, for it took place thirty years ago.

Sacrifice

Right now, however, this sacrifice thing is popping up again daily in the rhetorical altercations of our presidential contestants. This time, it relates to the presence of our troops in the streets of Baghdad and Kabul. The troops who are always pointedly and emphatically described by both candidates as the finest and most selfless and heroic fighting men (and women) that the world had ever seen (as many of them doubtless are). Our troops who are the only ones in the country now who are willing to make a sacrifice for the cause.

True, the rest of us are not engaged in very much sacrificing right now, although we have been exhorted by our commander-in-chief "to go shopping" for the sake of the country and its economy. But I find myself confused by all this political talk about sacrifice. In all my years in the army, I wore the uniform because I liked it.

It was my chosen career, and I never met any soldier who felt differently about it, except, of course, the ones who were drafted into serving against their will.

There was no more thought of sacrifice connected with being a member of the military service than it would occur to a lawyer, doctor, or policeman that he is sacrificing himself when he does his job, even though the pay was not yet comparable to civilian standards then. Neither can I imagine that an investment banker would feel that he sacrifices his life to the Mammon of his bonuses; or a priest, to the harsh demands of chastity. What they do is follow their calling for the satisfaction they get out of it and perhaps also for the rewards each one hopes to reap.

So I cannot help thinking of all this military sacrifice talk by our politicians as something they need to cultivate to cozy up to their patriotic constituents. As if true patriotism were not something entirely different! The real battle against terrorism will have to be fought on different fields than those of saber rattling and flag waving if we really aim to win it. But at any rate, the big presidential election (Obama vs. McCain) is coming up the day after tomorrow, and I expect that the pitch of the service-sacrifice dialogue will shift to a different key afterward.

Back on the LSU campus, the debate on sacrifice was equally serious. He and Marc knew that they were dealing with an important idea that may have been a formative one in the evolution of their becoming human. Yet they were not quite sure if the posit was really real. "You are attacking the very underpinnings of an age-old moral concept. You make it sound as if sacrifice were a form of horse trading. What about soldiers defending their country at great personal risk? Are they not obeying a societal imperative that is stronger than their own individual position toward it can ever be?" he (the biologist) might have advanced.

"Imperative: bullshit, and you know it. Try to recall how it all started. The priests would exhort their victim to sacrifice a kid goat on an altar to bribe some selfish god into sparing his crop from a hailstorm. Then you know who got to eat the roast," Marc may have teased him. "Don't get facetious with me, Marc! Think of your own tribal history. Was that the way a hundred-year-old Abraham felt when he got ready to pull the knife to his only son?"

Now Marc was secular. He did not claim to be a Talmud scholar, and so he gracefully demurred. "Hate to admit it, but I am not as much an expert on those things as I should be. But Abraham was experiencing the Shekinah when he had that knife in his hand; he was in God's presence. He really did not have much of a choice—you don't argue with God. That was not so much a human sacrifice. It was more of a divine imperative."

That was like oil on the fire. "Uh huh, here comes the imperative bubbling up again! You know what, old buddy? Maybe you are right. Maybe there is nothing more to sacrifice than the quid pro quo after all. I have no choice, so I do your bidding, God, Country, Society, Family (whatever), and obey, but don't forget that I do so in hopes of a commensurate reward. If this is so, then the concept of sacrifice as a selfless act rests on nothing but self-deception."

His buddy was dismayed at first. Self-deception! How can a normal, healthy mind deceive itself? The controller would have to turn against himself to do that, against the achievements of millions of years of evolution! If a computer were asked to go against its programming, it would have to crash. Strife between the controller and the controller's controller, between the brain and the mind? Conditioning, perhaps? Brainwashing? Marc was an inveterate civilian, but he (a biologist now) never stopped seeing things from the soldier's point of view. And so he is doing now, thirty years later, pondering the problems of our latest war.

The present intrudes

A big one of those problems is the patriotic mandate of supporting the troops. "Support the troops" is a slogan. Like all slogans, it tries to divert you from understanding the real meaning of the underlying cause. What exactly is that meaning? You sense that there is something there that is deep and strong under the surface of the slogan. Something visceral like a "gut feeling," red as blood, nonpolitically conservative, something you would feel compelled to agree with automatically if it were not for the slogan's obstruction. How could you *not* support the troops?

So let's think about it for a moment the way an open mind would. What does this "support" really mean? More ammunition, safer armored vests, and more steel plates under the humvees? Is that all there is to support? How about an honest examination of the reasons why those troops are in harm's way in the first place? And if the reasons fail to stand up to the logic of the facts that this examination reveals, what then? Leave them in harm's way anyway and send them turkeys for Thanksgiving? For that is what we are doing now. When the breaks of a freight train rolling downhill burn out, all you can do is blow the whistle at the railroad crossings. That is what we are doing now.

But let's stop waving the flag for a moment and be cold and cynical. Unpatriotic, if you want to call it, if only for the sake of a quick reality check on sacrifice. How many volunteers could we muster to go to Iraq or Afghanistan to sweat and die in the desert without a forty-thousand-dollar enlistment bonus and a ninety-thousand-dollar reenlistment bonus? Resent this question, if you like, but it is the acid test to see how genuine the sacrifice is!

As you can see, the here and now crept back into the flow of the story again. The events of the moment overpower the memories of the past. The cacophony of the present political theater is so atonal that it often drowns out the theme of the substance. "My opponent is against supporting the troops!" "No! I am against not supporting the troops properly!"

Over the seemingly never-ending continuum of these last two wars of ours, the substance is becoming ever more insubstantial with each passing year of them. Now it is no longer the early mirage of re-creating the world of Islam by Western lights; what is left of those grandiose goals is desperately little: an exit strategy. And what that amounts to is nothing more than training local folks to finish our purpose. Ask anybody, whether Petreus or McChrystal, and the answer is the same: train a local army and a local police, and bingo, problem solved; we can go home. It is slowly going on ten years now that we are training them, and it is like training water not to flow downhill where it wants to go.

"Train for what?" you might ask the experts. To fight? They know more about war than we ever will. What then? To support "their" government? And now we got it, that's the wrinkle in the dishdasha where the fleas keep hiding. The governments that we train them to support they clearly do not consider to be worth supporting. And how would we start convincing them that they are? By using unmanned drones to kill their leaders instead of learning Pashtun to be able to talk to them? You cannot convince people of anything by way of an interpreter, even if you have successfully polygraphed him.

"What's the use of all this?" you may rightfully ask. It does not belong here. The pundits have hashed it out ad nauseam in the media for years now. Chill out and let it rest. You are right about that, but this is the stretch of the road where I am now, and the search for its message is what this story is all about.

And the concept of sacrifice as it relates to the soldier's motivation to accept doing what he is told is part of the meaning that message conveys. What is the motivation of our troops now? I cannot help wondering. Although I am sure that many of them sincerely feel that they have a good one, I cannot help feeling that it is a misguided one. I was there myself, forty years ago. What was mine? Was it as mercenary as I do not wish to admit? This is a *Gestalt* that persists incomplete for me, and so it continues to reappear like the ghost of a haunted house; it keeps surfacing like the fins of a shark from the surface of an otherwise pacific sea.

Involvement

The little red Toyota made two trips to Oregon during that second year at LSU. Marina was coping well with the single-mother operation in Eugene, or at least so it seemed from two thousand miles away. With the preparation and teaching of new courses while she guided the kids along their unexpectedly meandering paths, she had more than a full-time job. He, on the other hand, missed out on another year of child development.

The Fox had a newspaper route and was making his own money for the first time. Schnuka had abandoned his attachment to the security of his *schnuckling* cloth by now, and so was ready to shed his old nickname. But he did not relate well to his real name either, only he did not say so yet. Robin. Maybe he did not see himself as a bird. He had become a little person of consequence with a firm footing on the ground.

His own relationship with his kids turned more ambivalent during that year. There was no real closeness and, consequently, little confidence. It was still better than just mere mutual tolerance; the ties were stronger than that. But not strong enough for the Fox to share how he felt about his early experimentation with grass. That had apparently the intriguing aura of something forbidden or at least not quite right, even though he was growing his plants in the closet with Marina's uneasy acquiescence. It was not something that had a place in exchanges of thought with a father who was not a close confidant. Solid, open reassurance of family support and belonging at this crucial time of early drug use might have averted much future suffering.

And he continued to be stricken by a blindness that took him two more decades to overcome, when it was way too late. One of his problems was that the circumstances of his own life on the road had led him early to the habit of self-sufficiency. He had no one to look to for help, so it was clear for him from early on that he had to help himself. Helping himself ranged from doing his homework for school well enough to earn a scholarship all the way to providing for all the necessities of life later on. He expected his sons to do likewise, as a matter of course, without his having to exhort them to be that way. What he refused to see was that the circumstances of their lives were entirely different. They had not lived through wars and refugee camps; they lived in a society where being provided for by parents was the norm, and they associated with classmates for whom homework was a nuisance.

He should have gotten involved. He should have gone to PTA meetings. He should have familiarized himself with the strange, nebulous world of the American school system. He had no excuse, for Marina had explained the situation to him repeatedly and emphatically. I have often tried to reconstruct the reasons for his intransigence. The fatal flaw was as I see it now, he did not and could not recognize the overpowering effects of peer pressure. Of peers who were products of a society where needs were satisfied as a matter of course, a society motivated and governed therefore mainly by its wants. One where shopping is the chief pastime and where buying and owning things under the relentless barrage of commercial wants creation is the dominant factor in the pursuit of an ever-elusive happiness that knows no contentment. He had not lived through such an experience as a child; peer pressure during his school years under postwar austerity was oriented toward goals like finding something to eat on the one hand and the ability to discuss the books one had read on the other.

He had the mindset of an old-fashioned alien outsider, and his children did not. Apparently knowing what doctor of philosophy meant in English was not enough to cope with his most important duties, those of a father.

But all this is a flash-forward. Back then, the problem was in its early stages and was not at all as clear yet as it is now. The Fox called just now from Las Vegas, where he lives. He has two jobs. They are empty chores that together do not pay enough to keep him afloat. He is depressed and feels like a failure. And so do I, for I am co-responsible for his plight.

The magnet of the Black Mesa

On the way back to Baton Rouge from the second trip to Oregon, the little red Toyota found its way again to the Black Mesa Country as if all by itself. Coming from the west, from Tuba City, he first stopped at Moenkopi. That means "Running Water," and so it is a place where plants will grow without the people having to do a rain dance to get the sacred corn crop irrigated. It is a far-outlying colony of Hopi Land proper, some fifty miles west of the Black Mesas. Sitting down on the bench in front of the little store that served the settlement that was nowhere near the growing town yet that it has become in the meantime, he turned to the toothless old-timer who was already sitting there gazing, as if he were sightless, out into the distance, unmoving as though he and the bench had been carved out of the same wood.

"How's the corn coming?" He (the biologist) ventured to break the silence. The man turned his head and focused on him. "I need nothing to buy from you." Well, being an introvert, he does not laugh easily, but being taken for a traveling salesman was a new experience. So it must have been with a big smile when he countered, "And I have nothing to sell to you. But I would like you to tell me about your corn plants." The Hopis don't mind selling you the silver jewelry they make for that purpose, but otherwise they prefer to be left alone by the Bahana since the real one, the white brother of the prophecy, the one they have been waiting for, has never returned.

Only they too are human, and if they have a story to tell they will share it with you, if you can somehow contrive to be lucky enough to gain their confidence. He wanted to know how that running water related to the role of the rain dance and the connection to the spirit world, and it seemed that this was something the old man on the bench had on his mind also as he was staring out into the past.

"This changing world is not easy for old people like me to come to grips with," he started, groping for words to express what had never stopped troubling him, and his story was indeed a troubling one.

His people, members of the Parrot clan, were of the first who moved to Moenkopi about a hundred years ago from Oraibi, led there by the promise of water available for farming from the Moenkopi Wash in good years. But "moving" is a white man's concept. At first it was just a sowing and harvesting commute, an arduous one on foot, but by the time that his memory was able to span, they were already living there. They were hardy, and their blue corn thrived. What did not thrive was the unity of their culture with their universe, the way they used to know it. For him, this was the trauma of his childhood, for the cohesion of their social structure had fallen apart, and they did not know how to cope with that.

That structure had been a simple one traditionally, if he understood the old man right. Theirs apparently had been a female-dominated society, where the women owned all property (the objects needed for everyday living), and also had control over the all-important necessities in life like housing, the cornfields, and the allocation of work in those fields. The men were in charge of all the religious rites and ceremonies; they were responsible for the contact with the Pure Spirit in its countless specific, material manifestations. When men married, they went to live in their wives' households (run by a grandmother-in-law) but returned to their original phratries for the ceremonies, and their children's upbringing was in the hands of the oldest brothers-in-law.

This was the way the world was organized in the original villages governed by the ancient clan structure, but it apparently did not work well in this new farming community where the rain dance was no longer needed and where the encroaching pressures of a more and more modern life were forcing the emigrants into a white, nuclear-family structure. The message of the old man's words were simple, eloquent, and sad. But he had not given up hope, he said, for there was a strong, new movement afoot now to keep at least their language alive.

Further down the road, as he passed the turnoff to Old Oraibi, he ran into a big signboard: "White man, you have broken our laws and you are even breaking your own. You are not welcome in our village." Disappointed, he stopped at the tribal headquarters in New Oraibi at the foot of the steep Third Mesa cliffs. There, an efficient-looking young woman explained to him patiently that she could not give him permission to enter the village for her office had no say in local governance. It served the villages and their clans as a liaison link with the Bureau of Indian Affairs, with the Navajo Nation, with the Mormon business people in Flagstaff and the like, but the village chief decided how to run the affairs of his community.

So he did what he always does; he walked the unpaved paths of New Oraibi and tried to make sense of how that unlikely, inorganically grown collection of houses, an undigested mix of old and new, might function with the words of his new friend from Moenkopi in mind. Then finding himself at the foot of the precipice on top of which the old village perched, what looked to him like a good few hundred feet above, he chanced on a footpath that appeared to wind its way up there. Maybe it was the path used to haul water up from below in the old days, but it was still well trodden. He followed it up to a high ledge from where he could see the village across a sizable, barren, flat but rocky outcropping dominated by what looked like the ruins of a small Mexican-style church. There he sat down in the shade of a large vertical slab of rock to rest and to ruminate over the day's events and lessons.

When he came to, there was an old couple squatting close by, looking at him. The woman nodded in a friendly way and said, "You can come in now. My brother does not mind." As it turned out, she was the chief of the village of Oraibi. Then the brother said, "And you may take part in the rain dance. You can dance or just watch, as you like." The Hopis have a lot of sacred ceremonies where outsiders are not permitted. Those are celebrated mostly underground in the *kiwas*, but the under-the-sun events may not be exclusive. That night, there came a nice, quiet, drenching drizzle, blowing in from the San Francisco Mountains. Maybe it came only by coincidence. Who knows?

On coincidences

There are people who claim to know that the notion of a coincidence is a misconception: nothing happens haply, only on purpose, by design. Einstein was one of these: "God does not throw dice." Not with the laws of nature, maybe. However, He might play games with people. Feel free to decide on that, but what happened to him a few weeks after that last Eugene-Oraibi rain-dance trip looked to him suspiciously like the mother of all designer coincidences.

Doing everything he could to get back to the West Coast to join the family there, he had applied for a job advertised at UC Davis. He made the short list and was actually invited to give an introductory lecture. The visit went well as far as that goes, but unfortunately, the Botany Department's selection committees were always excruciatingly selective. They had the annoying habit of finding more and better-qualified candidates, preferably ones who came from England or the Ivy League, ones who had apparently learned to levitate or walk on water while there.

He haplessly had to use an airplane for transportation to get to Davis, and this type of shortcoming must have caused some head shaking during the committee's deliberations. In short, someone else got the job. But on his way back to Louisiana, his airplane seat assignment happened to place him—or did it do so by design?—next to a smiling, mild-mannered gentleman. None other than Milford, a scientist at the WRRC.

The Western Regional Research Center of the US Department of Agriculture's Agricultural Research Service (ARS) is a big, diverse ag-bio lab in Albany, California. That is just north of Berkeley, the hub of the country's progressive universe. An hour's drive from Davis, he had looked for a job there repeatedly without success. So after a bit of conversation that clarified Milford's institutional identity, he did not hesitate to ask him about any positions that might have materialized in the course of the last two years.

"Sure," said Milford, "we just got a brand-new program in nitrogen fixation, and I am assigned to that CRIS also." As fast as he could get to the phone at his office, he called Glenn, the ARS research leader who ran herd on a few CRIS work units at WRRC. "I'll send you the application forms by tomorrow's mail. With your points of Veteran's Preference, you'll have no problem getting selected by the Civil Service Board. We'll be happy to have you" was Glenn's take on the matter. Well, that is the way things run sometimes in God's world. With some luck or by coincidence, if you work hard and assiduously at anything, be it some recalcitrant material like a slab of marble or a length of copper wire or something more esoteric like a manuscript or getting the job you want where you want it, in time the substance will tend to become malleable to your fingertips and yield to your will.

And that was that. The hardest part of breaking tents at Baton Rouge was leaving his good colleagues and friends at LSU. John, Freddie, Bill, and his philosopher buddy, Marc. He also knew he would remain homesick for all those weird climates of the Deep South, good or bad. *Partir, c'est toujours mourir un peu* was something that he had always experienced at leaving any place where he had ever been. Leaving, that's always dying a little. Move on and good riddance of what's left behind sounds to me like the extrovert's way, but I may be all wrong about this. Maybe it is the self-contained introvert who moves on more easily. But he was always prone to clinging a little, although he knew better.

California

When it was all done, house sold, household goods shipped, going-away party with the colleagues celebrated, and it was time to go, he came down with an ugly case of strep throat. It was the kind that feels like somebody slices your uvula with a razor blade every time you swallow. So he went to his doctor's office first thing in the morning in hopes of some miraculous quick fix, as a parting gift from Louisiana as it were, for he was all packed and ready to go.

Starting the trek back West

Once the course was set, he had never been one to linger. But it was his doctor's day on the golf course. The office help referred him to another doctor, but that one did not take new patients. The emergency room at the hospital did not think his was a case of emergency. By the time the morning was gone, he was thoroughly pissed off and decided to gut it out. He struck out heading West on US 190 toward Opalousas. But first he had to cross the Mississippi, which never failed to be a big event for him.

It was new every time, perhaps because each crossing at the present moment always evoked those moments of long ago when he first read and memorized the words that painted for him forever a picture of all great rivers. It was Goethe's poem, "Mahomet's Song." Those were words that conjured up a vision, prophetically I might say today, of the Father of Rivers:

Zedernhäuser trägt der Atlas	Cedar-houses bears the Atlas
Auf den Riesenschultern; sausend	On his giant shoulders;
Wehen über seinem Haupte	flutt'ring in the breeze above him
Tausend Flaggen durch die Lüfte,	Thousand flags are gaily floating,
Zeugen seiner Herrlichkeit."	Bearing witness to his splendor.

But this time the magic somehow did not work. Not because it was raining; the river was even more mysterious when shrouded in gray, for then it seemed to be even wider, as if it had no opposite bank at all. No, it was simply because he was hungry: his throat would not let him so much as think of swallowing a bite of food. So he missed his last good chance for a farewell crawfish pie in that cozy little riverside joint on the other side of the bridge.

By the time he had crossed into Texas the sky had cleared, the sun was westering, and it was getting to be high time to do something about that throat. On the outskirts of Tyler, the City of Roses, he passed a blue hospital sign, and he knew he had to give trusty, dependable, first-class, nonsocialist American medicine another chance to help him. The woman who manned the reception desk in that strangely deserted institution looked up from her *Reader's Digest*. "And what can I do for you tonight?" she offered. "Real bad sore throat," he croaked out in response, in a tone of voice that reminded him of the sound that the frogs made on the edges of the bomb-crater pools in Harthausen when he hit one with his slingshot.

She was a registered nurse as he could see on her name tag, but she carefully avoided volunteering to look into his throat. Instead, she picked up the phone and rang up the doctor on duty. "I can give you a penicillin shot," she summarized her instructions. "Do you have proof of insurance?" All his papers were on a moving truck en route to California, and he was not a card-carrying member of the new cashless credit economy yet. "That will be one hundred and seventy-two dollars," she clarified the situation upon seeing him hesitate momentarily. "And no out-of-state checks," she rounded out her exposition of the facts of life for the sick on the road.

"A hundred and seventy-two dollars for a penicillin shot?" his creaky, barely audible voice protested. "That includes the emergency room charge," she added reassuringly, as if suggesting that he was getting a good deal and could consider himself lucky. "But I've never come even close to your emergency room," he tried to persevere in a cold sweat with pain, glancing down to the other end of the long, dark corridor where the ER sign was displayed in big red letters. "You want the shot or not?" she shrugged, ending the negotiations and turning to her book again.

Fortunately, he always made sure to have plenty of old-fashioned, green folding money on him on long trips. Still, he felt outrageously robbed. But by the time he checked into his motel room that feeling had subsided and turned into one of incredulous gratitude, for the contents of the shot, administered out of a huge syringe into his bare butt right there next to the reception desk, almost immediately found its way to his throat, which then responded with a sigh of relief deep enough to be heard around the world (much like that shot fired at Lexington some two hundred years ago). So quick was the recovery that it was not too late to find an eating place still open and be served a juicy, rare, Texas-sized T-bone steak to celebrate the life of the healthy on the road.

Okeene

It was early evening again by the time he arrived at the small homestead just east of Okeene, Oklahoma. He had not been in a hurry, and his little red Toyota had not seen his old haunts in the Lawton area yet, for it had become a member of the family only recently, in Baton Rouge. So together they indulged a little in the exploration and research of the Lawton-Fort Sill past on the way to Romilda's house.

Originally a farmhouse, it apparently stood on a rise, there near the banks of the Cimarron River. I say apparently, for the lands of the Wheat Belt can be so flat that it takes a special event to make you aware of their gently rolling topography. Such an event occurred exactly at his arrival. And there, with uncanny precision, the full moon was rising as the sun was setting in such a way that both could be seen (from that suggestion of a rise) in their rotund entirety touching the horizon exactly at the same point in time. This is supposed to be a regularly recurring event, but be honest, how often have you witnessed it occurring with such glorious, fearsome symmetry?

Both celestial orbs were glowing red like the blood oranges that used to find their way every year without fail from faraway Sicily all the way to Léva, up to the time of the invasion of that island by the Western armies. After that, they abruptly stopped coming. That was in the summer of 1943, the time when his elementary school curriculum ordained that fourth graders were ready to deal with and to memorize the poetry that describes the Magyar landscape and countryside:

Mint kiűzött király országa széléről	Like an exiled king from his country's borders
Visszapillant a nap a föld pereméről...	The sun glances back from the edge of the world,
S mire elér szeme a túlsó határra,	And by the time his eyes reach the far horizon,
Leesik fejéről véres koronája.	His bloody crown drops from his head.

Well, the bloody crown of the exiled sun as it sinks below the horizon somehow blended itself into the dreams of his child's mind first with the fell omen of the abrupt disappearance of his favorite blood oranges and then with being exiled, driven from his home by a relentlessly advancing blood Red Army. It all became part on an archetypal, primal experience of the inevitability of something dreadful and unwanted. One that he never failed to relive upon seeing the sun set; only the substance of the experience became vague, subliminal, and fleeting, although it still remained palpable with the passage of time, in the same way as a coarse cotton shirt becomes soft and fine like silk upon having been worn and washed many times.

He was still standing there, entranced by the cosmic spectacle when he heard a woman's voice call out from the house that yes, he found it, and it was the right one. "So don't just stand there, come on in." Romilda did not seem to notice the sunset, although she was a cousin of Marina's, who always did and continues to do so. She was older than Marina by a generation, born some twenty years after the Sooners were given free license by the Great White Father to grab the land of the Red Man. There they staked out their claims, often at the site where their covered wagons happened to break down in the rush to a new life that was going to be based on the growing of wheat.

The Tautfests, recently immigrated Germans from Russia, made their stand on the erstwhile land of the Osage and the Kiowa at an auspicious place, on the river. It must have always been a big clan or had become one there on the Cimarron, for Romilda's living room filled up with a host of relatives before the evening wore out, to meet and inspect the guy who married Bud's daughter.

Bud

Bud was a living legend in Okeene; there could be no doubt about that, although sadly, he had died just before he (the biologist) had met his daughter. This legend had it that one day when he became tired of fighting his old-fashioned, conservative elders' resistance to embracing the cars and the tractors that were fast becoming both symbol and essence of the budding, brand-new American Century, he nailed metal plates to the leather soles of his boots in preparation for a long journey.

One that took him eventually to Chicago, a city that must have been then, before the Great Depression hit, the throbbing heart, the nerve center of hope-filled, dynamic, forward-straining, future-aching activity of country-and globe-encircling business; a cauldron; a melting pot where all the currents of the awakening giant's pith and vigor were swept together by the tornados of a manifest destiny that would last a hundred years, until the greed of Wall Street and the hubris of Pennsylvania Avenue finally shackled the dream in an ocean of debt that unleashed the first Great Recession of the twenty-first century. But all that came later. When Bud, his father-in-law, got there, it was still the

> Hog butcher for the world
> Tool maker, Stacker of Wheat,
> Player with Railroads and the Nation's Freight Handler;

Stormy, husky, brawling,
City of the big shoulders

There he became a captain of industry who later was to lead the activities of a large corporation in postwar Europe. He was the quintessential native son who made good, and so quite naturally, his son-in-law, a foreigner, outsider, Catholic, and an ex-soldier, was the target of some sharp, quizzical, and critical looks by the kinfolks who had never left home and to whom the wide world must have been a chimera at worst and a mirage at best.

At least so it seemed to him at first. But when they heard that he too was an Oklahoman in spirit who had topped his five years as an in-migrant to their state (as they all had also been not so very long ago) with a "Norman degree," he was quickly accepted. He was, as it turned out, the first one in the family to graduate from OU and with a solid engineering degree to boot.

The Menonites

He had known all along that the Tautfests had been, and some of them maybe still were, peace-loving Menonites, but it was at this welcoming party that the new relatives related the remarkable history of their clan. Theirs was a past that not only held strong convictions but had also the full measure of courage to go to the ends of the world to live them and to uphold them.

I don't know what makes a man a pacifist, for it is a philosophy that almost sounds like a genetic aberration to a soldier turned biologist. Unless, of course, you embrace the teachings of the Buddha and decide to follow his compassionate path. But in the latter part of the eighteenth century, that path had not yet made its way to what later became known as the Western World and especially not to rural Germany, where it was that these sturdy folks had decided not to bear arms under any circumstances.

The local, ruling creed there, on the other hand, must have been one of perplexing ambiguity to people of humble station, for it exhorted men of good will to love their neighbors as themselves. Yet when they looked to their betters for an example, to the mighty lords that ruled them by the grace of the same God whose Son had left them this legacy of love, all they could see was holy alliances resulting in unholy wars enforced and waged *ferro ignique* by the sword.

So when this revelation of nonviolence had jelled in their minds and the ruling lords called on them to participate in the next carnage of their choosing, they would have none of it anymore: they packed up and left. They were promised a peaceful existence by the Great Lady of the Eastern Empire, and so they moved to the uncharted wilderness on the banks of the mighty Volga River, which they then civilized. But with the change of times, the promises were forgotten, and they were to be pressed into military service again. Then they packed up again for another wilderness, this time the one on the banks of the trickle that the Cimarron is in dry years. And by the time he got there two generations later, they had that well civilized also. Now, that is what you can call the courage of your convictions.

Romilda

But the crux of his Okeene experience was Romilda herself. He had first met her during his tour at Fort Holabird. She lived on the other side of Baltimore and was married to Owen, who was an interesting mix of the kind and modest with the inquisitive and assertive. He taught high school and loved to tinker with used appliances, which he took apart to see how they worked and then demonstrated assembling them to his class. She, on her part, was the good genie of his house that she kept immaculate for him, a modest little red brick home on an elm-shaded, quiet, dead-end street of the typical Baltimore sort that maybe survives to this day if mercifully forgotten by the harsh, deceptive doctrines of economic growth.

Hers was a life in later middle age at a time when the darkening eddies of a remote farming past and of a small suburban present had slowed their swirling, as if asking her, "What now?" The answer soon came when Owen died of colon cancer: Romilda went home to that little farmhouse on the Cimarron that she had grown up in to take care of her aging parents. And there she did then what few European women would do at her age and under her circumstances: she went into business.

After the visitors were gone and he and Romilda finished washing the dishes, she promised to show him a few things the next day. "The business of America is business," she quoted some long-forgotten politician as they started out on their tour of a part of Oklahoma he had not known before. Driving down the main street of Okeene, she would point to a house here and a store there with a sly chuckle. "See this one? And that one? And that other one yonder? And that field there with cattle grazing on the winter wheat?" as they drove out of town.

She did not elaborate on how she acquired all that property, and he did not ask for details. But he knew now that he was an outsider in Okeene after all, as he sat there in the force field of this little old lady, who was pleasantly instructing him in what it was like to be a proper American without ever saying so out loud. He too would have returned to the ancestral homestead in her place but in order to contemplate the shifting of the clouds, the ripples on the river, and the growing of the grass.

They drove down to Watonga, the seat of Blaine County. Since it was Sunday, the place was a regular ghost town. A few wide, paved streets, a number of two-story, redbrick buildings. Nary-a-soul moving. Stores on the ground floor, some of them boarded up. The windows of the second floor: dark and hollow like the eyeholes in a skull. Is it really Watonga that I am seeing now with my mind's eye? He had seen so many of that kind by that time that his memory soon started mixing them up. Who knows, maybe the stores came alive come Monday morning like the hectic hustle and bustle of those young towns conjured up in the old, pre-high noon, black-and-white Hollywood Westerns. What kind of America could that have been, the one long ago, when live people were looking out of those second-story windows?

He tried to share with Romilda this fascination, this preoccupation, this morbid love affair of his with the American small town whose streets and alleys he walked whenever the road would take him there for a night's stay, but he soon stopped short upon meeting with a kind of blank, head-shaking incomprehension. To her, apparently, the place was as alive and well as the Yankee-doodle dollar itself that still greased its now squeaky skids, and why should it not have been? She was born and raised there, and there is no place like home.

Lunch at the Roman Nose Lodge came off better for him. They did not have the rattlesnake stew that was on the menu; it was not in season; the snakes had already gone into hiding and hibernation with the northwest winds blowing nippy. But the buffalo burger was good. Was it really tastier than the plain-old beef kind, or was it just the Wild West mystique? It did not matter, for the view was even better. The escarpments that lead slowly up to the eastern slopes of the great central mountain ranges make their first tentative appearance thereabouts. The Cheyenne lived here and made their stand against the invader, and none of them more bravely and fiercely than Woqini, the tall, strong warrior with the aquiline beak who gave the place his name.

Oklahoma, as I may have noted before, is not a first-rate tourist trap. But there is something about its harsh, shoulder-shrugging, puritan standoffishness that proved to be irresistible to the introvert that he was. He always regretted not having met his father-in-law, who had grown up there and whose character and values must have been formed by that land. He felt the two of them could have understood each other, sharing the silences of kindred spirits.

The Llano Estacado

Since he was between jobs at the moment and so in possession of a bit of freedom from the need or even from the want of doing something useful and productive, he let the little red Toyota make contact with US Highway Sixty and then encouraged it to head southwest on it toward the heart of the Llano Estacado. That was a strange, doubly foreign word that he had first encountered some forty years ago when America was nothing but a blotch on that large map that was his job to haul out of a closet in fourth grade to be unrolled from a hook on the wall for the geography class.

The place from where the Llano first popped up into that part of his mind that philosophers call "access consciousness" was a chapter in one of the two books that were his father's Christmas presents in 1901, at a time well before the first car had made its appearance in Bethlenfalva. His father clearly thought of them as treasures, for he selected them, ahead of hundreds of more important and practical items, to accompany the family into exile. An exile whose menace must have loomed up before the grown-ups who were doing the packing of essentials for survival as the blind darkness of some unknown hell.

The other book I still have, believe it or not. But this one he loaned out in Harthausen to Csicsa *bácsi*, the lieutenant colonel, who was in charge of the train that picked them up in the middle of that snow flurry near Linz. But the man disappeared before he could get around to returning it. Its title was *Villámsugár* or *Lightning Bolt*. It was an adventure story centered on the friendship of a Magyar, buckskin-clad, Wild West explorer with a great, noble, chivalrous, and diplomatic chief of the Apache Nation, and (if I remember this right) in riding together through this same Llano one day, they had occasion to spar with some hostile Comanche, who were the bad guys in the story and who pulled up the direction-guiding stakes (the *estacas*?) to lead them astray, away from the next water hole.

The name of the Indian was given in the book as Attakualla, and in writing it down here, it just occurred to me to check it out: was it a real name or just a fictitious sequence of letters? And here is what Google can do for you. Without hesitating one second, it produced pages of hits of which this one seemed most relevant:

> Six Indian chiefs accompanied Sir Alexander Cumming on his return to England. Noted among these was Atta Kulla Kulla, the Carpenter, so named for his ability to hammer together difficult agreements. On September 30, 1730, at Dover England, these six chiefs signed a treaty with the British government. This treaty declared that "the Chain of Friendship" between the King of England and the Cherokee Indians "is like the Sun, which shines here and also upon the great mountains where they live, and equally warms the Hearts of the Indians and of the English."

Well, well, what do you know! Did they write that treaty with foreknowledge, or did history just happen accidentally afterward? That friendship turned out to be a chain indeed, a prophetic bond that dragged the Cherokee directly to the Trail of Tears in the end. That was a path that ended not far from the Llano, where the sun still shone but less brightly now a century and a half after that treaty, on the Atta Kualla who lived in my book.

The description of that vast, empty, sere, high-mesa landscape, the Staked Plains, with its short grass undulating in the wind was vivid and compelling in that book, so that he could not help rereading those passages many times back then, on the sofa in his father's study in Léva. So much so that in the end, he had no doubt left in his mind that someday he would have to see and experience it himself. And this was to be that time: right now. Once he passed through Amarillo heading south toward Lubbock, he started looking forward to it with high expectations. But by the time he got to Roswell on the New Mexico side of the Texas Panhandle and had seen nothing but ploughed, harvested cotton fields, he knew he should have known better. Leave well enough alone!

> The meaning is live though its spirit is struggling,
> But in Lubbock, in Lubbock it's gone into deep hiding.
> Into hiding in the depths of Buffalo Canyon
> Where the Brazos is dammed and the bison extinct.
> Where the grass is now gray with dust—if there is any.
> Gray like the sobs of Chief Quanah's laughter
> Over the staked Llano, now all under the plough.

Passing on through Santa Fe next offered scant consolation. There were some real Indians on the plaza to be sure, but they did not seem to be Attakualla's descendants. They were selling Indian trinkets.

Solitaires

I have a difficult time getting on with this next chapter of my story—the years in what is known as the San Francisco Bay Area. It covers a long time, the longest stay in one place in my life. Twelve years! Is there anything I can say about them that my wife, my sons, or anyone who might want to follow me as I wind my way through them could use, perhaps to compare his own search of an america with mine?

So I sit here playing the spider solitaire on my computer. With real cards, it would take fifteen minutes to deal out the two decks. Now, pushing a button on my keyboard will do the trick in a second. The spider is the best of all solitaires. It is complex and therefore mind maintaining; it keeps aging neurons alive, their synapses sparking. It is also a form of meditation, like turning a prayer wheel or fingering the beads of the rosary. It is like life: its randomly assorted distributions may be influenced by the player to form orderly sequences, which when completed, drop out of the game like a *Gestalt* that effort had formed into a polished whole. Also, it saves me from having to write my next sentence, when I feel that I have nothing left to say.

It would have been too difficult for his grandmother to play though. She played a *Zopf* and a *tizenhármas* every evening after dinner, after the maid had cleared the table. The *Zopf* was easy; it "came out" almost always. The *tizenhármas* almost never. That one took two decks also, one of which was laid out in four groups of thirteen cards, hence its name, the "game of thirteens." She played these two games to the very end, to the very last day of life the way she knew and understood it, when she fell and broke her hipbone and was taken to the hospital a week before her daughter left with her family to follow their fate into exile, leaving her behind to suffer hers alone. The hospital was evacuated, and the patients were moved to the neighboring town of Ipolyság just before the Russians arrived. So she died there not only alone among strangers but also in a strange place, probably of bewilderment.

He found out about all this decades later. His mother might have died of self-blame for having left her mother behind, had she not soon died of leukemia instead. Even though she knew that she had no choice, she had to leave his grandmother behind for the sake of her family that could not stay. This was not a war like others; this war on the Eastern Front. Not like a normal war like that one in the West. The last "Good War," as Americans keep calling it. One whose horrors scar over and heal after it finally plays itself out, and then life goes on much like before.

It is human nature that leads to wars, and they are fought for economic gain, suggests Clausewitz. If that is true, they are the result of the analytical calculations of those who hope to benefit from them, while the actual fighting, suffering, and sacrificing is an emotional burden born by the victims. This war in the East, where it was his fate to be, went beyond profiteering by the elite. It was also a clash of ideologies and classes. Those of the old order, the ones on the losing side, his side, had to be eradicated, wiped out, preferably without a trace.

And so it happened, for instance, that Majláth Laci *bácsi* (his solitaire-playing grandmother's cousin), who stayed, was sitting in his office, resolved to face whatever would come (for his family had gone through this sort of thing on and off for a thousand years), his doors open as if he were waiting to surprise the boy with a new kind of candy bar, when the mob got him. It worked up its courage in the vacuum of power left in the wake of the Russians who passed through quickly. It dragged him outside, kicked out one of his eyes, and then left him frozen in his blood in the gutter. "*A szlovák komunisták kiütötték a félszemét,*" so reported the letter that his father got a few years later in Harthausen from some friend or relative who somehow survived eradication. The Slovak communists kicked out one of his eyes. Yes, dying in time can sometimes be merciful.

House hunting

Once Marina had made her move down to the Bay Area from Oregon, she quickly found a nice little house to rent on Ramona Street in El Cerrito, one of the East Bay communities north of Berkeley. Unlike most other houses in this area, this one was not open to the street, offering privacy provided by a courtyard and ample greenery in the front yard. It was within easy walking distance from his job at the WRRC. They rented the house and spent the next year looking for the right one to buy, being as picky and meticulous about the search as if they expected to stay in what they would find for a long time, a time as long as it would take for their solar system to be sucked into the galaxy's black hole.

In the process, they would have driven poor Mr. Daughtry, their real estate agent, crazy, had he not learned to endure, maybe even enjoy, the company of the most discriminating clients that he could ever fear to have. He even went through a buyer's remorse procedure with them and got their *earnest money* back after they changed their minds on the desirability or adequacy of one of the objects he had shown them. But when they finally found their dream house on Avila Street in El Cerrito, it was a sale by owner, and although the agent missed out on his commission, he was nonchalant about it and held no grudges.

The job scene

Work was slow to start at the WRRC. It was like trying to swim in syrup at first. The lab was old, ugly, and dark, and the little office, shared with Milford was totally inadequate. There was no equipment of any kind and no greenhouse to grow plants in, and being in the city, there was no access to natural soil to work with. WRRC was a postharvest, product-development center, large and bureaucratic, one whose more than a hundred Ph.D.-level scientists were expected to come up with value-added agricultural products like *shogun tofu* or *macho taco* that even the Japanese and the Mexicans would recognize as superior to what they invented and could produce themselves. The spirit of the people and the place was one of test-tube-oriented biology, and his was not.

But the nitrogen-fixation program was created and funded, although it was not yet operational, for no one knew what to do with it. Since the money was there, however, it needed to be spent, and so he was sucked into his new position as the project's leader and lead scientist as if by a vacuum, even before he found out where the water cooler, the coffee machine, and the outhouse were—by default at first, but soon by design.

As there was nothing in place for the proper spending of the funds allocated for the work, no people, no equipment, no plan, no experience, and no initiative even, all he had to do was outline his own vision of it to the chain of command, especially to the director of the center. That was a jovial but aloof civil servant, not given to back slapping but not to back stabbing either. His management style was to keep it a well-guarded secret whether he held any interest at all in the science and the operations of his center, a little empire of research scientists, research support technicians, and other administrative civil servants. True to his style, he accepted his new project leader's proposals without changing an iota; the director was an all-or-nothing guy.

The research leader, the immediate superior of a project leader in the chain of command, happened to be a lipid chemist who had some four projects under his care. One of these was this one on "nitfix," and the RL knew nothing about its science. He was not only jovial; he was outright jolly and personable instead of being aloof and officious. Glenn was a dream boss, for not only did he not know about any of the details that some of the work under him involved, he did not care either, as long as it produced publications to prove that something worthwhile was being done. So that when he (the biologist) gave the two bosses a little talk on what he wanted to do, they just nodded. He took that to be a glass half full: he could do with the project what he wanted on the one hand but without being particularly encouraged yet about his plans on the other.

To fill up his glass, he made a pilgrimage to Beltsville (Maryland). That is where the Agricultural Research Service has its national headquarters, and it was none other than that group of big, old, yellow, three-story brick buildings that he had driven by every working day for two years on his way from College Park to Fort Meade during his army days without knowing or caring what they were all about. Strange how things of total irrelevance can sometimes become central to one's focus later.

There he met with good fortune. The national program staff director of the ARS, whose area of responsibility covered nitrogen fixation was interested and found the time to hear his story. The ARS-NPS is the staff agency whose job it is to listen to the representatives of politically powerful farm-commodities groups, to deal with the members of the agricultural committees of Congress, to keep tab on scientific advances and projections that impact on agricultural production, and last not least, to keep an ear open to hear messages from the grassroots, from workers in the field like him. From all this input, the NPS then designs a multi-year plan of research priorities whose progress it monitors and guides. Gerry was the man's name. When he had *his* ear full, he said, "Gabe, what you tell me fits right into our plan. Now let's go and have lunch." From then on, he went out of his way to be helpful time and time again.

"I hear they liked you at Beltsville," said Glenn when he got back. "I'll assign a technician to you to get you started, and I just volunteered Milford to work for you." He started ordering equipment using the developing needs of the work as a guide as it slowly unfolded. Back then UC Berkeley had an agricultural field site next to the WRRC grounds, and there he found a collaborator who had plant-growth facilities, which he could use until his own outfit built a greenhouse on the roof of the huge WRRC building.

He gave talks on his project at in-house brown-bag lunches, and as people became interested, they wanted to join in. Postdocs were hired, and Gerry had a Ph.D. soil microbiologist assigned to what had become a recognized and successful research group in short order. He developed the program to fit his own interests (within ARS priorities) and planned, designed, and timed the experiments needed to produce the desired results.

Since he also wrote the publications and presented most of the talks at scientific meetings, it did not take long for the colleagues in his field to recognize his name worldwide. Since the local bosses and the faraway NPS had only a superficial grasp of the details of his project, they subsided into a state of benign neglect, which was just fine with him and which he tried to cultivate by presenting them with update summaries periodically. In these, he tried at times to amuse them with his newly developed symbiosis-centric view of the agricultural universe.

Symbiosis, tongue-in-cheek

Crop plants, he would say, are in reality just tubes designed by microbes who are only interested in serving their own purposes. Each microorganism has something important to offer to its specialized symbiotic associates and needs to receive something important from the others in return.

Take, for instance, the aboriginal cyanobacterium (formerly known as a "blue-green alga"). It lives and functions today in green leaves where it is now known as the "chloroplast." There it captures carbon dioxide from the air and reduces it to carbohydrates: the staff of life that virtually all other life-forms need as their basic food staple. It sends these products down to its associates in the root through a plant conduit, the phloem tissue of the bark.

In turn, bacteria of the genus *Rhizobium* take up residence in the roots of leguminous (bean family) plants, where they cause the root to form nodules to house its new residents. In these root nodules, the modified bacteria have ready access to the carbohydrates arriving from above, and there they return the favor by fixing atmospheric nitrogen into N compounds. These are known as amino groups, and their combination with the carbohydrates from the chloroplasts gives rise to amino acids, the building blocks of proteins. Proteins are essential to the functioning of all life, but one life-form that has direct access to them right down there where the nodules are is another microbe: a root microfungus.

These fungi belong to an ancient group that helped plants survive on dry land when they first washed up from the sea together eons ago. They colonize the cells of the root cortex but also range out far and wide into the soil. There they pick up essential mineral nutrients such as phosphorus (P). This P is always in short supply since most phosphates are just barely soluble, and both chloroplasts and rhizobia have super-high requirements for it. You get the idea: they supply the fungus with carbohydrates and proteins, and in return, they get some of the P that the fungus extracts from the soil. They need this nutrient, as their metabolic functions use up lots of ATP (adenosine triphosphate).

And the production of this ATP, the energy currency of life, is where the granddaddy of plant-associated microbes enters the currency-exchange system of the plant symbiosis (although he himself did not work on this kind). This one, the mitochondrion, is today an organelle that inhabits eukariotic cells, but its ancestor, the proto-mitochondrion, probably descended from the proteobacteria to become the intracellular powerhouse of all of us multicellulars, plants and animals alike.

"So from the microbes' point of view, the plant is nothing but a set of tubes and conduits that they use to share their products," he would educate his bosses. "And to perpetuate the existence of the tubing system that hosts them, they permit it to grow pods, whose contents, the beans, they let us have." "Okay, okay," the bosses would say, "just don't forget that the taxpayer pays your keep to do work and not to play games." That was fair enough, and so in time, he decided to refocus on agricultural problems.

The home scene

Yet it would have been a blessing had he found his work on the problems of agriculture less exhilarating, for then he might have been more open to problems at home. But his primary focus during this creative prime time of his journey on the road was on his work and not on his life, and he lost sight of the fact that the two of them were not one and the same.

There was no end to new experiments whose data wanted to be reported, technology transfer as it is called, and that meant talks at one conference after another, all over the country and much of the time abroad. This brought recognition and promotions, always *sui tempore*, at the right time, without having to wait a lot! But he would gladly give all of that back now could he only go back to Albany Middle School and help the Fox with algebra.

What made it unforgivable was that he knew his son had problems not only with math but with school in general. His hard-headed attitude still was "Nobody had to help me, so why should my son not be able to get it on his own?" Good question, that, and he could use it now as an excuse had not Marina clearly, urgently, and repeatedly explained to him the difference.

"When you were at this stage, life was one of postwar survival. School in rural Icking was not a battlefield of confused teenage mindsets like here in this largely affluent Bay Area metropolis. There were no cliques of preppies, geeks, jocks, and rockers and who knows what else in your teenage world in postwar Germany. You and your classmates had all seen the ruins of war and felt what it was like not to have enough to eat. You knew there was only one way to overcome the past. Maybe you were cheated out of your childhood, but you knew what you had to do and he does not."

He was too busy with his newfound success to hear what he heard. So the Fox ended up joining the rockers and adopting their ways without really being one of them in spirit. "Rockers rule" was their rowdy war cry. A geek, who in Icking was called a *Streber*, one who had fun in learning and therefore had good grades, was dismissed with contempt.

When rockers got together, they had to contribute something to the group. Those who could not pilfer booze from home had to prove themselves by stealing a bottle at the supermarket. So he found himself picking up his son at the police station, and it was more than once. They always caught him. "I had to have something to offer my friends," his son would explain.

It was always the same: the gang watched from the sidelines and disappeared when the guards caught him. "You call these assholes friends who run away when one of their own is in trouble?" he struggled with his son's value system. It was not the act of stealing *per se*, the huge supermarket chain could survive the disappearance of a few items as far as he was concerned. It was the defamation of the sanctity of friendship, the lack of understanding of what that word is meant to mean and had always meant to him, as he had learned to understand it in a culture that seemed to be alien where his son was growing up. By the time his thick head started to see that it was no one's fault but his own that his son chose the rockers as role models instead of him, it was too late.

By now there was nothing but resentment and resistance, and he had to admit that he felt quite powerless to deal with the situation. The dam was broken, and the consequences were rushing through it. The peers would show up at the house, at that detached garage on Ramona Street and at the in-law apartment on Avila Place with mean-looking faces on some of them. These friends stole his mountain bike and his record collection. He warned, "Watch out, that guy is trouble." No use. So he did the simple and easy thing that weaklings do when in trouble. He went into denial about it: "This is nothing but a transition phase. It will pass."

That was not the way Marina saw it, fortunately, and she took action by getting the family into counseling that went on for many weeks. At first, it really went against his grain. "What can this stranger tell me about myself that I don't know well enough already?" John was still a youngish man, but he had seen and experienced all of the conceivable problems that people could bring to him. "What you have to do is to make things work *for* you instead of letting them go against you," he counseled. "Look at me. While I am sitting here, I have bees working for me out there in the almond orchards of the Capay Valley. Then every week, I go out there and harvest the honey." That made sense, and so bit by bit, communication was starting to happen, conflicts were discussed and defused, and his sense of humiliation of having to turn for help abated.

In the end, when their allotted time was up, the Fox, who was at first an equally unwilling participant, suddenly appealed to John: "Why can't we keep on coming? How am I going to deal with these guys without you?" Rob acted like the wisest one in the family. Not too happy to be there either, yet he was insightful and conciliatory. And when they came home, their black cat was there waiting for them at the door and was passed from arm to arm and lap to lap, purring up a storm. It was as if the mostly unspoken love that held the family together had taken shape in her, a little guardian spirit of the household.

The next step Marina took was to find a school that would not replicate the same ugly patterns of clique formation that had the power to lock the kids into a fixed and limiting identity. She found a little private outfit that ran a school on the grounds of the Methodist Church on Bancroft Avenue in Berkeley: Maybeck. The classes were small; the students received personal attention; the teachers were young and enthusiastic. Some had credentials; others were grad students from the university up the street. For all of them, the goal was to keep the joy of learning alive in their students. They began each school year with a week camping out at the Feather River, a time devoted to an overarching topic explored together by all grade levels.

But the curriculum? Well, if there was one it was not apparent to him, so different was their approach from what he had known school to be in Europe with its rigid, mandatory set and sequence of subjects. But Maybeck was accredited to award a high school diploma, so presumably its graduates did get whatever students were expected to get in an American high school. It was a wholesome experience that changed previously negative attitudes; both kids liked the venue and did well after struggling through middle school in the public system.

Previously, Rob had even put in a stint at Saint Jerome's, the parochial school in El Cerrito, where Marina had moved him out of an uninspired class at the local grade school. But you have to start early if you want to swing to the tune of the Gregorian Chant, and Rob did not have the proper Catholic background and preparation for that. He felt that the way the sisters went about their business was "weird," and he felt out of place there. Why, he wasn't even properly baptized.

Baptizing Robin

He was, actually, but not with holy water under the fragrant clouds of the holy smokes. The water we used for that came from the clear stream of the *arroyo* that flows by Cataviña, Baja California. That is normally dry, but it was trickling happily then: a Christmas gift of the Pacific storm that the jet stream, in a rare good mood, had moved that far south just for that occasion the day before. That baptism had actually taken place back in their Davis days (1977) and it was during their second foray into Baja California, one they undertook to escape the commercial American Christmas scene that remained so foreign to them.

The first exploratory one was to Mulegé even before that. He had read about Mulegé in a travel magazine while sitting in his dentist's waiting room. The place was described in glowing terms, and it was not far from their Alta California, considering how far so many other places manage to be from there. The kids went off to grandmother in Munich for the summer, and so they were free to strike out on their own. They drove down that endless curvy spine of the great Baja Peninsula to what they thought would be their destination using the only paved road there, whose thousand-mile stretch had just been completed all the way down to La Paz the year before.

On the way, they stopped overnight in magic Cataviña and knew immediately that they would come back there many times. But as Mulegé was a hot and dusty disappointment at that time of the year, they soon went on to La Paz and not having found the real, romantic Mexico there either, they took the ferry, the *transbordador*, over to Mazatlán. That was an entire little ocean voyage of a day and a half across the Sea of Cortez. By then, their time was running out, however, and what was planned to be R&R in an idyllic spot turned out to be a roadrunner experience covering well over two thousand miles.

But such is the nature of coincidence: that chance magazine article in the dentist's office began a love affair that kept blossoming out with time. Marina studied up on Baja, and when Christmastime came looming up again on the calendar with the shortening of days, they decided that they would escape the incessant, mind-numbing repetition of Yuletide carols in the stores this time and spend it at the Molino Viejo on the Bahía San Quintín.

Now, you must know that Baja is not the average tourist's dream. It is stark, sere, deserted, primitive, and dust blown. You love it or you hate it; there is no in between. That is not a decision you make with your head; Baja leaps out to your heart. He loved it on first sight, and Marina did too, but at first perhaps only for his sake. You ramble along on that narrow, two-lane road without shoulders and banked the wrong way on curves where you cannot get lost as it is the only one there is, minding always that *este camino no es de alta velocidad*. And you really have to mind your steering wheel always, for the *camino* is indeed curvy and not built for high speeds. So you must watch out that your botanist's eye does not get lost in the most glorious desert vegetation on our blue planet. That our earthly spectrum of visible light that shimmers here in red-ocher-terra cotta to olive green hues is restful to the mind while the eye never stops searching for new and maybe even undescribed species of plants. Cacti, mainly.

When they got to the old motel that was a favorite stopover for both seafaring and landlubbing *norteños*, the sky was already gray and misting moisture gently but steadily as if in transition to the mild, subtropical, 100-percent-humidity kind that Pacific winter storms turn into that far South. They found a saltbush branch and set it up as a Christmas tree in their not very cozy, dampish, viewless room and decorated it with peppermint candy sticks.

The kids were as unenthusiastic and squirmy about all this as the larvae of may bugs are when you dig them up out of their cool, moist, underground habitat and put them into the hot sun (*kínlódik, mint pata a napon*, as this was called back in Léva). One could see how they were silently questioning their elders' competence and judgment. But dinner was a consolation; it was Christmas Eve, and the Viejo Molino had a tradition of not forgetting to celebrate it. Also the Baja lobster populations were not yet harvested to extinction, and generous portions of their tails were part of the feast. The Fox, in particular, was born with the ability to appreciate a tasty morsel.

In the morning, there was a surprise. The candy sticks had disappeared: surrendering their discrete entity to the humidity, they melted into little moist stalagmites under the saltbush branch. Exploring the beach, collecting sand dollars, and climbing the mounds of volcanic rock was okay, but the mood was bleak there in that drizzle; things simply had not lived up to expectations. To avoid open rebellion, they decided to go on to Cataviña.

That included lunch at El Rosario, at the Posada of Mama Espinosa, and consisted of none other than her famous *burritos de langosta*. They did not find it by accident; Marina's studies had revealed that Mama Espinosa was a living legend who had kept a guest book since the 1940s for the rough riders of the Baja cross-country stock-car race, when El Rosario was a flyspeck hamlet at the very end of the gravel road that led there from Ensenada. From there on south, Baja was a trackless wilderness up to 1973 when the paved road to La Paz opened: one year before they got there, that is. Mama, going on seventy, was still very much in evidence. On that day, she was chatting about change in a way that was uncharacteristically downhearted for her, so her daughter Rolli commented from the sidelines. She had a dream about that amply running well that was the chief (maybe only) supply of water for the village, and she had seen it gradually run dry as the village grew with all those trucks that were going to roar through it now. "Then, El Rosario would turn into a *pueblo de fantasma*—what is that in English? Yes, that's it, into a ghost town."

He wanted to check out that well, but it was said to be a ways down the *arroyo*, and they had no reservations at the Presidente. That hotel, then the only building of Cataviña, was connected to the world by radiotelephone and that was not working that day. When they got there, though, they were the only guests. "The Gringos," the bartender said with an ingratiating smile to imply that no slur was meant, "like to go to the Cabos by boat, so the government is losing a lot of money on this inn."

After a moment of reflection, he went on, oddly and out of context, "Like lobster-taco Mama in Rosario says, 'Bad road, good people. Good road, bad people.'" So-so road, so-so people, he (the biologist) wanted to add to complete that thought with a missing dimension and to pinpoint his own position on Mama's roadmap, but the man was mixing him a margarita already, and so he did not press the point. It was getting dark and quickly so, so they had dinner instead of rushing out to explore. He had a *pierna de pollo con mole poblano* that he had first tasted in Mazatlan and liked a lot. The Fox took a sampling of it and called it promptly what it was: stringy roadrunner leg in chocolate sauce. Marina ended the meal with the question "When are we going to go and explore the real Mexico?"

The next morning, upon noticing that they were now even further from *tout terre habitée* than ever before, the mood of the infantry turned decidedly glum. But the sun was out, and as they descended the rather steep banks of the *arroyo*, they found a streamlet running in it. That saved the day and the entire trip. Before long, beaver dams were being built. Water has built-in magic in it, and with the enthusiasm that grows as an integral part of any good enterprise, little eyes were opening to the strangeness, one might even say otherworldliness, of the surroundings. Huge gray granite blocks and boulders were strewn all over the landscape as far as the eye could see from the top edge of the *barranca*—like storybook castles and cities overgrown with a vegetation every bit as strange and outlandish as it really is, for much of it is endemic and does not grow anywhere else on the planet.

There was the *cirio* tree, or boojun, that looks like a giant, thirty-foot inverted carrot that branches out just enough on top to make its flame-colored flowers up there look as if it were burning like the candle for which it is named. There was the elephant tree, with its thick, fleshy trunk, elephant-leg-colored bark and gnarled contorted branches all greened out at the moment in response to the recent rains. There were the fan palms that send their tall spindly stems way high up in the air so that they may swing gaily in the wind with their little round crowns peeking out over the rims of the canyons in whose bottom they prefer to root near water. And there were cacti, too many kinds to count.

He gave a little lecture on the one to watch out for, the jumping cholla. Not that you did not have to mind the spines of all the others also, but this one breaks off from the main stem in small chunks, and if you walk heedlessly, you kick them up so that they get stuck in your pants. And then you are in trouble. For the tips of the spines of this one are curved like fishhooks, and as you try to get rid of it with one of your hands, the spines quickly embed themselves in your skin. Next, if you are not desert savvy, you try to free yourself with the other hand so that that one gets to be hooked by the spines also. Now you are doubly manacled, and painfully so, for the spines are working themselves ever deeper as you squirm and desperately try to wiggle yourself free from it. As a final recourse, it may then occur to you to use your remaining upper extremity, your nose, to budge the offending menace loose—do not do it!

It was a teachable moment, following which everybody was careful, nobody made contact with the cholla, and Marina, who is the mistress of ceremonies of the family, decided to take advantage of the happy and lighthearted mood of the occasion to make up for an old omission. Robin had never been baptized in church and had inquired sometimes why he was not "babitized." They made use now of a small cascade of water over a rock for a baptistery and pronounced him, with a sprinkling of that pure desert water, a free spirit in the name of the ineffable cosmic consciousness of the universe.

India

With the course of the kids' schooling now apparently running a little more smoothly or at least out of the rapids for the moment (we are back now in the mid-1980s), at Maybeck, he wasted no time in becoming fixated on his hobby again. At the time, the Indo-US Science and Technology Initiative was one of the vehicles that the great Indian agricultural revolution used to make that subcontinent self-sufficient in food. One area that the Initiative was particularly interested in was nitrogen fixation. Producing N fertilizer by the Haber-Bosch process is expensive, and legumes fix atmospheric N_2 for free.

The question was how to improve this biotechnology? His contribution was the use of root-colonizing microfungi. Unbeknownst to most people at that time, including those of the plant-science community itself, plants do not have roots. Instead, the vast majority of them have mycorrhizae (fungus roots), and the fungal component of this symbiotic organ is highly susceptible to agricultural abuse, such as mechanical soil degradation, compaction, fungicides, and the like. But the fungi are a main uptake agent of phosphorus that is especially important for nitrogen fixation, and in developing countries, where the peasants cannot afford fertilizers, they are a consequential aspect of successful crop management, hence the mutual interest of the Indo-US STI in him and his in it: it was a source of funds, connections, exchanges, and travel for him, and above all, one more way to make the world greener.

In the course of this involvement, Indian colleagues came to his lab, and he was invited to go to India. So it happened that he was sitting in the coffee shop of the Kanishka Hotel in New Delhi, having breakfast with Jim Trappe of the US Forest Service. Jim was the ultimate resource person. He was co-author of "Mycologia Memoir Number 5," the momentous paper that had defined the taxonomy of mycorrhizal fungi, and so had put them on the map of science in earnest. Jim not only knew everybody in the field but also was known to be able and willing to help anybody when it was within the scope of his science. So after having discussed the role of weeds in the survival of fungal propagules in crop rotation, he asked Jim if he knew of any good, friendly colleagues in Mexico.

"Sure," Jim said, "I will write to Ronald at the Agricultural University of Chapingo to expect you. He will pick you up at the airport in Mexico City with a big grin on his face." He put Ronald's address and phone number in his shirt pocket (this was way before the e-mail era), feeling assured that with a little effort in grant writing, he would now be able to show Marina the real Mexico more thoroughly than tourists do. Then he set out on foot in the direction of the Red Fort in old Delhi, a tourist destination he had seen in the distance from his tenth-floor window. He wanted to experience a bit of the real India on the way.

It was easy going along the shady, wide, empty avenues of New Delhi, the city the British had built. The heat was turned up high enough to roast a pig, but then for him, it could never be hot enough. As he trudged along, the scenery slowly changed. More than just the scenery. His eyes were expecting to perceive a different input on the other side of a not very wide belt of deserted, broken fields that seemed to be there as the transition zone between the new and old worlds (his nose was also keenly aware of the changes as he went on).

But there was also another perception, a nonsensory one, that he knew from the past without really knowing it and remembered in the undefinable, formless way in which wordless impressions perpetuate themselves like distant echoes of something real and actual in some lost, dead-end corner of one's subconscious. He had experienced a feeling like this that morning in the Mauthausen Camp and then again upon his first arrival in New York Harbor.

It was neither ominous nor expectant but more like messages sent without an addressee: "To whom it may concern," to be received by someone or anyone in the anonymous ether like what the world of the World Wide Web is today. Its texture was more like what his mood at the moment might make of it: kind of neutral. Based on his exposure to physics, his mental image of the phenomenon was most akin to what an antenna might feel when a transmitter sends out a signal of radio waves into the stratosphere from where these are bounced back diffusely, an antenna that not only happens to be in the way of the signal but is also tuned to its frequency: a receiver by chance.

Slowly, the path he followed, keeping the Red Fort always in sight up on that still distant rise, was filling up with life of all kinds. It was not quite clear if the path was along streets defined by buildings, for the throng that was closing in on him started to absorb his vision, shutting out everything else. The animals, stolid and stationary, caused him to deviate, but the mass of humans seemed to open a path. Not politely and certainly not deferentially but more as if compelled to do so by an aversion to be too close to him. They were very dark skinned, small, and sickly, and their faces seemed pinched by a world of needs and wants, hungry, he felt, for more than only food. Suddenly he became aware then that they were the source of that eerie message, and he felt shivering cold. Their collective signal was not directed at him; he just happened to be in its way.

He went on fighting an upwelling of panic, but by the time he thought he had that under control, the Red Fort was no longer there. The sun was overhead, all directions were the same, and the knowledge overcame him that if he got lost, he would never get out of there. They would not let him get out; they might eat him alive. He squinted his eyes half shut and, trusting his instinct of orientation, let it guide him without making conscious decisions at each turn. After a while he found himself back in the transition zone.

The Indian colleague at the reception that evening, to whom he related his experience, was aghast. "You must be crazy. Looking for the real India on foot! It is unforgiving. You Americans are like children. You with your romantic notions of august ashrams replete with luminous enlightenment! Okay, we will put out a warning immediately. If you guys want to see the Red Fort, you take an official tour bus from the Kanishka."

With the meetings over in New Delhi, he wanted to take the Rajdhani train to Bangalore to visit his friend and colleague, Joe Bagyaraj, at the Agricultural University and to see the countryside on the way. That was another little insight into the real India. You don't go by yourself to the train station there to get a ticket. If you do, instead of a ticket, you get practical experience in what theoretical physicists call the chaos theory. Lines in the thousands, shoving and pushing in seemingly random directions, all with imaginary hopes for reaching unattainable goals defined by a profusion of instructions on the grimy walls decipherable as to their meanings only by those in command of ancient Sanskrit, yet perplexingly, written in some form of present-day English.

"Oh, to get a reservation for a Rajdhani train, you need help from an important person," the organizer of the conference enlightened him. "I will get you one." But it was just as well that he forgot, for the airplane ride saved him two days.

The Bangalore he saw was the one before it became Silicon Valley East. What I remember of it was his third experience of the real India. He was giving a talk to Joe's grad students from behind a table in a chemistry classroom that had large sliding doors on each side, open for ventilation. In the middle of his spiel, a troop of some half dozen tall monkeys leapt in silently through one of the doors, much like a gust of wind can sweep dry leaves into your garage. It halted between the table and the front row of chairs.

Some sat down in vacant seats. The leader, an alpha individual of undisputed authority, hopped up on the table where he made himself comfortable, facing the class. He (the biologist) took a few steps back to be out of range of the monkey's long arms but also to the side to be able to observe the proceedings. Perceiving this, the monkey glanced back at him and nodded. There could be no mistaking the meaning of his message: "It's okay with me that you removed yourself, for I am the center of attention now."

He then turned his attention to the only object on the table on which he was squatting. It was a test-tube rack. With his thumb and index finger, he picked out a test tube, swirled it, slanted it to peer at the contents from the top, and finally sniffed at it. Then, with the tube still in his hand, he looked back a second time, caught the biologist's eye, and shook his head in an unmistakable expression of disapproval. Finished with it, he gingerly replaced the tube, jumped off the table, and in a second, the troop was swept out through the other door by a gust like the one that had brought it in.

Joe swore that he did not see the monkey nod or shake his head. The class, with remarkable self-control, had restrained the roaring laughter that broke out after the troop was gone. At first, he too had felt that the incident was exceedingly hilarious. But on second thought, he wondered why. Why would the event not have been funny had the inspector been a human?

I admit that the monkey may have seen a human instructor act in a similar manner and was just aping what he had observed before. But he had also connected with me personally beyond any doubt of that on my part. You see, sometimes I get up from this writing to putter around in the garden, and what I observed there just now fits in here.

There is a large, grass green juvenile-stage instar of a locust in residence on the front-yard passion-flower bush, on which live also a number of caterpillars of the fritillary butterfly, whose exclusive food this plant is. This morning then, the long-legged young insect started walking, slowly and ponderously, straight in the direction of one of the small caterpillars. There he stopped, and after a while, he raised his right front foot and touched the caterpillar with it. The caterpillar lunged out at him as is the custom of his kind when disturbed, but it did not seem to be further concerned, for it went right back to munching its lunch. The locust, in turn, did not take the caterpillar's gesture as unfriendly, for it raised his foot even higher and shook it up and down rhythmically a few times as if in greeting. Then he touched the caterpillar again as if he wanted to reassure himself of the reality of the event: with the same results. They went through this simple routine four or five times. Then the locust stopped to consider the experience. After that, he turned and walked away.

What was this all about? What sensory insight was transmitted to the brain of this creature by this encounter of his foot with a fellow being? Did the insight reach that quality of his that philosophers call his "phenomenal consciousness"? A quality that he is not supposed to have? Of this creature who doesn't even have a "real" brain! Was he in touch with some primary-principle mysteries while immersed into the impersonal essence of the Brahman? Mysteries that evolution regrettably blocked out, covered over by the cortex of our sophisticated, real learned brains, our *cerebra docta*?

> "Into blind darkness they enter,
> people who worship ignorance.
> And into still blinder darkness,
> people who delight in learning,"

admonishes the Isavasya Upanishad. If Andrei Linde's thoughts about consciousness being a fundamental dimension of our universe hold water, as I suspect they may, then perhaps it would be not only more modest but also more correct not to think of our fly-speck home in the greater multiverse as anthropic. Instead, maybe *all*, not only human life, should have a place in that elusive, cosmic component of consciousness.

His last stop in India was Hyderabad, where he had a research initiative pending with the international research institute ICRISAT. This grant, approved for funding by USAID, did not come to fruition because Indian bureaucracy took forever in making up its mind on the conditions of collaboration, and in the end, the funds were allocated to someone else. This was a crusher, but that came later. At the moment, Hyderabad offered a fourth insight into the real India.

His colleague and prospective Indian collaborator, a modest, bright, cultured, and affable young man, invited him for breakfast to his house. The apartment was clean, tidy, and functional, though bare and containing only the minimum essentials. But it was dark and damp, for it was half sunk into the ground, perhaps to keep it cool. For him, it had a murky element of unlivable discomfort about it that reminded him uneasily of how some of the destitute, so-called lower-class people, the proletarians, lived in prewar Magyarország, whose homes he would visit with his mother on her humanitarian errands.

The wife brought in the food from the kitchen that was devoid of any of the labor-saving devices without which Americans could not imagine life to exist and then retired there to eat her breakfast alone. A personable young woman, she was a practicing medical doctor.

"Krishna," he said after having taken store of the situation, "enlighten me. What is this all about? It is just the three of us here. Would it unhinge the axis of the earth if we ate together? Her being out there makes me feel acutely uncomfortable. If she does not join us, I will have to insist on washing the dishes afterward."

The man sighed but politely, not like someone who means to imply "Here we go again." "We are Brahmins," he said finally. "We do not live *by* the tenets of our caste. We live them. They are our life. So now, please, you enlighten *me*. How is life in a land where people belong to nothing that is greater than their own ego? By your country's creed, all men are created equal. But they are not. Even if they were, their lives' limitations force them into different pigeonholes, which they then deny. Everyone claims to be middle class. No cohesion of culture and tradition. Then when the storms of credit-card debt hit them, where is their safe harbor like our extended families, clans, and yes, castes? Then they move out, bankrupt, to live under the bridge. We here, we hang on to our anchor. To be a Brahmin has a price, and we are happy to pay it.

As to the dishes, the maid will come and do them. Do you want to make her unemployed?"

That was some twenty-five years ago. Who knows, maybe that is not the real India anymore. America has discovered outsourcing since then. Money is like the tides. It ebbs and flows. With us, it is seriously ebbing now and has been doing so for nearly thirty years. Nonetheless, let us wish those Indians well, the ones who are now benefiting from their rising tide. May they enjoy their new prosperity without losing their cultural anchoring. May they upgrade their kitchens now with the money that the global free market funnels their way by means of our outsourced jobs. It is an ill wind that blows no one any good.

Free market

And what was the free market doing locally in El Cerrito? There was a little grocery and general store just around the corner from Ramona Street on Stockton Avenue. It had served the neighborhood since the citrus orchards on the bay-facing slopes had given way to urban development in the wake of the war. You can still run into a house now and then that looks fifty years older than the ones next to it: boxy, live-in basement half-sunk into the ground, with steep cement stairs leading up to the main floor. Add-on, freestanding, afterthought garage. Those must have been the farmhouses, and the streets were then laid out so that they would fit in seamlessly.

The store gave up the ghost the year they moved in. The kids went there to help with the closeout sale and were paid in leftover toothpaste, shoe polish, and oranges. The business went to the emporium and to safeway down in the mall. The big fish were swallowing the little fish. Growth is unforgiving.

But things still felt kind of local, at least to newcomers like them. The rumblings of the real market earthquake that was coming were still too far away to be felt in El Cerrito. It is not only so with politics; life is also local. Life's attention was riveted for them on what mattered: the mostly frustrating school environment, the menacing gang and drug scene, the teaching of ESL at the adult school in Berkeley, and the developing of the research program at the WRRC.

Their television set was still the same little old black-and-white one, and when it showed the Great Communicator, now president, congratulating Sam Walton for being a paragon figure of American business, one whose superfish one day might swallow all the stores of the world, the picture on that small screen was too dim and distant to make much of an impression. How could they know that the policies of the new administration would let the up to then still solid US foreign trade balance slide into the red forever?

When they heard that theirs was a service economy now that did not need to manufacture goods anymore, they thought the leaders knew what they were doing: what was best for the country, of course. They did not ask what that meant: "service economy." Presumably, it was one made up of a lot of servants. And also a few masters to pay them. And where would the masters get the money to pay all those servants if they did not produce things that they could sell? Could they maybe borrow it from foreigners who continued to make things? At this point, the chain of thought ended, for nobody seemed to know or care either.

But they could not help noticing that everything they bought was made in China and Korea and that their gasoline came from the Middle East. The name of this game was *free trade*, they learned, and bully pulpit preached that free trade was intrinsically good.

However, there were specific examples in the political process that he felt really uneasy about. The one I remember most clearly was the convincing rhetoric of a clever, fiscally conservative candidate during the primary campaign that ended with the Great Communicator's first presidential victory. This rhetoric projected clearly that the economics proposed and pushed by the handlers of the frontrunner (who clearly did not understand them himself) would have disastrous effects in the long run.

Well, frankly, he (the Ph.D.) did not quite understand the nuts and bolts of that clever conservative's arguments either, but then that's what you elect experts for, experts you can trust. What really worried him was not so much the substance of the arguments that he did not get but something more fundamental. And that was that this same candidate, unlike the frontrunner, seemed to understand what he was talking about. Yet he immediately sold out to the views that he so aptly criticized during the primary after the frontrunner had won and picked him as his heir-apparent vice president. He seemed to show no shame in espousing now what before he had so clearly derided as "voodoo economics," policies that in the long run would harm the country.

It all seemed so disingenuous. Well, to put it more precisely and less politely, it was mercenary. If you can convince me that it was not for personal gain that the losing candidate adopted the winner's program, although he knew it was wrong, I will apologize happily. But now that the bitter harvest of those voodoo seeds is being gathered in almost thirty years later, it does not matter anymore.

What they concocted then was the snowball that got the avalanche rolling. And so the shining example for the world, the model for everybody else to follow, the rock-solid credibility and integrity of the US credit, banking, and financial systems, is now (AD 2008) in shambles, and the science of the free market concept has become a joke. And who are the ones left laughing? The ones whose bonuses in the untold millions continue to be paid but from my tax money now: the bailout barons. Rewards for having wrecked the system they were responsible to uphold!

That reminds me of Roger Smith. It is several years ago now that Paul Kangas of the *Nightly Business News* on PBS mentioned the retirement of this eminent businessman of Michael Moore movie fame. During his tenure at the helm of General Motors, this paragon of private-sector efficiency managed his company so well that its market share fell by some 10 percent by the time he left. Yet he received a golden-parachute bonus that was thought to be one of the most humongous in size of its time. Having reported on this, Paul paused for a second as if in deep thought and then commented, "I wonder how many more zillions he would have gotten had he taken GM all the way down to zero."

Well, let me insert an *ex post facto* note here. This follow-up happened months after this writing, which progresses at a snail's pace (I have just started with Twilight now). A successor genius of Roger's actually managed to drive GM down to business zero in the meantime, to bankruptcy. GM, the iconic symbol of almighty capitalism! And as a sign of changing times, the man got only a measly ten million dollars of a bonus for his accomplishment. Of course, he is also getting full pay for life, which might increase that number tenfold. And what do all the other retirees of GM get? Sympathy, at best.

A society that rewards failure is sick. A society that permits failure to reward itself while punishing the innocent is moribund. People today are not able to comprehend the enormity of this. General Motors bankrupt? General Motors *was* the America of the American Century! Not *an* america, the one he keeps searching for though. It was *the* America whose greed and violence its betrayers cover up with blankets of hypocrisy.

Cuernavaca

No doubt the handwriting was on the wall in the 1980s already, in large letters but in a script that folks like he could not read. Economics was not his racket, and his attention was on other things anyway. He was a latecomer in his field and wanted to make up some of the lost time but not only by pushing the buttons of the instruments in his lab. So he contacted Ronald in Texcoco and set up a visit with him in Mexico to discuss collaboration.

Sure enough, Ronald was at the airport to pick them up, with the characteristic, big endearing grin on his face that seemed to say something like "I hope I will continue to be happy to see you after I have come to know you." "Them," for Marina came along on most out-of-country business trips. Her presence made him feel stronger and more confident, and with her there, things were not only more fun but could be experienced more fully and deeply. This one, however, was mostly a vacation trip, for after social contact in Texcoco and professional discussions at the Agricultural University of Chapingo, they were off to Cuernavaca for four weeks of an immersion Spanish course.

They picked Cuernavaca not only because of its easy access by bus from Mexico City but mainly because of a book Dante had recommended sometime ago. Dante has read every book there is and has half of them on the shelves of his library, and so when he calls and says "Read this," they do it.

As expected, *Under the Volcano* was an important experience. The volcano itself, Popocatépetl, is almost too far in the distance from this erstwhile summer residence of the gold-crazed former *matamoros*, the *conquistador* Hernán Cortéz, to be in evidence at all, but the book is aptly named regardless, for its pages are filled with the looming presence of something big, foreign, enticing, and ominous at the same time. Some still latent, pent-up force under a surface of genuine cordiality, endearing simplicity, and gracious hospitality that could erupt nonetheless, well, like a volcano, lofty and picturesque though it is to look at from afar, and snuff you out traceless, you, transient, ignorant, out-of-place intruder, if you do not watch out. And maybe even if you do. The real Mexico.

The book was written a generation before their first visit, and since then the growth rate of Mexico's population had been logarithmic. Cuernavaca was not what they expected, it was already overrun by the culture-killing effects of traffic. If you sat in an outdoor café, you quickly learned not to focus your eyes on one of the ever-present street urchins selling chicklets, for if you did, dozens of them would descend on you from nowhere buzzing like swarms of mosquitoes. As long as you still wondered, "My god, why are those kids not in school?" You had not even started to understand it. It, this real Mexico, that you are so anxious to experience.

The language school was fine. It was on the other side of the big, deep *barranca* with a mucky *arroyo* meandering in its garbage-strewn bottom that separates the traffic-choked main town from some quieter, residential developments on the other side. Students were placed with local families for the sake of language immersion. For him, this arrangement would have been more effective had he not had Marina to speak English to, while she picked up the lingo effortlessly in spite of it.

At first, they had a very nice landlady from a more modest social stratum with whom they got along so well that contacts persisted even after they left. But their room opened on a large inner courtyard where the dogs started barking on cue, as if by design, when people turned off their lights to go to sleep. They did not tire of it until dawn when the roosters took over. They did not know yet that this was the norm to be expected everywhere except in the cities. Mexicans groove on noise, it is their heritage from their Spanish fathers, while their Indian mothers suffer it with placid equanimity, though underneath that perhaps with silent despair. But Marina is not placated easily when something interferes with sleep, and soon they transferred to yet another setting of the real Mexico but without the nocturnal symphony.

It was a great mansion still owned by a family with a historic name. But it was crumbling, complete with overgrown park and dysfunctional swimming pool replete with moldy organic matter. If you want to get a clear idea what it looked like, check out *Sunset Boulevard*, the fifties movie with William Holden and Gloria Swanson from your neighborhood Blockbuster Video store. Long extension cords brought electricity to their reading lamp in their stately, high-ceilinged bedroom, for a leaking roof had inactivated some of the wiring in that wing of the house.

The lord of the manor was absent, a circumstance that apparently had a bearing on the encroaching state of decay of the place. The lady of the castle, their hostess, and her teenage children seemed to live there in a way that reminded him of someone who is caught by a thunderstorm without an umbrella somewhere, in a library or coffee shop, and is obliged to wait it out until the weather blows over. They were just passing their time, these people, well mannered, nonchalant, and unconcerned, as if frozen in an act of *encojerse de hombros*, of shrugging their shoulders and yet suffering from some vague upper-class malaise or malady, purposelessness perhaps.

They were the first paying guests in this house, a circumstance that must have caused quite a bit of emotional discomfort there, and so they were treated as if they had been real guests. That made things easy and comfortable for them; he played *ajedrez* with the son, and Marina practiced her rapidly improving Spanish with the lady and her daughter. Graciella had written a book on her insights into the political and societal *mores* of her social class and that was their first reading in this new language of theirs. Also, her cuisine was exquisite. It gave them a first glimpse into real Mexican cooking: there was far, far more to it than just the tacos and the tortillas that one finds in Mexican restaurants in the States.

With the Cuernavaca experience, the die was cast; they wanted to see more of this land so near and yet so distant, and Mexico became a main item on their agenda. To arrange for that, he needed extramural funding, and so grant writing became an important part of his routine back at work. He found that the reading and research needed to formulate the thoughts essential for obtaining a research grant was most helpful in designing his ongoing experiments also, and in time, the US Agency for International Development provided the money for some fruitful collaboration with Ronald's *Colegio de Postgraduados*.

Family storm clouds

He had seen whitewater trips on television but had never been on a real, risky riverboat ride himself. Imagining what it must feel like to emerge from the rapids wet, but paddling safely and happily painted for him an even more vivid mental picture than the experience itself may provide for extroverts who actually do such things. These years, this decade, in that house on Avila Place with the grand view of the Golden Gate were for him like floating in a fast-moving current but one with a calm and smooth surface now for a stretch of unknown length and duration between the rocks and the rough spots of the past and those that lay ahead, waiting. Now, he could pull in the paddles and enjoy the scenery for a while.

Introverts are not bad people; they mean no harm, but it can be their lot and their nature to be self-centered like he is. Not that they would mean to take advantage of others; no, their problem is more that they do not go out of their way to volunteer help; they just assume others will shift for themselves, pull their own weight, and make their own way like they do themselves. And so he felt that he was justified to be absorbed by his work that advanced smoothly, swiftly, and with considerable exhilaration without having to pay much attention to how exactly the others in his boat were faring.

The fatal flaw in this attitude was that although he was still responsible, he did not fulfill the demands and duties that go with that. Somehow, he failed to see and consider the consequences. And unfortunately, it is the nature of responsibility that he who is responsible must suffer the consequences, if not immediately, so surely in the end. Karma. As his old Latin teacher in Léva would cite: "*Quidquid agis, prudenter agas, et respice finem.*"

Not minding the doings of the family was a big mistake, for the signs for concern were there, impossible to overlook. He had seen the movie version of Arthur Miller's play, *Death of a Salesman*, back in his army days, and it had left a deep impression on him.

Should he ever have children, he determined, he would make sure they would not end up like Loman's sons, the streetwise but incompetent pushover candidates to become subordinates of the much-disdained, studious, goody-goody neighbor kid, who unlike them, made good and became their boss. Had he only known and foreseen then how hard it would be for him thirty years later to find the words to describe his failure as I sit here now trying to do it! He surely would have changed his spots, for he was certainly no leopard. How ye sow, so shall ye reap.

On being cooped up

As he sat in his office running statistical tests of significance on his jumble of empirical data, trying to arrive at some hermeneutic interpretation of their meaning in a greater context, his mind dwelt very much less on his son's problems with things like algebra and marijuana than on his own problem with being cooped up in an ugly little office.

He did not like to be cooped up anywhere, and whenever the feeling, the threat of claustrophobia overcame him, he invariably recalled spending all those afternoons in that small children's playroom in Léva, facing the task of rewriting in his own words some German poem or story, not only in German but also in the Gothic script that was in those days a must-know symbol of cultural correctness for those who had to deal with anything German. His German governess absolutely insisted on this.

But her approach to language training was a good one, for having to write something down points out clearly what one does not know or what one knows only vaguely; the gaps in one's grasp of the matter to be dealt with, that is. And one's grasp of German grammar is not an easy grab, especially when you come from a language that knows no grammatical gender, which is a totally superfluous nuisance. Thus, for instance, the German word for city is *Stadt*, and because a *Stadt* is feminine, it is *die Stadt*, *die* being the definite article for feminine nouns. When you go *to* the city, you say, "*Ich gehe in die Stadt*," which is okay so far. But when you get there, it becomes "*Ich bin in der Stadt*" ("I am *in* the city"), which is not okay for *der* is the definite article for masculine nouns.

So you see already, it can take quite a while to sort out this jumble. Now, when you say a sentence like that, it is no big problem for you can slur and fly over the rough spots quickly, so no one might notice. But writing is a tough taskmaster (*verba volant, scriptura manent*) and if you want to pen your piece correctly, you can spend a lot of time chained to your desk when the sun is shining out there and all you want to do is be out there (and not in here) with the plants and animals that interest you much more than German grammar.

Like that one time that I remember most clearly because of the unusual coincidence of the subject of the rewrite (*Nacherzählung*) with a very special occasion. It was a glorious afternoon of early spring, the snow had just finished melting and was trickling away in rivulets in the vineyard (in full view of the window behind which he was fretting over his *der-die-das*), the snowdrops were already in bloom, and the first butterflies had also made their appearance. Especially that rare bright yellow one that hibernates in hidden places to emerge first, the *citromlepke*, whose caterpillar he had never been able to find.

The text he had to comment on came from the lines of the Hitler Youth's theme song that one could hear all the time on every Göbbels's *Schnauze* (as some disapproving Germans called their radio receivers) when tuned to a news station like the one in Vienna:

Vorwärts, vorwärts,	Forward, forward
Schmettern die hellen Fanfaren,	Blare the clear-voiced fanfares
Vorwärts, vorwärts,	Forward, forward
Jugend kennt keine Gefahren.	Youth is above the fear of danger.

Well, the heady occasion that day was created by the most welcome news that the fast-advancing German armored units, *die Panzerspitzen*, had surrounded a major Soviet army group that was now being annihilated somewhere near Minsk (or thereabouts) in a type of operation called a *Kesselschlacht*, a cauldron battle. And the song clearly called on fearless young people (like him, for instance) to be out there in the front lines of the advance and not sit in a darkish little room parsing the spirit of the occasion in hopefully correct Teutonic syntax.

I am sure you see where all this is leading: it was the very same thing that he was now doing in his darkish little office in Albany just then, massaging his data statistically by means of the analyses of variance and of regression. "Doggone it, what's wrong with me? I gotta get outa here" was his spur-of-the-moment reaction as the flashback of that *Vorwärts! Vorwärts!* scene played out in the circuits of his hippocampus.

He picked up the phone and called the ARS Lab in Reno, Nevada. "I'd like to determine how grazing-and trampling-mediated soil compaction impact the soil microflora around the affected plant roots," he told Ray, the leader of the Range Research Station there. "Would some of you guys be interested in working with me on that?" The following week, he and Suran were in Reno, Nevada, finalizing work plans, which centered on cattle exclosures within a heavily grazed area some forty miles north of town. Such an exclosure, where livestock had not entered for many years, developed vegetation of a distinctly different composition from that of the area outside.

Suran, Reno, and economics

Suran was an incidental, gratuitous addition to his group. A refugee from Armenia, he had worked his way through Eastern Europe, including a stint at the Agricultural Research Institute in Martonvásár, Magyarország, where he picked up some Hungarian, including, of course, the saucy and even gross expletives that seemed to have been much in vogue there (like *lófaszt a seggedbe*). These he used now as his form of friendly greeting when he showed up for work in the morning, much to the amusement of his boss who then responded in kind (*a tiedbe egy mégnagyobbat*).

I do not remember how he made his way to the United States, but once here, he proceeded, in advanced middle age already, to earn a Ph.D. in soil physics from UC Berkeley. Well, the employment climate in this land of opportunity to start a career past the age of forty-five is harsh, especially if you are severely overqualified to be a beginner. Suran was lucky to get a one-year temporary appointment with one of the research groups at WRRC, but interest in that line of work soon fizzled, and Suran, still paid because of his contract but now walking the hallways, was up for grabs. He (the biologist) grabbed him and together they developed a CRIS Work Unit on soil compaction.

If anything, Armenians love to talk. They are clever, witty, and astute, so much so that back in Magyarország, where their people skills were well known and appreciated, they were described in the following terms of high esteem: "A Jew can easily get the better of ten Hungarians, but an Armenian can bamboozle ten Jews without even trying." Well, the charm did not work now, not in America, not for Suran going on fifty.

They did an extensive soil survey on grazing-affected compaction, two doctors of philosophy working like chain-gang convicts with pick and shovel (the Fox came along to help) in the blazing semidesert sun, taking hundreds of soil cores to provide an adequate database for significant statistics. The agreed-upon deal was two publications, each one co-authored by both of them: his on the vegetation and the accompanying soil fungi, Suran's on the texture and structure of the soil. His was soon published, and Suran worked diligently to reduce his soil samples to a lot of promising data. But the data never got to see the light of print; they got filed away for years, and he finally dumped them when his program was transferred to Oregon and he moved along with it.

Writing a modest research paper requires a mindset different from the inspiration that great writers need to pen a masterpiece. What may lead to the work of art is often some harrowing or tragic experience like unrequited love, as in the case of Dante or Madách, that spurs them on to a creation of beauty and wisdom (as an exercise in self-therapy, maybe). Not so with that honest plodder, the pedestrian scientist. What he needs is peace of mind and concentration, not exhilaration or despair, to produce the terse, short, declarative sentences that his product requires and that describe and elucidate his tables of data (at least it is so in English usage).

Poor Suran did not have that luxury. After half a year's work, it was becoming apparent that WRRC, a postharvest, product-development lab, was less than keenly interested in continuing this work out in the field. It was too tangential to its mission, and so he was worried about his livelihood, for the pickings of work in the job market were slim indeed for soil physicists, even young ones. But his real problem lay elsewhere.

He had a son, his only child, who had come of age in the early years of the new supply-side, trickle-down, voodoo-economics era. And so, when he (the biologist) prodded Suran to sit down and take pen in hand (he needed this publication badly as ammunition in his campaign to show that this line of work had enough promise to continue), he would throw his hands up in despair and tell about his troubles with his son instead.

The young man, in his early twenties, could not appreciate his father's hard, honest, dedicated effort and sacrifice to achieve the status of a man of the mind. "He tells me," Suran was lamenting, "that if he is not a millionaire by the time he is twentyseven, he will be a failure like I am. An advanced degree? Look where that has got you! You are working day and night for a pittance, taking orders from other people in a herd of "sheeple!" All you need to succeed here in America is a flashy car, smart clothes and a risk-taker, devil-may-care, maverick's attitude."

Suran was not a central figure in his life; their association lasted only about a year, and they did not socialize other than having lunch sometimes at the Chinese buffet around the corner. But he was a man with a compelling presence; his conversation was wide-ranging, and his insights, especially in fiscal politics, were portentous. Compared to him, Suran was a recent newcomer to the United States, but his background, the tragedy of his people and of his extended family some two generations back under the horrors perpetrated on them by the Turks, his making his way as a trained technician through the vagaries of Soviet-occupied, communist-dominated Eastern Europe, and his dexterity in finding a ship to take him and his family legally to Ellis Island somehow must have honed his vision to see what was happening in the world around him with unusual clarity.

It was mostly depressing stuff he had to report about his findings. The politics concerned him less; the economic consequences of those policies all the more. Maybe that's the way Armenians have evolved under the selective pressure of their people's hardships: to have an innate understanding of and a keen insight into economics. We Magyars sure don't have it, even though we had our own share of trouble in the course of our history. We just keep humbly praying to that foreign God of the Bible, who for over a thousand years has never shown any interest in adopting us as his children for relief from adversity:

Balsors akit régen tép,	Beset by ill fortune as he is,
Hozz reá víg esztendőt!	Grant him a year of good fortune!
Megbűnhődte már e nép	For this people has already atoned
A múltat s jövendőt	For both the past and the future

Suran himself might not have known or cared what the name of the secretary of the treasury was or even to what party the president belonged, but he knew all about the important things. Like for instance that Jimmy Carter was the last president under whom we had a positive trade balance and that industrial production had started declining ever-increasingly since the onset of the era of voodoo reaganomics. And these early insights proved to be lasting.

Maybe it was his son's mentality in embracing this neo-conservative "make your bundle and run" spirit that opened his eyes and contributed to his interest in the goings-on on the national business scene: "Are you satisfied with picking up the crumbs that trickle down to you?" my son asks me; he would lament. "This world is going crazy. Instead of producing something of value, Americans spend their time speculating in worthless pieces of paper, trade them as if they stood for a share of something real, when in reality their worth is based on nothing but the greedy hope for highly leveraged, large, and quick profits. Service economy, my ass! You, you must make, you must produce something of value to be able to pay your servants' wages. Unless you borrow the money to pay for all that service. All Ponzi schemes crash in the end. Neither a lender nor a borrower be." And so he could carry on forever. As I said, Armenians like to talk.

It sounded quite disconcerting to be sure, but it was remote, really. It was none of his business. America had been good to him. What he had was a dream job; he went to sleep at night expecting to get up in the morning to go on doing what he liked to do and get paid for it. Medical care, vacation time, retirement benefits assured, house being paid off, the American Dream come true. That his own son was soaking up the same toxic atmosphere that had infected Suran's son should have made him think, but it did not. Experimentation with "grass" was a passing phase, a children's disease to be grown out of naturally. A "friend" stole all his records? That was tough, but it will teach him a lesson. "Don't push it, or else it may come to a shove"—that was his motto.

When Suran's son was killed in his muscle car, he expressed his condolences. And very sincerely so. Yours very sincerely! Sincerely, I remain a compassionate but ultimately uninvolved spectator of your hardships from above and from the outside. Namely, one who hopes and expects to remain immune to anything that may threaten his own orderly, well-swept island, his *tonal*, as don Juan, Carlos Castaneda's Yaqui *brujo*, describes it. The conservative approach of living in the security of those who have made it. Let the black *nagual* rage outside, none of his business, is it really? So forget it all, for the time being at least.

When the year was up without a paper published, the best he could do for him was a three-month extension, but by that time Suran's island was already swept over by a flood from the kind of rain that pours all at once and at the wrong time. In the end, he had to go into consulting, which is a hard life. But he was strong, had a good wife, and probably made out okay in the end. I hope. And now, twenty years later, reminded of him by this writing, I googled him up to see if he was still alive. And lo and behold, he has an address in Oakland. I need to ring him up.

Austin: an Eden?

The work in Nevada went on, however, although without the soil-compaction aspect now. It turned more into a hobby, a report on natural history, under the guise of stress ecophysiology. Fieldwork. Escape from office and lab.

These were the trips to Central Nevada in the little red Toyota, to the Grass Valley, always with an overnight stop in Austin. Austin, as you know already, is not a *Stadt*, it is not *die*, not feminine. Nor is it masculine, *der*, although many of its male inhabitants tend to avoid the razor blade and go stubbly faced as a real *macho* outdoorsman sees himself. It is a village, a *Dorf*, and *Dorf* is *das Dorf*; it is a neuter but not only grammatically so. So the first night, even the first few nights that you stay there, it evokes no particular emotions, no more than any other stopover would anywhere. It leaves itself open to interpretation, free of compulsion. It is up to you what you make of it, and it makes nothing of you; it leaves you alone; it ignores you; it comes across like you expect a proper neuter ghost town to be. But in time, it turns into your very own introvert's paradise.

Paradise. Before getting on with this bio, let's digress for a moment and stop at this word. The Magyar word for paradise is *paradicsom*. "So what?" you may say, and it's true by itself that means nothing, unless you know that the Magyar language is the last and only surviving heir of ancient Sumerian, the tongue of a people who appeared at the dawn of civilization to become the first to record their lives in writing and so transmuted legend into history. This relationship between what I call ancient and modern Magyar is, of course, stoutly and sharply ridiculed as pretentious, ignorant layman's nonsense by the professional experts of linguistics in general and of Sumerology in particular. So feel free to dismiss all this as nonsense also.

Be that as it may, let me only say right now (more of it may come later) that it is a characteristic of agglutinating languages like Magyar and Sumerian that the densely syllabic structure of their words, which are glued-together (agglutinated) composites of the root with a string of syntactic modifiers, is remarkably impervious to erosion and to change with time, unlike the case with inflective languages (like all the Indo-European ones). At any rate, to unravel the meaning of an old word, one can make use of the universally valid phenomenon of sound shifts that occur over time to arrive at the following simple etymology of the Sumerian-relic word *paradicsom* still in use in Magyar. This gives *paradicsom* (paradise) a surprising, present-day meaning:

> parad—ics—om → barat—os—hon, with the standard p→b, d→t, cs(ch) →s(sh), m→n sound shifts, and inserting the unaspired *h* which may not have been sounded or annotated in the original cuneiform. This results in: barát=friend, os~with, and hon=land/home, so the meaning

of "paradise" becomes recognizable again after the lapse of some five thousand years as the "land of friends" in modern Magyar.

And a nice place such a land must have been to live in: no wonder that its name had survived the millennia. The fact that he made no friends in Austin, his "land of the friends," is no reflection on its people; the ones he talked to were all exceedingly friendly. It was more a reflection on him.

The next time I go there, however, I must change my spots; I will extrovert myself into someone outgoing, communicative, and helpful. I will start by attending all the church services (there are at least five denominations present, all equipped with different, separate houses of worship), starting with those of the Saints of the Latter Day (if they will let me in). I will tell all of them that I agree with each of their diverse notions of God because I see the unity in all of their differences like a fly sees the oneness of the world in a many splendored way with each of its eye facets perceiving a slightly different aspect of the same totality. I will buy a trailer on the south-facing slope with a view to the Reese River Valley and will live there except for the season when the roads get icy. *Wer jetzt kein Haus hat, kauft sich einen Trailer, und wird auf den Wegen von Austin wandern bis sie vereisen*, to paraphrase Rilke's jewel of a poem about *Herbst* (autumn). Who has no house now buys a trailer and will roam the streets of Austin until they ice over.

The birth of the story

There was a large trailer already out at the Gund Ranch in the Grass Valley, owned and operated by the ARS station in Reno. It was not in much use anymore, but it was still functional: it had running water, a stove in the kitchen with a full propane tank, and bunks equipped with blankets. There were also parkas (it could get beastly cold there all of a sudden even in April) that served as a reminder that at some time in the past, people must have been working there regularly. Now, after Ray, the ARS research leader, had given him a key before going back to Reno, he was the only one around, which suited him just fine.

He did some observational work on crested wheatgrass (*Agropyron desertorum*), a deep-rooted bunchgrass that had been cultivated there by ARS colleagues to see if it could be used to control a noxious weed-pest introduced from Southern Europe called red brome (*Bromus rubens*). This species of brome grass is a spring annual and works much like wild oats (*Avena fatua*) do in California in that it outcompetes and displaces the native perennials. It takes over a habitat in wildly multiplying stands, and when it has depleted the soil of moisture by mid-spring, it dies and survives till the next rainy season as seed.

What are the native flora and fauna to do in the meantime, accustomed as they are to year-round, live, green presences? In addition, this red brome is not a very good host for those symbiotic soil fungi of his either. And that means that the soil-stabilizing function of these organisms, whose dense network of soil hyphae depends on the moisture pumped up by the deep roots of the native grasses, also becomes dysfunctional. He was being paid to mind these things, and so he worked on them diligently enough.

But he also traveled the side canyons that emptied into that Wide Valley and climbed a good number of its peaks so that he would not have to know them only from the road below. One of those canyons opened up at one point to form a large, flat, circular area that was almost completely occupied by a dense grove of old, sturdy palm trees. It gave him a jolt as he came upon it around a bend, for this was unexpected. It was unreal. This was not palm country. They should not have been there, but they were. Unnatural as their being there was, there was certainly nothing supernatural to it, except that it somehow made him feel as if it were so.

The Grass Valley canyons are (at that time of the year) tannish beige in color. With walls curving up gently, they have a completely different aspect from that of the rocky, steep-walled washes of the Anza-Borego Desert or of Cataviña, where he knew that his old friend, the fan palm feels at home. He sat down to contemplate the sight, and since the weird feeling did not subside, he decided to let it run its course. As it turned dark, he unrolled his sleeping bag to spend the night next to those palm trees.

Nothing happened; no eerie specters or fairy princesses arose out of that unlikely grove, not even a coyote could be heard in the distance. But he had a Kafka dream. It was one of that bland, colorless, uneventful sort whose impact lies not in drama but in a sequence of small, everyday events from which there is no escape that starts and terminates within itself again and again like a labyrinth with an entrance but without an exit and which is accompanied as a sound effect by a hollow, mirthless, impersonal laughter as if coming from some empty, indifferent void like an echo maybe from a cavity in one's own skull, from a sinus when you have a head cold.

He was driving along a freeway. It was drizzling, and his windshield wipers had trouble clearing the gray, sleety accumulation away. As daylight was already failing (things always happen when night is about to fall) he started looking for a place to stay. He saw a bright orange neon sign flashing not far ahead. It showed a bed with a pillow on a billboard. So he took the next off-ramp. It eventually led—there was no other way to go—to a typical American suburban development of one-family "homes" (houses). He erred around in it like in a maze, looking for that sign. Then darkness fell. He had glimpsed the sign again in the distance, but the bed seemed to beckon from the wrong direction, from the other side of the freeway. Or where he thought the freeway should have been, but it also had vanished.

In time, the windows of the houses went dark one by one (like they do in Hans Henny Jahn's story, Die Nacht aus Blei (The Night of Lead). By now he knew he was hopelessly lost. His trusty sense of orientation had totally deserted him. His growing feeling of unease had merged fully into the cold sweat of apprehension.

By this time, the streetlights blinked out also or were not there anymore. He was no longer among houses, perhaps. He could not tell for sure in the dark.

At the same time, the red "empty" light of his gas gauge started flickering menacingly. Not too long ago, there were hundreds of fellow beings, cars traveling with him on that well-lit freeway, all with a purpose and knowing where to go. Now it was dark and cold, and he was all alone stranded in the middle of nowhere. The road, turned gravel and then dirt, had come to a dead end in a swampy, streamside thicket just as his motor sputtered to a stop, out of gas.

The dream went on, but his controller did not record further details. Maybe they were too gruesome. He remembered only, and gladly so, that he did not remember them, for the controller was whispering in his ear that dreams are important: they are the shadows of something real. By midmorning at the latest, they were gone. What lingered on was the memory of his being lost: that is a feeling particularly painful to the erstwhile army map-reading instructor. Back in the trailer, he fixed a big breakfast for he was well provisioned; the grocery store in Austin was still in business.

But somehow he could not focus on the wheatgrass. He knew already quite well what he could say about the ecology of it, but in that manuscript, every sentence had to cite his own data or "the literature"; that is someone else's pertinent, prior observations on the subject. This constraint is a real nuisance when you come to think of it that way.

Then, out of nowhere or maybe out of last night's nightmare or out of the prospect of having to research all those pesky "lit-cites," a thought suddenly emerged, sprang forth, like Athena, the goddess of wisdom, out of the migraine-plagued, aching head of the boss-god Zeus. "I am going to write a story! My own stuff, anything I like, and no research and no citations! A real Kafkaesque one! Unreal like life itself!" With that, the search for a plot was on.

It led nowhere. He was not a writer, no Papa Hemingway to go dancing on the top of Mount Kilimanjaro or run with the bulls in Pamplona, watching the sun also rise. Scaling the Bishop's Peak and jogging around the yard of Bishop's Peak Teach School was all he would eventually be able to manage. He was an introvert. He did not have the kind of imagination that extroverts have, one that is fed and nurtured by free and spontaneous intercourse with other people by participating in their lives, their joys, and their sorrows, which is the stuff of a good story. He had nothing to write about.

In writing a scientific publication, it is often useful to do the introduction first, for it forces the author to make a thorough review of what had been found before by others and then to summarize it, so that the reader is prepared for the meaning of the new data that follow and is able to see them in a wider context. But now he was at sea with this newfound purpose of his. All he knew was that if he did not dare to write some kind of introduction, a prologue for the nascent story, if only for the sake of the idea of it, and write it soon, time would overtake it. In a minute, its time would pass and it would wither in the dry wind of procrastinations and indecisions like the brome grass does in the sere of summer after the last rain of the season had fallen.

> And indeed there will be time
> To wonder, "do I dare?" and, "do I dare?"
> Do I dare
> Disturb the universe?
> In a minute there is time
> For decisions and revisions, which a minute will reverse

So by way of his introduction to the he-knew-not-yet-what, he decided to describe the scenery that accompanied him on his trips to his Nevada field sites. He could do that easily, for it was something he knew—and knew well. And once written, he could then revise it and reverse it as often as he liked to the end of his days. Well, it did not take quite that long, but it did take fifteen more years, until he got around to really following up on the introduction, to the writing of the visions and revisions.

During those years, Marina kept nudging him to write down what he knew about his family, his life, his work, his country old and new, and out of that, a new idea gelled. Why try to reinvent something Kafka knew and he did not? For Kafka, even though he had never been there, knew America better than he did after more than half a century as an observer in residence. Instead, why not report on the only thing he knew something about: how an introvert and the road fight over who is boss?

In the end, the introduction stayed, and out of it grew the design of using the trips to the Grass Valley as a mnemonic device to unroll the scroll of the past to use them as flash-forwards in starting a new chapter. Then, as his time on the road lengthened, the tale outgrew the device, disrupting the unity of the concept. To borrow a Frostian metaphor, it had become "like a piece of ice on a hot stove that rode on its own melting." Although it is no poem to make a figure, still the tale "is running itself and is carrying away its writer with it."

Collaboration with Ronald

One of the perks of his dream job was that the authorities rewarded his efforts and productivity with generous concessions of freedom. So when the US Agency for International Development awarded him a sizable grant to collaborate with Mexico on a project of mutual interest, and to pursue this calling he had to leave his darkish office and lab and go, well, to Mexico for times on end while everybody else stayed on to continue pushing the buttons of their instruments, all they said to him was "Good luck with the curse of Moctezuma while you are down there."

The whole thing had been set in motion actually and essentially to satisfy Marina's interest in seeing the real Mexico, but in practical terms, it was justified by as yet unknown consequences of a new insight into soil microbiology that were of interest to him and to people who depend on the companion cropping of *maís y frijol*, that is, of corn and beans.

What happens in such an intercrop system is that the same beneficial soil fungi that colonize the roots of one host plant also become part of the roots of its neighbor. They do this by means of their soil hyphae, which then form a living bridge between the two plants. There is not much to this phenomenon under normal circumstances, for it is the norm in nature. But it becomes consequential if a *milpa* (that is *Nahuatl* for cornfield) is deficient in nitrogen as it almost always is, unfortunately. Then, a legume like the bean plant, which is able to fix N_2 out of thin air in its root nodules into an N-compound that it can assimilate, might be able to share this N with its nonnodulating neighbor by using the fungal hyphae as the means of transport. Whether it does so or not (so he thought, since no one knew yet) depends on what plant physiologists call source-sink relationships.

A source is a plant organ that produces some essential compound, such as the leaf that makes carbohydrates out of sunlight, air (CO_2), and water, or the root nodule that makes the ammonium ion (NH_4^+) out of air (N_2). A sink is any other plant organ that uses these products, the strongest sink being usually the developing fruit. To which of the possible sinks the source translocates its product depends on "sink strength," a property thought to be a joint function of sink size and sink activity. So in order for the N to flow via the fungal hyphae from the bean plant to the corn plant, two conditions need to be met (according to the hypothesis): the corn plant has to be a vigorous sink, and the bean plant an adequate, noncompetitive source.

The initial experiments soon revealed the first complication. For the bean to be capable of copious rates of N_2 fixation, the *milpa* where it grows must not be deficient in phosphorus (P), which it unfortunately almost always is. And when it is, the corn plant becomes a weak (P—and N-deficient) sink and the bean plant an inefficient source of N. *Ergo*: no transfer of N. Many of the *milpas* he had seen down there, especially the small plots of the *campesinos* engaged in subsistence farming, had such poor, overexploited soil, that it was a *milagro*, a miracle that anything grew on them at all. But a reintroduction of the fungi into such dead soils could help, for they are the main P-uptake organs of the plant (in addition to being possible transfer agents of N).

Which led to the next complication. The P in many such soils comes as ferric or aluminum phosphates or some form of calcium salt, such as rock phosphate or hydroxyapatite. Since all of these are as good as insoluble, the P they contain is not available to the plant. But it can be made available by lowering the pH (increasing the acidity) of the soil, which helps to solubilize the P-salts. This is a process that in a live soil is accomplished naturally by acid-forming bacteria. These, in turn, derive their energy from (are fed by) the fungi whose hyphae they encrust and with which they live in close symbiotic associations.

Which led to yet another complication. The soils of many *milpas* were so degraded by overuse and trampling that they lacked structure. And structure means micropores: tiny but habitable spaces in soil aggregates and capillaries. The bacteria that inhabit them just barely fit into these, and there they are protected from being eaten by protists. These are larger unicellular organisms, like the amoeba, and they like to "graze" on bacteria like cows graze on grass when they can get to them, namely when they find bacteria outside their protective micropores. So for acidification and P release to proceed, the bacteria had to be protected by a stable soil matrix.

In a word, there were problems galore to accompany the pleasingly simple hypothesis. No soil structure, few bacteria, few bacteria no accessible P, no P no N_2 fixation, no N_2 fixation no fungus-mediated N transfer from plant to plant. The sequences of these and other complications turned out to be not so much a straight chain of cause-effect relationships, as a veritable, multidimensional web of interactions, and they were fun to encounter and to try to unravel. His part was to do this under controlled conditions in the greenhouse in Albany; Ronald's to do the fieldwork at Montecillo, where the Colegio de Postgraduados (CP) had just finished moving from Chapingo on the outskirts of Texcoco, some five kilometers away.

Texcoco, Walmart, and the *mercado*

The first full exposure to the real Mexico that opened their (his and Marina's) eyes to the great luminous opaqueness that is Mexico was a stay centered on Texcoco. This visit served as a program definition meeting but turned out to be ever so much more. Texcoco is where Ronald lives, a bustling, busy, traffic-congested, commercial town of medium size on the *periférico*, the four-lane northwestern bypass road of the huge capital-metropolis to the southwest. It passes by Montecillo, Chapingo, and Texcoco and connects with the freeway to Veracruz near Chalco.

They stayed at the Posada Santa Berta on the Avenida de Nezahualcóyotl in a downtown as typical of nonpicturesque, nonstatelycolonialsilverminingtown Mexico as you can find, and yet it had the essential characteristics that are at the core of our neighbor world to the south. A world that could not be more different from the one we *norteños* inhabit if it were on the far side of the moon. Hidden on a side street, this nontourist Texcoco preserves the remnants of a pyramid from the time of yore when the great poet of pre-conquest America, Nezahualcóyotl, was the philosopher king of what was then a city state, a member of the Aztec Triple Alliance and the cultural center of that empire. From it, a five-minute stroll takes you to an impressive, huge, seventeenth-century, baroque church, *cathedra* of a bishop, whose see includes some of the *Estado de México*. As part of it, an early postconquest chapel that incorporates remnants of a preconquest palace maintains the continuity of history.

Directly in front of the cathedral is the plaza, or *zócalo*. Back in colonial times, its size may have sufficed to serve the cultural functions of that small town well enough: the fiestas, the processions, the promenading, and the social intercourse of a gregarious, interaction-happy people. Now the city has outgrown it, and dust and traffic fumes becloud the vision of a more gracious past conjured up only by the eye of the history-conscious visitor. But the real bridge to the aboriginal Aztec-Acolhua past, more so than the surviving stones of pyramid, church, and chapel, is the indoor *mercado* that abuts on the *zócalo* to the east.

This is where the echoes of the traditional, great marketplaces like that of Tenochtitlan, the capital of the bygone empire, resound with vibrant, present-day reality. Everything that the *dinero* of the descendants of Cortés and Malinche can buy and that they can produce themselves is offered up there for your use (things like motorcycles you get elsewhere). I searched for a while for the right word, and the best I could come up with was *offering* to juxtapose it with *selling*. The difference may be subtle, but essentially it comes down to what sets off such a *mercado* from a Walmart superstore. It is a difference in spirit, for the function is the same.

At a Walmart, you cannot get lost like you can in a *mercado*. The Walmart's island stacks of shelving, with each island devoted to a different type of merchandize, appear to sit there at random but are scientifically so organized as to prolong your search. That improves your chances to find what you were not looking for. Your large shopping cart rolls along the passageways that separate the islands, much like your SUV does on a freeway. Your field of vision is unobstructed; there may even be an exit sign somewhere far in the distance, and you wonder when you glimpse it, if it is your instinct of self-preservation that urges you to run for it along with your hoard of cheap items mostly made in China. Or maybe you just want to flee because you feel cold, remote, separate, and alienated in that impersonal, sterile world void of any human contact until a checker clicks off your items on a tally machine. But let's be fair and admit it, at least you leave feeling that you could not have gotten the things in your cart for less anywhere else.

That said, what sane mind would ever worry about the price you paid for that price you got? Like employee rights? Union representation? Manufacturing jobs outsourced? Production capacity destroyed? Downtowns boarded up? People alienated? Do you really have time for that? You got problems of your own. At least I do. Funny thing is, however, inconsistent though it seems, that I, the hermit, should feel right at home in the great loneliness of a Walmart—and I do not. I don't even know for a fact if the qualms I have about the price of the price are truly justified, for I have not checked them out myself. Like I haven't researched anything else in this story. But barely have I finished with the self-therapy that writing my objections to Walmart down may mean to me when I read the following snippet in today's *San Francisco Chronicle* (February 14, 2009):

> A federal appeals court gave Wal-Mart another chance Friday to derail the nation's largest-ever civil rights suit, a class action by 2 million past and present female employees who accuse the retail giant of discriminating in pay and promotions.

There you have it. As the saying goes, where there is smoke, there is fire. The people's representative, our government, gives the giant octopus yet another *chance* so sock it to the people in some remote court, distant, impersonal, untouchable.

Then on the other hand, consider the *mercado*. Go and see one while you still can if you have not experienced one yourself yet. Do not rely on me to describe it to you. You see, he cannot do it justice for you, for he is not a *mercado* person. Marina is. His heart was not in the *mercado* any more than in the Walmart; he would just tag along with her as a bodyguard. Although it was not necessary, really. Not in Texcoco, for where there are no tourists, picking scanty pockets is not a very lucrative trade.

No, it was the biology of it that attracted him. Look at it this way. The *mercado* is to a Mexican town what the ribcage is to a quadruped (or to a "quadrulimb" to properly include us bipeds in that taxon). It sucks in all the goods that people need and want from the surroundings like lungs suck in the air. It then holds all those goods in warm, friendly, life-liking spaces, arranged fondly like offerings by people who await your coming, browsing and choosing as if you were one of them (for you are one of them), just like the cells of your lung's alveoli expect the red cells of the blood to come and bring oxygen to them in those hollow little cavities that function just like the *mercado*'s booths. In plants, the process is also called "gas exchange," different in detail but the same in its end result: each party to the transaction has reason to feel satisfied and in the end even the goods themselves feel good about the way they changed hands and look forward to going where they will fill a need or satisfy a want.

It is in this way that the *mercado* fulfils its societal duty, buzzing busily with life like a beehive while it is at it. From the flowers on the eastern side to the fish on the western one: in between those extremes, it treasures the gamut of the human experience and productive spirit displayed in the full spectrum of all the colors and odors of sensory experience. Offered by live people to live people in each booth: Mom or Pop, or both, and maybe even an *abuelita* sitting in the corner smiling toothless with a couple of *nietos* wimmeling underfoot. Yes, *wimmeln* is in German what we Magyars call *nyüzsögni*, and it is what grandchildren do when they have nothing to do.

The booths are partitioned off, each one a separate unit with its own contents and centered within its own sphere of proprietary influence. Each one different in character and with its own competitive survival instincts very much intact but nonetheless structured by likeness like discrete plant cells grouped in distinct tissues, separate but connected by the transfluent plasmodesmata of the common interests of ultimate, cooperative interdependence.

The rebozos in one booth may reveal the weaving characteristics of Tlaxcala, in the next those of Calculálpan or Amecaméca. Nothing from too far away; the key word here is still *local*. By the time Marina has sampled all the *tejidos*, she has chatted with and came to know dozens of *gente*, talking to them in their idiom, for she would understand them even if they wanted to sell her their *nopalitos* in their native Nahuatl at the far end, the produce corner of the mart.

She was intrigued by the *nopalitos*, young, green, beaver-tail cactus "leaves" (branches, anatomically speaking) that come with their mean little bristles already shaved off and so are ready for cooking. They are of an unusual, slightly sticky and slimy consistency but have a pleasant sour taste like the *sóska*, the leaves of the sorrel plant that he and his brother used to gather in the shade at the forest edges in Harthausen in the days of hunger after the war. The *sóska* made a good *leves*, or soup, especially when fortified with the dissolved contents of some marrowbones that could be traded for the remaining leaves of cured pipe tobacco that they still had from home and treasured like the only surviving reserve currency of real value.

But the *nopalito* is just an aside, for the organic sequence of progress from the textiles is to the *calzados*, and Marina has an affinity for the *huaraches* more than for almost anything in that market. Sure, many of the shoes there are factory-made but the huaraches are not; they are mostly the works of locally known artists. If you looked closely, you could distinguish distinct styles of craftsmanship in the aesthetic arrangement of the thongs of leather before their ends were made to disappear artfully between the upper and lower layers of the sole.

Strangely, I must add here, it is below the dignity of middle-class Mexicans to wear these splendid sandals. These must have been what the *indigenas* wore when the *conquistadores* burnt their feet to charcoal to make them tell where they kept their gold, and so the *huaraches* may have remained associated with what became the lower class afterward.

A strange quirk it is of the Mexican mind that the grand history of the native *antepasados* is revered as are their artifacts and majestic monuments, but the surviving Indians themselves are generally held in disdain, much like the untouchables in India. Although that may be changing, hopefully, for the traditional native folk dances are much in vogue in the *Casa de Cultura*, down the street from the Posada Santa Berta.

Un poquito sobre la ciudad de México

Let me skip over the description of Mexico City. That's what guidebooks are for. Still, the stream of this tale's consciousness takes me directly to the *Palacio de Gobierno* on the huge national *zócalo*, for back then, one could just stroll in through the gate freely past the deeply dark-skinned guards (apparently the rank-and-file is recruited from the *indigenas*) and then gaze at the most marvelous set of historic murals in the world. It is all there, the whole tragedy of it in the vivid color of Diego Rivera's brush, on the walls that surround the great central stairway and the courtyard.

The history lesson it teaches starts with the tall ships arriving from beyond the limitless seas recalling the ancient prophecy that the benign white God Quetzalcóatl would one day return . . . Well, by the time the *Mexicas* woke up to the fact that it was a *demonio* who had landed instead, somewhere near the place that this devil later named the "Rich Town of the True Cross," it was too late. This Vera Cruz quickly turned into a veritable cross on the backs of the vanquished. But let me skip all that also, it makes me emotional, and it is really the job of history books to tell it anyway.

Let me just call your attention to the mesmerizing focus of this both huge and great work of monumental art. That central point is the pair of blue eyes that gaze down unfocussed on the tortured, dark, naked *indigenas* on foot and the merciless, armor-clad pale *jinetes* on horseback nearby, and on the emerging, smoke-belching cities and factories in the distance of the future. The eyes of the papoose who surveys his new realm from the cradle board that hangs from the back of Malinche, the native woman who follows Cortés on their way to conquer Tenochtitlán together. The tan child of the Spanish father and of the Indian mother.

Stepping out of the Palacio, you turn left and then follow Pawnshop Avenue north, past the archbishop's residence to the dead-end street Calle de la Republica de Guatemala. Along the way, you pass by a huge, ornate building, the *Monte de Piedad*, the national pawnshop. That means "mountain of pity," a name that originates from the *Monte di Pietà* movement started by the Franciscan order in *Perugia*, Italy, in 1450. Then it had the aim of providing financial assistance to people in the form of no-interest loans, a tradition that was continued in Mexico, for today's high-end pawnshop specializing in jewelry was started in the late 1700s as a charitable institution.

From the Calle Guatemala, there leads a long, dark passageway under the buildings that separate the two streets to the Calle Donceles, where their nice, old hotel, as yet unrenovated and patronized by locals, the Hotel Cathedral, awaited them. But in this *pasaje*, there is, among other shops, one that deals in medicinal herbs. Hundreds of them. Whether in brown bags or in crystal glasses, all are neatly labeled with their common and Linnean names and supplied with explicit explanations as to the lore of the origin of their use and with the scientific validation of their virtues that followed.

Herbs, like the ones in the Boleman *patika* in Léva. Old Boleman, the pharmacist, was a friend of his grandfather, the doctor. They used to play four-handed piano twice a week in the late afternoon, at dusk, in the room that overlooked the *kis erdő*, the grove of overgrown fir trees in the garden. Haydn mostly, but the one I recall best is "Variations on a Theme of Haydn" by Brahms. He also heard his grandfather mention that Liszt's compositions were too elaborate for their liking. *Kacskaringós*, he called it, or when the spirit moved them to speak German, it was *schnörkelig*. Boleman *bácsi* could sing, and he had a marked predilection for the *Lieder* of Schubert's romantic spirit.

>   Am Brunnen vor dem Tore   At the well before the gate
>   Da steht ein Lindenbaum.   There stands a linden tree.
>   Ich träumt' in seinem Schatten   I dreamt in its shade
>   So manchen süßen Traum . . .   So many a sweet dream

Then a small group would assemble to enjoy the *Hausmusik*. Not too many, for his grandfather was a shy and solitary man who had few friends, but these occasions taught him (the boy) to think of these songs as of his very own private property.

Small as the town was, it nurtured a large circle of old, homegrown but far-cultured intelligentsia, down there at the foot and under the aegis of the castle fortress, strong and protective during the Middle Ages, but that had, by his time, long been in ruins. The slopes of the hill on which it still stands were the best imaginable for bobsledding in the long, snowy winter months. But the town, as he knew it, had been razed by the Slovaks, and its ancient Magyar culture is gone with the wars, alive only in my memory. Besides me, nobody but my brother (who is once again in the hospital fighting for his life) still remembers where the Boleman *patika* once stood.

Going east past the Hotel Catedral, the Calle Donceles turns into the Calle Justo Sierra, and there the old and the new Mexico meet like nowhere else, perhaps. On the left, there are buildings of the university, of the Faculty of Law, if I remember it right. The buildings are new compared to what they face on the other side of the street, but by modern standards, they are nostalgic, antiquated, weather-and time-worn relics of the past already.

Compared to them, the "building" on the right is as young as living legends manage to stay as long as their magic keeps the imagination of their devotees alive. It is the great pyramid of Tenochtilán, or what is left of it. Some or most of its building blocks of old are now part of the new city that grew up around it. But while that city, which dried out and covered over the blue lagoon in midst of which the old shrine once stood at the center of its island capital, is already graying and crumbling under the sheer weight of its unsustainability, the pyramid made him feel as if it would remain there forever, outlast the new city, and watch it vanish into oblivion when its uncounted multitudes run out of water to drink.

But there is at least one place in this megalopolis of some twenty-five million people that is far from vanishing into the dust, and that is the Terminal de Autobuses del Norte. That is a bus station, one of the four major ones of the city. It is as big as an international airport, and at any one time may hold as many people as a small city in another country. Although there must be millions of cars dashing about in Mexico's Capital, it seems that they are not much used for travel outside its limits. You can drive along in this land, planning to reach a good-sized town shown on your map, but when you get there, there is no place to stay.

The saturation of the US roadside with motels is one of the most evident signs of its surplus (now borrowed) wealth. Whenever the mood strikes you, you stop, check in, and stay overnight, for you can afford it. Not so in Mexico. If you are rich, you fly. When you are not, you take the bus and get off at your exact destination and stay with relatives. If you are a foreigner in your car and you do find a *posada* when night falls, you are lucky. Hence, the bustling crowds at the *Terminal del Norte*.

However, unlike in India, you can locate your bus, secure a seat, and it will take you to San Miguel Allende, if it is a picturesque, statelycolonialsilverminingtown-type place that you want to indulge yourself in, after having experienced pedestrian Texcoco. San Miguel is wholesomely unlike Acapulco or Cabo San Lucas. It is real and endearing, and yet—how can I say it?—it had been discovered by many others before they got there.

Here, Marina had fun taking in the art scene, especially the *talleres de ceramica* for she has tried her hand at the potter's wheel herself. He, on the other hand, was enchanted enough to move there for good, having noted the presence of a sizeable American expatriate colony. She just shook her head indulgently at the rashness of his enthusiasm for radical relocation. "Think about it a little," she said. "We would always remain foreigners to the locals, and I cannot see how we would fit in with the aliens either. We would feel isolated from both. I need to have my roots in the soil where I live." That was that. They did not even try to make contact with the colony to find out if they were really that far apart from its view of the world as they thought they were.

When they left (after having enjoyed their stay), Marina forgot a pouch with valuables on the high shelf of their room's cupboard and discovered this halfway back to Mexico City. So they got off at Querétaro to take the return bus from there. That one came in a couple of hours, and they used the time to explore this new town. It was a delightful one. Halfway in its vibes between Texcoco and San Miguel, it had an air of quiet dignity. Busy but without a sense of haste; old and historic but without an all-out picture-postcard perspective.

In one of its cool and shady squares, they discovered the institution of the *paleta*. It was the first time they dared to buy anything from a street-side vendor to taste. But they looked harmless, those pieces of fruit juice frozen onto sticks to hold them. *Agua de melon, agua de limon, agua de piña, agua de guayaba.* They transported him right back to Léva with its creamless ice cream, the *fagylalt*. The great delicacy of a childhood which was wisely kept frugal by the grown-ups at a time long past, before Coca Cola, before french fries, fast food and Big Macs, before constant oral gratification, and before child obesity and attention-deficit syndrome.

The pace of the people of that shady square with the *paleta* vendor was like that of the people in Léva, measured and leisurely. There was next to no traffic (like in Léva), although that may have been only because it happened to be *siesta* time. He was ready to reopen the "let's retire here" theme when it was time to rush back to the bus station. The pouch was still where Marina had hidden it.

Jerusalem

Life is like a spider. It makes no exceptions; it cannot. It spins its webs in ways over which it has no control; it does what it cannot help doing. But its predetermined routines are still adaptable to the requirements of the moment. The webs can be traps, but they can also serve as benevolent systems of life support, depending on your relationship to them. His professional life was like that. It supported the family with the necessities and easily so, but at the same time it did not permit deviations from the course set. The course was fixed along the path of his research specialty.

He was not trained to do anything else, and no one but his organization was interested in employing and paying him, not at the present generous level at any rate. However, there were escapes from the work routine, and these were the professional meetings, where he would go to report his findings. The technical term the organization used to justify the expense connected with this type of travel was "technology transfer." Quite often, though, the organizers of meetings would invite him to come and contribute what he knew, and then they picked up the tab.

One of these events was an international symposium on arid and irrigated-land agriculture hosted by the Hebrew University of Jerusalem. For him, the science of this grand event was totally overshadowed by the emotional aspects of the occasion. He had grown up with the Bible constantly in the background. Now, the mythological character that the great stories of the Good Book had held for him for so long should take on the dimension of tangible, visible reality. The Via Dolorosa. The manger at Bethlehem. The Mount of Olives. And so, once there, he delivered his talk and listened to a few of the key presentations, but mostly, he cut class and spent the time wandering through old and new Jerusalem.

As expected, it was all a monumental experience of the kind where the mass of details is so great that it obstructs the formation of a unified, lasting picture. What he was left with in the end, then, were a few of these details, and they may not even have been the most important ones. But the controller is the decider over what is salient (for its own, often mysterious reasons). Like the hectic construction activity of what was becoming a splendid new metropolis, all built in the honey-colored Jerusalem Stone outside the walls of the old city. Like those walls, built in the sixteenth century by the Turkish *padishah*, the sultan Suleiman the Magnificent, a couple of decades after the *Mohácsi Vész*, the disastrous defeat of the small army of a weak, young Magyar king of foreign birth by the Turks at Mohács, that led to a century and a half of a genocidal occupation of that country. An occupation that left vast tracts of the land depopulated and that destroyed all the culture and cultural monuments of the Middle Ages, all the fruits of six hundred years of growth by the Magyars in that new home of theirs in the Carpathian Basin. In that, it was not unlike to what the Romans had done to the old kingdom of the Israelites.

What must it have been like to live, he was musing, safe inside those walls and yet under the Turkish yoke? For he could not help comparing that life in Turkish Jerusalem to life in Magyarország, where the walls around the fortresses were leveled one after another by the invader's siege guns. It was a land bleeding to death under the sword, which at the same time built a wall around Jerusalem to keep it safe! But still, he felt a kinship with those who lived in the Jewish Quarter of that time: safely inside the wall and yet a powerless minority in their own ancestral home. For the city of their great kings, of David and Salomon, the city of the Temple that harbored the Aron Kodesh, came to house foreigners in its Armenian, Islamic, and Christian quarters, just as the Great Plains of Magyarszag, a wasteland now, were recolonized by peoples of foreign tongues from the neighboring lands.

Such thoughts were not an abstract historical exercise for him. He understood those feeling well, for in the here and now, his own relatives in Fülek and Zetelaka were living just like that, an oppressed minority in their own ancestral land. So he could not help but feel as if he were at home in that old city with its people tested by ages of adversity, although there was a bit of jealousy mixed in it, for here the treasures of the past were preserved, including the Wall of Wailing, where they could go to pray, while in Magyarország, the Turks left a desert behind them once they were finally driven out.

Under the spell of the past he got thoroughly lost in the labyrinth of the Arab Quarter, and it was that feeling last experienced in Saigon, that of being followed, that jerked him back into the present. At a sharp corner that formed an acute angle, he glanced over his shoulder without actually turning, and sure enough, there were the three men advancing on him. The street was so narrow that a car could not have passed, and as it approached another turn, he could hear firm footsteps coming from the other direction. He kind of wished he had gone to listen to the lecture by Jerry Haas, who had invited him to the meeting, instead of facing something unknown, trapped between high walls left and right and robbers at best in front and rear. But it was a patrol of two Israeli soldiers that appeared around the bend, with their weapons hanging on long straps from their backs so that the rifles could be held crosswise in front of them, ready to fire.

"Hey, I got lost in this here maze! May I tag along with you until I get oriented again? And let me tell you, I am sure glad to see you." They looked at him, looked at the three men behind him who quickly disappeared into a side alley. Then they looked at each other and shook their heads. Not meaning "no" but clearly meaning "crazy tourist" in their silent way that spoke much louder than words. They said nothing but took him to (what I think was) the Jaffa Gate, even though they probably had to deviate from their prescribed patrol route. From there, one could see the meeting hotel, a fine modern building with each floor set back stepwise like a pyramid.

The Via Dolorosa is a string of souvenir shops. On Golgotha, the place where the cross stood is the church of the Holy Sepulchre. There a number of Christian sects fight each other jealously over the right to be in charge of the day's business. The Mount of Olives looks like olive groves on a hillside do anywhere else. But unlike most anywhere else, here the unmet expectations did not disappoint. The magic of the place was too strong. It was a power spot; one could feel it clearly.

Instead of going to the Dead Sea like everyone else, he took a tour south into the Negev, to the Desert Research Station Midreshet Ben Gurion. That was memorable. He would have loved to spend a research stint there, but Mexico was coming up. On the way, they passed by the outskirts of Beersheba, where an enormous new development was being built right on the edge of the desert. It was still completely empty. "For the Russian Jews who are coming soon," the guide commented. This was around the time when a ten-billion-dollar loan for getting the newcomers settled was being approved in Congress. There was quite a bit of debate on that, for back then, ten thousand megabucks were still thought of as a lot of loot.

It was dark already when they passed Bethlehem on the way back. Theirs was a little group, five colleagues with the driver and the guide (a local scientist), both of them armed with submachine guns. "No, you cannot go in there to see the manger," their guide said. "Not in the dark. This is a Palestinian stronghold. During the day, they are glad to collect money from the tourists. But not now. If I had known, we could have issued you rifles," he added with a wink. "Then you could have braved it, but on your own, without me, of course."

The next day, after getting up, he had his cup of coffee, read the paper, and then took a regular tour bus to Bethlehem. He got what he expected. The stable "where Christ the babe was born" was a dark, damp, cellarlike basement room under a large stone house, and the entrance fee to it was stiff. But his mind was really on something else. It was on what he had read in the paper that morning. Upon returning to Jerusalem, he got copies of the other four or five English-language publications to verify the story. It was the same in all of them.

Back home, apparently, the US government was again grappling with budget problems. So it decided (according to these local papers) to delay till July payment of half of the no-strings-attached, three-billion-dollar gift that Israel received each year from the US Congress.

The reaction to this was apparently one of outrage in Jerusalem. The US government has no right to do this to us, so the commentary went. The Congress has appropriated the money; it is ours on January first and not later, and if the Americans want to delay it, they should pay compound interest on the still outstanding half. This was the main theme, and the variations on it went on and on and left him annoyed. This was money deducted from his pay as taxes, which might have gone to schools and hospitals at home! He was indignant, I must admit, and that is an understatement. Interest was wanted on this gift that his Congress handed out without his approval! He was being taken for granted, and that is a feeling no one likes. It was a most unfortunate, somber undertone to the harmony of an otherwise exhilarating week.

And that now distant bit of discord reminds me of Pat Buchanan. Pat is a well-known columnist and commentator, one of the self-appointed spokesmen for the conservative far right like Rush Limbaugh. I still hear him advancing his reactionary worldview during those weekly political shouting matches of the McLaughlin Group on television. At one time, he even ran for the presidency, and I think it was in the course of that campaign that he came out with a statement relevant in this context: "The US Congress is Israeli-occupied territory." That, of course, caused quite a bit of grief and reaped him buckets full of the grapes of politically correct wrath for being flagrantly anti-Semitic. Yet frankly, for him, Pat Buchanan's gaffe seemed validated by the chutzpah of those papers in Jerusalem.

First trip home

Seeing the world in the vacuous ways tourist do, maybe observing strange alien cultures from a cruise ship as an upscale variant of consumption, is one thing, but it is quite another and a lot more gratifying to be able to do it with a useful purpose like in the course of exchanging hard-gained information of value with other scientists in order to face coming ecological challenges better informed and prepared. Yet his dream was not to visit exotic places like Machu Picchu or Iguaçu while working on the greening of the world at the same time. No, the one destination that haunted him that would arise, come to life, in his sleeping mind was more down to earth. It was always the forbidden land. The land one of whose great poets had admonished him, unforgettably, before he left it as a child:

A nagyvilágon e kivűl	There is no place for you anywhere
Nincsen számodra hely:	In this wide world, except here at home:
Áldjon vagy verjen sors keze,	May fate's hand bless or punish you,
Itt élned és meghalnod kell.	Here you must live and die.

At this time, the iron curtain had not lifted yet, but cracks were slowly being forced open. People had gone home from the West and came back alive! But things were trickier for him because of his military-intelligence background. It was a curious, quirky incident that called for care if he wanted to pass through that curtain by himself.

While he was stationed in Frankfurt, in charge of the MI outfit there, an agent of the Hungarian Intelligence Service had defected to the United States and was being interrogated in Washington by the CIA. But by inter-agency agreement, the other services could participate in such a process if they had reason to be interested. So since he spoke Magyar, he was summoned home to be the army participant.

By the time he got there, rapport was already established with the defector, and the meetings were casual, almost collegial. But when he introduced himself as Mr. Bentley, the man could not suppress a smile. "Good to meet you in person, Major Bethlenfalvay," he offered. "Your dossier is well known to me. It has some good snapshots of you in uniform."

So there, this was a useful pointer; it meant that they knew about him. Now, you must know that once you were a member of the intelligence system in the Soviet Block (unlike in the Free World), you could not just quit and leave. You could disappear from view for a while, maybe as a mole or a sleeper, but you were married to the system till death parted you from it, and they, over there, were convinced that this was the way we in the West operated also. Going home to Magyarország as a private American citizen therefore could have become problematic for him; they would have thought his new science career was nothing but a cover. He had to find some officially sanctioned crack to creep through the Curtain.

A splendid opportunity for this was offered by a program of the National Research Council that administered grants for exchange visits of scientists between the United States and Second-World countries. He got a grant for a one-month visit easily. Traveling with a red, official passport with an invitational visa from the Magyar government in it and with a detailed itinerary prepared by the Hungarian Academy of Science, whose guest he was officially, there could be no problem with encountering snoopy molestations by the *Államvédelmi Osztály*, the "Agency for Homeland Protection," as they called their secret political police.

The academy managed the trip almost too well: in thirty days, he gave some twenty talks at that many different institutes. All in all, it was a good experience. People were friendly, interested, and well informed; their science, especially on the practical level, was no worse than ours. Even their instrumentation was remarkably advanced, for they had a windfall gain in those years: poor harvests in the Soviet Union forced the Russians to import food from Magyarország, which they were obliged to pay for in gold. The Magyars used it to buy Western hardware, and they quickly upgraded their research equipment with that, for their theoretical preparation had always been first class anyway.

Marina came along gamely everywhere and was his support in times of stress, something that she has always been, going on fifty years now. That trip, however, was not very stressful but all the more emotional. Before it actually came about at last, during the long forty years of waiting and hoping, he had always felt like Jews must have when they greeted each other with the words "Next year in Jerusalem" in the course of their long years in the Diaspora. In these days of worldwide free travel, this feeling of being locked in—or in his case, being locked out—is difficult to conjure up. That you simply cannot go somewhere even if you have the means otherwise to do it is a failing, a frustration, and a pain the current generation is no longer familiar with, and the young ones therefore miss out on the exhilaration when the obstacles finally fall, the bar of the gate is raised, and the road opens up.

Like the bar of that massive roadblock at Hegyeshalom, strong enough to defy entry to a tank. The border guards made them wait for an hour, fretting over his passport, but then they waved them through. They were at a loss at first about the most elementary details of travel on the far side of the Curtain: did state-owned hotels, restaurants, and gas stations (if there were any) function by the same rules as in lands blessed by free markets? They just noticed then that they had not researched this problem; it simply had not occurred to them that there could be one. So by dark, they were lucky to find a room in a workers' recreation center in Esztergom, and a somewhat primitive *maszek* (that stands for *mag*án *szek*tor, private sector) eating place served them the only food they had: *frissensült*. That consists of small pieces of pork and beef thrown into hot lard for a minute or two like french fries.

No matter, once the Academy had them under its wings the next day in Budapest, their physical well-being was well taken care of. They were put up in a luxury hotel on the east bank of the Danube, every bit as plush as comparable ones in the West. Since that was not the right way to experience Magyarország as it really was, they requested to be transferred to a modest little apartment on the hillside in Buda (west of the river) that overlooked the City of Pest below. They noted the pockmarks all over the walls of the buildings there, some with the bullets still sticking in them, reminders of the siege at the end of the last war and of the bloody uprising of 1956.

But his problems were not with housing but with communications. To his acute chagrin, he found that he had to give his talks in English. His knowledge of Magyar, of fifth-grade level in the first place, not only lacked all the technical terms of his trade but had gone dormant and rusty on the conversational level also. Fortunately, the language of science had become English everywhere in the world, and so he was gratified to find that they generally understood his message and were genuinely interested in its insights. The intricacies of soil biology were not new to them, but they were more of a theoretical *abstractum* for them and not a modern, applied agricultural reality. The name of the game there was still chemicals: fertilizers and biocides.

Léva revisited

Important as the professional aspects of this scientific-exchange experience were for him and his career, let me skip over all of its remaining details, for he was about to come face-to-face with an existential trauma of entirely different proportions. *Das dicke Ende kommt nach*, so goes the saying in German vernacular: the bulky part comes last.

Business completed, the next stop on their Odyssey was none other than Léva. There was now a border to cross to get there, and for an avowed, unreconstructed national chauvinist and politically incorrect irredentist like him, it is no small matter to have to cross a foreign border before he can get home. Léva was now in Czechoslovakia.

A town is sturdy, its houses (in that part of the world) are built of stone and bricks. Such towns are old and rock-solid, one might say. There were some fifteen thousand people living there, in Léva, who all enjoyed the sweet melody of their mother's tongue when he left forty years ago:

Magyar vagyok, magyar.	A Hungarian, that is what I am.
Magyarnak születtem,	I was born to be Magyar,
Magyar nótát dalolt a dajka felettem.	My nurse sang Magyar tunes over me.
Magyarul tanított imádkozni anyám	In Magyar my mother taught me to pray
És szeretni téged gyönyörűszép hazám	And to love you, home of my reams

The rain-washed, clean air with the fragrance of lilacs and acacias wafting through the quiet, dreamy streets replete with the feeling of peace and harmony of childhood memories. Surely, if the reality of anything can be permanent and indestructible, these must be such things. Nobody can spoil them, erase them, destroy them.

Ah, but yes, they could. And they did. The first thing he saw was that the old streets of the center of town had disappeared. Gaping holes remained where those solid stone houses have stood. A few landmarks remained, the Catholic church with its two towers, the city hall, the school building. The Kákasor. They were left there to make this work of wanton destruction all the more confusing for him.

What happened was that his eye of the present, in its desperation, tried to compromise and to coalesce what it saw with what it knew that it should see, but his eye of the past was in shock; it denied reality and refused to cooperate. This was not urban renewal. This was the result of ethnic cleansing. The people were driven out, and their houses were then torn down. Where was the Boleman *patika*? Where was the Nyitrai *könyvesbolt*, the bookstore, and bindery that published his grandfather's novelets? They must have been there somewhere as one walked down that slight rise from the Kákasor toward the *nagymalom*, the mill on the old main street of the town that was no more. Just before one crossed the Perec *csatorna*, the swift-running, tree-lined canal that provided the power to the great gristmill, the town's main industry, one passed a quiet side street, the Petőfi *utca* with its hundred-year-old wild walnut trees whose stumps were still all there. That was where his grandfather's house had once been.

But by some malevolent quirk of fate, it had not yet entirely disappeared; it had waited for him to be recognized and cried over. The foundations were still there, showing the layout of the rooms, the room where his mother used to play Chopin. A few of the trees of the small park, the great elm tree on the far side, beyond the rose garden, were still there. The sidewalk was not yet bulldozed away, although the corner house, where his mother's piano teacher had lived, was gone.

In front of this house, there was an uneven place in the sidewalk that his mother had pointed out to him when they moved to Léva. She used to jump over this bump, she told him, when she was learning to walk. That must have been around 1905, when Léva got its first hardtop sidewalks. He used to jump over that bump also when *he* was five. And that bump in the asphalt was still there, whole and unchanged, exactly like he remembered it, but everything else was gone or broken. Instead, a half-completed, now deserted, huge cement structure, meant to become a high-rise obliterated what had been the street. It seemed to him that they had torn everything down to put that monstrosity there, but then they ran out of malice and abandoned it.

An old couple, country folk apparently on a rare visit to town, was walking along that still present sidewalk, and since they spoke Magyar, he followed them; he knew not really why. Believe it or not, this is what he heard the woman say, "*Jaj Istenem, a tótok hogy ledöntötték az öreg Karafiáth doktor úr házát* (My god, how the Slovaks have knocked down the house of old doctor K.)!" The *doktor úr* had died in 1943, and now in 1984, people still remembered his grandfather! She might have been a patient of his. But he was in such shock that he did not stop them. He was just crying like a child.

And over this nightmare hung like gun smoke over a battlefield the acrid reek that the razing of old structures leaves behind. For a moment, he was passing through Vienna again after that bombing raid. The fine particles of cement and other debris eventually settle out of the air, but every slight gust of wind swirls them up again, and so they hang on for a long time like a curse over a haunted house.

They did not linger. The old Denk Hotel with its twelve rooms and one bathroom down the hallway still stood but was closed, and in the new hotel of the newly emerging Slovak town, they had no room for them. They got into their Lancia, the big car that Chris, Marina's younger brother, had lent them, to head back to Icking via Nyitra, Szenc, Pozsony, Vienna, Linz, and Werfen, through all the memorable stops of that trek of the past into a then unknown future, when the world was still the unexplored promise of an america.

But since this is the first mention of Chris, let me just say here that he will come up again. He is the kind of guy who says, "So you are going to Hungary for a month? You will need a car. Why don't you take mine? I'll ride the bicycle to work while you are gone." That's the kind of bro-in-law a man needs. Always helpful, generous, good-natured, bright-humored, self-deprecating, tolerant of other peoples' shortcomings, and above all, willing to laugh at himself. Marina talks to him for half an hour across the Atlantic in these latter days every other night. He reports on the snowstorms in Bavaria, while here, in the shadow of Bishop's Peak, the apricot tree in the front yard has already finished blooming.

When the time came, they flew home again. He, with a newfound understanding of what it means not to be at home anywhere. This awareness had been there, lurking below the surface all along, but now it had molted and emerged fully like a night-flying moth, like the *halálfejes*, that had been incubating over winter in the moist darkness of its underground pupal shell. Ah, the uncritical, accepting identification that people are blessed with who are born, for better or worse, to be raised into an unquestioning commitment to the same ways and values of home for an entire, unqualified lifetime!

Back at "home" again, things were chugging along sometimes more and, at times less placidly. The Fox was now attending UC Berkeley and was encountering some initial hurdles in his choice of courses. But he was doing it his own way and paying for his tuition with a part-time job, signaling that he needed neither help nor advice. And again, he was just a distant spectator of his son's problems: "No one helped me, so the best lesson *he* can have also is the one taught by life: fight your own way through the briar patches."

While this was a genuine conviction on his part, there was quite a bit of alienation mixed in it by then. By now, his son was listening to him only to end up doing the opposite of what he might have done otherwise. So he just let things happen, hoping for the best. And good things did happen. Not quite like the Fox wanted them to happen, for calculus, as taught at the UC Berkeley level, closed the door to engineering for him. In preparation for calculus, your mind has to be focused on algebra, trig, and analytic geometry and not on being a badass rocker in junior high. And so, when the time came to build on that missed knowledge, it was not there and it was too late. He could have mastered calculus had his father been there for him when his help was needed with the basics.

But he continued to pursue his interest in technology by jumping at opportunities to work in that field. A long-standing job in building circuit boards for a physics professor at UC Berkeley qualified him to work as a technician for the Space Lab of UCB, and he contributed to the genesis of a satellite that may still be orbiting our globe. He took great pride in carrying out his responsibilities with enthusiasm and the utmost of conscientiousness, although it slowed his progress toward a degree in geography a bit, as did his fun endeavor of managing a band of rock musicians.

Meanwhile, Rob, who had also gone to Maybeck, finished high school and gave a splendid, thoughtful graduation address with the remarkable ease and aplomb that are among his many gifts. But that speech reminded him (and keeps doing so painfully every time I think of it) that he had missed his older son's graduation, where the Fox had given a splendid talk of his own, so Marina told him when he came back from some conference that at the time must have appeared very important.

The real Mexico

Then it was time for them to go and spend a real stretch of time in Mexico. The USAID grant, as approved, required both primary investigators to spend time at the collaborator's lab, and it was his turn to participate in the fieldwork at the Centro de Postgraduados. To accommodate them, Ronald arranged for a faculty apartment on the Chapingo campus, where they kept house for three momentous months.

But in reality, not much of that time was spent in residence. Remigio, Ronald's best graduate student was looking after the work, and he quickly realized that there was no need for him to hover over it. The complex problems that field experiments entail were well under control. To keep the local *roedores* (large gopherlike ruminants) in check, Remigio first enlisted some *urones* (a kind of weasel) to keep them away; by what form of persuasion, he never did come to understand fully. But the predators were unreliable, and their young and juicy corn and bean plants continued to be attacked. So Remigio hired two *campesinos* who spelled themselves day and night with pistol in hand, waging war on the root gnawers and other, above-ground menaces. Clearly, he was not needed as a further link in this defensive chain, and so he and Marina went off to do some serious *turismo*. This was accomplished *sub titulo*: cultural exchange, part of the grant's provisions and requirements.

First, they went back to San Miguel Allende, where they had dropped Rob off on their way down, for yes, they were driving this time. Rob was enrolled in a language school living with a family as they had done three years earlier in Cuernavaca. However, San Miguel was most famous for its art school, the Instituto Allende, and also had a thriving cultural center in an old convent. Rob discovered that they had pottery classes and spent more time on that than on learning *Español*. He made some interesting pieces modeled after ones he had seen at the *Museo Antopológico*. But he did not linger in San Miguel and went off on his own to discover his Mexico. He even lost his wallet to pickpockets but made it home safely and undaunted.

Meanwhile, they made a momentous roundtrip through the historic, old Mexico: Guanajuato, Celaya, Irapuato, Morelia. The southern states, Vera Cruz,

Oaxaca, and Chiapas, they saved for next year. Others like León and San Luis Potosí, they saved for even later, a later that probably will never come. For the country is sinking into drug-war-related ungovernability, while they themselves are developing the kind of timidity that comes with the golden age of life.

But in the late 1980s, the time of their stays, the onslaught of modernity, especially of traffic, had not yet been able to completely corrupt and debase the great, lapidary harmony of these monumental cities that are a lasting heritage of mankind's peak accomplishments. If you know a little of the turbulent, bloody, tragic ups and downs of Mexican history, you cannot help marveling how they were able to create these *Patrimonios de Humanidad*, these cities carved in stone that reflect in their arrangement the tri-partition of the great Gothic houses of God of Medieval Europe. For what the latter-day "Age of Enlightenment" liked to deride as the "Dark Ages" was really a time of a holistic, over-arching world view of unity.

A church had a part reserved for the representatives of the spirit, the clergy, arranged around the altar in the apse. Opposite, at the east end, often elevated on a high balcony, sat the also God-ordained guarantors of earthly law and order, the lords. And in between these pillars of support and stability was an honorable place reserved for the people in the main body of this ship of their state, the nave. Everybody knew his rightful place in this Old World Order.

The typical Mexican town was built to reflect this same idea. There is the *palacio de gobierno*, the always imposing seat of local authority. Opposite from it, on the other side of the main square, is the often even more ornate *iglesia* (like the churrigueresque jewel of Tepozotlán), and in between is the people-welcoming *zócalo* with a covered bandstand in the middle and tree-shaded all around, for the enjoyment of all comers. And the comers down there, south of the border, do enjoy. They do not sit at home in the evening in front of their stale television programs in homes that are very much less commodious than the ones up north. Instead, they go to frolic in their *zócalo*.

But you must not think that every Mexican town is like a jewelry case. Only a few are. In between those, as your car climbs a hill from where you may gaze down on what looks from afar like a splendid little undiscovered haven to spend the night, with a gleaming white church or two next to a promising green square surrounded by friendly, hospitable red-tiled roofs, all sitting there in the glow of the setting sun, laid out expressly for you like a well-phrased letter of invitation. And when you get there it is a dust-blown bit of desert desolation; garbage in the streets like a nest from which the mother bird had no time to remove the droppings. You look at your map carefully: how far is it still to Zacatecas? For you know that you must not be on the road at night.

It is not only the ever-present *topes*, the road bumps that are mostly marked but sometimes are not, which happens just often enough to make them all the more insidious. They serve very effectively as speed-limit enforcers, though. They can ruin your tires or break your axle, but they are impersonal and free of calculated malice. Not so the motorized speed guards. Of those there are not many on the open road. They like to lurk near stop signs and red lights. They see your American license plate and pounce. *Infracción*! You learn not to surrender your driver's license to collect it again, who knows when and at what out-of-your-way police station? But neither do you argue. Instead you ask them if they would be good enough to deposit your fine at the station for you: "*Se puede pagarle la multa a Usted? Para que la envie a la oficina.*" "*Si, si, claro, no hay problema.*" They take the bribe, and yet you know that they are not totally corrupt.

They got the job for whatever service they or their great uncles once rendered to some higher functionary, and they accepted it with the understanding that part of the *mordida*, the bribe, would be passed on along the chain of command, all the way to the top, perhaps. To all those honorable politicians who have earned the right to leave office with fortunes in Swiss banks.

Lately, the events that led to our Great Recession of 2008-20?? taught us that this is not so different from what we have here at home. Where do the bonuses come from that line the pockets of the bailout barons who run the companies that we, shareholders, think we own? Enron, AIG, Merrill Lynch, Citygroup, GM . . .

But what can the little Mexican policeman do? With him, it is a different matter. His family expects it of him. Now that the son, the *hijo varón*, has got to wear his police uniform, it is not only his but also the whole family's chance at last to make good. It all seems to be more of a cultural matter down there than one of ethics. You learn these big and little vagaries of the road not with rancor but with bemused wonder. They are all part of the local etiquette, and when abroad, you are a guest, not a reformer.

That first trip was too long and eventful to remember and to record in detail. Puebla, Xalapa, Vera Cruz, San Andes Tuxtla. Catemaco! Everywhere where there is water, Marina says, "*Gehen wir schwimmen!*" When she looks at a map, it seems to be mainly in search of bodies of water, and when they get to one, it's "Let's go swimming." Well, the Lago de Catemaco looked liked that on the map and also from the hill their car climbed before they got there. But can you imagine that you can drive around a nice, big, beautiful lake like that without a single place that looks clean enough to venture into it?

Four highlights

There are four things about this Mexico experience that I must mention in some detail, among the host of other pictures, that come to life again now and then, before the light in the storage bin between my ears blinks out for good. One is the Mexico City subway system. The other is the Museo Antropológico. The third is the Park of Chapultepec. Last not least, the river of Las Estacas.

The Metro is a marvel. It transported eight million people a day back in the late 1980s when they were among its passengers. You wait for no more than five minutes for the next car. It takes you to any important point in the city you want to get to. The system is so easy to understand that you cannot get lost even if you don't speak a word of *Español*. But you can lose your wallet even more easily. There are masters at picking your front pants pockets there, prowling the Metro. It happened to him twice. "Pick you once, shame on them . . ." After the second time, you learn to carry your moola, your passport and your credit cards in a flat pouch under your belt and over your belly button, with the small change in another pouch hanging from your neck under your shirt for easy access. Do not leave home without those pouches! After his memorable second time on his last day in the country, when his credit card was one of the casualties, he was lucky to have a knowledgeable and friendly expert behind the desk of the Hotel Majestic on the Zócalo to deal with. He had no backup info on the card (a real no-no), but the man ferreted out the necessary details on the phone, had the card stopped, and obtained the funds from the account to pay for his stay.

Finally, he put on a stern, paternal mien, one that you use when giving free advice, and spake thusly: "You look old enough to know better. You do not use the Metro when you don't look like a poor Mexican. You were lucky. They can push you into a corner and slit you open with a razor blade to get at your money with ten thousand people streaming by looking away (or at it) as it happens. If you survive and go to the police to complain, you might find the very same man who did you in, sitting behind the desk. Now, thank you for visiting my country, for using our great Metro, and for patronizing the Majestic."

Well, in reality, the picture may not be as grim as the man painted it. But the point here is not trying to duplicate any suggestions that you might or might not find in your travel guide. All I wanted to do was to bemoan the sorry state of our BART, the San Francisco Bay Area "Rapid" Transit System. How can it be that a country like Mexico can maintain such a marvel of engineering efficiency, while the richest and most powerful country in the world gives birth to gray mice? Think about it! Even the Budapest subway beats BART by far.

Now to the Antropológico! He is not a museum man. Definitely not. But when in Mexico, the Antropológico is like a magnet for him. Closing time is the time he leaves, and Marina would linger on all night if they let her. First, even before you get in, you pass the enormous, primitive, monolithic rock statue of Tlaloc, the rain god. Of course, we are the ones who call it the rain god. Can we know for sure how they who wrought that statue into existence thought about it? What we do know is that they were a sophisticated people, insightful enough to have come up with the concept of the mathematical zero. I like to think that they conceptualized their god as indescribable, but whose individual manifestations, as these impacted on human life, could and maybe had to be personalized to deal with them in terms accessible to humans. Such as that massive block of rock that stood for the thought complex of "Tlaloc."

Water from rain is one of the essentials of life, and life, within the as yet unspoiled natural setting wherein these people lived, was one with its setting. A great teacher of the Maya people, the *chilam* Balam, summarized this in the stark simplicity that is the most eloquent form of expression:

Toda luna, todo año,	Every moon, every year
Todo dia, todo viento	Every day, every wind
Camina y pasa tambien.	Makes its way and passes also.
Tambien toda sangre llega	So also all blood
Al lugar de su quietud.	Comes to its place of rest.

I wish I knew how this sounded in its original Yukatec, but I do not. Neither do I have the corresponding version of it in Magyar at my fingertips. But I do know how it sounds in German:

Über allen Gipfeln ist Ruh'.	Over all peaks there is peace.
In allen Wipfeln spürest du	Hardly a breeze is wafting
Kaum einen Hauch;	In the tree tops;
Die Vögelein singen im Walde.	The birds sing in the forest.
Warte nur, balde, ruhest du auch.	Just wait, soon you will rest also.

At this level, life experience is universal. The lines of Balam are like an incarnation of the spirit of the Antropológico in words, for this great codex-in-stone of the past is nothing if not a testimonial that all human endeavor, toil and striving indeed arrives in the end at its final resting place. In this case, in the exhibits of this marvelous museum. By and by, he and Marina made sure to visit most of the actual sites of origin of the incredible collection of artifacts contained within those walls. The Olmecs at Tres Zapotes and La Venta, the Toltecs at Tula and Teotihuacan, the Zapotecs at Monte Alban, the Miztecs at Mitla, the Maya at Palenque and Chichen Itza . . .

Chapúltepec Park. A chapulín is a grasshopper to this day in Mexican Spanish, and the top of Grasshopper Hill, surrounded by a huge park always jammed with throngs of cheerful, exuberant easy-goers, escapees from street life, all-week weekenders, had been home to the powerful throughout the ages. Toltec and Mexica kings, Spanish viceroys, and finally, the Austrian-import emperor of Mexico maintained their palaces there. This last one, the unfortunate Maximilian, put the most permanent stamp of his fleeting presence on today's Mexican culture, although unknowingly and unintentionally. With him came, from Vienna, the schmaltzy three-quarter beat airs of dance and entertainment that we still hear in the music of the *mariachis*, first played at the wedding parties (marriages) in the days of Maximilian.

As you stroll through the gaiety of the year-round carnival crowds in Chapúltepec Park, the dominant, all-pervasive *fluidum* that surrounds you is Maximilian's legacy, blaring from all portable radios and loudspeakers. Most are cheerful, *mariachi*-type tunes, although doleful lost-love ballads also adapt easily to what has become the prototypical Mexican music. If you spent some years of your life in the German-speaking regions of the Alps where it came from, it makes you feel right at home, although you do not see the connection right away. You feel very much in Mexico and nowhere else when you hear it, and especially when you are inundated with it as in Chapúltepec. But then you say, "Hey, I know where I heard this stuff before: at the *Oktoberfest* in Munich." With a few add-on variants, of course, like the vowel *o* sung at the end of the lines of the lyrics in a trilled, rhythmically outdrawn manner (the *o* is a naturally recurring rhyme in the Spanish of such songs).

But Chapúltepec is far from being only a pleasure park. When you stand at the edge of the cliff that looks down on the Paseo de la Reforma, from where the last of the *Niños Héroes* leapt to his death wrapped in a Mexican flag after he and his fellow child-cadets defended the fortress to the last against the US Marines, you cannot help feeling steeped in history. For what is now the traffic-choked "main street" of Mexico City was once a causeway to the capital of a vanished empire. An island city amid a clear, blue lake that reflected the surrounding green mountains of the great Central Valley on the silver mirror of its surface.

One of those causeways provided entry to the coarse group of adventurers lead by Hernán Cortés, who was received reverently as Quetzalcóatl, the returning White God, until he revealed the true color of his ravenous black feathers. Then he was driven out by the eagle and jaguar knights in what for the invaders became known as the *Noche Triste*. But all empires carry within them the venomous seeds of their own destruction: greed, violence, and the addiction to power. And so the surrounding peoples, subjects of the *Mexica*, thought that the magic newcomers with their instruments of death by fire and thunder, sitting high up on the backs of animals so strange that not even their myths spoke of them, had come to help them shake off the Aztec yoke.

It was Marina who first discovered Las Estacas on a field trip with the School in Cuernavaca, while he was off to a meeting in Rio. She was so enthused about it that they soon made a point of going there to experience it again. It is not far from Texcoco as the crow flies, but you have to navigate your way around Mexico City to get there, for driving through that maze is the last thing you want to do. So you take the *Periférico* south to Los Reyes, an important stop, for it had a (then rare) gas station dispensing *super sin plomo*, unleaded, a *sine qua non* for your precious catalytic converter.

Next, you drive up from Chalco to Tlalmanalco through the Valle de los Conejos (up because you are now approaching the great mountain of smoke), and although you don't actually see any *conejos* frolicking in the *milpas*, you stop for a delicious dish of stewed rabbit in one of the two roadside restaurants that specialize in it. He also would stop several times to collect root and soil samples from corn plants of the prototypical landrace Chalqueño and from a strange plant known as *teosintle*, supposedly the ancestor-precursor of today's *maíz*. Supposedly, for on the one hand, there are other taxonomic pretenders for the honor of being the progenitor of our modern corn plant, while on the other hand, *maíz* is a direct, personal gift of Centéotl to mankind by *de novo* creation. It therefore cannot be subject to any sort of man-contrived theory of evolutionary progression or of any cultural selection practices. But if you then take time out to wander through Tlalmanalco, you are rewarded by yet another gift (of the man-made kind).

This is a *capilla abierta* of the earliest postconquest vintage, when the *indígenas* still refused to enter the forbidding, roofed-over houses of the new, terrifying, foreign God. Sculpted by still heathen hands in the hard, volcanic rock of the arches of this chapel that are open to the sky above, you encounter Judeo-Christian motifs as interpreted by the minds and mythology of a culture alien to those concepts. A fire-and-brimstone hell, a heaven of harp-playing angels, Judgment Day, original sin, and more of the like.

From there, you pass through Amecaméca at the foot of Popocatépetl on your way to Cuautla, a *pueblo* with narrow streets zigzagging in every direction and large enough to get completely lost in. Now you are approaching the heart of historic, revolutionary Zapata country, centered on the town of Tlaltizapán. But before you get there, you turn right, off the main road, and there you are. Las Estacas.

There, in the middle of nowhere, a river erupts out of the earth. A current a good six yards wide and deep enough that you cannot reach bottom with your feet. Crystal clear like Lake Texcoco must have been before the progeny of Cortés scorched it dry. There it bubbles, that sparkling flood, cool and inviting in the subtropical sun. The swimming stream of the gods; Huitzilopotchli himself must have (I am sure) favored it for a skinny dip when he was not sitting in his temple on top of the Tenochtitlán Pyramid, right next to Tlaloc, or inspiring marauding Mexica armies riding on a black thunderhead above them. But now, it (the river) meanders through a pleasant park with carefully mowed lawns dotted with tall, graceful palms of silk-smooth trunks shining like gray, antique silver, trunks like those of the magical mallorn trees of Lothlorien, home of the elven-queen Galadriel.

Although he is not descended from the dolphin like Marina, he found that swim every bit as irresistible as she did. What's more, there were not too many people there either, at least not back then, now twenty years ago. Usually they had *no problema* finding shelter in one of the rustic cabins on the premises, although on one occasion, they had to stay overnight in the nearby village of Tecumán in the most seedy, literally down-to-earth accommodations of their traveling careers. There, the dogs and the roosters were not somewhere in a neighbor's yard but were camping on their doorstep.

That was on the weekend of a folk festival at Las Estacas. Food was prepared on the lawn, and since this particular chicken came right off the roast in front of their eyes piping hot and germ-free, they dared to accept its beckoning welcome. "*Con cabecita o sin cabecita*," asked the cook since they could choose the half of it with or without a head. "*Con cabecita, por favor*," he decided, for the brain of a roast chicken had always been his favorite, back in Léva, where people knew how to appreciate an *ínyencfalat*, or *Leckerbissen*. That is a concept without a special word for it English, the language of a culture whose *cuisine* has not come to be known as particularly *haute*. "A tidbit with the flavor of special delicacy" one may circumlocute it laboriously. So he was able to introduce Marina to this half walnut-sized treat, and she was duly appreciative.

Ash Meadows

Sometimes it happens by chance that this process that I am engaged in now, this love's labor of making the past present again by thinking of it and by writing it down, coincides with a similar experience in the "real" present, or more precisely, the more recent past, for by the time you think about it, it has already happened and is gone, even if it was only a blink of an eye ago. Well, this more recent time passed only last week, so let's not quibble; it is very much more present than Las Estacas is or was.

Having crossed Death Valley proper on their way to Las Vegas, they stopped, as they always do, in front of the Opera House of Death Valley Junction. Glancing at their map, they noticed a more recent addition to the main National Monument, a small, protected enclave in the otherwise barren desert. Its Crystal Springs oases are far enough off the road that you don't become aware of them as you zip past them on your way east. This time they decided to check them out.

And there, out of the desert floor, came crystal-clear springs. Not quite rivers like the one in Mexico, but sizable creeks rushing out of the green pools of their origin, creating verdant havens for wildlife along their course. And like gemstones of turquoise woven into a fine liquid-silver hishy necklace, there sparkled in the sun blue pupfish darting in and out of emerald mats of algae, their only food. About two inches in length, they are marvels of survival. Each of the several streamlets of the Ash Meadows Wildlife Reserve is home to a different subspecies of these fish that hung on to their ever-receding reach as the mountain ranges to the west rose higher and higher and the great body of water that gave rise to their being shrank to the tiny pools still fed by a bountiful upwelling of the stuff of life.

Karma

Mexico for most Mexicans is little more than a harsh reality. For him and for Marina, it is like a home in the clouds. It is like a return from the clean, impersonal, well-ordered chill of the *El Norte*, the land of the lawyer, to the warm muck of mankind. Las Vegas, on the other hand, the Strip, the lagoons of Venice on the fifth floor, each casino a self-contained dream city, is a Mecca of escape to unreality for the tourist, but for him and Marina, it has now become the touchstone of their remaining strength. It is the source of both their hopes and desperation.

It is their first son, the Fox, who was transferred to LV by his company, Acres Gaming, from Oregon some ten years ago. That is, earlier than the real time of this writing, but in the story that is still to be told, it comes later, for now we are in the middle of a flash-forward. So at this point in real time, we are arriving in LV, coming from the blue-pupfish experience in Death Valley. Now.

The Fox is forty-two years old, despondent, depressed—although the Lord be praised, no longer on drugs—unemployed, being evicted from his house, and going into his second bankruptcy. These are the times when I do not want to report anymore, although I must. I lapse back into doing the spider solitaire. The "Great Recession" of the world, of the country, and of this family all conspired to break out and descend on them at the same time.

He (the Fox) is laying on his couch all day watching television on his outsize, new, digital TV set bought on money borrowed from his credit card. But ah, a ray of hope, he is also reading a good little book on Buddhism that Marina gave him. He is uncharacteristically subdued and soft-spoken. For the first time, I wish he were the loud, abrasive, noncooperative, and often expletive-spewing but cheerful self that he was when things were going well.

By one definition (a very non-Buddhist one), happiness is nothing more than the feeling that things are going well. So when things are going against your expectations, you get unhappy and depressed.

He is preparing himself to move in with his parents as a last resort and dreads it. For he fears that the house is too small for three large people. He does not think that it can offer him the privacy that he needs. And worst of all, it has unwritten rules of conduct that promise to be incompatible with the person he has become. We shall see. Karma. The relentless effects of past causes.

But even though I know from experience that miracles do happen and keep hoping for them to happen again, I cannot help but feel depressed when I compare my son's road with mine, as I do so often. My road led me to understand that doing one's thing is no big deal. Mine was a simple world to live in. One gets one's education, one does one's job, and one lives one's life as best as one can, expecting nothing that one did not earn. One pays one's bills, one charges one's credit card with no more than one can cover at the end of each and every month. One does not expect to get a medal for any of it, for there is no one out there to give medals away. *Punctum*.

His son's world was no different, really, for reality does not change. But expectations can and do change when the forces of television-fed greed spin them relentlessly to become a new world of fantasy. It was my job to bridge the two worlds for him. And I did not do it.

His son's world, back then in the 1980s that were formative years for him, was not the one of the harsh, postwar realities that the father had known, where the road signs pointing to consequences were clear and easy to read: swimming this way, sinking that way. This new world of fantasy was a maze. The signs posted on television by the market pointed every which way, each one to a different distraction, to a different bypass around real commitment, to yet another easier way. And there was no wolf at the door; mother cooked dinner, and the room was rent-free. The "kid" needed guidance and did not get it, and had he gotten it, by this time, he would have gone off in the opposite direction.

The way I have come to see this new world from the outside, as it were, it was one where the satisfaction of needs is taken for granted, and so it becomes what is left of it, a world of wants. And in the eighties the message that came from the all-pervasive voices of the media and from the peer groups was one of illusion and delusion, the promise of the easy way, of the free lunch. And if that turned out to be elusive, there was always the choice of escape. Drugs.

The Fox fought this thing gamely; he worked his way through to a college degree, and he did it on his own. And after that, he went on to earn his keep. At the same time, though, he was open to all the devious influences around him, and in the end, he decided to distance himself from all that for which a coat and tie, a regular haircut, and a cash cushion in the bank stood as identifying symbols. Maybe because that was the growth medium that fed his parents, both with a Ph.D., whose road he did not wish to walk.

By and by, he cultivated himself into the persona of a maverick and then froze into it. He was going to be different. Clothes black, Hell's Angels style, with the long, shaggy hair of the rock musician. What he did not know and consider was that the original Maverick, a horse thief and cattle rustler, paid dearly for his choice of ways. There is always a price.

If you covet the good life that society has to offer, you have to compromise and fit yourself in. Unless you are a genius computer whiz, maybe. But if you choose not to fit in, you have to do without the perks and face consequences that can be very cold indeed. The Fox wanted the perks but on his own terms. So he played the game and did so honestly and diligently but uncompromisingly. Until society canceled the terms. The most important of these are the membership dues. You not only have to conform, but you must constantly struggle to do more than the next guy or you wash out. Going home after work to watch television bodes trouble ahead in the world of predatory capitalism.

Well, I know all this now, and more. But then (we are back in the past now) he just chose to surf on the crest of his dream job. He had a team pulling the cart for him, the work was getting done, publications were seeing the light of print, and technology was transferred to the user in meeting after meeting. He earned his keep. No one was telling him when to do what, and this was becoming easier with each passing year, for the organization was evolving in the same direction that he was heading for personally.

The ARS discovered sustainable agriculture in earnest during the eighties, and the priorities of its long-term plans were reflecting it. It was a perfect fit. The surface of the waters on the home front was or seemed unruffled. Marina liked her job teaching English at the Berkeley Adult School to people who really needed the knowledge to survive in America. She preferred feeling useful in this way compared to just earning a paycheck by putting affluent college students through the paces of a "language requirement."

Rob was always his cheerful and pleasant self. He was never a squeaking wheel, and this is perhaps the reason why he seems to receive relatively little of the grease of attention along the turning of these lines, paragraphs, and pages. He had come back from a semester of school in Germany with his hair cut short, and from then on he started pursuing his interests in a more focused way, keeping sight of his goal of becoming an engineer.

Maybe his attending my old school on the new campus of the *Realgymnasium* in Icking for half a year was a pointer, a *Fingerzeig*, for him, for what he found out there was that whatever education he brought along from his high school in Berkeley was way below the standards of his peer group in Germany. So he came back with the feeling or knowledge or purpose that his college education should teach him the skills he would need in his working life as an engineer. However, he did not become a geek, nor did he abandon the Maybeck ideal of a broader base. He continued to develop his skills in ceramics and fireworks, as well as swing dancing and skiing. And the workshop in kite building that he took during one January Program was clearly a step on the way to his later work designing airplanes.

Oaxaca

During this year, Ronald came to work at his lab, always cheerful, smiling, and appreciative; a real split personality, for basically he was a strict authoritarian who ruled his large *grupo de posgraduados* with an iron fist back home in Montecillo. But here the weight of leadership was off his shoulders, and he could bask in the mellow glow of the Jekyll side of his brain's right hemisphere. Except at rare slips, and one of these led, by pure accident (as is so often the case) to important long-lasting developments for his hosts.

It was at a party at their house and one of Marina's students, a young scientist from Oaxaca, jokingly kept correcting Ronald's fluent but grammatically less than flawless English. Ronald was senior, a full professor, and this kidding was clearly getting up his goat. But since his effort to keep himself safely domesticated was good enough, his hosts let it go on for a little while, thinking of Max und Moritz with hidden amusement:

Alles konnte Ron vertragen	Ron could tolerate it all
ohne auch ein Wort zu sagen,	Without saying a single word,
jedoch als er dies erfuhr,	But upon hearing this,
war's ihm wider die Natur.	His nature revolted.

In the end, Ronald had enough, and without further ado, he declared his aversion to being teased: "*No puedo aguantar que me corrijan*" ("I cannot stand being corrected"). The young man graciously apologized, though with a wink: "I am just passing on the English that I had learned from Marina." But he added, "Dr. Ferrera reminds me of an American back home in Oaxaca. Boone. He also has a hard time with being corrected."

One thing led to another, adding up to yet another Spanish language course in the end, in Oaxaca this time. There, of course, everybody knew about Boone. Boone was a local legend, whose fame in time spread well beyond his adopted state. I say state, for he adopted Oaxaca, not Mexico (which, you should know, is called the "*Estados Unidos de México*" by the Mexicans). In his days as a graduate student, he spent a summer in Southern Mexico collecting plants, and it changed his outlook on life. Leaving behind the abstractions and regimentation of academia and not without means stemming from his family's apple orchards near Sebastopol, he trekked south to do something real with his life. "To experience another economic model," as he puts it.

On the way along his rough road, long and adventurous through the years, he did not nail metal plates to his soles like Marina's father but adopted the open-toed *huarache* as his trademark, which he wore without socks everywhere and all the time, even to high-level meetings of science and administration. But unfortunately, it was not only the Oaxacan ruling class that took offense at this message of disdain for their ways of life by this *gringo* but also the old, established, tradition-bound hierarchy of the Zapotec town of Ixtlan, a picturesque place situated uphill from the high and dry Oaxaca Valley toward the misty mountains of the Sierra de Juárez Range.

Once Boone had found Ixtlan, there was no more thought of return for him. He married a Zapotec woman and built a model farm on the outskirts of town, the Rancho Tejas. It was a model, for though he meant to make it his home, he intended even more to use it as a practical tool for the teaching of a form of sustainable agriculture, which integrated modern techniques with age-old local practices of intercropping and seed selection, as validated by modern science as well as millennial local experience. He was trying to protect the campesinos from the intrusions of the Green Revolution and later of NAFTA and reconfirm for them the value and soundness of their own ways.

Unfortunately, that was *gringo*-style benevolence. It apparently gave no thought to consulting with the *alcalde* of the *pueblo*, a *cacique* of power who was used to being the fountainhead of guidance to his people, aided by the village council but still without competition. That led to problems of various orders of magnitude for Boone, and these were aggravated by his wife's own attitude toward his activities.

A cornerstone of that attitude was an ethos involving an entirely different outlook on the role of wealth in society from that practiced back home in Sebastopol, California. It decreed that it was not the mere possession of wealth that bestowed acceptance, respect, and influence on a member of a community but rather its proper use. And that was nothing less than spending it, all of it, on the needs of the community once it was acquired, maybe by accepting a position of responsibility and paying for everything that the duties imposed by that position entailed. Zanaida expected that of her husband, and when he showed no signs of conforming to the local views of proper societal functioning, it was she who had to suffer ostracism by her peers for having such a stingy foreign weirdo for a husband.

In reality, Boone was everything but a stingy weirdo. In the perspective of his surroundings he was, and still is, a giant. He made it his life's purpose to extol the virtues of the vast diversity of the plants of his State of Oaxaca and of the native knowledge of the people in using and protecting this storehouse of riches.

As you climb up the western slopes of the Sierra de Villa Alta, one landrace of *maïs* replaces the other with the change in altitude. The colors of their *mazorcas* shift from white to blue-black having passed through grades of yellow and red, each change in hue of the kernels suggesting and identifying some adaptation of the plant not only to climate as it changes with elevation but also to pests and pathogens whose attacks they have learned to withstand through evolutionary time.

The *campesinos*, who had cultivated them on their minuscule *milpas* ever since Centéotl gave them this gift, know and appreciate all this, "but both the germplasm and the knowledge to use it properly is getting lost," preaches Boone wherever he has a chance. "If they can buy the imported hybrid corn of Pioneer Hi-Bred International at the government-run CONASUPO store for less than their labor is worth to grow it, they will stop growing it, and then both the plant and the knowledge will be lost" (corn does not seed itself out without human help anymore).

As for him, rarely had he run into a person as compatible as Boone. "Damn NAFTA," they would intone together at the slightest provocation ever since that pact was perpetrated in 1994. Since then, with trade liberalization, the Mexican government has been closing down CONASUPO, the state-owned food distribution network and grocery stores, which for sixty years has provided cheap food for Mexico's poor. The result of the shutdown of this network is that the *campesinos* who produce and sell corn, beans, and other food products will be at the mercy of food monopolies and speculators. The private food distribution system will then be able to raise prices in the absence of competition.

As for Boone, he immediately understood the merits of soil biology that they started discussing promptly upon meeting, and he took him out that very same afternoon to collect samples in the fields along the Rio Atoyak that he knew so well. As they moved from *milpa* to *milpa*, he (the biologist) was puzzled to see the workers disappear, take off furtively but on a run, all in the same direction. Finally, they met up with a group of about two dozen dark-skinned, slightly built people, peasants equipped mostly with long, sturdy *coas*, or planting sticks. They started milling around excitedly when the two of them came into sight, in a way that would have made him apprehensive had Boone showed any sign of concern. He just stopped quietly and waited for a spokesman to come to them to explain deferentially that they did not think they were behind on their taxes or whatever dues they may have owed to anyone. "*No se preocupen* (Don't worry)," smiled Boone, "this famous *científico estaduniense* had come all the way here to see how you are doing, and he is satisfied," he was in the middle of explaining when a sudden cloudburst broke up the exchange.

Unfazed by being soaking wet, Boone continued the exploration, while he, for his part, felt distinctly uncomfortable, as the temperature at that altitude was not exactly tropical. That feeling was a mixture of both past and present, for the memory of being wrapped into cold, wet sheets whenever he came down with a sore throat as a kid in Léva was one of torture that will be with him to the end of his days. In Sebastopol, apparently, they did not deal the same way with bouts of tonsilitis, for instead of driving home to change into dry, warm clothes, Boone stopped for dinner at a rustic eating place in the next *aldea*, oblivious of the chills his new companion was suffering in his still damp underwear.

Boone apparently knew the only thing that was on the menu from long experience without having to ask: *carnitas, frijolitos negros y arroz* (chopped meat, black beans, and rice). That was delicious; the only thing missing was something hot to drink. It was late by the time they got back, and Marina was in a tizzy, for she had been in class when they left without advising her and did not know what had happened to him. He, of course, did not know yet that when you went on an errand with Boone, you would not come back before nightfall.

Totóntepec Mije

The next errand was even longer. It was the first of several expeditions to the land of the giant corn plant. If I recall this right, the road back then was not yet paved past Ayutla, where Boone filled his gas tank. You had to know how to do that, for there was no filling station in town. He went into a house that was in no visible way identified as a source of fuel and came out with a couple of buckets of the stuff.

This type of map reading is known as *dirección conocida*, or "address known," and it is also the designation by which mail might reach you, if your house has no street name and number. The locals know their neighbors. This was also the last stop of modernity, as I must call it, for civilization did not diminish as the road got worse, it only became older and more deep-rooted.

It was also the stop for a cup of coffee (although Boone himself was not into that sort of degenerate habit) and a *pastel de tres leches*. Well, let's admit it, Mexico is not Austria as far as the quality of pastries is concerned, Emperor Maximilian's influence notwithstanding. The trip from there up to the Mixe town of Totóntepec was breathtaking. The flora is incredibly diverse and Boone knew every plant by first and last name. Higher and higher along the side of a deep valley they climbed at first and then zigzagged through upland forests, fording crystal streams, and stopping at roadside hamlets for a sip of home-brewed *pulke*, until finally they arrived at the house of the parents of Juan Areli, Boone's friend and student from his Chapingo days.

If you think by now that every other Mexican place name ends in *tepec*, you are right, for people used to like living somewhere up high, from where they could survey the surroundings for trouble in the old days. So not surprisingly, *tepetl* means hill or mountain, and the terminal *c* in *tepec* is a particle that determines location, "on" in this case. It is a postposition affixed to the word stem, for Nahuatl is an agglutinating language like Magyar and Sumerian. Totóntepec therefore means "on the hot hill." Of course, it is hot only in comparison to villages at even higher elevations, for at eight thousand feet, it is blanketed by a cold drizzle over three hundred days a year. And under the benign influence of all that moisture, the kind of corn they grow there really grows: halfway up to the sky it seems, a good four yards tall.

If one could induce, engineer, and persuade this Olotón landrace of *maís* to bear *mazorkas* at every node all the way up to the top, Pioneer Hi-Bred wouldn't have a ghost of a chance to compete with Mixe agriculture. But no such luck. Four ears per plant at the very most. On the other hand, this Olotón has a curious adaptation of its own. At the lowest two or three nodes, it grows aerial roots that are covered with a syrupy slime. So there they were now, Boone, the agricultural extension agent; Areli (with an MS degree in agronomy from Chapingo, but in a wheelchair, tragically incapacitated by a car accident); and yours truly, squatting around one of these giant but spindly plants, contemplating those strange roots while shivering in the aforementioned cold drizzle.

"What do you make of that?" says Boone, tasting the oozy stuff with the tip of his tongue. "*Tenemos análisis del suelo?*" he asks in answer, deciding to start at the beginning. For him, things concerning plants start with a soil analysis. "*Si lo tengo, y dice que no hay nitrógeno,*" contributes Areli, whose thesis covered exactly that area of knowledge. It seemed then that all that rain was leaching the nitrogen out of the loose soil. Yet those plants showed no signs of N deficiency. They went back and forth on this for a while, and then a light lit up for him. It really showed what a one-track mind is good for. "*Permitanme proponer un apuesto*," he said (they were tolerant with his *español chapurreado* but were not the type of people to take him up on the bet he proposed), "that the ooze on these roots functions as a growth medium for associative N_2-fixing bacteria, and that is why these plants are so green."

Then and there the idea of a major collaborative grant program was born. He would provide the plant-soil biological project integration, Ronald in Montecillo would do the bacterial taxonomy and metabolism and Areli and the ag agent the field experiments right there in that same *milpa*. What followed is easy to summarize but took quite some time to accomplish.

He wrote the grant request and coordinated it with the collaborators, incorporating their input. Then he staffed it to the US Agency for International Development, mobilizing his contacts there. That resulted in an expedited approval with a promise to fund it fully.

When this good news arrived a year later, collaborators and grantor's representatives converged on Totóntepec to inspect the premises and to celebrate. Everybody who was anybody in the tribe was there also, and the famed Mixe *Banda Filharmonica* played its locally composed music. All were ready to show that the Mixe *Municipio*, the State of Oaxaca, and last not least, Mexico itself, harbored hitherto unknown riches in its biological resources: the newly to be discovered aerial root bacteria.

But then, alas, the Iron Curtain rusted into dust just at the wrong moment in history. It was the poorest of timing. The State Department decided that scientific collaboration in a big way with the newly emerged Russia was one of the methods to cement ties with it. So the USAID was told to scrape up the funds for that, and the way it did it was to scrap not only his grant but the entire program that funded work like his world-wide. It was a harsh blow. To make it even worse, he had another grant approved at the same time to collaborate with Hungary on putting N_2-fixing bacteria into mycorrhizal fungi. The resulting endosymbiosis (if successful) might have eliminated the need for chemical N fertilizers for all crop plants. That was scrapped also. *Es war zum Kotzen*. That is what Germans say when they are most thoroughly disgusted with something. Feel free to remember the saying and use it whenever circumstances call for it. Damn, damn, damn! Those damned Russians again! That Russian program must have been a total flop, for nothing was ever heard to have come out of it.

The vision

But all that came later. Right then, still squatting in that *milpa*, the sudden exhilaration of facing such a fine piece of work generated waves of energy in the atmosphere that broke up the cloud cover and let the sun touch the surrounding countryside that had hitherto been shrouded in that thick pea soup of a drizzle. He looked up to take in his surroundings, and there it was! The others kept carrying on in Mexican, and he tried to act as if he were with them. But there was no mistaking it.

Every contour of that bishop's hat—shaped rock, the *mitra* as the locals call it, was there perched high above the town, exactly like he had seen it in that meditative trance at the Ananda ashram some thirty years ago! This could not be; it was impossible. Now, impossible, that is a mouthful of a word, so let me define it here. Impossible is something for whose existence the mind cannot imagine an explanation within the realm of the elementary principle, the sum total of our knowledge in physics, chemistry, and biology.

Nevertheless. Nevertheless, that which he called "I," his trillion brain cells or his Atman maybe had perceived it from some two thousand miles away and recorded it with such precision that he could, without any doubt, superimpose that past nonsensory input on the present visual sight with flawless congruence. The experience must have released cascades of nervous impulses under his thinking cap, connecting perhaps centers of cognition there that are normally disjointed. He felt dizzy and disoriented, so that Boone soon asked if he felt okay.

The rest of the day wore on in the normal, nugatory ways of social intercourse with the hosts, made extra laborious by having to conduct it in a still very foreign language. But underneath, his mind was busy with its new experience trying to imagine the unimaginable.

Back at the Aloisius Kolleg in Bad Godesberg, his physics professor, a *doctor rerum naturalium* and respected expert in his field, would sometimes slip into metaphysics, and in the course of one of these lapses, he stated that one of the things he considered to be impossible was an electromagnetic transmission of visual images. That is a phenomenon that not much later materialized anyway and became known as television. That suggested that impossibilities were perhaps only figments of the imagination and were not frozen in ice. If someone in that class then had gone on to speculate that one could permanently embed reasoned, intelligent knowledge into an inert, dead magnetic disc and, then by pushing a button, transfer this packet of knowledge through an immaterial medium to another disc so that this same knowledge now existed in two places, the professor would have smiled, shaking his head: "*Ich bin kein Hindu, um an Seelenwanderung zu glauben.*"

But such an operation has now become commonplace also. Although a comparison of the wireless transfer of knowledge, or intelligence, between computers with the reincarnation of the Self in another material body is still a little too risqué to be proposed; except maybe by clairvoyant Hindu mystics, it opens the door to new imaginable mechanisms for old conventional impossibilities, my above definition notwithstanding. Like, maybe, discreet packets of reality not being localized uniquely in spacetime but accessible in some timeless and spaceless way to receptors of the right kind (like a brain) anytime and anywhere? A form of an as yet nameless, nascent, forcelike "motivator," that might become known, defined, and measurable in my lifetime, maybe?

At this point, however, that momentous day was far from being over. When Areli's mother asked what he'd like for dinner, he replied that anything was fine with him, but *carnitas, frijolitos negros* and *arroz* were his all-time favorites.

As silver-gray dusk was quickly falling from the unusually clear southern sky on that darkening mountain peak of Totóntepec, he wandered off by himself to clear his mind. Sitting on a rock with his back against the thick wall of the church (that was also part of that original vision), he was gazing at the *mitra* up there. And then, after a while, he lapsed into another experience that is hard to describe, for descriptions are chained to the sensory sphere, the things for which we have created a world of words. How then to convey a message of speechless speech and sightless sight? Still, it seems, lifelong habituation has taught us to interpret even the ineffable in real-life terms and in images that may be told.

So then, as he sat there, there arose in the darkness such an image. It was one of emptiness. Its enormity he understood by "knowing" that it was made up of all the galaxies of this universe, but to make it accessible to his own finite mind, his brain ordered all those infinite points of light into a shape with an outline ever so faint. The contours of that shape, he "knew," revealed the standing figure of Brahma.

The black and empty shape did not speak to him, but he could "hear" its thought, and this thought seemed to be directed at him or perhaps at all the live substance of the world that was like him or at all the substance of life of which he was part. "So you are now measuring the length of my day," he "heard," and he "knew" the god meant those fourteen billion years since the Big Bang and was amused by the presumption. "Still, as I inhale, you are and as I exhale you are not. That is my day and that is my night. You deduced that also. That is in order," Brahma's thought continued. "For it is life what connects the principle that I am with those points of light that you think you 'see.' That is your limit, for reality is emptiness sated with substance beyond your ken. You are given to grasp a little of that, some of the elements of my material manifestation. But what are my thought, my dreams, and my smile? They are not light or dark. They just are, and they rest in the Brahman, in whom your one universe of galaxies is but a speck."

That was all, the essence of it at least, as best as I can render now what he "heard" or perhaps overheard then. No bicameral, internal voices resounding in the left ear, no command to pass on what he saw, and no repetition of it, at least not so far. And there was nothing new in it for him, really, except that he had it now directly, from the horse's mouth. What did it have to do with seeing the *mitra* of Totontepec Mixe with his mind's eye long ago, before he ever saw it "in reality?" Was there a connection? Maybe an encouragement that imagining the impossible is in order, for it is also an attribute of life?

As the biologist that he is, it all reminded him of something biological. Like a kidney cell, for instance. Consider such a cell, endowed with the totipotent array of all the possibilities of the original stemcell that it sprang from, but with many of these possible expressions dormant after having specialized. So as it sits there, embedded within millions of other cells of its own kind which are all busily scrubbing toxins, at one point it steeps itself into a bit of existential fretting: "Wherefore am I? And wherefore art thou, oh great filter, who art I, and I who am thou? Hast thou a purpose beyond that which I do for thee day and night? And is there any sort of existence, really, beyond thy limits? As I surmise there must be, for there cometh from somewhere out there this fluid that feeds my functions."

The great filter does not answer, but a red cell ventures down to the end of the capillary near this fretter beset by the angst of being, and delivers like a mailman its prescribed subsistence rations of oxygen. While doing so, it overhears these musings and is happy to show off its own greater insights enabled by its mobile lifestyle: "There is indeed a world outside this filter of yours. The center of it is the throbber. Everything revolves around him; everything moves through him; everything depends on him. He is the lord of us all. I believe in that. That is, I mean, I suppose it might be so. There are other groupings of differentiated units like you, of course, for the world is great, but I do not know why they are all there. I just deliver their food."

A distal fibril of an axon that passes through the kidney tissue is listening in on this. It knows much more, for it connects to the thinker. "What you guys think is the world is just a speck," it feels called upon to contribute airily. "I don't do it myself. I just forward messages, but my cousins within the thinker reach out into spaces that are entirely out of this world where we live. And they do it without actually going there, if you can imagine that! They tell me that your throbber is not a lord but just a pump. But out there, beyond this world of work and pain of ours there are things of a different kind: like thoughts, dreams, and smiles."

An in-law

There are windows of freedom in life whose light one must not hesitate to take advantage of, for their shutters close again, slam shut, quickly. He often thought, smiled, and dreamt about a trip with his brother, retracing their steps that led into exile, revisiting all the stations on that road. Making this come true had always seemed unlikely for an untoward reason, and that was Marilynn's concept of a proper American husband. "Nick," she would admonish his brother, "forget the past. This is your home now, here where your family is. Don't even think (or dream) of ever going back there again."

This shuttered mindset of hers, of course, was by no means a typical attitude for a college-educated woman to take, and it had a long, sad history. The workings of Karma again. He didn't know how she managed to emerge from the multitude of tens of thousands of eligible young women that lived in Omaha at the time to make herself indispensable to his brother, for he was jumping out of airplanes at Fort Campbell while it happened. But when he came "home" on leave, he met her, and the only thing that both he and his father could do was to shake their heads sadly. There was a wall between them and her that they could not and she would not climb. And they felt that that was the way she probably wanted it to be. I know, I know, *de mortuis nihil nisi bonum*, but I can't help it, that was the way they felt.

Why was that wall there? Who knows what it is that opens you up to relate well to the reality of another human being! Maybe it is nothing more than this mysterious, sixth-sense organ, the *nervus terminalis* in the nose, that has nothing to do with smell but that determines whether that proverbial first sight is propitious or not. More likely, though, Marilynn built that wall to protect herself. Not consciously, on devious purpose, rather it could have arisen as an outgrowth of her loveless childhood as an adopted orphan that made her both jealous of her husband's past with its ties to a world unknown to her and fearful of its claims on him.

He and his father were parts of this past and therefore part of the feeling of unease that surrounded this menacing alien world like storm clouds on the horizon. Not that she ever projected distance by design; she never did. Instead, she distanced herself effectively by overgenerous recourse to the conventional chatter that may go on in American college sororities, that was, in turn, alien enough to them to keep them away.

Her chief weapon was the irresistible strength of weakness. As a child who grew up under the cold eyes and hands of a hateful, fairy-tale stepmother, she made sure that his brother did not ever forget all her sufferings. Being genetically challenged to be chivalrous, the guy felt obliged to stand by her, and even more so upon sensing the distance between her and his father and brother.

And this otherwise laudable attitude of solidarity then led, apparently, to acquiescence to her lead in matters of family, finances, and career. Military doctors, being a rare and precious commodity, have a greater say about their assignments than the general run of soldiers. He could have been sent to Europe, and he would have liked to, but the mere suggestion of it made Marilynn panicky. And that made her dread the thought that her house-broken husband could catch a breath of the air of freedom, even if only for a couple of weeks. She must have feared that once on his own, he would never return, though the way he was configured, he had no choice but to come back. Miklós was bound by Kant's old *moralisches Gesetz* in him. To his credit. Maybe.

Past revisited

Nevertheless, permission was finally granted. Miklós asked Marina to plead his case with his wife, and she undertook the mission. She explained to her sister-in-law that it was important for both brothers to make this journey into the past together.

That when you are cut off from your roots, it is more likely to haunt you than if you can go back and revisit it and in some way complete the *Gestalt* that was interrupted when the brothers, still in their teens, set off for the New World. And Marilynn listened. Maybe she also realized that at his age, pushing sixty, he could now be trusted not to escape.

At any rate, she said okay to his going home to Magyarország, and the trip was on. For him, trips to Europe had been frequent enough that he had lost count of his crossings of the Atlantic. But for his brother, this was the first real time in forty years, not counting one professional meeting that coincided with a class reunion. This was *az élmény, das Erlebnis, the* experience of a lifetime, something unreal and elusive that Miklós had been hoping and waiting for so long. A thing hard to imagine in today's unfettered world of globetrotters. First stop was the house in Irschenhausen, that of his brother's mother-in-law.

There they traveled together the forest paths of old, many of which had disappeared but some that were still there. And the backcountry dirt roads, to Dorfen, Bachhausen, and Aufkirchen, which were now all paved to accommodate big, elegant cars. At one time, Miklós saw a large, purplish brown vehicle approaching. "If I did not know that we are in the Ickinger hinterland, I'd think I see a UPS truck," he marveled. And that's what it was, for the spread of free-market globalization is irresistible.

They wandered over the hills to the Starnberger See and took the ferryboat to Starnberg. "How are we ever going to get home?" his brother wondered and was amazed how the *S-Bahn* whisked them back to Icking with only one change of trains at the *Ostbahnhof*. Nothing like that had existed back in their school days, but miraculously, the old building of the Schülerheim still stood there on top of the Walchstätter Höhe, although it was now uninhabited, waiting to be torn down to make place for some fancy *Wirtschaftswunder* villa. Then Chris, that prince of a brother-in-law, lent him his car again, and off they were in that little red Saab to rediscover the past.

They took the Autobahn to Vienna where he had business with a colleague from Australia who worked there with the Atomic Energy Agency in charge of the nitrogen isotopes used to quantify N uptake by plants via the bacterial fixation process.

But on the way they searched for traces of their tracks at Mauthausen. The first sign that he was on the right path was that road sign with the bullet holes in it: Pyburg. The one that he had glimpsed in passing more than forty years ago, shivering with the cold wind and with the fear of an unknown world lying ahead. By now, he had seen countless thousands of road signs in his life and had forgotten this one like all the others. Yet seeing this one again in passing, released cascades of memories.

But such is the nature and the force of habituation that the images of the past were now mixed in the strangest of ways with a pondering about the molecular nature of the phenomenon of memory. How did the controller fix that Pyburg sign into his circuitry? How did it get buried? How was it released and revealed in the process of recognition? Why it and not any number of other totally insignificant details? And his brother had not even noticed it! Not being able to share a memory is like a pang of pain, of regret. *Les souvenirs et les regrets aussi . . .*

From the Pyburg sign, it was not far to the railroad crossing. It was unchanged. The open spaces around it were not developed, and that grouping of houses in the distance was exactly like it was back then when he saw it first. Only now it was a pleasant summer afternoon without snow flurries, and they were well heeled tourists secure in a well-known world. His brother was not sure about the exact identity of the place. Once you had seen one railroad crossing, you had seen them all, to paraphrase a famous saying by a former governor of California. But he certainly remembered the train that stopped there to pick them out of the cold, and that was helpful, as sharing always is.

To recover from the stresses of the past, they stopped at a *Konditorei* for a cup of coffee with *Schlagsahne* and a slice of *Linzertorte* before going on. They did not find the hotel described and recommended by the colleague. Instead, they got so thoroughly lost in Vienna that no longer showed any signs of ever having been in a war that it was late at night until they finally found a place to stay. It was fiendishly expensive, but it was too late and they were too tired to do any more searching.

They spent the day in Vienna (it was not Bécs for them anymore) and, the next morning, found the border crossing to Pozsony, the Magyar city, that according to the redrawn borders is now part of Slovakia and goes by the Slovak name of Bratislava. That place was for them the official opening in that Curtain, whose iron mesh was already rusting terminally. For him, his last visit in Magyarország dispelled somewhat the mystique of that no longer impenetrable shroud whose shreds still darkened the lands on the other side.

The way the people had talked there, it was clear that the Evil Empire was about to collapse any minute now, and everybody knew it except the CIA. Who knows, maybe the CIA knew it also, but they felt duty-bound to keep it a secret from the Great Communicator, perhaps for the sake of the defense budget's inviolable continuity. A little later, after history had run its inexorable course, the Great Communicator was then duly given credit for victory over the rival Superpower.

That reminds me of that black-and-white movie about the black dragon who stands for the dark and evil past and the white-robed sorcerer and his apprentice, who represent the bright promise of a better future. Well, the struggle between the forces of darkness and light is always fierce. So it is in that story also. It also involves a king, the commander-in-chief, and his courtiers, all shadowy nonentities compared with the sorcerer but who are still empowered to do harm and make mischief. At the climax, in a pitched aerial battle, the sorcerer succeeds in bringing the dragon to a fall at the price of his own life. The enormous carcass of the dragon then lies on the ground, clearly dead now. Finding the fiend there, the courtiers drag that figurehead of a king to the scene, put a sword in his hand, and declare with great pathos, "Behold the great king! The Dragonslayer."

And that reminds me further of that oft-cited historical *dictum*: "Mr. Gorbachov, tear down this wall!" declared by the Dragonslayer from a secure place of safety. About the same time, another historic but obscure figure (Miklós Németh, Prime Minister of Hungary in 1989), unsung, unknown, and forgotten now, facing great personal peril under the guns of Russian tanks and under the hostile opposition of his own Communist Party stalwarts, ordered the barbed wire on the border between Hungary and Austria cut. That was an act of real courage and conviction, and it was the one set the Soviet East Block's disintegration in motion. That was what in the end brought down the Berlin Wall, not the Dragonslayer's well meaning but empty bravado.

But for his brother, the mystique was still intact with all its disturbing possible implications, and so he ended up going through a whole pack of cigarettes while pacing the floor of the border-post waiting room, waiting for the guards to finish with their passport ritual. Then it was on to Pozsony. That is a fine city on the Danube with a great castle fortress dominating its skyline. It had been the seat of the king when the city was the capital of Hungary for a while in the early Middle Ages. They had explored it quite thoroughly during their ten weeks there in the winter of 1945, while watching those hornets of liberation fly past overhead. But now they did not find their way in its changed, modern streets and squares anymore. What they were looking for, whatever that may have been, was not there. "Let's scoot," his brother decided. So they did not linger and drove on to Szenc that same day.

Szenc, the first stop on their westward trek as refugees, was about half an hour's drive away. All those places in the neck of the woods of their world of old were surprisingly close together now. But it was a world that had shrunk only in space. In time, in terms of a lifetime, it was a very distant one indeed. Space and time, funny concepts! They are not real. You cannot pick them up and take them to the lab for analysis. Yet we are surrounded and permeated by them like a fish is by water.

There was the *Török Ház* where they had spent that first week on the road of exile. The center of the village then, the manor of the nobleman whose ancestors ruled their little fief in the olden days but who still remained the dominant figure of civic influence among his people until the war blew that way of life away. There was the little bookstore whose empty shelves held all of three books then, one of which they bought. I think it was "János Vitéz," the versified tale of a Hungarian folk hero. There was the church on a small rise just off the road to the west of the village. It was already dark when they found it, after having checked in at a lakeside resort.

The resort and its lake were new; they had not been there forty years ago. And the check-in could be accomplished in Hungarian, to their great relief. They could not find that other gravel-pit lake that had that fish solidly frozen into the ice crust. At the church, the evening service was in Hungarian and they went in to participate. All the people were old like them. Later at dinner, seated with others at a long common table while listening to the news on Radio Budapest, they were told that all the young people had left. Under the pressure of heavy discrimination by the Slovak authorities, they had to move to Hungary to make a living. The old village of Szenc gave him the eerie feeling of standing on a flat island surrounded by a rising sea. Ugly, gray, socialist housing blocks full of newcomers surrounded the island now, commuters to Bratislava outnumbering its dwindling people many times. And the newcomers did not speak Hungarian.

Léva

In Léva at last, they first drove to the new hotel, and to their delight, the management, or at least the receptionist was Hungarian. They were welcomed heartily instead of being sent off to Nyitra like he was the last time. By this time, the destruction of the town that he was already prepared for had accelerated significantly. His brother was therefore spared the sight of the ruins of his grandfather's house. In fact, its entire street, the Petőfi *utca*, had disappeared to make way to a bypass road that was being constructed just then. So Miklós just stood there in silent consternation and disbelief, even though his brother had done his best to prepare him for what was awaiting him.

It would have been easier, perhaps, if everything had vanished, but there were still those few leftover reminders of the past, the mill, the church, the school, the hospital, the villas of the Kákasor, they all stood there amid all that ruin, like forgotten gravestones in an abandoned cemetery. They made it back to the scenes of their childhood just in time to see the beacons of the past in their final state of decay. The Rákóczi *fa* at the end of the row of those old willow trees (remember the hornets?) was cut down with its stump still there next to the memorial chapel that was in ruins, and the surrounding open spaces, fields and vineyards were being built up with a disorderly sprawl of urban growth.

This is not an uplifting account; I admit it. Perhaps it is even a bit pathetic: what's the big deal? Changes occur everywhere. Houses, even landmarks, are torn down, cities get firebombed, mountaintops are leveled, forests are clear-cut, whitewater is dammed, and species of life are hunted to extinction. But you can face all that with more detachment if it is not your own childhood memories that are buried. It is also easier to take when everything gets wrecked, but that was not the case here. It was their town that had been singled out, perhaps because it was a focal point of Hungarian culture and ethnicity in the area.

"Let's scoot," his brother said as they were sitting in that public-sector eating place, looking with distrust at that socialist menu written in a language they could not read and brought on by a waiter whom they could not understand. "Scoot where?" he asked. "This is what we waited for forty years to come and see and experience together." But to tell the truth, that was the way he felt also. It was a full-blown flight reflex.

The window of the restaurant looked out on the old main square, on the *városháza*, the city hall, on the opposite side, where their father's office had been on the third floor. But now a foreign flag was waving from the flagpole in front. And from what I hear today, having become members of the European Union did not help any, as far as the treatment of the surviving Hungarian minority there is concerned now. But that came later, at the moment they ordered the only two things they could decipher on that menu: *Sztrapacska* and *lecsó*.

Just north of Léva the foothills of the Northern Carpathians begin rising to the first one of several mountain ranges, the Selmeci Hegység. That is where Slovak country began back then; it was a region of transition between the ethnicities, a peaceful and essentially amicable one for a thousand years all the way to the end of the era of the two great wars, when the spirit of harmony was shattered.

Many ties had developed during that neighborly millennium and one of the influences from that northern march on the people of Léva was a culinary one. Domestic servants in town were mostly folks Slovak of tongue though Magyar of identity and persuasion, and the cook in his grandfather's house was one of them, a kindly older woman with a round, always smiling face and the funniest accent imaginable. She was the one who introduced *sztrapacska* and *lecsó* to that house of yore that had now disappeared. Simple peasant foods, they were served as separate, stand-alone dishes.

Sztrapacska is a sort of dough whose bits are boiled in water to a chewy consistency and then made palatable by the addition of bacon grease, cracklings, and sheep curd, while *lecsó* is a thin, watery stew of several mixed vegetables. Nothing much to write home about, but since they had not tasted either for four decades now, those servings opened the floodgates of memories like only the combination of smell and taste together are able to. So they sat there, each one immersed in his own, separate thoughts trying to sort out the unsortable. It is said that a final sorting can only take place in the moments before death, when all the brain's circuits fire at once, unimpeded by all the controls of a lifelong habituation, whose fog then mercifully lifts.

So scoot they did, but not before having done a bit of exploring, a thing that had always been his thing. To the north of the town, past the Kákasor, the main road splits, the right fork leading to Kereskény, which they knew well from many trips there by horse-drawn carriage. But the left one pointed toward the unknown, a circumstance disquieting enough that he had dreamt about its promising vagaries now and then in the course of the past decades, usually whenever the apprehension that precedes another move or a new job portended as yet unmet challenges. And now they had a car and could go and see where it led! That in itself, having a car in Léva, being no longer a dust-of-the-road-bound pedestrian kid but free to float where he wanted, was such a novel experience that it enhanced his overall feeling of being in a time warp manyfold.

This way, they made it to Garamszentbenedek. It was not very far but special enough that they did not feel like going on beyond it. There, on the river Garam, is a surviving jewel of the past the like of which he had not yet encountered anywhere within the historic boundaries of the old, greater Hungary. A gothic church of the fourteenth century that survived the devastation left behind by the long terror regime of the Turks! This Abbey of Saint Benedict was founded by King Géza in the eleventh century, and the entire layout that makes up a monastery was there, restored here and there but essentially untouched by time. He had seen such monuments often enough in the rest of Europe, but here this relic of the past was a rare, a unique, event of the moment of time transformed into the stone of permanence:

Nur allein der Mensch	It is man alone
Vermag das Unmögliche . . .	Who achives the impossible . . .
Er kann dem Augenblick	He can bestow permanence
Dauer verleihen.	On the moment.

And not only was the permanence of the past there written in stone, but the crown and coat of arms of Hungary were present everywhere on the walls and in the colored-glass windows. His brother is not a national chauvinist or a lover of antiquities like he is, but they were both touched to the core by this discovery.

It led them back to Léva, to the cemetery, where Miklós found their grandfather's grave after a long search. Such old, Central European cemeteries are rarely the manicured preserves of pedantic piety one finds in the West. Once there, you are left to stay with the parting wish of *requiescat in pace*, and they really mean it. And if all your survivors are driven out, made to go away, like it was the case in Léva, why then, the unattended sections become overgrown by the jungle of time like the ruins of Ankor, as was his grandfather's headstone.

So then, when his brother had finally lifted it out, dragged it back, from the depths of the past, he took out his pocketknife (one could still take one with you on an airplane back then) and scratched his name and address into it without really knowing why. Maybe it was a flashback to what he had seen the homeless refugees do after the war, when people were tacking notices of their whereabouts, or just of their still being alive, to telephone poles in hopes that someone they knew would chance by and find it. But at this time, they were not aware of any surviving kin behind the Curtain who might still remember them.

With that they did scoot, heading east to Losonc where their uncle Sörös Béla *bácsi* had been bishop, presiding over the Episcopal See of the Reformed Church of northern Hungary. In Hungarian usage *református* means Calvinist, and *evengélikus* means Lutheran. They found his house and his church, although it took some looking, for they had been small children when they visited there last. All through the search, he had a strange feeling that something was different here, until he realized all of a sudden what it was: Losonc was whole. It had not been destroyed like Léva. Why not? It was also a Hungarian town. I will never know why my hometown was singled out. And I do not want to know it, for it would not help anyway. Some people in power probably got together in a smoke-filled room and, after downing some glasses of *slivovic*, decided: this one must go, that one can stay. That is probably all there is to it. There are probably plans and studies dealing with such matters drawn up by technicians everywhere in the world. Reams of paper based on earnest research. Required formalities. But do the deciders ever read them? The decider likes to make emotional, gut-feeling decisions in the end. Like Mussolini did in Ethiopia. Or Hitler in Poland. Or Johnson in Vietnam. Or Bush II in Iraq.

In Losonc, however, unlike in Léva where they knew for sure they had no one left, Béla bácsi had left behind three daughters, Lilla, Zsuzsi, and Márti, their cousins. Yet somehow they felt an inexplicable reluctance to do a determined search to find them like making inquiries at some competent public office. Let this part of the past remain buried. Nonetheless, they did go to the cemetery to look for Béla bácsi's grave, and also, perhaps, because this whole mission to dig up the past put them in a generally cemeterial mood.

The Losonc graveyard was better kept than the one in Léva, maybe because ethnic cleansing had not been as thorough here. One of the graves was being tended by three old women dressed in black, as they walked by. His brother shared the same eerie feeling he had himself: would it be possible? How could those old women be the young girls we had known? His brother's comment was very à propos: "We should have a mirror to look at ourselves. Then it would be easier to make the connection." But the name Sörös was not on that headstone. It could not have been, for this was the Catholic cemetery. They had forgotten that in that part of the world the denominations do not mix even in death.

They entered Hungary at the Salgótarján crossing and had passed the little town of Fülek on the way without knowing how often they would return there in the future. In Budapest, they rented the second floor of a Villa near the Városmajor Station of the rack-and-pinion mountain railway in Buda. There was a filling station on the other side of the street, but traffic was still very benign. He wondered if Hungary would learn from the abhorrent example of rush-hour traffic jams in Los Angeles and New York and go the route of reliable, cheap public transport.

But the discussions on television, led by *elvtárs* Grósz, the comrade party chief, about the coming *beruházások*, the investments, that they were planning to make, did not bode well. Aping the West, growth, free-market capitalism, living well on borrowed money, and the like was already on their minds, one could sense it—between the lines. Although I remember well Grósz declaring repeatedly, almost as if in defense of his having already committed ideological treason while the red star was still waving over the Royal Castle: "*Én kommunista vagyok . . .*" Who knows, maybe he really was a committed communist, as he professed to be, only he did not want it forced down his throat by Russian tanks.

They rediscovered Budapest, although his recollections of it were very spotty; he was six when they moved to Léva. They lived on a quiet street, the *Család utca*, that changed its name to something I forgot. A two-story house with too tiny a yard to merit the name garden. Walks to the nearby *Városliget*, the huge City Park, with a grown-up now and then. Once all the way to the railroad bridge over the Danube. Maybe it was these walks as a five-year-old through quiet, featureless, unexciting, suburban landscape, often in dreary, gray winter weather over sooty snow that fixated him forever on walking the streets of every town, large and small, where ever he stopped, even if only for a night. He was easily impressed by everything, for he was a lonely child; one cooped up on that second floor of the house at *Család utca* 10.

The institution of the kindergarten was not in vogue yet then, although it did have a Hungarian name: *óvoda*. Child psychology had not yet made its way into the mainstream consciousness of people even like his parents. That kids should interact with others of their age is so much the norm today that it is hard to imagine times when the need of it was not recognized.

The quiet household in the *Család utca* was one of adults: his parents and the two servants. His brother was not much of company, for at the time he was almost twice his age and had other interests when he came back from school. So by the time he arrived in Léva, where the limitations of city existence opened up to the great freedom of a countryside without No Trespassing signs, he was already a shy introvert when all of a sudden, he saw himself surrounded by a rowdy bunch of tough kids in first grade. At first, he was not sure at all if he liked it, and it took him some time to adjust to having peers around.

Jet lag

From then on, adjusting had become his way of life in earnest. Of course, there is nothing special about that. Everyone has to adapt his ways to new circumstances much of the time. But still, it is fair to say that his case was somewhat atypical since so many of the adjustments he had to face and then digest had unusually large gaps to span, comparatively speaking that is, as opposed to other lives that run more in the routine channels of conventionality. So to come home now to California, USA, he had to leave the old home, Hungary, Europe, behind yet again and readjust now to homelessness with a new level of understanding.

Now, normally, there is nothing special about coming home from a trip abroad, except maybe for the rueful feeling that a long-awaited vacation is now over. For him, it turned into a form of identity crisis every time. Everywhere he went, it seems to me now, he was looking for his childhood vision of America, which then was never quite there. Each new place always offered some desirable novelty, while at the same time, it was lacking something else that he had come to appreciate in the place he just left. This is a feeling not unlike jet lag. After having shorted out the time zones by flying over them at near-sonic speeds, you are upon arrival, wherever that may be, not quite yourself. You feel disoriented, out of sorts, and sleepy without being able to sleep. You don't hurt physically, but somehow the person inside your skin is not really you, until you get over it. It is the same thing with this sense of not belonging anywhere. With time it wears off, but never does so completely.

To get a feel for this, think of that caterpillar you caught and played with as a child. When you touch him (the caterpillar), he curls up in a spasm and "plays dead" for a while. But after having gone through this routine a few times, he quits playing dead. "See," you say, "I tamed him. He is not afraid of me anymore." Of course, what happened was only that his rigidity-producing hormones had worn off.

And so it is with this jet-lag feeling of adjusting to homelessness. It dulls in time. It spins a cocoon around itself for protection, but it does not go away. You cannot become a citizen of the world. Maybe your head can, but your heart and guts cannot. Your home is the place that your habit of being used to it had imprinted on your mind. It is a haven. Real or imagined, that is where you want to be, not floating loose like in a balloon around the world.

The readjustment of coming home to El Cerrito after that trip with his brother was particularly disquieting. This was brought about perhaps by the fact that it was not a business trip like that first excursion to Hungary. A business trip has the reassuring quality of structure. It has limits, it has agenda that have to be accomplished within externally imposed boundaries and requirements. It is carried out in the businesslike way. In a word, it is essentially unemotional, even if emotional aspects bubble up in its course.

This second trip, on the other hand, had been pure emo-tourism. The emotional kind that looks backward, that people, particularly those well past their prime undertake to complete a *Gestalt* by shedding emotional baggage or maybe in hopes of fixing, reconnecting broken threads in the torn fabric of half-forgotten yet treasured memories. He and his brother succeeded in neither. Instead, they ended up loading on more baggage (at least he did), and they carried it "home" with them. So were Marilynn's fears justified? However unsettling many aspects of this trip had been, the whole thing was a closure of sorts, and that is of value.

But once at home, life and work went on as before, and the jet lag of adjustment wore off. And then again, it did not. There was a deeper adjustment to the past in the works this time: Magyarország, which had now fully reemerged into the present, was shifting its place on the slowly drifting tectonic plates of his consciousness. It was crunching and grinding itself into a new place called Hungary. That is the name of the place as foreigners see it.

Birds leaving the nest

It was a hidden, private process he did not even notice at the time under the impact of the more important, current events of every new day. The Fox now called himself Steve and was working for a Berkeley professor assembling electronic gear. He and Marina were uneasy about this for it was no career path. It was leading nowhere at a precious time of life when a man is laying the foundations for his professional future. But they did not dare interfere. Steve was satisfied with himself. He told them how his buddies, who did not graduate, admired him for being a paid person involved in electronics. They were afraid of pushing him into something else, something more promising in their eyes, an initiative for which if it failed, he could blame them. So they let him tread water in place.

Robin started out with courses at the community college but at a snail's pace that was alien to his father. It was just dawning on them then, that something might be amiss with his health that explained his slow, hesitant steps. But those steps were goal-oriented nonetheless; he mastered calculus and was heading toward an engineering degree. And Rob, just like his brother, did it on his own like a man should. He was proud of that. This was the time when Rob formed a long-lasting alliance with Angie, a strong-willed, deliberate, and very pretty young lady, with whose mindset they had little in common but whom they gladly accepted for she evidently wished their son well.

The most important person in his life, for whom the term *better half* had been most appropriately coined, the right hemisphere of his mind, was the glue that held the family together, kept him motivated in his work, looked after the welfare of the kids, shone light on and added color to the every day, also seemed to be content so much so that she found the energy to undertake a major renovation of their house there on Avila Street.

Once it was finished, the house became very much more commodious, and its new second story had an even more commanding view of the Golden Gate. If such a task had been left up to him, he would never have gone through with it, for he saw it as a hassle. It would never have occurred to him to do it in the first place.

Ambiance

It is always easier to remember the highlights than the routine: there was yet another trip to Mexico. A business one, but Steve came along. It was a father-and-son thing, the only big one like that they had undertaken together. It was moderately successful, and I will not give up hope of reading his own account of it one day to make me understand how he felt about it. To him, it was another revelation how different the two of them really were.

Steve would display very little enthusiasm for roughing it under primitive circumstances, especially when the ultimate goal was only "do-gooding." Doing good in this case was bringing the recognition of international science to the *campesino* growers of Olotón corn in the remote Mixe Mountains, with the added advantage that it would bring them some financial gain. Although his son went along gamely, it was more with the attitude of "what the hell am I doing here?" He would clearly have been happier around the resort hotels of Acapulco or Cancun.

One time, driving back to civilization from Totóntepec with Boone, they stopped at the Zapotec village of Yalalag because Boone gets his custom-made *huaraches* there. By the time the transaction was finished, it was getting late, and they discussed their next move. Boone said he would let them decide. As to him, he was intrigued with this remote, isolated Indian settlement and wanted very much to stay and explore it, to sense the sounds, the smells and all the signs of its life at night. Steve clearly regarded such an attitude as an incomprehensible, quirky aberration. "Let's get out of here," he said. "The place simply does not have the *ambiance* of the Zócalo of Oaxaca."

Ambiance! Well, that's the way things go. He found the use of that term particularly irksome, even though Boone kindly refrained from shaking his head. People have different values and outlooks on life, even if they are as closely related as they can possibly be. They did stay at Yalalag because it was really late by then, and Boone, who knew the road to be muddy, curvy, washed-out one-lane in places and precipitous in others, advised against taking it in the dark. So they stayed in the hostel that reminded him of his old army barracks in basic training. Cots lined up side by side in a common room with primitive bathroom facilities at the far end.

Yet another lesson of life for Steve came later, on their excursion from Oaxaca City to Puerto Angel on the Pacific Coast. When you look at a Mexican map, you think you can make it, those 200 kilometers, in three or four hours on what looks like a good, paved road on paper. But when they did it with Marina the first time, it took a whole, long day, and they got there late at night. By some miracle, she managed to find a room, but it was one where the dog and the rooster did not camp out on their doorstep but in the bed right next to them, it seemed.

Why does time pass so slowly on Mexican roads? He thought this would be a good lesson for Steve to learn, and besides, that passage over the Sierra Madre del Sur is as real a Mexico as anyone could hope to find. So they set off early in the morning (being awakened before noon made Steve grumpy in those days), heading southwest via Ocotlán, Ejutla, and Miahuatlán, places that no one has ever heard of but whose remote, serene, simple solitude his controller tucked away carefully it his memory pouch because they were so very real in their sleepy liveliness that his heart ached for not being able to set anchor there and then not move another inch anymore.

But they did move on and then stopped on a high ridge somewhere near Tres Cruces (or maybe it was Salchítepec) to have something to eat at a roadside joint. The something was *huevos*, eggs, and they were not completely fried through as *huevos revueltos* are. They had a soft core, which they did not notice maybe because they were fighting clouds of flies the whole time. They crossed the mountain range in good time, without the mixed snow drizzle of the previous run, and got to Puerto Angel still in daylight, in time to find the only hotel in town. It was a nice old one on a dirt road across a *barranca*, complete with a pleasant sitting room, and an eating facility, on a rise looking down on the ocean. But by this time, Steve was greenish yellow in the face.

The one-day bug is an awesome experience, even if you have had it before and therefore know that it too will pass. Maybe it will linger on for two, perhaps even three, days but rarely so. However, for the first-timer, it is no joke; you think you will die right then and there. And so Steve had no eye for this splendid, old-fashioned relic of a hotel of days when Mexico was a dream of tranquility. *Como en las películas . . .*

But that line is a fragment from yet another trip, I don't remember which one of the several, when they took out time for a few days to attend a sustainable energy workshop of the Zopilote Association at the Rancho of Don Caballero near Tlazco (not Tazco). It was organized by Ianto Evans of the Cob Cottage Company of Cottage Grove, Oregon, who was in the middle of demonstrating the virtues of a bread oven self-built out of a mixture of sand and clay, when about fifty yards further down the pleasant, wooded stream where they were working, three *jinetes*, horsemen, were crossing a bridge, in sombreros and stately traditional *haciendero* dress and all, playing the guitar. Not for an audience but just so naturally. Everybody watched the scene raptly, with the *compañeros*, mucky with mud to their elbows, shaking their heads: "*Como en las películas*"—they sighed—"like in the movies." Ah, that Mexico of old like the one in the movies! But that hotel in Puerto Angel is gone also now, just like the old Mexico it evoked. A Pacific hurricane took it down a few years later, along with much of the town, if you can trust the weather reports on TV.

The next day, Steve recovered on schedule. Back at the Hotel Majestic, on the zócalo in Mexico City, they rehashed the highlights of their travels. "You know some of Mexico now that a tourist rarely gets to see," he commented. "A tourist!" Steve exclaimed. "Not even a native Mexican ever loses his way into those wilds!" That was a redeeming thought: adventure substituted for *ambiance* in retrospect. They parted at the airport. Steve flew home, and he went on to Guatemala to discuss another research venture for which USAID required the participation of a Third-World partner.

Then in the end, his good days at WRRC came to en and. The organization decided to do some reorganizing. The center was to revert back to its original mission of doing research only on postharvest product development. Like tackier tacos for Mexico and tastier tofu for Japan. His work on fungi to improve plant growth did not fit into that particular mold (no pun intended), so they transferred his program to a location where similar work was already in progress. That is the old principle of business administration: collocating like units of activity for the sake of greater efficiency. He already knew Corvallis, Oregon, having visited colleagues there, Jim Trappe, the godfather of mycorrhizal taxonomy, at the USDA Forest Service, and Bob Linderman at the ARS Station, his new boss. Both salt-of-the-earth characters.

Don't take me wrong with what follows; there is nothing wrong with Corvallis. It is as fine a spot on earth as the Good Lord created in the best of His moods. If you were born and raised there and knew the dozen different words for the dozen different kinds of rain that falls there nine months out of twelve, you would be heartbroken if you had to leave it. But coming from Berkeley, the hub of the universe, it is a town, well, a little remote, even though there are no cows roaming its streets, only deer. So he went to Beltsville to talk his top leadership out of this idea of sending him there.

He encountered no sympathy. "People come here begging us to be assigned to Corvallis before they retire. It is one of our choicest, most desirable locations. Or would you rather have us send you to Fargo, North Dakota, or to Stoneville, Mississippi? No? That's settled then. We would love to be transferred to Corvallis ourselves. So if we understand you right, you do consider yourself lucky? Thank you! Now, let's go and have a cup of coffee." Large organizations have a way of not seeing things like little people do. There is more to successful work than the efficient organization of collocating like work units. But he was trained in the facing of adjustments. And Marina, the darling, heaved her sigh with a smile on her face. All in all, it was a new experience, and it turned out all right.

Oregon

Oregon is not only a state in the sense of a sizeable landmass; it is also a state of mind. One with a split personality, for better or worse. One that he found to be not so different from his own, and that familiar feel eased the havoc that a move always is and smoothed the process of settling in again one more time yet, an experience he needed by now like a hole in the head. But there is a saying that summarizes a common human reaction to being displaced against one's will: "People try to make a home for themselves, even if it is in hell." Well, Oregon, at least the western part of it, is as far as you can get from the Semito-Christian concept of the fire-and-brimstone type of hell, the kind that dwellers of hot deserts envision as fitting punishment for ill deeds.

The big picture

It was certainly not its unhellishly cold, gray, foggy drizzle that helped him make a home for himself there but the fact that Corvallis is located in the heart of the vale of the Willamette River, centered in the left hemisphere of the bicameral mind of Oregon. And the left hemisphere is where he is also when he tries to conduct his business cerebrally, which is most of the time. So there he was now in a mentally familiar place: the green, moist, liberal, cismontane side of Oregon. He, a rational, reasoning, intellectual, progressive, innovative, hermeneutic, teleological, pro-choice, pro-people, eco-active, free-thinking, man of a carbon-clean, wind-and-sun-embracing, hopefully-nascent renaissance.

A state of existence that is, where people pine for the chance of trusting their government bureaucrats to manage their single-payer health care. In other (simpler) words, an era of well-regulated banks, local markets, benignly but firmly controlled sustainable growth (if that is possible), and a brand-new sort of neo-socialist, unwaveringly people-friendly, progress-promoting, and entirely reinvented governance. An Eden, where even the little people feel sufficiently empowered to force their government to spend their hard-earned tax money wisely making love, not war. The America of the dream.

But then again, his brain has another side also, and so does Oregon. That one is the side of a dusky, mysterious zone of emotional twilight, as popular, pseudoscientific thought ideates the cerebral lateralization of the way one experiences the world. The world of emotion rather than logic, of imagination rather than facts, of images instead of words and numbers, and of fantasy replacing reality. A world that can be warm and benign but also scary and nightmarish that connects to the supernatural, conserves tradition, and treasures values that it has accepted as true. It is the introspective, contemplative, compassionate, holistic complement to the analytically active, forward charging left side.

But still, it is one that in all its mellowness is not above passing judgment on things it does not approve of. Oregon has a sizeable hemisphere like that. It is its transmontane half, or two-thirds rather, on the other side of the great north-south mountain range that sheds its waters east and west. These are streams that all find their way to the ocean at the end of the day, but during the day they do not mix; they are at odds; they are like its people who do not see eye to eye on most of the things that do not matter and unfortunately also on some of the important ones that do.

What introduces you to this Eastern Oregon when you cross the crest of the Cascades is an eerie greeting by a brown forest of conifers (by now, maybe they have been cleared away). All those trees are dead or dying. That blight is blamed on the bark beetle. When there is not enough rain, as has been the case lately, the sap is not flowing in the bark, and so resin is not produced plentifully enough to freeze up the insect's inroads, an invasion that includes a fungus that the beetle brings with him. The two together then kill the tree. At least, so goes a straightforward, scientific, left-brain analysis of the problem.

Yes, but that brown forest is not amenable to analysis: it is vast and ominous, and for him it defies simple cause-effect reasoning, factual though that might be. It whispers, it rumors of forces of fate, and if you are in your "right mind," you need not analyze them to know how sinister their portent is for the future. There is a bane on the loose there on the other side, and it has a spirit that is beyond the control of progressive technology to which it is hostile and which it threatens with its own persistent validity, perhaps only because it feels threatened itself. You enter a dry country over there, one in the rain shadow. If you live in the west, you do not go there very often.

But he did, and he liked it, and by the time his seven years up there in the northern diaspora were over, he had explored much of it. It felt immediately familiar to him like gut feelings do. Somehow it felt more secure, reassuring, and even heartwarming than all that activity of exploring progress back there in that cold, wet, green world that abuts on restless, ever-moving tides and on-rushing waves driven by fierce Pacific storms, that in time threaten to erode any safety that its coastal cliffs might offer. It felt more safe and solid to him in its penchant for stability, for conserving what was proven practical in the past: the values of experience and tradition. For that is what he had sprung from himself.

Back home, in Hungary, very much unlike in America, military officers were a dominant class of society. Many were landowners, and they all wore their uniforms with pride off duty also, for the cloth of honor was, complete with a sword worn when out of doors, the visible veil of patriotism. The enemy was real and lived next door, not self-contrived and to be invaded oceans away. For festive occasions, the uniform had gala versions of a different, distinctive color for each combat arm (cavalry, infantry, and artillery) and adorned with plenty of gold braids intricately woven. Those looked so splendid that in America owners of upscale clubs and hotels adopted them for their doormen to entice people to come in.

Hungarian parents of lesser station strove to get their sons to don those uniforms exactly as Americans strive to get their offspring accepted by Ivy League colleges. But unlike the output of Harvard and Yale, which has a choice to go red or blue, the stratum that his kin belonged to did not seem to have one. "*Aki a hazát szereti, a jobb oldalon áll*," he remembered his father saying time and time again. He who loves his country stands on the *jobb oldal*, the right side!

Now, the words *right* and *left* do have qualitative connotations in English (and in many other languages) that come perhaps from the fact that most people carry out their daily tasks with their more dexterous right hand. But there is something definitely negative about *left*. Just think of our word *sinister*. It comes from Latin *sinestra*, which originally only stood for the direction left but acquired its current ominous connotation already in ancient Rome. At the same time, *right* is always connected to concepts like justice and correctness.

But in connection with left, right is neutral. When the sergeant counts cadence: "left, left, left right left," to keep the troops marching in step, he does not think politics in using those words. One might speculate, tongue-in-cheek, of course, that since a column of soldiers always starts out with its right-hemisphere-motivated left foot to do what soldiers do, like defending their flag's sacred honor, or the dominant position of their empire, for instance, it is the right hemisphere that is ultimately responsible for the soldiers' actions.

Strictly speaking, however, the sides on which partisans of the opposing ideologies, the Jacobines and the Monarchists, sat in the Revolution Era French Assembly, where this political left-right terminology originated, was accidental.

Not so in his own, personal usage of Hungarian. There, *jó* means "good," and *jobb*, its comparative form, means "better." *Jobb* also means right (as opposed to left), and so the *jobb oldal* is both the right side *and* the better side. Not surprisingly therefore, when he heard this term as a child knowing nothing of politics, he naturally deduced from the context that the side, the *jobb oldal*, where his father, his family, all the people of his life's sphere stood, was the *better* one, certainly better than those Russian communists and terrorists that the heroic *Magyar Királyi Hadsereg*, the Royal Hungarian Army, was so gallantly fighting and with whom they, those on the left, tried to make despicably unpatriotic common cause.

And somehow, strangely or perhaps consequentially, this by now subconscious emotional distinction carried through all his life and now all the way into those conversations on the politics of national security with confused fanatics who, the Lord only knows how, managed to be pro-gun and pro-life at the same time in bars and at lunch counters in the Oregon of Burns, Vale, and Wagontire, whose convictions, however, were gut-level familiar to him, even though there was a world of difference between the left and the right of his childhood's Hungary and his present's Oregon.

In Hungary, then, the difference was simple. It was a matter of money and of status. In eastern Oregon, now, it was a matter of a convoluted complexity that somehow persuaded poor people to side with the power groups of the rich elite that were obviously hostile to their own economic interests. Why, it even involved the Holy Bible as interpreted by the Jerry Falwells of the politico-religious world, who were so eloquently pious that the Almighty Himself must have dropped in on them for a cup of coffee now and then to have a neighborly chat, one among likeminded cognoscenti. How else could Jerry have been so intimately privy to the Good Lord's mind to know that "God loves homosexuals but hates homosexuality," a dogma that he overheard the great guru promulgate while tel-evangelizing on the tube one evening.

Even Saint Thomas Aquinas was more careful in using God's name in vain. He just said that the *church* welcomes the sinner but rejects sin. I will not try to resolve this conundrum here. I am not a theosophist and have no mystical insight into the nature of God and the soul like Jerry and his kind. Let me leave it to the rhetoric of the Limbaughs and the Palins and of the Olbermanns and Obamas to explain it to you.

As far as he himself was concerned, however, he thought he had rationalized and understood both sides, and so he was not surprised to find this saddening sense of distance and even disdain for Western Oregon in the casual conversations along the road in the east. This sense was more subtle but not unlike the gut-level distrust and hostility that the national borders of the past have evoked in Europe and in many places there still do. The winds of politics blew drier and hotter over there in the rain shadow, and when gays, guns, and God were mentioned, the mood turned strident and passionate, leaving no room for a rational give-and-take. A muddy moral clarity was the motto there; it seemed to be etched in stone with acid, and sometimes it made his prized political correctness shake in its boots, for he had started life in the large footsteps of similar values. But then, he only went there to explore. He did not have to make a home there.

Closer to home

Making a home in Corvallis, on the other hand, was easy. The folks at the ARS headquarters had been right. Corvallis was one of America's prime retirement garden spots. To be sent there was like being decorated with a Medal of Merit. It was a place where the American Dream was being lived in real time. That American Dream is a "many splendored thing," and everybody develops his own private definition of it. Old as he is now, the concept was put into words even before he was born. When the term was first coined (by J. T. Adams in 1931), it meant:

> The American Dream is that dream of a land in which life should be better and richer and fuller for everyone, with opportunity for each according to ability or achievement.

Since then, it had been reinterpreted widely and more narrowly to mean owning a big car or two and a comfortable house and believing in retiring early enough to enjoy a long string of golden, work-and worry-free years that are associated in the minds of many with the favorite though elusive national pastime of fishing. But not even the Great Gatsby had a firm faith in its attainable reality, for what he saw was "the green light, the orgastic future receding year by year before him." Corvallis, however, seemed to be populated by true believers in a then still Golden Age of dreams come true. Excepting, of course, such marginal folks as illegal-immigrant Mexican janitors who were visible to Marina for she taught them to speak English but who were invisible to most others since they worked at night.

In the 1990s, when they lived there, the dream was still very much alive, and it could not have flourished in a more idyllic place than the home of Oregon State University. Although not particularly distinguished by its architecturally unremarkable, eclectic mix of buildings, the campus is essentially a great, wide-open park awash with an abundance of flowers in most seasons and blessed by a veritable forest of stately old trees from many of botany's 270 plant families. It is uplifting and mind soothing to walk its byways, as he always did, especially when the wording for his next paper's introduction would not gel in his mind as he sat by his huge, antique desk in his tiny, modern office. Walking helps to organize your thought. People can still be found walking to this very, gadget-driven day, only the young ones all have their ears plugged into some source of electronic output to hear stuff produced by others. But then, maybe, that is the way to stay connected these days.

It was Lorna who connected them to Corvallis first by showing then all the "homes" that were for sale on their house-hunting trip in the fall. Corvallis had built itself into the forest on its outskirts, making for an exceptionally pleasant, livable environment for all the upscale folks, hundreds of professors among them, who inhabit it. Their own house abutted on a patch of leftover woods on McKinley Street so that many a day, a small family of deer would spend the night on the grass between their back porch and the tall trees beyond. The deer roamed freely, and because they had developed a taste for tulips and rose blossoms, the city organized an opinion poll on what to do about them. Shoot them, tame them, or put them in a zoo were some of the choices. But the answer of all those gardeners who refused to erect anti-deer fences to protect their flowers regardless was unequivocal in its blue-green Oregonality: "They were here first, so leave them alone."

He moved up to Corvallis in the crisp but still mellow midwinter of an exceptionally dry year. Marina and Rob stayed in the Bay Area to finish their terms teaching or studying and followed a few months later. ARS agreed to move them twice, first the few items that he needed right away, and the whole household later. He organized one of the six bedrooms of the oversized house that they had picked as his temporary quarters and bought a refrigerator, a white wool Berber area rug, and a small electric blower of warm air to make things livable for himself. The refrigerator is now, eighteen years later, an energy inefficient but still working relic. The heater has never been used again, but the rug is doing well and is determined to serve them out in this lifetime, although it needs to be cleaned professionally now and then to stand up to Marina's standards of spot-intolerant perfection.

Angie, footloose and not enrolled in classes at the time, moved up next in anticipation of Rob's impending transfer and promptly found work, as she was a paragon of self-sustaining resourcefulness. Sometimes she came over to check out his dinner, which consisted invariably of bread, cheese, sausages, and raw greenstuff, such as yellow bell peppers, white cauliflower, orange carrots, purple kohlrabi, and red radishes, all procured from a small hippie cooperative on the other side of the bridge over the Willamette River, the Corvallis Food Coop, which was central to making this type of permanent picnic dining very pleasant with its selection of local bread, and imported cheeses and olives.

They carried items like French Roquefort, Italian gorgonzola, and British stilton, and when Peter came to visit on one of his rounds of journalism covering the American scene for the readers of his Berlin newspaper *Die Tageszeitung* (called simply *TAZ*), he acted much impressed that such a distant outpost of the just recently tamed Wild West should show such a flair for *Esskultur*. That is another short but much-encompassing *terminus technicus* used by the palate-oriented German *Feinschmecker*, people who like the French *gourmet* have developed a taste for the noble culture of savoring exquisite victuals. A thing that English-speaking peoples are just now are discovering (their stilton notwithstanding), as I may have mentioned before.

The conditions for his work were unchanged. He designed his own program and nobody interfered with it, even though unlike at the WRRC, the local boss, Bob Linderman, knew exactly what he was doing. But Bob was another one of those salt-of-the-earth people that populated ARS, a dedicated and enlightened public servant, one who knew how to appraise people correctly and to treat them accordingly to nurture their loyalty to cause, country, and to the greening of the globe. And as a consequence, also to him personally, which he deserved. He was also a good friend and scientific peer, met before at innumerable meetings, some of whose colloquia they had co-organized. Bob was also a specialist in plant-microbe interactions, but his training and interest centered on the pathological aspects of that field, while his own were those of physiology.

But somehow, all that freedom notwithstanding, the transfer had taken the wind out of his sails. He had half a dozen initiatives in the works back at the WRRC, and all held promise to produce breakthrough results. They were terminated. He adjusted, as always, but he knew that from here on, he would be on the downhill slope in his organization, marginalized, relegated to a back eddy.

Organizations are not like machines; they *are* machines. And the larger they are, the more like that they get. That applies also to the people who tend them. The higher their station in the organization, the more they get enthralled by the rhythm and the vibrations that emanate from what they think is *their* toy. But the toy has its own mind and momentum like rogue elephants or runaway freight trains do, and after a while, it is no longer clear who runs whom. When they become aware of that, the tenders get scared and they decide to regain control. That process is called a reorganization. Ostensibly, that is done for the sake of improving efficiency. In reality, it is the high-level tender's way to show that he is still alive, active, and in charge and that he therefore merits a final promotion, maybe to the highest rung of his ladder.

What usually happens in the course of such a process is that the useful output of the machine declines, for it is now spinning its wheels. If the machine is big enough, the losses are difficult to measure, at least in the short run, and therefore they are easily overlooked. But the grinding down which results from the spin can be painful to the cogs on those wheels, and he was one of those cogs. A good organization (his, for instance) means no harm, it just does what it somehow cannot help doing. How could it possibly keep in mind all those cogs individually? They are small and there are many. A full understanding of what is happening materializes only further down, at the level of the wheel itself (which knows it would be useless without its cogs). That is where things within an organization become personal, and it was at that level that his transfer to Oregon was facilitated. And it was done gracefully, which he appreciated greatly.

Part of this facilitation was that the area director (a wheel) agreed to transfer Keiko, his chief technician, along with his program, a concession that is against the rules, for normally ARS only pays for moving category one scientists. Keiko was a microbiologist of the most excellent kind. Her joining his group was an event of true serendipity. She became disaffected somehow with her previous assignment and, on her own initiative, got herself reassigned to the Mycorrhiza Project. She was most welcome there, and it was largely her expertise that helped the project expand into one of a more broadly based scope. One that included and later centered on generalized plant-soil interactions with the soil microflora as the agent of the processes involved. Had she not been willing to move to Corvallis, the project would have not only lost her solid, pleasant, personable presence, but also its scientific double edge.

It did not take long for the little group to grow again. Paul joined as a postdoc and brought with him from Penn State a large store of up-to-date head knowledge, deft, ambidextrous fingertip know-how, two green thumbs, and yet another solid, pleasant, personable personality. Now, things started to look up again. Then Joyce came looking for a microscope to continue her work on the taxonomy of arbuscular-mycorrhizal (AM) fungi.

She and her husband, Jim, had retired from their pro-humanity labors in South America, and they decided to settle in Corvallis for an unlikely reason: because Jim Trappe had his lab there. Trappe was the granddaddy of AM taxonomy and Joyce had thought that she could work with him. But he was off to Australia and on the verge of calling it quits after some four decades of work.

At the same time, his local USDA Forest Service unit was fighting for its financial life. It seems that the FS was yet another entity with a split personality. The research arm, the people who understood the nuts and acorns of forest biology, were at odds with the management arm that was reputed to be deep in the pockets of the logging industry. And indeed, Oregon forests were being clear-cut in a hideous, huge checkerboard pattern. It seemed that the two did not speak to each other, and when things came to making funding decisions at the Department level, the research arm tended to loose out, and Jim's lab was sinking with that boat.

So Joyce came to work at his new lab, more as a pastime and on her own interests to be sure, but those fitted in nicely. She and her husband Jim had built a gorgeous house amid all that greenery, and when visiting, talk would always touch on what one does with those long, golden days after retiring. "Write stories, a story, the novel of your life," he suggested, and Jim laughed. "I hear a lot of talk about that," he said, "but I have never seen or heard of anyone who has actually done it." Well, that was the straw that broke this obstinate, procrastinating mule's back. He took that as a challenge, and here I sit now wearing out my old Dell Inspiron 2650.

The one that Steve gave me, for I have two of them now. I hope Jim lives to see the end of my story, for if he won't read it, I'll make him eat all these reams of paper. I'll leave the choice up to him.

Marina and Rob moved up in June and started a new life in what is the paradisian climate of the three-month-long Oregon summer. Marina went into teaching English and French again, and Rob took up the study of engineering, in earnest now. He set up house with Angie, and the two of them seemed to be doing well together. Steve stayed in the in-law basement apartment in El Cerrito, and news from him was spotty but not disquieting—yet. He had never been a great communicator of his affairs. Things were turning placid again, so time was ripe for him once more to think about searching for his elusive america. By this time this search was turning into nothing more than a recurring dream about exploring new bridges to the unknown, to new cities and countries that lie there beyond the next bend of the road:

Und schon sah er bei dem nächsten Biegen	And already he saw beyond the next bend
wieder Wege, Länder, Brücken liegen	new roads, countries, bridges looming
bis an Städte, die man übertreibt.	even up to cities that one exaggerates.

I am not quite sure what Rilke meant by this strange "exaggerate," here, in this sparkling, opalescent poem about "The Stranger." It was one that the great poet "condensed" clearly and directly with him in mind, for Rilke was not one who fitted in words merely because they completed a rhyme or a rhythm. Poetry is called *Dichtung* in German, but *dichten* translates as "to make dense" or "to render substantial," and in the realm of Erato's art that means to condense or substantiate the wispy, loose ends of the shimmering tapestry of life until the pattern stands out clearly, outlined in a few, terse words that rest in themselves forever and can be felt only, for they are above exegesis.

Granada

But there is nothing that one can exaggerate about the city of Granada, for Granada is exaggeration itself. That is where this next search took him. Or rather it was re-search, for they had been there before, on vacation while stationed in Frankfurt. Now, with half a year rather than two short weeks to look forward to, it would be a true search and research at the same time, as this trip was based on work proposed, funded by the Organization for Economic Cooperation and Development. The OECD had its origins in the sorting out of the ways and means of the Marshal Plan, the rebuilding of war-torn Europe. Now, among its many functions, it also provided for scientific exchanges between collaborating countries, and he had little trouble in being accepted when he applied for membership.

If I have time left for it, later, I'll write an elegy about having had time only for fleeting waftures of hello and then of good-bye to El Andaluz, for six brief months of stay there are no more than that. Everyone who has ever been there heaves the sigh repeating the *Suspiro del Moro* again upon leaving, upon looking back on his brief stay in that enchanted place, and so he learns to understand Francisco Icasa's advice when seeing a blind beggar:

Dale limosna, mujer	Give him a gift of alms, woman,
Que no hay en la vida nada	For there is nothing in life
Como la pena de ser	Like the sorrow of being
Ciego en Granada	Blind in Granada

And so it is. When they arrived in November, fresh snow was already gleaming on the northern slopes of the Sierra Nevada, of which they had a guarded view from their fourth-floor apartment. That was in a modern section of the city on the busy Avenida Cervantes, just past the Estación Experimental del Zaidín, the Institute where he got himself invited to work.

Breathtakingly beautiful as Southern Spain is even to the locals who are used to it, it is not at all like California climatewise. In winter, it is wintry in earnest, and the abodes of the general populace seem to lack some of the cozy *Wohnkultur* practiced in the more decadent reaches of the First World. *Wohnkultur*, that is yet another expression of the German preoccupation with culture, this time with the refinements lavished on one's living space. And that is important, for shivering does not mix with *Gemütlichkeit*, which (the latter) is the crux of domestic bliss, and especially for him, for whom no climate can never be warm enough:

A warmer Ofen, a Schalerl Kaffee,	A warm wood stove, a cup of coffee,
A guats Buach zum Lesen am Kanapé,	A good book to read on the couch,
Das Radio g'stellt auf leise Musik,	The radio tuned to soft music,
Was fehlt denn noch zum häuslichem Glück?	What else is there to domestic bliss?

as defined by one of Hermann Leopoldi's Austrian-accented songs about his pre-television, pre-holocaust world. And the central element of it is clearly that *warmer Ofen*, the lack of which is like a little green worm in even the reddest and juiciest of pomegranates. Their apartment building did have central heating but it had the peculiarity that the furnace was only turned on from late afternoon until ten at night. After that one went to bed or joined the rest of the population in the cafés and bars.

Why do I get hung up here on that retarded central-heating system in all that glory that is Granada? He did not suffer from cold when he was a child; his deep aversion to shivering did not carry over from there. There was a great big *csempe kályha*, an oven built of ceramic tiles glazed in different colors on the outside and reaching all the way up to the ceiling in each and every room, in which blazes were set every wintry morning by a servant. It must have been a vague, child's inkling not tainted yet with the guilt of privilege that it might not be so for many other people, even though he did not know any of those, but who, he knew, must have wished very much that they had a warm oven also, even if only a tiny little one.

Megölte valaki magát,	Someone killed himself
az hozta ezt a rút időt.	That's what brought on these icy times.
Fú a szél, táncol a tányér	The wind blows, the plates dance
a borbélyműhely előtt:	In front of the barber shops:
Hol a boldogság mostanában?	Where to find happiness these days?
Barátságos, meleg szobában!	In a friendly, warm room!

There it is again, the friendliness (*barátság*) of a warm room. Who knows how much more poetry is devoted to this deeply felt *desideratum* throughout the destitute globe? Well, anyway, in Granada, it was the custom to turn on that central heat not one minute sooner than at five o'clock *en la tarde*, which in winter is more afternoon than evening, but in either case, too late for much of the day's *felicidad domestica*, or domestic bliss.

But they spent little time in those rooms that were otherwise quite acceptable, for there were worlds to explore outside. The place of work, the *Estación Experimental*, did not measure up to American standards, yet a lot of substantial work had emerged from there. Maybe his hosts were used to visitors asking to come to "work" with them who were more interested in spending some time immersed in the mystique that is Granada than in doing a bit of serious science there.

Be that as it may, the hosts were less than eagerly forthcoming with integrating him into what they were doing, although he would have welcomed that. So he felt somewhat out of place at first, but surely that was due only to the long warm-up time that his introvert persona always needed when dealing with new people close up. He did not quite know how to hook into the conveyor belt of the local routine. Everyone was already doing his or her specialized thing, a circumstance that was aggravated by a lack of resources for his line of work. Then, as always in his experience, change came from an unexpected quarter. That quarter was Galdino, a graduate student from Londrina, Brazil.

A young man of herculean stature, with an always smiling, happy face and huge paws for hands, he was more like a bull in a china shop than someone whose vocation it is to do the most careful and meticulous type of work with the tiniest form of life there is. Gal was a microbiologist. But apparently one with sharp eyes for the problems of the macroscopic life-forms around him also.

Coming back from a vacation trip, Gal brought with him an unasked-for present, a large plastic bag full of exactly the thing he needed. It was a poor, yellow, clay soil of a well-described type that was the perfect complement and comparison to the local black soil for microbe-mediated soil-aggregation studies. With that, he had no problem in pulling off a respectable four-factorial experiment with plants, AM fungi, bacteria, and soil types as factors. The results showed that soil stability is significantly affected by the soil biota and differently so by different microbes in substrates of different chemical and physical soil characteristics. The data that resulted from this work sufficed for three publications!

There was even a fourth one produced in collaboration with Juan Antonio about biocide effects on the plant-soil-microbe system. Antonio, a much-published expert on the subject, apportioned and mixed the poison. "*Cuidado con tu leche de cabrón,*" the guest cautioned his host in his well-meaning manner as his colleague was applying the vile-smelling, yellowish-milky potion to the soils of the potted plants, but his elementary Spanish may have had some hidden, unsavory meaning, for the man shook his head disapprovingly when he heard him say it.

A bit of *turismo*

With all those results, his conscience was appeased; he had earned the trust OECD had placed in him in financing his trip and ARS in letting him go, and they were ready to make the most of this splendid opportunity to cross a bridge to what was for them a new world. The great tourist attractions like the Alcazaba, Alhambra, and Albaicín I leave to you to experience for yourself. His interest of old standing, however, in roaming the byways and alleys in search of the serendipitous effusions of life, was fulfilled here more than anywhere else. When tired of it, his steps would lead him to magic hide-outs like the Mirador de San Nicolas, where the bar had a few tables outside so that he could savor the *tapas* while getting engrossed in the full view of the effulgent Sierra in the distance and the Alhambra close by.

The *tapas* must have been a parting gift of the *Moros* to the Iberian Peninsula after the *Reconquista* by the barbarian white knights, who instead of being grateful for not having been wiped out completely by the rule of the Arab Caliphate, in time rose up against it, and eventually wiped out its culture so thoroughly that only a precious little of it is left. And he thought a bit of this precious little might have been this unique, endemic *Esskultur* of the *tapas* that he had not encountered anywhere else. They are savory tidbits of diverse kinds that one normally enjoys with a glass of foaming *cervesa* standing at the counter, and when you have sampled most of them, it is like having had the main course of your meal and not needing anything else.

But sometimes these tidbits are more substantial like the *sopa de rabo de toro*, and this was his favorite, a thick stewlike concoction the way that bar on the *Mirador* prepared it. You could tell that the chunks in it were transverse cuts of the tail of a split-hoofed ungulate, such as the cow, or more precisely, the male of the species, the *toro*. And that invariably reminded him of a then popular parody of that famous aria from Carmen that he heard one time on *Rádió Budapest Egy* half a long lifetime ago:

Ó toreádor, öld meg a bikát,	Oh, toreador, do kill the bull,
De jól vigyázz:	But take good care
A farkát le ne vágd!	Not to cut off his tail!

Well, Ronda, the picture-postcard town, where bullfighting had been perfected to an art form by Pedro Romero, was one of the highlights of their excursions to the more distant surroundings. They did not sympathize with the tormenting and killing of animals for sport no matter how artfully it is executed as a national pastime, and so they did not try to get tickets for one of the events. This was just as well, as they were fiendishly expensive, and it gave them more time for other things. Like watching a flock of rooks perform aerial acrobatics from the porch of a nice little restaurant in the deep *barranca* of the Rio Guadalevín near the arches of the old bridge.

There were many others, in fact, all the surrounding towns were highlights, even though I do not recall in detail anymore why they stood out. One should write things down on the spot, but he was the kind that carries no camera with him (let alone a pen), for it is a distraction, and besides, he is afraid of memories fossilized into photo albums that result from that sort of activity. Baeza, Úbeda, Almuñécar, Mojácar. Fascinated by the cave dwellings, they visited Guadix several times.

In Alcalá la Real, the church was being renovated, and in raising the stone floor of one of the side chapels, the workers were just uncovering a mass grave containing a jumble of human skeletons. It was probably a gruesome memento of the *Reconquista*, which was particularly tumultuous in this frontier area, for the final assault on Granada was unleashed from there in the decades before Columbus first landed on what he named Hispaniola.

It seemed to him that the victorious Christians must have slaughtered the *Moro* inhabitants and then raised a monument over their remains in thanks to their God for having sided with them. Of course, it might not have been this way at all, but he found himself on the side of the *Moros*, and taking sides always colors one's perception by reinventing or at least distorting reality.

Maybe he identified with the *Moros* because of what he knew about Mexican history, where these same *matamoros*, or Moor killers, having run out of victims at home, sailed across the ocean to wipe out another great culture in their quest of gold and their craving for power. Like the Turks had done in Hungary at about the same time. There was also a grandiose fortress there that had seen better days, the *al qal'a*, built right after the *Moro Conquista* in the sixth century.

Last not least, there were Las Alpujarras, a region of mountain villages with an elaborate system of terracing and irrigation that had turned rocky slopes into fertile orchards. Here some of the *Moro* presence persisted long after the last effeminate Arab king of Granada left, was permitted to leave in shame, heaving a great sigh on top of the hill to the south that offers a last glimpse of the City, a place called to this day the *Suspiro del Moro*. In a word, you could easily spend a lifetime in El Andaluz, especially if you were born and raised there. If you were at home.

But his favorite place was Alhama de Granada. It was very special, maybe because there was nothing spectacular about the town itself. Sure, the *al hammam*, the baths, outside town, are a glory of Arabic architecture, and the distant view to the Sierra Nevada is grand. But it is more likely that he liked it because it reminded him of Léva. Not that it was laid out the same way; it was not. It was very different in fact. And it was not that it too had a fortress that in the end fell to the enemy like Léva *vára* fell to the Turks a few decades later.

It was because of the way the sun shone there, because of the way the shadows fell, and because of the way the wind blew and seemed to offer up like a sacrifice of the past to the present, a fragrance of lilacs and acacias, even though there were none, at least not at that time of the year. People moved in the streets, in the main square, unhurried with the easy and stately grace of the knowledge of being safely at home like they did in Léva. Or so it seemed to him, and he felt like he owned all of this present and all of that past again for a brief moment in a time that had blurred its sharp, nonexistent borders:

Doch auf fremden Plätzen war ihm eines täglich ausgetretnen Brunnensteines Mulde manchmal wie ein Eigentum.	Yet sometimes in the squares of strange towns he felt as if the stone slabs of a fountain worn hollow by use were his very own.

Here I go again. On rereading my last paragraph, I notice that I called the armies of the most exalted catholic majesties of Castilla and Aragon: "The enemy!" Now, why is that? It slipped in naturally, without my intending it. But I think it is quite clear to me now. In his mind's eye, he saw those Christian armies marauding, looting and torching the treasures of a higher culture as he had always seen the hordes of savage Turks doing the same thing in the Hungary that had just reached a climax of cultural rebirth under its great king, Mátyás *Király*. It is not easy to relate to history dispassionately, not to one's own. And why should it be? It is not a subject of cold, dark, impersonal, distant-cosmic chill like astronomy. Its pages are written in hot, red blood, and he had felt as if he had seen it flow himself.

Only, the Spanish Christians had permitted traces of the past to survive, while the Turks did not. And some more of these traces they were set to discover when the Fox, now Steve, came to visit. Chief among them was the great mosque of Cordoba, a forest of painted pillars with a lost and forlorn Christian church inserted into the middle of it. Then they zipped down to Jerez and Cádiz, which Steve wanted to see, bypassing Sevilla for lack of time. But they toured some of the small towns of the *Frontera* region, where frontier warfare had dragged on for a long time. The precious little late-Gothic church in Medina Sidonia de la Frontera gave a hint as to the historic time frame: further east, toward the heart of the rest kingdom of Granada, the churches were renaissance, postreconquest structures like the great cathedral of the city of Granada itself. Sidonia must have been reconquered a little earlier, when the spirit of the time still saw God's house in clean, straight, vertical lines soaring to the heavens rather than in the solid elegance and later in the gilded pomp of the ages that followed during the long time while it was a-building.

After a night's rest in Tarifa, from where you could throw a stone over to Africa over the Straights of the Rock if you tried hard enough, they took the Costa del Sol route back. That was a good preview of what a burst real-estate bubble looks like.

In the first decades after the war, fed among other things by the German *Wirtschaftswunder*, the folks north of the Alps found that their rapidly increasing wads of cash were burning ever-larger holes in their pockets. And so, like a modern phoenix, hedonism started to raise its environment-disdaining head out of the ashes of war. The money needed to be spent, and with that the genteel pastime of "traveling abroad" enjoyed earlier by members of a more decorous old-money club, now became a tourist onslaught of hordes of semi-*arrivés* yearning for a tan on foreign beaches of the sun. It must have been a real field day for the developers! But as the ugly concrete high-rise hotels began taking over the coastline from Algeciras to Málaga, the increasingly sophisticated crowds of tourists started looking for as yet unspoiled shores, and by the nineties, when they were there, some of the Costa had become a deserted asphalt jungle.

It was not yet so a quarter century earlier, when they first explored the area with Torremolinos as their base. It was then as charming a spot as you could hope to find for a two-week vacation. From there, they took public transport everywhere, and going to Granada, they got wet in the cold rain (it was March) before getting on their drafty, unheated bus. En route they saw a sign in big, black letters on a firewall: *Velcom Mommlers*. Well, whatever *mommler* may mean in whatever language, it found its way as a new term into their family vocabulary where it is in use to this day. Their new verb *mommeln* (or "to mommel," for they speak a mixed German-English *Gerglisch* at home) came to mean to be cold and uncomfortable, especially with wet and freezing feet, and not being able to do anything about it like when riding on a bus. It is a good term for people to remember who travel a lot but do not do it first class.

This time, however, they had a great, big luxury car at their disposal, a Lancia, no less, that their dear friends, the Guerras had loaned them for their entire six-month stay! "*Tienen que ser muy amigos*," they must be very good friends, remarked their host at the Estación del Zaidín, José-Miguel, when he heard of it. And that is a fact. Marina had met María back at the Berkeley Adult School in her English as a Second Language class (when Luis was on a one-year physicians' fellowship in California), and they formed a friendship of the most rare kind, one that knows no secrets. Still, depriving yourself of the use of your car for half a year to make life more pleasant for a friend is an act of solicitude and generosity that surpasses all norms of normality (i.e., impulses of customary hospitality).

But the Spanish are a special people; they (all of the ones they had the pleasure of meeting) are imbued with a special kind of *grandezza* that is mellowed to human size by a down-to-earth, genuine, warm cordiality. With the Guerras as expert guides, they did visit Sevilla and the El Escorial and the Prado and the Sierra de Guadarrama north of Madrid.

Also, with a good half year's work already done, they made a grand tour of the Extremadura region: Zafra, Mérida, and Cáceres, where storks nest on all the spires, battlements, chimneys, and even the eaves of the taller buildings. Finally, it was time to go, and they rented a car for the cruise to Munich and to Slovakia via Andorra, the Provence and Switzerland, visiting the laboratories of colleagues on the way.

Fülek

One day, still back in California and long before the move to Oregon, the US Postal Service delivered an envelope with a strange address on it. But the name of the addressee was undeniably his, so he opened it. There is no telling how the mail men managed to locate him, for the address that he had scratched lightly into the surface of his grandfather's headstone in the Léva cemetery years ago must have eroded to near illegibility with time. But Karafiáth Jenő *bácsi*, then an octogenarian, copied it off when paying a last visit from Budapest to the grave of his uncle. He then passed it on to Márti in Fülek, a Hungarian town now in Slovakia, just across that unfortunate border and on the wrong side of it. Márti is his cousin and the youngest of the three daughters of Sörös Béla *bácsi* of Losonc.

When he knew her as a little girl back in Léva on her occasional visits to their grandfather's house in the Petőfi *utca*, she was certainly not someone a boy who was a boy scout could relate to, for she was given to complaining much of the time. That is called *nyafogni* and is a no-no; in a word, she was known in the family as a *nyaffancs* (pronounced ñah-fanch).

However, life had taught her how to grow out of that childhood affliction thoroughly and in a hurry with the onset of those trying, hard times of the Russian-Slovak occupation of Losonc and with the concomitant shattering of the economic basis of her family's life. She grew into what is called in old Hungarian usage a *"nagy asszony,"* which means "grand woman" translated literally: a *materfamilias*, a female personage whose sphere of influence of loving authority extends well beyond the limits of her family to her entire community. A role that she shared with her no less impressive *paterfamilias* of a husband, Frédi.

They were the first living relatives that emerged from the oblivion of nearly fifty years, thanks entirely to that sequence of chance events: his impulse of self-identification at the gravestone, Jenő *bácsi*'s noticing and copying it, and Márti's initiative in following up on all this by writing a letter to the phantom address. Well now, there he was on his third visit to the homeland of his childhood, the Hungarian *Felvidék*, or Uplands, that was settled by one of the seven confederate tribes of the young Magyar nation after they conquered the Carpathian Basin. This *Felvidék* is represented in the coat of arms of Hungary by three green mounds (symbolizing the Carpathians), upon which stands the apostolic double cross of its first king, Szent István (Saint Steven) crowned in the Year of the Lord 1000.

Henceforth, the home of his relatives in Fülek, a ten-minute drive from Losonc, proved to be an anchor in his attempts to refamiliarize himself with his roots. It was built from scratch by Frédi himself, the work of his own hands, masonry, plumbing, roofing, everything, while he was earning his living as a science teacher of the only Hungarian-language high school that was tolerated by the Slovak authorities in this area north of the border, home of close to a million Hungarians before ethnic cleansing dwindled their numbers. I cannot help but calling this type of cleansing, this slow and merciless deprivation of an ethnicity of its right to its language and to its identity: cultural genocide.

But Frédi and Márti, together with a small group of dedicated colleagues, somehow managed to set up their school in the old Berchtold Castle, where they then succeeded to teach a high school curriculum in their mother tongue. I can only hope that this description of their struggles will not result in repercussions for them in what is now part of a liberal-minded, free, new European Union.

I do not recall in detail how the momentous first meeting with the long-lost relatives went, but he and Marina were showered with the most lavish hospitality imaginable, even though their hosts were struggling on their meager Second-World state salaries. The customs were those of the old times: breakfast started with a swig of *barack pálinka*, the hundred-proof, transparent, yellow-tinged, fruit-fragrant distillate of apricots.

Zsuzsi, the middle one of the three sisters, played the piano after dinner and they all sang Magyar songs, of which he remembered quite a few, having amused his steering wheel with them on his solitary drives on another continent. There was no television, and it was not needed for entertainment. The old times awoke anew from their deep sleep in the telling, and the tale of the new times demanded and received undivided interest and attention. And let's not forget grandmother's cookies that sweetened all that talk. Márti knew how to prepare them the same way, as if sixty years of adversity had not passed to make her forget the folk art of the *magyar konyha*, the Hungarian cuisine.

More soil biology

Science at the Corvallis lab had not been asleep in the meantime. As usual, it took first place with him to cook up the recipes for coming experiments. Paul, his postdoc, had been busy working with fungi. He was spraying his *Glomera* (that's the Latin plural for *Glomus*, or ball, the main *genus* of mycorrhizal fungi) with fungicides. Knowing how these poisons affect the good guys, the symbiotic fungi, is important for reasons that neither the chemical industry nor the growers like to consider if they happen to think of it at all. Interest at their level is focused on the bad guys, the pests and the pathogens, because they are the ones that affect their profits directly.

It takes a long time and a lot of money to formulate and bring to market a specific killer compound that targets the enemy life-forms successfully. If a captain of the chemical industry or a mogul of agro-business had to include in his research budget funding of the collateral damage, the effects of their products on beneficial organisms, the expense might become prohibitive. So having found the antidote against *Verticillium* or *Fusarium* for instance, fell fungal crop banes both, can you expect them to spend another three years to find out if it kills the symbiotic fungi also? That's why his lab was involved in looking at fungicides.

To illustrate this, consider the following as a simple example of the string of complexities that even a monoculture like a soybean field can pose.

Its lonely plants yearn for the diversity of their native habitat and so they try to attract any companions they can find close by. Like the lowly cocklebur, for instance. This particular weed has a special affinity for the soybean, for its growth habit is very much like that of its favorite cultivated associate. Once it has snuck in between those tidily sown rows of soy, it promptly becomes locked into the larger system by the web of AM-fungal hyphae. These are hair-fine filaments (just to remind you of it) that interconnect all the roots down there in the soil, regardless of species-identity differences and of human use-value discrimination.

Now, noticing the unwanted plant, the grower promptly dumps a weed-specific herbicide, such as bentazon (☻ mention of a brand name does not imply endorsement by the author or the publisher ☺) on his field. As it takes effect, changes start occurring. The crop plant is safe, but the weed starts suffering; its still vigorous roots draw reserves from the moribund shoot to itself in an ultimately futile attempt at survival. Sensing this via the interconnecting hyphal network, the soy plant now regards the struggling weed roots as a source of sugars and amino acids. Soon subtle commands go out to the hyphae, which then start transporting the goods to the strong survivor sink. This is a process that can be monitored and measured using nitrogen isotopes.

But what if the good fungal hyphae are not there anymore because they have been wiped out by fungicide poisoning aimed at pathogenic fungi? Well, the agricultural soil system will do what our own bodies do also under the influence of all the medications that we swallow these days. It struggles and tries to adjust to the chemicals. But eventually those connections, the links in the topsoil food chain, may succumb to the poisons, in what is not unlike to what happens to our nervous system under the influence of drugs, however enticing their use may appear at first.

We have a hard time understanding that the soil is a living organism, just as we are reluctant to grasp that our brains are not test objects for hit-and-miss experimentation with mind-and mood-altering substances. But how did I lapse into this out-of-place comparison of fungicides with drugs? I did not consciously channel my stream of thought to lead here. My keyboard did it on its own, seemingly, sensing that I was really preoccupied with trouble on the home front while I was trying to discuss soybean fields.

For this is what was really on my mind, and this was where all this was leading up to: Abe's warning call to Rob that his brother was in deep trouble.

Black clouds

Rob was quite upset with his father that he had been doing nothing besides passively watching the El Cerrito scene deteriorate while sitting in his office focused on himself. He should have occasionally visited that in-law apartment in the basement of the house on Avila Place to make sure things were in order. But he had not. His elder son was now a grown-up, one who knew he had to face life on life's terms. If his education did not provide the skills needed for the standard of life he desired, it was up to him to go out to acquire them without any prodding. Like he had done himself.

But things were clearly not going well. There was always a need for more money back in El Cerrito. At one time, Marina sent a large check in token payment for the tuitions that Steve had always paid himself: "As you know, we welcome independence, but we also value education and are proud that you were able to earn your degree yourself. This sum is intended to repay debts incurred in the process," the letter said, but in reality it was in response to a feeling that things were going desperately astray in El Cerrito. Instead of repaying debts, the money helped to add the cost of a big new car to his already hopelessly overcharged credit cards.

Abe was a Maybeck High School classmate, a rare bird of a true friend. "You must come now and do something immediately," his message said.

What had happened to set off the long overdue alarm? They were sitting one evening there in the basement, so it seems, a small group of dropouts, Steve's groupies in a way, for they knew that he had a little money now and then. Also, unlike them, he had a part-time job, and he provided the shelter for hanging out together. They were just sitting there chewing the fat and using whatever substance they had available, and there was a little stash of it in the fridge at this crucial point in time.

That was the scene when it happened. Another member of the clique dropped in suddenly, in an agitated sort of way, and was followed very soon by disaster. The law descended on what was really nothing more than a harmless get-together. It seems that this last comer had stolen a car, which was immediately reported, and the police simply followed him to the basement of that dead-end street house on Avila Place. And that was the end of it.

Steve did not try to hide what was obvious anyway and admitted what could not to be denied. He thought the law would look upon cooperation favorably. Big mistake! The law does not care. It is like a cold November rain; it drops on everyone, whether you have an umbrella or not. When you admit, you are guilty by default, and no lawyer can undo that, no matter how many hundreds of dollars he is raking in per hour for trying.

It seems I have suppressed most of the other details, for I do not remember them. I hope that Steve will one day write the story of his experiences with drugs. His tale, told honestly and self-searchingly and, in the process, fleshed out to correct the details of this episode also. It would do him good to write it, and others would benefit greatly from hearing it. A tale that includes also his near-miraculous recovery. But that came much later, after much more learning, growing, and *suffering*.

When the family drove down to the house in El Cerrito following Abe's warning, the little apartment was flashing the symptoms of disease like a red light. It was filled halfway to the ceiling with an assemblage of junk, barely leaving room for people to sit and do their thing. While the ability to tolerate disorder can be a sign of creative energy, the unchecked accumulation of unneeded things is usually a sign of a deeper disorder. Poor Steve. It must have been a sore trial for him, the way he had lost control of his life with the merciless market stuffing his pockets with credit cards and his head with the alluring promises of an easy life.

Always a headstrong manager of his own affairs, he offered no resistance this time to being packed up and moved to Corvallis. He saw for himself that a major change was needed. Without Rob's help, they could not have managed it. But Rob felt that his brother's predicament was aggravated by his father's negligence, and this damaged the father-son relationship for a long time. At least that's the way I see it now.

The false friend

What more can I say? Once in Corvallis, Steve got his act together. He went to work immediately. He did not want to move into the family home, however. That told volumes about the state of family affairs. Instead, he moved in with Rob and Angie for a while, and then rented his own place. After a bad year under a bum boss, he found work that he liked with Acres Gaming, an outfit that appreciated his talents. He was now doing well, taking computer-related classes at the community college and developing new skills. He is one who grooves on appreciation, and now he was earning that from all sides.

They attended rehab meetings together, an experience from which the father learned more than the son. In fact, those meetings were much more than educational. That woeful assembly of addicts broken by one unmanageable misfortune or another who were all earnestly trying to turn their lives around sat there and told its tales and shared its lives with such total sincerity that it opened up new worlds of insight for him. But it was a world too alien to be fully understood and internalized. So although he had become aware of the chasm between their worlds and his now, he did not yet succeed in bridging it emotionally.

For him, it was an alien scene, one that he identified as escape. And that is something for which he could muster little sympathy. There is no escape. That was the lesson life had taught him. But was it not possible that other people learned other lessons from their lives? Lesson plans that defined the rules of an exotic game that his own life did not teach him to play? One that he was spared to play, thanks to the good fortune that accompanied him on his road. No credit to him for that; he was just lucky.

Escape from what? He kept shaking his head whenever he thought of it. From emptiness, disillusionment, purposelessness? Because the roast duck was not flying into the escaper's mouth like in the *Schlaraffenland* of Grimm's fairy tales? Maybe. That is probably how it starts with most. But later, out of the teen stage, comes stress, more intense than that of the schoolyard. A mean boss. Neglect by the parents. A failing relationship. The real world closes in. And then the friend makes his appearance.

Not a stranger perhaps, but now his company is not playful experimentation with grass anymore, for slowly want becomes need. At first the friend is gentle and enticing. "Come to me. Come to me, and I will tuck you in like your mother did when you were little. Come to me, and I will open doors for you to bright new worlds without fear. Come to me, and I will show you the ecstasy of being. I am the measure of your real self. Trust me. Trust me, for you are the real you only when you are with me."

How could he know anything about it, he, who had used nothing more than an occasional, fleeting puff of grass? It was the hard-core addicts who told him about it, whose meetings he frequented later, in that building by the San Luis Obispo

Railway Station. Later, when things really turned grim. How trust turns into tyranny and the friend became a fiend and finally a ghoul.

Come to think of it, however, Steve used different words for his experience, which may be a rare variant of the drug story, the run-of-the-mill way the literature of the subject describes it. Or perhaps it is the central one. Only it takes a man as gifted with words as he is to tell it that way. I would not know. "It is a state of exaltation that provides an otherworldly norm or standard, against which the vicissitudes of normal life may be measured," he said. And in the end, Steve learned to turn that norm into a useful tool to gain mastery over the friend. Believe it or not!

Times of yore

Sometimes, in the process of fixing my thought permanently on paper, a stream that flows reluctantly like a thick, viscous fluid out of my fingertips, an innocent turn of a phrase can lead me to the next, unpremeditated paragraph. "Come to think of it."

Come to think of it, I have been saying little about his real, everyday life, as its milestones wore on inch by inch, at home on McKinley Street and on Orchard Avenue, his workplace. It is only the highlights that occupy the spaces in the darkening caves of my memories. The travels that throw floodlights of different color on his search for an america, the place that was hiding everywhere and nowhere, often even in America itself. Besides the highlights, it seems that it is only the fun at work that takes up some space and then the shadows of personal failures that sometimes fall on the sunlight of his honeymoon, the life that Marina's smile kept unchanged, now going on fifty years.

But as he walked through the quiet backstreets of Corvallis to work or to the downtown Beanery for his newspaper and cup of coffee, he never stopped wondering, as has always been his wont, when passing by one quiet, tidy little home-house after another, what made those people inside tick? If he was that interested, why did he not reach out to get to know them? Well, that's how introverts are. Like his grandfather, whose story, *Az Életem Regénye*, *The Novel of My Life*, would have accompanied him on those walks had he known of the book, for *ópapa* had walked the same way to work, up the rise from the Petőfi *utca* to the hospital on the Kákasor through those quiet, traffic-free streets of another age.

Fifty years of quiet, meticulous service dedicated to the well-being of the people of his little town, with two or three excursions to points of interest nearby as the only highlights. Yet full of the joys and sorrows that make up life and that the old man perhaps felt even more acutely as they were not dulled by the hectic distractions of this new age of constant moving. From my involuntary vantage point as a roadrunner, I stand in awe of that life, and if I had not had a glimpse of it as a child, I might think it could not have been real. It could have been nothing but the type of fiction that one reads in old books.

But now, that I have read those handwritten pages, my grandfather's life in Léva comes across to me like a sun fleck. Like a bright spot of light on the gray marble floor of a church of yore whose solid, cold, enduring Romanesque arches entombed its interior, the vast, silent space around that glittering sun fleck, in a hushed twilight. A darkling space, except for that beam of light that found its way first through the clouds and then through a small round window to cast a glow of reality on the spot where he stood for a moment in time. And then the vision was gone never to return again the way it was, for an earthquake of history had rent those arches that framed his existence.

Hazatérés—Homecoming

This was the trip that produced grandfather's book. They were celebrating the homecoming in earnest this time. Everybody was there, almost everybody, that is. His mother's two sons, for Miklós made it also, and his aunt Zsuzsi *néni*'s three daughters, Márti, Zsuzsi, and Lilla. Lilla, the eldest, bent with age but smiling, came up from Kecskemét, Hungary, for the occasion. Her two children were teachers and could not come, and Steve and Rob were missing also. Márti's and Zsuzsi's children, the locals, were there. Missing was also the offspring of the other aunt, Bözsi *néni*. They could not come because they had vanished in the turmoil of history into the distant vacuum of timespace, lost though not yet passed out of memory: Laci, Ila, and Bözsi. Very much missed were also his cousins on his father's side, the children of his two uncles of Bethlenfalva, Jenő *bácsi* and Gyula *bácsi*. They could not come because they were not born: their fathers had fallen on the Russian front during the first months of that War of 1914, before they could have children.

But for those who were there, it was a real celebration, one of the joyfully solemn kind. Young Frédi, then the administrator of the Hungarian Radio Station in Bratislava but already preparing to become a man of God in the footsteps of his grandfather, Béla *bácsi*, the bishop, produced a cassette, whose playing brought him and his brother to tears. It was a poetically crafted tale in which history, exile, and family were interwoven with the melody and text of Vörösmarty's *Szózat* (Appeal) fading in an out at the appropriate narrative passages:

A nagyvilágon e kivűl	There is no place for you in the world
Nincsen számodra hely.	Except for here.
Áldjon vagy verjen sors keze,	May fate's hand bless or punish you,
Itt élned, halnod kell.	This is where you must live and die.

It was during this moving episode that old Frédi got up and pulled out grandfather's writing from a long row of other books, sprinkled with the dust of years of waiting for its moment, like a precious bottle of old vintage vine.

Like that bottle that his grandmother in Bethlenfalva opened on the last day of their last visit in the summer of 1944. It was the last one of thirteen from the harvest of currants in 1894, from the first year that those bushes had born fruit, and his father mentioned that he remembered that occasion of crushing the red berries that had been exceptionally sweet that year, for he was already six years old at that time. The bushes were still there fifty years later, edging in long rows plots of different varieties of apple trees in the huge orchard behind the house, the orchard where rows of ugly socialist blockhouses now stand. But that comes later. Back then, in 1944, the grown-ups were making ecstatic faces sipping the dark orange-colored liquid, *ribizli bor* (currant wine) they called it, that poured out of that dusty bottle, while discussing that harvest of old, and somehow all that got stuck in my memory.

That was what went through his mind as Frédi silently handed the dusty book to Márti, for it was hers to give. It took me a long time to open it, for I was afraid to face the world it would describe. I am not one to voluntarily stir up the past, for that is what I cannot help doing all the time anyway. Nowadays, when there is nothing to traveling freely anywhere, the fuss I am making here of these homecomings must seem odd. But those who still remember the Berlin Wall and the Iron Curtain might relate to the feeling of being cut off from one's roots and kinfolks for long decades.

Young Frédi then gave a moving speech to celebrate the occasion and the passing of the book as a bridge between the worlds, the old and the new. And because he was preparing to become a man of God, he was able to suggest between his lines that hidden dream world, that America that exists only in dreams and in prayers. He is good with words, for he means them. I trust he will become a bishop, like his grandfather. He is now minister of the village Apácaszakállas, and his flock thinks the sun cannot rise before he awakens. But he is also active in the affairs of the Reformed Church nationally, and many threads in the fabric of that bi-ethnic society run through his hands.

Let me just add here that Marina was sitting through all this with both empathic joy and bafflement, for she was not yet able to piece all those many words (that she already knew) together when they are, as they were, spoken rapidly. It was simply impossible to stop and translate them in the middle of all that emotional happening. A dearer treasure than she is, is not imaginable.

Whatever else may have happened in the course of this memorable trip, the one of consequence for him was a chance visit to that little bookstore in the historic Castle District of Budapest. It is in the Fortuna courtyard off the András Hess *tér*, right next to his favorite restaurant. There he found a book by Dudás Rudolf:

Földrajzi Neveink Szumér-Magyar Nyelve (*The Sumerian-Hungarian Tongue of our Geographical Names*). It was published 1992 in Madeira Park (Canada?) by *Szikamber Kör* with copyright number 417911 C, but it has no ISBN listing and I cannot find it on Google.

It shows hundreds of present-day Hungarian place names and details their etymology from their original form, complete not only with ancient word stem and agglutinated modifiers, but each of those syllables is reflected also in both its Latin-letter transliteration and Sumerian cuneiform equivalent. Here are two examples of names mentioned in the present writing: (the following is given in sequence: today's proper name; Sumerian transliteration; translation): Eger; E-GUR$_{10}$; harvesting plain; or Léva; L(i)—É—Ú-A; grove of the plains temple. I am omitting the cuneiform, for I would have to draw in those crowfeet by hand as Dudás had done, and I can tell you that they are formidable. But he found all this too fascinating not to follow it up, even though those place names had no recognizable meaning in Hungarian. But their etymology indicated that they had an ancient origin that predated a later Slavic or Vlach colonization of much of the area in question.

The Sumerian connection

Once back in Corvallis, he made a beeline to books like Samuel Kramer's definitive, although already somewhat dated treatise on the subject (*The Sumerians, Their History, Culture and Character*, 1963). He was captivated by the story and the findings and awed by the difficulty of the work, which was all presented in a most pleasantly readable prose (see also *SCYTA szó—és mondattár*, Scythian Word and Sentence Collection by Dudás Rudolf, Vancouver 1998, Copyright No. 470403 C).

According to Kramer's summary of this arduous process, the eventual decipherment of the Sumerian script came about in a three steps, a sequence in which the discovery of Rosetta Stone-like texts written in three different, at first unknown languages and symbols were crucial.

One of these texts, made up of only some forty recurring characters appeared to be phonetic and turned out to be Old Persian, an Indo-European, inflective tongue. Once this code was cracked with the help of modern Persian, it then served as the bridge to the others.

Unlike the first, the second of the trilingual texts consisted of a large number of recurring units indicative of syllabic writing. With the help of known proper names from the Old Persian text, this second version was eventually also elucidated in the course of many decades of hard work by a string of dedicated scholars. It came to be known as Akkadian, an ancient Semitic and likewise inflective language.

The third segment of these trilingual documents was the hardest nut to crack. Since the syllabic values of the cuneiform signs did not trace well to Semitic words, it seemed to be reasonable to assume that the cuneiform system of writing, used and adapted later by the Akkadians, was invented by a non-Semitic people, one whose existence was totally unknown and unexpected up to that time. Comparative studies of the by then quite well-known bilingual texts with the third and unknown one showed no linguistic affinities with the latter, and analyses of its structure revealed it to be an agglutinative language like Turkish or Hungarian. The entire process of elucidation took well over a hundred years and continues to be in progress.

This whole intricately interwoven detective story would have been fascinating for him even without the Hungarian connection, however fragile that looked, but with it, he had no choice but to read the whole 300-page book from cover to cover. And there it was, at the very end, in the appendix, that he found the key reference that really sparked his interest anew. Not that the story itself was lacking the motivation to keep on reading. The history, theology, rites, myths, literature, societal organization, and legal codes of this people who were the first to develop and institute civilized life and then invented the means to create a record of it all on sun-baked clay tablets to make their moment in history endure and who spoke a language similar to his own was for him more captivating than science fiction.

But always a stickler for detail and a skeptic, he kept on wondering throughout the book, how all those ingenious elucidators of Sumerian were able to assign present-day sounds and phonemes (as represented by the letters of the Latin alphabet) to those arcane symbols of old made up of a collection of interconnected wedges, when all of it had to be first pressed through the sieve of an Aryan and then a Semitic inflective language. For the only thing they had to go on at first were proper names in Old Persian (had they not?), and I dare guess that even today's scholars of Modern Persian have only slight clues to what their predecessor tongue may have sounded like. And from there they had to make the great leap forward (actually backward) to Akkadian and assume that those names of kings and gods may have had similar sound values in both languages. But for Akkadian at least, there are known, Semitic survivor tongues for a remote, yet existing reference. Not so for the final, greatest of leaps to this third, unknown language that they had named "Sumerian" somewhat arbitrarily, it seems to me, and that they declared extinct, without successors!

What came to his mind, of course, was the possibility, the game, of making comparisons between Hungarian and Sumerian words and never mind that they were separated by some five millennia, based, however tenuously, on that near-imperishable permanence of the consonant sequences in agglutinative word structure. He read some of the secondary literature on this and found that other nonprofessionals have already tried this and had met with the expected disdain and ridicule on the part of professional philology.

The gist of this experience was a bitter pill for him; for the first time in his life, he met up with the realization that something was "too late" for him. He should have started with Sanskrit, Hebrew, Farsi, Greek, and who knows what else no later than in kindergarten in addition to a most thorough study of Hungarian to undertake a meaningful reexamination of the soundings and meanings of those cuneiform symbols to see if the idiom of their writers was really extinct as the specialists claimed. To see if perhaps mistakes had been made in the beginning of the elucidation process that then carried through the building of this still only precariously balanced edifice.

Because once a scientific structure is in place, the workers who built it resist any change to it fiercely. The ruling paradigm permits no challenge, for that would invalidate the proud accomplishments of its creators. Well, too bad! He realized regretfully that for him it was too late for a serious involvement.

But it was not too late for a bit of dilettantizing, just for the fun of it. The *dies faustus* came for this when he finally arrived at the aforementioned appendix, where he found something that anyone who does not speak Hungarian would readily overlook:

> In addition to the main Sumerian dialect, which was probably known as *Emegir*, "the princely tongue," there were several others which were less important. One of these, the *Emesal*, was used primarily by female deities, women, or eunuchs.

Now, women today, maybe not deities but women of respect and social standing like one's favorite aunt for instance, like Bözsi *néni*, aunt Liz, do not speak a "less important dialect," at least not in Hungary. Instead, what they do is something very important. Something that Bözsi *néni* did on her visits to Léva, when she would sit with him and his brother in front of the fireplace in the evening, while the snow was blowing outside. She told fairy tales. A fairy tale is called a *mese*. *Mesél-ni* means to tell fairy tales (*ni* is the infinitive ending in today's usage), and the one who does it is always a *néni*: "*Néni mesél*" ("Aunt tells a tale"). In Sumerian, the corresponding female personage is called *nin*, of whom, when she is telling a story, we can say the same thing (if Kramer is right) as we did in Hungarian: "*nin [E]mesal*" (woman speaks). Now, this uncanny correspondence may rest on nothing but a coincidence: the chance, that the consonants of both subject and predicate happen to be the same and that the sentence happens to have the same meaning in both languages. But it does not end there. There is also the other "dialect" to consider, the princely one, the *[E]megir*.

Megir, of course, looks similar to *magyar*. But drawing inferences of equivalence from this similarity is a risky assumption, for different morphemes that are transliterated the same way (from the Sumerian) may not be phonetically identical, although they could be, of course. The sound value of this *g* in *megir* is therefore in question, as is perhaps that of its other consonants also. The *g* in *magyar*, on the other hand, is not the *g* as we know it; it is part of the digraph *gy* which is a distinct consonant peculiar to Hungarian and is denoted with a separate symbol (ɟ) in the International Phonetic Alphabet. It is written as *gy* only because of the dearth of sounds and therefore of letters in Latin, on which our script is based. But what expert can say today what the *g* in *megir* sounded like, and that it did not sound like the *gy* in *magyar*?

As to the Sumerian "prince" with his *[E]megir* "dialect," we can surmise that he used it to explain things to his people, exactly what the word denotes in Hungarian today: *magyar[áz]* (*[E]megir*), which means "he explains" or more simply, "he speaks." And he does it today with his Magyar tongue, as he did five thousand years ago with his Megir one. I may add here that the Hungarian *gy* sound is rendered by many different symbols in texts written by peoples of different tongues who came in contact with the Magyars in the course of history. So it may well have been the sound that Sumerologists decided to denote with a Latin *g*.

There were many other examples of such comparisons that he found, all closely similar both in form and meaning, but none were judged to have credible etymologies by the experts whom he consulted. To show you a few, there is Sumerian *udug* meaning "evil spirit" with its Hungarian equivalent of *ördög* meaning "devil" (*r* and *l* are often elided before dental stops like *d* in speaking and therefore may not be notated in writing). There is Ishk-ur, the rain god, with the Hungarian equivalent of esők ura (s=sh), *lord of the rains*! Another one is Sumerian *'lil* which is interpreted as air, breath, or spirit. This comes in several forms in Hungarian like *lél-ek* (soul) or *lél-egzet* (breath). Or take *birdu* in Nunbirdu, "Nippur's stream," where Enlil (the air god) fell in love with Ninlil (*néni lélek*, "lady spirit") as she was bathing there. Well, *birdu* translates simply to *fürdő* (bath) in Hungarian, and Nun(?)-birdu may therefore not have been the proper name of a stream but just a water hole for bathing.

And so it goes, on and on. The singing of hymns was accompanied by the instrument *adab* interpreted as "drum" that is called *dob* in Hungarian to this day. But the best example to illustrate the problem with such layman's comparisons is given by the early historical kingly name *Mesanepadda*. This one he interpreted as mesa-nep-adda, in Hungarian: *mező-nép-attya* (*mező* = plains, *nép* = people, *attya* = father of; hence, "father of the prairie people,") a splendid name to be called by one's subjects at the dawn of history. But no, the truth of the professional Sumerologist is different: the correct etymology for him is *Mes-ane-pada*, which is thought to mean "hero chosen by the god An."

Be all this as it may, we have another, as yet unused key here to the door of understanding Sumerian: the Hungarian language. A door that is still only barely ajar. Why not use this key to help it open more widely? It seems to me, that it is a shady side of Hungarian mentality that prevents this from happening. The inflective-language-speaking scholars, who did all that fine work up to now are understandably happy with their status quo. It is now up to the Hungarian Academy of Letters and Sciences, and to the Cathedra of Finno-Ugric Languages of the

University at Budapest, to make use of this key that only they possess. But they are bending over backward to avoid doing so. They are worried about the disapproval of their foreign colleagues. They are afraid of looking ridiculous, as if they were in search of more noble ancestors than the primitive, fish-smelling Ugrians. And so they choose to stay stuck in the rut of the language-family scheme that locked them into the Finno-Ugric group where they have learned to feel safely at home over the last hundred years.

They forget that the scientific method is not to accept a hypothesis on the authority of others and then spend lifetimes to prove it (as they have done), but to question the accepted paradigm and then attempt to disprove it as new insights arise. *Dixi*! I said it! And I feel good about it, and never mind my quaint derivation of paradise from *paradicsom* (remember?), which was a bit tongue-in-cheek, I admit. Detractors may even argue, for instance, that *barát* is not Hungarian but an Indo-European loan word, where it occurs in several forms: b-r-t (brat), b-r-d (Brud-er), or f-r-t (frat-er).

How to get to Baja and stay for a while

That is Baja, California, and unlike the city of Baja (pronounced baya) near the tragic, sixteenth-century battlefield of Mohács on the Danube, its "j" is pronounced as "h," the Spanish way. It is the Baja where we had already been, but this time it was to be in earnest. It all started out at a meeting in Banff, Canada, where he first made friends with Yoav. Dr. Bashan is a bundle of chutzpah, as used in the positive American sense, one of nonconforming, gutsy audacity, a true extrovert that is, who had set up shop at the Centro de Investigaciones Biológicas del Noroeste (CIB for short) in La Paz, near the southern end of the Baja Peninsula.

It all began with chats on nitrogen fixation—Yoav is the world authority on the diazotrophic bacterium *Azospirillum*—and then progressed along more personal lines. It turned out that Yoav was also an ex-soldier turned scientist, a desert and nature lover, and a greener of our abused planet. He himself, in turn, always careful not to let his introverted side show at scientific meetings, found this guy's exuberance appealing, and so he dropped the word, though innocently and without any ulterior motives, that he always wanted to do some work in Baja ever since he first experienced its serene beauty some twenty-five years ago. And it seems that Yoav took note of that comment.

But good things take their time to ripen. Time went on, work went on, Gal finished his degree in Granada and came to work at his lab. While there, his *alma mater* in Londrina happened to organize a symposium on global warming, and Gal mobilized his contacts in Brazil to invite him (me) for a keynote talk. Now, Londrina is in the State of Paraná and so are the Waterfalls of Iguaçu. So the colleagues in Londrina set them up for a trip there (after the meeting was over) by bus, so that they could see the countryside. He had already seen Niagara Falls and so he did not expect much, while Marina, who studies up on such things beforehand, knew better. The trip was not exciting but insightful; the towns they passed through reminded him of Hungary and Mexico at the same time, but there was something wrong with what he saw there.

The bus wound its way through farmland, which could not be true since he distinctly remembered reading in a magazine, fifty years before this bus ride, a fascinating, contemporaneous adventure story of explorers passing through a virgin jungle that they called the *Zöld Pokol* (Green Hell), while he was sitting in an easy chair looking out on the apple orchard in Bethlenfalva, when a large branch loaded with his favorite, almost-ripe apples broke off a tree nearby. They were the *erdélyi jónatán* (Transsylvanian Jonathan) variety, a loss but it mattered little, for there were many more. But that broken branch somehow connected to the explorers slashing their way with their machetes through the dense vegetation of the *Zöld Pokol*, of which there was also plenty more, and he could not help feeling protective of the forest, and he wanted it left alone, unslashed.

That article left a picture of the Mato Grosso fixed in his child's mind, of a three-canopy jungle-forest that should have been where the plowed fields now stretched to the horizon, obscured only by the dust cloud of his bus. Yes, all that destruction had happened during his lifetime, while he was busy with other things. They had come from Europe, from Germany and Italy to slash and cut all the trees down and to create yet another man-made semidesert as far as he was concerned, although for the slashers, it may have become a new home, a kind of paradise. One of which they were now mighty proud.

It is a miracle that Gaya did not make the great cataracts of Iguaçu dry up in revenge! She might be saving that for later. They are indescribable; at least my computer is not capable of finding words for it. They are one of the greatest wonders of the world, and they are one of the few things that I would really like to experience again. We have a big picture of them hanging on a wall, and when we happen to look at it together with Marina, we just nod silently. That trip to Brazil was an intense and glorious two weeks with flashes of insight into many things, even though it was one of those that did not take long to ripen, it came and went in the flick of an eyelash. But the Baja episode took its time to gel. The next event leading to it was in Mexico City, a rare foreign jaunt in which Marina did not participate.

It was yet another meeting, for his work was productive and there were always new results to report. The foreign participants were housed in the plush Zona Rosa District, in an old hotel graced with the kind of elegance paneled in dark wood that is now considered faded, but whose *ambience* he can appreciate, for he grew up with it as a child. I do not remember the details of the meeting, but its scheduling was such that both he and Yoav found themselves with time left over at the end before the scheduled flight home. Now, Yoav had met a young colleague at a session that he chaired and since she also had time on her hands, he promptly invited her to an excursion to Tepozotlán.

At breakfast of that day off, Yoav suggested to his friend (me) to come along with them. The friend declined; he already knew Tepozotlán and had planned to explore this new part of the city around the Zona Rosa. Also, he had the feeling that something was afoot between Luz and Yoav that might need some early privacy to get growing and did not wish to be in the way of it.

And right he was; the excursion turned into an adventure and that adventure soon matured into an enduring bond. Had he gone along, it might not have turned out that way, and he kept reminding Yoav of it jokingly: "Don't forget, *amigo*, you owe me one." So it became Yoav's turn to reciprocate and he did it in style.

He obtained a grant from CONACyT, the Consejo Nacional de Ciencia y Tecnología, to invite a scientist to work with him on soil restoration in Baja! Needless to say, he jumped at the chance; it was something he had dreamed of doing for twenty-five years! And to top it all off, not only did ARS come through with enthusiastic support for the idea, but Marina felt intrigued by this next adventure also.

The recurrent Dream

As I am writing this, I am not sure why, but I am suddenly aware again of having realized the American Dream. I own a nice house, two nice cars, am totally debt-free and enjoy the luxury of a generous retirement check that arrives regularly at my bank account. And all that in the middle of the Great Recession with the news reporting half a million people losing their jobs each month for almost a year now and with hundreds of thousands being evicted from their homes as a consequence.

Capitalism seems to be going the way of communism: down the drain, that is, even though (or perhaps because) the chief executives of the financial companies are still, or again, paying themselves their obscene tens of millions in bonuses as a reward for having wrecked the economy, while they are firing tens of thousands of their less fortunate employees in order to line their own pockets with the loot so saved.

And I, I hike up Bishop's Peak in the morning and then go to read the *LA Times* at my favorite café, water my plants, harvest my apricots, and nectarines (*my* for all these things is only a euphemism; they are really all Marina's) and then have time to read and write. The only thing I do not do is go fishing, but that is only because I admire fish; they are weightless, otherworldly marvels of silvery moonshine down there in their cool element, and I wish people would leave them alone. I keenly feel my bond of direct descent from them, even and perhaps especially when Marina prepares red snapper for dinner the way only she can. My irrational rationale is that I did not catch and kill him (it), and if *I* did not eat him, someone else would.

"This rationale is not only one of the many ways in which we do not live up to our convictions, but it is a blatant example of bad faith and a blot on this manuscript," Marina added in with red ink, upon reading it. "Our patterns of consumption have a direct effect on the supplies made available to satisfy consumer demand. If we ate less fish (or beef, or *foie gras*), supplies would adjust to demand and the oceans would continue to be alive with fish."

On to La Paz

If people who go to Baja listened to Marina, many of them might not go, for they go there to fish. That is called sportfishing as if killing animals for fun were a sport. But back to the tale. It was more than ten years ago now that the Baja adventure was ready to start. The last thing they had to do before taking off now was to find a four-wheel drive vehicle, and there was little time left for shopping. The choice was limited; American cars were known to have abandoned any claim to reliability decades ago (Ford seems to be coming back of late), and Nissan had the only authorized Japanese dealership in La Paz. They found a solid-looking, white Pathfinder at the Nissan place in Albany (Oregon) and made a quick decision.

It must have been too quick and easy for the normal sales routine, for the salesman, having consulted with the boss, came running back to announce that they had made a mistake, the price tag on the car was in error, and the real price was three thousand dollars higher. They got up in disgust to leave, for they knew well what was going on. He was particularly upset, for it made him feel as if he looked like a pushover. You do not want to be taken for a fool. But barely had they left the building and the same salesman was already running after them to offer a good deal after all. Having signed the papers, he could not help adding something like "You are lucky we had little time for this, or you'd get a false advertising suit instead of a deal," for which he earned a disapproving look from Marina. She is confrontational only when it really matters.

Then, they were finally off. First stop was in San Diego, to visit with Kathrine and Gordon. Kat is a classmate of Marina's, back from schooldays in Kaiserswerth, who somehow found Marina by way of Peter (who, of course, still went by the name of Tautfest) on the Internet. Kat achieved her own version of the material American Dream by dealing in real estate. While making a bundle in the booming housing bubble, she also found personal happiness by marrying a businessman in computers who is the only Republican I know but who is a kind, compatible, interesting, and hospitable guy, really pleasant to be with, a swell type in every respect, except for his misguided politics. Well, no one is perfect.

On the way south, the road eventually leads to Santo Tomás. It is the first logical spot for an overnight stop south of the border, especially if you cross it at Tecate, the thing to do if you want to avoid Tijuana, which by now has become a battlefield of warring gangs of *narco trafficantes*. Upon crossing Santo Tomás

Creek, a great valley opens up to the east, and every time he passed it, he wished for time to explore, to follow it upstream rock hopping, and to search for the things of the sort that he finds on his roamings through the worlds.

A red wine is grown there. One without pretensions but one that is savvy rather than naive. It is just good and earthy: no hints of peaches or gooseberries but very gulletable. Its bottles are identified on their labels simply as "Santo Tomás," and you can drink it with your first authentic Mexican dinner at the equally down-to-earth but cozy restaurant of the motel there. Your room then introduces you to what is coming. Baja is not for the finicky tourist. You love Baja or you hate it.

It is a thousand miles long, and if you are crazy you can drive it in two dawn-to-dusk days. Unfortunately, but it may be only he who feels that way, that paved road has done much to make its dust-blown settlements grow during the past quarter century. A few have now become good-size towns. I will mention only San Ignacio on the way down this time, for it is not quite a town yet, but it is another one of those places where he could have lived for the rest of his days, given a chance. You drive along on the high and dry central plateau of the peninsula crossing it from west to east without any hint of its coming, until you descend all of a sudden into an oasis of palm trees. That is San Ignacio.

Regretfully and shame faced, I admit that he never took the time for exploring the area around it. That kind of time you do not take, you make it. Off hand, the oasis looks like a sizeable rift valley with a running stream in the middle. You cannot see the tops of its tall palm trees until you drive down into it. It was always only a point of transit for him, and in that respect, it resembles life itself. Maybe that is its chief attraction, come to think of it: it is lifelike. But then again, it has all the traits of endurance that one misses in life so much. One would like to hang on to something lasting, and so when you chance into San Ignacio, you envy the locals for being surrounded by things that have been there for a long time now. Unchanged, paved highway notwithstanding, which mercifully passes it by. You have to get off the main road to get in, and once you are in, you'd better have a mindset that appreciates little things, or else you may not see how big the things are that you found.

Those sorts of things are a matter of perception. The sensations your eye registers upon stopping your car at the curb in the little *zócalo* are individually not all that appealing. Everything is pretty run down as old things usually are. A store or two that have nothing you want to buy, an eating place that does not make you feel hungry (there is a much better one a little off the *zócalo*), a graffiti-covered community building whose business is none of yours, and a weather-beaten church whose message you may not agree with. If you look at it that way, you have missed seeing what is there and you quickly move on, unless you stay overnight at the Presidente (now the La Pinta), which is not on the *zócalo*. But in contrast to this town square it is new, and strangely, it is this very newness that is in an unseemly hurry to point out to you how rapidly it is aging already. But it still has a swimming pool, and for Marina there is no better welcome mat than that. And the welcome mat, if it means its message, can color the mood of your stay.

Now, how we actually perceive our world much of the time, is the way that traveler did it, who stopped, looked around, saw only the disparate, unappealing detail, shook his head, and left in a hurry. That is how the receptors in our eyes do it, the rods and cones that register individual, disjointed bits of information, photons reflected to them from unknown, alien surfaces. They register massive globs of brown and diffuse splotches of green actually when what we really "see" is a tree. The finished percepts that our brains are creating for us are miracles of unreality, but how exactly those come about, we do not fully understand yet. Are they formed and completed from simple sensations by some sequential process of integration, or are they basic to experience, do they leap out in an *a priori* way as preformed shapes, *Gestalten*, from the world that surrounds us? Who knows?! Couldn't it be that different brains do not go about perceiving the world the same way and therefore come up with different results, maybe because their past experiences from early on channeled their functioning differently?

His brain, at any rate, works the unified *Gestalt* way; he did not even notice the parts that make up the San Ignacio *zócalo* when he first stopped there. He just thought, *I like this place*. The pieces fell in place later bit by bit into what was already an unshakably complete whole.

First, there was the refreshingly cool ambiance of those stately, old Indian laurel trees that managed to shade out any appearance of neglect that might otherwise have hung over the place like rags from a scarecrow. All right, so there was neglect in evidence, but it was not the same kind that American highways showed before Lady Bird Johnson had the litter cleaned up. It had an endemic feel to it; it belonged there. Like a garage whose venerable contents have, after decades of stratification, out-accumulated the family car from its home. It did not feel impoverished because it was not. Whatever surplus means San Ignacio may (or may not) have for shoring up appearances is spent instead on priorities known only to itself, and those are not geared to satisfy finicky strangers with alien standards who might (or might not) chance by someday.

Then there was that church of hand-hewn stone that has looked down on the square for some two hundred years now. It had buried the bodies and the language of its builders and sent their souls to a heaven where they did not wish to go. But after that, it had also helped new generations to be born, to live, to grow old and to die. It, in turn, had never asked for help from anyone. Did it turn cold of heart in its loneliness as it grew old? He would have liked to know, and he knew that he knew the answer already while he was still wishing to find it. Just looking at that church made him feel the unknowable, the smile of the sphinx. Nat King Cole's velvet voice bubbled up in his ears as he pondered the message of those stone walls:

> Is it only 'cause you're lonely, men have blamed you
> For that Monalisa strangeness in your smile?
> Are you warm, are you real Mona Lisa,
> Or just a cold and lonely, lovely work of art?

That old general store! It must have been kept stocked before the occasional truck started to make the run there from north or south on the new road, for people need shoes, knives, and everything else that they cannot make themselves. Or did they make everything themselves that they needed then? Or did it all get there on the backs of burros from five hundred miles away? It must have, how else? What kind of community centered there on that square when those old trees were just starting to grow? What kind of music did they play for their fiesta to celebrate Ignacio's Day? The square had been there a good hundred years before the Emperor Maximilian brought his Austrian tunes with him, whose melodies and rhythms then pervaded Mexico like the smell of *carne asada* pervades the noses of hungry people. What came before that? Did the aborigines who built the church leave behind echoes of their drumbeat for a while? Did early settlers from outlying ranchos come in on market day and did they eat at that ancient eating place where today's visitors dare not touch the food? Did they take deep draughts of a drink fermented from the sweet dates that the padres had ordered from Spain by caravel mail, expressly to build a local economy?

I really got stuck in San Ignacio, didn't I? And I must get on, for sometimes I feel that I am running out of time. This is not a travel guide, so let me just say that he savored the glories of the Baja road from the last earth-bound barrel cactus to the first sky-seeking candle tree. And that includes even the Viscaino Desert, which is so truly dismal that he did not pause to identify its plants that hang on there somehow, even though the jet stream-driven rains from the north do not dip down that far south, while the southern monsoons run out of steam before they can get all the way up there.

From there on, however, the gray-brown world of Central Baja started greening out, little by little ever so lowly, of course, for there were still a few hundred miles to go to La Paz. The southern rainy season, made up of a few hurricanes that usually move north way offshore but still provide the needed moisture, was late that year, it seems, for by the time they passed Loreto flowers and greenery were in increasing evidence.

El Comitán

Once they arrived in La Paz, Yoav first put them up in the guesthouse of the CIB (Centro de Investigaciones Biológicas). That was not bad, but it was in the middle of nowhere, and so they were in a hurry to get settled. After a thorough survey of the range of local housing two possibilities offered themselves as most likely.

One was a fancy and expensive modern apartment in the Lomas de Palmira area, on the left-hand side of the Paseo Alvaro Obregón after that main drag leaves town toward the harbor of Pichilingue. On the fourth floor, facing the bay with a full view of the sunset over the water and furnished in the vivid colors of the Mexican spirit. An unseasonal squall was just reflecting a rainbow over this bay called locally the Mar Bermejo, the Vermillion Sea, when they first surveyed the scene from the balcony, and so it was a sore temptation not to fall in love with it and move in without further ado like the swallows that had just completed their migration from the north. Had a band been serenading in the park below, it could have played to celebrate the occasion nothing but the song that they had first heard in Oaxaca:

De colores,	Of colors
de colores se visten los campos en la primavera.	Full of colors the fields turn in the spring
De colores,	Of colors
de colores son los pajarillos que vienen de afuera.	Bright of colors are the birds from afar.
De colores,	Of colors,
de colores es el arco iris que vemos lucir.	A gleam of colors is the rainbow above.
Y por eso los grandes amores	And therefore the great loves
De muchos colores me gustan a mi.	Of splendid colors are the ones I like.

Well, fortunately, one of them had a mind of good, common horse sense, and it was not his, although his childhood nickname was *ló*, and that means horse, adopted and used by Marina to this day. "*Nada de tus tonterias pour moi, mein lieber ló* (None of your foolishness for me, my dear horse)," she declared (for by this time she spoke the lingo fluently enough to mix any metaphor in four foreign languages) after having considered the situation. "I prefer not to be stuck here with expatriates, tourists, and local upper class, while you drive twenty miles every day clear across town to your institute to do something useful." And that was that, no arguments. One of his better character traits is that when he senses horse sense in something, he can also admit it and adapt to it cheerfully.

As it happens, the institute, the CIB, sits on the shore of the large inlet that is pinched off from the Bahia de La Paz by the Mogote, a wide strip of land shaped like a thumb, west of the city. And right next to the CIB is a settlement, semiprimitive and inhabited mostly by winter nomads from the north but also by some locals, who live in accommodations ranging from a few new and elegant houses to old and semidecrepit trailers, that is to say no longer mobile "mobile" homes. This is El Comitán. Or was then, without telephone or mail service or garbage pick-up but with a truck driving by once a week with large *garrafones* of bottled water.

Its streets of sand were cut out from the semiarid tropical forest, which forms a transition zone there between the Sonoran desert scrub and the sarcocaulescent scrub, as these formations are known to plant geographers. But with rainfall mostly upward of ten inches a year, this is no longer real desert vegetation. On the contrary, the plants that make up the flora here create a botanist's paradise; they come in all sizes and bloom in all colors. The stateliest ones were left in place by the developers to embellish the plots where they hoped people would settle, while the lesser ones came back quickly on their own. On one of these half-acre plots stood the trailer, the other one of the two possibilities of Marina's short list for housing, and that was where they dropped anchor. It also had the important added advantage that living a frog's hop away from the institute easily permitted Marina to tutor the colleagues in English. That is very important for Mexican scientists, for only international publications (written in English) count for professional advancement and promotion.

From their front porch, it was a leisurely five-minute walk to his desk that looked out over that wide expanse of the inlet across to the Mogote. And what was he expected to do there? That was entirely up to him. That sounds fine on the surface; it is a very gentlemanly way to do work, but in actual fact, it is much easier to follow an agenda already laid out for you. There is always a price to pay, and the price of freedom in such a scientific environment (and maybe others also) is responsibility, the expectation weighing on you to produce something worthwhile and preferably in an expeditious manner. Since it was clear that the year he was to spend there was not enough for field experiments focused on revegetation, especially as there were neither funds nor facilities available to conduct them, he had to come up with a reasonable alternative in focusing on a problem to solve.

One of the problems in the La Paz area was people. There were some twenty thousand of them when they saw it first, but in the next twenty-five years, the population of the city had grown to over three hundred thousand. People, a problem though they may be, cannot be solved, but the mess they sometimes get themselves in can be worked on. Such a mess was the vast tracts of land that had been bulldozed free of vegetation to accommodate this frantic growth. But the vagaries of an unstable economy often forced the developers to abandon their projects, leaving the broken surface of the land open to the wind. And the wind then picked up that surface and blew its now unprotected topsoil as dust into the city, where it created respiratory problems, especially for children, and the city government was called upon to find a remedy.

The answer to such a plight, of course, is to reestablish the *status quo ante*, namely to put the plants back where they had been. But the plants were uncooperative, even resentful, it seemed. They did not like the dead, mineral soil that was left there by the wind, for it was pretty much baked free of microbial life by the subtropical sun, and, as you already know by this time, only a few hardy weeds can grow in places like that. This then was the situation to be addressed, although a solution was clearly out of his reach.

People, however, were not a problem in El Comitan. There were few, and they left you alone, unless you yourself chose to socialize with them. Still, they were a bit surprised by the friendly attention of their welcoming committee as they woke after their first night's sleep, which was restful for the mice had not moved in yet to rustle between the walls. As they stepped out on their porch, there was the committee, three large, black *zopilotes*, smiling at them with open arms from their perches on a giant Cardon cactus a few yards away. That apparently is a habit of El Comitan vultures, they check out newcomers. And if they drop in for inspection in the early morning, they open their wings arched forward to dry them in the sun from the night's fall of dew.

It was an auspicious omen of welcome, but the birds seemed disappointed, for they never came back. Who came back to stay was a sizeable, active and persistent Gila woodpecker. He did not deem the newcomers worthy of notice; instead, he was preoccupied with their metal mailbox and their equally metal rain deflector on the kitchen chimney. On these he practiced his staccato rhythms taking turns with each instrument, for they produced different tones that echoed out into space for miles. Like Pityu *kakas* in Léva, he was a character actor. His message to the whole community was "I am Geronimo, the most *macho* of all peckers (of tin), so take note of my glorious presence."

Behind the trailer there were three large *pinos salados*, or salt pines, so called locally for the ability of tamarix to tolerate and take up salt and to drip any excess of it back on the ground below. Because that was the only shade within sight and hearing, they parked their Pathfinder there until they knew better. There was always an excess of salt around; it came with the water in the pipes. This had not been so when the settlement was first established and the wells were dug, but it is in the genes of the white man to exploit and ravage his environment without bothering with foresight. "*Quidquid agis, prudenter agas et respice finem,*" his Latin teacher would have told them, I am sure, for he repeated this favorite adage of his in class whenever the occasion called for it (as I do also in these lines, for it cannot be said too often).

No, the first colonists overplanted; they started with palms, no less, and palms suck up water like a fire hose. So by the time they got there, the communal water supply was pleasantly saline, just the way those *pinos* like it. There was also a large, old Pitaya Dulce (organ-pipe cactus) in front and an equally impressive Garambullo (old-man cactus) in the back, next to the palm-frond covered *palapa*. This is a screened gazebo-like structure, often used by folks who have no air-conditioning to spend the night in it. Oh yes, there was also a small pepper tree, a red-blooming oleander by the gate, a palo fierro by the back steps, and a couple of almendros, but otherwise, the whole half acre was as bare as a *zopilote*'s red pate.

Is work that is fun work?

In the morning, walking to work, he would cross the paths, sinuous grooves in the dust that the rattlesnakes had made while hunting at night. He adopted Yoav's informal, Israeli style of a work uniform, best for the climate but an eyebrow-raiser for the spiffy local colleagues: shorts, toeless sandals, and no socks. On his own, he would not have dared to violate the local dress-code, but Yoav was like a duck in water in this and most other matters. He did what he liked and let disapprovers stand on their heads and turn purple. And they did so frequently. Did he really not care, or did he crave acceptance secretly, hidden deep down as most people do? If so, it did not show. It's the work, and its results that matter, was his philosophy, not how dignified you make yourself look. He must have been a sore vexation for most locals, although he met a few *investigadores* there who did have a compatible northern work ethic.

Some of these went out of their way to be helpful. There was for instance José-Luis León de la Luz, who did honor to his splendid name by being a lion of a light, a *lumen et auctoritas*, in plant taxonomy. There was no plant in Baja that he did not know, not only by first and last name, but he was also thoroughly familiar with its preferences for climate, water, and soil, as well as its competitive or co-operative lifestyle. This knowledge came in very handy, for what he (the biologist) decided to do when he finally had his mind made up was to look into some of the mechanisms that individual plants use to establish themselves on their own on barren, mineral soil and how they then form the nucleus of communities. This by observation only, of course, for an experimental procedure would have taken at least several but more likely many years.

The observations showed that a chance presence of propagules of mycorrhizal fungi (spores and fungus-colonized root fragments) on a site of seed dispersal is very helpful for successful seedling establishment. In the absence of such propagules, survival of early colonizer plants appears to be unlikely, unless spores are soon provided, born to the site perhaps by the wind, but also by biological vectors (birds, rodents, and bats). As the plants then grow, some remain solitary introverts depending on the nature of their characters, but others like mesquite (*Prosopis articulata*) or lomboy (*Jatropha cinerea*) become what is known in the jargon as "nurse plants."

Such plants are also called keystone species; they are crucial to the formation of some semidesert plant communities. They develop dense canopies early and those act as windbreaks. As wind speed drops between their leaves and branches, wind-borne dust particles drop to the ground below the canopy where they accumulate to form a mound. Their surface films are laden with nutrient ions, which attract plant-growth promoting bacteria (like Yoav's nitrogen-fixing *Azospirillum*) and stimulate copious growth of the fine, symbiotic hyphae of mycorrhizal fungi that help to establish their host plant in the first place. The hyphae permeate the growing mound of dust and stabilize it by exuding gluelike substances (e.g., glomulin), which cement the loose particles into water- and wind-stable soil aggregates that are no longer subject to easy erosion.

The biological system so established is called a "resource island." Taproots are then able to penetrate deep down to water-bearing layers of soil, and transpiration from the leaves helps to pump the moisture up to quench the thirst of the entire island. For by this time, the nurse plant is no longer alone as it is well on its way to fulfill its function: under the cool shade of its canopy and in the fine aeolian soil around it an increasing number of nursling plants have found shelter, waiting to grow to adulthood while the nurse senesces and eventually dies. In time, the islands may coalesce and barren ground is transformed into a live, green carpet. To recognize and describe this process was what he could do toward solving the people problem of La Paz mentioned above.

This process of resource-island formation could be read like in a book from the disturbed, semi-disturbed, and undisturbed plots in and around the El Comitan settlement since these areas displayed a succession of plant establishment and development over two decades. The lesson learned was readily applicable to any large-scale future effort in revegetation by the city. It was simple: if you want your plants to survive and thrive, you need to recreate a natural, live, microbe-inhabited soil that they depend on. If you don't, you can plant them but they are not likely to survive long. As for him, the whole process was nothing but fun, all day long. He came to know every perennial plant in a square mile area (*mas o menos*), counted them, determined their relationships to each other, evaluated those statistically for significance, and kept his eyes peeled for rattlesnakes while doing so.

The subtropical tip of Baja

Life was not all work in El Comitan, however, far from it. The part of Baja south of La Paz is a brick-shaped area fifty miles across and a hundred miles long. It is bisected north to south by the Sierra de la Laguna, whose highest peak reaches up to a little over seven thousand feet. It is a lush, green paradise that produces veritable clouds of the most colorful butterflies toward the end of the rainy season. But the lushness is not overabundant; it is a one-canopy affair, for water even this far south remains limiting. It is on the subhumid side of being semiarid, as climatologists like to call such precipitation patterns. And best of all, it is still mostly wild (or was back then) for mercifully it holds little interest for the hordes of tourists that come to stay in Cabo San Lucas. The Cabo—that is a maze of bars and hotels at the southernmost tip of the peninsula, at land's end, another Costa del Sol.

Of course, a few of the tourists will get in a cab or rent a car and venture away from the Cabos (there is another Cabo also, a nicer and friendlier one, that of San José). But they stay on the road and do not get any further than Todos Santos. This village town of All Saints is a little jewel, a miniature Zacatecas or Guanajuato, but is so in all innocence and simplicity and in spirit only, for there was no money around from silver mines when it was founded. The money just started trickling in of late, when the town made a start toward becoming an artist colony—but it is trying to do so without losing its rugged Baja-Mexican soul. They never managed to stay there for a night or maybe even a week so they could really get the feel of it. But they will remedy that should they ever manage to go and visit there again, as they keep promising themselves: "Let's just hop in the car and drive down to Baja."

Family visits

The family came to visit, Rob and Angie, Peter and Sabine, and Steve.

They were all duly taken to the gorgeous water holes, little known even to the locals, that are formed by the Rio San José, that comes down the eastern side of the Sierra de la Laguna. Not from the *laguna* itself though, for that is only a mountain meadow now, and uphill from the village of Miraflores, where the water holes are, it is not a *rio* but only a trickle of an *arroyo* most of the time. But it has carved large, rounded swimming-pool hollows out of the granite rock, watched only by a few stately *zalates*, what *castillano* Spanish calls *higueras*. Through their long association, these wild fig trees had themselves learned to imitate their arroyo, for they grow their stems and aerial roots smoothly following the contours of the rock faces, as if they wished to embrace them, the same as waterfalls do.

Then they took the boat ride to Isla Partida to snorkel with the *lobos marinos*, or sea lions. He himself is somewhat wary with water adventures like that, maybe because of his empathy with the fish, from whom he claims his lineage. The sea lion must have taken a different route and is no kin of his. But Peter was enthralled by his close encounter with them; he said they seemed to single him out for play and tugged at his fins and fingertips. He felt like he was meeting long-lost relatives. Seems like extroverts relate to each other easily, doesn't it? For the sea lions are no brooders, they go with the flow. Like the dolphins who followed the boat on the way back and had enormous fun ducking in and out of the waves that the fast little vessel made in its wake.

With Steve they made a special excursion to Loreto, up north. Loreto is where the padres made their first stop in conquering California, which some thought at that time to be an island. The mother church of all the later missions was established there, and it is now a regular town, one rightfully sought out by discriminating tourists, for it has not succumbed to the excesses of the Cabo. On the way there they stopped for brunch at his favorite joint in Ciudad Constitución. The only thing they serve at that little rustic restaurant (besides Cidral and Coke) is *bíria de chivo*. This is a soup of goat meat cooked with chilies and herbs. You can get the meat swimming in its broth or separately; then you drink the juice from a cup. The kitchen contains nothing but an open fireplace with a huge metal cauldron over it in which the goat is simmering. The *cocinera* lets you have a spoonful of a taste right out of the pot, to which you say: "*Muy rico*!" for it is truly rich, tender and spicy.

It was Ernesto, his soil-expert technician, a native of the town, which had grown to size during his lifetime, who took him to the *bíria* place. On his own it would never have occurred to him to stop there. Steve surveyed the scene warily at first, and at his father's prompting: "Goat is good," he just shook his head. But then he tried a forkful from his mother's plate, and the lights of understanding were turned on. "Goat is good" had become kind of a family expression.

They stayed overnight in Loreto and then moved on to the adventure. The graded dirt road inland to the Mission of San Javier is kept passable today, for a few of the visitors to the resorts around Loreto find it worth their while to undertake that side trip. What they find there is the most significant monument of the Californias, both Baja and Alta. A church. It is dwarfed by the steep, barren, gray-black slopes of the towering rock formation right next to it, and yet it looms as large as any cathedral considering its place in its unlikely history. After the trek to get there, which is arduous even in a four-wheel drive SUV, you cannot believe what you see. The village around it holds maybe two or three hundred souls who live there in their remote, self-sufficient solitude like in a separate reality. The church, complete with gargoyles, tall, solid, angular, granite-gray, timeless, does not seem to be part of the village; it feels more like a ship left over on the sere bed of a dried-up sea.

Three hundred years ago, when Padre Píccolo arrived there with a couple of mules and an assistant from Loreto, the Cochimí had already heard of the strange newcomers who had started squatting on their favorite fishing spots on the coast. They had a hard time figuring out what made these pale-skins tick, as they watched them from afar: they liked to break their backs baking clay to form, and then piling this *adobe* up in formations that in the end shut the sun and the moon and the stars out of their sight. In such a dark and forbidding cave they then set up crossed pieces of wood to which they nailed the carved effigy of a naked, suffering man. They went on their knees in front of it and sang to it while producing suffocating gray smoke in a shiny vessel, apparently in its honor but more likely to appease it.

When the paleface in his robe and sandals came to them also, they learned to talk to him in time. Then it started dawning on them that the effigy was big magic. It had something to do with the new beasts that they had never seen before but on which a man could ride, and also with those heavy, hollow sticks that made a loud noise and could kill them from afar. Soon they found that the pale faces did not really like to break their own backs cutting, hauling and piling up stones, but preferred that it be done for them by others. For this "it" they had no word yet but were soon to learn one. It was "work." And then they realized that they were the only others around.

They did not go for that at all. Neither could they see why the new big magic wanted to have a stone cave built for itself to hide in, when their own spirit lord, the one they had known from the time before time started, was everywhere and was one with the plants and the animals and the mountains and the sea and with Viggé Biaundó, the sweet water of the spring that was the life-giving center of their world.

What they did see was that the servants of the new big magic, who called themselves *sacerdotes* in the language in which they spoke to it, were followed by others, the ones with the thunder sticks, and if they did not do as they were told, the sticks might thunder at them. So they rose up against this new big magic to drive it out and its followers with it. But then plague and pestilence broke out among them whose horror was unknown and unmatched in the lore of their kind before the coming of the new big magic, and they sent their elders across the hills to the sea where the priests had come from to ask them for help. And the priests came back and said unto them: "See, God is punishing you for not wanting to build his house."

All right, the chronicles that the Jesuit *padres* wrote, do not mention their having used this tactic to gain the natives' cooperation in hauling granite blocks to the site of the present church on their bare backs from a quarry twenty miles away, so I am making this up.

Nevertheless, then, as it is now, it was a sin against God and a crime against man to make a gain or profit from people's fear of pain and death (a tenet that comes to my mind often these days that are full of the discussion how our American health insurance companies are doing just that). Well, the gain was made, the blocks were hauled, and the church stands. By the time *padre* Miguel del Barco finished building that jewel of the California Missions, fifty years had gone by, and the recalcitrant natives had been cowed into abject submission by the plagues. Or maybe they were converted instead to a joyous acceptance of the new work ethic? You decide.

Be that as it may, that church sits there determined to outlast those gray-black cliffs next to it that are ten times its height but are dwarfed by it nevertheless, as if its gargoyles were speaking for it in tongues, repeating words like "*Himmel und Erde werden vergehen, aber meine Worte werden nicht vergehen,*" as *pater* Schuhbauer, the monk from the abbey of Schäftlarn who baptized the little Fox and taught religion at the school in Icking, liked to end his short, pithy, and memorably deep sermons in the old church of Icking, before he built a new one up on the hill.

Yes, the God-Man effigy had promised that his word and with it the realm of his stone church would outlast heaven and earth, and so its servants, with the motto of their order of "*ad maiorem dei gloriam,*" on their lips closed their eyes so that they would not have to see what they could not help seeing, that they had wrenched their hapless charges out of a Garden of Eden into a hell on earth in which they were withering away on their way to an alien paradise where they did not want to go, and all that for the greater glory of God.

Or did they just want to set a monument to some glory for its own sake, their own perhaps, deceiving themselves in the process without ever thinking of it that way?

On self-deception

Self-deception had always been much on his mind. He had been arguing about it with his friend Cohn at LSU, and he discussed it a lot with his friend, Dante, who as a student of philosophy at UC Santa Barbara, had written his thesis on the subject and later published a definitive paper that proved the possibility of this strange quirk of the mind. But he (that's me) could not help holding that a sane mind cannot deceive itself. It was the old problem: can the mind exist independently of the biological machinery that makes up the trillion nerve cells of the brain? For if it can, it is much like an outside observer, like an impartial arbiter maybe, of the conflicting inputs and interests that affect the machinery in its passage through the constant controversy that every living day brings. "Am I doing good or bad by the poor heathen souls and bodies of these deplorable Cochimí, for whom I have made myself responsible?"

The machinery of the nerve cells has evolved to decide matters of daily life not based on some lofty, superordinate principles but on the effect of its decision on the survival of the organism that it serves. Therefore, should a conflict arise between the demands of the organism and the precepts of the principles, there is a problem. Its solution requires a decision on a higher level, the one where the impartial arbiter resides. And the arbiter, who observes the problem as if from above, cannot possibly convince itself that there is no problem; it cannot deceive itself that the problem's reality does not exist while maintaining its sanity. He (that's me again) still clung to the idea of such an arbiter's existence and identifies it with his Atman. That's why he cannot subscribe to the validity of self-deception.

Of course, if there is no Atman, then everything is left to the machinery to sort out, and the machinery is anything but impartial. Its guiding principle is that of *Realpolitik*. Compromises and cost-benefit analyses are the world where it feels at home. "The rocks they haul for me may break their backs, and they are dying of smallpox, but I am sending the souls of my Cochimí to my heaven, so where is the problem? I've done good."

Thoughts of this sort often took him back to Hungary, to one or another episode of its history and the role that Christianity had in shaping it. The story and the fate of the Cochimí and the deeds of the savior of their souls, Juan de Ugarte, reminded him of Vajk, the son of Géza. Géza was the last heathen leader of the seven Magyar tribes at the turn of the first Christian millennium.

This Vajk married a Bavarian princess, and she brought German knights and German priests with her. Was it her influence that led an enamored young Vajk to abandon his ancestral culture and god and to eradicate, with the help of the foreigners, the lore, the history, the records of old in runic writing, and the identity of his people in bloody battles against the past? He even abandoned his name to become crowned as the "apostolic" King István, canonized soon after by the pope as Saint Stephen. Or was it the demands of statesmanship, as the official line of latter-day history claims, that made him do all this to secure a safe place among enemies on all sides by accepting and adopting their foreign ways and religion? Who knows?

Fact is, however, that the gradual decline of the power that Hungary was then (it even had invincible kings, as is noted in the Motivation) began in the year of the Lord 1000 with the conversion of Vajk to something he was not. Conversions are risky. The Cochimí did not survive theirs. And the Hungarians better stop their decline if they want to continue their great adventure that brought them to Europe and to escape the fate of the Cochimí.

Poor road

But an adventure does not have to be a great undertaking to earn the name. All it needs is an element of risk to make it so. He knew that he would be facing one if he did not return on the safe tourist road to Loreto. If instead he took the only other way out, the one heading west past the village. For the Baja map described that way clearly as "poor road." And when the triple-A Baja map says that, it means it. But then he had this four-wheel drive car, and he felt that this was the time to give it a chance live up to its name, to show its quality in finding the less-traveled path.

Well, by the time he had serious qualms about the wisdom of the undertaking, it was too late. The "road" was not poor. It had lost the last suggestion of being one at all. The only clue to its being there were the boulders left and right of it. They were bigger than the Pathfinder itself. The smaller ones in between them were all so arranged that when one wheel found traction in a space between two of them, the opposite wheel spun freely in midair, with only the muffler and the catalytic converter providing some stability by resting precariously and then scraping ominously on one or another sturdy formation of granite below. And all this, of course, going down the ungentle slope of a deep desert wash. What an *asquerosa pinche chingadería* it was (don't look this one up, it's not in your dictionary nor in my glossary)!

Steve, who had gone into this trusting the good sense of his father, thought at first that the route was well known and explored though maybe a little rough, but by the time it was clear that a turning around could not even be thought of because of the large boulders that flanked the "road," he started raising his eyebrows. But he kept his cool, acting gamely as if he enjoyed this fine example of obstacle-course driving. What he could not know was that had an axle snapped, and it was a miracle that it did not, the car would have had to stay there until it rusted out of the way, for although the institution of the *grua* is well known in Mexico, no tow truck in its right mind would have thought of venturing out there, even if there had been one within a few hundred miles, for it would not have gotten out either.

But as we already know, miracles do happen. After a while, and it was an endless and grueling while, the path turned into a dirt and then into a gravel road. "*Noch einmal glimpflich davongekommen*" was the thought that rose up from a recess of his mind. *Glimpflich, glimpflich,* where have I heard that word the last time, he was wondering, as he chugged along, leisurely now on that graded gravel. Where, where? It must have been another age, another adventure, one having to do with some car or truck also. Escaped once more by the skin of my teeth, once more, *noch einmal . . .*

It was Steve who shook him out of his pondering the past, thinking perhaps that he was in some mild form shock. "I say, you have a car that can do what few other cars can," he said, and the compliment (to him by way of the car) was most welcome. But just imagine the *chingada* for a second, had they gotten stuck for good out there in the middle of trackless Baja. Abandon the car, hike back to the Mission, hitchhike back to La Paz, shop for another car, etc. Would life not be so much more peaceful if the imp in charge of the urge of looking for trouble were not always at work, if one just stayed at home safely sitting by one's cozy fireplace,

Beatus ille homo,	Happy is that man,
Qui sedet in sua domo	Who sits in his house
Et sedet post fornacem	And sits by his fireplace
Et habet bonam pacem.	And is at peace.

as students and journeymen used to sing in an era, a long-past romantic one, ages ago now even before his time, when they left home on foot with only a knapsack on their backs to see the world?

The road imp again

When midsummer came, Baja turned too hot for comfort for Marina, and she decided it would be a good time to visit the family in Munich, where the weather can be wintry even in August. Well, wintry at least compared to that in La Paz. And he decided this would be an equally good time for him to drive up to Tucson, to the University of Arizona, to do some library research in preparation for the upcoming writing of manuscripts.

The prospect of a thousand miles of open road, and then one as wide-open as the Baja highway, always made him feel ecstatic. How many thousands of miles long a trek had it been for the Hungarians from the Caspian Plains to the Carpathian Basin? Toward the end of the first millennium, a time when the whole world was an open road! And then on horseback! And to add spice to that fine affair of an adventure conquering a new homeland, they had all that fun of fighting off the pesky Besenyő nation that pushed them from the rear and clobbering the Bulgarians and Moravians in front who seemed to resent their coming.

Was it dreaming of ancient Hungarians on horseback or being kept awake by that truck dieseling all night right outside his motel window in Guerrero Negro that wore him out enough to make it easy for the aforementioned imp to go to work on him again? At any rate, before he knew it, the Pathfinder decided once more to find a new path and turned off the hard top to a gravel top, one going east, following a sign first to Coco's Corner, but then on to San Felipe on the Sea of Cortes side of Baja. To be sure, there was a left-brain rationale also behind this new *desafio*, for this route seemed to be a shortcut on the map, like the hypotenuse of a right triangle, on the way to Yuma and Tucson. But mostly, it was the imp's work, who having taken the safe path a good number of times already, was getting bored. Well, what can I say? The graded, smooth gravel became dirt past (or was it just before?) Coco's Corner.

That alone would have been okay, but with time, the road turned into a deep sunken track, the kind of one-lane job that does not permit passing from either direction. Even that seemed to be okay, for people, either in the know or else in their right mind, apparently did not take this road often, so traffic was so light that you could safely say there wasn't any.

The trouble was with the terrain. It was so configured along this stretch that no all-terrain vehicle could have negotiated a passage anywhere but where the road was, which was where it was because of that very circumstance in the first place. Trouble was then compounded by the efforts of some philanthropists with foresightful business acumen to fill up the bottoms of this hollow road, which must have turned to mud baths after a rare *chubasco*, with crushed rock. And crushed rock has sharp edges, which when your tires are not inflated to the max, find the soft underbellies or sides of the latter and shred them, a threat that he had not been aware of before.

Sure enough, after a while on this type of rock, he noticed that the Pathfinder had a hard time moving, so he got out to see what was wrong. It was the right rear tire. More precisely, it was its absence, for it was not there anymore. It had been shredded to bits by that crushed rock. He must have been rolling on the rim for quite a while by then. And now he had come to rest like Noah's Ark on Mount Ararat in such an awkwardly slanted way, that no jacking-up could be attempted with any hope of safety. He was in the middle of assessing the situation when a GMC Jimmy rode up from behind.

A crusty old Baja gringo got out and joined him in his silent contemplation of the scene. "Well," he said finally, "I hope it will make you feel better if I tell you that you are not the first green tourist whom I have gotten out of a fix hereabouts." Fortunately, his callow greenness was seasoned enough to let him take that complimentary epithet with a grateful smile, and then the man went to work. He dragged the car with his winch to a position where the two jacks that were now available could be applied at the right points to lift the chassis sufficiently off the precariously loose roadbed. This then permitted putting the small spare in place. "You got to drive real slow now," he advised, "for otherwise the difference in size between your rear tires will wreck your differential. And it is a good hundred and twenty miles yet to San Felipe," he added with a wink. Well, he had not known that about the differential either and felt duly and abjectly humble as a confirmed green tourist by now.

But then the imp must have gone to sleep (in spite of the old Hungarian insight that the devil never takes a nap, *az ördög nem alszik*), for the road turned gravel again, and after a while there appeared before his unbelieving eyes, like a mirage of an oasis in the middle of the Sahara Desert, the large sign of a *llantería*. But it was not an illusion, it was real, the tire shop of Rancho Grande, equipped with all sizes of the rejects for which US service stations charge you a ten-dollar disposal fee. "*Tiene Usted buena suerte que la grava ha 'basurado' solamente una de sus llantas*," reassured him the grinning mechanic. So he was lucky that the gravel had "garbaged" only one of his tires! And this was the case indeed, for he had only one spare and the shop had only one of the over-sized tires he needed.

The Rancho Grande operation was well planned, for there was a joint close by that offered ice-cold *cervesa* for waiting tire clients. There he ran into his rescuer again, who explained that the crushed rock was placed there expressly for green tourists like him, a business that kept the shop going. But by this time, he had heard his new moniker once too often to be amused.

Decisions jelling

Tucson was as scorching hot as he likes it best, but he had been there before only to meetings, and now he felt strangely structureless or unstructured, without a set schedule to follow. He finished with the library and set out west, but the Pathfinder, instead of heading for Tecate to cross into Baja, veered north as it passed the Salton Sea. He himself was puzzled by this, for it had been the old red Toyota that knew the way to Pismo Beach, where the Dolphin Cove Motel used to be the last overnight stop before hitting home in El Cerrito, coming from meetings at UC Riverside. He tried to talk to the steering wheel about his strange new feeling, but that relationship did not have enough depth yet to enable the wheel to explain.

The feeling was something a brand-new butterfly must experience when he crawls out of the chitin corsage of his last formative stage equipped with eyes and antennae, able now to pick up signals that he had never sensed before but unable yet to make any sense of them yet, especially as those unfamiliar appendages on his back are still wet, crumpled up, and useless so that he is not yet ready to take to the air.

As he walked along the beach and then all around San Luis Obispo the next day, he knew already how to write up his remaining publications based on the library research and his work at the CIB, and that felt comforting and satisfying. But at the same time, this new feeling was dawning on him. And it was disconcerting. He noticed that his head had stopped formulating new research plans for the future, when they would finally get back to Corvallis. This state of affairs was disturbing, even threatening. He was used to having a long string of new project for future experiments in his mind and could hardly wait to finish the current ones to get on with the ones waiting down the road. Now he felt like having arrived at a waterhole in the desert, only to find it dried up. To divert him, he took to discovering San Luis Obispo, a place of many meetings he had attended before, those organized by the California Plant and Soil Society.

Wandering aimlessly through the streets, he discovered the new rust-brown bridge over the railroad tracks near the railroad station and climbed up on the open-space of Terrace Hill from the north, from Ella Street, for that tract was not built up yet back then in 1998. The hill opened up a gorgeous view of the town below with Bishop's Peak in the background. How about that? he thought. I never saw it like this before when I came here for those meetings. What is going on with me? Am I sprouting new sense organs, or what? Then he caught himself wondering if Marina would fancy retiring in San Luis Obispo.

The experience of having seen SLO in this new light left him with a feeling that an important mission had been accomplished, and now he was ready to head back to Baja. And so he did, but as he turned south from the Ventura Freeway to I-405, progress turned into a crawl. He tuned his radio to the traffic station to hear what was going on. "Nothing is going on," the station kept repeating all day. "There is no accident on the San Diego Freeway, and there is no construction activity. It's just that there are too many cars, and there is no place to put them."

And so it went on, believe it or not, for eight hours running. A Sunday it was. He had gotten up early to get to Santo Tomás by sundown, but he was lucky to reach Chula Vista near the border as night fell.

This america I have been looking for all my life is becoming more unmanageable every time I have to pass through this asphalt jungle, he was musing while listening to the station commenting on a driver trying to fix a flat in the center one of the five lanes going north, with all lanes bumper to bumper and moving fast, as he could see across the center divide. "Don't do that," the station admonished. "Don't do it. Wait for a tow truck!" Will a time come when it becomes also ungovernable? his chain of thought went on. But it was just a fleeting reflection; 9/11, the second Iraq War and the Great Recession were still to come. The peace and the serenity of the Baja highway was beckoning. It was promising safety and sanity in comparison to the havoc on I-405.

Phasing out

With the Baja experience all wrapped up, they enjoyed the ride back north somewhat nostalgically. When they hit Pismo Beach, it was late, and Marina did not particularly look forward to a motel search in the dark. She was pleasantly surprised when he pulled straight into the Dolphin Cove parking lot right next to the breaking waves like someone heading for a familiar place. The Dolphin is one of the last cozy, old-fashioned motels left in Pismo, now surrounded by big, new, fancy, upscale establishments that leave him (and her also) cold with alienation. But young folks seem to like their america that way. Ah, the homemade cherry pie of those vanishing mom-and-pop coffee shops at off-the-freeway corners of this road that he liked to stop at! When the last one is gone, he will not linger either.

The Dolphin was a hit with Marina and a good starting point after a stroll out to the end of the pier to rediscover SLO. What are the things a town needs to offer for her to be content with it? A fresh, cool, close-by ocean breeze, a university with cultural events, a good public library, a farmer's market, a cinema offering non-Hollywood movies, a good Thai restaurant, a friendly bookstore equipped with easy chairs, and open space behind her house with a great mountain view, where wild turkeys, California quail, deer, rabbits, foxes in addition to cows and horses make her feel at home.

Furthermore, humanely tolerable traffic, no traffic noise, and above all, kind, friendly neighbors, ones who are also of her political persuasion. An airport, a train station, year-round cool weather, a group of friends practicing the Buddha Path . . . A few of these things, of course, may be found elsewhere also, as they well knew, after all, they were not exactly new travelers of their road. But all of them like in SLO? And to top it all, it was already familiar, a part of both of their past professional life, not simply an ideal place to which they had no connection.

That settled it. Back in Corvallis everything was like it was before they left. The only thing different was that they knew, not for sure yet (for what is ever sure in life?) but quite decidedly anyway, that their time there was up anytime they chose that it be so. Having a choice is reassuring, although leaving always leaves a lot behind. They had been there for seven years by the time the time came, and that is a long time. He wrote the three manuscripts on the data collected in El Comitan and felt homesick for it as I feel now. He also started to feel homesick for Corvallis, while he was still there, knowing full well that he could have stayed there, and it would be the sensible thing to do. But somehow, Corvallis never really became home; I do not know why.

After the papers were written, he coasted on for a while, perhaps quite a while, but it was not in him to start another experiment. He did design a follow-up research plan to continue the work in Baja, and it was a good one. In hopes that it would be approved, he kept the gas-guzzling Pathfinder, which by now had become an expert on handling the Baja rough patches. Then Rob finished school and moved to LA, and Steve got himself transferred to Las Vegas. It was time to say good-bye to the mists of Avalon. Marina sold the house that was all paid off by now. It was poor timing; houses did not sell well in Oregon and were becoming priceless in California. But it could not be helped. What was to be his last move was on.

Chapter 10

Twilight

In the heady days of America's golden Empire Age, the quarter century that followed World War II, Americans still believed—in fact, were more sure than ever before—that their children, each new generation to follow them, would lead happier, wealthier, and more secure lives than those of their parents. With the competitive industrial bases of the enemy destroyed both to the east and the west of the two Shining Seas, the world, free of economic rivals now, had become one great, big, free consumer market for everything "made in America."

These were good times for all. Everyone who was willing and able to work had his chance to lay the foundations for his dream. This was especially true for all those who were identified by their blue collars as part as the great American working class. Well-paying jobs and guaranteed health and retirement benefits were the rock on which their fortunes were founded. From there, they moved up steadily to become members of the middle class, formerly the exclusive domain of professionals like doctors, lawyers, and businessmen. As their skills as plumbers, carpenters, and auto mechanics were much in demand, they could now move up easily, without having to break the back of a book in college. They did not even have to exchange their blue collars for white ones.

And so many of them, to their credit and as behooves savvy people with foresight, prepared for their golden years by setting up a retirement dream home somewhere where they expected to be happy after having finished with their work-lives. One of his ARS buddies, an agronomist, with whom he liked to go out and have a glass of beer when visiting Brawley, a sun-baked small farming town in the irrigated desert of the Imperial Valley of Southern California, was one of them.

The guy would gush about his cabin and garden in verdant Sweet Home in faraway Oregon, a place worthy of its name, not far from Corvallis, where Marina helped some Russian immigrants with their language problems for a while.

The colleague, having worked at the Brawley Station for decades without ever feeling at home, was a cheerful, clever, and resourceful fellow, and now, in his early sixties, was finally ready to move to that Garden of Eden place of his choice to be finally at rest there. Dream fulfilled, one might say, textbook story of late mid-twentieth-century America.

Big decision

But he missed his chance to cash in on those heady days; he wore the sweaty, colorless collar of the assembly-line worker and then the khaki one of the soldier and finally the collarless tee shirt of the student, and by the time he was finished with all that the bang of the booming, postwar economy was starting to turn into a whimper, there was no retirement dream home to repair to when he would decide that it was time for him to go.

He did not have to go when he went; he was neither senile nor decrepit yet. He too could have stayed on if the spirit had not moved him to move on. Bob Linderman decided to stay and to go on enjoying his experiments, while Yoav had already told him that he intended to die in his lab.

There is everything right with an attitude like that of his colleagues. People like that are lucky; they were born with a true calling and were lucky to find it in the course of their search for their america. He, however, was one of those without such a calling. What he had found in his biology was his path. And it was a good path to follow, for it let him soar with the warm updrafts of keeping busy with something that was of interest to him and of use to others. An activity where effort is not a chore but a challenge and any little bit of success is its own reward. But it was not a true calling. Such a calling is the certainty that one is made and intended to spend one's life exactly that way and no other way.

What he might have called his calling was not something one does, but something one is. For him, that would have been being a Hungarian army officer and landowner. That sort of existence is like the mystical quintessence; it flows on like whitewater, a river left undammed, turbulent through the rapids of war, and placid through the quiet, unruffled depths of peace, the way the world is when you are in harmony with the laws that rule your own little private universe.

So in a nutshell, biology was no less but no more than his favorite hobby. And it still is in a quiet, gardening and science-reading way, only back there, at work, he was paid for having fun with it. And he still is being paid and will continue to be, unless the politicians find all of a sudden that they have spent his nest egg that he had paid into the Federal Retirement Fund on some war or on tax cuts for the very rich or on bonuses for the bailout barons and then send him a note by e-mail not to expect another annuity check.

His freely elected politicians and their appointees, who fumble around in consternation and incomprehension with their beloved Free Market and the deficits that it always produces of late, but that now, in the wake (or still in the middle?) of the Great Recession, grow at the rate of logarithmic progressions. "And why shouldn't we have spent your nest egg?" the politicians might add by way of explanation. "The retirees of General Motors got theirs spent also, and what is right for GM is right for the USA." But here I go again, I am ahead of myself, for the Great Recession came eight years later, and even now, the check is still coming, miraculously perhaps.

So when the time came and he knew for sure in his bones that the active, formal part of the hobby has played itself out, he called it quits and Marina nodded assent. Then they set out to survey the likely spots along (or at least not far from) the California Coast. Eureka, Davis, Santa Cruz, San Luis Obispo, Santa Barbara, San Diego. SLO won hands down, and not the last reason for this choice was that the pace of life seemed benignly slow and that traffic was tolerable there.

They stayed at the Dolphin Cove Motel again while house hunting and were joined there by Peter and Sabine and their (now grown) kids Ben and Jupp. There was little socializing during the day, for finding a place to live was not easy and they had a deadline. The house in Corvallis was sold, and the moving of their household goods was scheduled.

On greed and bubbles

Now it would have come in handy to have a retirement dream home all ready to move to. But no such decision had been made or could have been realized before hand, and now, in SLO, unlike in the backwaters of Corvallis, there was a wild seller's market raging in housing. It was the era of the dot com stock-market bubble, which was rapidly coming to a head.

Fortunes were being made on the tech stocks and the overflow of new wealth from the trading them was frothing into real estate. "Populations are inexorably growing and the land available on which to house them is fixed and limited," was the conventional wisdom. "Therefore, real estate prices can only go up," declared a newfound law of nature. Milton Friedman's economic theories had produced physics-mimicking equations for the ways of the market, and Alan Greenspan, a true believer and the chief conductor and regulator of the nation's money matters, proclaimed them as the gospel.

Accordingly, prices continued to soar for a few more years. These were also the heydays of the derivatives. These are, if you still don't know, worthless pieces of paper that derive their spurious value from some form of risky speculation that promises their holders a hasty, hefty, and highly leveraged gain. A casino chip might be an easy-to-touch example for the concept. Deceptively, it has the exact shape of a silver dollar. At the gambling table of the house that issued it, you can use the chip to multiply your ante manyfold if you are lucky. So also, you can lose it all in the blink of an eye. But off the premises, it is not a silver cartwheel; it is only a worthless piece of plastic.

Such then were the conditions of the housing market in which they were still determined to find their dream house. While they were spending their day trying to find a place to live, the Peter family went hiking in the hills near Lopez Lake. There one of them met up with an inquisitive wasp and tried to slap it away. Wasps do not like that in general, and this one in particular was annoyed and felt moved to discharge an attack pheromone into the air. Before they knew what they were up to, her sisters, cousins, and aunts taught them a painful lesson. Fortunately, such a wild clan of yellow jackets is not large. It does not have to be to function and to survive, for it is made up of the quickest and meanest creatures on earth when provoked. They could easily take over the world if they wanted to, if something were not holding them back from doing so.

Biologist though I am, I do not know for sure what that something is. But I do know what can hold back the wasps of the business world, the ones who dream up, issue, and deal in these derivatives. It is called strictly enforced government regulation. Of course, you cannot regulate the real cause of the pernicious activity that these sharks engage in; you can keep in check only the practices that are derived from it. This real cause is avarice. And that is primal. So what's the big deal? Greed is always present in some more of less subdued form everywhere. The problem was that at the moment greed in SLO was not subdued but unbridled, and people were asking a fortune for their houses and you could not blame them, for they were getting it.

They got their first taste of this state of affairs after they had found a nice one to rent on the southern edge of town for a mere thirteen hundred dollars a month. But by the time they came back after lunch to sign the papers, the price had risen to sixteen hundred, accompanied by stiff, new lease provisions. "Why not?" the owners who were in the full swing of pursuing their happiness were telling them. "The business of America is business." And they were right.

They, on the other hand, knew by now that to find what they wanted would take time, and so they moved their search for a rental out of town. There they found an acceptable stopgap solution for their immediate problem on a quiet side street in Arroyo Grande, just south of SLO, where the market was a little less frenzied. And there they stayed for a year without unpacking most of their two hundred cartons, driving up to SLO almost every day, looking for something that approximated their dream house. Looking at all those boxes gathering dust, they always reminded him of old Dr. Schlusnus, who liked to quote famous people. And whenever he came up with a bit of wisdom of his own, he then attributed it to Confucius: "If you own stuff that you did not use for a year, relieve yourself of its burden."

I do not remember what exactly he did all that year, short of looking for a house in SLO that fitted their specifications. On many mornings, he went for a run on the beach. He also walked or drove down to the village of Arroyo Grande to read the paper with a cup of coffee and a cookie at the Café Andreini.

The "Village" is a real village, two blocks of genuine, pleasant, leftover Old Americana of stores and restaurants (even a butcher shop) on the one side of the great *arroyo*. This is a year-round stream at the bottom of a deep ravine and is spanned by a wooden pedestrian bridge, which hangs on cables and swings up and down when you walk across. It leads to an equally pleasant area of small houses on the other side, very much villagelike but without open space and view and pretty much encroached upon by a burgeoning growth of modern developments.

That eliminated it from their short list of prospects. He also went to the library there to read the *Wall Street Journal*, for their investments had participated in the dot com boom, only to collapse with it in the end. He kicked himself for not having seen it coming, as did so many others who called themselves professional experts. Like the aforementioned Al Greenspan, the Chairman of the Federal Reserve. There is no escaping it: greed is a devil, and he never sleeps. You know by now what that sounds like in Hungarian: *Az ördög nem alszik*.

On the way to the roots

Then a phone call came from Budapest, and it injected new reality into the somnolence of retirement. The man identified himself as Márton Zsolt. Márton, Márton! The name sounded like an echo from the other side of the Grand Canyon. There had been a distant cousin somewhere in Germany with whom his father had been corresponding in his Harthausen days, a refugee like themselves. And another one, a priest or monk, the *fehér csuhás*, the one with the white robe.

But these were relatives from Zetelaka, and Zetelaka had become too distant to be real. It seemed to be very far away even back in childhood days, although it was only a few kilometers from Bethlenfalva. Back then, when they spent the last summer there in that big house with the apple orchard, the red currants and the butterflies. They had written all that off, he and his brother, for they did not know anyone there. It was like the Island of Atlantis, sunk into the black shadows of the *nuit froide de l'oubli*. So much so that they did not even attempt to rediscover it when they visited everything else, Fülek, Léva, Eger, Miskolc, and Debrecen in the red Saab that Chris had lent them.

"*Szervusz, Gábor bácsi*," this Márton Zsolt's voice said, "*remélem jó egészségben találom.*" *Szervusz* comes from the Latin *servus* or servant and is an abbreviated way of saying "I am at your service." It used to be a common greeting but only among people with whom one was on familiar terms. Such people accosted each other with the personal pronoun of the second person singular, the familiar *te*, the *thou* that had regrettably died out in nonbiblical English usage. It was practical, this *te*, for members of a certain social class (theirs) could apply it to each other as a sign of mutual recognition of "likekindedness," even if they had never met before. For you would only offer to be someone's servant if he belonged to your own stratum of society. Younger people could greet their elders with *szervusz* but then revert to the formal, respectful third-person appellation, and this was what this Zsolt had done.

"Yes, thank you," he answered, "you did find me in good health," but the socio-idiomatic implications of this first sentence put him in a time warp, for he had been living in a world of social intercourse at the American business-communications level for the last several decades, and even German seems to lack this level of finesse. Needless to say, he was at once highly expectant of what might follow. Then Zsolt identified himself as the great-grandson of his (my) grandmother's sister. "I have been searching for you everywhere," he explained, "for the Romanian government decided to return real estate expropriated by the communists to its owners, and that includes your house and land in Bethlenfalva."

Their follow-up to this initiative came soon. By late August, he and his brother were in Munich again, and after having discharged all their customary reverences to their common past in Icking, they hopped on the train, the Béla Bartók, to Budapest. It was the first such train trip that Miklós participated in, and they enjoyed it. The familiar scenery of turquoise forests and emerald meadows undulating up to the steepening foothills of the Alps, all free of barbed wire, was floating by as they were sipping their coffee and savoring their *palacsinta* after a meal of *kolozsvári rakott káposzta* in the train's elegant dining car.

This is a dish of the type that is called an *Eintopf* in German. *Eintopf* means "one pot" and suggests that it is a multicourse offering, all in one. It was a favorite of his mother's, who liked it so much that she always prepared it herself. He was fond of it also, back then in Léva, so much so that he would go to the kitchen and watch its evolution from its constituent raw ingredients, *káposzta* (cabbage), *bárány hús* (lamb), and *rizs* (rice). Each of these are prepared separately as if to be served individually, but then they are layered (*rakott*) on top of each other (the same way a proper chocolate cake, like the *dobos torta*, becomes a work of art) in a large pot with generous servings of sour cream between the layers. Then the pot goes into the oven without a lid, until the top layer of the sour-cream-soaked shredded cabbage turns golden brown.

So they were sitting in the dining car after it had emptied out past Vienna, holding a leisurely hour of recounting, of delving into the now deep and darkening pools of their past. He stuck with the time-honored way of flavoring *palacsinta*, that is, with raspberry jam rolled into it, while his brother tried a (for them) new-fangled Gundel version with chocolate cream. Hungarians claim the *palacsinta* to be their very own invention, which was adopted later and then popularized by the French as *crèpe*. They agreed that the *ízes,* fruity kind was more genuine and that a chocolate topping somehow harmonized neither with the underlying thin, pancakelike substrate nor with all the memories that their favorite desert awakened in them anew.

In the meantime, the landscape outside flattened out and took on a flavor of its own, an Eastern one. What that is is hard to explain, for it is difficult enough to feel and experience it, obvious though it is. It is not only a concept, for it is real, and so it should not depend entirely on how perceptive the beholder's frame of mind is when he sees it. It has historical, political, cultural, economic, climatic, biogeographic, and who knows how many more defining aspects.

Some ten years had already passed down into the Black Sea with the now murky waters of the once Blue Danube since the end of the Soviet Empire, but the drop in the wealth gradient past the border station at Hegyeshalom was still as sadly evident as ever. Austria had become one of the most prosperous countries in the world, while Hungary had been left behind.

Over fifty years of apathy, neglect, and exploitation under foreign occupation leave long-lasting wounds that do not heal quickly. That would have taken time, even if new vultures had not descended on that hapless country. The Western capitalist interests that had an easy time buying up everything worth having with their hard currencies would have alone been a burden too heavy to bear. But even worse was the plague engendered at home. The local communist rulers had not been in power by accident prior to the dawn of the New World Order. They were experts at their business of ruling. And so when freedom at last broke out, they blithely took over again, expropriated and divided up much of "their" country's meager, remaining wealth among themselves, reinventing themselves in the process as the new political, capitalist right, a *parvenu* upper class of a tainted ownership elite.

That these new lords were not much interested in improving the people's lot, they (he and his brother) could easily deduce from the neglected state of the gray, forlorn buildings with their peeling paint revealing shell marks and bullet holes from guns silenced long ago that they saw moving by their window now and that replaced the cheerful hues of Austrian houses, the orange-yellow that had been the favorite color of Maria Theresia, Empress of Austria and Queen of Hungary. And that was his favorite color also.

It was the light reflected from the colors outside that they were really interested in, not the politics that they were not aware of then and that would have left them cold at the moment even if they had known about it.

There were no forests in evidence anymore by now, and the fields all had a touch of gray mixed into their verdure if they were not all-out brown, for the season was past the national holiday of the Twentieth of August, the day of the Harvest Festival and the feast of that sainted king, Stephen, the one who had first invited in the foreigners a thousand years ago.

It was not that many of those fields had been fallowed because of a persistent drought that seemed to add an element of melancholy to their touch of gray. Those fields simply did not have the signs of the purposeful, robust, rectangular regimentation as they do in Iowa or in Bavaria. Their edges were fuzzy and overrun by weeds. They tended to be bounded by balding hedgerows irregularly spaced and often dotted with a few acacia trees, the very same that are so fragrant in spring but that become scraggly by the end of summer. The rural countryside looked a little as if it were ready to revert to its aboriginal state before the axe and the plow but was now stuck in its rut full of resentment for being half-heartedly hindered from doing so.

This was still Central Europe, but a breath of the endless, desolate Russian Steppes had reached out and touched it to dull its luster a little. But do not get the idea now that this "Eastern flavor" is not beautiful, for it is and is so even to a judgmental eye as long as it is willing to be open to things different and foreign. And for some reason, he was afraid to ask his brother if he saw it that way also. Maybe because his eyes rarely strayed outside the confines of the railroad car, as if his mind were somewhere else.

The Mártons

Zsolt picked them up at the *Nyugati Pályaudvar*, the still ornate but now sadly neglected Western Train Station. He said he recognized him immediately as family, while his brother, with his six-foot-three mundane elegance and aristocratic hook nose looked like a stranger, so that he was at first hesitant to accost them. This reminded him of the people with whom they shared a restaurant table in that *Halászcsárda* on the Margit Körút the first time they returned to Budapest who thought he was the local tourist guide and his companion (his brother) a wealthy foreign visitor. They spent the night at the Márton home way out on the green northern fringes of the city.

The Mártons had ended up in some other part of Germany after the war, and there had been an exchange of letters between Papa Márton, Zsolt's father, and his father. I do not know how they found each other, but they were out of visiting range, for money, even only for a train ride, was something his father did not have after the *Währungsreform* introduced the new German currency.

Papa Márton, as I try to piece the fragments together now, was young enough to call my father "*bácsi*" and old enough to be called Jenő *bácsi* by me, only I had never met him, so I cannot call him uncle here either. A young army lieutenant at the end of the war, he decided to become a veterinarian and studied in Munich at maybe a year or two before he (that's me) tried his hand at physics there. What a pity that he spent those years in Munich without any inkling that he had live relatives nearby. Contact with the Mártons at that time might have given a significant change to the direction where he was heading.

As a professional civilian now, Zsolt's father married Etelke and settled into a postwar, middle-class existence in Germany. Zsolt attended a Hungarian language school that apparently existed somewhere in Germany unbeknownst to the Harthausen diaspora. Had they been aware of this, his search for an america might never have ended up in the actual America itself. For the special brand of National Catholicism that some Hungarians like to practice is a powerful bond, and with the mutual support of like-minded relatives, the need for the great leap across the ocean may not have been so urgent.

The Mártons had demonstrated how to resolve the identity problem: they became German citizens without becoming German nationals in spirit. They gave no thought to ever abandoning their Hungarian identity so that when the Evil Empire finally imploded, they packed up, sold their houses, and moved home to Budapest.

On the road to Bethlenfalva

The next morning, they were off in Zsolt's car, heading for Nagyvárad, a city of Hungarian history, traditions, and tongue at the eastern edge of the Great Plains of Hungary, the Magyar Nagyalföld. He had read all he could find about the storied beauty and substantial cultural presence of this city, more Hungarian in its historical unity than Budapest perhaps. For the capital had rapidly outgrown its traditional bounds in the process of turning into a metropolis, unfortunately. Nagyvárad had still maintained its age-old identity during its foreign occupation between the two Great Wars. He knew of this, for he had passed through it as a boy several times and in 1944 for the last time.

Back then, there was no border there to cut it off from its past. Now, there was. It is a pity that there is no English translation of Tibor Déry's book, *Mr. G. A. in X* (there is one in German and French), for it describes in suffocating detail the desolation of the approach to a dystopian, socialist city much better than I ever could. Maybe the Romanians have cleaned up by now the shuttered, rusting factories along the road and replanted the desertlike, weed-infested, and refuse-strewn approaches to the city from the west that disfigured the formerly shining face of the city. But the ugliness of those huge, gray structures everywhere, erected hastily to house the tens of thousands of immigrants shipped in from Walachia, was overpowering for him.

He could see the consternation in his brother's face also, although he was not quite sure if he was fidgeting so desperately in the back because of his dismay with what had become of Nagyvárad or because he was overdue for a smoke break. Sad to say, Miklós was a chain smoker. And Zsolt had made it clear that there was to be no lighting up in his car. But he was clearly in a hurry to get out of Nagyvárad also, so there was no stopping for a while.

They followed the course of the Körös River at first and then drove up to the historic pass across the mountains, the *Király Hágó*, the gateway to Erdély, Transylvania, the Land beyond the Forest. The route was Romania's Highway One, a road that appeared to be in the experimental stages of road building, and Zsolt was navigating it like a pilot would handle his plane through extreme turbulence.

I will spare myself further details of the anguish that he felt in passing through this Third World that opened up on the other side of that border. If there was quite a gradient in prosperity noticeable between Austria and Hungary, this one was like the drop off a cliff. Hungarian small towns were clean and well kept, brimming with hope and life in comparison, while here, the Balkans were rampant. Of course, maybe it only appeared to him like that, for he saw it all through his childhood's nationalist eyeglasses.

Well, enough of it. Let me just mention by way of comic relief the enormous mansions of strange and exotic design with balconies, towers, balusters, arches, and turrets, unfinished yet, as if in the process of being conjured up by Ali Baba's genie according to plans by an architect from the fairy tales of mystical Araby, and all topped by silver roofs gleaming in the sun from far away. Wealth in the midst of neglect: the palaces of the King of the Gypsies and his retinue, who levy taxes on their people like a state within the state. Should you ever pass through Bánffyhunyad, you can't miss them on the eastern outskirts of it.

In the end, they arrived in Zetelaka by darkness, so the sights of childhood memories had to wait till morning. Overnight, a cold drizzle, an early harbinger of winter, moved in over the mountains from Russia, the kind of weather that they had never experienced during their summer vacations there. It produced an unwelcome feeling.

Enikő, their landlady, a niece once or twice removed, said a few words about the state of affairs in Bethlenfalva to prepare them for what was coming, but she, being of the next generation, had never known and seen with her own eyes the past that they were expecting to find. Also, when you have lived through the changes yourself, their end result does not surprise you; it looks natural to you as if that were the way it should be. So when she said that the village of Bethlenfalva, swallowed up by the growing town of Székelyudvarhely, did not exist anymore with its name almost forgotten already; it not only sounded ominous, but it also made him feel as if he had lost his bearings and his way, like that lost, ancestral horseman of yore:

Hajdani, eltévedt utas	A traveler of old who has lost his way
Vág neki uj hináru útnak.	Starts out on a new, tangled path.
De nincsen fény, nincs lámpa-láng	But there is no light, no shining lamp
Es hirük sincsen a faluknak.	And vanished are the villages.

The news conjured up the vision of developers on the loose. And that was what the next day brought after an uneasy night in a damp and cold room where you could see, if you had the eyes of a mycologist, the molds in the crevices release their spores into the air currents stirred up by the rare visitor. For that is how guest rooms tend to become that are in use only once in a blue moon.

Paradise lost

Houses, no matter how stately, used to be built near the road in that part of the world, separated from it only by a row of trees and a formal garden complete with a fountain, roses, and boxwood hedges edging its pathways, even if there was plenty of hinterland belonging to it in the rear. That was in order then, for the slow-moving horse- or ox-drawn carts did not stir up any dust, and the occasional elegant, swift carriage that might have usually considered such a house its destination anyway.

But now that road had evolved into a traffic artery frequented by trucks, for an industrial park had made its appearance right next door. And where the hinterland had been, those meadows of wildflowers blessed by butterflies, a development had sprung up of the same kind that had given him the shivers in Nagyvárad. And the first of those large, gray, square, two-story buildings, forlorn and forbidding at the same time and radiating the sadness of a socialism gone astray, sat in the middle of where the apple orchard had been, surrounded now by a wasteland of weeds. School was still going on inside the house that by law, now should have been theirs, and looking at it from the street, recognizing its old outlines but not comprehending the new injuriess that fifty years of diverse communal uses had inflicted on it, he was at a loss of what to feel, besides feeling numb inside.

It was almost a relief that he could not do anything at the moment, for as his cousin Móka explained, the mayor, who had jurisdiction over it, was not in a hurry to give it back, citing loopholes in the law. Móka had spent his professional life in Bukarest as an engineer and, having returned home in retirement, spent much of his time as a resident amateur paralegal helping people to find their way in the Byzantine labyrinths of local law.

"Let's scoot," his brother suggested as was becoming his habit by now, echoing his own feelings. But they were stuck, for Zsolt was driving and he had things to attend to; he was building a tourist hotel in Zetelaka. So they contemplated "their" house for a while from the street in the cold drizzle until it was finally time to go.

Settling in for good

So it was not a placid dream, this retirement life, for as you can see, it had some excitement left in it: those trips to the roots were always a challenge. But there was challenge enough at home also, for the dream house was still a dream; they were still renting a nondream one in Arroyo and not in the Village but in one of those new developments. The search was still on, and searches always involve an element of excitement, especially if they are frantic like the housing market was now in San Luis Obispo.

It had reached a state of such frenzy that their agent could show them a house newly up for sale in the morning, and by the time they had decided on it after lunch, it was not only sold but sold usually for more than its original asking price. Believe it or not, they spent a whole year looking for the right house, as if they, well in their golden years now, were expecting to occupy it forever.

And in the end, they found one. It was far from being a dream house, but it had potential, for it abutted on open space. That was Cerro San Luis itself, a picture-postcard example of a little mountain, surrounded by a storybook forest of gnarled old evergreen oak trees and by meadows below it that were inhabited by all the wild and tame animals that they expected to find there. Geologically speaking, their mountain is a pluton, formed by a huge upwelling of magma back when the earth was young. The house is on a rise formed by the foot of the mountain so that it has a wide, panoramic view with Bishop's Peak at its center, and that was the decisive factor for their choice.

Then Marina went to work remodeling the house to make it more dreamlike. She hired an architect and a contractor, and by October, the contractor's crew had succeeded in tearing two-thirds of the house down to the ground. That does not say much, for an American house is a house of cards by European standards. They had moved their belongings to the remaining three small rooms, stacking all that stuff up to the ceiling, leaving a cavelike opening in one of the rooms for them to live in. From their door that opened to the open sky at first, they could then observe the morphogenesis of a modern American dwelling.

Such a house rests on a precariously narrow outline of concrete poured between boards into ditches in the ground. Iron rods are frozen into this foundation, which help to stabilize the structure of wooden two-by-fours (the cross-section of a board measured in inches) and a few four-by-fours, boards that make up the skeleton of the walls, floors, ceilings and roofs. Onto this skeleton are then applied and affixed various layers of plaster, sheetrock, and the like, after the wiring and plumbing has been put into place within the holes of the skeleton. Then a layer of stucco is added to serve as the outside surface. Slap a coat of paint on all that and, bingo, you have a house.

Nowadays, of course, the building code also requires earthquake stabilizers, insulation, and some fluorescent lighting in a token gesture to safety and energy efficiency. But put a match to it, and it's ashes in ten minutes, even though it took several months to assemble all the pieces during which time they, the cave dwellers, cooked their food on a hot plate and washed the dishes in a bucket on the lawn outside.

Compare this to that house in Bethlenfalva. You can't. The same word simply does not apply to the two. There, a cellar of rock and brick, vaulted in Romanesque arches, formed a foundation built by some ingenious wizardry in such a way that its rooms were cool in summer and warm in winter, and they were so dry and airy that you could have easily lived in them had they not been in use to store the apples from the orchard and other goodies from the field.

The feature that stood out for him most on the main floor was the unique arrangement for heating the central part of the house. It consisted of two rectangular, hollow columns, each five by five feet in size that ran the height of the house to provide heat for the upstairs also. The columns were placed at the four-corner intersections of adjacent rooms so that the five-foot walls of these "places of fire" cut off a corner of each of those rooms, making them five-sided. I call them that not to confuse them with the open American fireplace. Once fires were lit in these columns, they heated their four adjacent rooms all at once. Their doors were kept closed for best heating efficiency, unless a fire worshipper like him wanted to sit in front adoring the blaze.

Alas, he had not seen these places of fire in use, as he had never spent a winter in Bethlenfalva. And now they are gone, for the building was restructured for a succession of public uses. They must have burnt up a small forest in the course of a long winter, and the forests are now dwindling in Erdély as everywhere else in the world. But the house still stands, and so much so that the local paper, the *Udvarhelyi Hiradó*, occasionally prints an article about it, "The Haberstumpf Ház," describing it as one of the most noteworthy structures in town, while bemoaning its sad state of disrepair.

Austin, an america

Starting with his first retirement year, he made regular pilgrimages to Austin, Nevada, for a few days during the first two weeks of June. That is the time when the acacias and the yellow roses bloom there.

As you wind your way down the road from Austin Pass, coming from Tonopah or Eureka, the first thing you see in town on the right side of the road is an extensive junkyard. An old couple used to run it. They are storied old-timers. The role Ray played in the history of Austin is written up in a book on Austin he found in the library of Ely, a town some two to three hours of drive to the east.

I say "used to," for I have not been back for two years now. Irene, who was running the show there, even had a computer and a credit card machine to relieve customers from the bother of having to carry cash with them, for there is no bank in town. But that last time he was there, she was facing a cancer operation, and if she went, Ray would soon follow, I am sure. I should have kept up with them, but people like me, we live in our heads. As it happened, these two old people, besides living in a trailer next to that picturesque, live American junkyard at seven thousand feet of elevation, were also in the hotel business. They owned the Pony Express House (PEH) that they rented out to transients like him. That's how he met them.

The PEH is one of the oldest original buildings in town. It is a oner, as genuine as a silver cartwheel. It is not nailed together from two-by-four-inch matchsticks. It is solid stone and brick, built by the miners of old, and if the pinion pine logs that hold up its roof (there is no ceiling) should burn one day, those walls will stay and outlast the planet and will then circle the sun as asteroids. The door opens into the living room that is equipped with a black-and-white television set, one of the first ever made, one, however, that is somehow able to reach PBS. That is the broadcasting station that used to be public but is of late sponsored by Walmart, Chevron, Boeing, Intel, and several others of that sort of benevolent funder. It seems to me that their spirit now colors the message of what used to be my station, and it overrides the impact of the contributions of "viewers like you," as the announcer still likes to call me generically, even though there is no one else like me.

The PEH has a bedroom with an old wooden wardrobe, where he left a faded pink, short-sleeve shirt of his on a hanger the first year he slept there because it had served out its use. Each year thereafter, he found his shirt still hanging in the exact same place where he left it. There is also a kitchen with a refrigerator—all the comforts of home—and as you sit in front under an acacia tree, transferring the contents of your mind to the hard drive of your computer, you can look out on the chapel of the Latter-Day Saints on the other side of the Loneliest Road.

What you do in Austin is hike, and the glory of it is unparalleled. That dirt road that veers off the highway as you reach Austin Summit going east (the one I must have mentioned before) runs on and on endlessly from vista to vista, looking down on the Valley of the Reese, and between vistas, there are hollows and depressions, some with springs feeding stands of aspen, small mostly, but also regular little forests, home to hawk, owl, rabbit, and deer. As you go on, the land rises and forces you off the beaten path, for following the ridge line south leads to peaks snow-capped in good years. The ground tends to be rocky but easily passable cross-country. The vegetation is no more than knee-high, but on north-facing slopes can be bushy.

In good years, that is when the wet Pacific winter storms are mighty enough to pass all the intervening mountain ranges to reach the Toiyabe and leave snow behind, or when local thunderstorms bless the land frequently, that knee-high vegetation is a painter's palette with the blues and reds of the lupine and the Indian paintbrush predominating. It is a psychedelic experience.

Hidden meadows in the hollows that are moist following the snow melt, harbor patches of a pale-lilac hued iris, the favorite of large moths with pink-and gray-striped lower wings that whizz around the flowers like hummingbirds do in milder climes or like the *halálfejes* moth did around the deep purple, fragrant petunias in Sándorhalma.

If you decide to sit down and contemplate this bit of america of yours from the cool, shady edge of your favorite aspen grove, you may become aware of a solitary mourning-cloak butterfly who is patrolling his beat there, passing tirelessly back and forth on his dark, sad, yet silver-lined introvert's wings without minding your presence, for this is truly free country. Here is an america without barbed wire, the real, mythical America envisioned by all emigrants who go through life in search of it.

Nine eleven

But the real America is many-faceted, and it ferments its way through the dough of global society on many levels: it is generous and benevolent on some; sinister and selfish on others. Since these societies are many-tiered, they rise and fall in response to the yeast of world banks, international monetary funds, military bases, and commercial missions differently, each according to its own gospel and level of wealth or marginalization. The responses to largess by the affluent are expected to be those of grateful appreciation by the givers of this "foreign aid," but sometimes the recipients see the underlying intent in a different light, and then their reaction to it can be violent.

So it came, while they still lived in their cave with their small TV set so fitted into all that ceiling-high stuff that he could watch it from bed, that Marina shook him out of his morning slumber. Fortunately she is an early riser; otherwise, he would have slept right through the event of the age. "Look at this," she said in a tone of voice that got him wide awake instantly. And there it was, just in time, one of the hijacked planes crashing into the second World Trade Center tower of New York City.

That same evening or maybe a day or two later, Val Zavala and her male companion were discussing the event on their show after the *NewsHour with Jim Lehrer* on PBS. I think they might have been interviewing someone who suggested timidly that this nefarious attack may not have come entirely out of the blue but might have been possibly provoked by Western capitalist practices aimed at some third part of the world and that it might therefore be to our benefit to find out what grievances they might possibly hold against us.

That was exactly what he would have proposed had he been Vice President Cheney's advisor on foreign policy. But it was not where the mind of Val Zavala's suave, older middle-age journalist companion was. "They attack us, take American lives, and we try to find out why?" was the gist of his comment, delivered with a smile but with a head-shaking, soft undertone that accentuated the razor's edge of his real meaning admirably.

Well, we do not seem to be interested to find out why. Why should we? We do not have to. We have the most sophisticated modern weaponry that ever existed, and we are using it to teach them a lasting lesson. But maybe we will be the ones who have to learn the last lesson in the end. Ominously, these are a people that had defeated all comers, from Alexander of Macedonia to Leonid of the Soviet Union.

These wars, the one in Afghanistan and the other one that is hopefully winding down now in Iraq, are an impasse that can drive anyone in search of his america desperate. And we do not even have the excuse that the problem is a new one for us. We had been there before; he had been there before himself, in Vietnam. We seem to be unable to learn, so we are repeating history. I can write polite letters to the president and say, "The terrorists that aim to attack us are not training to do that on monkey bars in Kandahar. They are training there all right, but that is for local control. The ones who might hit us again train in Saudi Arabia and in Germany and in England and in Detroit and in Los Angeles. And lately also in Pakistan. You do not fight hatred with brigades of infantry. Instead, you do go and find out what their grievances are, and if they are justified, you alleviate them."

And then a polite answer by Chief Presidential Advisor Axelrod does come from the White House to ease his worries, and its gist goes like this: rest assured, we are working day and night to keep you safe. Our soldiers are valiant, our intelligence reliable, and we know much more than you do. Our strategy is flexible. We hit their villages using blind drone aircraft now to take out their leaders in order to win their hearts and minds and also to save American lives, all in one fell swoop. So therefore trust us and never stop hoping for the best, for yes, we can! May God bless America, and don't forget that when an army unleashes terror on a people, that is war, and when that people makes war on that army, that is terrorism. Of course, this is no direct quote, so there are no quotation marks. But as I said, it is the gist of the message.

But I am some six years ahead of myself, am I not? It is so easy to mix up the present with the past when it comes to thinking about all these American wars of ours at this very moment. Why do we not mind our own business? There is always money for a war, but when it comes to the people's most elementary needs, clean air, clean water, clean energy, poison-free food, and nonprofit health insurance, all of a sudden there isn't any. Because we have an empire to defend? May God help America, indeed, for the Chinese will soon get tired of helping.

The neighborhood

Hermosa Way, in the northwest corner of San Luis Obispo, is a quiet backwater like Afghanistan was before the whole world started making war on it. It leads nowhere even though it is not a dead end; it is a curved offshoot of Luneta Street, which does not go anywhere either. Instead of going anywhere, it abuts on a wide *open space*, as wide-open land exempt from development is called around here. This open space starts on the other side of their fence and is a meadow, which slopes up to the live-oak forest on the north-facing side of San Luis Mountain. This sizeable piece of grassland is kept free of introduced, invasive weedy species like wild oats, crane's bill, and yellow-star thistle by the cows and horses of Madonna's Cattle Ranch, which owns and operates most of it.

It took them a while to realize that this Madonna was not the Mother of God, but the father of US Highway One-O-One, a four-lane freeway, which he built and which now odiously bisects the small city of San Luis Obispo. Sometimes they climb this moutain through the forest, for Madonna, who owns all of it, does not mind trespassers. From up there, you can see the city to the southeast and have an overview of the row of plutons to the northwest, all the way to the last one, Morrow

Rock, from where a cool and refreshing though sometimes outright cold ocean breeze blows most of the time.

Two five five Hermosa Way had become a livable place after Marina's remodeling. Its focal point is a little black woodstove with a clear window in front so that fire worshippers can watch the action inside. Such stoves are no longer legal in California, but this one was grandfathered in because it was already present in the old house before the remodeling. It keeps the house pleasantly warm on the coldest of days, even the new upstairs, from where the view is grand.

He moved his computer up there, for looking at the mountain clears his mind, although that unfortunately does not speed up his writing. How it is dragging on! Maybe it is so because he has little immediate incentive for it. He remembers so well how he was urging his father, back during their days together in Fort Sill, to write the story of how he experienced the era that spanned the two Great Wars. "Who will read it?" his father shrugged, and that was the end of that. Maybe you should write your memoirs before you had lived them; that way, you'll still know some live people who might open its pages when it's finally finished.

At any rate, while he was writing, Marina was planting flowers everywhere, in front and in the back, without much input from him. He too was doing some planting, but his plants were fruit trees, and always with her help. By now those have become a little orchard. An apricot tree, a nectarine tree, a lemon bush, an avocado tree, a cherimoya bush, two apple trees, a tangerine and a guava sapling, an olive tree, and about five varieties of grape. These grapes are not the seedless and tasteless but supersweet kinds that are the only ones you can buy nowadays in the grocery stores but the fragrant muscat ones that grew in the table-grape section of the vineyard behind the house in Léva, where they were called *saszla* or *muskotály*. One of these he imported to SLO from Chris's vineyard from Montalcino, Italy.

In all this fruiting and flowering, however, they have some unfortunate problems, and those are with the soil and the rain. There is very little of either of it, for the jet stream prefers to funnel clouds from the Pacific to Orgon, while their backyard slopes up quite steeply, and there is bedrock below a few inches of topsoil. So it takes a real root expert like him to handle the gardening. If you sprinkle irrigate a bit too much, you can leach all the nutrients out of that bit of topsoil very easily. You must feel and sense how far the roots of each plant will reach and leave the surface over that area bare. But it is not in Marina's constitution to leave open spaces in the space that her planting spirit occupies. This is apparently hereditary, for her two sons are both overplanters, as was her mother. Rationality has nothing to do with this, for she fully understands the mechanics and the mechanisms of root growth and water and mineral-nutrient economy and ecology.

Up and down their street that was chiseled and developed out of the mountainside some fifty plus years ago, there are some front yards like theirs, with flowering bushes and maybe a lawn in an anglophile imitation of what Americans like to cultivate as their role model, the British one. Then there are front yards that are completely overgrown with ivy, a plant that the developers must have first put there to give the brand-new houses some immediate green curb appeal. Ivy grows fast.

This variant of low-maintenance gardening must also have come from England, for the plant is called English ivy. And it just so happens that they did not come to meet and know any of the folks who like ivy. They themselves had theirs taken out upon arrival. Ivy, he feels, is like Baja. You love it or you hate it. Maybe it is the control freak in him that makes him rip it out wherever he finds it. It is as if ivy spoke to him thusly: "It's you or me. You can fight me, but in the end, I'll win. I am one of your hopeless fights." But they made some good friends with some of those with flowers in their front yards.

The neighbors

From one end of the street to the other, there is Dick, the conservative Republican. He first met him on his way down to the schoolyard some fifteen minutes of a walk away to do his daily five-mile jog there, for this was also Dick's time to walk his dog. To his credit and his dog's delight, he does that every day. One cannot hope to meet a more cheerful, likeable, and personable person than Dick. To stop and have a chat with him is a pleasure even for an introvert all turned outside in, and he would never have guessed the truth about Dick's regrettably misguided political affliction, if Rudi, his next-door neighbor, a Democrat, had not told him about it, for Dick clamps down when it comes to politics, as if he felt that the stone walls of his tenets might crumble if he put them to the acid test of an open-minded analysis.

Rudi himself is every bit as friendly as Dick but decidedly less approachable. He has a large Stars and Stripes flag displayed in front of his house all the time, perhaps to leave no doubt in anyone's mind that he, the Democrat, is no less patriotic than any of the gun-toting, saber-rattling, union-busting folks on the other side of the aisle. He really does not have a good reason or need for this ostentation, for he has some highly honorable service under his belt. He too is an ex-paratrooper. Not only that, Rudi also wore the winged patch of the Eleventh Airborne Division on his shoulder and at the very same time as he did. But they did not know each other, for there were some twelve thousand extroverts assembled at Fort Campbell at the time. Too many to know them all.

My goodness, that was more than fifty-six years ago! And Rudi had been living in this house on Hermosa Way ever since that time! But he was an infantryman with the Five-Eleventh Airborne Infantry Regiment, the one that his new neighbor's artillery battalion, the Eighty-Ninth, would have supported had they been in combat together. Because of this affinity (old soldiers not only never die, but they also relate to each other), there is no strife afoot with Rudi, even though his lot encroaches on a five-foot strip of land that actually belongs to them, Rudi's new neighbors. The developers somehow put the fence in the wrong place although the survey clearly shows where the right one is, and the finances involved in this are a good sign of the times.

When first confronted with the discrepancy, Rudi was disconsolate, for he has an avocado tree growing on that strip that is not his and he is fond of his alligator pears. Also, when you have turned eighty and are used to the way things have been for over fifty years, you have a hard time adjusting to changes like moving fences. "My neighbors came and went and none of them wanted that five-foot strip," he remonstrated.

When told that that narrow border strip was worth more in today's money than his entire lot and house were when he bought them, he refused to believe it. "The taxes I am paying on that strip, Rudi," he informed his neighbor, "are more than you pay on your entire lot and house." To which Rudi could only shake his head in disbelief. "But I won't move the fence as long as you are here," he reassured the old man. "And who knows, maybe I'll croak before you do." But Rudi is not into discussing politics either. He is a Democrat because he liked the way Roosevelt handled the Great Depression not because the spend-and-borrow ways of the Republicans disturb his philosophical equanimity.

The other next-door neighbor, downhill, is Bonnie. Life took her through some tragic events, and she responded to that by outgrowing the pain and disappointment and becoming a bigger and better person for it. It may be because of this education she received of life that she has turned apolitical or at least independent and unaffiliated. At any rate, she is not into discussing politics, although she is clearly on the correct side of the issues of the day, for there is always one. But she keeps a dog, although she is not a dog person, and for him, who is certainly not one either, that is a little like a bone of contention, one to pick or gnaw on. He simply does not trust dogs, no matter how soulful-eyed and reassuringly tail wagging their presence may be to others, not since that one back in Léva scared him badly, when he was seven, acting like he wanted to eat him alive with his bared teeth.

But Bonnie also has two Siamese-descended cats that associate only with her. Being a cat or a dog person is a watershed of personality, and it is not easy for him to understand how someone can relate to both. Maybe she just tolerates the dog. He is a cat person only, and it saddens him a little when Bonnie's Siamese give him only glances of distrust as they pass through his backyard where they make life difficult for the many different kinds of birds that live there. Marina brings Bonnie flowers from the farmer's market, and Bonnie has a nice tree of juicy lemons that are always appreciated in return. She is fun to talk to, and it is good to have her close by.

One house over from Bonnie live Michelle and Bob. They are a rare breed; they are real cat-and-dog people all at once. That is a feat like being able to be in two places at the same time. To my knowledge, only Roger Bacon, the Doctor Magnus, could pull off something like that, but that was eight hundred years ago and may therefore be only hearsay. What is credible about Roger's legacy, however, is that he was an alchemist, a Franciscan friar, and an Aristotelian philosopher—again all that at the same time, and those three things seem mutually exclusive, at least at first glance. It must not have been easy for him to reconcile such disparate callings harmoniously, hence the epithet of *Doctor Magnus*, I take it, for what is great cannot be easy by definition.

How does this apply to Michelle and Bob? If we choose to look at them as a family unit, they embody all three of these somewhat contradictory aspects of Roger's career. Bob, with Michelle's tacit support, took on an infernal-combustion-engine-driven vehicle and converted it to one moved by electricity, the clean, ethereal power of the flowing electron. That is alchemy, not unlike making gold from iron. Then, in their undiscriminating attachment to all creatures that accompany us here on our planet, cats and dogs alike, without ego-tripping in favor of one or the other, they follow in the footsteps of Saint Francis, whose reverence of all that lives contrasted sharply with the rigid dogmas of the anthropocentric theologies of his time. Finally, Michelle, in harmony with Bob, works with people in helping them to realize their potential on their way to a right life, practicing what Aristotle recommended in his discourses on ethics. Imagine the fun having neighbors who reembody the essence of that great doctor of old!

Last of the series in another Bob, as colorful an extrovert as you can hope to associate with. If somebody asked you to describe the typical professor of mathematics, what would you say? Especially if math ranked low in your choice of subjects you had to face in school? I bet it would be the opposite of what I just said of him. Since he retired from Cal Poly, he has done everything from green community service to acting at SLO's Little Theater. A master not only at chess but also at ping-pong, he is a benign tolerator of a boa constrictor, a wash-tub sized turtle, and a menagerie of other animals with whom he shares his home. And the ivy in front of his house does not bother him, for he is not a control freak. Different people simply have different priorities. Person-oriented folks often do not notice the plants around them, and Bob is fun to be with, even though he is so very different.

One more trip to Bethlenfalva

But as time goes on, even in idyllic places like Hermosa Way, things do not stay the same; they change their sense and substance like falling leaves at the end of their day, when the time is ripe for it in climes with seasons. Like in Léva . . . or in Icking . . . or in Oklahoma . . . or in Oregon.

Zöld erdo harmatát	The green forest's dew
Piros csizmám nyomát	The traces of my red boots
Hóval lepi be a tél,	Are covered by the winter's now,
Hóval lepi be a tél	Are covered by the winter's snow

So also his travels that used to be an undivided source of joyous anticipation are changing their allure and are taking on never before experienced side effects. Like seing himself turned into a sardine in an airplane's tourist-class cabin for endless hours. He never noticed this aspect of crossing an ocean before and so did not suffer from it. But now it is time again to go and see if that sad affair of grandfather's house in Bethlenfalva, stuck in the bureaucracy's rut, could be budged a step closer to closure. The mere prospect of it stirs up his by now dormant Hungarian chauvinist's subconscious:

Hogyha megyek Románia felé	When I am o my way towards Romania
Még a fák is sírnak	Even the trees are crying

This is as far as he recalls the text of what used to be a folk song. The rest of it refuses to resurface from the pools of the past, but the melody of it is very much alive in his ears. Nobody else remembers it anymore, and political correctness seems to have kept it even out of Google. This is the day of the European Union now, but Union or not, if he cannot read the telephone book in his very own home village for it is printed now only in a foreign language there, then he simply cannot fight down and lay to rest the upwelling of the nationalist malaise that is encoded in his DNA.

The people who live there do not speak that new language at home, although they have learned to use it whenever their business calls for it. But he does not understand it, and why should he? His ancestors, the Székely, lived there and spoke Hungarian when they rode out into the great plains east of their mountains to meet and greet the last wave of conquering Magyar horsemen eleven hundred years ago. They themselves had come with a previous wave, maybe that of the Huns or the Avars (the historians cannot agree), but they could understand the language, the language of the newcomers, for it was theirs.

These are feelings that only people understand who have a reason to understand them. The Israelis and the Palestinians, they both understand them. The Serbs and the Croats understand them. The Kurds and the Turks understand them mutually also. Americans don't, and how could they? But the Germans and the French have learned to transcend them, so there is hope. These feelings are old and go deep, and to make matters worse, in our times, in the times of modern history textbooks used in our schools, national histories are written and often invented to pour oil on the flames of ethnic strife in the name patriotic pride.

So it happened (to give an example) that a Romanian scientist was visiting the Botany Department in Davis at the time when he was in the middle of writing his dissertation there. The chairman, a jovial, kindly gentleman, seemed pleased to introduce them. In his well-meaning, naive, genuinely American way, with a mind void of any misgivings as behooves a Ph.D. botanist without any insight and interest in the affairs of remote and obscure corners of the globe, he offered, "You two are from the same part of the world, so you should be delighted to exchange thoughts and experiences."

Well, inevitably, the subject of Erdély, the bone of contention, soon arose in that exchange. It was a delicate matter for him, for the Romanian was a guest, and he, as the American, was a host bound by the laws of courtesy and hospitality. But upon hearing that Erdély had never been Hungarian, he could not help opening for his guest an American history book that showed the area as the "Kingdom of Hungary" through the centuries. This book included the following passage:

> The Latin-speaking Wallachians and Moldavians, inhabiting modern Rumania, are first mentioned at the beginning of the fourteenth century. Their later claim to be descendants of the Roman colonists planted there in the second century AD seems sententious and improbable, for the Roman withdrawal from Rumania [Dacia] in 270 and the appearance of the Vlach states are separated by a millennium in which the country was the property of Slav and nomad and which is devoid of all evidence of roman survival. Almost certainly the Vlachs came from the western Balcans and only migrated into [present-day] Rumania as the nomads abandoned it in the late thirteenth and early fourteenth century.

The man was furious, derisive, and incredulous. "This is an insidious, ignorant fabrication," he shouted. It was clear that his worldview was formed by facts of local manufacture and that he was unaware of how the rest of the world viewed his facts. But his guest's reaction made him think. Was his own worldview also the mirage of an artifact, a Hungarian one in his case? But the pictures in his several non-Hungarian history books showed battles, migrations, and boundaries that seemed real, if any past beyond the present moment has any reality at all, any reality worth getting upset about.

Well, they survived this ocean crossing again without undue health effects. They rented a car in Budapest and made it to Bethlenfalva again, with him driving and Miklós navigating over those roads that were still in the experimental stage. Twice they drove around a policeman standing in the middle of the road demanding a bribe. In Mexico, the police at least claimed that some *infracción* had been committed to obtain their *mordida*. Here not even that. Had Zsolt not instructed them to ignore this type of local law, they would probably have obeyed the custom and paid.

This time, they checked into the Hargita *szálloda*. It is owned and operated by a Budapest company, and the quality of service and also the level of the prices were up to European standards. And what did they do there, at home again, at last? All they did really was feeling oddly out of place. They drove out to the old Spa of Homoród with their cousin Móka. It is a place of vivid childhood memories, of playing at being scouts in the forests. But Homoród, although there was a road sign pointing to it, was simply not there anymore, not the way they remembered it. Communism apparently had not been kind to bourgeois diversions like tourism.

There was a problem, though, with any real exploration of the past together. Miklós has a bad back, and after a hundred yards of walking, he is ready to give it a rest. So he had to leave him behind to be able to walk every street of the town as is his custom, to look at every gravestone in the old cemetery overgrown by huge old trees, to explore new sights, and to grieve over old ones that he remembered but that were no longer there. But he felt guilty about leaving his brother behind on the one hand, and a little resentful that he showed only a strange sort of guarded, superficial interest in being there, on the other. It was as if his umbilical had been severed, perhaps by the different paths his life has lead him. Maybe Miklós had been searching for an america entirely different from his, or maybe he was satisfied by the one he found. He suggested to his brother to rent a place and stay for a while to see if the fractured past would heal up a bit if they gave it a chance to do so. But Miklós just shook his head incomprehendingly. "Let's scoot," he said. And so they did.

Bush era politics

Having scooted back to Hermosa Way, where life is generally placid and in tune with his temperament, he went back to watering the garden. Marina, however, seeks to get involved in this life. She needs and finds human contact and volunteers for the care of the sick and dying with the local hospice organization. She also rediscovered Buddhism in earnest, has become a practicing member of the local *sangha*, and is gaining new, like-minded friends.

He finds all this activity enviable, but his tongue has run out of words, and he was born with only a very few to start with more than seven decades ago. Now, unfortunately, when you are with people, you have to have something to say to them, and for him that something can only be something that matters, for he is and has always been incapable of small talk. I think it was his brother who got him that way, for he always made fun of everything he tried to say when he was little. That made him feel as if anything he could say was wrong and not worth saying. Strange how such banter can become a lasting handicap that you cannot ever overcome.

But his silence does not mean that he is through with the affairs of the world as they are brought to him on television. They continue to interest him very much, but do so in an increasingly remote, abstract way. There is politics, for instance: the increasingly bitter infighting between the two factions that toss the structures of power back and forth between them in the Land of the Free every few years like a ping-pong ball. Why should it matter to him at this stage of his life which side should be hitting the ball at the moment? As long as they do not perpetrate some crime by covert action or overt omission that makes the stock market crash. The market that provided them half their income in dividends before its latest crash.

So he walks or drives down in his gas-guzzling pathfinder SUV to his favorite café, Rudolph's, on Higuera Street, almost every day to have his cup of coffee and to read the *San Francisco Chronicle*. He is what the British call a "Mediterranean man" who can enjoy reading his paper only in a public place, even if it is not on a picturesque promenade looking out on the sea. The news matters, and it is the nefarious conduct of the people in power, "them," the other side, that make it matter these days, in the early ones of the new millenium. Central to it all are those inane economic policies that they tolerated and those tragic wars that they have unleashed.

As he is uneasily pondering all these imponderables while sipping his coffee, people drop in sometimes for a word, interrupting his preoccupation with timing the speed at which he solves his crossword and sudoku puzzles. They are not much into the wars; those are too remote to be real for them. All the more, however, they are into worrying about the economy. The stock market carnage following the dot com bubble was by then history, although a painfully recent one. But the next bubble, the one involving real estate was rapidly ballooning out to its final, irrationally exuberant proportions.

One of his good neighbors, the biologist, was involved in that himself, personally. He lent his lifetime savings to developers who paid him 12 percent interest while an empty lot, say, was being developed into a modern mansion with that loan. Those mansions were selling like hotcakes, and when sold, the speculator (called investor at the time) got his money back plus his part of the profit made on the deal. Everybody was doing this. It was a racket that had become a sure thing in peoples' minds since the boom that had now turned into a bubble had lasted for years already. What if the mansion did not sell? That was not part of the equation yet, and doomsday thoughts were out of style.

Then there was one savvy guy at Rudolph's who could not stop talking about the speculation with all those worthless derivatives that was fueling stock prices, which were not supported, he claimed, by the moribund US industrial production base. This one was on neither side politically, maybe because his mind was too abstract for that. He was a computer nerd, one who puts all the available historical data into his programs in attempts to model future events. One morning, he came in to proclaim his computer's vision of what was to come: "What will the next administration do, the one that must sweep out the present discredited one with promises of change?" he said. "It will escalate the war and aggravate our economic demise. And my computer does not lie." Hearing this, he relapsed back into working on his puzzles.

Las Vegas

Newspaper puzzles are not real, although they are black on white, but he thinks they encourage his brain to function, so he does them. Then there are enigmas that are even less real. Questions like "Why is there anything?" or "Could nonexistence exist?" These are easy, for you can leave them alone. But there are others that you cannot. Those are the problems of finding solutions for things one is unprepared for. Or if not a solution because there may not be one, at least the right attitude to face the problem and bear its consequences. Let me explain.

On the surface, their golden years at the foot of San Luis Mountain were uneventful. This is the reason, perhaps, why their trips, short in time compared to all that day-to-day placidity, take up most of the space of this narrative. Likewise, the tale of their younger son's life earns far less mention than it merits, for its course runs in straight and narrow channels, varied and exciting though it is. The creaky wheel is that gets the oil, and so their eyes rest mostly on that family outpost in Las Vegas, where their older son, the dean of the family's next generation, had been leading an independent, productive, and drug-fee life since he moved there about the same time as they moved back to California from Corvallis in 1999.

His was an activity that he liked and was good at, albeit it was in the service of an endeavor frowned upon by some: gambling. Or gaming, as that industry had renamed itself. Just give the beast a more savory name and, bingo, the stigma is off. What's in a name? Everything. And true enough, all those untold thousands of slot machines in all those huge, small-city-sized casinos on the Strip of LV apparently fulfill a societal need, as uncounted multitudes throng through the plush premises day and night where the slots are lined up as far as the eye can see to plug some hole or satisfy some urge that their users suffer from at home. So they go to Vegas to game, and many of them, I am sure, return home satisfied.

Now, back in the days when he was passing through Reno on his way to the outback of the Grass Valley some twenty years ago, he was not above stopping at a casino either. Only he did not go there to shake hands with the one-armed bandits a dime at a time. Instead, he was studying stress psychology at the blackjack table. At that time, the bandits still had a redeeming side effect. To make them work, you had to pull a lever, and that built up the biceps of your punching arm. But now the bandits do not line up their cherries or plums mechanically anymore, the times of progress have passed them by, and they have all been moved to a junkyard or to a museum. Electronic machines line up now in endless rows on the red carpets of the gaming floors, and they have to be administered, serviced, and their malfunctions corrected. That is the line of work that Steve had grown into.

It was a real growth process. He started out as a parts clerk and solderer of electric junctions in Corvallis with Acres Gaming, a people-oriented small outfit where the employees liked to do whatever they were doing, for they were treated right, treated as people. He soon moved up to building circuit boards for the next-generation, brainy bandits by computer-aided design and then further to interacting with casino staff on the various problems that their installation, maintenance, and trouble-shooting entails. And that included even travel to distant continents. Then Acres moved to Vegas, and he was enthralled, at first, by the ever-glittering flimflam of that metropolis of make-believe.

Meanwhile he had become a respected presence in his company and had earned the freedom to come to work and go home at his own daily rhythm, which was that of a night owl. This confirmed him further in his self-image of a maverick, someone who is different (and perhaps better) than just a run-of-the-mill, coat-and-tie establishment man. Life was good; he rented a nice apartment, and Bethany, his girlfriend from Corvallis, came to live with him. Bethany was a fine young lady, and they liked her. But she had her own mind and needed her own space, and her space and his were different spaces. To their regret, things did not work out.

He was only marking time. A relationship is a growth process, a more intensive one than life alone as a bachelor, and growth involves pain. No pain no gain, remember? Relating to one's work is also a type of relationship. It also requires growth. Especially in American business. There, you cannot be content with staying in place, in the niche that fits your needs and wants at the moment. You can do that in government work and still be good and productive, but in business, you wash out before long if you do not strive for advancement, and do it successfully.

And when Acres was taken over by a large corporation, the ice age of impersonal, cold-eyed management descended on the few who survived the merger. Steve had to come to work when everyone else did, and the bosses looked at mavericks with jaundiced eyes. With his own eyes newly opened up to reality by reality, he started asking himself why he was selling the days of his only life so that others could profit by his labors. He became disillusioned by the life that he felt locked into, for he had no marketable skills in anything but the highly specialized work he had been doing for the gamers. He had all kinds of good, salable talents and a gift of empathy, communications, and leadership, but he did not seem to have the self-confidence to put them to use. And moving on had never been easy for him, his outgoing, charming demeanor notwithstanding.

Then there was the new relationship. It started at Rob's wedding, where Lindsey was one of the bride's maids, and it blossomed into a real love affair. And it was for a good reason, for she was a lovely lady, cheerful, caring, and warmhearted, and a hard-working one on top of it, one competent with her finances. Again, they really liked her and did their best to make her feel at home in the family, a welcome to which she responded in kind. Watching it from a distance, the affair seemed to be going well until she moved to LV to share Steve's life in a common household.

The new house, which Steve had bought, was fun to visit for a day or two; he was always a perfect host. It was spacious and let in the clean desert air and the bright desert sun. It was the opposite of a badger's den, but only in its physical layout. Of course, I had never experienced living in a badger's den, but knowing something of badger idiosyncrasy, I assume that badgers arrange and furnish their living space to suit their solitary and uncompromising ways. Ways that admit no permanent concessions to another badger's needs. So how could a substantial woman with a clearly space-requiring temperament like Lindsey set roots and grow there? History was repeating itself, and when that happens, it is meaningful. It means there is a lack of growth.

He, as always watched and waited from afar—Las Vegas is a full day's drive from SLO—hoping that the cold collections of antique slot machines, defunct computer consoles, unused tool sets, and other disorderly heaps of things that his mind summed up as "junk" in that house would melt away under Lindsey's sunny, life-loving influence. Of course, one person's junk is another's treasure.

But the zephyr winds, the currents of Steve's life, that blew warm and strong for years after he had exorcised the demon the first time must have turned into gusty turbulence at some point during this time, for the news from LV, sporadic as it was, did not speak of the blossoms of spring. And the streams of discontent at work and at home were emptying in the end into a dead sea like that dried-up one in Russia, where hulks of stranded boats lie now on their sides on the desert floor, where waves were not long ago playing with the wind. The sea of escape, methamphetamine.

The demon reappears in Budapest

Miraculously, the stock market recovered after the implosion of the dot com bubble, and they felt safe enough financially to pay yet another visit to the past. They decided to invite Steve so that the next generation could experience the roots for the first time, but even more to get him out of the rut in LV. Getting a glimpse of something new, they naively hoped, might clear his mind.

The kid, pushing forty, had dark rings around his eyes when he arrived in Munich, and it was not just from jet lag. He was edgy and touchy and in need of sleep, a lot of it, or so it seemed, but eventually he rallied and they set off for Hungary. He enjoyed the train ride from Munich to Budapest; the luxury of a good Hungarian meal in the elegant dining car of the Béla Bartók (they eliminated that in the meantime and relaced it with an ugly modern buffet) while the scenery was floating by outside was a first for him. It was a good experience. They had good talks, and the shadows lifted for a moment. Budapest was a success; he was entranced by it during his week there.

He tried to impart to his son what little he knew about this new city, regretting all the time that he missed his chance to plant the seeds of the past much earlier, stories that might have connected his son more harmoniously with his roots. Looking down on Pest on the other side of the Great River from the ramparts of the Castle of Buda, he tied to outline a bit of the history of the city below.

When the Turks were driven out at last toward the end of the seventeenth century by a European coalition army, all that was left of the Renaissance splendor of the court of the last great Hungarian king, Mátyás Király, was a small, muddy village, from where you could look up the hill on the Buda side and see essentially nothing but devastation even inside the walls of the fortress city up there. And what followed then was not a rebirth in freedom but more hard times now under Austrian domination. It was the time of the first fight for independence (that lasted some forty years and ended in 1711) from the Austrian Empire to reestablish the ancient glory of a sovereign past in freedom. It was the struggle of groups of dedicated patriots, a mostly ragtag force facing the overwhelming superiority of a well-fed, well-equipped, armed and trained professional occupation army. The freedom fighters were called the *Kuruc*, and some of their songs that survived reflect the mood of a people after defeat:

Nagymajtényi síkon leborúlt a zászló,	The flag fell down on the plains of Nagymajtény,
Rászállt tollászkodni egy fekete holló	A black raven alit on it to preen himself.
Tépi sötét szárnyát, hull a tolla rája,	He rends his dark wings with a falling of feathers
Szegény kurucoknak tépedt zászlajára.	On the tattered flag of the poor Kuruc.

The songs were accompanied by the *tárogató*, a woodwind instrument of the oboe variety, one of a plaintive but also raucous and vigorous timbre, an instrument that the Kuruc cavalry used to signal the attack on the Austrians and on the traitorous Magyar allies of the enemy, the *Labanc*.

In time a new city was rebuilt in the plains, at the foot of the *Várhegy*, the Castle Mountain, and on the hills of Buda that surround it, and now it is a veritable metropolis, far too big for the small country to maintain. The rest country that was left of the old Hungarian Kingdom after the Trianon Peace Dictate following the first Great War. And so on close inspection, let's admit it, it looks somewhat neglected by Western standards. Western European ones, that is, for parts of many an American city could consider itself lucky to be that well maintained.

But Steve did not do any close inspecting; he just gazed down from the ramparts of the *Halászbástya* on the city below, pulsating peacefully in the amber glow of the setting sun at the hour when the Great River's beginning and end vanish in the mists of falling dusk, and he liked what he saw.

In fact, he liked it so much that he felt at home enough to dress one morning as some American teenagers think is fashionable. Sloppy tee shirt and ragged, holey blue jeans. What now? He tried to explain to his son that he, a grown man in that kind of getup would be picked up by the police as a vagrant, especially up there, in the upscale atmosphere of the *Várhegy*.

The reaction was unexpected. It was that of a rebellious child. This behavior should have been a flashing red alarm light for them. But while they were troubled and saddened as well as upset by it, they still recognized it as their older son's characteristic moodiness and sensitivity to anything he perceived as criticism. He half apologized by muttering darkly about "I am having a hard time" and "Lindsey's family is down on me" and "You don't know what I've been through," but he refused to actually talk about it.

In retrospect, it is clear that his parents should have seen the proverbial writing on the wall. They should have suspected that this emotional volatility was more than remnants of past drug use, which they knew had left him somehow stuck at the emotional age when it began, when he was a teenager. When they learned a few months later, from Lindsey, that their son's life had fallen apart and that there had been a long lead-up to the final collapse, they thought back to that week in Budapest and recognized the signs in retrospect.

But at the moment, on the evening of Steve's last day in Budapest, the country celebrated its Harvest Festival with a Fourth of July style show of fireworks over the Danube. A huge crowd was assembled along the eastern walls of the Castle District to watch it, and then a swift-moving thunderstorm of bright lightning from black clouds moved in rapidly to snuff out the festivities. There were even a couple of fatal accidents resulting from it. They got home before the first drop fell, for their apartment was just a block or two away from the *Halászbástya*, but the black cloud was to linger over them after that for some two years.

There was a misunderstanding with Steve's return date; he had inadvertently extended his leave by one day, and his company used that as a pretext to fire him. But they probably have been intending to do so for a while, for his supervisors must have seen the signs as well.

Relating to realities

They took Steve to the airport in the morning, and Márti and Frédi arrived by train from Fülek that same afternoon. They rented a little apartment in the Castle District on the *Várhegy* of Buda, and the relatives from across the border commented with pleasure on this experience of staying up there, where every house is a *műemlék*, a registered, historical reminder of the past. They felt it was their time to invite, for they had enjoyed their cousin's hospitality many times by then.

For the occasion, they organized a get-together of the Karafiáths, those that could be assembled. Jenő *bácsi*, in his midnineties now, could not come, but his brother, visiting one last time from Florida, was there. He died shortly after he returned to America. And so did Jenő bácsi. He promised Klári *néni,* Jenő *bácsi*'s wife, the aunt who had written to Márti about having found his scribbled address on his grandfather's headstone, that they would come to see his uncle after they returned from Erdély but then did not follow up on it. The visit there had taken longer than they planned, and there was no time. Or so they thought. But they heard later that Jenő *bácsi* was very upset about it. This was a man, still alive, who had officiated at his parents' wedding! And they did not find the time to see him before he died!

Then they drove to Erdély, and there they went to see everybody. They stayed in Szováta for a second time with Bandi *bácsi* and Berta *néni*, his father's first cousin, both pushing ninety, at that strange house filled with antiques. Old Bandi is a collector, and he was wistful about the fate of all his treasures after his death, for they have no children. He offered his house for sale with the provision that they could stay in it until they died. "And that won't be very long now," he smiled, looking fondly at the arrays of antique plates that covered the walls, as if he were praying for tender loving care for them in all perpetuity. His visitor almost slipped into his "don't cling" lecture, thinking of Marina's Mexican weavings on their own walls, which his sons will not know what to do with, when they themselves go. Each of us is saddled hard enough with our own collections.

But this visit was a good one; he experienced his hosts as kindred spirits. At one point in the evening, by a glass of *barrack pálinka*, Bandi offered to read his favorite poem. He did not mention the title, for that would have given it away (he said), but as the unique rhythm of the masterpiece progressed with its double rhymes in each line, the listener had a distinct experience of *déjà vu*. Then it clicked. *A Holló! Persze, világos, ez a holló*! "The Raven"! Of course, it's clear; this is "The Raven"! Poor Poe, he caught himself thinking, this sounds even better in Hungarian than your own original version." For the translator, Babits Mihály, was a great poet in his own right. Bandi was elated about the success of his favorite, and for him, this excursion into the music of that poem's drumbeat was a special treat. To make all this more lifelike, there was a stuffed raven sitting on a ledge, but it did not contribute its favorite prognosis of the future this time, at least not audibly.

Unfortunately, the mayor of Székelyudvarhely was not that accommodating. Móka set up an interview with the man to discuss the fate of the family house in Bethlenfalva. Heavy-set, with feisty eyes that blinked noncommittantly in a broad, beefy face, the mayor displayed a cold and professional air, and although he did not actually say "nevermore" a single time, his message was clear. He was reputed to be involved with a private foundation whose business it was to acquire real estate of legally undetermined ownership at cut-rate prices. It was his duty to preserve his city's property for public use, was his line, and behind this official facade, he thought he could sense the hidden glee, the man's obvious pleasure in his position of power as he was restraining with difficulty his urge to gloat: "I have other plans for your house."

For him, the petitioner, the experience was one of revulsion, and it was so strong that it triggered a distant, seemingly unrelated association to surface. It was the face of that conservative radio talk show host of the Institute of Advanced Conservative Studies, whose voice is on all morning aired on Premiere Radio Networks, the one on whom he tunes in when driving up to the trailhead at the foot of Bishop's Peak for his morning hikes. His only exposure to that face was its brief appearance on television, when the news of the man's addiction to some drug broke.

But all of a sudden, while the mayor was thinking his "nevermore," that forgotten dream face emerged from nowhere, the one of that brown animal in the forest of Kereskény, the mountain lion, with the bloody piglet between his feet. It was the face of that radio host, beyond any doubt, looking out at him at the moment with the mayor's narrow, squinting eyes. It was very disconcerting, for he had to talk business with a savvy adversary, and he could feel his cousin Móka's disapproval of his distraction.

But Móka was not distracted, fortunately. He knew that while the mayor was in office, nothing much could be done. He just appealed the case through the courts all the way to the supreme one in Bukarest, and as a fast-forward footnote here, that court just decided, at long last, to dismiss the objections of the now deposed mayor of Székelyudvarhely to give us our old house back.

It was a long journey, that one in Europe. It ended with the traditional grape harvest at Chris's place near Montalcino in the Toscana. But eventually, they got home to San Luis Obispo, and I will skip describing in any detail the dark years that followed.

Marina stopped smiling. They went to the meetings of recovering addicts and consulted back and forth with their shrink, Bud, a charismatic old retired professor of history and self-declared unreconstructed socialist. He wished he could have had him for a friend, but that is apparently against the professional code of psychiatric practice. Bud described the risks of what is called an "intervention" in drug treatment. They decided against it.

Their visits to Las Vegas were heartbreaking. Steve had withdrawn his retirement savings from his IRA account and was living from day to day spending that. He had ideas for a great screenplay that would highlight crucial moments in human history, illuminating human evolution and destiny. Big sheets of paper with the film's timeline covered his living room walls.

His friends around him abandoned him. Lindsey, in a last desperate attempt to save him, threatened to leave him if he did not give up his drug use, and when that did not help, she left to save herself. It was heartbreaking. Bud said that he knew of no published, credible case where a confirmed methamphetamine addict had ever recoved fully. Yet Steve was sure of himself that he could stop anytime he felt that the time was ripe for it. Enough of that. I do not want to go there again. Today I keep trying to convince him to write his own story. He is good with words, and the world can benefit from the wisdom his experience has taught him.

The cloud is lifting

His own story, told in his own words, for miracles happen. One day, he simply stopped. No detox, no nothing. Just like that. He recognized that his erstwhile friend and ally, the dependable one, the one that was always there to help, to ease the pain of stresses and disappointments, had abandoned him. What the friend had to offer turned bitter. He had revealed himself as a false friend, a dark angel. Can you believe it? It happened. And he did it all by himself, on his own.

He trained himself in printing tee shirts and then got a job selling them for a regular company. In the process, he turned into a resourceful salesman. But the timing was off. This was the beginning of the very end of the great secular real estate bubble whose implosion also triggered what has in the meantime been dubbed the Great Recession. People were losing their jobs, over half a million of them a month for a while. So they stopped buying anything but essentials, and you can do without printed tee shirts. His new company sank into bankruptcy, while his beloved house, his castle, sank "under water": It was now worth less than the mortgage he owed on it. He took in housemates, but they also lost their jobs and quit helping him with paying the rent.

He struggled on for a while, and apparently, because one miracle begets another, he did not lose his spirit and did not return to the false friend for solace. In the end, he made the right decision, let the courts clear his debts, and came home to the house on Hermosa Way. And that time is now.

The days dwindle down

Winter is coming again even if only mildly, Central California style. The wind from the North Pole that blows straight down on Bishop's Peak from across the ocean is becoming cooler with every passing day, even though the ice of that Pole is said to be melting. But around here, November is interspersed with many halcyon days. Yet they are getting shorter each time the sun rises. That old Sinatra song that sounded so far away when he first heard it, but that has been haunting him most of his life, is moving in on me ever closer, looking at me from the front row now, just below the stage where the last scene of my play is acting itself out:

> And the days dwindle down to a precious few
> September, November . . .
> And these precious days I'll spend with you
> These precious days I'll spend with you

Yes, with you. And she is now smiling again. Marina is smiling again, now that her son has come back, back to her and to life. That is the only thing that counts. Steve has turned into a different person. He is no longer only cheerful and personable, he goes out of his way to be helpful in every one of the many big and small ways of living together in the same space. He reads, hikes, and even took up cooking with gusto. He also took the first chance that offered itself and went to work in solar installations. And there is promise that the miracle will last.

There has been no more news about that court decision in Bukarest, and Móka says things take their time in Romania. But when the time comes, I will have to go back there once more to take possession, maybe even this summer? That might add yet another scene to the last act. I would like to see my people again, one last time. I would also like to be buried there, in the cemetery of Bethlenfalva. But last night, I had another Kafka dream. It suggested a different scenario, perhaps a more realistic one. And it was one with a good ending, as good as anyone can hope for.

Epilogue

—Nachwort—Utószó

Dreams often do not spell out all their details exactly in sequence; you just "know" what's behind the settings of the stage; the events of the previous acts are well in your mind while the here and now of the present moment's action plays itself out. So he "knew" in that dream that Rob was off to Naples to work on his airplanes there, and Steve had just moved to Guadalajara to start putting solar panels on Mexican rooftops. As to himself, the memory of Marina was accompanying him with every step he took, was with him in everything that he still did. So he knew that it was okay with her to buy a first-class ticket to Hungary so that he could go there in comfort and style this last time, to experience at last what winter was like in Bethlenfalva and to let his days then dwindle down, there, at home, to the end of his December.

But a couple of days before he was to leave, he fell ill. He could not walk, let alone drive, and so he was quite emaciated by the time his dear neighbor Michelle found him a week later, sitting in the leather easy chair downstairs in the living room, behind the picture window looking out on Bishop's Peak that he used to climb every day in the days when he could. She got worried when he did not pick up the local paper that she left daily in his mailbox after she was through reading it herself. She called an ambulance and had him taken to the hospital in Arroyo Grande, on Halcyon Street. There they kept him for a whole week but not being able to tell what was wrong with him and what to do for him, they decided to send him home. "You are ready to go, young man," they said. "Call your folks and have them pick you up."

It was November again, and since the afternoon had worn on by the time the staff had made its decision, it was turning dark. The volunteer in charge of the wheelchair rolled him out to the curb. No one was coming, and the old attendant was shivering in the thickening, cold fog. So he told him to go on back in and let him sit on the covered bench in front while he was waiting for his pick-up. The man protested; it was against the rules to leave a patient alone, but in the end, his discomfort persuaded him to leave.

Then silence fell. A streetlight gave off a hazy, washed-out substance that felt like a tempera rainscape by a dilettante painter looks. The monotone, dark fog was swirling around him and limited the contours of visibility to those of a small room. He felt content. He had his gray, warm windbreaker on and Rob's blue ski cap over his ears. He was at ease; fear had subsided. He would not see the sun rise again, an inner voice assured him of that.

It was the voice that counts the hours, the hours of that borrowed time whose far horizon now was within an arm's reach all of a sudden, and it was no longer a secret what it was really counting,

Der uns die stunden zählte,	He, who counted the hours for us
er zählt weiter.	he keeps on counting.
Was mag er zählen, sag?	Tell me, what is he counting?
Er zählt und zählt.	He just counts and counts.

for there was little left to count. Even change itself ceased shifting its shadows now; the cold, dark, damp fog around him was motionless,

Nicht kühler wirds	It does not become colder
nicht nächtiger	nor more darksome
nicht feuchter.	nor more damp.

and only the solitude of silence was left over to go on listening to itself:

Nur was uns lauschen half:	Only that which helped us hark
es lauscht nun	it now listens
für sich allein.	alone, by itself.

But *he* was not quite there yet. A pang of anxiety sprang up as if from nowhere: had he left the sprinkler on in the back? The chirimoya bush always wanted watering, but the water bill could be stiff. All in all, however, sitting there like that was not different from what introverts do all along, only it was disquieting that the pictures, plans and expectations of future events had dried up, and he, accustomed to live in his head, perceived this spectral vacuum now in its essence, as that which is imperceptible, like emptiness. And really, it was not an unpleasant feeling at all, not wishing for anything.

Pictures of the past soon arose, however, and put him at ease. That faint light out there somewhere—a streetlight maybe?—almost looked like a candle, a candle in a small, deserted, dark room. Like the one Petőfi told him about when he foresaw his own death as a hero on the battlefield, and all the kids in fifth grade wanted to die like him while listening to the air-raid sirens:

"... Egy gondolat bánt engemet,	One thought keeps haunting me,
Ágyban, párnák közt halni meg ...	To die in bed among cushions!
Elfogyni lassan mint egy gyetyaszál	To burn down slowly like a candle stick
Mely elhagyott, sötét szobában áll ...	That stands in a deserted, dark room ...
Ne ily halált én Istenem,	Do not give me such a death my God!
Ne ily halált adj énnekem ...	Do not let me die like that!
Ott essek el én	Let me fall out there
A harc mezején ...	On the battlefield ...

"*Suum cuique*," my son, "*Suum cuique*," the Latin teacher of Léva chimed in. "It was not your lot, though you tried. Of course, you could have tried a little harder. But neither do I see any cushions around, come to think of it, if that hard bench you sit on is a source of consolation for you." "But the war zone where they sent me was not the kind of battlefield where I wanted to fall, sir," he tried to interject, only Schlusnus cut him short, "What is this 'sir' stuff at this point in time? Where our parallel lines are about to meet now, in infinity, we are all alike. No excuses now. High time to clean up your act and get on with it. *Nur forwärts gibt es einen Weg*!"

"But it's not up to me. Nothing was ever up to me," he tried to explain only to be consoled by a friendly, benign voice. "*Úgy van kis fiam, az igaz*," his father was saying. "*De most azért nem szabad mindjárt elszontyolodni.*" That was about some problem long forgotten, but that word of encouragement on their way home to their refugee room in Harthausen in that cold winter night remained with him forever, and now he wished he could share that comfort with someone when another voice asked him: "What took you so long?" It was none other than Natty Bumppo, the old trapper, sitting next to him. "I've been waiting for you here since I met you last time in Budapest. Remember? In that hospital, where you lost your tonsils." He tried to sort this out. "You have? But that was seventy years ago, and this bench is new! Well, anyway, I am so happy to have you here! You of all people! The one who can really understand my tale of the road!" He was starting to tell Bumppo about it, when a real, harsh voice interrupted.

"Move it! You can't sit here!" Well, well, look at that, he thought. One last challenge is coming my way. "And why not?" he said aloud and thought, Should I have added: May I ask you, sir? but he did not say it for the sake of being decisive, concise, and to the point. Like an extrovert, this last time. The man was elderly and portly, dressed in the uniform of a private security guard, and his voice was beery. "Because this is private property, and vagrants may not sit here at night," he said.

Well, well, he thought again, a challenge indeed it is. "How do you define a vagrant?" he demanded firmly, but with a hidden, inward tinge of amusement. "You wanna argue with me?" the man pointed to his side arm, only he had been too much of a gunman in his day not to recognize a fake pistol. "No, I do not want to argue with you," he said, "but let me tell you what a vagrant is. He is an introvert who wanders the byways of this Earth in search of an america. Like you and me both." The man backed off. "What is this stuff! You a philosopher or something? I don't give a rat's butt. I'll just call the police. You and me both! The gall! They'll show you an America! In jail!" And he disappeared into the fog.

Silence fell again, but the incident left him exhausted. One last social intercourse, he thought. And what an ugly one! That was all I needed. Now it is really time to go. But oh my god, did I pay the long-term care insurance back in September when it was due? And why did I not get some more firewood before that first rain of the season fell?

Then he heard the air-raid sirens wailing in the distance, coming closer with the red, white, and blue lights of exploding bombs flashing. And after a little while, a round disc appeared pointing at him, glowing orange in the thick fog. Orange! How come there was no real Magyar word for that? Maybe because nothing had that color until someone brought that first golden apple with him from the Land of the Hesperides. And then they called the color by the name of that fruit! *Narancs-sárga. Orangen-gelb.* Orange-yellow. Always his favorite color! Except for that long moment, the time when mountain-lake blue had him confused. Hare-Krishna yellow, yes, that's what it is, Hare-Krishna-orange-yellow. Wow! That is a concept that did not exist until it did. A new color! How many more new colors will Krishna show him now?

"Never mind the firewood, the insurance, and the water bill!" rang out a voice like one he had never heard before. "Your search is over. You can stop clinging to the road now."

"Krishna!" he said. "Krishna! I *did* remember your name! Like you told me in the Gita. But I do not deserve you. I was not good. I was not kind, I was judgmental, and I played the spider solitaire and the stock market instead of seeking you." But Krishna smiled. And then, indulgently, his orange shroud enveloped him.

Hungarian Pronunciation

All words are emphasized on the first syllable. Doubled consonants are pronounced double like in Italian; they do not shorten the preceding vowel like in German. Consonants expressed by digraphs are doubled by doubling the first letter of the digraph (e.g., szsz → ssz, gygy→ggy). Accent marks do not denote emphasis as in Spanish but indicate differences in sound quality for a/á and e/é, and lengthen the other vowels. Consecutive vowels constitute separate syllables; there are no diphthongs. Symbols of the International Phonetic Alphabet are shown in parentheses when no comparisons are available.

a—like u in but, but more guttural
á—like a in father
c—ts, like z in German Zeit
cs—like ch in church
e—like in get but more guttural (æ)
é—like in fate
gy—d and y completely amalgamated (ɟ)
i—like i in hit (short)
í—like ea in heat (long)
j—like y in yet
k—k but not aspirated
ly—like ll in Spanish llamar
ny—like ñ in Spanish año
o—like o in British not (short)

ó—like o in rose (long)
ö—like eu in French jeune (œ, short)
ő—like ö in German schön (long)
r—like r in Spanish rojo
s—like sh in shirt
sz—like s in sit
th—archaic, pronounced as t
ty—t and y completely amalgamated (c)
u—like in soot (short)
ú—like in boot (long)
ü—like u in French musique (short)
ű—like ü in German grün (long)
y—archaic, pronounced as the i in in
zs—like j in French jour or English ple*as*ure

Glossary

F-French, G-German, I-Italian, L-Latin, M-Magyar (Hung.), N-neologism, S-Spanish.

A

AARP: American Association of Retired Persons.
Afoot and light-hearted . . . : From "Song of the Open Road" in *Leaves of Grass* by Walt Whitman, 1900.
A nagyvilágon e kivűl . . . : From "Szózat" (Appeal) by *Vörösmarty Mihály,* 1836. The official anthem (Himnusz) is sung at the beginning of ceremonies, and *Szózat* at the end. M
À propos: With regard to. F
Aber sie sind doch . . . : But you are not really and American, since you speak German. G
Abschiedsschmaus: Farewell feast. G
Abstractum: A theoretical and not a concrete entity. *Abstracta*: plural.
(mit) Ach und Krach: By the skin of one's teeth. G
Actinomycetes: Unicellular, prokaryotic, and microscopic soil organisms.
Ad majorem Dei gloriam: For the greater glory of God. L
Ad nauseam: To the point of vomiting. L
Adlai Stevenson: Liberal, scholarly politician; Eisenhower's losing opponent in two Presidential campaigns.
Agendum: That which is to be done; singular of agenda. L
Agricola terram arat: The farmer ploughs the field. L
Agua de . . . : Water (ice) of melon, of lemon, of peanut, of guava. S

Ahol nincs, ott ne keress: Do not search where there is nothing. M

Aida: Opera by Giuseppe Verdi.

Aki a hazát szereti, a job oldalon áll: He who loves his country stands on the right side. M

Alcalde of the pueblo: Mayor of the town. S

Aldea: Hamlet. S

Alexander: That's King Alexander III of Macedon (the Great), conquered half the known world back in the fourth century BC.

Alger Hiss: An influential state Department Official, accompanied Roosevelt to Yalta. Was later accused of being a Soviet spy.

Alice: Whose *Adventures in Wonderland* were written in 1865 by English author and mathematics professor Lewis Carrol*l* (C.L. Dodgson).

Állami szektor: Public sector. M

Alles in Ordnung: Everything is okay. G

Alles konnte Ron vertragen . . . : From *Max und Moritz* slightly changed to fit the context.

Alles war verrückt . . . : Everything was crazy. G

Alma mater: School, college, or university that one has attended or from which one has graduated. L

Am Brunnen vor dem Tore . . . : From "Der Lindenbaum" ("The Lindentree"), by Wilhelm Müller, 1822. G

Ambiance: Feeling or mood associated with a particular place, person, or thing: atmosphere. F

Americanity: The process as well as the product of assimilating the essence of being an American, especially by one not born into that essence. N

Amor omnia vincit: Love conquers all. L

And indeed, there will be time . . . : From the poem "The Love Song of J. Alfred Prufrock" by T. S. Eliot, 1917.

And the days dwindle down . . . : From "September Song," an *American pop standard* by Kurt Weil, with lyrics by *Maxwell Anderson*. Introduced in the 1938 broadway musical *Knickerbocker Holiday*.

Angle of Repose: Novel by Wallace Stegner, 1972.

Anno domini: In the year of the Lord (AD). L

Ante, apud . . . : Latin prepositions requiring the accusative case. L

Antepasado: Ancestor. S

Anything that can go wrong will go wrong: An *adage* or *epigram* known as Murphy's Law.

Ao-dai: A Vietnamese national outfit primarily for women. In its current form, it is a tight-fitting silk tunic worn over pantaloons.

A priori: "From the former," involving deductive reasoning from a general principle to a necessary effect; not supported by fact. L

ARS: Agricultural Research Service, an agency of the US Department of Agriculture.

Arrivé: One who attained success, mostly used in a derogatory sense; a parvenu. F
Arroyo: Creek. S
ATP: Adenosine triphosphate, the main molecule of biological energy storage.
Autobahn: Freeway. G
A Világ: The World. A poem translated from Wordsworth, an original of which I cannot find.
Az óperenciás tengeren is túl: Even beyond the Sea of Operencia. M

B

Babe Ruth: American baseball legend.
(Mihály) Babits: Hungarian, writer, poet, and translator.
Bácsi: Uncle, also respectful title of an older man of one's acquaintance. M
Bahnhof: Railway station. G
Balsors akit régen tép . . . : From "Himnusz" by Ferenc Kölcsey, 1823, Hungarian national anthem. M
Barack pálinka: Apricot brandy. H
Barranca: Ravine. S
(Fulgencio) Batista: A US-backed Cuban general, president, and dictator. He served as the leader of Cuba before being overthrown by the Cuban Revolution.
(Béla) Bartók: Hungarian composer and pianist, considered to be one of the greatest composers of the twentieth century.
Beetle Bailey: Perennial comic-strip character of a private and draftee in the old army of wooden barracks days.
Bellum Gallicum: Gallic War. An account by Julius Caesar of his exploits during the conquest of what became the Roman Province of Gallia. L
Bethlenfalva: Hungarian (Székely) village now incorporated into the town of Székelyudvarhely. Location of the Bethlenfalvay family home. Now in Romania. M
Bhagavad Gita: "Song of *God*." One of the most important Hindu scriptures and philosophical classics of the world. Sanskrit
Biblician: Tongue-in-cheek reference to the true believers who claim that every word of the Bible was dictated by God. N
Bilbo: Bilbo Baggins, the adventurous protagonist of J. R. R. Tolkien's book *The Hobbit*.
Bildung: This German word has more than a dozen translations. In the sense used here, it means the possession and mastery of the culture of an educated European middle and upper class.
Biotroph: An organism that can live and multiply only on another living organism.
Birken Allee: (The one between Bad Aibling and Harthausen) A path for pedestrians and bicycles shaded by evenly planted birch trees. G

Bishop's Peak: One of the groups of plutons between San Luis Obispo and Morro Bay, California.

Black Goya: Ominous and gloomy paintings by Francisco Goya, some showing atrocities of The occupation of Spain by Napoleon's armies; early nineteenth century.

Blasé: World-weary, worldly-wise, and sophisticated. F

(Niels) Bohr: Danish physicist, one of the fathers of our understanding of the atom.

BOQ: Bachelor Officers' Quarters.

Botfülü: "Stick-eared"; someone who cannot carry a tune. M

Bőség: Plenty. M

Bourgeois: Wealthy middle-class person.

Boys' Town: A Catholic institution located west of the City of Omaha. Engages in the rehabilitation of vagrant, homeless boys.

Brahma: *Hindu* god of creation and one of the *Trimurti*, the others being *Vishnu* and *Shiva*. Sanskrit

Brahman: In the Hindu religion, Brahman is the unchanging, immanent, and transcendent reality which is the divine ground of all matter, energy, time, and space. Sanskrit

Brujo: Sorcerer. S

BS: Bachelor of science.

(Martin) Buber: Jewish philosopher of religious existentialism.

Bud lite: Mass-produced, erstwhile American-icon beer a little short on taste. The Budweiser Company, maker of this "King of Beers" was sold to a Dutch brewery in 2009.

Bundeswehr: Post—World War II German Army.

Bundesgrenzschutz: Federal Border Guard; a special unit of the Bundeswehr.

Burrito de langosta: Lobster burrito. A burrito is a *flour tortilla* wrapped or folded around a filling. S

C

C: A passing, average grade in school or college.

Cacique: Title for the leaders of indigenous Mexican tribes. S

(Julius) Caesar: Roman general, conqueror of Gaul, aspiring to become hegemon of Rome. L

Calzado: Shoe. S

Campesino: Mexican peasant. S

Carne asada: A roasted beef dish, mainly consisting of pieces or thin cuts of meat. S

(Johnny) Cash: American singer-songwriter and one of the most influential musicians of the twentieth century. Primarily a country music artist.

(Carlos) Castaneda: A Peruvian-born American author. Starting with *The Teachings of Don Juan* in 1968, he wrote a series of books about his purported training in Mesoamerican shamanism.

Cave canem: Beware of the dog. L

CCC: Civilian Conservation Corps, one of Roosevelt's New Deal programs.

Centeotl: Aztec god (also goddess) of maize (corn).

Centro de Investigaciones Biologicas del Noroeste: Center of biological Research of the Northwest, CIB for short. S

CEO: Chief executive officer.

C'est tout . . . : That's all. That's all for you, poor schlemiel. F

C'est le ton qui fait la musique: It is the tone that makes the music.

(Richard 'Dick') Chaney: Executive vice president of the United States, formerly CEO of Halliburton, a global oilfield services corporation.

Chaos theory: A field of study in mathematics, physics, and philosophy on the behavior of dynamical systems that are highly sensitive to initial conditions.

(Ernesto "Che") Guevara: Argentine Marxist revolutionary, physician, author, intellectual, guerrilla leader, military theorist, and major figure of the *Cuban Revolution*.

Chesire Cat: An image from *Alice in Wonderland*.

Chilam Balam: A chilam is a teacher or priest. Balam is a commonly used name meaning "jaguar." Yucatec

Chubasco: Cloudburst. S

Churrigueresque: Spanish architectural style with extreme elaborate and florid detailing. S

C-in-C: commander-in-chief.

Cidral: A Mexican soft drink, mostly apple-flavored.

Científico estaduniense: American scientist. S

Civitas Societatis Jesu: The community of those belonging to the Society of Jesus. L

Citrom lepke: Lemon butterfly, a beautiful, yellow, early-spring insect (*Gonepteryx rhamni*). M

(Carl von) Clausewitz: A Prussian general, military historian, and military theorist, most notable for his military treatise *Vom Kriege*, translated into English as *On War*.

Cochimí: Member of the Yuman linguistic family whose tribes occupied an extensive territory in the extreme southwest portion of the United States and Lower California.

Cocinera: Female cook. S

(Nat 'King') Cole: American musician hailed as one of the best and most influential pianists and small-group leaders of the swing era. He attained his greatest success as a vocalist specializing in warm ballads and light swing.

Comme il faut: In accord with conventions or accepted standards; proper. F

Como en las peliculas: Just like in the movies. S

CONASUPO: Compañía Nacional de Subsistencias Populares: National chain of state-owned grocery stores. S

Con cabecita o sin cabecita: With or without the (small) head. S

Condicio sine qua non: Or simply *sine qua non*, a condition without which it could not be. L

Conejo: Rabbit. S

Conquistador: Conqueror. S

Conundrum: A riddle, a puzzle, a difficult problem. L

Corso: Concourse. I

Couramment: Fluently. F

Credo in unum mercatum . . . : I believe in one market, the all-pervasive lord and regulator of peoples' lives. L

CRIS: Current Research Information System, the *US Department of Agriculture's* documentation and reporting system for research and education projects.

(Bing) Crosby: Popular crooner and movie star of the 1940s and 1950s.

Cui bono?: For what benefit? What is this good for?

Cuidado con tu leche de cabron: Careful with your billy-goat's milk. In Spanish slang, a cabron is not only a male goat but mostly something like a "fucking asshole." S

CWO: Chief Warrant Officer.

Cs

Csak egy kislány van a világon . . . : Hungarian folksong. M

Csatorna: Canal. M

Cserebogár: June bug. M

Csöbörből vödörbe esett: He fell from a pan into a pail.

D

D: A just barely passing grade in the evaluation of course work in school.

Darumadár útnak indúl . . . : Hungarian folksong. M

Das Kapital: "Capital," an extensive treatise on political economy by Karl Marx and edited in part by Friedrich Engels. A critical analysis of capitalism, first published in 1867. G

Das Schicksal setzt . . . : Fate applies the plane and planes us all the same. From the Viennese couplet "Das Hobellied." See "Der Verschwender" by Ferdinand Reimund, 1834.

Datum: Derived from the Latin verb *dare*; to give. It means "something that is given." It is the singular form of *data*; things given. L

Dawn came in a russet mantle clad: *Hamlet*, act 1, Shakespeare.

D.C.: District of Columbia.

Decider: A word popularized by George W. Bush (US president, 2000—2008), who liked to call himself one.

De colores . . . : "Of Colors" is a traditional folksong that is well known throughout the Spanish—speaking world. Brought to the Americas from Spain during the sixteenth century. S

Demonio: Demon, devil. S

De mortuis nihil nisi bonum: Of the dead nothing, unless something good. L

De most azért nem szabad . . . : That's no reason to get discouraged right away. M

Denouement: The final resolution or clarification of a dramatic or narrative plot.

De novo: Anew (from nothing). L

De Revolutionibus Orbium Celestium: *On the Revolutions of Celestial Orbs* by Nicolas Copernicus, 1543. L

Der, die, das: German definite articles (masculine, feminine, and neuter). G

Der uns die Stunden Zählte . . . : From the poem of the same title by Paul Celan, 1955.

(Tibor) Déry: A Hungarian writer, first a supporter of communism, who later wrote a *satire* on the communist regime in Hungary. *Georg Lukács* praised Déry as "the greatest depicter of human beings of our time."

Desideratum: Something desired as a necessity. L

Deus ex machina: "God from a machine." It denotes a sudden and unexpected resolution to a seemingly intractable problem in a plot line; used as a theatrical or literary device. L

Diazotrophic: Nitrogen-fixing.

Dictum: Something said, i.e., a pronouncement. L

Die Köpfe kühl . . . : "Heads cool, feet warm: that makes the best doctor poor." G

Die Luft is kühl . . . : From "Die Lorelei," by Heinrich Heine, 1822.

Die Nacht aus Blei: The Night of Lead, novel by Hans Henny Jahn, 1956. G

Die Nazis brachten uns . . . : The Nazis brought us vitamins, the Amis (Americans) brought us calories, who will give us something to eat? G

Die Temperatur . . . : "Temperature is not a property of matter, it is only one of the possibilities to measure its state of energy." G

Dieser drohende . . . : This menacing, red aircraft carrier in the middle of the Black Sea. G

Dies faustus: A day of favorable omen. L

Divide et impera: Divide and rule. L

Dixi!: "I have spoken!" From *dicere*, to say or speak. Roman orators used to end their speeches with that word to indicate that they had finished. L

DNA: Deoxyribonucleic acid, large organic molecule, carrier of the genetic code.

Dobos torta: A cake named after the famous Hungarian confectioner, József Dobos (1884). It is a five-layer sponge cake, layered with chocolate buttercream and topped with thin *caramel* slices. The sides of the cake are coated with ground hazelnuts, chestnuts, walnuts, or almonds. M

Doch auf fremden Plätzen . . . : From the poem "Der Fremde" ("The Stranger") by Rainer Maria Rilke, 1908.

Doctus: Learned. *Doctor* is its comparative: more learned. L

Doctor rerum naturalium: Doctor of natural things; doctor of science. L

Doing the garden . . . : From "When I am Sixty-Four," by the Beetles.

Domine, non sum . . . : "Lord, I am not worthy that you enter under my roof . . ." L

DP: Displaced person.

Du bist eine rein theoretische Begabung: Your talent is purely theoretical. G

Du hast begonnen . . . : From a poem by a classmate given as a parting gift to the author in Icking. G

(John Foster) Dulles, President Eisenhower's secretary of state; architect of American foreign policy during the eight years of that administration.

Durch die Wälder . . . : "Through the forests, through the meadows we wander around with the Fox on our backs." A family adaptation of the operatic text of the *Freischütz*. G

Durch die Wälder . . . : From the German romantic opera *Der Freischütz*, by Carl Maria von Weber, 1821.

Dürer: Medieval German artist of Hungarian origin (Ajtós).

E

Ég a napmelegtől a kopár szík sarja . . . : From the epic poem *"Toldi,"* by Arany János. M

Egy gondolat bánt engemet . . . : From the poem of the same title by Petőfi Sándor, 1846.

Egy magyar diák élete . . . : Life of a Hungarian student during the times of [King] Mathew. H

Emeritus: Retired from professional life but permitted to retain as an honorary title the rank of the last office held. L

Eisriesenwelt: World of the Ice Giants. G

Elvtárs: Comrade. M

Er allein kann dem Augenblick dauer verleihen: "He alone can bestow permanence on the moment." From the poem "Das Göttliche" ("On the Divine") by J. W. von Goethe.

Erdély: Transylvania, a Hungarian province for a thousand years; now in Romania. M

Erdély felé mutat . . . : From the poem "Mikes" by Lévai József. Mikes Kelemen (of the village of Zágon) was a freedom fighter with Prince Rákoczy Ferenc against Austrian tyranny, early eighteenth century. M

Érettségi: Test of Maturity, exam taken at the conclusion of studies at the secondary-school level. M

Ersatz: Substitute. G

Erstes Physikalisches Institut: First Institute of Physics (there are also others). G

Es lagen noch im Zeitenschoße . . . : From the poem "*Die Glocke*" ("The Bell") by Friedrich von Schiller, 1799. G

Es kommen härtere Tage . . . : From the poem "*Die Gestundete Zeit*," by Ingeborg Bachman, 1953. G

Español chapurreado: Broken Spanish. S

Esprit de corps: Morale of a group. F

Esskultur: The cultivation of and predilection for fine food. G

Estación experimental: Experiment station. S

Este camino no es de alta velocidad: This road is not for high speed. S

Este van . . . : From the poem "*Családi Kör*" ("Family Circle") by Arany János, 1800. M

Et habeat bonam pacem . . . : "And let him have sweet peace, he who sits by the stove." From the Romantic poem "Wanderlied der Prager Studenten" ("Roaming Song of the Students of Prag"), by Josef K. B. von Eichendorff.

Eula (Varner): Earth-goddess figure from William Faulkner's Snopes trilogy, 1940-1959.

Exec: Executive officer, second in command of a battery.

Ez a mauthauseni . . . : This is the Mauthausen concentration camp. You may not exit from the train. You may not look out of the window. H

F

Facetiae: Witty, odd sayings. L

Factotum: An employee or assistant who serves in a wide range of capacities. L

(Jerry) Falwell: American televangelist, conservative commentator, founding pastor of a megachurch in Lynchburg, Virginia, cofounder the Moral Majority in 1979.

Farm (The): An intentional community in Lewis County, Tennessee based on principles of respect for the earth. Founded 1971 by Stephen Gaskin and 320 San Francisco hippies.

(William) Faulkner: Nobel Prize-winning American author. One of the most influential writers of the twentieth century.

Fear fear itself: "The only thing we have to fear is fear itself," from Franklin Delano Roosevelt's first inaugural address, 1932.

Felicidad domestica: Domestic bliss. S

Ferro ignique: With iron and fire. L

Fidel Castro: One of the primary leaders of the Cuban Revolution, served as the prime minister and then as the president of the Council of State of Cuba.

Fillér: Cent. M

Finegan's Wake: A novel by Irish author James Joyce, with a reputation as one of the most difficult works of fiction in the English language.

Fingerzeig: Hint, cue, tip. G

(Die) *Fledermaus:* (The) Bat, operetta by Johann Strauss II.

Fluidum: Liquid; a special atmosphere that emanates from a person or thing. L

(Jóska) Fischer: Erstwhile Revoluzzer, later became foreign minister of Germany.

Föhn: A strong warm downhill wind, so called on the north-facing slopes of the Alps.

(Milton) Friedman: American economist, statistician, and *Nobel Prize winner* in Economics, known among other things for his political philosophy that extolled the virtues of a free market economic system with little intervention by government.

Française: Stately French dance; of the quadrille form. F

Fräulein: Miss. G

Frissensült: A freshly baked or prepared meal. Mostly unlike the dish described in the text. M

(Erich) Fromm: A German social psychologist, psychoanalyst, *humanistic* philosopher, and democratic socialist.

Frontera: Frontier. S

Fugit Amor: Love Flees, sculpture by Auguste Rodin, Musée Rodin, Paris, France. L

Funker Bunker: Communications bunker. *Funke* = spark; commo specialists were called "sparkers" in the German military of Morse-code days. G

Führer: Leader. G

G

Gallia divisa est in partes tres: "Gaul is divided in three parts" is the first sentence of Caesar's book, *Bellum Gallicum,* The Gallic War. L

Gazember: Scoundrel. M

GED: General Educational Development; a test for nongraduates of high school, showing an education equivalent to that of graduates.

Gedächtniskirche: Church of Remembrance. A bomb-damaged church left standing as a ruin as a memorial for the destruction caused by war at the Beethoven Platz in Frankfurt am Main, Germany. G

Gehen wir schwimmen: Let's go swimming. G

Gelt, man kann . . . : "Isn't it true, you can go steal horses with them." G

Gemütlichkeit: A feeling of comfortable, cozy, stress-free, happy contentment. G

Genus: Kind or race, taxonomic unit (taxon) between species and family. L
Gestalt: Shape or form. Gestalt therapy is a psychological system and procedure that stresses the development of self-awareness. G
Gestapo: Geheime Staats Polizei, the notorious Nazi secret police.
GI: Government issue. Everything connected with the army came to be called GI, including the soldiers themselves.
GI Bill: The Servicemen's Readjustment Act of 1944 (GI Bill) provided for education expenses for World War II veterans and was extended to Korean War era soldiers.
Gita: See Bhagavad Gita.
(Das) *Glasperlenspiel:* Game of Glass Pearls, novel by Hermann Hesse, 1943.
Gloire de la patrie: "Glory of the fatherland." The French cult and concept of the *gloire* is not quite known, felt, and practiced elsewhere as it is in Fance. F
(Doktor Joseph) Göbbels: Hitler's Minister of Propaganda, 1933—1945.
Göbbels Schnauze: Primitive radio receiver that could be tuned to only one station, often the one on which propaganda by Göbbels was aired. G
Grandezza: Grandeur. I
Gratulálok . . . : I congratulate you—this lad is a real *stüszi* hunter. M
Gravitas: A quality of substance or depth of personality, including dignity, seriousness, and duty. L
(The) Great Gatsby: A great American novel by F. Scott Fitzgerald.
(Alan) Greenspan: American economist, served as chairman of the Federal Reserve of the United States from 1987 to 2006.
Grua: Tow truck. S
Grupo de posgraduados: Group of postgraduate (students). S
Guernica: The results of the bombing of the town of Guernica by fascist warplanes as depicted by Pablo Picasso, 1937.
Gulletable: While palatable implies a savoring process that squishes wine around below the palate; this new word signals enjoyment by downing (gulleting) it a little more deliberately. N
Gulyás leves: Goulash soup. M
Gute Leut': Decent folks. G
Gutes Geld . . . : To throw good money down the throat of the owner. G
Gymnasium: Secondary ("college preparatory") school, for the academic training of the mind, not of the body as in US usage. G&M

H

Haciendero: Lord of a large Mexican estate. S
Hajdani eltévedt utas . . . : From the poem "Az Eltévedt Lovas" ("The Horseman Who Lost His Way"), by Ady Endre, 1914. M
Halbbildung: A superficial, shaky possession of Bildung. G

Halálfejes (lepke): "With a death head" (butterfly) literally; a large, night-flying moth that shows a skull on its thorax (*Acherontia atropos*). M

Halász bástya: Fisherman's Tower

Halász csárda: Fisherman's restaurant.

Hausmusik: Playing of music, also singing, in a private home, often as a formal or semiformal presentation by artists or other adepts. G

Haushaltskasse: Household's cash box. Equally contributed money to be used for shared expenses. G

Haute cuisine: High cooking; an elaborate and skillful manner of preparing food. F

Heathcliff: Eerie character from *Wuthering Heights*, a novel by Emily Brontë.

Heil-Hitler Gruß: "Hail Hitler" greeting; right arm held out at a forty-five-degree angle, palm down. G

Herr General, der heisse Kaffee . . . Sir (Mister General), the hot coffee is waiting below in the communications center. G

Herr Professor Doktor: American academics like to make fun of the German predilection of this double title. In America, professor tends to have a negative connotation in the general populace.

Himmel und Erde werden vergehen . . . : Heaven and earth shall pass away, but my words shall not pass away. From the New Testament, Mark 13:31. G

Hirngespinst: Whim or chimera. G

Himmler: Heinrich Himmler was chief of the German police and Minister of the Interior. He oversaw all internal and external police and security forces, including the *Gestapo*.

Hog butcher for the world . . . : From the poem "Chicago," by Carl Sandburg.

Holzweg: Logging road. G

Hongrois: Hungarian. F

Honvéd: Protector of the homeland; a soldier of the Hungarian army. The honvédség or

Home Defence Force was first established during the Revolution of 1848.

Horribile dictum: Horrible to relate. L

Huarache: Mexican sandal. The word is of Tarascan (Purépecha) origin. P is a small language family still spoken in the highlands of the Mexican state of Michoacán.

Huitzilopochli: Aztec god of war. Nahuatl

Hundertwasser: Friedensreich Regentag Dunkelblut Hundertwasser, twentieth century Austrian painter and architect.

Hunyady: Historical figure, Prince of Transylvania and Regent of Hungary; he stemmed the Turkish advance in the fifteenth century by repeated significant victories. M

Hypha: A long, thin, branching filamentous cell of a fungus. In most fungi, hyphae are the main mode of vegetative growth and are collectively called a *mycelium*.

I

Ich bin kein Hindu um an Seelenwanderung zu glaubem: I am no Hindu to believe in reincarnation. G

ICRISAT: International Crops Research Institute for the Semi-Arid Tropics.

Iglesia: Church. S

Ihr führt ins Leben uns hinein . . . : From *Wilhelm Meisters Wanderjahre*, by Goethe.

Il pleuvait sans cesse sur Brest: It rained without stopping at Brest. F

Il pleuvait sans cesse sur la Bavière: It rained without stopping in Bavaria.

In a lonely shack . . . : From "The Wayward Wind," by Herb Newman and Stan Lebowsky, 1956.

Indigena: A native or aborigine. S

INS: Immigration and Naturalization Service.

Intelligencer: My word for soldiers playing at intelligence, after the now defunct daily newspaper, the Seattle Post-Intelligencer. N

IRA: Retirement Investment Account.

Iron cross: High German military decoration. G

Isartalbahn: The suburban railroad line from Munich south through the Isar Valley. G

Is it only 'cause you're lonely . . . : From "Mona Lisa," an Academy Award—winning *song* sung by Nat King Cole and written by Ray Evans and Jay Livingston for the Paramount Pictures film Captain Carey, USA (1950).

Isten áldd meg a magyart . . . : "Himnusz," by Ferenc Kölcsey, 1823, Hungarian national anthem. M

Ist es möglich, Stern der Sterne . . . : From "Wiederfinden" in *West-Östlicher Divan*, by Goethe, 1819. G

Iter militaris septentrionalis: Northern military road. L

I've been everywhere man: The song "I've Been Everywhere" was written by Geoff Mack in 1959 and made popular by the singer Lucky Starr in 1962.

J

Ja, in Stalingrad . . . : Yes, in Stalingrad, that's where we lost the war. G

Ja, wo nicht geschossen wird . . . : Yes, where they don't shoot, that's where they buried the mines. G

Jambalaya and a crawfish pie . . . : From "On the Bayou" done by Hank Williams Sr. who copied The Jambalaya musical melody from an earlier tune recorded in Cajun French called "Grand Texas."

Jambalaya, des tartes d'ecreuvisse . . . : Cajun-French original from which "On the Bayou' was transmogrified. Cajun-F

Jinete: Horseman. S

Jó: Good. M

Jó kedv: High spirits. M

Jobb oldal: Right side. M

Joie-de-vivre: Joy of life. F

Jongleur de mots: Juggler of words. F

(Carl Gustav) Jung: A Swiss psychiatrist. He emphasized understanding the psyche through exploring the worlds of dreams, art, mythology, religion, and philosophy.

Just So Stories: Tales centering on Maugli's adventures in the Indian jungle, by Rudyard Kipling.

K

Kacskaringós: Convoluted. M

Kaffee und Kuchen: Coffee and cake. G

(Franz) Kafka: One of the most influential writers of the twentieth century. The adjective kafkaesque refers to his nightmarish style of narration where the characters are ensnared in hopeless circumstances from which there is no escape.

Kaiser: Emperor. G

Kaiserschmarrn: A desert well known in Hungary and Austria. It's worth your while to look up its story and recipe in Google. G

Kakas: Rooster. M

(1901) Karácsonykor kaptam ezt a könyvet: I received this book for Christmas 1901. M

Karma yoga: The path of selfless action. Sanscrit

Katze: Cat, especially their cat to end all cats. G

Kennst du das Land . . . : From the poem "Mignon," by Johann Wolfgang von Goethe. G

Kereskény: The village where his maternal grandmother's family, the Majláth, had their estate. It is now nationalized in Slovakia. M

(Jack) Kerouac: American novelist; reference is made here to his account *On the Road* (1957).

Kilátszik a lóláb: "The horses hoof is showing," referring to the devil's foot peeking out from under a monk's cassock. M

Kínlódik, mint pata a napon: Hurting like a grub in the sun. M

Kis kakas: Small rooster. M

Kis erdő: Small forest. M

Kirchhoff's Laws: Rules on the conservation of charge and energy in electrical circuits.
Kiva: A Hopi word for an underground ceremonial room.
Kohldampf: "Cabbage vapors," slang expression for feeling hungry. G
Kolozsvár: Capital city of Transylvania. Now Cluj-Napoca in Romanian. Its Hungarian
population has been mostly replaced by Romanians through ethnic cleansing following World War II. M
Kolozsvári rakott káposzta: A dish made up of cabbage, rice, and lamb, as prepared in Kolozsvár. M
Konditorei: Pastry shop. G
Könyvesbolt: Bookstore. M
KP: Kitchen police performing menial jobs in the course of food preparation in an army mess hall. It was part of the private's way of life, now outsourced to civilian contractors.
Kumpel: Comrade; a term used among miners to refer to their co-workers, which eventually came to denote "miner" to nonminers. In this sense, it also came to be used in a pejorative meaning as one of the lower class. G
Kuruc: Name of the fighters for freedom against the Austrian Empire, at the turn of the eighteenth century. M

L

La donna è mobile: "Woman is fickle," aria from the opera *Rigoletto*, by Guiseppe Verdi. I
Lady Bird Johnson: President Lyndon Johnson's wife.
Laissez faire: Non-interfering or tolerant. F
Lapis philosophorum: The philosopher's stone is a legendary alchemical substance capable of turning base metals into gold and serving as an elixir of life. L
Lapsus memoriae: Slip of memory. L
Lara: Female protagonist of Boris Pasternak's novel, *Doctor Zhivago*, 1957.
Le baiser: *The Kiss*, sculpture by Auguste Rodin, Musée Rodin, Paris, France. F
Lengyel shopos: Polish shopkeeper, the Hungarian—*os* ending affixed to shop is an early adaptation of English words by the brothers into their Hungarian usage.
León de la Luz: Lion of light, real name of a botanist colleague at the CIB. S
Leonid: Leonid Ilyich Brezhnev. He led the Soviet Union during the last part of the Cold War.
Le Penseur: *The Thinker*, sculpture by Auguste Rodin, Musée Rodin, Paris, France. F
Les sanglots longs . . . : From "La chanson de l'automne," by Paul Verlaine

(Rush Hudson) Limbaugh III: *A*merican radio host, conservative political commentator, and highly influential opinion former in the conservative movement in the United States.

Limes: Boundary. The Romans built a few extended "limes" walls in the North, perhaps more to mark the "limit" of their empire than to keep the barbarians out. L

Llano Estacado: Staked Plains, high mesa country in Western Texas. S

(Jim) Lehrer: Respected anchor of the NewsHour with Jim Lehrer on Public Television.

Les souvenirs et les regrets aussi: The souvenirs and also the regrets, from Les Feuilles Mortes, see "Oh, je voudrais tant . . ." F

Léva: Small town in Northern Hungary, now in Slovakia; was subject to near complete ethnic cleansing following World War II.

Liebesträume: "Dreams of Love"; piano solo works by Liszt Ferenc, 1850. G

Likekindedness: Formed after "likemindedness" refers to people of similar social values. N

Limey: Also lime juicer, as Americans may call the Brits due to their use of lime on sailing ships to prevent scurvy.

Little Big Horn: This battle, also known as Custer's Last Stand and as the Battle of Greasy Grass Creek by Native Americans, was a fight between a Lakota-Northern Cheyenne combined force and the Seventh Cavalry of the *US Army* near the Little Bighorn River in Montana Territory, 1876.

Logos: Word, law, source, and fundamental order of the cosmos. Greek

Loneliest Highway, or Loneliest Road: US Highway 50, so called as it crosses the State of Nevada.

(Konrad) Lorenz: Nobelist, father of the science of animal behavior.

LSU: Louisiana State University.

Lumen et auctoritas: Light and authority. L

M

Mac the Knife: Allusion to the main character from the *Dreigroschenoper* (*Threepenny Opera*), by Berthold Brecht.

(Niccolo) Machiavelli: Of fifteenth century Florence, he is associated (perhaps mistakenly) with the justification of corrupt, totalitarian government.

MACV: Military Assistance Command, Vietnam.

Madjaren: How Germans sometimes call the Hungarians. G

Magic Mountain: *Der Zauberberg*, novel by Thomas Mann, 1924.

Magnum opus: Great work. L

Magyar: Hungarian. M

Magyarország: Hungary. M

Magyar Tudományos Akadémia: Hungarian Academy of Sciences. M
Magyar vagyok, Magyar . . . : From the patriotic poem *"Magyar Vagyok"* by Petőfi Sándor. M
Maikäfer: May beetle, june bug, or cockchafer. G
Maíz y frijol: Corn and beans. S
Mammon: A term derived from the Jewish-Christian Bible, used to describe material wealth or greed, and often personified as a pagan deity.
Man soll eine Beschäftigung . . . : One should have an occupation, but it should not degenerate into work. G
Marquis: High rank of French nobility. F
M*A*S*H: A television series adapted from the 1970 feature film *MASH*, a medical drama and black comedy recalling the Korean War.
Mas o menos: More or less. S
Mason-Dixon Line: Originally the boundary between free and slave states, it now symbolizes a cultural boundary between the Northern United States and "the South" (Dixie).
Matador: Killer; the toreador of the bullfight. S
Matamoro: Killer of moors, a Spanish reconquista term of the fifteenth century. S
Mátyás Király: King Mathew. King of Hungary during the second part of the fifteenth century.
Local tradition remembers him as a great, just, and beloved ruler. M
Maximilian: Maximilian I of Mexico, a member of the Imperial House of Habsburg-Lorraine. He was proclaimed Emperor of Mexico with the backing of Napoleon III of France and a group of Mexican monarchists on April 10, 1864.
Max und Moritz: An illustrated story in verse, a blackly humorous tale, told in rhymed couplets, written and illustrated by *Wilhelm Busch*, 1865.
(Samuel) Maverick: A *Texas* politician and landowner. His name is the source of the term *maverick*, first cited in 1867, which came to mean "independently minded." Left his cattle unbranded using this as a stratagem to misappropriate other unbranded calves.
MBA: Master [degree] of business administration.
Mazorca: Corn cob. Mexican S
(Douglas) McArthur: Five-star general; was relieved of duty by President Truman apparently for insubordinate behavior while in charge of the Korean War.
(Joseph) McCarthy: US senator; launched a political witch hunt, making accusations of disloyalty and un-American activity often without evidence.
Megölte valaki magát: From the poem *"Téli Világ"* ("Winter World") by Petőfi Sándor, 1845. M
Mei Ruah': My peace and quiet (Bavarian dialect). G

Mensch, gib acht . . . : "Human being, pay attention! What speaks the deep midnight? From *Also Sprach Zarathustra* (Thus Spoke Zarathustra), by Friedrich Niezsche, 1885. G

Mention of brand name . . . : This is inserted here facetiously; it is a requirement in scientific publications as a disclaimer of advertisement.

Mercado: Market. S

Merde: Shit. F

(K. W. Prince von) Metternich: German-Austrian politician and statesman (1773—1859). One of the most important diplomats of his era, a paradigm of foreign-policy management and a major figure in the development of diplomatic praxis.

Miatyánk Úristen ki vagy a mennyekben . . . : Church hymn. M

Michael-Moore movie: The documentary by MM referred to here is *Roger & Me*.

Military crest: The shoulder of a hill or ridge rather than its actual or topographic crest (highest point). Troops occupying the military crest tend not to be silhouetted against the sky as they would be if they were on the topo crest, making them more difficult to spot.

Mille miles de toute terre habitée: A thousand miles away from any human habitation. F

Milpa: Cornfield. Nahuatl

Mint kiűzött király . . . : From the poem "A Puszta Télen" ("The Plains in Winter") by Petőfi Sándor, 1848.

Minutium: Minor detail. L

Miraculum miraculorum: Miracle of miracles. L

Mitra: Bishop's hat. L

Mogote: A prominent feature in the landscape of the city of La Paz (Baja California) is the Mogote, a barrier beach that lies adjacent to the city and protects the Bay of La Paz connected to in the Sea of Cortez by a narrow inlet.

Mohácsi vész: The disaster of Mohács; defeat of the Magyar Army by the Turks, 1526.

Moro: Moor. Populations of Muslim people of Berber, Black African, and Arab descent from North Africa, some of whom conquered and occupied the *Iberian Peninsula* for nearly eight hundred years. S

Moralisches Gesetz: Moral law; allusion here to Emmanuel Kant's *Kritik der Praktischen Vernunft* (Critique of Practical Reason), 1788. G

Mordida: Bite, meaning here "bribe." S

(Bill) Moyers: Journalist and public commentator, extensive involvement with public television, documentaries, and news journal programs, well known as a trenchant critic of US policies and vocal proponent of worthy causes.

MP: Military police.

My heart knows . . . : From the poem "The Cry of the Wild Goose," by Terry Gilkyson, sung by Frankie Laine and Tennessee Ernie Ford, 1950.

My heart's in the Highlands . . . : From the poem by Robert Burns (same title), 1789.

Mycelium: The *vegetative* part of a *mushroom*, consisting of a mass of branching, threadlike *hyphae*.

N

Nada de estas tonterias, mein lieber ló: Let's not get carried away, my dear ló. S G M

NAFTA: The North American Free Trade Agreement is a pact signed by the governments of The United States, Canada, and Mexico, creating a trilateral trade bloc in North America, 1994.

Na, sie sind wohl . . . : So, you seem to be proud of your ancestors. G

Nächtlich am Busento . . . : From the poem "Das Grab am Busento" ("The Grave at the Busento"), by August Graf von Platen, 1820.

(the) Nam: Common abbreviation for Vietnam.

Nagy Magyarország: The historic, greater Hungary, prior to the end of World War I. M

Nagymajtényi síkon . . . : Kuruc song, lamenting the fateful defeat of a fight for freedom. M

Nagymalom: Big gristmill. M

Nahuatl: A group of related languages and dialects of the Nahuan (Aztecan) branch of the Uto-Aztecan language family.

Nappali pávaszem: Peacock's eye of the day, a colorful butterfly. The peacock's eyes of the night are large night-flying moths. M

Narcissus: A *hero* of Greek myth renowned for his beauty who falls in love with a reflection in a pool. Not realizing it was his own, he perishes there not being able to leave it.

Narco traficante: Drug dealer. S

NCO: Noncommissioned officer.

(Mikós) Németh: Prime minister of Hungary; opened the Iron Curtain in 1989, an act that eventually brought down the Berlin Wall. For the story in a nutshell, see Newsweek,

May 4, 2009, page 36.

Néni: Aunt; also respectful title for older women of one's acquaintance. M

Neocon: Neoconservatism is a political philosophy that emerged in the United States and that supports using American economic and military power to bring democracy to other countries.

Neptune: Greek god of the sea.

Neureich: Newly rich, like self-made but with a derogatory connotation. G

Never Never Land: It was introduced in 1904 performances of the theater play Peter Pan or The Boy Who Wouldn't Grow Up, by Scottish writer J. M. Barrie.

New World Order: A term often used in history. Here it refers to the post—Soviet Empire era as expressed by President George H. W. Bush in his "Toward a New World Order" speech (September 11, 1990) to a joint session of the US Congress on his objectives for post—Cold War global governance in cooperation with post-Soviet states.

(Friedrich Wilhelm) Nietzsche: Nineteenth-century German philosopher; wrote critical texts on religion, morality, contemporary culture, philosophy, and science.

Niños héroes: Heroic youths. S

Noch einmal glimpflich davongekommen . . . : Escaped once more by the skin of my teeth. G

Noche triste: Sad night. S

Noncom: Noncommissioned officer like a sergeant.

Novus ordo saeculorum: The new order of the centuries. L

Nuit froide de l'oubli: Cold night of oblivion, from the song "Autumn Leaves." F

Nur allein der Mensch . . . : From the poem "Das Göttliche" ("On the Divine") by Goethe. G

Nur forwärts gibt es einen Weg: Only forward is there a way. G

Nyaffancs: Habitual complainer and whiner. M

O

Obersturmgruppenführer: Chief storm group leader, an officer's rank in the Waffen-SS. G

Oberrealschule: Secondary school (fifth through twelfth grade) that follows elementary school (first through fourth). The "real" designation indicates emphasis in the natural sciences. G

Oh, Mensch gib acht!: Human being, pay attention!

Oh, je voudrais tant . . . : From the poem "Les Feuilles Mortes" ("Autumn Leaves"), by Jaques Prévert first sung by Yves Montand in the film of Marcel Carné, *Les Portes de la Nuit* (The Doors of the Night). F

Oh, to be in England . . . : From the poem "Home Thoughts from Abroad" by Robert Browning, 1845.

Offen: Open. G

Ohm's Law: States that electric current is directly proportional to voltage and inversely proportional to resistance in a circuit.

Oktoberfest: Go to Munich and experience it!

On the road again: From the piece "On the Road Again," by Willie Nelson but enjoyed especially as sung by Johnny Cash.

Ópapa: Version of *nagyapa*; grandfather. M

Oregonality: The essence of a progressive-minded, environmentally active Oregonian. N
Orioles: Famous Baltimore baseball team.
(Harvey) Oswald: Man who supposedly killed President Kennedy and was himself shot in public at the Dallas, Texas, Courthouse.
OU: Oklahoma University.
Oubli: Oblivion or forgetting.
Overdog: The opposite of underdog. N

P

Padishah: Great king.
Palacio del Gobierno: Government palace. S
PBS: Public Broadcasting System; used to be supported by the US listener donations but sponsored lately by Big Business.
Partir, c'est toujours mourir un peu: Leaving, that's always dying a little. F
Parvenu: A person who has suddenly acquired wealth or power but is not fully accepted socially by the class associated with the higher position; an upstart. F
Pastel de tres leches: Cake of three milks, a Mexican dessert. S
Paté de fois gras: Goose-liver paté. F
Pater: Father, title of the catholic priests. L
Patika: Pharmacy. M
Patrimonio de Humanidad: Heritage of Mankind. S
Peckee: The one being pecked like a chicken lower in the pecking order. N
Penes, pone . . . : Latin prepositions with the accusative case. L
Per aspera ad astra: Through hardships to the stars. L
Permanently viciate: That's how the bicolored python rock snake talked in the *Just So Stories* of Rudyard Kipling.
Permítame proponer un apuesto: Let me propose a bet. S
Per quem omnia facta sunt: By whom everything was made. L
Petőfi Sándor: Hungarian poet. Died in a cavalry attack against the Russians (1849).
Pfc.: Private first class, low US Army rank.
Platz: Square. G
Polis: A city and also citizenship and a body of citizens. Greek
Pontius Pilate: Governor of the Roman province of Judea. Washes his hands of Jesus, but sends him to his death anyway.
Ponzi scheme: A fraudulent investment operation that pays returns to investors from their own money or money paid by new investors rather than from any actual profit earned.

(Karl) **P**opper: Sir Karl Raimund Popper is widely regard as one of the greatest philosophers of science of the twentieth century.
Post mortem: After death. L
POTUS: President of the United States.
Pozsony: Hungarian city, now Bratislava, capital of Slovakia. M
Praestet fides supplementum . . . : Literally "Faith provides a supplement for the imperfections of the senses." L
Prima donna: First lady; principal woman singer (opera). I
Prof: That's what a professor is normally called, as if it were a word in its own right.
Prometheus Bound: An Ancient Greek tragedy attributed to Aeschylus.
PTA: Parent-Teacher Association.
Punctum: Period. L
(Vladimir) **P**utin: Erstwhile KGB agent; later became the president of Russia.

Q

Quid pro quo: this for that. L
Quidquid agis . . . : Whatever you do, do it prudently and consider the consequences (ends). L
Quo usque tandem . . . : "How long will you abuse our patience, Catilina?" From an oration by Marcus Tullius Cicero in the Roman Senate, 63 BC. L
Quintessence: From the Latin *quinta essencia*, the fifth and highest element in ancient and
Medieval philosophy that permeates all nature.

R

Rs: The three Rs are reading, (w)riting, and (a)rithmetic.
R&R: Rest and recreation. Military term for time off from War Zone deployment.
Rántott csirke: Fried chicken. M
Rappelle toi!: Remember! F
(The) **R**aven: Poem by Edgar Allan Poe, 1845.
Reconquista: Reconquest (of the southern part of Spain still occupied by the Moors, fifteenth century). S
Reichsmark: Currency of the Third Reich of the Nazis). It was replaced by the Deutsche Mark soon after World War II. G
Remélem jó egészségben találom: I hope to find you in good health. M
Requiescat in pace: May he rest in peace. L
Revoluzzer: A name for those in the counterculture student-protest movement in the Germany of the 1960s.
Rheinländer: Stately yet lively German dance. G

Rókagomba: Fox-mushroom, chanterelle. M
Roosty: Small rooster. N
RVN: Republic of Vietnam.

S

Sacerdote: Priest. S
Saddam Hussein: President of Iraq, 1979—2003. Overthrown by US invasion in 2003.
Saint Thomas Aquinas: One of the greatest and most influential theologians of all time. Author of the *Summa Theologica*, thirteenth century.
(Antoine de) Sainte Exupéry: French aviator and writer, real-life hero who looked at adventure and danger with a poet's eyes, sometimes from the viewpoint of a child.
Sándorhalma: A settlement near Léva where land was awarded to the author's father for merits in World War I under the auspices of the *Vitézi Rend*, the Order of Valor. M
Sangha: Association, assembly, company of community, as it refers to Buddhist groups. Sanskrit or Pali
Sárga: Yellow. M
S-Bahn: The *Berlin S-Bahn* is a rapid transit system operated by *S-Bahn Berlin* GmbH, a subsidiary of the Deutsche Bahn (German Railways).
Schäflarn: Schäftlarn Abbey is a Benedictine monastery on the Isar south of Munich, Bavaria, about half an hour's walk from Icking. The city of Munich was founded by its monks.
Schlager: Popular song. G
Schlauch: Hose, also a narrow (darkish) passageway, in family usage. G
Schlechte Zeiten: Hard times. G
Schloss: Castle. G
Schnörkelig: Loaded with florid, capricious ornament. G
Schnuckeltuch: Security blanket; often used by kids as an adjunct to thumb sucking. G
(Carl) Schurz: German revolutionary, American statesman and reformer, and Union Army general in the American Civil War.
Schülerheim: Students' Home. This one was run by the Lutheran organization of the Internal Mission (Innere Mission) and included, besides room and board, supervision, and twice-daily mandatory devotions with Bible reading and psalm singing. G
Schwanz: Nineteenth century usage for the penis, derived from Yiddish via the German meaning "tail."
Sea to shining sea: From "America the Beautiful," a patriotic American Song.

Semmeln und Leberkäs': (Bread)rolls and a Bavarian sausage specialty literally "liver-cheese," although it contains neither. G

Se puede pagarle . . . : May I give the fine to you? So that *you* can take it to the office.

SFC: Sergeant first class.

Shlemiel: A bungler; an unfortunate, hapless person. Yiddish

Shogun: A military rank and historical title for a military dictator of Japan.

Si, claro, no problema: Yes, sure, no problem. S

Si, lo tengo . . . : Yes, I have one, and it says there is no nitrogen. S

Si tacuisses . . . : Had you kept your mouth shut, you would still be a philosopher. L

Sie hatte die Nase voll: She had her nose full; she had enough of it—had it up to here.

Sierra Nevada: Snow-covered mountain range; *sierra* means "saw."

Silent Spring: This book by *Rachel Carson* is widely credited with helping launch the Environmental Movement, 1962.

Slivovic: Plum brandy. Slavic

(Tavis) Smiley: Contemporary talk-show host on the Public Broadcasting System.

Solch eine feige Kapitulation . . . : Such a cowardly capitulation is out of the question. We fight to the last drop of blood. G

So prüfe wer sich ewig bindet . . . : From *Die Glocke*' (the Bell), by Friedrich von Schiller. G

So, und das . . . : So this just came to your mind exactly when I wanted to call it quits. G

Sopa de rabo de toro: Bull's tail soup. S

Sozialistischer Deutscher Studentenbund: German Socialist Student Federation. G

Spatenbräu: Well-known Bavarian brewery. G

Spec4: Army pay grade higher than Pfc but without noncommissioned officer status.

Spoon River Anthology: A collection of epitaphs of residents of a small American town by Edgar Lee Masters, 1920.

Stamperl: Shot glass. Austrian

Status quo ante: Previous state or the last uncontested *status* of an *entity* before the *current* one. L

Staub und Asche: Dust and ashes.

Strich darunter: Done with it; it's over.

Sturm und Drang: "Storm and stress," an expression of the late eighteenth century German literary movement of emotional and rebellious feelings. First used as the title of a play by Friedrich von Klinger, 1776.

Sub rosa: Under the rose; in secret. L

Sudoku: Single Number. A *logic*-based, combinatorial number-placement puzzle. Japanese

Suspiro del Moro: Sigh of the Moor. S
Suum cuique: To each his own.
Swami: Hindu honorific title.
Sweet scent: Refers to the song "Sweet Violets" from Joseph Emmet's play Fritz among the Gypsies (1882) recorded also by Dinah shore (1951).

Sz

Székely: Name of a large Hungarian-language group in Transylvania (now in Romania). M
(János) Székely: Hungarian novelist.
Szép vagy . . . : Nostalgic patriotic song by Köteles István. Popular with Hungarian expatriates who tend to be touched to tears when they hear it or sing it. M

T

(die)Tageszeitung: *(The) Daily Newspaper* (this one is published in Berlin, Germany). G
Táltos: A *Táltos paripa* is a magical flying horse. *Táltos* may also mean a seer or wizard. M
Tapa: The name of a wide variety of appetizers or snacks in Spanish cuisine. S
Tarhonya: A grated fresh egg pasta. M
Tejszinhab: Whipped cream. M
Tejszínhabos kávé: Coffee with whipped cream. M
Tele van a város . . . : Hungarian folksong. M
Temps perdu: Time lost; gone by. Allusion to Marcel Proust's epic novel. F
Tenemos análisis del suelo (?): Do we have an analysis of this soil? S
Te quiero, dijiste . . . : From "Muñequita linda," by Mexican songwriter Maria Grever. S
Teosintle: The teosint[l]es are a group of large grasses of the genus *Zea* found in Mexico, Guatemala and Nicaragua. They are critical components of maize evolution. Nahuatl: *teocentli,* from *teotl* (god) + *centli* (dry ear of corn).
Terminal del Norte: Huge bus station in Mexico City that serves traffic going north. S
Terminus technicus: Technical term. L
The grace that God has shed on thee: Allusion to the poem by Katherine Lee Bates, "America the Beautiful."
The Latin-speaking Wallachians . . . : From The Penguin Atlas of Medieval History, by Colin McEvedy (1961—1969).
The lowest boughs . . . : See "Oh, to be in England."
Tiene Usted Buena suerte . . . : You are lucky that the gravel "garbaged" only one of your tires. S

Tienen que ser muy amigos: They must be very good friends. S
Tizenhárom: Thirteen, tizenhármas; a solitaire played with four groups of thirteen cards. M
Toda luna...: From the Mayan Chilam Balam books that consist of nine manuscripts named after small Yucatec towns such as Chumayel, Mani, and Tizimin. S
Töltött csirke: Stuffed chicken. M
Tonal: A concept in the belief systems of Mesoamerican cultures involving a spiritual link
between a person and an animal. Castaneda's concept is different from this.
Tope: Mole hill; in Mexican usage: speed bump. S
Tora Bora: Mountains in Afghanistan.
Torte: Layer cake. G
Török ház: Turkish house. M
Tu deviens responsible . . . : You become responsible forever for those whom you have tamed. From The Little Prince, by Saint Exupéry. F
Two-by-four: A board two by four inches in cross-section.

Ty

Tyúk udvar: Chicken (hen) yard. M

U

Über allen Gipfeln . . . : From "Wanderers Nachtlied" ("Wanderer's Night Song") by Goethe, 1780.
UC: University of California.
UCSB: UC campus at Santa Barbara.
Úgy van, az igaz, kis fiam . . . de azért nem szabad mindjárt elszontyolodni: That's right, it is true, my little son . . . but that's no reason to get discouraged. M
Un poquito sobre la Ciudad de México: A bit on Mexico City. S
Und schon sah er . . . : From "Der Fremde" ("The Stranger"), by Rainer Maria Rilke, 1908.
Unternehmungslustig: Enterprising, given to starting things.
UM: University of Munich.
Upanishad: Short summary of a Veda, sacred text of Hinduism. Sanskrit
UPS: United Parcel Service.
U of M: University of Maryland.
USAID: US Agency for International Development, an agency of the State Department.
USO: The United Service Organizations Inc. It is a private, nonprofit organization that provides morale and recreational services to members of the US military.
Utca: Street. M

V

Vár: Castle, fortress (vára: fortress of, like in Léva vára, fortress of Léva). M
Vaterland: Fatherland is the nation of one's "fathers" or "forefathers," a nationalist concept. G
V-8: A car engine with its eight cylinders arranged in a V outline.
Verboten: Forbidden. G
Verschmitztheit: Craftiness, slyness, or mischievousness. G
Verrücktheit: Lunacy. G
Vitézi Szék: A vitéz is a valiant warrior; the Vitézi Rend is the knightly Order of Valor, and a Vitézi Szék is an administrative region of that order. M
Vorwärts, vorwärts . . . : Marching song of the Hitler Youth by Baldur von Schirach, 1933. G
VSOP: Very special or superior old, pale (cognac).

W

Waffen-SS: The black-uniformed, politicized German military force. G
Währungsreform: Switch from the worthless Reichsmark to the valuable Deutsche Mark. G
Waiting in the front yard . . . : From "Louisiana Saturday Night," a country song written by Bob McDill.
(Sam) Walton: An American businessman and entrepreneur born in Kingfisher, Oklahoma, founder of the retailer giant *Walmart*.
Wanderlieder: Hiking songs.
Was bringt die tiefe Mitternacht?: What brings the profound midnight? G
Machen die monkeys?: [What] are the monkeys doing? (Fox used to elide first syllables). G
Watergate: The Watergate scandal (1970s) led only to the resignation of President Nixon, but it resulted in the conviction and jailing of several Nixon appointees.
Wehrmacht: Defense Force, name of the gray-uniformed regular German Army as opposed to the politicized, black-uniformed military force of the Waffen-SS. G
Weltanschauung: Worldview. G
Weltschmerz: World woe or weariness or sadness on thinking about the evils of the world. G
Wer einmal lügt . . . : If you lie just once, people will not believe you, even when you tell the truth.

Wer jetzt kein Haus hat . . . : He who has no house now will buy a trailer and will wander the streets of Austin until they turn icy. Paraphrasing Rilke's poem "Herbst" ("Autumn"). G

(William) Westmoreland: General, commandant of the US Military Academy—West Point, later became COMUSMACV, commander, US Military Assistance Command, Vietnam.

Where are Guisztó . . . : From the *Spoon River Anthology*, with names replaced.

Whittaker Chambers: Renounced his membership in the Communist Party and became notorious by his testimony in the perjury and espionage case of Alger Hiss at the beginning of the Cold War.

Wiedersehen (das): Reunion.

Wiener Schnitzel: Veal cutlet. G

Wilhelm Busch: German author of what may be the first book written in comic-strip style, nineteenth century.

Wir sind ein Stück: We are one piece. G

Witschaftswunder: The economic miracle of German reconstruction after World War II. G

Wo der deutsche Soldat einmal steht . . . : Where the German soldier once stands, there he stays.

Wohnkultur: The culture of cultivating cozy, well-appointed habitations. G

Wuthering Heights: Novel by Emily Brontë, 1847.

Y

Yogananda: Indian yogi and guru who introduced Westerners to the teachings of meditation and *Kriya Yoga* through his book, Autobiography of a Yogi. Founded the Self-Realization Fellowship in Los Angeles.

Yucatec: A Mayan language spoken in the Yucatán Peninsula, Northern Belize, and parts of Guatemala.

Z

Zalate: A tree of the fig family. Nahuatl

Zedernhäauser träagt der Atlas . . . : From the poem "Mahomet's Gesang" (Mahomet's Song) by Johann Wolfgang von Goethe. G

Zigeuner Bengel: Gipsy urchin. G

Zócalo: The main plaza or square in the heart of the historic center of Mexico City. The word means "base" or "plinth." Plans were made to erect a column as a monument to Independence, but only the base, or *zócalo*, was ever built. The plinth was destroyed but the name has lived on. Many other Mexican towns and cities, such as *Oaxaca*, have adopted the word *zócalo* to refer to their main plazas.

Zöld erdő harmatát . . . : Song of the Kuruc refugees from Austrian tyranny, turn of the seventeenth century.
Zopf: Plait, a kind of solitaire with the cards placed in the form of a plait. G
Zopilote: Vulture. Nahuatl
Zum Teufel: To the devil. G

Zs

Zsidó bácsi: Uncle Jew. M